The

WISDOM

of

PROVERBS

BOB BEASLEY

LIVING
STONE
BOOKS

THE WISDOM OF PROVERBS: An Essential Guide
by Bob Beasley

ISBN 978-0-9890922-0-3
Copyright ©2016 by LIVING STONE BOOKS

Previously Published in 1999 by Legacy Press of San Diego

Cover Illustration: *Netherlandish Proverbs* by Pieter Brueghel the Elder; completed 1559

Dedication

For my daughters, sons-in-law, and grandchildren:
Ally, Beth, and Brooke;
Mark, Don, and Chuck;
Willem, Hannah, Cian, Luke, Gabe, and Brienna.

"Children are an heritage of the Lord."
Psalm 127:3 KJV

About the Author

Bob Beasley lives with his wife, Amy, and three cats in Hartville, Ohio. He is the author of *101 Portraits of Jesus in the Hebrew Scriptures*, *The Commandments of Christ*, *Wisdom for Women* (with Amy), *Proverbs for Promise Keeping*, and has edited Flavius Josephus's *The Jewish Wars* and *The Life of Josephus* into modern English. He is also the author of the soon-to-be published, *Loving King Jesus: The Joyous Freedom of Obedience*, and *Proverbs 3:5&6: The Distilled Essence of the Christian Life*.

Bob is a graduate of Westminster Theological Seminary in California and teaches regularly in Ukraine at RITE Seminary.

Acknowledgments

(Original Publication 1999 by Legacy Press, San Diego)

A number of friends deserve special thanks for their help with this project. First of all, Art and Dan Miley at Legacy Press made the book's publication possible by first believing in the manuscript and then by putting their expertise and financial support behind it. Ron Durham made many helpful suggestions and lent substan- tive theological insight, and Christy Allen was indefatigable in her efforts to clean up my many errors and imprecisions.

Throughout the nine years from the book's inception as an idea to its publication, many encouragers stepped forward to keep me going. Special mention should be made of my dear pastor and his wife, George and Londa Miladin, who took me under their wing when I was going through difficult times. At one point, a simple note from Beverly Buffini was powerful enough to encourage me to finish the book's final 200 pages. And, of course, my wife, Amy, never ceased to be a help and encouragement to me.

Some others who deserve mention are, in alphabetical order: Bill Abrell, Michael and Laurie Arabe, Jerry and Teal Archer, Todd Archer, Ned Banning, my brother and his wife Bill and Roxanne Beasley, John Carson, Kim Cheatum, Chris and Jane Crane, John Cully, Joe Cusumano, Craig and Carol Farrington, Gene Getz, Dwight Johnson, Walt Henrichsen, Mike McFarland, Trudy McCoy, Jerry Moser, Andy Peterson, Phil and Mary Reinheimer, Steve Sammons, Rick and Jan Sanborn, Nova Smith, John Sowell, Tom and Cookie Sudberry, Skip Tschantz, and Jon and Trudy Verdick.

Thanks a lot, friends. This book belongs to us all.

Table of Contents

9

Preface

The Book Of Proverbs

Proverbs is a book of godly wisdom. Someone once described Proverbs as "the Ten Commandments in shoe leather." It often contains the very practical and homespun wisdom of secular proverbs, such as "a stitch in time saves nine" or "a fool and his money are soon parted." But the wisdom of Proverbs goes far beyond mere worldly wisdom. It contains the revealed truth of God, Creator of heaven and earth. Thus, as with any other of the 66 books of God's Word—the Bible—Proverbs needs to be approached with reverential awe, as we prayerfully ask the Holy Spirit to make it real to us that we might make application of its teaching to our daily lives. In doing so, God will guide our decision-making to His glory.

The book of Proverbs was written and/or edited principally by King Solomon hundreds of years before the birth of Christ. Nevertheless, it is a book in which Christ—the wisdom of God (1 Cor. 1:24)—is magnified. As in all of the other Old Testament books, Christ reigns preeminent. As you study, look for Him. (For a full examination of Proverbs' authorship and background, see the *Expositor's Bible Commentary*, in the bibliography.)

The Wisdom of Proverbs

While some groups of proverbs deal with a common subject, most proverbs stand alone. That is, the subject matter differs from one verse to the next. Most of Proverbs' verses are parallelisms, either antithetical, synthetic, or emblematic. For instance, Proverbs 10:4, "Lazy hands make a man poor, but diligent hands bring wealth," is an example of antithetical parallelism. Its two lines call our attention to both the good and bad results of some activity or truth. The second line of synthetic parallelism simply repeats the thought of the first line using similar words. For instance, Proverbs 11:7 says, "When a wicked man dies, his hope perishes; all he expected from his power comes to nothing." These types of parallelism, along with others, are typical of ancient Hebrew poetry.

The verses in *The Wisdom of Proverbs* are organized as they appear in the Bible. Each page features either a single verse or a group of verses sharing a common topic. The title of the page is a principle drawn from the verse or verses that states the central teaching. For instance, the main principle of Proverbs 10:4 is "Practice the Wisdom of Diligence." It is not the only principle that could be drawn from the verse, but it is intended to help you understand what the verse is calling you to do. Look for both the practical and the eternal lessons God has for you. Where a proverb has been repeated—such as those in 21:9, 21:19, and 25:24—separate principles have been drawn for each in order to focus on a different aspect of the proverb's lesson for us.

Next, a short devotion is followed by scriptural examples featuring men and women of both the Old and New Testaments who show us the results of following or ignoring the principle. Paul tells us in 1 Corinthians 10:6-11 that the personal examples given to us in Scripture should be a warning to us. The prophets, James says, should also serve as our examples (James 5:10). And Jesus, of course, is our shining example for righteous living (John

13:15; 1 Tim. 1:16; 1 Pet. 2:21).

Finally, a short prayer has been placed at the end of each page. This prayer makes application of each lesson and sums up what I believe the proverb is telling me. It may speak to you differently. That's great! Let the Holy Spirit speak to you and show you the proverb's proper application for your life. My suggested prayer is only a guideline for you.

Proverbs' Two Major Themes

Two major themes of Solomon's book are central to one's understanding of Proverbs. While other minor themes like the family, work, adultery, authority, gossip, etc., are woven throughout the book, these two themes are at its heart. They are "God and humans," and "the righteous and the wicked." To lack understanding of these central themes is to miss the point of most of the book and, indeed, the message of the entire Bible.

God and Humans

No study in anyone's life is more crucial than that of understanding who God is and, conversely, who humans are. Much of what ails our churches today can be attributed to our maunderstanding in these two areas. We typically attribute too little power to God, and too much to ourselves. We attribute some goodness to ourselves when there is none at all save that which God bestows (Matt. 19:17; Mark 10:18; Luke 18:19; Rom. 3:10-18). Only God is good, as Jesus testified to the rich young man.

On the pages of Solomon's book, you will see a God who is altogether infinite and holy. He is perfectly just and righteous, all-seeing and all-powerful. He is accomplishing His immutable purposes in every detail of His creation. People, on the other hand, are the "simpletons" of Proverbs to whom both the calls of wisdom and folly are made in chapter 9. Left alone—aside from the salvation provided by Christ—people want nothing to do with the holiness and goodness of God. Terms like "fool" and "wicked" and "scoffer" and "sluggard" are used in Proverbs to describe us. We humans are ultimately powerless—having only the power that God gives us—and yet we lift up our noses in pride and arrogance against Almighty God. Humankind's basic problem stems from this pride. We neither glorify God nor give Him thanks (Rom. 1:21). But it wasn't always this way. God created us in His own image (Gen. 1:26) for fellowship and friendship, with dignity, worth, and purpose. We were created to worship and glorify our Creator. But by one man's sin our anarchy against God began (Rom. 5:12). So, too, by one man's righteousness—the God-man Jesus—the grace of God overflowed into the world (Rom. 5:15). That brings us to the second of our two major themes.

The Righteous and the Wicked

As you study Proverbs, notice that there is no middle ground between these two categories of people. A person is in either one category or the other. He is either righteous or he is wicked. There is no one who is semi-righteous or somewhat wicked. (Compare these categories with those of Jesus in Matthew 25:32-33.)

Today's non-Christian might confuse the "righteous" or "wise" person of Proverbs with himself. He is greatly deceived. There is no person who does good. No, not even one (Rom. 3:12). Then who are the righteous? Those who have been reconciled to God through Christ's death. They are holy in His sight; justified before Him and without blemish; free from accusation and condemnation (Rom. 8:1; Col. 1:22). People are not righteous because of something they do. They are only righteous if God imputes to them by grace the righteousness of Christ (Eph. 2:8-9).

Christ offers His righteousness to all who simply believe on His name (John 3:16; Rom. 1:16-17). He died for sinners. If you are not now a believer, but feel drawn to Him, humbly repent of your rebellion. Ask Christ to enter your heart by faith and cleanse you from sin, giving you eternal life as a free gift of His grace. You will receive a new birth—a spiritual birth—which is the only qualification for being the "righteous" person of Proverbs (John 3:3-8).

This same grace which is offered freely to all now was also available to Solomon. In fact, we read in Genesis 15:6 that "Abram believed the Lord, and he credited it to him as righteousness." Trust in the Lord Jesus Christ and you will be saved. That is the key to righteousness. Faith's fruit is obedience, and the fruit of obedience is peace. Jesus offers to all who would call on His name the peace that passes all understanding (Phil. 4:7). Proverbs shows us pathways of that peace, through assisting us in making wise decisions in the daily struggles of our lives.

My former pastor, George Miladin, likens Proverbs to the "hard candy" of the Bible. He says that the verses of Solomon's book are not to be chewed up quickly and swallowed. Rather, they are to be turned over and over in the cheek, their sweetness and wisdom allowed to glide slowly over the tongue's taste buds. They are to be savored as we are given the Spirit's insight as to how each verse is best applied to our lives. All *The Wisdom of Proverbs* seeks to do is to remove the wrapper from the candy. I hope that the pure sweetness of God's Word will guide you all the days of your life down His straight and righteous paths of peace.

Bob Beasley
Hartville, Ohio

Chapter One

Wisdom: What Is It and Why Do We Need It?

Godly wisdom brings joy. It's as simple as that. I define godly wisdom as "doing the law of God." James said in 1:22, "Do not merely listen to the word, and so deceive yourselves. Do what it says." Likewise, Jesus said, "If you love me, you will do what I command" (John 14:26). Why? So that we might be burdened with a bunch of rules and regulations? No. Jesus came that we might "have life, and have it to the full" (John 10:10). In other words, Jesus came that His sheep might experience the joy of fellowship with God. That is the greatest joy imaginable and the only joy really worth having. This joy comes through obedience to God's law.

In Old Testament days, many people got the idea that one had to keep the law of God perfectly in order to be saved. Paul calls those who believed this way "prisoners" of the law (Gal. 3:23). But Christ came to set us free from such slavery (Gal. 5:1). If we "are led by the Spirit, [we] are not under law" (Gal. 5:18). Those who belong to Christ are saved by faith and not by the works of the law (Rom. 3:20, 22). Therefore, the law is no longer our master. Rather, the law is our friend. It is our trusted guide to a life filled with indescribable joy. As you travel the pages of Proverbs, I pray that you will do so in anticipation of the joy that is yours in Christ Jesus.

Decide to Walk the Road of Wisdom

1) The proverbs of Solomon son of David, king of Israel: 2) for attaining wisdom and discipline; for understanding words of insight; 3) for acquiring a disciplined and prudent life, doing what is right and just and fair; 4) for giving prudence to the simple, knowledge and discretion to the young— 5) let the wise listen and add to their learning, and let the discerning get guidance— 6) for under- standing proverbs and parables, the sayings and riddles of the wise (Prov. 1:1-6).

Many roads in life promise a future of success and happiness. But there is only one road of sure success. It is found in God's Word—and particularly in the proverbs of Solomon. Other roads lead ultimately to difficulty, defeat, and despair. They promise excitement, peace of mind, and fulfillment, but they deliver the opposite. Only the wisdom that our Creator has for us bears the ultimate fruits of joy, peace, and life.

Many benefits of godly wisdom are listed in the verses above. They all boil down to one: good decision-making. An older person looks back to see that life has been a progression of many decisions. Some seem unimportant, but even those "small" decisions are extremely important, because they team up with other decisions to become pathways, then highways.

Study the proverbs and hide them in your heart. Put them into practice daily, praying for God's guidance. Your godly decision making will put you onto the higher road of obedience that leads to the joy and peace that pass all understanding.

Scriptural Examples

Rehoboam. As Solomon was David's son, Rehoboam was Solomon's son. What a difference a generation can make! Faced with a decision that would determine the future of Israel, this foolish young man tossed aside the wise teachings of his father, and of the elders, and traveled his own road to ruin (1 Kings 12).

Prayer of Application

Father, thank You for Your Word that speaks its truth so clearly to us. Please send Your Spirit, Lord, as we begin this study of Proverbs, to the end that Jesus may be glorified.

Fear the Lord

The fear of the Lord is the beginning of knowledge, but fools despise wisdom and discipline (Prov. 1:7).

In verses 1 through 6, we looked at decision making. Here we come face to face with our first decision. What shall we do with God? If one doesn't get this decision right, all the decisions that follow will be wrong as well.

As people study the Bible they begin to see something startling about our Creator. There is no middle ground with God. On the one hand, He is a God of ultimate wrath, and on the other, a God of ultimate love. Our God is altogether righteous and holy, and He demands that we reflect His character.

What does it mean to "fear the Lord?" That day when He opened my eyes and I first beheld His holiness over my sinfulness, I shivered at the realization that there was nothing I could do to avoid His wrath. Then, when I understood that God Himself had provided the solution in Jesus Christ, and He lovingly held out His salvation to me as a free gift, my trembling fear turned to an affectionate reverence and awe.

Many who are in pews today are practical atheists. They don't tremble at God, and neither do they hold Him in affectionate awe. They are the fools of whom this proverb speaks. Don't walk with them. Fear the Lord, and be obedient to His every commandment. That fear is the beginning of wisdom's path.

Scriptural Examples

Korah. This Levite and his followers despised the leadership of Moses and Aaron. In their insolence, they showed their lack of fear of God. God opened the earth and swallowed Korah, as his followers faced fire from heaven (Num. 16:1-34).

Judas. There has never been a greater fool than this. He walked with the Lord throughout His earthly ministry, and yet despised His wisdom and discipline (Matt. 27:3-5).

Prayer of Application

Dear God, thank You for Your Word that makes us tremble at Your power and wrath. But thank You most of all for Your Son who gives us His righteousness. May I follow Him always.

Heed Your Parents' Instruction

8) Listen, my son, to your father's instruction and do not forsake your mother's teaching. 9) They will be a garland to grace your head and a chain to adorn your neck (Prov. 1:8-9).

I have a younger sister who lives in Hawaii. One of the great joys of visiting her there is to receive a beautiful, delicate lei. These are chains of aromatic flowers, strung together as garlands to grace the neck of the wearer. This proverb likens our parents' instruction to such fragrant and colorful leis.

The fifth commandment of God, found in Exodus 20:12, is the first that deals with our relationships with other humans. It is the foundational commandment requiring obedience to all those in authority over us, whether they are in the family, the church (Heb. 13:17), or in the secular government (Rom. 13:1). Those in authority over us are God's earthly representatives to us.

As adults we are no longer under parental authority. Still, we should not forsake our parents' wise counsel. I grew up in a Christian home, and though my parents are now with the Lord, their teachings still echo in my ears.

What a responsibility we have both as parents and children. As parents, we are to raise our children in the knowledge and admonition of the Lord, and as children, we are to obey the teaching of those who raise us. May God help us and have mercy upon us as we commit this process to Him.

Scriptural Examples

Hophni and Phinehas. These wicked men disgraced their righteous father, Eli, by their ungodliness. They would not listen to their father's rebuke, so God eventually put them both to death (1 Sam. 2:12, 22-24; 4:11).

Adrammelech and Sharezer. These wicked sons of King Sennacherib committed the ultimate sin against their father when they cut him down with the sword (2 Kings 19:37).

Prayer of Application

O Lord, thank You for godly parents who raise their children in Your ways. Help us children to be obedient to their teaching, and to the instruction of all those in authority.

Don't Get in with the Wrong Crowd

10) My son, if sinners entice you, do not give in to them. 11) If they say, "Come along with us; let's lie in wait for someone's blood, let's waylay some harmless soul; 12) let's swallow them alive, like the grave, and whole, like those who go down to the pit; 13) we will get all sorts of valuable things and fill our houses with plunder; 14) throw in your lot with us, and we will share a common purse" — 15) my son, do not go along with them, do not set foot on their paths; 16) for their feet rush into sin, they are swift to shed blood (Prov. 1:10-16).

I saw a TV show recently about Sicily, the island at the southern tip of Italy. Young men there will sometimes commit murder to prove themselves worthy to join organized crime. I thought of the gangs here in America, the membership requirements of which often include sinful acts. I also thought back over my own life and the influences of youthful "friends" that led to habitual sin in my life.

When God took the nation Israel into the Promised Land, He told them to be careful to drive the pagans that were there out of the Land (Num. 33:53-55). If they didn't, the pagans would become a snare, and lead Israel astray. So also we Christians should beware of developing intimate friendships with non-Christians (2 Cor. 6:14). We should be diligent to teach our children to choose their friends carefully. Today's choices will bear tomorrow's fruit.

Scriptural Examples

The crowd in the desert. Aaron foolishly went along with the crowd and made a golden calf. After they had worshipped the calf, they indulged in pagan revelry (Ex. 32:1-6).

The crowd in Jerusalem. Many who welcomed Jesus as a king now turned against Him and shouted, "Crucify Him!" They were swept along by the others, not realizing what they were doing (Matt. 27:15-26).

Prayer of Application

Father, help me to discern evil paths and avoid them. Instead, help me to walk the pathways of Your wisdom and find my close friends and associates among Your people.

Don't Set a Trap for Yourself

17) How useless to spread a net in full view of all the birds! 18) These men lie in wait for their own blood; they waylay only themselves! 19) Such is the end of all who go after ill-gotten gain; it takes away the lives of those who get it (Prov.1:17-19).

"What goes around, comes around" is a modern-day secular proverb that speaks to this principle. It means that whatever you do, your behavior will eventually catch up with you. Establish this principle early on in life: "You can never, ever get away with sin." The one we truly hurt when we sin is ourselves. You spread the net in full view of the one bird it will catch — you! Remember this and don't be deceived: "God cannot be mocked. A man reaps what he sows" (Gal. 6:7). Hosea 8:7 says of sinners, "They sow the wind and reap the whirlwind."

Today in our land, many who have sown the wind of sexual sin are reaping the tornado of AIDS. What those who disregard God's law against adultery and fornication fail to see is the advent of new diseases like AIDS and some strains of herpes that thwart the efforts of modern medicine to find a cure. Stay on the straight path, and don't follow those who only set a trap for themselves in their disobedience of God's law.

Scriptural Examples

Ahab and Jezebel. This wicked pair conspired to take Naboth's vineyard. By false witnesses they had Naboth stoned to death. Both reaped the tornado of death (1 Kings 21:4-24).

Haman. This vile character built a gallows on which to hang Mordecai. Ironically, King Xerxes used the same gallows to stretch Haman's neck (Est. 7:9).

Judas. Spreading what he thought was a net to catch the Lord Jesus, Judas only netted himself, and became a paradigm throughout the history of the world for treachery and deceit (Matt. 26:14-16; 27:3-5).

Prayer of Application

Sovereign Lord, help me to fully understand that any sin in my life is cosmic rebellion against You. Help me to warn others of the foolishness of wandering from Your righteous pathway.

Heed the Shouts of God's Wisdom

20) Wisdom calls aloud in the street, she raises her voice in the public squares; 21) at the head of the noisy streets she cries out, in the gateways of the city she makes her speech: 22) "How long will you simple ones love your simple ways? How long will mockers delight in mockery and fools hate knowledge? 23) If you had responded to my rebuke, I would have poured out my heart to you and made my thoughts known to you" (Prov. 1:20-23).

Who is this "Wisdom" who calls? It is the very voice of the God of creation. David speaks of the elements of the created order literally shouting of God's existence, of His personhood, omnipotence, oneness, reason, holiness, and beauty (Ps. 19:1-4). Many people choose not to hear this voice that goes out even to the uttermost reaches of the universe (Rom. 1:20).

If, by grace, you respond to God's natural revelation, God will make more of His thoughts known to you (Prov. 1:23). He will reveal His special revelation to you: Jesus Christ and the Holy Scriptures. These Words make people wise unto salvation (2 Tim. 2:15). But even the knowledge of this higher level of revelation is despised by fools.

How long will the simple love their ways? Until the Spirit of God gives them new birth. I thank God that He did that for me. How about you? Have you responded to Wisdom's shouts?

Scriptural Examples

John the Baptist. John urged people to turn from their simple ways and their foolish mockery. Likewise, the whole creation shouts of the One who brought it all into being, and sustains it by His powerful Word (Luke 3:4; Heb. 1:2-3).

The truth suppressors. These people know the truth of God but suppress it in unrighteousness. So God gives them over to their own ways and they enter a downward spiral of their own making. They reject Christ (Rom. 1:20-32).

Prayer of Application

Creator God, for many years I chose my own simple ways which mocked You and dismissed Your very being. Thank You, Lord, for opening my ears and giving me new eyes to see Jesus.

Beware of the Laughter of God's Wisdom

24) But since you rejected me when I called and no one gave heed when I stretched out my hand, 25) since you ignored all my advice and would not accept my rebuke, 26) I in turn will laugh at your disaster; I will mock when calamity overtakes you — 27) when calamity overtakes you like a storm, when disaster sweeps over you like a whirlwind, when distress and trouble overwhelm you. 28) Then they will call to me but I will not answer; they will look for me but will not find me. 29) Since they hated knowledge and did not choose to fear the Lord, 30) since they would not accept my advice and spurned my rebuke, 31) they will eat the fruit of their ways and be filled with the fruit of their schemes (Prov. 1:24-31).

There is a sense in which God gives every man and woman on this earth exactly what he or she wants. God plants in some a desire to know Him and His wisdom. For these, every event in their lives moves them closer to that desire being fulfilled, as they draw closer to their God (Rom. 8:29). But God allows some to follow the natural desires of their own hearts and even though He holds out His hand to them and tenderly calls (v. 24 above), they "ignore His advice and reject His rebuke" (v. 30). In the end, they will "eat the fruit of their ways and be filled with the fruit of their schemes" (v. 3). God will laugh at their disaster (v. 26). Don't be like them. "Choose to fear the Lord" (v. 29), and receive His free salvation.

Scriptural Examples

The Idolators. This huge group of people refuse to worship the Creator, preferring instead to worship objects that they have created themselves. Why? Because they want to be in control—to be a law unto themselves. Idolaters pick and choose the attributes of God that are appealing, then form an idol who bows down to them instead. They attempt to cast off all knowledge of the Creator, and hence His restraints, even though they know they invoke His laughter and His sentence of death (Rom. 1:18-32).

Prayer of Application

Sovereign Lord, enable me to heed wisdom's voice, and by it to warn those who would reject You. Strengthen me to tell them of the certain doom toward which their paths move inexorably.

Obey God's Wisdom and Live at Peace

32) For the waywardness of the simple will kill them, and the complacency of fools will destroy them; 33) but whoever listens to me will live in safety and be at ease, without fear of harm
(Prov. 1:32-33).

Here are the two marks of the fool. First, he is disobedient to the light God has given him. He is self-willed. This path will kill him, even as God has promised the "wages of sin is death" (Rom. 6:23). Second, the foolish person is complacent, or self-content. He has no need of a Savior. He thinks he's basically a good person whom God will gladly welcome into heaven.

But God's wisdom is diametrically opposed to this simpleton's. God demands righteousness of every person. And why not? How can a perfect, just, and holy God have fellowship with anyone who bears the stain of sin? The person who obeys God's wisdom has God's righteousness imputed to him as a gift of grace through Jesus Christ (Rom. 5:17).

This imputed righteousness restores fellowship between people and their Creator. Jesus Christ came to earth to reconcile us to the Father by "making peace through his blood, shed on the cross" (Col. 1:20; Eph. 2:15). We who have been saved by grace through faith need not fear harm (Luke 12:4-5).

Scriptural Examples

The home builders. One man built on the rock of God's wisdom. His house was secure even when the floods came. The other built on the shifting sands of man's wisdom. The onrushing waters brought disaster (Matt. 7:24-27).

The rich young ruler. This man trusted in his self-righteousness. He claimed that he kept the Law of Moses, but Jesus discerned that he loved the riches of this world more than the true riches of God. The man rejected Jesus' advice and went sadly on his way to destruction (Matt. 19:22).

Prayer of Application

Dear God, thank You for the imputed righteousness of Christ, without which there would be no fellowship with You, only a fearful expectation of the wrath which is to come.

Chapter Two

The Benefits of Wisdom

I have spent some of my working years in sales. We salespeople are trained to present the benefits of whatever we are selling in such a way as to provoke a positive response from potential customers. In addition to pointing out the benefits of our product or service, salespeople also answer questions (or objections), make known the negative results of inaction, and supply testimonials from third parties that reinforce the positive. Interestingly, these first chapters of Proverbs follow that same pattern. They are a glimpse of a father selling his children on the benefits of following God's righteous way rather than their own sinful way.

Notice in Proverbs 2:1-6 that godly wisdom is readily available. All one needs to do is to ask God for it. Memorization is a component of one's search (v. 1), but prayer is extremely important (vv. 2-4). Wisdom brings victory (v. 7), protection (vv. 8-11), and is "pleasant to [the] soul" (v. 10). Wisdom will protect one from the wiles of wicked people (vv. 12-15), and from the seduction of the adulterer whose pathways lead only to death. In verses 21-22 we see that wisdom brings stability in life. The wise in heart "will walk in the ways of good men and keep to the paths of the righteous." Such paths are stable and secure, free from ultimate trouble and full of joy.

Cry Out to God for His Wisdom

1) My son, if you accept my words and store up my commands within you, 2) turning your ear to wisdom and applying your heart to understanding, 3) and if you call out for insight and cry aloud for understanding, 4) and if you look for it as for silver and search for it as for hidden treasure, 5) then you will understand the fear of the Lord and find the knowledge of God (Prov. 2:1-5).

These verses are a map for the greatest treasure imaginable. The directional arrows are the verbs. Notice them. First, the treasure hunter needs to accept wisdom's words (v. 1). The serious student will diligently study God's Word and receive it by faith as truth. Next, he is to store up commandments within him (v. 1). He is to hide the Word in his heart (Ps. 119:11). Then, the student of the Word turns his ear to wisdom (v. 2), and applies his heart to understanding (v. 2). This is not academic research, but a spiritual quest. Then in verse 3, we find the student on his knees crying out in prayer for understanding and insight (James 1:5). Finally, in verse 4, he keeps on looking and searching for it as hidden treasure (Matt. 7:7).

And what is the treasure that the student so diligently seeks? It is to know the One True God. And what will we find when we come to know Him? We will find that His name is Jesus, who is the same El Shaddai and Yahweh of fearsome majesty. He is our shield, and our exceeding great reward (Gen. 15:1). He is the treasure hidden from the world (2 Cor. 4:3-4), but revealed to those who seek Him in His Word and in prayer. He is, in fact, wisdom personified (Prov. 8; 1 Cor. 1:30).

Scriptural Examples

Daniel. Here is a man who knew the fearsome majesty of God, and yet had an intimate personal relationship with his treasure—that same God. When people came to him, they found him in prayer, calling out to God for help (Dan. 6:11).

Prayer of Application

Father, how I want to know Jesus, to fix my thoughts upon Him and find the treasure of joy that He has for me. Dear God, supply me with the wisdom that can only be found in Christ.

Find the Key to God's Treasure

6) For the Lord gives wisdom, and from his mouth come knowledge and understanding. 7) He holds victory in store for the upright, he is a shield to those whose walk is blameless, 8) for he guards the course of the just and protects the way of his faithful ones. 9) Then you will understand what is right and just and fair — every good path (Prov. 2:6-9).

Suppose we find the treasure of the last verses buried in the sand, but the chest is locked. We need the key to it. Education and brains will not find the key. Those who have Ph.D.'s in theology can be further from opening the treasure than those who lack any formal education. What makes the difference? It is this: We are what we are only by the grace of God (1 Cor. 15:10). His free gift is the key.

I rejected Christianity in college because I saw it as a religion where people tried to climb over the backs of others to be saved by their good works. How wrong I was. Without the grace of God all our works are like filthy rags (Isa. 64:6). Unwittingly, I had rejected every religion *but* Christianity!

We can work and study until we're blue in the face, but if we don't have the saving grace of God, it will all be in vain. How does one get the key? Ask Him for it. It's free!

Scriptural Examples

The Pharisees. They looked beautiful on the outside. But Jesus showed us their insides which were full of "dead men's bones and everything unclean." Why? Because they sought righteousness not by God's grace through faith, but by their own works (Matt. 23:27-28; Rom. 10:1-3).

Paul. This Pharisee was, like the others, living on the basis of his own efforts to please God. Then by the grace of God on the Damascus Road he was given the key to real understanding and knowledge (Acts 9:1-15; Phil. 3:3-9).

Prayer of Application

Dear Lord, thank You for Your free gift of grace, which exceeds mere mercy by opening up the riches of your eternal salvation. Help me to tell others of the key to victory: Your wonderful grace.

Find Wisdom's Ultimate Protection

10) For wisdom will enter your heart, and knowledge will be pleasant to your soul. 11) Discretion will protect you, and understanding will guard you (Prov. 2:10-11).

Our diligence in mining the Word of God for wisdom brings knowledge. But notice that verse 10 says "wisdom will enter your *heart,* and knowledge will be pleasant to your soul." This is the work of God's grace, and it makes all the difference. Out of a person's *heart* come the issues of life (Prov. 4:23; Matt. 15:19).

And what are these "issues of life"? Several years ago, comedian Mel Brooks did a skit with Carl Reiner called "The 2,000-Year-Old Man." When Mel (who played the millenarian) was asked what motivated people 2,000 years ago, he replied, "Fear, mostly." For the unregenerate person, the fearsome issue of life is protection. That is one reason he seeks earthly wealth, desires job security, eats health foods, and the like, because he fears poverty, death, sickness, loss of love, loneliness, punishment, etc. He seeks protection in fleeting things that can never really protect him.

But the Bible tells us "perfect love drives out fear"(1 John 4:18). The Christian's motivation is to be this perfect love that God's grace has put into his quickened heart (Ezek. 11:19-20). This perfect love seeks to glorify God, to love Him with all of his heart, soul, strength, and mind (Deut. 6:5; Luke 10:27). He is to love his neighbor even as he loves himself. The love of Christ frees us to be the kind of people God wants us to be.

Ultimate protection for the regenerate person is guaranteed and is received by faith. We cry out "Daddy!" to our Protector-God (Rom. 8:15). And as our earthly daddies should protect us in our infancy and childhood, so our heavenly Father protects us through His marvelous grace. Does this mean we won't have trouble and problems in this life? No way. But through all circumstances we can trust in Him to accomplish His purposes (Rom. 8:28-29).

Prayer of Application

Heavenly Father, thank You for Your protecting fence around me. Even though I walk through the valley of the shadow of death, Your rod and Your staff will protect me forever.

Find Wisdom's Escape from Evil Men

12) Wisdom will save you from the ways of wicked men, from men whose words are perverse, 13) who leave the straight paths to walk in dark ways, 14) who delight in doing wrong and rejoice in the perverseness of evil, 15) whose paths are crooked and who are devious in their ways (Prov. 2:12-15).

In one sense, God's grace gives the regenerate person supernatural, real protection in this world and for eternity. But in another sense, God's practical wisdom seated in our hearts by study, meditation, and memorization keeps us from trouble.

Jesus told His disciples as He sent them out to the lost sheep of Israel that they should be as "shrewd as snakes and as innocent as doves" (Matt. 10:5, 16). We, too, are to lead innocent lives which allow us to live at peace with everyone (Gal. 5:22).

Verse 13 above, in speaking of those "who leave the straight paths to walk in dark ways," reminds me of some false preachers who distribute evil on television. Verse 14 speaks of those who get their kicks from their evil ways. Such people abound in our society. In God's practical book of Proverbs, we learn ways of avoiding the traps of these evil ones.

Scriptural Examples

David from Saul. King Saul was jealous of David. Saul had "left the straight path to walk in dark ways," and vainly sought David's life. By the grace of God, David's wisdom protected him from the evil king (1 Sam. 23:7-29).

Esther and Mordecai from Haman. Haman set out to kill all the Jews living in Babylon. But through a combination of Mordecai's foresight, Esther's fortitude, and the providence of God, the vile Haman was thwarted (the book of Esther).

Mary and Joseph from Herod. Herod, the wicked king, sought to kill baby Jesus. But Joseph was warned by God to take the baby and go to Egypt (Matt. 2:13-14).

Prayer of Application

Father, thank You for Your promise to keep us safe from the wiles of evil people. I pray that through Your Word acting upon my heart and mind, I will avoid the traps set for the unwary.

Flee from Both Kinds of Adultery

16) It [wisdom] will save you also from the adulteress, from the wayward wife with her seductive words, 17) who has left the partner of her youth and ignored the covenant she made before God. 18) For her house leads down to death and her paths to the spirits of the dead. 19) None who go to her return or attain the paths of life (Prov. 2:16-19).

As Jesus taught in Matthew 5:27-30, two kinds of adultery exist: the physical and the spiritual. In Jeremiah 3:8-10, God speaks of adulterous Israel defiling the land with gods of wood and stone. Idolatry is spiritual adultery (Ezek. 23:37), the worship of the created rather than the Creator (Rom. 1:25).

We live in a time when adultery of both kinds is commonplace. Spiritual adultery today is manifested largely in two ways. First, there is an overarching love for the material things of the world, its pleasures, comforts, riches, and power (James 4:3-5). Love of the things of the world is opposed to the love of the Father.

The other manifestation of spiritual adultery is in the smorgasbord approach to knowing God. Many people don't want to hear sound doctrine, but will hire teachers who will make them comfortable (2 Tim. 4:3). It's as if they were in front of a salad bar, i.e.: "I'll take some love, but I'll pass on the wrath. Mercy is nice, but I don't want any holiness." We either take God as He is in His Word, or we don't take Him at all.

Scriptural Examples

Joseph and Potiphar's wife. Today, we might call Joseph a "hunk." He was well-built and handsome, we're told, and far removed from family and friends. He was sold to a wealthy Egyptian named Potiphar who put Joseph in charge of Potiphar's entire household. Potiphar's wife tried to seduce him day after day. But Joseph ran out, saying, "How then could I do such a wicked thing and sin against God?" (Gen. 39:1-20)

Prayer of Application

Father, protect me from one who would lure me into sin and from the smooth talker who from his pulpit of lies leads people on paths to death.

Find Wisdom's Path to Eternal Life

20) Thus you will walk in the ways of good men and keep to the paths of the righteous. For the upright will live in the land, and the blameless will remain in it; 22) but the wicked will be cut off from the land, and the unfaithful will be torn from it (Prov. 2:20-22).

The hope of the Jew has always been in the land that God promised to Abraham, Isaac, and Jacob (Gen. 12:7). Aging Abramham was promised that he and Sarah would have a child from whom would come a people beyond number. All nations on earth would be blessed (Gen. 22:17-18). Abraham believed God and God counted his faith as righteousness (Gen. 15:6).

The writer to the Hebrews speaks of entering the Promised Land as entering "God's rest." Beginning at chapter 3, verse 15, he writes of those who rebelled against God and perished. He goes on to speak of a "new rest" for the people of God (Heb. 4:10). This rest is for those who, like Abraham, believed the words of God and were justified, saved by their faith (Rom. 3:20-22).

We are saved by faith just as Abraham and all of the Old Testament saints were (Rom. 4:16; Eph. 2:8-9). But saving faith is shown by what we do. As Abraham believed God's promise of a son and acted upon it, so saving faith always leads to works of obedience (James 2:14-26). They will "walk in the ways of good men and keep to the paths of the righteous" (Prov. 2:20).

Scriptural Examples

Joshua, Caleb, and the Israelites. At Kadesh-Barnea Moses sent 12 spies into the Promised Land. They told of a place of abundant harvests and wealth. But there was a hitch. The men in the land were giant, formidable opponents. Two of the spies, Caleb and Joshua, had faith in God's promise and wanted to lead the Israelites into the land, but the other spies discouraged the people. As a result Israel wandered in the desert for 40 years until that generation had died (Deut. 1:19-39).

Prayer of Application

Father, give me the faith of Joshua and Caleb, who when faced with the spectacle of a large and dangerous opponent walked by faith—not by sight—and entered into Your rest.

Chapter Three

More Advantages
of Being Wise

In Chapter Three, the father gives his child more reasons to search for wisdom. To remember the father's teaching and to internalize his commands is to find prosperity and a long life (vv. 1-2). To follow "love and faithfulness"—the summation of God's law—will win one "favor and a good name in the sight of God and man" (vv. 3-4). In verses 5 and 6 we are shown that faithfulness to God's ways will result in God's perfect guidance down the roadways of life. Godly wisdom will bring with it "health to your body and nourishment to your bones" (vv. 7-8). Verses 9 and 10 promise prosperity linked to one's honor of God with tithes and offerings.

The promise of God's loving discipline to those who delight Him is given in verses 11 and 12. In verses 13 through 18 wisdom is portrayed as more valuable than precious jewels, and we find the promise of the "tree of life." Wisdom will bring with it confidence and sureness of foot, and will allow its possessor fearless courage in the face of adversity (vv. 22-26). In verses 27 through 32 we are given some examples of wisdom in action. Given in contrast are the ways of the violent and perverse person. Finally, we see the ultimate results of wisdom versus foolishness. Wisdom brings blessing, grace, and honor while fools receive cursing, mocking, and shame (vv. 33-35).

Find Wisdom's True Prosperity

1) My son, do not forget my teaching, but keep my commands in your heart, 2) for they will prolong your life many years and bring you prosperity (Prov. 3:1-2).

The path of wisdom, with its admonishments to purity and moderation, may well lead some to longer life on this earth. But what does Solomon mean by "prosperity" in verse 2? Does God want us all to be rich in this world's goods?

The Christian has been resurrected to new life, a life of true prosperity (Rom. 6:4-7). No longer are we slaves to disobedience. No longer are we separated from the love of God (Rom. 8:39). No longer are we under the bondage of guilt (Heb. 10:26-27), or fear (Heb. 2:15), or the law (Rom. 7:4). And no longer do we walk under the shadow of eternal death (Ps. 23:4).

On the contrary, we have life as those who have already died and who have been resurrected to a new and living hope (Gal. 2: 20); to a new desire to follow after the ways of righteousness (Rom. 6:18); to fellowship with God (1 Cor. 1:9); to a lifting of guilt and shame(1 John 1:9); to an absence of fear (Isa. 43:1); and to an eternity as joint-heirs with Christ in all the riches of God's glory (Rom. 8:17). Now what could possibly constitute greater prosperity than that?

Scriptural Examples

Barzillai. This old man was not only blessed by the Lord with long life, but he was blessed with great wealth as well. His prosperit included friendship with King David, who blessed Barzillai for his faithfulness to the crown (2 Sam. 19:31-39).

Jehoiada. Jehoiada was a priest of the Lord and an advisor to Joash, king of Judah. During Jehoiada's life, Joash did what was right in the eyes of the Lord and prosperity surrounded Jerusalem. He was a man who understood the path to true prosperity (2 Chron. 24:1-6).

Prayer of Application

Father, what great and precious promises are in Your Word. You have given us an eternal prosperity that is beyond anything imaginable. Thank You for Your marvelous grace.

Find Wisdom's Good Name

3) Let love and faithfulness never leave you; bind them around your neck, write them on the tablet of your heart. 4) Then you will win favor and a good name in the sight of God and man (Prov. 3:3-4).

The "love and faithfulness" of verse 3 above is translated "truth and mercy" in the KJV. Jesus was full of "grace and truth" (John 1:17). Just as the Lord exhibited these virtues, so also are we to reflect them in all of our thoughts and actions. Together, they are the perfection and wisdom of God. Divided, as they may easily be, the lack of one lessens the efficacy of the other.

Suppose a person shows mercy but doesn't give out the truth? If we feed a homeless man one day, but then fail to give the man the gospel, our mercy is diminished. On the other hand, if we give out the gospel without a corresponding loving concern for an individual's physical needs, our words are as a "resounding gong or a clanging cymbal" (1 Cor. 13:1-3).

And what will be the end result of our binding these twin perfections upon our necks and writing them upon our hearts? It is to win favor and honor and "a good name in the sight of God and man." (See also Prov. 22:1; Eccl. 7:1.)

Scriptural Examples

The good and faithful servants. Three servants were each entrusted with large sums of money and told to invest it in their master's absence. The first two did as they were told, and received a good name. The master said, "Well done, good and faithful servant!" (Matt. 25:14-23)

The wicked, lazy servant. The third servant hid his master's money. He didn't even put it in the bank in order to draw interest. His faithlessness wasn't honored (Matt. 25:24-28).

Enoch. The father of Methuselah "walked with God." He pleased God by his faithfulness. God took Enoch home before he tasted death (Heb. 11:5-6).

Prayer of Application

Father, help me to reflect the mercy and truth of Christ in all of my dealings on this earth. I want to hear Him say, "Thou good and faithful servant, enter into the joy of your Lord."

Find Wisdom's Straight Path

5) Trust in the Lord with all your heart and lean not on your own understanding; 6) in all your ways acknowledge him and he will make your paths straight (Prov. 3:5-6).

Many of us list these verses as some of our favorites. And yet, do we really understand what they are saying to us?

First, we are to trust the Sovereign Lord with every fiber of our beings, putting the full weight of our cares, worries and problems on Him (1 Peter 5:7; Matt. 11:28-30). We are to place our trust solely in God Almighty and His Word (Job 13:15a). This is easy to say, but very difficult to do. It runs counter to our sin nature and upbringing. Many are raised to be self-reliant, but self-reliance is condemned by God (Prov. 28:26). Self-reliance is the province of the fool, not the wise man. It is idolatry.

How can we trust Him fully? Verse 6 shows us the way. The word "acknowledge" in that translation is better rendered "know"(Kidner, p. 63). To "know" God is to have intimate fellowship with Him. In prayer, we are to consistently study and ingest His Word (2 Tim. 2:15), growing daily in our knowledge of Him (2 Peter 3:18). The more we truly know Him, the more we will trust Him, and less in ourselves or others.

We who have trusted God for our salvation and our eternal security, how can we not therefore trust Him for all things (Rom. 8:32)? Let us then get up on our feet and run the straight path set out before us, trusting only in Jesus, who is the author and the perfector of our faith (Heb. 12:1-2).

Scriptural Examples

Daniel. Daniel's trust lay completely in his God. Three times a day he prayerfully sought God's face for help and sustenance. Wicked men tried to use his faith against him, but even in the den of lions God had Daniel on a straight path. Later, Daniel's enemies and their entire families found themselves on the lions' menu (Dan. 6:11-24).

Prayer of Application

Dear Lord, help me to grasp the truth of these verses in its full meaning and power, to the end that I would trust You fully in every area of my life. Help me to know You more each day.

Find Wisdom's Healthy Body

7) Do not be wise in your own eyes; fear the Lord and shun evil. 8) This will bring health to your body and nourishment to your bones (Prov. 3:7-8).

We've all known someone who was "a legend in his own mind"—wise in his own eyes. But the command is to "fear the Lord and shun evil." These are opposite sides of the same coin. If we honor the Lord, we will hate sin. When we turn to Christ for salvation, we turn away from sin (Prov.14:27; Rom. 12:9). Christ and sin are like oil and water; they don't mix.

God's love always seeks what is best for us. Sin does not. There are both eternal and temporal consequences of sin. For instance, drunkenness can produce cirrhosis of the liver, cancer, car crashes, divorce, and abuse toward others. The list could go on and on.

Health clubs abound in America as people seek physical fitness. These places look to me like 14th century torture chambers with their heavy iron, stationary bicycles, and rowing machines. Now all this is fine, but I belong to a different kind of health club. It's called a church. Within my health club I learn to fear the Lord and to live according to His commandments. While this doesn't guarantee that I'll always be in good health, it's a far better way than any that will ever be invented by humans.

Scriptural Examples

Gehazi. After Elisha's healing of Naaman, the prophet's servant ran after the visitor seeking the payment that Elisha had refused. Because of his sin, Gehazi was stricken with leprosy, like Naaman, who had been healed. Gehazi did not "fear the Lord and shun evil" (2 Kings 5:1-27).

Uzziah. This king of Judah had feared the Lord, but became prideful in his latter years and sinned when he burned incense in the temple. God sent upon Uzziah the same leprosy that Gehazi had received, but it never healed (2 Chron. 26:5; 16-23).

Prayer of Application

Father, help me to meet You each day in reverence and awe, and to follow Your leadership in all things, not allowing sin a foothold in my life. Surely it will mean health and peace for me.

Find Wisdom's Secret to True Riches

9) Honor the Lord with your wealth, with the firstfruits of all your crops; 10) then your barns will be filled to overflowing, and your vats will brim over with new wine (Prov. 3:9-10).

The "first fruits" (or tithes) were consecrated to God by the Israelites under the Law of Moses. It was a testimony to God's mighty hand in bringing the nation out of the land of bondage and into the Promised Land (Ex. 13:11-14). The offering brought rich temporal blessings from God. But what about today? Should we tithe, and what benefits are we promised?

There are two sides to the question. While some say that the tithe is still in effect, others disagree. They argue that under the Law, the Israelites were like children under a schoolmaster (Gal. 3:24 KJV), while the new covenant treats us as adults (Gal. 3:25). They say the matter is left up to the individual's circumstances and conscience. God no longer wants a mere 10 percent, He owns it all, they argue, and the question is, how much shall we keep?

Unlike Israel, we are not promised worldly wealth. In Luke 16:11, Jesus makes a distinction between temporal wealth and "true riches." True riches bring understanding of God's mysteries (Col. 2:2); met needs (Phil. 4:19); strengthened inner beings (Eph. 3:16); an eternal inheritance (Eph. 1:11); and the wisdom and knowledge of God (Rom. 11:33). This is the bottom line: that we affirm our trust in God by generous giving to His kingdom. Thereby we know the true riches of Jesus.

Bless your pastor, your congregation, yourself, and indeed the world, as you honor God by your faithful giving.

Scriptural Examples

The poor widow. She put in only a fraction of what the rich were contributing, but Jesus honored her as He said that in her poverty she had put in more than all the others. She had given all she had. Should we do less than she? (Mark 12:41-44)

Prayer of Application

Dear God, keep me from presuming upon the freedom that I have in Christ and forgetting that I owe You all that I am and ever will be. Open my heart and my wallet, that I may honor You.

In Discipline, Find the Father's Love

11) My son, do not despise the Lord's discipline and do not resent his rebuke, 12) because the Lord disciplines those he loves, as a father the son he delights in (Prov. 3:11-12).

I once heard someone say, "Come to Jesus, and all your probe- elms will be solved." That is very misleading. Nowhere are we told that we will not have problems on this earth. In fact, Jesus says, "You will have trouble" (John 16:33). I saw my earthly troubles increase when I became a Christian at 33. I wondered, "Why doesn't God just take me home and spare me from this?" Since then, I've discovered He keeps us here in part to make us into the persons He wants us to be. We are disciplined for our good, even as children beloved by the Father (Heb. 12:5-11).

God disciplines those He loves in two ways. One way begins with our "I'm going to do my own thing" attitude. If you get away with it, and don't experience God's discipline, you should tremble, because this is like you are an illegitimate child and not a true child (Heb. 12:8). If you are disciplined, take joy in your misery because you are a true child of God (James 1:2). But there is a better way.

The other way to find the Father's love is by the study and ingestion of His Word (Ps. 119:11). Scripture is given to us by God to train us in godliness (2 Tim. 3:16), and to cause us to grow to maturity in Christ (Heb. 5:14). By either path, God will get you where He wants you to go; but believe me, the latter is the much more pleasant route.

Scriptural Examples

The Laodicean church. This lukewarm church was rebuked by Christ for its lack of commitment. They were neither cold nor hot. He stood at the door of their hearts and knocked. Those who were genuine Christians would hear His voice and open the door, receiving His discipline and the joy of His subsequent fellowship (Rev. 3:14-22).

Prayer of Application

Lord, thank You for Your hand of discipline, as You have guided me into Your truth through the years. When I leave the path, You turn me back to the true way.

Find Wisdom's Invaluable Wealth

13) Blessed is the man who finds wisdom, the man who gains understanding, 14) for she is more profitable than silver and yields better returns than gold. 15) She is more precious than rubies; nothing you desire can compare to her (Prov. 3:13-15).

Over 25 years ago, God opened my spiritual eyes so I could gaze upon the incredible riches of His treasure house. Now, years later, I look back and realize I only saw a small portion of God's treasure that day. I know there are vast portions of it I won't see until death (1 Cor. 13:12).

Jesus spoke of a man who sold all he had to buy a field that contained a hidden treasure, and likened it to the treasures of heaven (Matt. 13:44). Another parable told of a man who sold all he had to buy a fine pearl of great value (Matt. 13:45-46). So it is with God's wisdom, which is found in the person of Jesus Christ (1 Cor. 1:24). His wisdom says that we are not to put our trust in treasures on this earth like silver and gold and rubies. Conversely, we are to put our trust in God, and lay up for ourselves treasures in heaven (Matt. 6:19-21). Does this mean earthly wealth is a bad thing? No, but we should fix our eyes on the only One who is able to supply all our needs.

Scriptural Examples

Solomon. The king and author of these proverbs had lots of wisdom and wealth. The former he counted as treasure, while the latter were but a chasing after the wind (Eccl. 2:8-11).

The Idolators. God said their treasures were worthless. There is but one Rock. All other rocks, such as rubies and precious metals, are nothing compared to Him (Isa. 44:8-9).

The rich young man. Jesus saw through his covetousness, saying, "Go, sell what you have and give it to the poor, and come, follow me." The man went away sorrowful. True riches eluded him because of his idolatry (Matt. 19:16-22).

Prayer of Application

Heavenly Father, thank You for allowing me to see Your riches in Christ Jesus. Help me to wisely mine those riches, to the end that I would glorify You, and receive a rich eternal inheritance.

In Wisdom, Find the Tree of Life

16) Long life is in her right hand; in her left hand are riches and honor. 17) Her ways are pleasant ways, and all her paths are peace. 18) She is a tree of life to those who embrace her; those who lay hold of her will be blessed (Prov. 3:16-18).

The riches and honor of wisdom's way mentioned in verses 1-2 are repeated in verse 16. In verse 17, the path of wisdom finds pleasantness and peace. But the really striking thing about these verses is the phrase "tree of life" in verse 18. The phrase is only used in three books of the Bible—Genesis, Proverbs, and Revelation. The Tree of Life was placed by God in the middle of the Garden of Eden next to the Tree of Knowledge of Good and Evil (Gen. 2:9). Anyone who ate from it would live forever (Gen. 3:22).

After the Fall, God sent cherubim to guard the entrance to the garden, lest anyone would eat of the Tree of Life (Gen. 3:24). In Revelation, the Tree of Life is in God's paradise (Rev. 2:7), and the way to it is opened to those who have been washed in the Lamb's blood (Rev. 22:14). The Tree of Life is a wonderful figure of the Lord Jesus, our "Root of Jesse" (Rom. 15:12), and the vine of which we are branches (John 15:1-8). Only by abiding in Christ do we find the pleasant and peaceful path.

Scriptural Examples

Adam and Eve. The couple was free to eat of any tree in the Garden of Eden except one. They were foolish to forsake the fruit of the tree that promised long life, riches, and honor, to choose the disobedient path of pride, arrogance, and death (Gen. 2:16, 17; 3:6).

The Blessed Man. David wrote of this man in the form of a tree, planted by streams of water, yielding fruit in season, and whose leaf did not wither when the heat was on. What made the difference in this man's life? He was a man who delighted in the law of the Lord, meditating on it both day and night, and embracing it in an unending search for its wisdom (Ps. 1:1-3).

Prayer of Application

Dear Lord, thank You for planting me by the river of life, which is the Word of God. Help me to drink deeply of its clear pure waters so that I might reflect the Tree of Life.

In Wisdom, Find the Secret Things of God

19) By wisdom the Lord laid the earth's foundations, by understanding he set the heavens in place; 20) by his knowledge the deeps were divided, and the clouds let drop the dew (Prov. 3:19-20).

If you think that the universe, in all its power, majesty, orderly- ness, and beauty, is incredible and vast, then you should read the Bible. The Word is unmatched in its revelation of the glory and plan of God. While much may be known of God through His creation, such as His power, unity, knowledge, wisdom, grace, and beauty (Rom. 1:20), it does not speak to us of His most wonderful essence and plan.

Only through the Word do we learn why things go wrong in God's world. Only through the Word do we learn of God's love for us, and the gospel which is able to save us from our sin. These proverbs point to the wisdom and understanding of God as He established the earth, as He set each star of the firmament in position, and as the seas were formed and the ecosystems set up. What a mighty God we serve!

Read the Word. Study the Word. Meditate on the Word. Memorize the Word. Share the Word with others. In it, we are given the knowledge of the secret things of God, established since the foundations of the world (Deut. 29:29).

Scriptural Examples

Job. This godly man suffered for his faithfulness at the hands of Satan. But Job knew of these secret things of God and glorified his Creator and Redeemer (Job 26:1-14).

Jesus. How often we think of Jesus as the humble little baby, the itinerant preacher and healer, or our Savior. But He is also the great "I AM" of the burning bush (Ex. 3:4), and the El Shaddai of infinite power. The entire Bible speaks of this Word who was made flesh and dwelt among us. All history is His story. All wisdom is His wisdom (John 1:1-14).

Prayer of Application

Father, thank You for Your self-revelation through creation. Further, thank You for Your wonderful Word which reveals so much more. Help me to know the Word and teach it to others.

Find Wisdom's True Confidence

21) My son, preserve sound judgment and discernment, do not let them out of your sight; 22) they will be life for you, an ornament to grace your neck. 23) Then you will go on your way in safety, and your foot will not stumble; 24) when you lie down, you will not be afraid; when you lie down, your sleep will be sweet. 25) Have no fear of sudden disaster or of the ruin that overtakes the wicked, 26) for the Lord will be your confidence and will keep your foot from being snared (Prov. 3:21-26).

I have a close friend who has endured some rough times in the California real estate market. He once told me that his portfolio was so shaky that if one property fell into foreclosure, the rest would surely follow. I have been in a similar situation, so I know the gnawing fear that tried to draw him in.

But he has not succumbed to that fear. Rather, he has confidence in the One who will see him through this crisis, and through all of life's crises. Whatever happens to my friend's development business, he knows that God has his family's best interests at heart, and he finds real confidence in that fact.

Notice that these proverbs speak of our walking and our lying down. That's how we spend most of our time — in one of those two postures. Our confidence in God's providence should take away our sleepless nights of worry and anxiety, because during our walking hours we are confident of His tender care. The Lord upholds us with His mighty hand (Ps. 37:23-24).

Scriptural Examples

David. What confidence David had in the Lord, his God! He wrote in Psalm 23:4 that even in the valley of the shadow of death he would fear no evil, for God was with him.

Peter. At Pentecost, Peter preached with superb confidence in his God (Acts 2), and while in prison at the hands of King Herod, Peter slept like a baby (Acts 12:6-7).

Prayer of Application

Father, thank You for the confidence that You have given to us. You love us with an infinite love, and protect us in Your infinite power. Help me to trust You more each day.

In Wisdom, Find Compassion for Others

27) Do not withhold good from those who deserve it, when it is in your power to act. 28) Do not say to your neighbor, "Come back later; I'll give it tomorrow"—when you now have it with you (Prov. 3:27-28).

Not only are we obligated to seek kindness and mercy for our neighbors, we are to seek it in a timely manner. One who says, "Come back tomorrow" is being devious in hoping that the needs of his neighbor will somehow disappear, be forgotten, or that his neighbor will find help elsewhere.

The very foundation of wisdom, and of God's law, is that we love God and love our neighbor as ourselves (Lev. 19:18; Matt. 5:43-45; 22:38-39; Luke 10:27; Gal. 5:14). This foundational commandment leaves no room for selfishness or procrastination. We are to seek the highest good for our neighbor, not as a secondaryl motive behind that of serving self, but as a primary goal that influences all of our actions on earth.

The world's wisdom says, "Look out for number one"—yourself. Selfishness is the root of pride, which is the root of sin, which is the root of all of the problems the world faces. Only in the selflessness of living to meet the needs of others may we find the peace, joy, and fulfillment that Christ brings.

Scriptural Examples

The old man in Gibeah. He came in tired from a long day's work in his fields and met a traveler in the city square. He knew there were wicked men in his city just as there were in Sodom in the days of Lot. In kindness and true hospitality, the old man took the traveler home and fed him and his donkeys (Judg. 19:16-21).

Boaz. The Law required that field owners allow the poor and alien to glean the leftovers of the crop (Lev. 19:9-10). Ruth, who was both poor and an alien in Israel, came to glean in the field of Boaz. He went beyond what the law required (Ruth 2).

Prayer of Application

Father, help me to gain more empathy for my neighbors and to look for ways to be of service to them, particularly those who are my brothers and sisters in the household of faith.

In Wisdom, Find the Path of God's Love

29) Do not plot harm against your neighbor, who lives trustfully near you. 30) Do not accuse a man for no reason—when he has done you no harm (Prov. 3:29-30).

The treachery described in these verses is condemned even by the non-Christian. Christians should hate it all the more. The difference in the outlook of the natural person versus the spiritual one lies in the phrase "for no reason." The natural person may conceive of harm done against him that actually never took place. He may rationalize that his accusations have merit and that therefore his actions are justified. But we are never to take revenge into our own hands, even if there is substantial reason for it (Rom. 12:19a).

On the contrary, the Bible tells us that "love does no harm to its neighbor" (Rom. 13:10). This doesn't mean that if we find our neighbor dealing in drugs we shouldn't call the police. Perhaps the highest good for our sinning neighbor would be to call for his are- rest. But we are not to take matters into our own hands. Revenge and "getting even" are in God's hands. That's His business, not ours (Rom. 12:19b).

Scriptural Examples

Jacob's sons. Following the seduction of their sister Dinah, these boys tricked the men of Shechem into being circumcised, and then in the middle of their pain, murdered them and carried off all their wealth. Their revenge grossly exceeded the crime, and brought the ire of their father, Jacob (Gen. 34:13-30).

Saul. David was loyal to his king, but Saul accused and attacked the younger man because he was afraid of the former shepherd and his vast popularity with the people of Israel (1 Sam. 19).

Joab. Seeking to avenge his brother Asahel, Joab stabbed Abner in the stomach while pretending to be Abner's friend. David cursed this sin of his commander-in-chief (2 Sam. 3:37).

Prayer of Application

Dear Lord, You are in control of every circumstance of my life, and in You alone do I trust. May I never accuse someone falsely or try to take matters into my own hands in revenge.

Worship God in Intimate Fellowship

31) Do not envy a violent man or choose any of his ways, 32) for the Lord detests a perverse man but takes the upright into his confidence (Prov. 3:31-32).

The chasm that separates the natural person from his Creator is extremely wide and deep, and no one can cross it on his own (Luke 16:26). Only when the Lord makes us "upright" can we be reunited in friendship with the Holy God. A similar gulf exists between the ways of one who follows God's wisdom and the one who does violence to it (Ezek. 22:26).

Christians are dead to sin and to the ways of violence, but alive unto intimate fellowship with God, the most wonderful treasure imaginable. We have His close friendship (John 15:13); communion (John 14:21-23); peace (Phil. 4:6-7); joy (Neh. 8:10); assurance (Rev. 2:17); instruction (Matt. 11:25); confidence (John 15:15); providence (Ps.107:43); and all the blessings of His eternal covenant with us (Ps. 25:14) (Bridges, p. 40).

In Psalm 51:11-12, David cries out for God to restore him to the joy of his salvation. Sin breaks our intimacy with God, even though He still loves us as His children. If you find that the fellow ship between you and God has been interrupted, search your heart for the sin that has done it, confess it, and turn from it. Then you will return to that sweet and intimate friendship with the Creator and Sustainer of the universe.

Scriptural Examples

David and Goliath. What a contrast between these two men! Goliath was a violent bully, prideful and arrogant. David, a shepherd boy, dared to stand up to Goliath, killing him with one well-placed stone. While David later became known as a man of violence (1 Chron. 22:8), he nevertheless enjoyed an intimate confidence with God, and penned many wonderful psalms attesting to it.

Prayer of Application

Sweet Lord, You have lifted me up from the mire and placed my feet upon a rock. Keep me in intimate fellowship with You, Lord, as I seek to serve and worship You, glorifying Your name.

In Wisdom, Find the Grace of God

33) The Lord's curse is on the house of the wicked, but he blesses the home of the righteous. 34) He mocks proud mockers but gives grace to the humble. 35) The wise inherit honor, but fools he holds up to shame (Prov. 3:33-35).

Notice first the contrasts of these verses. In verse 33, the homes of the wicked are cursed while those of the righteous are blessed. In verse 34, God mocks the proud but "gives grace" to the humble. And finally, in verse 35, the inheritance of the wise is "honor," but that of fools is "shame."

The fool mocks the things of God. He is in turn mocked by God. There but for the grace of God go all of us. In His infinite love and mercy, God calls men and women to salvation by His grace alone. He blesses the homes of those who walk in His wisdom.

Notice also, there is no middle ground and no intermediate steps between wickedness and righteousness. You either have Christ and His righteousness, or you don't. You either humble yourself before the Living God, or you don't. Ultimately, there is either eternal honor and glory on the one hand or shame and death on the other.

If you have never before done so, cast yourself by faith at the feet of the One who can save you with His grace alone, and not by anything you have done (Rom. 3:24; Eph. 2:8-9).

Scriptural Examples

Saul/Paul. Saul was a zealous Pharisee, a group that mocked the Lord Jesus during His earthly ministry. He imprisoned Christians and even killed them. Then one day on the road to Damascus, Saul was confronted in grace by the resurrected Christ. While blinded temporarily he received spiritual sight. Within days, God's grace had transformed Saul from an apostle of Satan into the great apostle of the Living God and minister to the Gentiles of His gospel of grace (Acts 9).

Prayer of Application

Father, what can I say but "thank You" for Your grace that reached down to an undeserving sinner like me and snatched me from the jaws of hell. Help me to tell others of new life in You.

Chapter Four

Summing Up Wisdom's Benefits

In Chapter Four, the father recapitulates his arguments for the many benefits of obtaining wisdom. It seems he is answering his son's objections as he moves toward closure. Notice in the first few verses the father actually gives his own testimony as he harkens back to the day when his father had this same talk with him. He says in verses 3 and 4, "When I was a boy in my father's house, still tender, and an only child of my mother, he taught me and said, 'Lay hold of my words with all your heart; keep my commands and you will live.'" Now grown with a son (or sons) of his own, he is giving him the same talk.

In verses 5 through 9 his own dad stressed the supremacy of wisdom over every other commodity in life. Now he urges his son to pay whatever it costs to get wisdom. The father then proceeds to sum up the life of wisdom in verses 10 through 19, and compares the end of a life of wickedness to that of wisdom. The balance of the chapter is a father's impassioned plea to follow wisdom. Wisdom is not just something that is nice to have in life, it is life itself (v. 22). He instructs his sons to guard their hearts, mouths, eyes, and feet as they walk through life. What his dad told him was true, and he wants to pass the same truth on to his sons after him.

Get Christ: Whatever the Price

1) Listen, my sons, to a father's instruction; pay attention and gain understanding. 2) I give you sound learning, so do not forsake my teaching. 3) When I was a boy in my father's house, still tender, and an only child of my mother, 4) he taught me and said, "Lay hold of my words with all your heart; keep my commands and you will live. 5) Get wisdom, get under-standing; do not forget my words or swerve from them. 6) Do not forsake wisdom, and she will protect you; love her, and she will watch over you. 7) Wisdom is supreme; therefore get wisdom. Though it cost all you have, get understanding. 8) Esteem her, and she will exalt you; embrace her, and she will honor you. 9) She will set a garland of grace on your head and present you with a crown of splendor (Prov. 4:1-9).

When I was a child, my mom would call us to the dinner table with her familiar cry, "Come and get it!" We would all rush to the table, hungry for the good food she had lovingly prepared. Like my mom, wisdom cries out to us, "Come and get it!" But few are hungry for wisdom's food. Most want to be fed with the foolishness of the world. In these verses, we have a father pleading with his children to get wisdom regardless of its cost (v. 7).

Why is this page titled "Get Christ"? Well, let's play a little game. In place of the words "wisdom" and "understanding" in the verses above, put "Christ." Also, replace "she" with "he" and "my" with "his." In Christ we have the distilled and personified essence of divine wisdom. When Christ calls to you, "Come and get it!" go for it! Love Him and get His wisdom. It is the only true wisdom and its benefits are eternal.

Scriptural Examples

The merchant and the treasure hunter. Jesus told the parables of these men who found, respectively, a pearl and a treasure. Each sold all they possessed to acquire these treasures— symbols of divine wisdom. Get it at all costs (Matt 13:44-46).

Prayer of Application

Dear Lord, thank You for showing me that all I had to offer You was brokenness and sin. I exchanged that for Christ and the joy and security of His wisdom. Guide me into His wisdom daily.

Get Christ: Hang on to Him for Dear Life

10) Listen, my son, accept what I say, and the years of your life will be many. 11) I guide you in the way of wisdom and lead you along straight paths. 12) When you walk, your steps will not be hampered; when you run, you will not stumble. 13) Hold on to instruction, do not let it go; guard it well, for it is your life. 14) Do not set foot on the path of the wicked or walk in the way of evil men. 15) Avoid it, do not travel on it; turn from it and go on your way. 16) For they cannot sleep till they do evil; they are robbed of slumber till they make someone fall. 17) They eat the bread of wickedness and drink the wine of violence (Prov. 4:10-17).

Have you ever lost sleep because of some sin or stupid thing you had done? Well, in these verses we see that for some, insomnia is caused by *intent to sin* (v. 16).

The depth of the wickedness of the heart of people is unsearchable (Rom. 3:9-23; Col. 3:5, 7; 1 John 3:10). If we could see ourselves as we really are, we would understand that we are each thousands of times closer to being like Adolf Hitler than like our Savior. But thanks be to God who reaches down and saves us by His grace.

Jesus said, "He who endures to the end will be saved"(Matt. 10:22; 24:13). But can we really hang on to Him to the end? No. It is Christ who hangs on to us for our dear lives. He will not allow even one of His sheep to be lost (John 10:27-29).

Scriptural Examples

The rootless man and the man in the thorn bush. These two men in the parable of the sower and the seed both received the gospel with joy. The rootless man suffered persecution and fell away, while the man in the thorn bush was choked into unfruitfulness by life's worries and the deceitfulness of riches. Don't be like them. Be like the soft and fertile soil, and hang on to the Savior for dear life. He'll hang on to you (Matt.13:18-22).

Prayer of Application

Father, thank You that You have not left it in my hands to endure to the end, but have committed my eternal security into the hands of Him who died for me. Help me to hang on to Him.

Get Christ: Let Him Illumine Your Path

18) The path of the righteous is like the first gleam of dawn, shining ever brighter till the full light of day. 19) But the way of the wicked is like deep darkness; they do not know what makes them stumble (Prov. 4:18-19).

Notice here that the path of the righteous begins with the first glimmer of dawn. It begins with a small ray of light and progresses to the fullness of noonday. Christ is that dawn's early light, as He is our "bright Morning star" (Rev. 22:16). In Matthew 7:13-14, Jesus speaks of the narrow and broad gates, the former leading to life and the latter to destruction. Let's look closely at the proverbs above and see if they can help us define the narrow versus the broad gates.

Imagine a funnel that is narrow at one end and broad at the other. Entering at the broad end, the way gets narrower and narrower, darker and darker, until it finally ends in destruction. This is the way of the sinner who does not repent. It is also the way of the legalist who thinks he can justify himself by good works.

Now turn the funnel around and enter at the narrow end. It is narrow because one can only enter it by the gate marked "The Lord Jesus Christ" (John 14:6; Acts 4:12; John 10:9). He is our light (John 8:12), and as we walk with Him down His path, the funnel gets wider and wider as we find truth, joy, fulfillment, and the divine wisdom, grace, and mercy of God.

Scriptural Examples

The Pharisees. These men represented themselves as lights of Israel, but in reality they were blind guides. They were legalists, men who placed extra-biblical requirements upon those who fool- lowed their ways. They entered at the broad gate and stumbled in the darkness (Matt. 23).

Satan. Satan is also known as Lucifer, which means "angel of light." He poses as an angel of light (2 Cor. 11:14), but is in fact the author of darkness and blindness (2 Cor. 4:4).

Prayer of Application

Heavenly Father, thank You for opening the door to salvation in the person of the Lord Jesus Christ. As I grow in Christ, how warm the light of His brightness is to me.

Get Christ: Let His Words Illumine Your Heart

20) My son, pay attention to what I say; listen closely to my words. 21) Do not let them out of your sight, keep them within your heart; 22) for they are life to those who find them, and health to a man's whole body (Prov.4:20-22).

In 1 Corinthians 1:24 Paul seems to identify Christ as the "wisdom" spoken of in Proverbs. In the verses above we are told to listen closely to His words. We are to keep them in our hearts. The heart is the very seat of our being, "it is the wellspring of life" (Prov. 4:23).

And what are these words? They are all the words of God's book, our Bible. They speak of the knowledge of God and His divine wisdom, and are profitable for us in every way (2Tim. 3:16). But we have to work at it. We need to get it off the shelf, read it, study it, meditate upon it, memorize it, and let its wisdom seep into the very core of our being. Most importantly, we need to be willing to do what it says (James 1:22).

Many scoff at the inerrancy and inspiration of Scripture. Others say the Bible needs a priest to interpret its meaning. Still others will subject the Word to private interpretation rejecting the historical teaching of the church fathers. All those who would denigrate the Word, or the Holy Spirit's ability and desire to make it real to us, walk in darkness.

The prophet Jeremiah wrote of a time when a new covenant would put the law in the hearts of God's people. That time is now, and all who know God seek to know His word and to hide it in their hearts (Jer. 31:33-34; Ps. 119:11).

Scriptural Examples

Satan. The central focus of his attack is upon the Word of God. Satan aroused doubt in Eve's mind, saying, "Did God say...?" In the desert, Satan distorted Scripture, but Jesus countered with the true Word of God (Gen. 3:1; Luke 4:1-13).

Prayer of Application

Father God, thank You for Your Word and for the illumination of it to my heart by the power of the Holy Spirit. Your Word provides supernatural light to guide my every step.

Get Christ: Let Him Guard Your Life

23) Above all else, guard you heart, for it is the wellspring of life. 24)
Put away perversity from your mouth; keep corrupt talk far from your
lips. 25) Let your eyes look straight ahead, fix your gaze directly before
you. 26) Make level paths for your feet and take only ways that are
firm. 27) Do not swerve to the right or the left; keep your foot from evil
(Prov. 4:23-27).

In the 17th century William Harvey discovered the importance of the heart in the circulation of blood. But long before Harvey's day, God spoke of the spiritual heart of people: the seat of our personality, character, and will. Before regeneration, our hearts are exceedingly wicked and deceitful (Jer. 17:9; Matt. 15:19). No one seeks God unless regenerated by God.

Following the new birth, a struggle begins between the new desire of the believer's heart and the sin nature that remains in him. He discovers that he has no power to keep or guard his heart so that all his ways are righteous (Rom. 7:19). He finds that only by giving his heart over to Christ and submitting to Him can he have any success at all (Rom. 7:20-24; 1 Peter 4:19).

Notice that the heart is not the only body part of which these proverbs speak. There are also lips, mouth, eyes, and feet. If the water from the wellspring is polluted, so too will be a person's words, that which his eyes drink in, and the paths down which he walks. We need to keep our eyes fixed on the One who can keep our whole body full of light (Matt. 6:22).

Scriptural Examples

Eve. Eve gazed upon the fruit and lusted after it with her mouth, with her eyes, and finally with her heart (Gen. 3:6).

Job. This righteous man made a covenant with his eyes, that he would not look lustfully at a girl (Job 31:1; Matt 5:28).

Daniel. This exile resolved in his heart not to defile himself with the king's food (Dan. 1:8).

Prayer of Application

Sovereign God, I am powerless to keep Your commands without Your Spirit working in and through Your Word. Help me to submit fully to the authority of the Spirit and the Word.

Chapter Five

An Example from Real Life

In Chapter Five the father uses a testimonial from real life to convince his child that obtaining wisdom is a matter of life and death. He knows that one temptation his child will encounter about the time he reaches puberty is that of adultery or fornication. Those sins are representative here of any sin that promises fulfillment and excitement but delivers just the opposite. Notice in verses 3 and 4 that "the lips of an adulteress drip honey, and her speech is smoother than oil; but in the end she is bitter as gall, sharp as a double-edged sword."

The child is warned not to even go near the door of the adulterer's house (v. 8). He may well be saying, "Don't even think about sex outside of marriage" (Prov. 6:25; Matt. 5:27-28). Verses 15 through 20 speak of the marriage union and the joy of sex in that context. God's wisdom of a lifelong relationship with a spouse of the opposite sex is seen as a thing of beauty and fulfillment.

Finally, the father gives an overarching reason to avoid adultery. Perhaps he remembers once thinking, "Who's going to know if I mess around a little?" God will know. He sees everything (v. 21). The adulterer ultimately hurts only himself as he is trapped in the cords of his own sin, cords that drag him down to the grave (vv. 22-23).

Avoid Fornication Like the Plague

1) My son, pay attention to my wisdom, listen well to my words of insight, 2) that you may maintain discretion and your lips may preserve knowledge. 3) For the lips of an adulteress drip honey, and her speech is smoother than oil; 4) but in the end she is bitter as gall, sharp as a double-edged sword. 5) Her feet go down to death; her steps lead straight to the grave. 6) She gives no thought to the way of life; her paths are crooked, but she knows it not. 7) Now then, my sons, listen to me; do not turn aside from what I say. 8) Keep to a path far from her, do not go near the door of her house, 9) lest you give your best strength to others and your years to one who is cruel, 10) lest strangers feast on your wealth and your toil enrich another man's house. 11) At the end of your life you will groan, when your flesh and body are spent. 12) You will say, "How I hated discipline! How my heart spurned correction! 13) I would not obey my teachers or listen to my instructors. 14) I have come to the brink of utter ruin in the midst of the whole assembly" (Prov. 5:1-14).

These fourteen verses really need no comment; they may be understood by any mature person. But there are some interesting features. Notice first the contrast here between the lips of knowledge that protect us (v. 2), and the lips of the adulteress that ooze honey (v. 3). Although her lips promise sweetness and her voice is smoother than oil, in the end she is as bitter as gall. All sin is like this. It looks good, feels good, tastes good, and sounds good, so it must *be* good. Right? Wrong!

Extramarital sex, including homosexuality, is destroying the American family. If left unchecked it will destroy our entire society. Abortion, incest, disease, divorce, and suicide are all manifestations of its bitter gall. Unwanted children, born out of wedlock, become victims of abuse and their unwed mothers wind up on welfare rolls. Fornication tears at the social and economic fabric of America. Christian, avoid it like the plague that it is.

Prayer of Application

Sovereign Lord, enable me to see the awful consequences of extramarital sex and avoid it at all costs. Let me not even think about sex outside of the context of marriage.

Know the Ultimate Joy of Sex

15) Drink water from your own cistern, running water from your own well. 16) Should your springs overflow in the streets, your streams of water in the public squares? 17) Let them be yours alone, never to be shared with strangers. 18) May your fountain be blessed, and may you rejoice in the wife of your youth. 19) A loving doe, a graceful deer—may her breasts satisfy you always, may you ever be captivated by her love (Prov. 5:15-19).

Recently, the Mississippi River and its tributaries flooded the upper Midwest states, and floodwaters tainted with sewage flowed in the streets. God is telling us in the verses above that adultery is like that dirty flood when a person rejects the sanctity of marriage.

In the marriage covenant, God has provided us with a picture of Christ and His Church. It is to be a relationship marked by deep intimacy and a nakedness before one another in both body and soul. What a wonderful gift to mankind marriage is, and what a major error it is to violate its exclusivity.

Husbands and wives, rejoice with the spouse of your youth, regarding him or her as God's gift to you (Prov. 19:14), each cherishing the other with gentleness and purity. Be satisfied with one another as your bodies merge into one (Gen. 2:24), and each seeks the highest good for the other. Only in that kind of relationship may the true joy of sexual intercourse be known.

Scriptural Examples

The loving couple. The last verse here contains language remit- nascent of another place in Scripture: the Song of Solomon. In it, a couple who is very much in love find great pleasure in their romance. For many years, the erotic language there describing the sexual delights of marriage was held by many to be taboo. But its graceful descriptions lift married love to a highly elevated plane, and remind us that God meant the marriage bed to be a source of joy and wonder.

Prayer of Application

Dear God, bless our marriages and help us to remember our vows to You. Thank You for the intimacy between husbands and wives, and for its metaphor of Christ and His bride.

Remember, Your God Sees Everything

20) Why be captivated, my son, by an adulteress? Why embrace the bosom of another man's wife? 21) For a man's ways are in full view of the Lord, and he examines all his paths. 22) The evil deeds of a wicked man ensnare him; the cords of his sin hold him fast. 23) He will die for lack of discipline, led astray by his own great folly (Prov. 5:20-23).

A man was trying to seduce a woman. He said, "Come on, who's going to know?" She replied, "There are three who will know: You will know, I will know, and God will know."

Few people are foolish enough to be atheists. Creation gives us ample reason to suspect and to even posit a Creator. But many, including some who call themselves Christian, live as if there is no God (Ps. 14:1-3). These "practical atheists" think God is in a deep coma. If they would just open the Bible, they would see the great error in their thinking.

There is another principle here: we are snared by our own evil deeds (v. 22). An innocent fib becomes a lifelong habit of lying. A seemingly innocent puff of marijuana at a party begins an addiction to drugs. A sexual encounter at a young age may bring on a guilty conscience, but the next time it happens there's less guilt. Each time the sin is repeated the conscience is seared, causing a thicker and thicker scar, and finally is hardened to the sin. Repetition of any practice forms a habit, and the habit becomes our master, or the cords that hold us fast.

Scriptural Examples

Jesus. On several occasions, Jesus read the very thoughts of the Pharisees and others. His omniscience was a clear indication of His deity, for no mere man can see into the mind of another. When we confess our sins to God, even those of the heart, we aren't telling Him anything He doesn't already know (Matt. 12:25; Mark 2:8; Luke 5:22; 6:8; 11:17).

Prayer of Application

Father, I want to make every thought and deed captive to Your Word. I am comforted by Your omniscience as You are holding me in the palm of Your hand. Thank You, Lord.

Chapter Six

More Practical Examples

Now the father begins to deal with examples of other situations and habits in life that can trap a young person. The first trap is one that involves money. He warns his child about cosigning a note with a neighbor and putting his family at risk (vv. 1-5). Next, in verses 6 through 11, he warns of the trap of the sluggard. Poverty awaits the slothful person who likes his bed too much. Then the father moves to warn his child about the trap set by people who, through guile and subtlety, lead others astray. He has much to say about this evil person, whose deeds are detestable to the Lord (vv. 12-19).

Ultimately, the father returns to the sin of adultery and gives his child some advice about how to avoid the seduction of the immoral person. In verses 20 through 25 he urges him to remember his mother and father. Let their words be his guide. Next, in verse 25, he advises his child to not even think about sex with a person not his spouse. Avoid looking at her beauty. In modern times, we might think of the proliferation of pornography in the context of his warning. Finally, in the remaining verses, the father argues that his child will avoid the evil adulterer by considering the consequences of his actions. He compares the result of illicit sex with hot coals in one's lap, and speaks of the revenge of an angry spouse.

Steer Clear of Risky Entanglements

1) My son, if you have put up security for your neighbor, if you have struck hands in pledge for another, 2) if you have been trapped by what you said, ensnared by the words of your mouth, 3) then do this, my son, to free yourself, since you have fallen into your neighbor's hands: Go and humble yourself; press your plea with your neighbor! 4) Allow no sleep to your eyes, no slumber to your eyelids. Free yourself, like a gazelle from the hand of the hunter, like a bird from the snare of the fowler (Prov. 6:1-5).

Years ago my dad received a late night call from some of his employees who were in a Tijuana jail for gambling. He had to go down to Mexico that night and post bail of about $300 each. (Some may remember the Kingston Trio tune commemorating the event.) He put up a pledge for his friends. It was okay, for he knew the bail money was the extent of his risk.

Years later, I became involved in the real estate development business and had to make a pledge. I signed personally on a large construction loan. By signing, I knew if the deal soured I would have to pay back the loan and the lender could seize all of my assets. That's effectively what happened. This pledge was wrong. It got me in lots of trouble.

Don't make the same mistake I made. Know the downside limits to any pledge. If you cannot afford to lose that amount, don't sign the papers.

Scriptural Examples

Reuben and Judah. They pledged themselves as security to Joseph. They knew it might mean their very lives, but they were willing to do it (Gen. 42:37; 43:9; 44:32-33).

Paul. Paul wrote to his friend Philemon on behalf of his runaway slave Onesimus, promising to repay what Onesimus owed his master. Notice that Paul didn't offer to pay Onesimus' future debts, only that owed to date (Philem. 1:18-19).

Prayer of Application

Heavenly Father, help me to remember I need to avoid any undertaking or pledge where the downside risk is too large. Help me to discern greed in my motive to take on debt.

Answer God's Call to Diligence

6) Go to the ant you sluggard; consider its ways and be wise! 7) It has no commander, no overseer or ruler, 8) yet it stores its provisions in summer and gathers its food at harvest. 9) How long will you lie there, you sluggard? When will you get up from your sleep? 10) A little sleep, a little slumber, a little folding of the hands to rest — 11) and poverty will come on you like a bandit and scarcity like an armed man (Prov. 6:6-11).

An ancient philosopher is reported to have said, "It is a shame not to learn morals from the small animals." But actually, it's a shame that people made in the image of God need to observe tiny creatures for instruction in righteousness. These little ants have no commander to direct their work, no overseer to inspect their work, and no ruler to call them into account. Yet they do their work diligently and in proper order.

To make diligent use of the tools God has given us, our minds, muscles, talents, educational opportunities, and especially our knees, is to honor Him (Prov. 10:5; 24:27). Unlike the ants, we Christians have a commander and guide: the Holy Spirit. We also have a ruler who will one day call us into account. Yet many of us still neglect the study of the Word, the employment of our spiritual gifts, and our duties that fulfill the multiple roles in the life to which God has called us.

Avoid the way of the sluggard who is glued to his bed, or to his favorite chair in front of the TV set. Let's use every day of our short lives to honor God with our diligence.

Scriptural Examples

The temple builders. These diligent men rebuilt the temple in Jerusalem. They made financial arrangements and hired workers. They even finished the work under budget! The money left over was used to make articles of service and for burnt offerings. Let's be diligent like them (2 Chron. 24:12-14)!

Prayer of Application

Father, thank You for the lowly example of the ant and its illustration of hard work and diligence. Help me to continually practice good habits of that same work and diligence.

Beware of Scoundrels in Your Congregation

*12) A scoundrel and villain, who goes about with a corrupt mouth,
13) who winks with his eye, signals with his feet and motions with his
fingers, 14) who plots evil with deceit in his heart—he always stirs up
dissension. 15) Therefore disaster will overtake him in an instant; he
will suddenly be destroyed—without remedy (Prov. 6:12-15).*

This chap is no sluggard! In fact there are no limits to his diligence, nor to the evil in which he delights. These people abound
outside the church, but Jesus reminds us in His parable of the
wheat and the tares (Matt. 13:24-30) that these people may be
part of the visible church also. We need to watch out for them.

Notice that this deceiver uses a lot of body language to distribute his poison. Compare this list of mouth, eyes, feet, fingers,
and heart to the list Paul gives us in Romans 3:13-17. Paul sums
up his list with the statement, "There is no fear of God before
their eyes." That, of course, is their basic problem.

The love of Christ promotes unity, but Satan stirs up dissension
(1 Cor. 1:10). Love is the glue that binds us together, even when
differences exist between brothers (Eph. 4:3; Phil. 2:2). But the
devious devices of the scoundrel can destroy a congregation — if
his actions don't destroy him first.

Scriptural Examples

The God haters. These scoundrels were described by David
as men who did not fear God. They practiced self-flattery and
deceived themselves into believing that they had no sin (1 John
1:10). The words of their mouths were wicked and deceitful, and
all their ways were evil (Ps. 36:1-4).

The Roman deceivers. Those God haters must have had
descendants who moved to Rome. At the end of his letter to the
church there, Paul urged the brothers to beware of those who
would blow the church apart with smooth words and flattery.
These men served themselves, not Christ (Rom. 16:17-18).

Prayer of Application

Father, help me to be as innocent as a dove in my dealings
with others, but at the same time as wise as a serpent. I pray for
Your love to prevail in my congregation, binding us together.

Look into the Mirror of God's "Hate List"

16) There are six things the Lord hates, seven that are detestable to him: 17) haughty eyes, a lying tongue, hands that shed innocent blood, 18) a heart that devises wicked schemes, feet that are quick to rush into evil, 19) a false witness who pours out lies and a man who stirs up dissension among brothers (Prov. 6:16-19).

Although the number seven usually means completeness, this list is far from a complete list of sins. It is merely representative of some of the sins we commit. Like the FBI's Ten Most Wanted criminals, this list may be God's seven most hated sins.

Notice that God uses members of the body to describe these sins: eyes, tongue, hands, heart, and feet. The list is headed by the sin of pride. God hates the proud look that thinks too highly of self and too lowly of others and of Him. Pride is the main sin that estranges us from our Creator (Job 20:4-8; Ps.10:4). Because of pride, people don't see a need for Christ.

Next, we see a lying tongue, then murder. I'm reminded of the innocent blood of millions of little children who have been aborted throughout America and the world. The list continues with scheming hearts, and evil feet that put the evil scheme into shoe leather. Finally, perjurers and people who stir up dissension among others are added to this hall of infamy. How do you look in the mirror of God's "hate list"?

Scriptural Examples

The Nicolaitans. In His letter to the angel of the church in Ephesus, Jesus stated He hated the practices of these men. Who were they? Little is known, but they are mentioned in Revelation 2:14-15 in the context of the Balaamites who were Idolators and sexually immoral people in Moses' day. They may have been a pseudo-Christian sect that expressed its freedom in libertine behavior, or Gnostics who worshiped the emperor (Rev. 2:6).

Prayer of Application

Search me, Lord, and know my heart, test me and know my anxious thoughts. See if there is any offensive way in me, and lead me in the way everlasting. Keep me on the right path.

Internalize the Commands of Christ

20) My son, keep your father's commands and do not forsake your mother's teaching. 21) Bind them upon your heart forever; fasten them around your neck. 22) When you walk, they will guide you; when you sleep, they will watch over you; when you awake, they will speak to you. 23) For these commands are a lamp, this teaching is a light, and the corrections of discipline are the way to life, 24) keeping you from the immoral woman, from the smooth tongue of the wayward wife (Prov. 6:20-24).

Until the day we die, we will be influenced by our parents' early training and teaching. For some, that training placed in us the very words of the Master, our Lord Jesus Christ. For many who were drawn to Christ later in life and without the instruction of a godly upbringing, salvation's road may be much tougher, and the lessons learned much harder.

God's lessons need to be fixed in the learner's heart if they are to be effective. We must internalize them by contemplation and memorization, and then apply them to all of the situations we encounter in our daily walk (James 1:22). Memorization of Scripture is one of the most worthwhile of all endeavors.

Jesus said, "If you love me, you will obey what I command" (John 14:15). If you love Him, you will also submit to His righteous correction and discipline (Heb. 12:6; Prov. 3:12). And what practical benefits are there for the person who internalizes and obeys the commands of Christ? I think verse 24 above gives us the answer. God's discipline keeps us from sin.

For a young man entering adulthood, every fiber of his being seems to yearn for sexual fulfillment. That's good, because God has made him that way. But human sexual fulfillment was meant for the married couple, and not for extramarital union. Beware of this woman and her false promises. Internalizing and keeping Christ's commands will keep you from obeying the sin that is in your body (Rom. 6:17-23).

Prayer of Application

Father, how I need Your Word to guide me through the treachery and deceitfulness of sin on every side. May I hide Your Word in my heart that I might not sin against You.

Don't Even Think About Sexual Sin

25) Do not lust in your heart after her beauty or let her captivate you with her eyes, 26) for the prostitute reduces you to a loaf of bread, and the adulteress preys upon your very life. 27) Can a man scoop fire into his lap without his clothes being burned? 28) Can a man walk on hot coals without his feet being scorched? 29) So is he who sleeps with another man's wife; no one who touches her will go unpunished (Prov. 6:25-29).

In the businessmen's Bible study that I lead, we once embarked on a topical study of the commandments of Christ. One of our first topics was "thought life." The first discussion was of our Lord's command in Matthew 5:27-28. Like verse 25 above, He said that even to lust after a woman was tantamount to adultery. The command should hit us right between the eyes. But outward sin always begins in the mind. That is why Proverbs 4:23 insists we guard our hearts with diligence.

Scriptural Examples

David. It was apparently a warm evening in Jerusalem. King David got up from his bed and took the stairs to the roof of his palace in search of a cooling breeze. He looked down from the tall building and saw on a nearby rooftop a beautiful woman bathing in the afterglow of the hot day. The vision of her body aroused a desire in him to have her. Undisturbed that she was the wife of one of his army commanders now out fighting in the field, the passion that stirred within him caused him to send for her. Obedient to her king, Bathsheba went to him.

Even though David would later confess his sin and receive forgiveness, its effects haunted him the rest of his days. His sinful thoughts had turned to action and brought an avalanche of burning coals into his life. Solomon, who penned these verses, knew this story well, because the participants were his mom and dad (2 Sam. 11:2-4; Ps. 51).

Prayer of Application

Heavenly Father, may the meditations of my heart always be acceptable in Your sight. May I honor You not only with my words and deeds, but with my every thought.

Pray for Adulterous America

30) Men do not despise a thief if he steals to satisfy his hunger when he is starving. 31) Yet if he is caught, he must pay sevenfold, though it costs him all the wealth of his house. 32) But a man who commits adultery lacks judgment; whoever does so destroys himself. 33) Blows and disgrace are his lot, and his shame will never be wiped away; 34) for jealousy arouses a husband's fury, and he will show no mercy when he takes revenge. 35) He will not accept any compensation; he will refuse the bribe, however great it is (Prov. 6:30-35).

Like burglary or theft, adultery is epidemic in America today. It is condoned on almost every secular front; in the daily press and in magazines; in novels, in movies, and on TV.

The commandment against adultery (Ex. 20:14) carried with it strict regulations against incest (Lev. 18:6), homosexuality (Lev. 18:22), and all kinds of perversions. Today, we see an almost complete collapse of these restrictions as adultery in all of its forms, has become commonplace. Unlike the thief in verse 30 above, who may steal to provide food for his family, the adulterer sins only out of his lusts and depravity.

But don't be deceived. What society condones, God still condemns. Men like Wilt Chamberlain, who brags of his sexual exploits, will ultimately tremble before the Husband whose fury knows no bounds. Let's join hands and fall to our knees in prayer for America and the other nations of this world who foolishly thumb their noses at God.

Scriptural Examples

Amnon. David's sin of adultery with Bathsheba continued to bear bitter fruit in the lives of his children. His son Amnon fell in love with his half-sister Tamar, then forcibly raped her. Amnon infuriated his father by his incestuous act, and Absalom, Tamar's brother, like the husband above, struck Amnon with fury (2 Sam. 13).

Prayer of Application

Dear Lord, as Isaiah said, "I am a man of unclean lips, and I live among a people of unclean lips." We also live among a people of unclean practices. Father, save us from our lusts.

Chapter Seven

More Warnings About Seduction

The wise father knows that sin is very seductive and his child's natural inclination is to follow after it. After once again urging his child to remember his commands and to "write them on the tablet of [his] heart" (v. 3), the father concentrates on the tactics of the one who lies in wait to seduce.

He tells the story of a young man "who lacked judgment" (v. 7) who walked toward the seductress' house in the early evening. Perhaps it was a true story, an encounter the father had actually observed. Nevertheless, stories or testimonials are very powerful in making a point. And the father does have an essential point to make, the essence of which is a matter of eternal life or death. Notice in verse 14 that the woman has a form of godliness. She speaks about fulfilling her vows. The woman is a hypocrite. She makes her appeal very personal in verse 15 and then speaks of the romance and joy she has in store for the young man. He is assured that no danger is lurking in the form of a jealous husband as she lures him with persuasive words into her lair (vv. 19-21).

The chapter ends with the chilling threat of "the grave, leading down to the chambers of death" (v. 27). This is not just the threat of bodily death. At stake is the eternal death of the enemies of God.

Love the Commandments of Christ

1) My son, keep my words and store up my commands within you.
2) Keep my commands and you will live; guard my teachings as the
apple of your eye. 3) Bind them on your fingers; write them on the
tablet of your heart. 4) Say to wisdom, "You are my sister," and call
understanding your kinsman; 5) they will keep you from the adulteress,
from the wayward wife with her seductive words (Prov. 7:1-5).

In verse 2 here, Solomon uses the phrase "the apple of your eye." I heard that phrase often while growing up. It always described something or someone that was adored. God uses it in that sense in Deuteronomy 32:9-11 in describing Israel, whom He kept under the shadow of His wing.

Jesus said, "If you love me, you will obey what I command" (John 14:15). We are told to love God and to love our neighbor, as these are the two commandments upon which all the others rest (Matt. 22:37-40). Should we not also love the commandments He gives us to keep? But how are we to do this?

When you love something or someone, you want to spend time in activity or with that person and get to know all you can about the object of your love. So it is with Christ's commandments. How can we love them if we don't know them? Christ says in effect, "Love me, love my commandments." Study them until, like the psalmist, you can say, "For I delight in your commands because I love them" (Ps. 119:47).

Scriptural Examples

The lover. In Solomon's "Song of Songs" he describes a lover as an apple tree. Delight is found in its shade and its fruit is sweet to the taste. A man takes a maiden to a banquet, and his banner over her is love. Likewise, what a Husband and Lover we have in the Lord Jesus Christ, who sets us down to feast at His eternal table under the banner of His love. Love Christ and His commandments (Song 2:3-6).

Prayer of Application

Lord Jesus, thank You for Your protecting banner of love over me. May I in turn live for You, and in living, love You and Your wonderful commandments for me.

Avoid the Way of the Simple Man

6) At the window of my house I looked out through the lattice. 7) I saw among the simple, I noticed among the young men, a youth who lacked judgment. 8) He was going down the street near her corner, walking along in the direction of her house 9) at twilight, as the day was fading, as the dark of night set in. 10) Then out came a woman to meet him, dressed like a prostitute and with crafty intent. 11) (She is loud and defiant, her feet never stay at home; 12) now in the street, now in the squares, at every corner she lurks.) 13) She took hold of him and kissed him and with a brazen face she said: 14) "I have fellowship offerings at home; today I fulfilled my vows. 15) So I came out to meet you; I looked for you and have found you! 16) I have covered my bed with colored linens from Egypt. 17) I have perfumed my bed with myrrh, aloes and cinnamon. 18) Come, let's drink deep of love till morning; let's enjoy ourselves with love! 19) My husband is not at home; he has gone on a long journey. 20) He took his purse filled with money and will not be home till full moon." 21) With persuasive words she led him astray; she seduced him with her smooth talk. 22) All at once he followed her like an ox going to the slaughter, like a deer stepping into a noose 23) till an arrow pierces his liver, like a bird darting into a snare, little knowing it will cost him his life (Prov. 7:6-23).

Derek Kidner views this drama of the simple young man and the seductress as taking place in four acts; The Victim (vv. 6-9); The Huntress (vv. 10-12); The Tactics (vv. 13-21); and The Kill (vv. 22-23). The victim is a simpleton, walking naively down the street whistling a happy tune. The huntress is dressed to kill, so to speak, and has a hard and unyielding heart. She is loud and defiant. What a contrast with the gentle and quiet spirit that is so valuable in the sight of God (1 Peter 3:1-4). The kill takes place as the simple-minded youth goes to her home, not knowing that he has made a fatal mistake.

Prayer of Application

Dear Father, sin speaks so sweetly and promises so many benefits. But I love Your commandments, Lord, and they are in direct opposition to sin. Through them, keep me from sin's door.

Flee from Spiritual Prostitution

24) Now then, my sons, listen to me; pay attention to what I say. 25) Do not let your heart turn to her ways or stray into her paths. 26) Many are the victims she has brought down; her slain are a mighty throng. Her house is a highway to the grave, leading down to the chambers of death (Prov. 7:24-27).

Proverbs has a lot to say about physical adultery, but spiritual adultery is much more serious. In fact, God uses physical adultery as a metaphor for its spiritual counterpart, the false gospel (Hos. 1- 2). These are not really gospels at all, but lies that lead the unwary to death (Gal. 1:7).

Like prostitutes hanging from their doorways in any red light district, spiritual prostitutes visit doorsteps with their false doctrines, seeking to lead people away from the Savior. They preach a different Christ than the One of Scripture (Luke 21:8), and lure the unwary with lies and half-truths that sound good to the spiritually gullible. Beware of people like these. Don't let your heart turn to their teaching.

Recently, a cult that is growing rapidly throughout the world built a multimillion-dollar "temple" near my home. It is beautiful in its stark whiteness against the blue sky, and its presence has lured many visitors to hear the cult's false teaching. That temple is a concrete prostitute, standing at the side of the interstate highway, seeking whom she may devour (1 Pet. 5:8). Avoid the spiritual prostitute. All her paths lead down to the chambers of death.

Scriptural Examples

Gideon. This man was chosen by God to be Israel's judge. He was used to lead a tiny force to victory against a huge army of Midianites. In spite of seeing the power of God at work in this victory, and in his life, Gideon turned to spiritual adultery. He made a golden idol, and Israel then prostituted itself by worshipping the idol in Gideon's hometown (Judg. 8:22-28).

Prayer of Application

Father, thank You for teaching me Your truth through the Word. But many in our land are teaching falsehoods about You. I pray that You would protect the unwary from them.

Chapter Eight

The Ontology of Wisdom

Perhaps the child has now raised a question. "Dad, how do I know that what you say is true? I've heard that 'if something feels good, it must be good.' What makes wisdom so all-important?" Just as a salesman might build confidence in his product or service by giving the history and reputation of his company, so the father in chapter eight speaks foundational truths about wisdom. He tells of its "being"—what wisdom is in its essential nature. He speaks of wisdom's ontology.

He begins in verses 1 through 5 to tell of wisdom's universal call. Wisdom is not known only to a few. Its call extends to the whole world. He goes on to speak of the worthiness of wisdom (vv. 6-11). Godly wisdom is truth. That which is not wise is crooked and perverse. Beginning in verse 12, wisdom begins speaking in the first person. It tells of its mighty power and understanding. Then in verse 22 wisdom begins to speak of its antiquity. This is not something that has been cooked up by humans who want to keep their children from having fun. No, wisdom has been "appointed from eternity" (v. 23). Finally, from verse 32 on, the father speaks again. He tells his child of the blessedness of wisdom and reiterates the eternal stakes involved in its seeking.

Know the Perfect Word of God

1) Does not wisdom call out? Does not understanding raise her voice? 2) On the heights along the way, where the paths meet, she takes her stand; 3) beside the gates leading into the city, at the entrances, she cries aloud: 4) "To you, O men, I call out; I raise my voice to all mankind. 5) You who are simple, gain prudence; you who are foolish, gain understanding. 6) Listen, for I have worthy things to say; I open my lips to speak what is right. 7) My mouth speaks what is true, for my lips detest wickedness. 8) All the words of my mouth are just; none of them is crooked or perverse. 9) To the discerning all of them are right; they are faultless to those who have knowledge. 10) Choose my instruction instead of silver, knowledge rather than choice gold, 11) for wisdom is more precious than rubies, and nothing you desire can compare with her (Prov. 8:1-11).*

Godly wisdom is found in the perfect Word of God: The Bible. The Bible stands at the crossroads of life (v. 2b) and cries out to all (v. 4b): "Open me, read me, study me, love me. Because in me you will find what is right, and true, and just. My words are without fault or error, and for the one who truly seeks, they are easy to understand. They are more valuable than any other treasure. Nothing can compare to the riches of the Word of God" (vv. 4-11, author's paraphrase).

For me, all theology may be rendered down to this little verse of a child's hymn: "Jesus loves me, this I know, for the Bible tells me so." Know the perfect Word of God. Read it, study it, trust it, and above all, obey it. In it is God's perfect wisdom.

Scriptural Examples

Paul. He knew and lived the Word of God. He also was an instrument of God to write down its truth for all generations. Follow Paul, as he followed Christ in believing and obeying the very Word of God (John 10:35b; 17:17; Phil. 2:8; 1 Tim. 3:4-16).

Prayer of Application

Dear Father, thank You for Your Word and for the Holy Spirit who guides me into its depths. Your Word is truth. I pray that through it I will be fully equipped for every good work.

Know the Way of Holiness

12) I, wisdom, dwell together with prudence; I possess knowledge and discretion. 13) To fear the Lord is to hate evil; I hate pride and arrogance, evil behavior and perverse speech (Prov. 8:12-13).

With these verses wisdom begins to speak in the first person; it is personified. We saw wisdom in verses 1-11 as the Word of God in its printed form. Here it is found in its embodied form: the person of our Lord Jesus Christ (John 1:1-14).

Jesus said that throughout history many would come in His name, saying, "I am Christ," and would deceive many (Matt. 24:5; Mark 13:6; Luke 21:8). In fact, many different "Christs" are being preached throughout the world today (1 John 4:1-3). But the true Christ, the Christ of Scripture, is distinguished by His call to holiness. This call is expressed in two ways.

First, there is a call to understand who He is. He is the majestic God, Creator (John 1:1-3), and Sustainer (Heb. 1:3) of all that is visible and invisible. He alone is worthy of our worship. He is altogether righteous and holy, set apart, transcendent in utter wisdom, knowledge, perfection, and power. He hates evil and every evil work, and will one day destroy them by the power of His coming (Mal. 3:2; 2 Thess. 2:8).

The second form of the call is to understand who we are. We are prideful, arrogant, and full of evil behavior and perverse speech. The way of holiness leads only by the cross of Christ, where the holiness of God met the sinfulness of man.

Scriptural Examples

Isaiah. God's prophet saw a vision of the Lord in His temple. Angelic beings sang out, "Holy, holy, holy is the Lord Almighty." In contrast, Isaiah saw himself as a man of unclean lips, of perverse and evil speech, living among a people of uncleanness and perversity. But, by grace, God seared Isaiah's lips and took away his sin and guilt (Isa. 6:1-8; Eph. 2:8-9).

Prayer of Application

Heavenly Father, thank You for the sacrifice of Your Son, which provided the payment for the crime and debt of sin and imputed unto men the righteousness of His sinless life.

Know the Source of Power and Authority

14) Counsel and sound judgment are mine; I have understanding and power. 15) By me kings reign and rulers make laws that are just; 16) by me princes govern, and all nobles who rule on the earth (Prov. 8:14-16).

One big question that came out of the Gulf War a few years back was, why didn't George Bush give the order to go in and eliminate Saddam Hussein's perverse government? The reason may be found in these verses. For some reason, God still has a role for Saddam Hussein, and He will use that madman just as He used Pharaoh prior to the Exodus from Egypt. God raised Pharaoh up for His own immutable purpose: His own glory (Rom. 9:17). God is the invisible King of Kings and Lord of Lords (Rev. 19:16), who will one day establish his visible reign on earth in the person of the Lord Jesus Christ.

In the United States, there is a growing concern that we have lost all of our statesmen, those men and women who served our people by principles rather than politics. Our government officials desperately need the wisdom and justice of God in their law making and administration, but seem to have sold out to the poll and the ballot box. Our leaders seem to be more interested in re-election than they are in revival. But be of good cheer; Christ has overcome the world system (John 16:33).

Scriptural Examples

Nebuchadnezzar and Belshazzar. This father and son were kings over Babylon. Daniel made it clear to them that it was God who had elevated them to their positions of power. Due to their pride and arrogance, God also brought them down (Dan. 5:18-28).

Pilate. At his trial before this Roman procurator, Jesus refused to defend Himself. Pilate spoke pridefully of his power over Jesus, but our Lord said that Pilate would have no power at all if he did not receive it from above (John 19:10-11).

Prayer of Application

Lord God, thank You for the peace that comes from un-derstanding that You are sovereign over all the events of this world. Not even the most minute occurrence escapes Your eye.

Know the Love of God's Wisdom

I love those who love me, and those who seek me find me
(Prov. 8:17).

Here again, wisdom speaks from the first person. In the title of this principle, we could substitute the name of Christ for "God's Wisdom." Truly, He is the wisdom of God (1 Cor. 1:24). He loves those who love Him, and all who seek Him will find Him (Matt. 7:8). In Galatians 2:20, Paul speaks of "the Son of God, who loved me and gave himself for me." Did Paul love Christ before Christ loved Paul? No. Paul was an enemy of Christ. It was Christ who sought Paul and found him on the Damascus Road, blinding him with the glory of His presence. If Christ sought the great apostle, does He not also seek us? (See Luke 19:10.)

"The heart is deceitful above all things and beyond cure"(Jer. 17:9). None of us has perfectly loved God or sought His face (Rom. 3:11). Rather, we hated God and ran from Him just as the first couple did (Gen. 3:8). Only God in His grace can make us seek Him and love Him. While we were yet sinners and powerless, Christ died for the ungodly (Rom. 5:6). We were dead in trespasses and sins, following Satan and objects of God's wrath. But because of His love for us, we were made alive with Christ (Eph. 2:1-5).

Now saved by His grace, we are called to love Him and seek His face. We are to love His wisdom and seek it. And how do we go about this? Jesus said, "If you love me, you will obey what I command" (John 14:15). To love Christ is to obey Him.

Scriptural Examples

The sons of men. The Lord looked down upon these folks to see if there were any who understood, or sought God and His wisdom. He didn't find one (Ps. 14:2-3; 53:2-3).

The non-seekers. God later spoke of people who found Him even though they did not seek Him. How did this happen? God revealed Himself to them (Isa. 65:1; Rom.10:20).

Prayer of Application

Sovereign Lord, what great grace that Jesus would lay down His life for His enemies. Thank You for the love of Christ and His wisdom that has caused sinners like me to seek Him.

Know the Wealth of God's Wisdom

18) With me are riches and honor, enduring wealth and prosperity. 19) My fruit is better than fine gold; what I yield surpasses choice silver. 20) I walk in the way of righteousness, along the paths of justice, 21) bestowing wealth on those who love me and making their treasuries full (Prov. 8:18-21).

Why do people strive to get rich? Some want power and prestige. Most want contentment, freedom from worry, and happiness. But can money really supply these things?

As temporal wealth increases, so does our desire for more. Likewise, a rich person's worry increases as he fears losing what he has. And happiness? At best, the happiness that money might bring is fickle and fleeting. Money, when set up as an idol, cannot deliver what it promises. Only God and the wealth of His wisdom can truly satisfy and fill all our needs.

So what is this wealth that is better than silver and gold? James tells us that it is pure, peace-loving, considerate, submissive, full of mercy and good fruit, impartial, and sincere (James 3:17). Paul says it is love, and seeks what is best for its neighbor (1 Cor. 13). It is joy, a deep-seated happiness that transcends temporal blessing (Ps. 21:6). It is peace (Phil. 4:7), patience (James 1:2-3), kindness (Col. 3:13), goodness (Prov. 2:9), faithfulness (3 John 1:3), gentleness (1 Thess. 2:7), and self-control (1 Cor. 7:5). This is the wealth God brings, wealth that satisfies and brings contentment, freedom from worry and fear, and happiness. It is more precious than all of earth's treasures

Scriptural Examples

The trees by the river. Ezekiel spoke of fruit trees by the river of life. Their fruit was for food and healing (Ezek. 47:12).

Dorcas (Tabitha). This fine woman and disciple of Christ was known for the fruit of wisdom in her life. We're told that she was always doing good and helping the poor (Acts 9:36).

Prayer of Application

Lord God, You have filled me with Your Spirit and ordered that I bear fruit. You are the Vine and only through You can I bear such fruit. Let Your wealth flow through me to others.

Know the One Who Was Before All Things

22) "The Lord brought me forth as the first of his works, before his deeds of old; 23) I was appointed from eternity, from the beginning, before the world began. 24) When there were no oceans, I was given birth, when there were no springs abounding with water; 25) before the mountains were settled in place, before the hills, I was given birth, 26) before he made the earth or its fields or any of the dust of the world. 27) I was there when he set the heavens in place, when he marked out the horizon on the face of the deep, 28) when he established the clouds above and fixed securely the fountains of the deep, 29) when he gave the sea its boundary so the waters would not overstep his command, and when he marked out the foundations of the earth (Prov. 8:22-31).

Think, if you will, about the home or apartment where you live. It doesn't take much of a leap of faith to imagine that a developer planned it, an architect designed it, an engineer laid out its foundations, a bank financed its construction, and a builder built it. It stands and has structural integrity because it was built with wisdom. It literally reeks with the wisdom (or lack thereof) of the people who were engaged in its creation. In like manner does this world speak loudly and clearly of its Creator (Rom. 1:20). The truth of the Creator is self-evident in what He has created. Yet people suppress this truth, and the other truth that God has revealed to them in their unrighteousness (Rom. 1:18).

Who is this Being, this Person who started it all? Can we know Him? Yes. He is the Lord Jesus Christ (John 1:1-3), who created all things and ordered them (v. 29) according to the natural laws that we observe every day. From His creative wisdom and power comes everything that is or ever will be. Because He created us, Christ has all authority over us. His ultimate wisdom and plan of salvation was put into effect before anything was (Eph. 1:4). And that plan saw the Creator's humiliation through His birth in Bethlehem (John 1:14) and death on a Jerusalem cross.

Prayer of Application

Dear Creator of all that is, thank You for Your wisdom that saved me even from before the creation of the world. Because of Your recreation of me, I will live eternally with You.

Seek God in Your Daily Quiet Time

32) Now then, my sons, listen to me; blessed are those who keep my ways. 33) Listen to my instruction and be wise; do not ignore it. 34) Blessed is the man who listens to me, watching daily at my doors, waiting at my doorway. 35) For whoever finds me finds life and receives favor from the Lord. 36) But whoever fails to find me harms himself; all who hate me love death (Prov. 8:32-36).

Jesus said in Luke 9:23, "If anyone would come after me, he must deny himself and take up his cross daily and follow me." In Galatians 2:20, Paul says that we have been crucified with Christ, and we no longer live unto ourselves. Christ has become the central focus and purpose of the Christian's new life, a life that is lived by faith in Him. We can bear our cross only by faith, and we are to live moment by moment in it, from faith to faith, step-by-step, on a daily basis (Rom. 1:17).

The verses above state two of the great blessings that have been promised to the person who will listen to the instruction of God's wisdom and keep God's ways. He will find life and favor (grace) from the Lord. These come by watching daily at His feet and waiting at His doorway (Rev. 3:20).

Those who say "I'm too busy" or " I don't have the time" to meet with God are really saying "My priorities don't allow time for You today, Lord." If your earthly boss asked for a 30 minute meeting each morning, could you find the time? I imagine that you could. Just as we need food daily to meet our physical needs (Matt. 6:11), so we also need our daily feeding from the Vine of spiritual food. Without it, you'll be a frail and fruitless Christian. Seek the blessings of God in your daily time with Him.

Scriptural Examples

The Bereans. The Bereans examined the Scriptures to see if what Paul said was true. What's more, the Scripture tells us that they did it on a daily basis (Acts 17:11).

Prayer of Application

Dear Lord, You provide all things richly for our enjoyment. Help me to recognize You as the giver of all things and to make time for prayer and for Your Word on a daily basis.

Chapter Nine

The Calls of Wisdom and Folly

Chapter Nine completes the introduction to the book of Proverbs. In the preceding chapters the father has given his child the benefits of wisdom, and he has recited examples of the traps in life that wisdom will help one to avoid. He has shown the life and death struggle between wisdom and folly that is unleashed upon every human and, finally, he has given his child the distilled essence of the wisdom of God. Now, he summarizes his arguments and boils it all down to a choice his child must make. There are two feasts going on in life, and two calls go out to those feasts. Which way will the child go?

Everybody in the world is going in one direction or another. When I was a teenager we used to sit on the front porch and play a game called "cars." We would try to name the make, model, and year of each car that passed by. Back then, we knew the difference between a Chevrolet and Cadillac, even between a 1955 Impala and a 1949 Coupe de Ville. But I always wondered where people were going. Some were heading east and some west. The game of life is like that. Some people are heading toward the feast of wisdom and some are heading toward the feast of folly. The father of Proverbs wants to make sure his children are heading the right way.

Enter the Feast of Wisdom

1) Wisdom has built her house; she has hewn out its seven pillars. 2) She has prepared her meat and mixed her wine; she has also set her table. 3) She has sent out her maids, and she calls from the highest point of the city. 4) "Let all who are simple come in here!" she says to those who lack judgment. 5) "Come, eat my food and drink the wine I have mixed. 6) Leave your simple ways and you will live; walk in the way of understanding" (Prov. 9:1-6).

In this final introductory chapter before we enter the next section of the Proverbs of Solomon, we find two invitations. One is from wisdom, the business of God; and the other from folly, the business of fools. This is the crossroads of life. There is only one way to God. We see it here.

The house that wisdom has built is none other than the temple of God, His church (Matt. 16:18). Its foundation rests on pillars which represent the completeness of the revealed truth upon which the church is built (1 Tim. 3:15; Matt. 16:17), and its apostles and prophets, with Jesus Christ as the chief cornerstone (Eph. 2:20-21). A feast has been prepared for those who would enter (Matt. 26:26-29).

In verse 4, we see that the sole qualification for those who are invited is that they must be simpleminded, totally lacking in judgment. That describes every man and woman on the earth. Only by God's opening our spiritual eyes in rebirth can we even see the door to the house of wisdom (John 3:3).

Scriptural Examples

The wedding banquet. Jesus told the parable of a king who prepared a wedding banquet for his son. One of the guests didn't have the proper clothes. He was thrown outside as one who was invited but not chosen. The wedding clothes are provided only by God to His bride, and that by grace alone (Matt. 22:1-14; Rev. 19:7-8).

Prayer of Application

Gracious God, thank You for inviting me to the feast of wisdom when I was dead in trespasses and sins and blinded by the god of this world. You have given me all things in Christ.

Discern Between Wisdom and Folly

7) "Whoever corrects a mocker invites insult; whoever rebukes a wicked man incurs abuse. 8) Do not rebuke a mocker or he will hate you; rebuke a wise man and he will love you. 9) Instruct a wise man and he will be wiser still; teach a righteous man and he will add to his learning. 10) "The fear of the Lord is the beginning of wisdom, and knowledge of the Holy One is understanding. 11) For through me your days will be many, and years will be added to your life. 12) If you are wise, your wisdom will reward you; if you are a mocker, you alone will suffer" (Prov. 9:7-12).

This chapter is something like a sandwich, with the bread of the feast of wisdom on one side, and the bread of folly's feast on the other. These verses are the peanut butter and jelly and speak of the minds of those called. Everyone in the world will attend one feast or the other, and all are on paths in opposite directions.

The directional test is one's response to the rebuke of God's Word. Notice that responses vary, and reveal just how far down the path a person is. In verse 7 we see that a mocker responds to rebuke with an insult, but as he moves down folly's path his response enlarges to abuse and then to hatred.

On the other hand, a wise person will love the rebuke of God's Word (v. 8b). He walks down wisdom's path increasing in wisdom (v. 9). His reward is in the eternal feast of God (vv. 11-12a). The mocker will suffer the consequences of his responses and enter alone to the feast at the house of his mistress Folly, not aware that eternal death awaits.

Scriptural Examples

David and Nathan. Following David's sin against Bathsheba and Uriah, the prophet Nathan rebuked David in the name of the Lord. David, like the wise man in these verses, confessed and repented. Restored by God's grace, he continued down wisdom's path (2 Sam. 12:1-13).

Prayer of Application

Lord and God, may I always respond in repentance at the faithful rebuke of the Word of God. May I walk the path to Your eternal feast confident that You will keep my feet from slipping.

Flee from the Feast of Folly

13) The woman Folly is loud; she is undisciplined and without knowledge. 14) She sits at the door of her house, on a seat at the highest point of the city, 15) calling out to those who pass by, who go straight on their way. 16) "Let all who are simple come in here!" she says to those who lack judgment. 17) "Stolen water is sweet; food eaten in secret is delicious!" 18) But little do they know that the dead are there, that her guests are in the depths of the grave (Prov. 9:13-18).

In utter contrast to Lady Wisdom, here Fraulein Folly sits as a prostitute next to her door and invites those same simpletons in for her feast of stolen water and secret food. Folly promises sweetness and delicacy but delivers death and hell. That is what sin always does. It promises excitement, glamour, and fulfillment, but delivers just the opposite.

Folly is just like those she calls, and she's heading ultimately to the same place (Rev. 20:10-15). She is undisciplined and knows no shame (v. 13b, RSV), nor has she knowledge of the Holy One.

Lord Byron, who was blessed with talent, wealth, fame, and good looks, was a man who evidently responded to Fraulein Folly. At the end of his life, he penned these verses (quoted from McGee, p. 36):

> "My days are in the yellow leaf,
> The flowers and fruits of love are gone;
> The worm, the canker, and the grief
> are mine alone."

Scriptural Examples

Jezebel of Thyatira. In His letter to the church at Thyatira, Jesus rebuked this woman and her followers. She called herself a prophetess, but was really a prostitute who led others astray in sexual immorality and eating food sacrificed to idols. He promised death to her and her children (Rev. 2:20-23).

Prayer of Application

Dear God, thank You that while I was on my way to the feast of Folly, You stopped me and put my feet on the path of understanding. Help me to warn others of Fraulein Folly.

Chapter Ten

The Proverbs of Solomon: Antithetical Parallelism

We now begin the proverbs of Solomon. The first thing we notice is the verses seem to bear little or no connection with those before or after. They are simple sayings that usually stand alone. The "wisdom literature" of Proverbs is written in Hebrew poetry. Their poetry didn't rhyme or have meter like ours sometimes does, but there were poetic forms nonetheless. Often, Hebrew poetry employed brief sentences of roughly the same length, set parallel to one another and containing visual images. Parallelism, referring to complementary phrases of a poem, is very prevalent in Proverbs.

Of the many types of parallelism, the most prevalent in Proverbs is antithetical parallelism. Proverbs 10:1 provides us an example: "A wise son brings joy to his father, but a foolish son grief to his mother." Notice that the thesis of the first phrase is positive, while that of the second phrase is negative. The second is against the thesis of the first, or, in other words, its "antithesis." Hence, it is "antithetical." The second phrase repeats the thought of the first phrase from the opposite perspective. Usually antithetical parallelism may be spotted by the word "but" at the start of the second phrase. Chapter Ten is full of examples of this type of Hebrew poetry. In the next chapter heading, we'll discuss two other forms of parallelism.

Bring Joy to Your Mother and Father

A wise son brings joy to his father, but a foolish son grief to his mother
(Prov. 10:1).

There is a sense in which the Bible is a record book of wise and foolish sons who either blessed or cursed their parents. On page after page we find examples of men and women who either brought joy or grief to their moms and dads.

Adam, the son of God, grieved his Father. Adam was in turn grieved heavily by Cain, but blessed by both Abel and Seth. The patriarch Abraham was blessed by Isaac, who in turn was grieved by Jacob. The list goes on.

Notice it is the wise son who brings joy and the foolish son who brings grief. Proverbs 1:7 and 9:10 say that wisdom begins with the fear of the Lord. All wisdom flows from that spring. The foolish son, on the other hand, despises the Lord and His instruction. And so it is in our relationship to the Lord that we bring our parents joy. Someone says, "My parents couldn't care less about God. They are upset about my faith in Christ. Have I failed to honor them?" No. You owe more allegiance to your Father in heaven. To bring Him joy is your greater calling.

Scriptural Examples

Ham, Shem, and Japheth. These sons of Noah are the acnestors of all who walk the earth. Following the Flood, Noah foolishly got drunk and lay naked in his tent. Ham disgraced his father by looking at his nakedness and joking about it to the others. But Shem and Japheth backed into the tent and covered their father, thereby honoring him (Gen. 9:21-23).

Noah. We're told in Genesis 5:28-29 that Lamech named his son Noah because Noah would comfort him and his wife in the labor of the soil that God had cursed. Noah did prove to be a wise son who feared the Lord, preached of His righteousness, and followed His instructions to the letter (2 Peter 2:5; Heb. 11:7).

Prayer of Application

Dear God, comfort and strengthen parents who must suffer in the wake of a child who runs from You. At the same time, help us children to honor our parents out of love for You.

Seek the Treasure of Righteousness

Ill-gotten treasures are of no value, but righteousness delivers from death (Prov. 10:2).

When a person is converted to Christ he is given — over time — a new perspective on life. This new worldview has many facets, but chief among them are these two: First, our God loves us and reigns in absolute power and sovereignty. Second, the life we now lead has eternal consequences.

As we grow in the Lord, we begin to see Jesus' point that earthly treasures are of little value (Matt. 6:25-26). But eternal treasures are of great value, and Jesus commands us to store them up. In this verse, we see that "ill-gotten treasures are of no value." That is a gross understatement. Treasures gotten by theft, extortion, fraud and the like are really treasures of wrath, and not "treasure" at all (Rom. 2:5). The true treasure of this life is the righteousness of Christ.

He is an eternal treasure for those who love Him, serve Him, and want to be like Him. As we grow in His grace, we see more and more clearly the heavenly treasure that is ours, far removed from the treasures of death that the non-Christian seeks.

Scriptural Examples

Enoch. Enoch treasured walking with God. God treasured Enoch for his faith. They walked so closely together that God took Enoch from the earth. He never tasted death (Gen. 5:24; Heb. 11:5-6).

Abraham. By faith Abraham left his home and journeyed to a land he had never seen. He and his family lived in tents as they looked forward to an eternal treasure "with foundations, whose architect and builder is God" (Gen. 15:1-6; Heb. 11:8-12).

Moses. Adopted into a family of great earthly treasure, Moses nonetheless preferred to value "disgrace for the sake of Christ." He persevered because he saw a heavenly storehouse of invisible and eternal riches (Heb. 11:4-28).

Prayer of Application

Father God, thank You for the eternal riches You have stored up for us in Christ. Help me today to exhibit the treasures of peace, joy, and contentment that only You can give.

Trust God for Your Physical Needs

The Lord does not let the righteous go hungry, but he thwarts the craving of the wicked (Prov. 10:3).

God created us with certain physical needs. We need food and drink, clothing, and a place to be sheltered from the elements. Additionally, we need meaningful employment, companionship and community, security, and hope for the future. God declares in many places in His Word that He will provide for those needs (Matt. 6:25-26 ; Phil. 4:19). In this verse is another such promise.

We Christians often worry and fret over these things as if God were faithless or powerless to deliver on His promises. In Numbers 11:22-23, Moses questioned God about the vast quantities of food it would take to feed Israel. God answered, "Is the Lord's arm too short?" God will not permit the righteous to "famish" as the KJV puts it in Proverbs 10:3. We ask Him for our daily bread, the supply of all our physical needs (Matt. 6:11), and He delivers.

Although the non-Christian often seems to have more of this world's goods than does the child of God, there is a problem with his craving. His perceived "needs" grow faster than his ability to supply them, so he is never satisfied or content. But God, in His mercy, puts our feet on a higher path. The godliness of Christ should bring contentment (1 Tim. 6:6).

Scriptural Examples

Shobi. This Ammonite brought food and other necessities to David's men. Our needs are often supplied through unexpected sources (2 Sam. 17:27-29).

Elijah. God's prophet was fed by ravens at the Kerith Ravine as famine ruled in the land (1 Kings 17:1-6).

Dives. This former rich man begged God that Lazarus be sent to hell to put just a drop of water upon his tongue. His request was refused. Even in hell the wicked will be denied and thwarted in their eternal cravings (Luke 16:24).

Prayer of Application

Sovereign Lord, thank You for Your great and precious promises. How can we who have trusted in Your eternal salvation not trust You for all our needs in this life as well?

Practice the Wisdom of Diligence

4) Lazy hands make a man poor, but diligent hands bring wealth. 5)
He who gathers crops in summer is a wise son, but he who sleeps
during harvest is a disgraceful son (Prov. 10:4-5).

These two proverbs display the compound fruits of sloth. On the one hand, in verse 4, we see that laziness can make a person poor. Then verse 5 tells us that sloth brings disgrace. Sloth therefore becomes not just a material problem, but a moral one as well.

God commanded the Jews to rest on the Sabbath. But the other side of that commandment is that they were to work six days before resting (Ex. 23:12). Laziness impoverishes in every way—materially, spiritually, physically, and mentally—and makes us unprepared for the challenges that lie ahead.

The wise son in verse 5 labors in preparation for the long winter ahead. Then he and his family will dine on the fruit of his summer's labor. So, also, you who are young need to store up knowledge and wisdom in preparation for your maturity when the opportunities may be limited. But even when we are older we should never stop learning and growing, applying our minds, hearts, and bodies diligently in all things.

Scriptural Examples

Adam. Adam was given fruitful labor in the Garden of Eden, to tend it and to name its creatures. We're not told how diligent he was in his administration, because he soon became the first man to be fired from his job (Gen 2:15, 19; 3:23).

Joseph. He diligently gathered the crops of Egypt during the time of plenty. When famine came, the wisdom of his diligence became apparent (Gen. 41:46-56).

The Athenians. They had nothing to do all day long but sit and listen to the latest gossip. They were the first-century equivalent to soap opera and talk show junkies (Acts 17:21).

Prayer of Application

Father, help me to be diligent in all things, in whatever role to which You have called me. Your Word says that You love diligence. Help me to walk in it, forsaking all sloth.

Seek the Lasting Blessings of Godliness

4) Blessings crown the head of the righteous, but violence overwhelms the mouth of the wicked. 7) The memory of the righteous will be a blessing, but the name of the wicked will rot (Prov. 10:6-7).

These proverbs run counter to Marc Antony's requiem for Julius Caesar in Shakespeare's play. He said, "The evil that men do lives after them; the good is oft interred with their bones." Here we see goodness living on while the evil man's name rots.

While the world might remember the evil that people do, their names rot in infamy. From evil men like Judas, Nero, and Herod, to Hitler, Stalin, and Idi Amin, their memories do not invoke blessing but a curse.

The evil men listed above are considered paradigms of wickedness by even the non-Christian. But God sees as evil even the little old lady who lives down in the corner house, who volunteers with the hospital auxiliary, who is delighted by visits from her grandchildren, and who is always kind and gracious to everyone she meets, if she remains estranged from Christ. We men and women, in the cloak of self-righteousness, are many times closer to these paradigms of evil than we are to Christ. First, we need to put on His righteousness by faith, and then the world will be blessed through us.

Scriptural Examples

Jacob and Esau. Esau seemed like a good guy, his brother Jacob was a liar and a cheat. But Jacob was chosen and blessed by God's grace and his imputed righteousness became a foundation of Israel. From his seed would come the One who would truly bless the world (Gen. 25:21; Matt. 1:2, 16; Rom. 9:8-16).

Ruth and Orpah. These Moabite women both married Isaelite brothers who subsequently died. Then, by God's providence, Orpah's name died and its memory faded, while the other lived on as a shining star (the book of Ruth).

Prayer of Application

Lord, You are the righteous God who lifts some up and leaves others where they are. Who can fathom the depths of your mysteries? Thank You, Lord, for Your great grace.

Let the Word of God Sink In

The wise in heart accept commands, but a chattering fool comes to ruin (Prov. 10:8).

At one time I was in the home-building business in California and Florida. Soil conditions, which are important in designing foundations for homes, vary widely. Compaction tests determine the soil's ability to bear weight. Drainage is necessary to carry water away from the foundations. Percolation measures the ability of the soil to drain water down into the ground.

In Florida, the sandy soils on which I built homes percolated water so fast that the soils-engineer's instruments couldn't measure it. But in Southern California, where the composition of the soil tends to be decomposed granite and clay, percolation may be very, very slow.

People's hearts are like soils, as we're told by Jesus in Luke 8:5-8. Some hearts receive the Word and, like water on sand, it sinks deep. These people grow in the Word and become sound in the faith. They become obedient to the indwelling Word.

The chattering fool is just the opposite. He may be continually exposed to the Word, but it runs off his mind without ever getting to his heart. He may even chatter on about creeds and doctrines and theology, but without any real evidence in his life of the indwelling presence of the Word as applied by the Spirit. As the proverb anticipates, this person will come to ruin.

Scriptural Examples

The Thessalonians. Paul thanked God for those who had received the Word of God, which had gone to work in their hearts through faith (1 Thess. 2:13).

Diotrephes. This malicious person, a chattering fool, was opposing the apostle John and refusing even to welcome brothers in the faith. John said that his evil actions indicated that he had not seen God (3 John 9-11).

Prayer of Application

Dear Lord, thank You for godly people like my pastors who feed me with the truth of Your Word. But hearing isn't enough. Help me to allow the Word to penetrate deep into my soul.

Walk the Straight Path of Integrity

The man of integrity walks securely, but he who takes crooked paths will be found out (Prov. 10:9).

My dictionary defines "integrity" as "soundness of moral character; a sound, unimpaired condition, or wholeness and completeness." A man or woman of integrity is one who has adopted certain moral principles in life and then walks according to them. For the man or woman of God, the Bible forms the basis of those principles. The Bible is the Christian's only authority for faith and life. Only the Bible can bind his conscience. Therefore, if the Christian is to walk in integrity, he must walk in conformity to God's Word. To do so is to walk securely, without fear of failure or shame.

How do we obey this proverb's principle and keep on the path of integrity? The bad news is that we can't on our own. However, the good news is that the Spirit of God working in our hearts by faith can! We can do all things through Him (Phil. 4:13).

Scriptural Examples

Enoch and the antediluvians. Enoch walked so closely in integrity with his God that God took him home. He never tasted death. All the while, he had lived among men who walked in crooked paths (Gen. 5:22-24; 6:5; Heb. 11:5).

Hanani. Nehemiah put this man in charge of Jerusalem because he was a man of integrity and feared God (Neh. 7:2).

Job. God commended Job as a man who feared God and walked in integrity. Job would be the first to tell us that his integrity came only from God (Job 1:8; 2:3; 2:9; 6:29; 27:5).

Ananias and Sapphira. This couple was on a crooked path. God took them home, but not like Enoch (Acts 5:1-10).

Peter. Peter was one who got off the path. Paul found out and rebuked Peter because he had left the true gospel in order to appease the Judaizers (Gal. 2:11-14).

Prayer of Application

Sovereign Lord, thank You for Your Word and for the Holy Spirit who helps me to follow its secure path. May I always walk in its light, to the end that You will be glorified in me.

Beware of Evil Conspirators

He who winks maliciously causes grief, and a chattering fool comes to ruin (Prov. 10:10).

Here is a contrast of two wicked men. On the one hand, we see a man who in conniving maliciousness causes grief to others. On the other hand, we are brought face-to-face again with the chattering fool of Proverbs10:8, who hurts only himself.

Evil men are comforted by an evil companion, just as surely as the righteous seek the fellowship of a brother or sister in Christ. Recently, America has witnessed the phenomenon of gangs in our cities. These young men and women have grouped together in malicious conspiracy. As these birds flock together, we can see their feathers match.

At the foundation of a conspiracy to do evil is our enmity with God. Without the comfort of fellowship with God, the conspirator seeks out others with whom he can face an angry God. In the judgment, what the conspirator fears will occur. He will stand naked and alone to face the Righteous Judge (Acts 17:31), and a lonely eternity of weeping and gnashing of teeth (Matt. 13:49-50).

Scriptural Examples

Adam and Eve. At the prompting of Satan, the first couple conspired together to reject God's Word. They ate of the fruit and thus began a race of many malicious and cunning fools who continue to deny the wisdom of God (Gen. 3:6).

Rebekah and Jacob. They connived to steal Esau's birthright and blessing. In so doing, they questioned the Lord who had said, "The older will serve the younger," and thought it best to take matters into their own hands (Gen. 25:21-23; 27:6-24).

Jonadab and Amnon. David's son Amnon lusted after Absalom's sister Tamar. This pair schemed together. The subsequent rape of Tamar caused grief for many in David's family, and spelled death for Amnon (2 Sam. 13:1-14).

Prayer of Application

Heavenly Father, thank You for the warnings in Your Word of those who conspire to do evil. Protect us from malicious people, and keep us from the chattering fool who is coming to ruin.

Let Living Waters Flow from You

The mouth of the righteous is a fountain of life, but violence overwhelms the mouth of the wicked (Prov. 10:11).

Water is an element that is often used metaphorically in Scripture. For the Jew, the wide and flowing river was a picture of eternity and peace. Ezekiel 47:1-12 speaks of a river issuing forth from the Temple of God that becomes so wide and deep that no one can cross it. Trees lined its banks and its waters teemed with fish and swarms of living creatures.

Water also speaks of judgment. Noah and his family rode safely in the ark through the waters of judgment, while everyone else perished (2 Peter 2:5). After the Red Sea opened to allow the Israelites to pass through on its dry bed, it raced back in judgment against Pharaoh and all his army (Ex. 14:27-28).

But perhaps water's greatest significance is in its representation of the Holy Spirit. Jesus said in John 7:38-39 that "Whoever believes in me, as the Scripture has said, streams of living water will flow from within him." By "living water" He meant the Holy Spirit. As believers, we are His temple. From us should flow His living water, a fountain of mercy and forgiveness, a flood of graciousness and kindness, a tide of joy and thanksgiving, a river of peace and patience, and a geyser of the gospel of truth. Let His Spirit flow through you and refresh the world.

Scriptural Examples

The Israelites. God spoke through the prophet Jeremiah about His people who had forsaken Him, the Spring of living water, and had dug their own cisterns that couldn't hold a drop. They were backslidden and idolatrous, prostituting themselves under every spreading tree (Jer. 2:13-20; 17:13).

The woman at the well. This Samaritan woman learned of the living water that Christ gives. Such water would become "a spring of water welling up to eternal life" (John 4:9-14).

Prayer of Application

Lord, thank You for the living waters that flow so freely. May there be in me a spring welling up toward others, inviting them to come, to taste and see that the Lord is good.

Seek Peace in All Your Relationships

Hatred stirs up dissension, but love covers over all wrongs
Prov. 10:12).

Another way to state this proverb is: "Sin separates; love unifies." Sin separates us from intimate fellowship with both God and our neighbors. Love reunites in its perfect bond.

In a parallel verse in 1 Peter 4:8, we read that "love covers over a multitude of sins." Does this mean that love hides sin? No. While love never gossips about the sin of another, there are times when love sheds light on sin. In such cases, our goal is to be reunited with our sinning brother or sister (Matt. 18:15).

Our local church congregations should be models of unity. But we often hear of a congregation torn apart by divisiveness. God hates this (Prov. 6:19). Does this mean that we should allow essential doctrine to be polluted in the interests of unity? Never. Rather, we are to consider our brother or sister first, submitting to one another in love, out of reverence for Christ (Eph. 5:21).

Scriptural Examples

Satan. Why did Satan seek to cause dissension between Adam, Eve, and God? Satan hated all three and opposed the purposes of God. By his hatred and lies, Satan stirred up dissension where there had been unity (Gen. 3:1-6).

The Creator. When Adam and Eve sinned, their bond of intimacy slipped away. They covered their nakedness with fig leaves, the works of their own hands. But God, in His love for them, covered them with the skins of animals, slain in anticipation of the One who would be slain for their salvation and eternal unity with Him (Gen. 3:7, 21).

The Corinthians. There were dissensions in this church caused by petty jealousy and bickering. As he wrote in Colossians 3:14, Paul urges us all to put on the love that binds us together in perfect unity (1 Cor. 1:10-13).

Prayer of Application

Father God, help me to be a true minister of reconciliation. In my congregation of believers, help me to be a part of the glue that binds us all together in the love of our wonderful Savior.

Let Your Lips Speak from a Godly Heart

13) Wisdom is found on the lips of the discerning, but a rod is for the back of him who lacks judgment. 14) Wise men store up knowledge, but the mouth of a fool invites ruin (Prov. 10:13-14).

When I was in high school, I knew a fellow who was always getting into fights. I asked him one day why this was so. He replied that he had a problem with his mouth. Before he could stop himself, some insult or slur would rush out and the other guy would take a swing at him. He didn't understand that he really had a heart problem, not a mouth problem.

Our Lord said, "Out of the overflow of the heart the mouth speaks" (Matt. 12:34). He said it in the context of calling the Pharisees and scribes a "brood of vipers." The fool's speech invites ruin, as did that of the scribes and Pharisees of Jesus' day.

Like my high school acquaintance, one of the surest ways into trouble is with a foolish and unruly tongue. How quickly can the words of our lips overflow from the heart and show others what is really there. Let your words come from a heart that has stored up wisdom and knowledge of the One who has called us to give Him glory (1 Cor. 10:31). Let them be words of kindness and truth, welling up from a godly heart.

Scriptural Examples

Solomon and Rehoboam. Solomon, on the one hand, asked God for wisdom so he could govern Israel with justice (1 Kings 3:8-9). God granted Solomon's request, and with his wisdom, gave him unparalleled riches and honor (1 Kings 3:12-13). Solomon had the horse rightly before the cart. Wisdom does not flow from riches and honor, but vice versa. Solomon's son Rehoboam, however, did not understand this principle and sought power at the expense of godly wisdom. He rejected the sage advice of the elders of Israel and sought to rule tyrannically. The kingdom was forever divided (1 Kings 12:13-19).

Prayer of Application

Gracious Father, You provide us richly with all things for our benefit. Create in me a heart of wisdom so that my speech might reflect Your glory. Forgive me for foolish words.

Don't Romanticize Poverty

The wealth of the rich is their fortified city, but poverty is the ruin of the poor (Prov. 10:15).

When I was in college, a security guard who had been on campus for years gave us some advice. He said that we should "get a solid education, because without it, the road of life is long and pretty much uphill." Looking back after almost 40 years, the wisdom of his advice rings crystal clear.

The middle class in America is wealthy beyond the wildest dreams of most of the world's population. It is very difficult for most of us to imagine living with gnawing hunger as a constant companion. We need to thank God daily for our wealth, our homes, our jobs, and perhaps most of all, the freedom to pursue wealth and to fail.

There is a real sense in which the fleeting riches of this life protect us from very little. But we shouldn't disdain wealth, or "embrace poverty out of laziness or romanticism" (Kidner, p. 87). Rather, if called to riches in this life, we should be careful to share with those who are poor (Prov. 22:9), and to understand that wealth is the blessing of the God who calls us to accountability for its wise use (Matt. 25:36-40).

Scriptural Examples

The prophet's widow. This woman illustrated the condition of the poor who are largely unprotected from the vicissitudes of life. She cried out to Elisha that a creditor of her dead husband was coming to take her sons in slavery to pay his debt. Through Elisha, God met her needs (2 Kings 4:1-7).

The Shunammite. In the very next verses of 2 Kings, we are told of a well-to-do woman who was also a friend of Elisha's. However, even in her wealth there were things missing that money could not buy. In her case it was a son, for which she longed. God allowed her to become pregnant (2 Kings 4:7-17).

Prayer of Application

Holy Father, help me to have mercy on the poor, and never to criticize their plight. Bring me to a better understanding of their misery and allow me to never romanticize such misery.

Labor for the Wages of Eternal Life

The wages of the righteous bring them life, but the income of the wicked brings them punishment (Prov. 10:16).

Out West we call Las Vegas, "Lost Wages." It is also labeled "Sin City." Like sin, Las Vegas makes many promises that it can't fulfill. Tourists go there lured by the glitter and glamour, hoping to "break the bank." Most go home poorer and sorrowful. Those fancy casinos don't pay their light bills with losses.

Paul says that the "wages of sin is death" (Rom. 6:23). The proverb above gives the other side of the story: that is, "The wages of the righteous bring them life." Now, we know that this righteousness only comes as the gift of God (Rom. 6:23), but we are called to labor in it (John 6:27). We are to put God and our neighbor first in our lives, and labor with a new motivation. The Lord commits to us that a sure reward awaits our faith and service, even a "crown of life" (James 1:12; Rev. 2:10).

The non-Christian labors only for himself. His mind is hostile to the things of God and does not submit to righteousness (Rom. 8:7). Lured by the glamour and glitter of the "good life," he receives instead the wages of the "bad death." What shall it profit someone if he "breaks the bank" in Las Vegas, but loses his own soul (Matt. 16:26)?

Scriptural Examples

Demetrius. This Asian idol-maker started a near riot among his fellow artisans because Paul was saying that their idols were worthless. Surely the income of the Idolator will be counted to him as ultimate debt (Acts 19:24-41).

Balaam. This false prophet loved the "wages of wickedness." Balaam knew the God of Israel, but chose instead his own madness. Peter tells us that his ultimate wages were the "blackest darkness" reserved for him and those like him (2 Peter 2:15-17; Num. 22-24).

Prayer of Application

Lord God, thank You for the righteousness that comes only by the free gift of Your grace. Give me the power to labor in the new life, warning others of the wages that lead to death.

Be a Good Example

He who heeds discipline shows the way to life, but whoever ignores correction leads others astray (Prov. 10:17).

It has been said that some people are placed upon this earth only to serve as a bad example. The Bible is full of bad examples, beginning on the very first pages. Satan, Adam and Eve, Cain, the pre-Flood people, Ham, the Babel builders, and Joseph's older brothers — the list goes on and on.

But we are called to be good examples for others (1 Tim. 4:12). We are to follow a long heritage of good examples, beginning with Abel, Enoch, Noah, Abraham, Joseph, Moses, Joshua, Caleb, Ruth, David, Jonathan, and so on. Of course, our great example is the Lord Jesus (John 13:15; 1 Peter 2:21; 1 Tim. 1:16). Paul is another, and he enjoins us to follow his example as he followed Christ's (1 Cor. 11:1). Even today, each of us knows of good and bad examples. Our pastors should be good examples to us, because the writer to the Hebrews commanded that we imitate the faith of our leaders (Heb. 13:7).

What makes the difference between the good and bad example? It is in the life of discipline; a life dedicated and consecrated to the ways and wisdom of God.

Scriptural Examples

Joash. Amaziah became king of Judah when he was 25 years old. He did what was right as he followed the example of his father Joash, who was king before him (2 Kings 14:1-3).

Nehemiah. This godly man was an example to those who had returned to Jerusalem. He showed them the right way to treat their brothers and sisters of Israel (Neh. 5:1-19).

The nation Israel. Israel was a bad example. As Moses met with God, these undisciplined people were scheming to do evil. In the desert, they lived in a cycle of rebellion and trouble, repentance and peace, rebellion and trouble (1 Cor. 10:1-11).

Prayer of Application

Lord, thank You for the many fine examples on the pages of Scripture. Help me, Lord, to set an example of Your Word in action, so that others might see and want to meet my Savior.

Avoid the Way of Hypocrisy and Slander

He who conceals his hatred has lying lips, and whoever spreads slander is a fool (Prov. 10:18).

The hypocrite and slanderer here are one and the same person. In your presence, the hypocrite hides his hatred of you, and may even speak words of friendship. But when your back is turned he slanders you like you are his worst enemy. Why? Because he wants to be thought well of, even by those he hates. Sometimes he covers his true feelings behind a mask of a smile or flattering word, yet in others he spews out vindictiveness like a live volcano spews molten lava.

The Christian is called to love his neighbor. (Lev. 19:18; Matt. 19:19; Mark 12:33; Gal 5:14). That is, we are to seek what is best for him, and to be reconciled to him. How can we then harbor hatred? We may not like what someone does, but we must not forget that the sinner knows no other way but sin. The follower of Christ knows the higher way of righteousness. He should be rebuked for his sin, but not hated for it.

If you have bitterness in your heart against anyone, confess it to the Lord (Heb. 12:15). God has called us to be ministers of reconciliation (2 Cor. 5:18). How can we, who are ministers of unity, practice the hypocrisy and slander of division?

Scriptural Examples

Joab. Joab hated Abner for his part in the death of Joab's brother Asahel. While in Hebron, Joab took Abner aside as if to speak to him quietly. Instead he stabbed the unsuspecting Abner in the stomach, mortally wounding him (2 Sam. 3:27).

Tobiah, Sanballat, and Geshem. These men sent a message to Nehemiah wanting to set up a "friendly" meeting. All the while they plotted to harm him (Neh. 6:1-2).

Judas. He concealed his hatred of our Lord and the other disciples after walking with them for three years in apparent friendship and camaraderie (Luke 22:47-48).

Prayer of Application

Lord God, search my heart and see if there is any bitterness there toward another individual. Remove it from me, Lord, and give me a heart that stands ready to be reconciled.

Watch Your Words

When words are many, sin is not absent, but he who holds his tongue is wise (Prov. 10:19).

James' epistle has much to say about the tongue. He says in 1:19 that we should be quick to listen and slow to speak, and in 1:26 that if we consider ourselves to be religious, and yet do not keep a tight rein on our tongues, our religion is worthless. The tongue is a fire (3:6), corrupting a person, setting him ablaze.

My friend Walt Henrichsen uses the analogy of the volcano. As we grow in the Word and in the control of the Holy Spirit, we undergo the process of sanctification. We begin to filter our words through a biblical grid, which serves like a cap on Mt. Vesuvius. The old volcano deep within us still seeks to blow out words of anger, sarcasm, and the like. But as we grow in Christ, we should begin to speak sanctified words. As the old self in us is crucified (Rom.6:6), and the new self is given a new desire and perspective, we should produce godly speech. The volcano is capped.

How are we to practice reining in our wicked tongues? Before you speak, pause and ask yourself, "Is it kind? Is it true? Is it profitable? Is it necessary?" If the answer to those questions is "Yes," then go ahead and speak. If not, hold your tongue.

Scriptural Examples

Miriam and Aaron. They began to speak against their brother Moses because he had taken a Cushite wife. They were also jealous of Moses' special relationship with God. Read Numbers 12:1-9 and see why God was upset with them.

Job and friends. Elihu accused Job of multiplying words of emptiness (Job 35:16), and Job accused his friends of the same (Job 27:12). As usual, God had the last word (Job 38:2; 42:7).

The praying pagans. Our Lord spoke out against those who would multiply their words in prayer, thinking they would be heard for their verbosity (Matt. 6:7-8).

Prayer of Application

Heavenly Father, thank You for delivering me from the power of sin in my life. Continue to work in me, Lord, to the end that the words of my mouth would be few and pleasing to You.

Seek Silver Lips of Eternal Nourishment

20) The tongue of the righteous is choice silver, but the heart of the wicked is of little value. 21) The lips of the righteous nourish many, but fools die for lack of judgment (Prov. 10:20-21).

The Old Testament is a rich treasury of the person of Christ. Some say He is to be found on every page. I wouldn't bet against it. One of my favorite pictures of the Lord is found in the tabernacle. God saw to it that it was made precisely according to the plan which He set forth (Heb. 8:5). God intended it to be a shadow of the real tabernacle in heaven, even our Lord Jesus (Heb. 9:24). Perhaps its gold spoke of His deity, while its wood foreshadowed His humanity. Silver was used in the bases that supported the tabernacle walls, as well as in other ornamentation and utensils. Silver speaks of redemption.

In Matthew 17:27, Jesus told Peter to go fishing. Jesus said he would find a coin in the first fish he caught. He was to use the coin to pay the temple tax. This temple tax dated back to the wilderness journey in which God had imposed a half-shekel "ransom" on all those counted in the census. The silver half-shekel was to be an offering to atone for their lives (Ex. 30:12-15). What irony that the Savior of the world paid the atonement tax that He didn't owe.

So it is that we have been appointed heirs of the atonement that Christ purchased for us and His ministers of reconciliation. Our tongues should be of choice silver in speaking of the eternal nourishment He gives through His body and His blood.

Scriptural Examples

Phillip. Phillip's tongue was indeed of choice silver. He journeyed into Samaria and there proclaimed Christ. He healed many and brought great joy with the news of salvation (Acts 8:3-12). Later, Phillip led an Ethiopian eunuch to Christ by explaining to him what the eunuch was reading (Acts 8:28-39).

Prayer of Application

Glorious Savior, help me always to speak words of nourishment. To Christians, may they be words of encouragement and joy. For the lost, may they be words of eternal hope.

Understand the Source of All Wealth

The blessing of the Lord brings wealth, and he adds no trouble to it
(Prov. 10:22).

Proverbs 10:4 says that the "hands of the diligent bring wealth."
Here, we're told that wealth comes from the Lord. Which is true?
They both are. It is the combination of our diligence and God's
blessing. The slothful person seeks wealth without diligence. The
practical atheist seeks wealth through his own diligence. But God
distributes wealth as He sees fit.

My friend Walt Henrichsen once startled a group of businessmen by saying, "There is no correlation between how hard a person
works and how much money that person earns." His statement
went against everything we had ever learned about wealth creation.

But the person who understands that God is the true source
of wealth has a humble dependence upon his Source and a call to
diligence that leaves the results to God. He understands that riches
are used as a blessing for one's family and for Kingdom work,
not for vain exercises of egotism. In this way, wealth becomes a
blessing and not a curse.

But for the slothful one who wins the state lottery, or the dili-
gent atheist who strikes it rich, wealth can bring trouble in spades.
It is worthless compared to the incalculable riches of knowing the
One from whom it comes (Jer. 9:23-24).

Scriptural Examples

Job. His story makes it clear that it is God who bestows the
blessing of wealth. Job's riches were from God, who took them all
away and then restored them two-fold (Job 1:10; 42:12).

The rich young ruler. This young man asked Jesus, "What
must I do to inherit eternal life?" Seeing his covetousness, Jesus
told him to give all his wealth away. The young man didn't realize
that he was talking face-to-face with the One who had given him
his riches in the first place (Matt. 19:16-22).

Prayer of Application

Sovereign God, You are the source of all blessing. Help me
use the blessings You provide as a blessing to others, as I provide
for my family, and for those who lack this world's goods.

Delight in God's Wisdom

A fool finds pleasure in evil conduct, but a man of understanding delights in wisdom (Prov. 10:23).

A young man was saved at a revival meeting one evening. The next day he was telling all his friends about his experience when someone asked, "How do you know you were saved?" The young man answered, "I was there when it happened."

I was "there" when I got saved too. And what happened was shortly made clear to me. My mind began to be transformed by the power of the Holy Spirit from a mind that took pleasure in evil conduct to a mind that delighted in God's wisdom.

I have always been a person who loves to laugh and have a good time. Before that day 22 years ago, that laughter and all those "good times" came in coarse joking, obscenities, sexual immorality, impurity, drunkenness, and the like (Gal. 5:3-5). Then, miraculously, my life changed and I began to delight in God's Word, the joy of walking with Him, and in the fellowship of other believers. Over the years, His wisdom has grown to be the delight of my heart and those other sins only a dim regret.

Someone may ask me, "Bob, how do you know you were saved?" Well, I was there when it happened, and I am here as it continues to happen. Only by God's Spirit working in my mind and heart could these things be so.

Scriptural Examples

Men of Sodom. They came to Lot's door seeking their evil pleasures. They demanded that Lot's visitors come out and have sex with them. God rained down fire and brimstone upon the city in judgment of its sinfulness (Gen. 19:1).

The Benjamites in Gibeah. These men raped a young woman who was the concubine of a visitor to their city. Because of their foolish evil conduct, judgment came upon the tribe of Benjamin, which suffered near annihilation (Judg. 19).

Prayer of Application

Precious Savior, thank You for giving me new birth. Since that day many years ago, You have changed me from one who delights in sin to one who delights in Your wisdom and Word.

Prepare to Meet God

24) What the wicked dreads will overtake him; what the righteous desire will be granted. 25) When the storm has swept by, the wicked are gone, but the righteous stand firm forever (Prov. 10:24-25).

What do the wicked dread? They dread the God who will ultimately overtake them and sweep them away like a storm. People hide themselves in religion, good works, temporal wealth and position, revelry and promiscuity, drugs and alcohol, and other diversions. But whatever they try will not extricate them from the coming storm of God's wrath. All paths lead to God in this respect; that God will one day judge all people in justice by the One he has appointed (Acts 17:31). Only by faith in Christ will any person find shelter from the coming storm (Acts 2:21).

What do the righteous desire? The same thing that the wicked dread—to meet God face to face (1 Cor. 13:12; 1 John 3:2). When we are born again, we are born into an inheritance that shall stand firm forever (Rom. 8:35).

Scriptural Examples

Adam and Eve. The first couple tried to hide from their Creator in the garden. Later, God would provide a covering of animal skins to hide their shame. The death of those animals spoke of the death of the One who would be slain to provide a covering of the sins of all who would believe (Gen. 3:6-10, 21).

The Babel builders. These men sought to avoid God and make a name for themselves. But God confused their languages and scattered them over the face of the earth (Gen. 11:4-8).

Sennacherib. This Assyrian king flaunted his power against the God of Israel. His entire army was swept away by the storm of God's angel of death (2 Kings 19:35).

Stephen. The first Christian martyr saw heaven opened and his Lord standing at the right hand of the throne of God. Surely his desire was granted as the stones struck (Acts 7:55-60).

Prayer of Application

Father, thank You for saving me from the wrath that is to come. In doing so, You put my feet on a path that leads to the desire of my heart. I will meet You face to face one day.

Don't Hire (or Be) a Sluggard

As vinegar to the teeth and smoke to the eyes, so is a sluggard to those who send him (Prov. 10:26).

There is vivid imagery here. Vinegar will truly set your teeth on edge, and acrid smoke stings and blinds the eyes. A slothful employee is like these distasteful elements.

A central principle of a successful business is to hire good people. Without able employees your business is doomed from the start. We who are employers, or who hire employees, need to take this responsibility very seriously.

In today's society, lawsuits are common, so proper hiring is even more important. Firing those who set our teeth on edge or blind our eyes with smokescreens is becoming more perilous daily. Take your time in the process. Get a consensus from others on the job. Don't fill the position too quickly. Review resumes and check references. You cannot be too careful.

What are the spiritual implications of this verse? We, too, are sent ones, as Jesus sends us in Matthew 28:19-20. Are we vinegar to God's teeth and smoke to His eyes? Or are we taking an integral and productive part in the Great Commission for which our Lord has "hired" us? With God's help, let each of us follow Christ's command with diligence, and avoid the path of the sluggard who displeases his boss.

Scriptural Examples

The reluctant son. Jesus told the story of a son who refused to go to work for his dad, but later went. The other son said he'd go, then refused. How this latter young man reminds me of employees who promise so much in the interview, but deliver so little when the chips are down (Matt. 21:28-31).

The Laodiceans. Christ addressed one of His seven letters to this church. They were a bunch of "sluggards" whom Jesus promised to "spit out of [His] mouth" (Rev. 3:15-16).

Prayer of Application

Father, You have called me to be diligent in all things and to do the work to which I am called in a profitable manner. Help me to fulfill that role at my job and in the Great Commission.

Fear the One Who Gives Life

The fear of the Lord adds length to life, but the years of the wicked are cut short (Prov. 10:27).

There are perhaps three senses in which the fear of the Lord brings long life. First, our actual number of days on this earth may be lengthened by a life led by the Holy Spirit. Our habits will be purer and our minds will not be beset with worry and anxiety. Second, the days themselves will be longer, as we are given a fuller, more meaningful life by our Savior (John 10:10). The third sense, of course, is that our years will never end if we continue in the fear of the Lord (Heb. 6:11-12).

The wicked person's years are cut short. His worldliness and bad health habits may do it. Even if he should live many years, they will be years filled with the guilt and sorrow that accompany unforgiven sin. He never knows the new life which God provides by grace, and chooses instead to cling to his worthless idols (Jonah 2:8). When the unsaved man does die, his death, unlike that of the Christian, is an eternal death.

Scriptural Examples

Jehoram. This wicked king's life was cut short at age 32, but more importantly, we're told that his death brought no one's regret. He wasn't even given the honor of being buried in the tombs of the kings of Israel. He, like many other kings of Israel, failed to fear the One who could bring life (2 Chron. 21:6, 20).

Jesus. Weren't His days cut short? Yes, but only because He took upon Himself our wickedness and died in our place upon the cross, to the end that we might have life. He is the Way, the Truth, and the Life (Isa. 53:4-6; Heb. 1:8; John 14:6).

Judas. His days were cut short as he threw himself over the precipice of suicide into an eternity of darkness. He walked the dusty trails of Judea with the One who gives life, yet he chose instead the way of death (Matt. 27:1-10).

Prayer of Application

Eternal God, thank You for the new life that You have given me by grace alone. I deserved death, but in Your infinite mercy You resurrected me to a new and living hope. Thank You, Jesus.

Make Your Joyous Hope Certain

The prospect of the righteous is joy, but the hopes of the wicked come to nothing (Prov. 10:28).

Hope for the future is the fuel that drives every man and woman on earth. Hope drives us on and spurs us to work hard, to go to school, to save, and to make plans for a better tomorrow. Hope that sees only darkness and destitution ahead is no hope at all. True hope, however, has as its basis a solid foundation, and it is at this point that the hope of the wicked and the hope of the righteous part company.

The solid foundation of the Christian is Jesus Christ and His Word. It is a joyous hope built on the historical truth of the resurrection of our Lord (1 Peter 1:3, 21). We are born again to this new and living hope, and receive faith as the sure evidence of it (Heb. 11:1). Our hope is that we, like Jesus, will be resurrected bodily, and reign eternally with Him in the Kingdom of heaven at His coming. We need to make our "calling and election sure" (2 Peter 1:10).

The hope of the wicked is based upon nothing. He hopes for a life after death, yet sets his feet on the shifting sands of his own good works to get him there. He hopes for good things in this life, while all around him he smells the aroma of death.

Scriptural Examples

The weeping sowers. Though we may shed many tears, as did the sowers in Psalm 126, there is a sure joy set before us, and them, just as there was before Jesus (Ps. 126:6; Heb. 12:2).

The Christian make-believers. These people called Jesus "Lord" and even preached, drove out demons, and performed miracles in His name. But Jesus said He never knew them (Matt. 7:21-23). These verses tell us that there will be many who will come in Jesus' name, but would not be His true disciples. Are you one of these, or have you taken steps to make certain your calling and election? If you are unsure, see your pastor for help.

Prayer of Application

Lord God, thank You for the sure hope You have given me of resurrection. I accept it by a faith based on the solid foundation of Christ and His Word. Thank You, Lord.

Walk in the Strength of the Lord

29) The way of the Lord is a refuge for the righteous, but it is the ruin of those who do evil. 30) The righteous will never be uprooted, but the wicked will not remain in the land (Prov. 10:29-30).

The KJV renders "refuge" here as "strength," a term Derek Kidner translates "stronghold." But, of course, the Lord is all of these things. As the psalmist wrote in Psalm 46:1, "God is our refuge and strength, a very present help in trouble"(KJV).

What is the way of the Lord? It is the path of righteousness upon which each saved person should have his feet firmly planted (Jer. 6:16). But it is an alien way to us, and to attempt to walk it in our own strength is futile. Only God can supply the means to keep His way (2 Sam. 22:33-34).

And how are we to appropriate this strength? It is only through faith in the One who says He will give it to us (Eph. 1:18-20; Phil. 4:13). We need to walk daily by faith, trusting in the One who can deliver us from evil. We need to be rooted and grounded in the Lord Jesus and His Holy Word. But the wicked do not even see their need for strengthening, because there is no inner conflict between evil and righteousness within them.

Scriptural Examples

Babylon and Tyre. These ancient cities typify the wicked who trust in their earthly wealth and power. It was only a matter of time before they met ruin and destruction (Jer. 51:49-54; Zech. 9:3-4).

Nicodemus. This high-ranking Jewish official timidly came to Jesus to ask about the Kingdom of God (John 3:1-21). Later, we see him strengthened in his faith as he tended to the burial of his Lord by his gifts of myrrh and aloes (John 19:39).

The Old Testament saints. These people accomplished all sorts of incredible things because "through faith" their "weakness was turned to strength" (Heb. 11:32-34).

Prayer of Application

Sovereign God, Your ways are so much higher than my ways, and Your thoughts so far above mine. Teach me Your ways, O Lord, and strengthen me in the path of righteousness.

Speak Wise and Appropriate Words

31) The mouth of the righteous brings forth wisdom, but a perverse tongue will be cut out. 32) The lips of the righteous know what is fitting, but the mouth of the wicked only what is perverse (Prov. 10:31-32).

Wisdom has many sides. It's not just what we say that shows forth wisdom, it's how we say it, when we say it, where we say it, and to whom we say it. In Ephesians 4:15, Paul tells us to "speak the truth in love." Our words should well up from a heart that knows God and seeks to please Him.

The wicked person will only speak that which is self-serving and perverse, as he seeks to elevate himself at the expense of his neighbor (Rom. 3:11-14). He will use innuendo and gratuitous flattery to serve his own purposes. The Bible teaches that the non-Christian cannot help but sin in all he does, and bears only corrupt fruit (Matt. 7:17).

But the righteous person speaks with gentleness and mercy. He speaks at the fitting time, and doesn't blurt out in public those things that are best said in private. The righteous man seeks out the proper person to whom to speak, and doesn't spread gossip. He doesn't slander others or belittle them to attempt to show himself in a better light. His words transmit at all times the sweetness and grace of his Savior.

Scriptural Examples

Daniel. What wise and fitting words poured from Daniel's lips. In these verses, he told Nebuchadnezzar his own dream, then interpreted its meaning to that king of Babylon. His words were fearless, yet full of tact and grace (Dan. 4:4-27).

Nebuchadnezzar. But the foolishness and wickedness of Daniel's listener soon was apparent as he did not repent before the Living and True God. God took his kingdom and sent Nebuchadnezzar out like a wild beast (Dan. 4:28-33).

Prayer of Application

Lord God, help me to speak only appropriate and fitting words, so that the sweetness and grace of Christ may be reflected in me and that He might be glorified in all that I say.

Chapter Eleven

Parallelism: Synthetic and Emblematic

In the Chapter Ten heading we discussed parallelism in Hebrew poetry and specifically antithetical parallelism in which the two phrases of the terse Hebrew poem are given from different perspectives. Chapter Eleven contains examples of two other types of parallelism observed in Proverbs: "synthetic" and "emblematic."

Synthetic parallelism occurs when the second phrase of the proverb supplements or completes the thought of the first phrase. An example is Proverbs 11:30: "The fruit of the righteous is a tree of life, and he who wins souls is wise." We learn in the second phrase what the "fruit of the righteous" is. It is a soul-winning ministry of witness. The "tree of life" bears the fruit of salvation.

An example of emblematic parallelism occurs in Proverbs 11:22: "Like a gold ring in a pig's snout is a beautiful woman who shows no discretion." Emblematic parallelism typically employs a visual image to illustrate the point, and compares it to the subject. In this case, an indiscreet beauty is compared to a pig with a gold ring in its nose. Just as a gold ring doesn't fit with a pig's nose, neither does indiscretion fit with beauty. They just don't mix. Look for the key words "like" or "as" at the beginning of a proverb. They usually tip off the fact that it is an emblematic parallelism.

Deal Honestly with Everyone

The Lord abhors dishonest scales, but accurate weights are his delight
(Prov. 11:1).

One of the greatest mistakes we can make in our Christian walk is to compartmentalize life. We must take the ways of God into every detail of our work and leisure activities, and not just into our times of formal worship, study, and prayer. What this proverb tells us is that if you own a grocery store and you falsely weigh the tomatoes to get one penny more from a customer, it's not just bad, it's an abomination to the Lord. On the other hand, an accurate scale isn't just good, it is His delight.

Greed is terribly shortsighted. The love of money produces evil (1 Tim. 6:10), and ends not only in shipwrecked faith, but in all manner of sorrow and grief. If you are tempted to cheat, even just a little, pause and ask yourself, "Why?" See the greed that is there and forsake it. Seek the path of the righteousness of Christ, and everything you truly need will be supplied to you (Matt. 6:33). God will be delighted.

Scriptural Examples

Jacob and Esau. While it is true that Esau held his birthright in contempt (Heb. 12:16), he was nevertheless cheated out of it by Jacob, who was egged on by his mother (Gen. 27:5-17).

Jacob and Isaac. Then Jacob pretended to be his older brother. He prepared some tasty barbecue and put goatskin on his hands and neck to deceive his father, Isaac. By his treachery, he stole the birthright that was Esau's (Gen. 25).

Jacob and Laban. By skillful manipulation, Jacob later dealt deceitfully with his father-in-law, Laban, and increased the size of his own herds at Laban's expense (Gen. 30:31-43).

Jacob and the silver. In his old age, Jacob was changed by God. He showed honesty with the Egyptian rulers by requiring that his sons return the silver in their sacks (Gen. 43:12).

Prayer of Application

Dear Lord, deliver me from any attempt to cheat others for monetary gain, or for any reason. Help me to be content to have what You choose to give me, Lord, and thereby reject greed.

Beware of the Pride that Brings Shame

When pride comes, then comes disgrace, but with humility comes wisdom (Prov. 11:2).

The common denominator of all sin is pride. Paul says that the love of money is the root of all kinds of evil (1 Tim. 6:10). But money is coveted in order to exalt the greedy. So we might paraphrase Paul and say that pride is the root of the love of money. Pride exalts self. In Christ, we are to humble self and exalt others (Phil 2:3), just as it is by Christ's humility that we are exalted.

Jesus did not give the invitation to salvation to those who had no need of a physician (Mark 2:17), but to those who were heavily burdened. He is gentle and humble. He is lowly in heart, and offers people rest for their souls (Matt. 11:29). God takes up the cause of the lowly and downtrodden and gives them His wisdom. But to the arrogant, and those who are exalted in their own minds, He brings shame.

Scriptural Examples

Adam and Eve. In pride, the first couple disobeyed God and ate the fruit that He had forbidden them. Shame followed immediately, as they hid their nakedness, and were ultimately driven from the Garden of Eden (Gen. 3:6-8).

Men of Babel. In pride they built a tower to make a name for themselves. God then scattered them in shame throughout the world (Gen. 11:1-9).

Uzziah. His pride caused him to usurp the prerogative of the priesthood by offering unlawful incense in the temple. The Lord brought a shameful disease of leprosy upon him, which he had for the remainder of his life (2 Chron. 26:16-21).

Nebuchadnezzar. The king of Babylon pridefully surveyed all he had built. The next moment, the Lord brought him to shame as he was driven from the palace to the field, to eat grass like the cattle (Dan. 4:29-32).

Prayer of Application

Father God, I confess that at times I have sought honor for myself. This was a wrong attitude, and one that caused me shame. Help me to walk in meekness and humility like Jesus.

Be Delivered by Righteousness

3) The integrity of the upright guides them, but the unfaithful are destroyed by their duplicity. 4) Wealth is worthless in the day of wrath: but righteousness delivers from death. 5) The righteousness of the blameless makes a straight way for them, but the wicked are brought down by their own wickedness. 6) The righteousness of the upright delivers them, but the unfaithful are trapped by evil desires. 7) When a wicked man dies, his hope perishes; all he expected from his power comes to nothing. 8) The righteous man is rescued from trouble, and it comes on the wicked instead. 9) With his mouth the godless destroys his neighbor, but through knowledge the righteous escape (Prov. 11:3-9).

These seven verses all speak to the same central theme: righteousness versus wickedness. Righteousness delivers one from evil, while the wicked are trapped in their own deceit. One key to understanding the Bible is in these two terms.

Only God is righteous. Any deviation from His righteousness is wickedness, or sin (James 2:10). Humans, in rebellion against God, are altogether wicked (Rom. 3:10-12). How then can a wicked person become righteous? Only by Christ's righteousness imputed to him (John 3:3-6). The righteousness that God brings delivers us from many troubles (Matt. 6: 22-23). It will ultimately deliver us from the wrath of God (Col. 3:5-6).

Scriptural Examples

The Israelites and Pharaoh's army. God opened the way of deliverance through the Red Sea. His people walked on dry ground, but Pharaoh's army was trapped (Ex. 14:21-28).

Mordecai and Haman. Haman built a gallows for the righteous Mordecai, but it was the vile Haman who would ultimately have his neck stretched upon it (Est. 5:14; 7:10).

Daniel's accusers. The same lions' den from which righteous Daniel was delivered sealed their doom (Dan. 6:22-24).

Prayer of Application

Lord, thank You for delivering me from the wrath that awaits the ungodly. My only hope is that Christ died for me and has become my righteousness and my sure deliverance.

Bless the Community by Your Faithful Walk

10) When the righteous prosper, the city rejoices; when the wicked perish, there are shouts of joy. 11) Through the blessing of the upright a city is exalted, but by the mouth of the wicked it is destroyed (Prov. 11:10-11).

There are many today who say that Christians are a plague upon society, not a blessing. They hate the moral law of God and would erase it from the public consciousness. Christians are ridiculed for their stands against the evils of abortion and homosexuality, to name only two issues, by those who would call evil "good" and good "evil" (Isa. 5:20).

Throughout its history, Christianity has been a blessing to society. Hospitals, schools, and orphanages, as well as the rights and dignity of women and the abolition of slavery, are only a few of the areas where Christian wisdom, work, and prayer have made a difference. We need to get involved today in the political process by supporting those who are on the side of righteousness and who know of its role in the stability and welfare of the community.

Bless your community by your faithful walk and involvement in the political process. Write letters or telephone your legislators and other leaders. Stand against those whose wicked mouths would overthrow and not build up.

Scriptural Examples

Sodom. The sins of Sodom were many and are duplicated to the extreme in American society today. The city was not blessed by God, but was destroyed by Him (Gen. 19).

Mordecai and Susa. The evil Haman plotted genocide against the Jews in Babylon. But Esther and her cousin Mordecai won King Xerxes' favor in the matter and Haman was hanged. Mordecai was elevated in the government, and the people of Susa and all the Jews in the land had a joyous celebration because of the victory of good over evil (Est. 8:7-17).

Prayer of Application

Father God, by Your grace enable me to be a blessing to my community here on this earth. Strengthen me, Lord, to work and to pray for those in authority that Your will may be done.

Respect the Dignity of Others

12) A man who lacks judgment derides his neighbor, but a man of understanding holds his tongue. 13) A gossip betrays a confidence, but a trustworthy man keeps a secret (Prov. 11:12-13).

We all know people who love to hear juicy gossip and can't wait to spread it. They don't even consider whether it is true or whether they may harm someone. They just open their mouths and out it comes. What motivates these people to do this?

As usual, pride is the principle culprit. A gossip wants to feel superior to his neighbor. By debasing his target, he thinks he is elevating himself. Gossip is cheap and fraudulent. The gossip may even reveal secret things that were given to him in strictest confidence, simply to gain this self-exaltation.

Gossip and slander are the "safest" ways to attack someone. To confront a neighbor directly is too perilous. How much safer it is to secretly sneak behind his back! We must be discerning of this foolishness and rebuke the gossip. To listen to gossip is to give credence to it. The gossip is a coward and only exhibits a low opinion of himself in his madness.

But the person of wisdom holds his peace. Why? First, wisdom implies self-knowledge. A person of wisdom knows that he is not superior to his neighbor. Second, wisdom brings the love principle. Love does no harm to its neighbor (Rom. 13:10). We are to love our neighbor as ourselves and treat him with dignity. With God's help, may we act only in love.

Scriptural Examples

Tobiah and Sanballat. These evil men tried to frighten Nehemiah into thinking they were coming to kill him. They showed their lack of wisdom as they spread their lies (Neh. 6).

Judas. What a picture of some gossips! They kiss you when in your presence, telling you what a fine person you are, but stab you in the back when out of earshot (Matt. 26:47-49).

Prayer of Application

Dear Lord, by Your Spirit keep me from listening to or spreading gossip. Help me rather to live by the law of love that seeks no harm for its neighbor, only that which is good.

Get Advice from Many Sources

For lack of guidance a nation falls, but many advisers make vice- tory sure (Prov. 11:14).

In seeking advice the temptation is strong to seek only the advice we will like. However, the purpose of advice is not to confirm our thinking, but to establish our thinking. We seek advice from several perspectives. In doing so, we are able to uncover the blind spots in our own thoughts.

In forming a board of directors for a corporation, different disciplines are sought in board members because they will all approach decision-making from different angles. From a team of diverse counselors, a business can establish a foundation that will chart a profitable and safe course through today's competitive environment.

We each need to seek counsel from many sources. Have a friend play "devil's advocate." Look for the downside potential of any course of action. Seek professional counsel. Whatever the decision to be made, the chances for it to be a right decision increase in direct relation to the solid advice one receives.

Scriptural Examples

King Rehoboam. Solomon's son chose to follow the advice of his friends and to scourge the people, rather than showing them kindness as his father's counselors advised. His problem was not that he didn't seek advice, but that he rejected the best advice and followed his own selfish motives. Because of his decision, the division of Israel ensued (1 Kings 12:6-19).

Ahab. This king of Israel sought advice about going to war. His 400 yes-men all told him to go. But Jehoshaphat suggested Ahab listen to Micaiah, the prophet of the Lord. Micaiah said he could only give God's advice, and that defeat awaited Ahab and his army. The lesson? Even if hundreds stand against the revealed will of God, choose His Word (1 Kings 22:1-38)!

Prayer of Application

Dear Lord, as I make decisions that affect my walk with You, help me to remember to seek out godly counsel. Thank You for those who will give me honest and competent advice.

Discern Between Grace and Mercy

He who puts up security for another will surely suffer, but whoever refuses to strike hands in pledge is safe (Prov. 11:15).

God calls every Christian to be a vessel of mercy and kindness (Matt. 9:13; 18:32; 23:23). But we need to see the limits of mercy. Nowhere in Scripture are we called upon to go into debt for another, particularly strangers. Why? Because not knowing what the future holds, we may get ourselves and our families into trouble and suffer for our actions in a way that is not pleasing to God. Surely we are called to suffer for the sake of Christ (1 Peter 1:21), but not in this way.

God is omniscient and knows all things—the future and even our very thoughts. He is also in control of all things. Therefore, only God can administer grace. Grace goes above and beyond what mercy requires, and we are never asked to be in the grace business. That's God's business.

Therefore, if a stranger, or a friend, comes to you and asks you to co-sign a loan, don't do it. But, if your finances allow you to lend the person the money — and you can afford to lose it — go ahead and make the loan, or simply give the person the money. God never calls us to take on unreasonable debt, and even commands us here not to do it.

Scriptural Examples

Judah. Joseph instructed his brothers not to return to Egypt unless they brought Benjamin (Gen. 42:19-20). Later, when their grain was gone, Israel would not send their younger brother. But Judah uttered an oath of surety to his father, guaranteeing Benjamin's safety (Gen. 43:8-9). He put himself and his family at significant risk.

Jesus. Jesus was surety for others and is the divine exception to the rule. As God, He redeemed strangers by taking our debts upon Him and suffering for us (Gal. 3:13).

Prayer of Application

Father, help me to understand that You want me to practice mercy but there is a limit to my resources and knowledge. Help me to know my limitations and not put my family at risk.

Seek the Wealth of a Good Name

A kindhearted woman gains respect, but ruthless (KJV: "strong") men gain only wealth (Prov. 11:16).

The contrast in this proverb is between the honor or respect of the kindhearted woman and the mere wealth of the ruthless or strong man. Respect does not necessarily bring wealth, nor wealth respect. To have a good name is far preferable to even great riches (Prov. 22:1).

In our materialistic society, there is a real tendency to equate wealth with honor. Back in the 1980s there was a wealthy couple in San Diego who were always being honored for their substantial gifts to charity. Then it was discovered that their wealth was obtained through a Ponzi scheme, an illegal pyramid that bilked naive investors out of millions of dollars. Their previous respect from the community came crashing down in the revelation of their ruthlessness.

Respect and honor are the result of a spirit of kindness and mercy. To have respect, even without riches, is of inestimable value. To have riches without respect is the worst of foolishness. To have both riches and respect is truly a blessing, and that is the state of every person who is born of God.

Scriptural Examples

Ruth and Boaz. What kindheartedness Ruth displayed in her faithfulness toward Naomi. Boaz was a strong man who was both rich and respected. He was kind and generous to all. This gracious woman and this strong, gracious man received good names that have been immortalized on the pages of Holy Scripture (Ruth 2:1-18).

Jezebel. This infamous woman was most ungracious; in fact she was downright mean. She killed the Lord's prophets and threatened to kill Elijah (1 Kings 18:4; 19:1-2). Ultimately her ruthlessly-obtained wealth could not save her, as she was thrown from a window and eaten by dogs (2 Kings 9:33-36).

Prayer of Application

Heavenly Father, thank You for the honor and riches that You have bestowed upon me in Your gracious salvation. Help me to live a life that brings honor and glory to Your name.

Know the Righteous One: Reap His Reward

17) A kind man benefits himself, but a cruel man brings trouble on himself. 18) The wicked man earns deceptive wages, but he who sows righteousness reaps a sure reward. 19) The truly righteous man attains life, but he who pursues evil goes to his death (Prov. 11:17-19).

These proverbs state a principle almost universally understood: eternal justice. Before I became a Christian, I dabbled in the Eastern religions, and knew the principle of karma, that a person will reap in this life—or the next—that which he has sown. But with Hinduism or Buddhism, the principle operates as a natural law and not as the result of the judgment of a personal God.

When God saved me, I began to see that karma, like many concepts of false religions, was a half-truth. What karma didn't tell me is that without the intervention of God, no one is capable of sowing righteousness. Righteousness only comes through Christ (Eph. 2:6-9). He is the "truly righteous man" of verse 19 above. It is by His righteous life that we are given righteousness. We have any good reward only because of Him. Romans 1:18 tells us that people suppress the truth in unrighteousness. The unrighteous half-truth of karma is one way they do it.

Scriptural Examples

Adoni-Bezek. Following Joshua's death, the Israelites defeated the Canaanites and Perizites. The enemy leader Adoni-Bezek was captured and his thumbs and big toes were cut off. Before he died, he confessed that he had done the same thing to 70 kings, and now God had paid him back (Judg. 1:1-7).

Cornelius. This Gentile centurion was commended by God for his generosity. He and his family were devout and God-fearing but had not heard the gospel. An angel told him to send to Joppa for Peter. Peter ultimately went to Caesarea and led Cornelius and others to a saving knowledge of Christ (Acts 10).

Prayer of Application

Dear God, thank You for the salvation that is mine only because of the truly righteous man, Jesus. Any good that comes from me is only because the Holy Spirit is working in me.

Praise God for His Righteous Deliverance

20) The Lord detests men of perverse heart but he delights in those whose ways are blameless. 21) Be sure of this: The wicked will not go unpunished, but those who are righteous will go free (Prov. 11:20-21).

In these verses we again see the contrast between the righteous and the wicked. Sometimes I am tempted to look upon a wicked person scornfully. But then the truth of God comes to me, and I realize "there but for the grace of God go I." The only thing that stands between the saved and the sinner—the blameless and the perverse—is the grace of God.

Look back to your own conversion. Did not God reach down and deliver you from your perverse heart of stone and put in you a heart of flesh (Ezek. 11:19)? Did not Jesus say to Nicodemus that unless a man is born again he cannot even see the kingdom of God (John 3:3)? In the final analysis, there is only One who is blameless. He is the Lord Jesus. By Him alone are we freed from the punishment to come (Rom. 5:6-8).

Scriptural Examples

The pre-Flood people. In the days before the Flood, people were going about their daily lives following their perverse hearts (Gen. 6:5). The Flood came and swept them away (Matt. 24:38-39). Unfortunately, people haven't changed. Then, only eight escaped the flood waters. But today many more are escaping. God still invites them into His ark, the Lord Jesus Christ.

Job. God said of Job that there was no one else on earth like him who feared God and shunned evil (Job 1:8). God put a hedge around Job and his household (v. 10). That hedge was the same hedge God now puts around the Christian. Job had a heart that loved God, and in fact made his suffering so much more painful, for he could not see the justice in it. In the end, God delivered Job from his afflictions (Job 42:12).

Prayer of Application

Father, I cannot imagine how You could love me when I was Your enemy. Even now I have a propensity to drift back into my old ways, but Your love and grace bring me back on track.

Seek the Inner Beauty of Wisdom

Like a gold ring in a pig's snout is a beautiful woman who shows no discretion (Prov. 11:22).

When I was a child, my family used to visit the farm of my great aunt and uncle in Tennessee. One of the most fearsome sights was that of pigs in their sty. I kept a safe distance as they rooted around in the mud and the slop. It's hard to imagine one of those porkers with an expensive gold ring in its nose. Why would God use such a hideous example to describe a beautiful woman who is devoid of wisdom? Perhaps it's because that's exactly how He sees her.

The swine is doubly horrible as an example because it was held in scorn by the Israelites—its flesh was restricted to them by the Law of Moses (Lev. 11:7). The gold ring in her flat snout only mocks the reality of who this woman really is. Charles Bridges put it this way: "Many a lovely form enshrines a revolting mind" (p. 123). To have external beauty without its corresponding inner quality is a mockery.

Scriptural Examples

Michal. Saul's beautiful daughter was in love with David (1 Sam. 18:20), but they must have had a stormy relationship. One day David danced openly before the Lord (2 Sam. 6:16). Michal despised him for what she thought was an outrageous display of worship and zeal. God made Michal barren (2 Sam. 16:23).

Abigail. The wife of the foolish Nabal was blessed by David for her discretion and wisdom. Her quick thinking in bringing food to David and his men following her husband's scorn of them kept David from vengeance (1 Sam. 25:32-33).

Ruth. I believe Ruth was a knockout. She would have been a shoo-in for the title of Miss Moab, and Miss Bethlehem since it was her adoptive home. But Ruth's true beauty resided in her heart as a woman of loyalty and character (Ruth 2:11-12).

Prayer of Application

Heavenly Father, keep me from putting too much emphasis upon physical appearance. Rather, may I value the true inner beauty only Your Spirit gives to both women and men.

Expect War Between Your Spirit and Flesh

The desire of the righteous ends only in good, but the hope of the wicked only in wrath (Prov. 11:23).

Once again the righteous and the wicked are contrasted. Here it is the "desire" of the righteous versus the "hope" of the wicked. The righteous person is that way only because God made him righteous. Therefore, the desire of his heart is God. In Genesis 15:1, God says to Abraham that He is Abraham's reward. He is our reward also as we are Abraham's seed. To be like Him, to please Him, to live with Him eternally—these are our heart's desires.

Our flesh has not yet been redeemed as have our hearts. We still have a sin nature—which I refer to as "the flesh." So while our hearts desire only good, our flesh desires only evil. Although I believe that the second part of this proverb deals primarily with those who reject God's salvation, there is a sense in which the only expectation of our flesh is wrath as well. Its end is corruption and death, while our souls will live on and will receive an imperishable body at peace with the good desires of our hearts (1 Cor. 15:42).

Scriptural Examples

The desert wanderers. Following God's divine deliverance, the Israelites still murmured against Him. They wished they were back in Egypt where they had meat to eat. So the Lord gave them their desires, but He sent a plague among them because of their wickedness (Ps. 106:15-23). Time and again they sinned against God, and time and again His wrath was revealed. Surely the wrath of God became the firm expectation of these wicked men (Num. 11:7-33).

Paul. In Romans 7:22, Paul stated that in his inner being he delighted in God's law. But then he said that there was another law at work in his body that warred against his mind. How was he to be delivered from conflict? Only Christ Jesus and His salvation gave Paul—and gives us—the victory (Rom. 7:22-25).

Prayer of Application

Father, how I sense this warfare within me. While I want to follow You and do good, I feel an opposition pulling me another way. I pray for Your strength to follow Christ in all I do.

Be Generous

24) One man gives freely, yet gains even more; another withholds unduly, but comes to poverty. 25) A generous man will prosper; he who refreshes others will himself be refreshed. 26) People curse the man who hoards grain, but blessing crowns him who is willing to sell (Prov. 11:24-26).

In agricultural communities, a greedy person might buy a poor farmer's crops for a low price, then withhold that supply of food from the market. As demand increases in relation to the shortened supply, the price per bushel would be driven higher. The greedy person would then wait for the perfect time and sell for an exorbitant price.

But the Christian is called to use God's system of economics. First, he is to recognize that God is the source of all things. Second, God honors the one who shares generously of the goods, talents, and money that God has entrusted to him. In feeding the 5,000 and again the 4,000, Jesus showed His ability to provide all the food the people needed. In God's economy, there is no lack of supply. Someone has said, "You can't out-give God." I believe that is true. God will richly reward the person who steps out in faith and generosity, trusting in the One who freely gives him all things (Phil. 4:19).

Scriptural Examples

The money changers. Jesus entered the temple area and drove these men out. Apparently, they were taking advantage of the worshippers by setting unfair rates of exchange for the temple currency. Jesus' zeal for His Father's house matched His distaste for those who made it a den of thieves (John 2:15-16).

The early church. The early Christians practiced great generosity so there were no needy brothers and sisters among them. As needs arose, some sold lands and houses to provide funds for distribution (Acts 4:34).

Prayer of Application

Lord God, help me to understand that all things are provided by Your mighty hand. Teach me to be generous to those who are in need and to use my resources for Your kingdom.

You'll Get What You Seek for Others

He who seeks good finds goodwill, but evil comes to him who searches for it (Prov. 11:27).

This proverb puts teeth in the Golden Rule. Jesus tells us, "Do to others as you would have them do to you" (Luke 6:31). This is no pious platitude. It is the law (Matt. 7:12). Don't be deceived, God is not mocked. Whatever a person sows, that shall he reap (Gal. 6:7). The person who seeks good for his neighbor finds goodwill in return. He that seeks evil will find evil.

If you've been alive for more than 10 years, you know that what I've just said isn't always the case. Volumes could be written about wives and mothers who have devotedly served their families for years only to receive scorn and beatings in return. Husbands who have diligently worked to bring good things to their families, and who have tried to lead their families in the ways of God, have been mocked by overbearing and ill-tempered wives.

It is important therefore to recognize that God does not settle all of His accounts in this life. Our motive in serving others should always be to serve the Lord and expect *His* good will, not that of the person we're serving. To do otherwise is shortsighted and may end in disillusionment and cynicism. As Paul says, "Let us not become weary in doing good, for at the proper time we will reap a harvest if we do not give up" (Gal. 6:9).

Scriptural Examples

Ruth. She clung to Naomi in love and devotion and was repaid for her kindness by Boaz, and by God as well. Her offspring was the grandfather of David the king, and ancestor of our Lord Jesus (the book of Ruth).

Haman and Mordecai. Haman sought evil against Mordecai and the Jews living in Babylon. Ironically, Haman was hung on the same gallows that he had prepared for Mordecai, while Mordecai was honored by the king (Est. 7:10; 8:2).

Prayer of Application

Lord, give me the perspective that sees Your sovereign hand over all circumstances in this life. You will not be mocked. Every person will be repaid for the way he has treated others.

Be Secure in the Riches of Christ

Whoever trusts in his riches will fall, but the righteous will thrive like a green leaf (Prov. 11:28).

As I began to study the Bible, I marveled at the foolishness of pagans who worshipped gods of wood, stone, and metal. What advances we have made, I thought, to rid ourselves of these idols of superstition and impotence. I was the foolish one.

As I grew in the Word, I began to see that idolatry has taken many forms in history. Today, it is still practiced throughout America and the world, even among professing Christians. In one way, the pagans were more enlightened than we moderns. At least they worshipped gods of gold. Today, we worship a paper god: the Federal Reserve currency, the almighty dollar.

But God demands unswerving allegiance. To put any object, commodity, or person in His place is idolatry (Col. 3:5). Paul says in Philippians 4:19 that God will supply all of our needs through His riches in Christ Jesus. Do you believe that? Or do you just play the game of lip service, trusting instead in your bank account, stocks, real estate, or Social Security check? Trust Christ alone. Be attached as a branch to the Vine. His riches satisfy like no other and endure to eternal life.

Scriptural Examples

Abraham. Abraham was one of the wealthiest men in the ancient world, rich in sheep, cattle, camels, donkeys, servants, gold, and silver. But all of his wealth he attributed to the gift of God (Gen. 24:35-36).

Job. Job was also rich beyond measure and knew God as the source of those riches. In the midst of his affliction, he said that he would trust God even if God took his life (Job 13:15).

The rich young man. This young man asked Jesus how to get eternal life. Jesus struck to the heart of his problem when He told the man to give up his trust in riches (Matt. 19:16-23).

Prayer of Application

O Lord, teach me to trust You for all my needs. I have trusted You for eternal life, why is it so hard to trust You for my day-to-day sustenance? Give me the faith of Abraham and Job.

Seek Harmony in Your Family

He who brings trouble on his family will inherit only wind, and the fool will be servant to the wise (Prov. 11:29).

To cause division in the home is to inherit the wind of the fool and not the blessings of the wise. The common denominator of unity is love, while the common denominator of division is sin. Sin always causes division as surely as the love that Jesus teaches us brings peace and harmony.

A short time ago in San Diego, a young police officer was shot to death while responding to a domestic violence situation. Violence in families is now a common occurrence throughout America and can be directly attributed to sin. Drugs and alcohol abuse, adultery, and slothfulness are just a few of the sins that torment the American home.

The Christian family, both in the home and in the church body, is to be a place of peace, rest, and sanctity. Harmony is to be protected and encouraged. Selfishness, pride, gossip, envy, covetousness, and the like are great dividing principles. Love, joy, longsuffering, gentleness, kindness, and the fruits of the Spirit like them are the principles of peace (Gal. 5:19-6:2).

Scriptural Examples

Korah. His foolish murmuring against the Lord and his complaining of the leadership of Moses and Aaron brought death to Korah and his entire family as God opened the ground under their tents and swallowed them up (Num. 16:1-33).

Achan. Like Korah, this man also foolishly destroyed his own family. God had directed that all of the spoils of Jericho be reserved for Himself, but Achan covetously hid some of the plunder in his tent (Josh. 7:11-25).

Cornelius. This Roman centurion feared God and gave gennervously to those in need. His entire family was blessed with the ultimate gift of God's salvation (Acts 10:1).

Prayer of Application

Merciful heavenly Father, may I manifest the fruit of Your Spirit as I seek to live out my new life in Christ, to the end that there would be unity in my home and in the body of believers.

Be a Soul Winner

The fruit of the righteous is a tree of life, and he who wins souls is wise (Prov. 11:30).

The Tree of Life is seen in the Garden of Eden (Gen. 2:9; 3:22-24) and in the book of Revelation (2:7; 22:2, 14, 19). It holds out the promise of eternal life to whoever eats of its fruit. (Besides Revelation, the phrase "Tree of Life" is seen only here, and in Proverbs 3:18; 13:12; and 15:4.) Following their eviction from the Garden, Adam and Eve looked back and saw cherubim with flaming swords guarding the gates to the Garden and the Tree.

In Revelation quite a different picture is given. Those whose robes are washed are allowed to eat of the fruit of the tree. Oh the marvelous grace of our God, who turns our sin, rebellion, and consequent death into the joy of eternal life with Him!

As bondslaves of Christ, He calls us to bear the fruit of righteousness that only comes through Him (Phil. 1:11; Gal. 5:22-25). As it were, we are trees of life planted in this world, and as Christ's ministers of reconciliation (2 Cor. 5:18), we are to show forth the fruit of eternal life to all people everywhere.

Scriptural Examples

Jonah. Jonah was called by God to go to Nineveh and be a tree of life. Instead, he rebelled and ran away. I'm afraid we are often like Jonah, refusing to hold out the Tree of Life (Jonah 1:1-3:10).

The apostles. When told not to preach the gospel, Peter exclaimed they "must obey God rather than men." With joy they held forth the Tree of Life (Acts 5:16-29, 40-42).

Paul. Paul won many souls for the Lord. He hoped his ministry to the Gentiles might cause his own countrymen to respond in repentance and faith (Rom. 11:13-14).

The righteous wife. Peter advised wives how to win their husbands to the Lord: through the purity and reverence of their lives, as they exhibited the fruits of the Spirit (1 Peter 3:1-2).

Prayer of Application

Father, thank You for Your gospel of grace. Not through any works of mine am I saved, but only through the life and death of Christ my Savior. He is truly a Tree of Life for me.

Don't Think You Can Get Away with Sin

If the righteous receive their due on earth, how much more the ungodly and the sinner! (Prov. 11:31).

There is a great misconception in some Christian circles that because we are no longer "under law but under grace" (Rom. 6:14), we can sin without any fear of discipline or recompense. Don't be deceived by those who would foster this nonsense. It presumes upon the riches of God's grace.

The truth might be stated like this: Those under the law found that they had no power to obey the law, and so the law for them was a harsh taskmaster which begged to be broken. The sinner couldn't do anything but sin (Rom. 7:8-9) The Christian is not given the freedom *to* sin, but the freedom *not to* sin. In fact, he is given a desire not to sin, and it should pain him greatly when he does violate God's commandments.

Scriptural Examples

Moses and Aaron. The Lord told them to stand before the grumbling Israelites and speak to the rock, out of which would flow drinking water. But in his anger at the people's folly, Moses struck the rock, not once, but twice. Water did gush forth, but God disciplined these two by not allowing them to enter the promised land (Num. 20:8-12).

Eli. The Lord let the Levite have it with both barrels because of his lax fatherly discipline. Because of his sons' sins, God took Eli's priesthood away and gave it to Samuel (1 Sam. 2:27-36).

Solomon. As Solomon got older, he followed after other gods. God's punishment was to take the kingdom from him and give it to a subordinate. For the sake of David, God waited until Solomon's death to do it (1 Kings 11:9-13).

Ananias and Sapphira. This couple lied to the Apostles—and to the Holy Spirit—in the matter of some real estate. God's discipline was immediate and extremely harsh (Acts 5:1-11).

Prayer of Application

Father God, thank You that I am no longer a slave to sin, but a slave to Jesus. Help me to walk in the way of His commands, being obedient to Him in every thought, word, and deed.

Chapter Twelve

The Temporal and the Eternal

One of the most interesting aspects of the book of Proverbs is that it often gives us truth on two levels, the temporal and the eternal. For instance, Proverbs 12:17 tells us that "A truthful witness gives honest testimony, but a false witness tells lies." On the surface the proverb seems to be a common truism. On the temporal level we can simply say we know a truthful witness by his honest testimony. But on the eternal level we know by other Scriptures more is at stake here.

In John 8:44-45 Jesus confronted a group of Jewish leaders with some strong words: "You belong to your father, the devil...there is no truth in him. When he lies, he speaks his native language, for he is a liar and the father of lies. Yet because I tell you the truth, you do not believe me!" On the eternal level of Proverbs 12:17, Jesus is the truthful witness and Satan is the false witness. Our Lord speaks only the truth and Satan speaks only lies. We humans sin because we are sinners, not the other way around. The non-Christian may often tell the truth, but he has based his entire life and worldview on a lie. The Christian may sometimes lie, but he has based his life on the truth of God's Word. Look for both the temporal and eternal meanings as you study Proverbs.

Seek a Teachable Spirit

Whoever loves discipline [instruction] loves knowledge, but he who hates correction is stupid (Prov. 12:1).

There is a modern saying to which this proverb speaks: "My mind is already made up, don't confuse me with the facts." Know anyone with a mind like that? The kind of knowledge to which the proverb refers to as loved, is knowledge of one's own self and the ultimate knowledge of the state of one's heart.

The non-Christian thinks he's good. Oh, he'll admit he's not perfect, but he's improving daily. But the Bible views humans as radically corrupt (Gen. 6:5), and getting worse every day (Titus 3:3). The non-Christian will shut his ears to this teaching even though the daily news, and his own conscience, scream of its truth.

Only God can show a person the truth about himself. Only God can provide the remedy. Once the need for and the way to a Savior is revealed to us, we should gladly seek the instruction that leads to righteousness. We need to search the Scriptures, for it is there we look into the mirror that shows us our faults. In His discipline is peace and life everlasting.

Scriptural Examples

Moses. Moses was teachable. He originally balked at God's plan to release His people. But from his humility and teachable spirit, God raised up one of the greatest leaders this world has ever known (Ex. 4:10-14).

Pharaoh. Pharaoh was thoroughly brutish, hating instruction and not recognizing his own corruption. Time and again God revealed His mighty power to Egypt's king, only to be rebuffed by this foolish man (Ex. 7-14).

Saul (Paul). At first Saul was unteachable in the true ways of God. But unlike Pharaoh, God chose to circumcise, not harden, Saul's heart. By grace on the Damascus road, Saul received a new destiny, and a teachable spirit (Acts 9:3-8; 13:9; 26:13-18).

Prayer of Application

Thank You, Lord, for opening my eyes to the awful truth about myself. Help me now to be taught by Your Word and to obey its instruction, that I might grow in Your love and grace.

Praise God for the Goodness of His Favor

A good man obtains favor from the Lord, but the Lord condemns a crafty man (Prov. 12:2).

Here is a question worth pondering: "Which comes first, the good man, or the Lord's favor?" Does the Lord bestow favor on a person because he is good, or does the Lord's favor make a person good? The Bible teaches that a person only has goodness by the grace of God. But it is amazing how many believe the opposite. There are three views of people in Christendom: that they are *well*, that they are *sick*, and that they are *dead*. Only the third is the correct view. People are dead in trespasses and sins and humanly unable to respond to the gospel (Eph. 2:1, 5; Col. 2:13).

The man condemned here is of wicked devices, and crafty by nature. He is the non-Christian. But God, who is rich in mercy, resurrects us to a new and everlasting life of goodness (Eph. 2:4-5). His favor, or grace, is not bestowed upon good people, but upon ungodly people and sinners (Rom. 5:6). We should praise Him always that we are no longer of the craftiness of the world, but rather we are of the goodness of Christ.

Scriptural Examples

The wicked servant. In Jesus' parable, this fellow owed about $5 million to his king. He begged for patience and his king forgave the entire debt. Then the wicked servant began to enforce the debts owed him, showing no mercy or forgiveness. The king discovered this crafty man's devices and unforgiving spirit, and threw him to the royal torturers, until he "paid" all that he owed (Matt. 18:23-35).

Barnabas. He is one of the few men in the Bible spoken of as a "good man." Why was he good? He was full of the Holy Spirit and of faith, both of which are gifts of God (Acts 1:4-5; Eph. 2:8-9), and only they make a person "good." What was the fruit of Barnabas' goodness? He encouraged Christians to remain true to the Lord and brought others to know Him (Acts 11:22-24).

Prayer of Application

Father, thank You for the grace that saved me from my own crafty ways. I was blinded by the ways of the world that are so enticing and seem to be so true. Thank You, Lord, for Your favor.

Be Rooted in the Righteousness of Christ

A man cannot be established through wickedness, but the righteous cannot be uprooted (Prov. 12:3).

My family and I lived in Florida in the 1970s. One of the trees of coastal Florida is the Australian Pine, an import from Down Under. The Australian Pine has a shallow root system, so when a hurricane swept through our area in 1979, those trees went down like pins in a bowling alley. Their support structure was not deep enough to withstand the high winds.

The root of the righteous is Jesus Christ. He is described in Scripture as the Root of Jesse (Isa. 11:10) and the root out of dry ground (Isa. 53:2). He is the solid rock (Ps. 62:2; Matt. 7:25). Those who have been grafted into the Tree of Life have Christ as their deep-rooted foundation against the ravages of the winds and tides of this world (Rom. 8:38-39).

Not so the wicked person, who is left exposed to the elements. He stands over and against Almighty God. How could he be secure? Wicked people will come and go, but those rooted and grounded in the Lord will be established forever.

Scriptural Examples

Abimelech. Gideon's son committed treason against the Lord. He slaughtered his 70 brothers in his plan to be king over Israel. But God had the last word. During the siege of the city of Thebez, a woman dropped an upper millstone on Abimelech's head, leaving him to die in his own search to be established in wickedness (Judg. 9).

Caiaphas. The high priest at the time of Christ's trial sought to establish the nation of Israel by an act of wickedness. Caiaphas said it was better that one man die for the people than the whole nation perish. Ironically, in one breath he both prophesied of Christ's atoning death on behalf of many and of his nation's peril because of its general rejection of that atonement (John 11:48-50).

Prayer of Application

Sovereign Lord, thank You for the solid rock who is Christ. I was like a house built on the shifting sands of my own sin, but You saved me and made my foundation secure.

Wives, Honor Your Husbands

A wife of noble character is her husband's crown, but a disgraceful wife is like decay in his bones (Prov. 12:4).

What a great gap divides the two women of this verse. The disgraceful wife seeks her own honor. She provokes arguments. She cares only about what her husband can do for her. Her love is contingent upon his performance. Her eyes may wander to other men. She may be sloppy in her administration of the family. But her main problem is she has no interest in the things of God. The love of God is not in her.

The virtuous woman is faithful to her husband (Prov. 31:11-12). She is pure (Titus 2:5). She delights in being under her husband's care and teaching (Eph. 5:25-27). She loves her husband and seeks his highest good. She is affectionate to both him and her children (Titus 2:4). She manages her household carefully (Prov. 14:11). She is considerate of others and kind to the poor (Prov. 31: 20, 26b). Finally, and most importantly, she reverences the name of the Lord God (Prov. 31:30). Future husbands, look for that last quality first. Without it, you are certain to find your bones decaying.

Scriptural Examples

Eve. Eve was created by God as a helper for her husband, Adam (Gen. 2:18). But Satan made her into Adam's temptress. She was tempted by pride, led astray by her own appetites, and gave some of the fruit to her husband (Gen. 3:1-6).

Ruth. This fine and virtuous Moabitess became a crown to her husband, Boaz. He became her kinsman-redeemer. The book of Ruth is a picture of Christ and His Church, a bride for the Lamb (the book of Ruth and Rev. 21:9-11).

Gomer. God told Hosea to go and take a vile and adulterous woman to be his wife. So he married this woman. She is a picture of the adulterous nation Israel (the book of Hosea).

Prayer of Application

Father, encourage and strengthen the godly women in the church who are seeking to obey Your Word in their homes and families. May they shine brightly in this dark society.

Be Righteous: In Thought, Word, and Deed

5) The plans of the righteous are just, but the advice of the wicked is deceitful. 6) The words of the wicked lie in wait for blood, but the speech of the upright rescues them. 7) Wicked men are over- thrown and are no more, but the house of the righteous stands firm (Prov. 12:5-7).

Here again, we see a progression to either honor or dishonor. Both begin in the thought life, then emerge through the lips, and finally result in action. There is honor for the righteous person, and dishonor and disaster for the wicked.

The righteous one is righteous only in that he has put on the righteousness of Christ (2 Cor. 5:21). Christ's thoughts and plans —not ours—are right. We should, therefore, seek the mind of Christ (Phil. 2:5); then the words of our mouths will deliver us. If we confess Him as Lord and Savior (Rom. 10:9), we will be delivered from death and deliver others as well (Matt. 28:19-20). We will stand secure eternally (John 10:28).

The wicked man's plans and thoughts are deceitful all the time (Col. 2:8), and are opposed to the truth of God. His deceitful words seek to trap the unwary. Although he may often give the appearance of righteousness, his motives are always sinful. In the end he will be overthrown (Rev. 20:15).

Scriptural Examples

Sanballat and Tobiah. These wicked men ridiculed Nehemiah and the men who had returned with him to Jerusalem (Neh. 4:1-3). Sanballat falsely accused Nehemiah of setting himself up as king. Nehemiah prayed God would remember their actions (Neh. 6:1-16).

Herod. The wise men followed the star, looking for the baby Jesus. Herod invited them to return, saying he, too, wanted to go and worship the child. God helped them to avoid his wicked advice and return another way (Matt. 2:1-12).

Prayer of Application

Father, thank You that Your Word and Your Spirit work in me the righteousness of Christ. Forgive me for my repeated failures. I long for the day when I will stand complete before You.

Seek Praise Only from the Lord

A man is praised according to his wisdom, but men with warped minds are despised (Prov.12:8).

The world sometimes honors those of godly wisdom, but not often. Typically, it gives lip service to godly wisdom but won't take it to heart. I think of the evangelist Billy Graham. Rarely has a godly man been commended by the world like Billy. Yet how many of those who honor him are willing to accept his wisdom and repent? Few.

Interestingly, worldly people will truly despise those with a heart more warped than their own. They elevate themselves in their own eyes so that their perverse hearts will seem less so.

The only praise that counts is the praise of God. He will commend all those who obtain godly wisdom, and eternally despise those whose hearts remain perverse. I have a hope for the day I meet the Lord face-to-face. My hope is that He will hug me and say, "Well done, good and faithful servant" (Matt. 25:21). Do you have such a hope? What could be better?

Scriptural Examples

Joseph. In the foreign courts of Egypt this godly man's wisdom was revered as he was elevated to the highest office in the land, just short of that of Pharaoh himself (Gen. 41:39-40).

Nabal. Abigail's husband had a warped mind and was despised by his household as a fool (1 Sam. 25:17).

David. David's wisdom elevated him in the eyes of his own people. He was well-known for his abilities, his bravery, and his manner of speech (1 Kings 16:18; 2 Sam. 5:1-2).

Daniel. Like Joseph before him, Daniel also served in a foreign land. In the midst of opposition, his God-given wisdom elevated him to a high post in Babylon (Dan. 2:48).

Jesus. Even from His enemies Jesus drew honor and commendation (John 7:46). Of course, the crowds that praised Him one day condemned Him the next (Matt. 21:9; 27:20-23).

Prayer of Application

Heavenly Father, while a pat on the back from humans is very helpful sometimes when I'm discouraged, I pray that I will seek praise from You alone. Only You can rightly judge me.

Beware of Praising Yourself

Better to be a nobody and yet have a servant than pretend to be somebody and have no food (Prov. 12:9).

Being originally from the South, I heard many stories of the fabulously wealthy plantation owners before the Civil War. Following the war, many of these families were virtually penniless, yet they tried to maintain appearances of wealth. Humbled by God's frowning providence, they refused to be humbled in their own minds. What foolish vanity. But many in America do exactly this today. They mortgage themselves to the hilt to impress others with their possessions, but hardly have enough money left after all their payments to buy food.

To seek praise and honor for one's self is always foolishness because it impresses no one. But how much more foolish to promote one's own honor when there's nothing to honor. Such is the plight of anyone who finds himself a slave to the opinions of others. So anyone who is a nobody, but has some personal possessions, is better off than the proud boaster who doesn't even know from whence his next meal is coming.

Scriptural Examples

Mephibosheth. This grandson of King Saul had been left destitute, humbled by a crippling childhood injury. David sought to honor him and to return to him all of the land his grandfather Saul had owned. Mephibosheth humbly bowed down to David and called himself a "dead dog" (2 Sam. 9:6-8).

Wedding guests. Jesus said that if you go to a wedding feast, take the lowest seat. The host may ask you to take a more elevated place. But if you take the best seat, he may ask that you give it up to a more highly honored guest (Luke 14:8-11).

Paul. Paul gave a number of valid reasons why he might boast in himself. But he found that all of his deeds were rubbish compared to the surpassing greatness of knowing Christ (Phil. 3:8-11).

Prayer of Application

Lord, grant that the same mind which was in Christ Jesus be also in me. He made Himself of no reputation, but humbled Himself, that He might accomplish our salvation.

Treat Animals with Kindness

A righteous man cares for the needs of his animal, but the kindest acts of the wicked are cruel (Prov. 12:10).

The animal kingdom has suffered greatly under fallen humankind. They have been under a curse because of our sin (Gen. 6:7,17). Even today, the whole creation groans under the burden of human rebellion against God (Rom. 8:22).

People are not to add to this suffering by cruelty to beasts, be they livestock or pets. The dumb animal cannot testify to its master's cruelty, so the wicked person thinks he can get away with it. Even his tender mercies are cruel. A person who chains a dog tightly so that it will not go into the street, and leaves it with no attention, performs a cruelty to the dog that may be worse than death under the wheels of a speeding car. Or perhaps he beats his dog, thinking it will benefit the dog as it learns to obey. All the while, the dog has no understanding as to why it is struck and the beating is in vain.

Beware, wicked person! Every animal belongs to the Lord (Ps. 50:10-12). He knows every bird and fish and creeping thing (Matt. 6:26), and He expects us to treat them with kindness.

Scriptural Examples

Jacob. On their return to meet Esau, Jacob's family drove large herds that included ewes and cows that had young. He moved slowly on his journey, and upon arrival built shelters for all of his livestock. He explained to his brother that if he drove his animals too fast, they would die (Gen. 33:13, 17).

Balaam. His donkey saw the angel of the Lord in the road, holding a drawn sword, and veered off into a field. Balaam beat his donkey to get it back on the road. The donkey pressed against a wall, so he beat it again. Finally, the donkey lay down under Balaam. He was so angry, the wicked Balaam beat the donkey mercilessly until he, too, was confronted by the angel (Num. 22:22-31).

Prayer of Application

Dear God, thank You for the pets that we own, and also the animals which provide the meat that we eat. Help us never to subject animals to pain or torment, but to respect Your creation.

Let Christ Define Success for You

He who works his land will have abundant food, but he who chases fantasies lacks judgment (Prov. 12:11).

This proverb, as does the entire Word of God, calls the believer to diligence. While farmers can till, plant, and water their fields, if they fail to follow the Lord's instructions, as in not allowing their fields a Sabbath year (Lev. 25:4), their diligence will ultimately fail. Diligence and industry alone will not provide one with real success. A Christian should seek the Lord's leadership over non-Christians who define success in worldly ways. We need to recognize that it is God alone who gives us good judgment and all good things, remembering that God calls us to faithfulness (1 Cor. 4:2), and not to worldly "success."

This is particularly true in spiritual matters. What lack of judgment there is in much of the visible church today, as people follow fantasies (2 Peter 2:3). True believers are exploited while the gospel of Christ is hidden from the unsaved. Beware of those who lack judgment. Instead, follow Him who has called you to righteousness. Be filled with His Word (Ps. 119:11) and diligently till the soil of eternity, satisfied with the abundant food of the Bread of Life (John 6:35). Let Christ define success for you.

Scriptural Examples

Cain. Cain worked his land as a farmer but was void of understanding. He brought some of the fruits of his labor in worship of God, but it was not what God had ordained, and was therefore rejected (Gen. 4:2-8).

Uzziah. This king loved agriculture and became very successful as a result. In the end, his power was his undoing. He had not followed God (2 Chron. 26:10-21).

Peter. When Christ confronted him in his fishing boat, he left all and followed his Lord. Peter did not follow fantasies, but let Christ define success for him (2 Peter 1:16).

Prayer of Application

Father, how often I look to the world to define success. But You are my Creator, and only You have the proper definition. Help me to seek Your will, and not to chase worldly fantasies.

Bear Fruit that Comes from Christ Alone

The wicked desire the plunder [KJV: "net"] of evil men, but the root of the righteous flourishes (Prov. 11:12).

There are two metaphors here, the "net" and the "root." They speak of the differences in thinking between the wicked and the righteous. The wicked person believes that he will find success in the ways of other evil people who have become "successful." Several years ago, the savings and loan crisis was in the headlines, and with it the prosecution of those who had imitated one another in deceit. They devised a *net* for the unwary and figured that they would get rich from the plunder. People will emulate the cunning plans of others, but they all lead to destruction.

The righteous person thinks in terms of the vine, or tree. The root and trunk of the tree or vine is Christ and each believer is a branch (John 15:5). Branches *bear* fruit, but roots *produce* fruit. The branch, unattached to the root system, will wither and die. It has no life in itself, but must look for its success and fruit-bearing in the life support of its attachment to the root. It is imperative for the Christian to recognize his or her powerlessness apart from the sustaining power of Christ.

Scriptural Examples

Haman. This wicked man sought for a net wherewith to destory Mordecai and the Jews (Est. 3:6). He built a gallows but he himself was hanged upon it (7:10).

David. David spoke of the cunning plans of evil men who sought his life. He described their plots against him as a net that had been hidden in a pit they had dug in the ground. He asked the Lord (his root) for their downfall. David's enemies were trapped in the same net they laid for him (Ps. 35:7-8; 57:6).

Daniel. Daniel was rooted in the love of God. As a branch, he resolved in his heart that he would bring forth fruit unto God and he did so abundantly (Dan. 1:8).

Prayer of Application

Dear Lord, thank You for grafting me into the Tree of Life. By myself, Lord, I am nothing, and can do nothing. But because I am attached to the Vine, I can do all things through Him.

Seek the Rewards of Righteousness

13) An evil man is trapped by his sinful talk, but a righteous man escapes trouble. 14) From the fruit of his lips a man is filled with good things as surely as the work of his hands rewards him (Prov. 12:13-14).

A common theme in Proverbs is that of the justice and mercy of God in rewards. (See 13:21, for instance). Here we see the wicked man sinning by his words, for which God will justly repay him; maybe in this life, but certainly in the life to come (Matt. 12:36-37). The righteous man may also transgress. But God rewards him with mercy and brings him out of trouble.

This righteous man, justified only by the atoning work of Christ, should seek to be satisfied by the fruit of his lips (Prov. 13:2) and his hands. In other words, he should be concerned only with the rightness of what he says and does, not with what specific reward he will get for obedience. Jesus commands us to seek eternal, permanent rewards (Matt. 6:19). Seek God's reward.

Scriptural Examples

Caleb and Joshua. These men urged the people to believe God and go in and take the land. Caleb and Joshua were saved from trouble by the fruit of their lips and were rewarded with entrance into the Promised Land (Num. 14:6-10, 24).

The Amalekite messenger. This man, apparently thinking he'd be rewarded, ran to David in Ziklag to tell him of the deaths of Saul and Jonathan in battle with his countrymen. As David questioned him, he discovered that the messenger himself claimed to have delivered the *coup de gras* to the mortally wounded Saul. The messenger, trapped in his own words, was struck and killed on orders from King David (2 Sam. 1:1-16).

Moses. He preferred to be mistreated with the people of God rather than enjoy the treasures of Egypt because he looked forward to his reward (Heb. 11:24-28).

Prayer of Application

Heavenly Father, forgive me for not seeking reward from You alone. Help me to trust You more and not to seek earthly rewards, but only those rewards in the life to come.

Be Willing to Be Wrong

The way of a fool seems right to him, but a wise man listens to advice
(Prov. 12:15).

Have you ever known a person who would not respond to proof? Some refuse to acknowledge the facts because their minds are already made up. Such people are puffed up in their views of themselves and think that clear teaching is beneath their dignity to consider. This verse says that such persons are fools.

The church has its share of those who are not teachable. They may know Christ as their Savior, and are therefore not fools in the full sense of the word, but they cling to dogma that has no scriptural basis. They refuse to change their position on some matters, doggedly clinging to their own ideas, even though valid proof exists that refutes them. But we are called to humility and a teachable spirit (Matt. 18:3-4; 5:3). Be solidly grounded in the Word, but also seek the input of godly people, and of the Holy Spirit. Don't adopt every wind of doctrine that comes down the pike, but be ready to change your mind if necessary.

Scriptural Examples

The rich young ruler. This man asked what he had to do to inherit eternal life. When Jesus told him to keep the Law of Moses, he responded that he had. But Jesus saw his covetousness. The young man wouldn't be instructed in the truth he claimed to seek, and went away sad and unsaved (Matt. 19:16-22).

The prideful Pharisee. The Pharisee thanked God that he was more righteous than others, that he observed the law in detail. The tax collector just beat his breast and asked for mercy. Jesus said that it was the latter who was justified (Luke 18:9-14).

Apollos. He was thoroughly trained in the Scriptures but knew only the baptism of John. Paul's friends Priscilla and Aquila took him into their home and explained to him the gospel of Christ. Apollos was teachable (Luke 24:41).

Prayer of Application

Dear Heavenly Father, thank You for Your Word and for its counsel in my life. Keep me teachable, Lord, so that I don't become wise in my own eyes and depart from Your truth.

Respond to Others in Godliness

A fool shows his annoyance at once, but a prudent man overlooks an insult (Prov. 12:16).

In a real sense, our sanctification as Christians centers on God changing our responses to false accusations and insults. You may not have a problem with proper responses to contrary people, but I do. To become angry when provoked is always a sinful response. The prudent person will overlook an insult and respond in a way that promotes peace.

In Southern California, God has given us a training ground for practicing godly responses. It is called a freeway. There is something about being cut off by someone who changes lanes at high speeds in heavy traffic that always brings out the worst in me. I don't often respond in a godly way.

God is not pleased by angry responses, and now the minute I even think wrongly of the other driver, I am convicted of it. May God help us to respond in godliness and Christlikeness, and with a blessing as opposed to a curse.

Scriptural Examples

Moses. At Meribah, God commanded Moses to answer the people's rebellious murmurings about their lack of water by speaking to the rock, and water would pour forth from it. Moses gathered the people together, but was very angry and sarcastic, calling them rebels. Then he angrily struck the rock twice with his staff and water gushed out for the people to drink. The Lord accused Moses and Aaron of the same sin of which they had charged the people: not trusting Him (Ex. 20:2-13).

Jesus. Jesus showed us precisely what our response should be when attacked or accused unjustly. He was held up to scorn and bitter reproach, yet He remained calm and silent (Matt. 26:63; 27:14) and did not seek to retaliate. Instead, He trusted God, who knows human hearts and is able to judge justly (1 Peter 2:21-23).

Prayer of Application

Father, teach me the proper response to those who rankle me with contrariness. Change me, Lord, into the likeness of Your Son who answered His accusers calmly and peacefully.

Speak with an Honest Tongue

A truthful witness gives honest testimony, but a false witness tells lies
(Prov. 12:17).

The ninth commandment (Ex. 20:16) teaches us not to bear false witness. That is, we are not to seek to injure anyone by lying. But it goes beyond just avoiding injuring another. We are to speak the truth and even rejoice in it (1 Cor. 13:6). The truth should be spoken in love. We need to keep firmly committed to the One True Witness, who came seeking our best.

The false witness speaks lies. Or he will use half-truths to deceive others. By taking the truth out of context, or by only giving a portion of the truth, he deceives. That is the wicked person's intent. The spiritual person should seek the whole truth, and speak it in love and righteousness.

When a person is called as a witness in a court of law, the bailiff will ask him to take an oath that goes something like this: "Do you promise to tell the truth, the whole truth, and nothing but the truth?" We should always do that, speaking the truth in love.

Scriptural Examples

Doeg the Edomite. David lied to Ahimelech the priest that he was on a mission from King Saul, and asked for food and a sword. Ahimelech gave both to David. Doeg overheard all of this, but when he reported it to Saul he deceitfully left out parts of the whole story. At Saul's command, Doeg killed Ahimelech and 84 other priests (1 Sam. 21:1-7; 22:9-10).

The false witnesses. The Sanhedrin looked for some false witnesses to trump up charges against Jesus. Many were apparently rejected because of their obvious error and conjecture. Two witnesses came forward who spoke part of the truth. Jesus had indeed said, "Destroy this temple and in three days I will raise it up" (John 2:19), but never in the context of anarchy or blasphemy against God (Matt. 26:60-61).

Prayer of Application

Father in heaven, place in my heart a true spirit of love for others and help me never to lie. Strengthen me in my love for them, so I will seek good for all and harm for none.

Speak with a Kind Tongue

Reckless words pierce like a sword, but the tongue of the wise brings healing (Prov. 12:18).

I have never been pierced by a sword, but I did put a telephone pole climber's spike through my foot as a boy and I understand the pain that is involved. I have also received harsh words from a loved one that put a pain in my chest like that of a sword's piercing. It took several hours for the pain to subside. I pray that I will never hurt someone like that. Words can cause deep wounds, and there are reckless people who use such words without compunction.

But God calls us to kindness (Gal. 5:22). Our first consideration must always be for the glory of God, and then for the welfare of others (Matt. 22:36-40). God has treated us with incredible kindness. How then can we treat other human beings with anything but the same? Shall we not rebuke others? Yes, we must rebuke them when necessary, but in kindness, hoping for reconciliation between parties (2 Cor. 2:5-7).

Scriptural Examples

Jesus. Our Lord was often the recipient of reckless words. Because He associated with people of low estate, and attended banquets and parties, the Jewish leaders falsely said of Him, "Here is a glutton and a drunkard" (Matt. 11:19).

Jesus. As He stood before the Sanhedrin, and truly testified of Himself, He was falsely called a blasphemer (Mark 14:64).

Jesus. They accused Him also of sedition (Luke 23:5) and of anarchy in plotting the destruction of the temple (Mark 14:58).

Jesus. But our Lord always spoke with kindness, except in moments of righteous rebuke (Matt. 23). Even then, His were words of truth, not slander. Our Lord spoke words of comfort and encouragement to the poor and the sick. We are called to walk in His steps.

Prayer of Application

Father, thank You for the example of Jesus, who spoke words of life and salvation. Help me, Lord, to treat all people with kindness. Not because they deserve it, but for Christ's sake.

Speak Words of Eternity

Truthful lips endure forever, but a lying tongue lasts only a   moment
(Prov. 12:19).

Truth is like an endless river, flowing crystal clear in an uninterrupted eternity of time. The same truth in Noah's day is true in our day and will be true for the ages to come (Heb. 13:8). The lying tongue wants to darken the truth, as mud or pollution in the river. This is the basis of Satan's work. He is intent upon damming, diverting, or dimming the river of truth. He pours his lies into the river because he is the father of lies (John 8:44).

Today, many deny the existence of the river of truth. Like the scorning Pilate they ask sarcastically, "What is truth?" To them, all truth is subjective, and is to be determined by each individual for himself. But in spite of them, the river flows on. Those lips will speak only for a moment and then pass away.

The Bible admonishes us all to speak its truth in love (Zech. 8:16-17; Eph. 4:15) and avoid that which would hide or darken it. Delight yourself and refresh others in the clear and eternal river of truth, which is the Word of God (John 17:17).

Scriptural Examples

Shimei. Shimei cursed David (1 Sam. 16:5) but David let him live. Upon Solomon's ascent to the throne he sent for Shimei and allowed him to build a house in Jerusalem while restricting him to the city. Shimei agreed, then broke his word three years later and went out in search of some runaway slaves. Solomon found out about it and confronted Shimei. The king then put the liar to death for the wrong he had done to his father, David (1 Kings 2:36-46).

Peter. Jesus asked, "Who do you say that I am?" Peter answered, "You are the Christ, the Son of the living God." Jesus blessed Peter and told him that the truth had been revealed to him by the Father. This revelation of truth was to be the "rock" upon which the eternal church is founded (Matt. 16:15-18).

Prayer of Application

Father, thank You for the certainty of Your enduring and perfect Word. Help me to know the Word, Lord, so that I may be able to speak its truth to others who need it desperately.

Joyfully Rest in the Truth, Delighting God

20) There is deceit in the hearts of those who plot evil, but joy for those who promote peace. 21) No harm befalls the righteous, but the wicked have their fill of trouble. The Lord detests lying lips, but he delights in men who are truthful (Prov. 12:20-22).

The non-Christian's heart is inclined toward deceit. He is a slave to his imaginings of evil (Gen. 6:5; Eph. 2:1-2). He is filled with trouble, and indeed born to it (Job 5:7). His lying lips are an abomination to the Lord. Except for the gracious intervention of God, he will die in that condition (Eph. 2:4-5).

The Christian seeks peace for his neighbor. He delights in the truth, and does not lie. At least he should know better (Rom. 8:6). He receives the joy that comes from a clear conscience (2 Cor. 1:12). He does not fear evil (1 John 4:18), because all circumstances, even the lying lips of the wicked and their abominable deeds, will work to his eternal benefit (Rom. 8:28).

This is the one who delights God: the one whom God has called to salvation and who rests in and obeys the truth of God. He produces a crop of righteousness (Matt. 13:23) through faith in Christ. God seeks these people to worship Him (John 4:23), to glorify Him in all that they do (1 Cor. 10:31).

Scriptural Examples

Ananias and Sapphira. This early church couple joined others in selling their property and distributing the proceeds among the poor (Acts 4:32). However, they deceitfully withheld a portion of the proceeds from a sale, retaining it for their own use. There was nothing wrong in doing that, but they had apparently led others to believe that they were actually giving it all. In fact, they lied to the Holy Spirit, who knows our every thought and motive.

God dealt very severely with them. First, Ananias fell down dead. Later, his wife, Sapphira, also perished. God used their example to train others in His church (Acts 5:1-11).

Prayer of Application

Dear Lord, I humbly ask You to take away the vestiges of evil that remain in my heart. Crowd them out with Your truth, Lord, that I might bring You joy in all that I do and say.

Speak with Discernment

A prudent man keeps his knowledge to himself, but the heart of fools blurts out folly (Prov. 12:23).

A few years ago, my older brother Bill was on a summer mission to Qingdao, in China. In his letters to me, he used such phrases as "think about my bad knee." I knew that he was using a code because he knew that his letter was being censored, so he used "think" instead of "pray." His ministry among the people was his garden, where seeds were sown and a harvest was taken. He had to be particularly discerning when talking to the Chinese people about Christ. His group could get into much trouble by looking like they were proselyting.

We may not live in a country where such concealment is necessary or where such a code would be advisable. But we do need to be discerning about our speech, particularly with those outside the church. To discuss with them deep truths regarding Christ is not prudent when they will not even accept the elementary truths about Him. Keep it simple, and always pray for, and rely upon, the leadership of the Holy Spirit in all your conversations with unbelievers.

Scriptural Examples

Abraham. The patriarch kept quiet about the mission to Mt. Moriah on which God had ordered him to go. He spared his family great stress by doing so (Gen. 22:1-7).

Joseph. When he first received his brothers in Egypt, Joseph chose to keep his identity a secret. By doing so, he disciplined them and heightened the suspense and impact of his ultimate unveiling (Gen. 42:7).

Esther. In the court of a foreign king, Esther prudently concealed her identity as a Jewess (Est. 2:10).

Jesus. Jesus often cautioned the disciples to keep the truth about Him secret until the timing was right (Matt. 16:20.).

Prayer of Application

Father, I find that too often my mouth speaks before my brain is engaged. Give me a tongue of discernment, one that will have wisdom to speak only words that bring glory to You.

Prepare to Reign with Christ

Diligent hands will rule, but laziness ends in slave labor
(Prov. 12:24).

We have here two polar positions in life—a ruler and a slave—and two reasons for it. The businessperson who has laid the foundation of a solid education, then diligently applied his time and intelligence to the solution of problems, should move up in the ranks of leadership. Conversely, the person who was slack in his educational efforts and who does not apply himself to the job may never be promoted, and may even be fired. We all know of instances where a slothful person has been elevated, but that is the exception and not the rule.

As Christians we have another eternal sphere in which we are focused, and where it is imperative that we show diligence. Paul tells us in 2 Timothy 2:11-13 that we will live with Christ eternally if we died with Him, and if we endure in patient and faithful service, we shall also reign with Him. However, if we disown Him, He will disown us. If we are faithless, He will remain faithful, but what a scourging rebuke to be found faithless in God's sight. Be diligent in His work and look forward to your reign with Christ.

Scriptural Examples

Joseph. Pharaoh looked for a diligent man to rule. Who else should it have been but the man who had shown himself wise and discerning (Gen. 41:39-41).

Joseph's family. Upon their arrival in Egypt, Joseph's brothers and their families were assigned to the land of Goshen as their home. Because of their experience, Pharaoh entrusted them with his cattle (Gen. 47:6).

The wise and faithful servant. This servant was diligent and obedient, even in his master's absence. When he returned, he would put the servant in charge of all he owned (Matt. 24:45-51).

Prayer of Application

My Lord and God, please give me the desire and then the strength to diligently serve You every moment of my life. May the diligence of my life bring honor and glory to Your name.

Speak Comforting Words

An anxious heart weighs a man down, but a kind word cheers him up
(Prov. 12:25).

A few years ago, I went through a very difficult trial in my life. I was weighed down in sorrow. Thank God for His Word, which lifted me up and took the weight off my back. The Word reminded me of my hope in Christ, and gave me courage to keep on keeping on. I used to go to sleep reciting the 23rd Psalm. His rod and His staff comforted me. Jesus commands us not to worry (John 14:1). His instruction is precious and always comforting.

But also precious beyond words is the comfort offered by other believers during times of trials. Sometimes we can get so discouraged that we don't even want to open the Bible. Then, the comforting words of a dear brother or sister are sweet indeed. God has sent us His Comforter and I believe that He speaks through the mouths of people like you and me. Open your heart to the Holy Spirit and ask Him to make you His vessel of comfort and encouragement to those around you.

Scriptural Examples

Ruth. All of the men of her family died in Moab, leaving only Naomi and her two daughters-in-law. Only Ruth stuck by Naomi, offering her comforting words (Ruth 1:16-17).

Elijah. Elijah was feeling alone and discouraged. "I am the only one left," he said, "and now they are trying to kill me, too." But God came to him with encouraging words. He said that He had reserved 7,000 who had not bowed their knee to Baal. Refreshed, Elijah got up and into action (1 Kings 19:9-21).

The Philippian jailor. Paul and Silas were thrown into jail in Philippi. That night, an earthquake opened the doors of the jail. The jailor was about to kill himself when Paul spoke comforting words to him. No one had tried to escape. Later, more comforting words brought salvation (Acts 16:12-34).

Prayer of Application

Dear Father, how I need the comfort and encouragement of Your Word and of Your children. Help me through my experience to be one who is able to comfort and encourage others.

Beware of Being Misled by Wicked Friends

*A righteous man is cautious in friendship, but the way of the wicked
leads them astray* (Prov. 12:26).

The righteous person differs from his wicked acquaintance in
his relationship with God. He is called into a more excellent family, set on a more excellent path, fed food and clothed in a more
excellent way, and is given a more excellent hope. The Christian
should therefore be careful not to rush into friendships where his
moral insight into appropriate behavior would be harmed.

Satan was led by his insatiable quest to war against God, and
therefore tempted Eve to commit a seemingly innocent act of
eating a piece of fruit. Although warned, Adam and Eve couldn't
fathom the fatal consequences that would follow. And so it is, that
we, too, are potentially blinded to the consequences of sin in our
lives. One way to avoid sin is to avoid friends who would lead you
to violate the clear teaching of God's Word.

Scriptural Examples

Abram. The patriarch was circumspect in his association
with others. Following his rescue of Lot from Kedorlaomer and
the kings associated with him, Abraham was met by the king of
Sodom. The Sodomite monarch told Abram he could keep all of
the plunder stolen from the city if he would return the people. But
Abram told the king he would not so much as keep the thong of
a sandal so it could not be said that Sodom made Abram rich. In
this way, Abram distanced himself from the city and its sin (Gen.
14).

Lot. Conversely, Lot lived among the people of Sodom. He
apparently was the city's only righteous man (2 Peter 2:7-8). Peter
tells us how Lot was distressed and even tormented by the awfulness
of the deeds of the Sodomites. His problem was he settled there
in the first place, instead of distancing himself from it as Abram
did (Gen. 18:16-19:38).

Prayer of Application

Heavenly Father, others who do not know Christ may seek
to mislead me into sinful ways and habits. Protect me from their
deceit and wickedness and lead me in the way everlasting.

Conserve God's Precious Resources

The lazy man does not roast his game, but the diligent man prizes his possessions (Prov. 12:27).

This verse has always reminded me of bird hunting in Mexico. We always brought home dove or duck, but we rarely brought back any quail. They were so precious to us and so good to eat that we would clean them in the field, stuff them with tomato and onion, wrap them in tinfoil, and throw them on the hot coals of the fire. Soon there was a feast fit for a king.

The lazy man here has enough energy to go hunting. It's his attitude that is atrocious. He doesn't hunt for food. Maybe he just goes out to be with the boys and have a good time. Whatever his reason, he leaves God's resource to rot on the ground.

God's common grace has bestowed upon humankind many vital and precious resources. Unfortunately, many have done their best to exploit and destroy them. God gave us authority over the earth, but that authority carries with it responsibility. If we are truly God's servants we will conserve His precious resources.

Scriptural Examples

Esau. Here is a man who loved to hunt and who prized his kill. But there was a more substantive gift which he cared less about: his birthright as the first born son of the patriarch Isaac. He was a godless man who sold his precious birthright for a bowl of red stew (Gen. 25:29-33; 27:30-36; Heb. 12:16-17).

The Egyptians. Warned by God through Joseph, the Egyptians conserved the first seven years of harvests. By the time the famine arrived, they were ready for it (Gen. 41).

The manna. God sent the Israelites manna each morning. On the sixth day, they would collect enough for two days, so that on their Sabbath day, they wouldn't have to work in gathering it. By the manna, God taught His people to trust in His provision, and to follow His orders precisely (Ex. 16:22-23).

Prayer of Application

Dear Lord, we are often a wasteful people, and consume more than we ought. Help me to see areas in my life where I can be more diligent in conserving the gifts You so graciously give.

Walk in Christ, Your Pathway of Righteousness

In the way of righteousness there is life; along that path is immortality
(Prov. 12:28).

I once thought Christianity was a matter of religiously keeping a set of laws, living a righteous life, and observing certain sacraments. If you did it right you might get to heaven. But Christianity is a person; the God-man Jesus. Christianity isn't even a religion in the normal sense. Christianity is Christ!

Religions claim to be pathways to God. But Christ isn't just the pathway to God, He *is* God, and as such He is the pathway of righteousness. In the person of Jesus, God came to this earth to live a perfectly righteous life. He died as an atoning sacrifice on the cross in order to secure our salvation. Through Him we are regenerated (Titus 3:5-6), reconciled (Rom. 5:10), justified (Rom. 5:8-9), sanctified (Eph. 5:25-26), and glorified (Rom. 8:30). He imputes His righteousness to us. We haven't any of our own!

Christ rose from the dead to seek and to save the lost (Luke 19:10) and to give them power to walk the path of righteousness by living in them. Only through Christ can a sinner's feet even hit the pathway to righteousness. And in that pathway there is no death. There is no other way to God (John 14:6).

Scriptural Examples

Jesus. Just who did Jesus claim to be? Let's look at some verses where Jesus uses the phrase, "I am." John 6:35—"I am the bread of life." John 8:12—"I am the light of the world. Whoever follows me will never walk in darkness." John 10:9—"I am the gate; whoever enters through me will be saved." John 10:11—"I am the good shepherd. The good shepherd lays down his life for the sheep." John 11:25 —"I am the resurrection and the life. He who believes in me will live, even though he dies." John 14:6—"I am the way and the truth and the life." John 15:1—"I am the true vine." Only through Jesus may we branches bear the fruit of righteousness.

Prayer of Application

Father, thank You for the unspeakable gift of salvation through Your Son, who as both truly God and truly man, lived and died that I might walk the pathway of life and righteousness.

Chapter Thirteen

The Law of God: Its Three Uses

As mentioned in the Preface, the book of Proverbs has been called "the Ten Commandments in shoe leather." That is because it shows us how to apply God's moral law to our daily lives. Much confusion about the role of God's law exists today. Paul says, "You are not under law, but under grace" (Rom. 6:14). Does that mean we put aside the law? Paul answers that question in Romans 6:15: "By no means!" But what role does the law play for the Christian?

No one was ever saved by keeping the Law (Rom. 3:20). It can do nothing to justify the sinner or to relieve his bondage to sin. Only grace can do that. The Law's first purpose was to restrain sin in society by providing a ground for all moral laws and ethical decisions. Secondly, the moral Law was intended to drive people to their knees, pleading to God for mercy, by exposing their sin and their inability to consistently keep its commands. Thirdly, and most importantly for the Christian, the moral Law of God gives us a rule by which we may shape our lives and find happiness.

The Law is to be the delight of the redeemed heart (Ps. 1, 119:97; Rom. 7:22). The Law is a gift of grace (Ps. 119:29), a way of life and the road to the blessings of God (Deut. 28:1-14; 30:11-20) that has been given for our own good (Deut. 10:12).

Open Your Ears to the Father's Instruction

A wise son heeds his father's instruction, but a mocker does not listen to rebuke (Prov. 13:1).

When I was a new Christian, I used to wonder at the words of Jesus when He said, "He who has ears to hear, let him hear." (See Mark 4:9, 23; Luke 8:8; 14:35, for instance.) Ezekiel 12:2 explains it. The people had ears, but they were rebellious. They just didn't want to know the truth. Know anybody like that?

What does it really mean to "hear" in the biblical sense? Hearing in the Bible connotes receiving the message with the heart as well as with the brain, and acting upon the message in repentance and faith. The scorners of Jesus' day didn't want to repent and turn to Him, and it's the same way today. Many people don't have the spiritual ears to hear.

But we are exhorted to hear and be obedient to our natural fathers, and more so to the Father of our spirits (Heb. 12:9). We do it so that we may share in His holiness (Heb. 12:10), and be conformed to the image of His Son (Rom. 8:29).

Scriptural Examples

Isaac. He opened his ears and willingly obeyed Abraham on Mt. Moriah. Like Christ, Isaac was obedient even unto death, although God provided an alternate sacrifice (Gen. 22:6-12).

Er and Onan. These sons of Judah were so disobedient that the Lord put them both to death. When told by his father to lie with Er's widow, Tamar, and fulfill his duties under the law (Deut. 25:5-6) Onan spilled his semen on the ground. Read this entire story, and you may get some insight about the man from whom these boys inherited their disobedience. Tamar ultimately had a son, Perez, an ancestor of Jesus (Gen. 38).

Jesus. Faced with unimaginable suffering as He prepared to bear the sins of His people, Christ heard His Father and was obedient (Luke 22:44).

Prayer of Application

Heavenly Father, thank You for Your Word and for its rule over me. Open the ears of my heart, Lord, that I might hear and respond in obedience to the proper activity for my life.

Be Blessed by Your Own Words

From the fruit of his lips a man enjoys good things, but the unfaithful have a craving for violence (Prov. 13:2).

I see three ways in which God's people will enjoy good by the fruit of our lips. First, we are often edified in what we say. I am sometimes amazed at what I say in a Bible class I'm teaching. Something I haven't planned just comes out; words that are fitting to the situation, and true, but not planned. I know instantly the Spirit put those words on my lips. Second, we are saved if we believe in our hearts God raised Jesus from the dead and if we confess Him with our lips (Rom. 10:9). Our words in that case bless us eternally. Third, the fruit of the lips of a righteous person is sanctified by the Spirit of God. The love, joy, peace, longsuffering, gentleness, goodness, faithfulness, kindness, and self-control (Gal. 5:22-23) of a person's lips produce friendship, righteousness, and peace in his life, and in the lives of others as he comforts and encourages them.

Scriptural Examples

Korah, Dathan, and Abiram. These men exalted themselves and questioned the authority of Aaron and Moses. God caused them to eat violence, and a lot of sand to boot, as they were swallowed up by the earth (Num. 16:1-32).

Simon Peter. Jesus asked the disciples, " Who do the people say that I am?" Then He asked them, "Who do you say that I am?" Peter said, "You are the Christ, the Son of the Living God." Jesus blessed his words and told him that he had spoken what could only have been revealed by God (Matt. 16:13-17).

The Pharisees and teachers of the law. Jesus pronounced seven woes upon these blind guides. They denied they would ever strike down a prophet of the Lord. Jesus scathingly rebuked them, stating they would eat the violence their words and actions brought about (Matt. 23:29-36).

Prayer of Application

Father God, having confessed my faith in the Lord Jesus with my words to You and to others in my church, grant that I might confess Him and glorify Him always with my words.

Guard Your Lips

He who guards his lips guards his life, but he who speaks rashly will come to ruin (Prov. 13:3).

During World War II, the War Department put this principle into a short rhyme: "Loose lips sink ships." They meant that secrets shared with others would hurt the war effort. As Christians, we too are at war—spiritual warfare—with eternal souls at stake. We need to be cautious in what we say, and not babble on with the disease of fools (Eccl. 5:3) often known as "diarrhea of the mouth."

Economists speak of the law of supply and demand. The higher the supply of something, the less value each unit of it has, assuming demand remains constant. I think that economic principle applies to words, too. The more words you speak, the less potential value each of your words will have to the hearer. When the immediate listener is God, as when you pray, Jesus cautioned us not to babble on like the pagans, who thought they would be heard for their many words (Matt. 6:7).

Scriptural Examples

Ham. Following the Flood, Noah planted a vineyard and drank some of its wine. Apparently he drank too much, because he passed out naked in his tent. Ham, seeing his father's nakedness, ran outside and couldn't wait to tell his brothers, Shem and Japheth. Because of his big mouth, Noah cursed Ham's son Canaan, a curse that is still having serious effect upon the course of world history (Gen. 9:20-22).

Hezekiah. Following an illness from which the Lord cured him, Hezekiah proceeded to show all of the nation's treasures to men from Babylon. I imagine that he "babbled on to the Babylonians" about the wealth of the land. The prophet Isaiah scolded the king about his serious lack of judgment in the matter and predicted that it would cause the ruin of Jerusalem and the captivity into Babylon (2 Kings 20:12-19).

Prayer of Application

Sovereign Lord, I pray as the psalmist prayed that You would set a guard over my mouth and a watch over my lips. Give me wisdom in my speech, that it would be restrained.

Be Diligent in Spiritual Things

The sluggard craves and gets nothing, but the desires of the diligent are fully satisfied (Prov. 13:4).

I am reminded of the man who approached the piano virtuoso following his concert and said, "I'd give half of my life to play like that." The pianist responded, "That's exactly what I did." The man had the desire, but desire alone wouldn't teach him to play the piano. He needed the diligent study and practice of the concert pianist to reach his aspiration.

Although diligence is profitable in many areas of life, it is indispensable in spiritual things. The Bereans, we're told, didn't just take the things they heard Paul say as the gospel truth. Rather, they searched the Scriptures daily to see whether or not they were true (Acts 17:11). Doctrine is important. It is only through doctrine that we can have assurance of salvation. We're warned many times in Scripture to beware of false doctrine. (See Matt. 24:11; 24:24; 2 Cor. 11:13; Gal. 2:4; 1 Tim. 1:3, for instance.) But the study of the Scriptures isn't the only way we're to be spiritually diligent. We are to be diligent in prayer (1 Thess. 5:17), in obedience, in making our calling sure (2 Peter 1:10), in guarding against defilement (Heb. 12:15), in good deeds (1 Tim. 2:10), and in instructing our children (Deut. 6:7). God will reward our diligence as we seek to know Him.

Scriptural Examples

Ezra. This man of God returned to Jerusalem to begin reforms among the people. We're told that Ezra was blessed by God as he devoted himself to the study and keeping of God's law, and in teaching it to others (Ezra 7:9).

The Pharisees. These men were commended by Jesus for their diligent study of God's Word. Their problem was that they didn't combine their diligence with faith in Christ, and consequently missed the blessings of that diligence (John 5:39-40).

Prayer of Application

Father, thank You for giving me a desire to follow Your Word in obedience. Help me to make its diligent study and application the top priority in my life, that I may be satisfied.

Hate Falsehood

The righteous hate what is false, but the wicked bring shame and disgrace (Prov. 13:5).

I marvel at how some people can tell a bald-faced lie and not feel any guilt. If I tell a small fib, or exaggerate the truth a little bit, I feel the conviction of the Spirit immediately. I hate lying, as the proverb says I should, and yet for some reason from time to time I lie. Why do I lie if I hate falsehood?

There are many reasons that will tempt a person to lie, but they all center around selfishness. I lie to protect myself. I lie because I'm lazy and sometimes it seems easier than telling the truth. I lie to make myself look better in the eyes of others. But I've been born again of the Spirit of God! Why do I do these things? Paul says that he, too, loathed some of the things he did and he blamed the sin that was still in him (Rom. 7:19-20).

But the wicked person takes pleasure in deceiving others. Often, his lies will find him out and he will be brought to shame in this life, as Gehazi was when confronted by Elisha (2 Kings 5:27). But God doesn't pay all His bills in this life. The wicked one who brings shame and disgrace will be rewarded ultimately with eternal punishment (Rev. 21:8).

Scriptural Examples

Abraham. Abram lied about his wife Sarai to the Egyptians. He said she was his sister, because he was afraid if they knew she was his wife they would kill him. The deceit backfired as usual, and the Lord inflicted a disease upon Pharaoh and his household for taking Sarai into the palace (Gen. 12:11-19).

Satan. He is the father of lies (John 8:44). He lied to Eve in contradicting God's words (Gen. 3:4-5). He lied to God about Job's motives in trusting Him (Job 1:9-10). He lied to Jesus in the wilderness as he sought to tempt Him. Beware of his trickery. Satan still spreads his deceit in false doctrine and temptation (Matt. 4:8-9).

Prayer of Application

Sovereign Lord, Your Word is truth. Help me to seek the truth in all things, particularly in my own speech. May I speak the truth in love that it may bring healing to all I meet.

Persevere by the Righteousness of Christ

Righteousness guards the man of integrity, but wickedness overthrows the sinner (Prov. 13:6).

The Bible states emphatically that there are none who are righteous; no, not even one (Ps. 14:3). The person who is righteous in his own eyes is self-righteous, and therefore wicked (Luke 16:15). The only way a person can become righteous is if God imputes righteousness to him through Christ's atoning work on the cross (Rom. 3:2-24; 4:5).

Two things happen then. First, the sinner is justified or made to appear righteous before God, clothed in the righteousness of Christ. The second thing that happens is that the saved person wants to serve and obey God and turn from his wickedness. His life begins to prove out the righteous desires planted in his heart (James 2:24) in the process of sanctification.

When God imparts His righteousness to the sinner, He gives him eternal life (John 6:47; 10:27-30). The only righteousness that can guard the person "of integrity" is Christ's, who is the author and perfector of our faith (Heb. 12:2). He will finish what He has started. He imparts His righteousness to us and that righteousness will guard us all the way to heaven.

Scriptural Examples

Noah and the pre-Flood people. Noah was a righteous man and a preacher of righteousness (2 Peter 2:5). When the flood came, Noah and his family rode the ark to survival. The ark is a picture of the Lord Jesus, who keeps the upright from harm while the wicked are caught in their own net (Gen. 7:1).

Israel and the nations driven out. God promised Israel that He would drive out the nations that occupied the land. This was not due to any righteousness in Israel, but because of the wickedness of the other nations and because of God's covenant with Abraham, Isaac, and Jacob (Deut. 9:5).

Prayer of Application

Lord God, how marvelous is Your grace that saves without respect of persons. You give it freely to sinners, then You keep them in the way of righteousness by Your mighty power.

Exhibit the Riches You Have in Christ

One man pretends to be rich, yet has nothing; another pretends to be poor, yet has great wealth (Prov. 13:7).

In every city in America there is at least one section of town that is known for its fancy houses and cars. There's also a lot of fancy indebtedness in places like that. Many people who live there are living on the hope of future earnings and are really only pretending to be rich. Conversely, we sometimes hear of a person who lives like a hermit but is extremely wealthy. A woman named Hettie Green lived such a life in New York some years ago. She appeared to be poor, but died with a portfolio worth millions.

As Christians, we may be rich in this world's material goods, or we may be poor, but each of us has untold riches in Christ Jesus. However, here again deceit is often practiced. There are those who claim to know Christ and to be rich in eternal life, but are phonies and have nothing. Such people are like the Pharisees who sought God's favor through their good works. Then we have true Christians who are rich beyond measure in spiritual things, but who pretend to be poor by being "closet" Christians. Jesus commands people like these to put their candles on top of a stand, not under a basket. By letting your riches in Christ show, you bring honor and glory to your Father in heaven (Matt. 5:15-16).

Scriptural Examples

The Gibeonites. These men pretended to be something they were not. They clothed themselves with rags and carried moldy bread like people who had traveled a great distance. They were saved from certain death, although they served the Israelites as slaves from then on (Josh. 9:3-15).

The Pharisees and scribes. These men wore long, flowing robes and were Israel's spiritual leaders during the time of Christ. They pretended to be righteous but Jesus condemned them, calling them "blind guides" and "hypocrites" (Matt. 23).

Prayer of Application

O Lord, You have made me rich in the things of Christ. Help me to reflect those riches in my life by the words that I speak, and the actions that I take, and, yes, in my every thought.

Rest in the Ransom Paid by Christ

A man's riches may ransom his life, but a poor man hears no threat
(Prov. 13:8).

In this verse we have some good news and some bad news. First, for the rich man, the good news is that he can pay a ransom. The bad news is that someone will probably be lying in the weeds demanding money by extortion, theft, or some legal claim.

The poor man's bad news is that he is poor, but at least he doesn't provoke lawsuits and ransom notes. His poverty becomes a kind of sanctuary: "You can't squeeze blood out of a turnip." Those looking for the big bucks will apply elsewhere.

But beneath this aphorism's surface truth, there lies its spiritual "good news and bad news." The bad news is that no ransom is great enough to satisfy the wrath of God for humankind's rebellion against Him. What can a person give in exchange for his soul? (Matt. 16:26). Many think that by doing good deeds they are satisfying the ransom that God demands to be paid. Their "good works" are but filthy rags in God's sight (Isa. 64:6).

But there is good news! A ransom has been paid for humankind that is acceptable in God's sight. Jesus Christ gave Himself as a sacrifice to reconcile the creation to the Creator (1 Tim. 2:5-6). It was a ransom paid by God to God. The poor in spirit who receive His gift will not hear the threat or rebuke of God, but will share in the eternal riches of heaven (Matt. 5:3).

Scriptural Examples

Jacob and Laban. Jacob endured anger from his father-in-law because of the wealth he helped to create. Riches may pay an earthly ransom, but they can cause strife as well (Gen. 31:1).

Goliath. This giant taunted the Israelites demanding a ransom. The ransom was to be a man who would represent Israel in battle. David killed the giant. He foreshadowed Christ, who would represent many in the payment of *the* ransom (1 Sam. 17:1-52).

Prayer of Application

Dear God, thank You for the ransom paid by Christ for His people. You knew that we would need Your salvation and that it could only come from the depths of Your grace toward us.

Rejoice in the Light of Christ

The light of the righteous shines brightly, but the lamp of the wicked is snuffed out (Prov. 13:9).

Notice that the righteous have lights, whereas the wicked carry lamps. The light of the righteous is Jesus Christ and it is His light that is to shine through—or be reflected by—the righteous (2 Cor. 4:6). He created light (Gen. 1:3-5; Isaiah 45:7) and was transfigured in a blinding light (Matt. 17:2). He is the light of the world (John 8:12) and calls us to be the same (Matt. 5:14). Bathed in His light, we should serve Him joyously in purity and holiness and become as shining stars in His heaven.

The non-Christian carries a dim, flickering lamp of philosophy, works, religion, or worldview with which he seeks to illumine his path. It barely provides a glimmer on the trail ahead. He doesn't care how bright it is, as long as it doesn't shed light upon the real truth—that its carrier is wicked through and through. He walks his own path in darkness rather than step up to the highway of truth and righteousness (John 3:19). At death, he will be cast into outer darkness where he won't even have his little lamp to comfort him (Matt. 22:13).

Scriptural Examples

The wise and foolish virgins. In this difficult parable of Jesus, 10 virgins went out with their lamps to meet the tardy bridegroom. Five are wise virgins, while five are called foolish. What made the difference? First, the wise brought extra oil. Second, the bridegroom's arrival was unexpected. The foolish virgins' lamps went out and the bridegroom arrived while they were off buying more oil.

I believe the extra oil the wise virgins had was their God-given perseverance (1 Cor. 1:7-9). For them, the bridegroom's tarrying was not a factor because the light they had would never go out. The foolish virgins did not have this storehouse, only oil from the world's market (Matt. 25:1-13).

Prayer of Application

Father, thank You for the light of the gospel of Christ, which You have shed abroad in my heart. Shine through me, Father, so that others will know of Your precious love for them.

Humbly Seek the Advice of Others

Pride only breeds quarrels, but wisdom is found in those who take advice (Prov. 13:10).

Here is one of the principal ways pride manifests itself. When we were kids there was always some guy in school with a chip on his shoulder who dared someone to knock it off. His honor had to be maintained at all costs, and his was the final word. Ready to quarrel and fight if necessary, his pride stuck out like a sore thumb. Know any adults like that?

We are told to flee from such a mindset (Phil. 2:5-8) and adopt the mind of Christ. With an open mind and a humble heart we are to seek the advice of God, through His Word and godly men and women. The proud person considers himself too wise to do this. His "wisdom" is but foolishness. It results in the separation that is caused by quarrels. The true wisdom of Christ unifies.

Scriptural Examples

The men of Ephraim. In two instances, first with Gideon, then Jepthah, these men were filled with pride and complained bitterly that they had not been invited to fight for Israel. Gideon was able to bring peace with sage advice, but Jepthah put gas on the fire (Judg. 8:1-3; 12:1-4).

The disciples. The Grecian Jews complained against the Hebraic Jews that their widows were being overlooked in the distribution of food. In godly wisdom, which brought unity among brothers, the disciples met together and decided to elect deacons who would attend to the matter (Acts 6:1-7).

The Corinthians. Their church was suffering from divisions caused by pride which led to quarrelling. Paul, with godly advice, urged humility and peace (1 Cor. 3:3-7).

Diotrephes. This man had the desire to be preeminent and would have nothing to do with John or the other apostles. His pride bred quarrels and separated brothers (3 John 1:9).

Prayer of Application

Dear Lord, help me to set an example of humility among my brothers and sisters in Christ, willing to sacrifice my "rights" for those of others. Help me also to seek godly advice.

Learn One Secret of Material Wealth

Dishonest money [KJV: "gotten by vanity"] dwindles away, but he who gathers money little by little makes it grow (Prov. 13:11).

I believe that we can simply render the first phrase here in the modern vernacular: "Easy come, easy go." Or, as my dad would quote the old saw, "A fool and his money are soon parted." Money or wealth gotten easily or dishonestly will be spent in the same manner in which it was acquired.

There is a story in secular circles entitled "The Richest Man in Babylon." His secret of enormous wealth was that he saved and invested a portion of each month's earnings. Compound interest did amazing things with it, and pretty soon he was a very wealthy man. Of course, the secret to saving a little income each month is to budget your outgo prudently. The woman with the gift of wise administration of her household probably makes more men rich than any other means.

I have been guilty of trying to hit "home runs" in my business life. That is to say, I've bitten off big, risky projects. The result was that my wealth (such as it ever was) dwindled. In retrospect, how much wiser I would have been to have taken on smaller, more manageable projects where there was less risk. This proverb has some very practical lessons for us all.

Scriptural Examples

The people of Judah. God accused them of planting much but harvesting little, eating and drinking but never being filled, having clothes but never being warm, and earning wages but putting them in a purse with holes in it. They were shoddy in their administration of His gifts (Hag. 1:6).

The prodigal son. The son of a wealthy man asked his father for his inheritance. He then took the easy money and spent it vainly on wine, women, and song. He wound up getting his whipping in the far country (Luke 15:11-32).

Prayer of Application

Heavenly Father, all wealth comes from You. Teach Your people that the secret to earthly wealth is to put aside a little each month, then to put it to work in the marketplace to gain more.

Cling to the Blessed Hope

*Hope deferred makes the heart sick, but a longing fulfilled is
a tree of life* (Prov. 13:12).

The non-Christian has his hope in this world. He sees happiness as being just around the corner with his next promotion, his marriage, or in owning his own home. But the things his heart hopes for are rarely truly satisfying when the actuality arrives. Solomon says earthly hope is meaningless, a "chasing after the wind" (Eccl. 2:11).

The Christian, on the other hand, has an eternal hope, the end of which is truly a "tree of life" (Rev. 22:14). We wait for it, in the midst of the trials of this life, and our hearts sometimes grow sick longing for our Lord's blessed appearing, which will signal the end of the age. We know in the heavenly Jerusalem where the Tree of Life stands, we shall see our Lord face-to-face (1 John 3:2).

The Christian hope is not an uncertain hope, some "pie in the sky" hope. Rather, it is a sure hope, sealed by God's Holy Word (Heb. 6:13-19), and by the Holy Spirit's affirmation to our hearts (Rom. 5:5). It is a hope that purifies us (1 John 3:3) and prepares us for eternal communion with our Lord.

Scriptural Examples

Abraham. Though aged, Abraham was promised an heir who would be from his own body. Years later, Sarah, also well past childbearing age, gave birth to Isaac, the child of the promise. There was great joy when their hope in God's promise became reality (Gen. 15:4; 21:3-6).

Simeon. This old man waited in hope of another child of promise — the Messiah. When Mary and Joseph brought the baby Jesus into the temple courts, Simeon praised God, having seen the Lord's salvation as God had promised (Luke 2:25-30).

The disciples. Heartsick at their Lord's execution, their hope was fulfilled at His resurrection (Luke 24:41).

Prayer of Application

Father, how I long for the appearing of Jesus. Thank You for the firm hope You have placed in my heart. Help me to live each day in purity and humility as I wait for His return.

Stand in Awe of God's Holy Words

He who scorns instruction will pay for it, but he who respects a command is rewarded (Prov. 13:13).

As a young Christian, doubts would sometimes cross my mind regarding my faith. I would think of Jesus—His life, death, burial, and resurrection—and ask myself, "Is He really who He said He was?" At the same time, I would think about what I knew of Scripture, its law which makes so much sense practically and spiritually, its prophets who had spoken with such exactitude about Christ and other future events in the nation of Israel, and its book of Psalms which so accurately reflected the depths of my own soul. Soon, my doubts would leave and I would be rewarded with blessed assurance.

What I did in this exercise was to look to God's Holy Word in its two manifestations: His written Word and the Word that was made flesh and lived on earth (John 1:14). To scorn the written Word is to scorn the Word who came in the flesh. To scorn Christ and His instruction is to warrant eternal destruction. Receive the Words—Christ and the Bible—with gladness, and stand in awe of them. Your reward will be great.

Scriptural Examples

The pre-Flood people. Noah spent 100 years building the ark. He also preached to the people that judgment was upon them (2 Peter 2:5). But they scorned the Word as preached by Noah and were consequently destroyed (Gen. 6:9-7:7).

Jehoiakim. This king of Judah took the scroll containing God's Word and after portions were read to him he had them cut off and thrown into the fire. Jeremiah was told by God to rewrite the scroll and add words of a curse upon the king. Bitterly for Jehoiakim, God's words came true (Jer. 36).

The Ninevites. When they heard God's warning they feared His command and God rewarded them (Jonah 3:5-10).

Prayer of Application

Father, thank You for the Word in its two manifestations. I love them, Lord, because You first loved me and opened my spiritual eyes to the truth. Thank You for Your loving grace.

Trust in the Protection of God's Word

The teaching of the wise is a fountain of life, turning a man from the snares of death (Prov. 13:14).

The Law of God, as recorded by Moses in the first five books of the Bible, was both a spiritual and a practical law. It was spiritual in that its motif of sacrifice and cleansing set forth the type of atoning work of the Fountain of Life (John 4:14). Our Lord Jesus would ultimately come to perform, once and for all, the sacrifice of Himself on a Roman cross (Heb. 10:12). The Law was a mirror into which an Israelite could look to see that he was a sinner in need of a Savior. Practically, the Law was also a guide to a happier life, teaching God's people to avoid the many snares that awaited in the Promised Land.

Moses' Law was fulfilled by Christ (Matt. 5:17). He is the Savior to which it pointed. The Word of God, as we now have it, is complete and fully capable of keeping those who obey it from the snares of death and eternal loss.

Scriptural Examples

David. David loved the law of God and meditated upon it for wisdom in life's decisions. In Psalm 1:1-2, he described as blessed the man who does not follow the ways of the wicked but who delights in God's law. In Proverbs 4:4, Solomon told of his father David's teaching, which was a source of life to him.

Solomon. Solomon asked God for wisdom and God gave it to him (1 Kings 4:29). God's same gift is available to anyone who asks. It is found in His Holy Word, which will protect you and give provision for each turn in the road (James 1:5).

Paul. In 2 Timothy 3:15-17, he spoke of the Holy Scriptures, which are able to make a person wise unto salvation but which are also profitable for wisdom and instruction in righteous living. Read the Word of God, study it, and meditate upon it. Do it daily, that it may guide you all your life.

Prayer of Application

Our Father, how I love Your Word and seek its wisdom for my daily walk. Help me to apply it fully to my life, trusting that its eternal wisdom will keep me from the snares of death.

Get Wisdom Early in Life

Good understanding wins favor, but the way of the unfaithful is hard (Prov. 13:15).

Before I was saved at 33, my life was outwardly peaceful and calm. I had a good job, a fine family, and a nice home in the suburbs. But underneath the seemingly calm surface was inward turbulence, dissatisfaction, and fear. After I was saved, the surface of my life began to erupt in trouble and difficult problems, but down deep there was a peace that passes understanding (Phil. 4:7).

The decisions I had made in my rebellion against God, the bad habits, my sinful patterns of thought, and the relationships in which I found myself, all began to work against me in the new life as God set about to change me into the image of His Son (Rom. 8:29). Had I gotten "good understanding" early on in life, much trouble and discipline would have been spared me.

There are many who do not remember when they were not a Christian. If you have had that experience, praise God for it. He saved you from the hard path of the transgressor. The lesson? Teach your children the things of God from the moment they're born and pray God saves them early in life.

Scriptural Examples

Joseph. Joseph's upbringing under God's admonition stood him well even though he was called to suffer unjustly. The circumstances surrounding the incident with Potiphar's wife showed his good understanding. He increased in favor in the kingdom (Gen. 39-41).

Samuel. Left by his mother, Hannah, in the care of Eli, and dedicated to the Lord early on as a Nazarite, Samuel grew in favor with God and was a true blessing to Israel (the book of 1 Samuel).

Daniel. Daniel called upon the good understanding he had received in his youth and refused to be defiled with the king's royal food and wine. He, too, grew in favor (Dan. 1:8-9).

Prayer of Application

Father, thank You for saving me. The way of transgression is hard and Your discipline uncomfortable, but in the end there is the wonderful peace of knowing there was a purpose to it all.

Put Your Wisdom to Practical Application

Every prudent man acts out of knowledge, but a fool exposes his folly (Prov. 13:16).

It's one thing to have "head knowledge" of wisdom, but quite another to apply it to our lives. This is the essence of prudence. Otherwise, such wisdom will just puff up our pride.

Practical uses for wisdom are in training our children (Judg. 13:8-12); exercising caution against pitfalls along the path (Prov. 22:3); using wise counsel in discipline (Rom. 15:14); practicing moderation (Titus 1:8); organizing finances (Prov. 11:15; 22:26); and in decision-making (2 Thess. 2:15-17). The spiritual person's wisdom is shown in his prudent walk.

Conversely, the fool is a natural at manifesting folly. Like Balaam, he vents his wrath (Num. 22:29-30). Like Goliath, he boasts loudly in his vanity (1 Sam. 17:44). Like Herod, he is thoughtless in his promises (Matt. 14:7). Like Simon the Sorcerer, he'll do anything for a buck (Acts 8:9-24). Like so many other examples in Scripture, and on our streets, fools display folly.

Scriptural Examples

Abigail. Abigail showed great prudence in dealing with David and his men, and with her foolish spouse. When Nabal got drunk, she circumspectly waited until he was sober before confronting him with the events of the day. As it all turned out, Nabal was "dying" to hear Abigail's words (1 Sam. 25:36-37).

Ezra. This prudent man of God stopped by a canal to pray for a safe journey to Jerusalem. He had not wanted to ask King Xerxes for an armed guard because he had told the king that God would protect them. God did (Ezra 8:21-23).

Jesus. Once again our great example shone in His application of wisdom. He walked circumspectly to avoid His enemies (John 11:47-54). But it was in His teaching ministry that His great wisdom shone most clearly (Matt. 13:54).

Prayer of Application

Heavenly Father, may the prudent application of Your Word in my life keep me from sin and error and show others Your marvelous grace. Help me to glorify Christ in every way.

Be a Faithful Ambassador of Christ

A wicked messenger falls into trouble, but a trustworthy envoy brings healing (Prov. 13:17).

God has given Christians the ministry of reconciliation (2 Cor. 5:18), sending us as His ambassadors to a lost and dying world (2 Cor. 5:20). His Gospel brings healing and nourishment to their bones (Prov. 3:8).

Filling many of America's pulpits today are those who are not teaching the full counsel of God (Acts 20:27). They distort the Word of God, denying its power and truth (2 Cor. 4:2). They add some work that we must do to complement God's grace (Eph. 2:8-9). They betray the trust God has given in His Word and disgrace the name of Him whom they loosely call "Lord" (Matt. 7:22-23). These wicked messengers face trouble with a capital "T."

We can't lay all the blame at their feet, however. We evangelical laypeople are equally guilty and yet we are supposed to cherish the true Word. We are guilty of laziness and fear of criticism. Few of us witness as we should. Are you a faithful ambassador for Christ? I know I fall short of the mark.

Scriptural Examples

Eliezer. Abraham's faithful messenger trusted God's leadership fully in the selection of a bride for Isaac (Gen. 24:33-56).

Gehazi. This unfaithful messenger of the prophet Elisha tried to cash in on God's healing of Naaman's leprosy. He himself was stricken with the disease (2 Kings 5:26-27).

John the Baptist. Malachi predicted that the Lord would send a messenger before the coming of the promised Messiah (Mal. 3:1). Malachi's prophecy was fulfilled in John the Baptist, who preached repentance and baptized many (Matt. 11:10).

God's Prophets. These faithful men brought a message of health to Israel. But they were often killed by those they sought to warn (Acts 7:51-52).

Prayer of Application

Dear Lord, help me to be a trustworthy envoy of Your gospel of grace. The community in which I live needs it so much. Help me to understand You control the results.

Open Your Ears to Receive Instruction

He who ignores discipline comes to poverty and shame, but who- ever heeds correction is honored (Prov. 13:18).

Shortly after I was saved in 1972, I decided to go from the real estate brokerage business into real estate development. I was certain I would cut a "wide swath for God" (my exact words) in that lucrative but highly risky business. My first project was successful and, with God behind me, I was on a roll! Without seeking the counsel of others, but inflamed with the pride of my initial success, I embarked upon several large projects. Then came Watergate, the gas crisis, and spiraling inflation that took interest rates sky high. My great plans were sunk. Only by God's grace was I spared poverty, but there was plenty of shame to go around. It would be years before I recovered financially.

As essential as good advice and instruction is in the business world, it is absolutely essential in spiritual matters. The stakes are so much higher. The Christian who thinks he can stand on his own without the reproof of godly teaching and exhortation is headed for spiritual poverty and shame. The unsaved person who refuses the instruction of righteousness is headed for an eternal poverty and shame, and worse. But the one who opens his ears to instruction and learns from discipline shall be honored and saved from the fire of actual trial.

Scriptural Examples

David. Nathan reproved King David for his sin against Bathsheba and Uriah, and David openly confessed before God. David had to live with the consequence but his faithful regard for God's discipline ultimately brought honor (2 Sam. 12:1-14).

The prodigal son. Refusal to hear instruction took this young man of Jesus' parable to a far country where he got his fill of poverty and shame. His pride fallen, he headed home to seek a servant's job, but found honor instead (Luke 15:11-32).

Prayer of Application

Father, what foolish mistakes I have made that could have been avoided had I listened to correction. Help me to hear godly reproof in every area of life, that I might bring honor to You.

Long for the Sweet Taste of Righteousness

A longing fulfilled is sweet to the soul, but fools detest turning from evil (Prov. 13:19).

Evil is detested by God, yet fools detest departing from it. Why? The fool hates God. He is in bondage to sin. In the Fall, we lost our moral ability to choose God's righteousness over evil and now cannot depart from evil (Rom. 8:7-8).

But God, who is rich in mercy (Eph. 2:4), invades the hearts of evil people and regenerates us, giving us a new life in Christ. He places a longing in our hearts for righteousness, and righteousness in our lives that fulfills our longing is sweet to our souls. We still have the ability to choose evil, and we sometimes do, but we find no sweetness there; only the bitterness of a fearful expectation of judgment (Heb. 10:26-27).

The finishing line for evil is eternal destruction. The end of righteousness is eternal riches. What a great distance between the two (Luke 16:26). How the spiritual person's soul longs for the sweetness of the fulfillment of his ultimate longing—to meet his Lord face-to-face, and to live and reign with Him eternally.

Scriptural Examples

Adam. His rebellion against God's direct command brought sin and death to the human race (Gen. 3:6; Rom. 5:12).

David. David confessed the sin principle was working in his life and in the lives of all people from birth so they cannot do anything but sin (Ps. 51:5; 58:3).

Paul. The most dramatic picture of the new birth in Scripture occurred when Paul was confronted by the resurrected Christ, who chose him to be the apostle to the Gentiles (Acts 22:6-11).

Jesus. Just as Adam's sin brought death to all through the principle of representation, so Christ gave Himself on the cross as a representative of all who would believe in Him and be saved (Rom. 5:17-19; Acts 13:48).

Prayer of Application

Sovereign God, thank You for reaching out to me and making righteousness the longing of my heart. Help me to grow daily in Your Word and live in the sweetness of Your will.

Choose Your Friends Wisely

He who walks with the wise grows wise, but a companion of fools suffers harm (Prov. 13:20).

There are few principles more important to one's life than this one. While we need to recognize the impact our lives can have upon our unsaved friends, it is important that we not walk with them, or as the Bible states, be "unequally yoked" (2 Cor. 6:14-17). We may be led into unrighteousness.

New life in Christ has not just changed our philosophy of life. We are radically changed. God has put His Spirit within us and we are headed toward a different eternal future than many of our friends. Those paths get farther and farther apart each day. To keep company with sinners is to invite trouble (1 Cor. 15:33). If you find yourself married to an unsaved person, the problem is even worse.

The Christian needs the fellowship of believers for edification, encouragement, true joy, and growth toward maturity (Eph. 4:15-16). It is extremely important to join a Bible-honoring church where you are exhorted toward righteous living. Choose your friends and closest companions, your wife or husband, and your business partners only from among those with whom you share a common language and destination.

Scriptural Examples

Joash. This young king of Judah befriended Jehoiada the priest. While Jehoiada lived, Joash did what was right in the eyes of the Lord. When he died, Joash befriended fools. They abandoned God and worshipped idols. In the end, Joash was murdered by the same foolish friends (2 Chron. 24:1-27).

Peter and the disciples. Throughout Acts, Peter and the disciples preached to the unsaved, but assembled together only with believers. The call of God is to "leave and cleave." Just as we leave our parents and cleave to our spouse, so we leave our old lives and cleave to the new (Acts 2:28-42).

Prayer of Application

Father, give me discernment to get close enough to people to show them the difference You have made in my life, but not so close as to be drawn back into the cares of this world.

Seek a Reward of Grace, Not Justice

Misfortune pursues the sinner, but prosperity is the reward of the righteous (Prov. 13:21).

God told the Israelites to set aside six towns in the land as cities of refuge. If a man accidentally killed someone, he could flee to one of those six cities and be afforded refuge from the "avenger of blood" (probably the victim's close relative) until he had a chance to have a fair trial (Num. 35:11-12). If he was found guilty, the avenger would put him to death (Num. 35:19).

The avenger of blood pursued the sinner. The city of refuge provided a covering of grace and was a temporary refuge for a murderer. In that way it was like the world in general—before justice is ultimately served in God's eternal court. The guilty will then be rewarded with condemnation, and the innocent set free.

In eternity, however, the righteous or innocent person—justified through faith in Christ—will not merely be set free. He will be given a reward far in excess of mercy; namely, eternal treasures and a brotherhood with Christ as heir of all things (Rom. 8:17). Justice is getting what we deserve. Saving grace means not only that we don't get the punishment we deserve, but that we are lavished with gifts and treasures far beyond what mere mercy would bestow. Prosperity will truly be our reward.

Scriptural Examples

Cain. Following the murder of his brother Abel, God cursed Cain and drove him out to be a restless wanderer. God put a mark on Cain that protected his life, but he was to be pursued by evil for the rest of his days (Gen. 4:11-16).

Achan. Following the defeat at Ai, the Lord told Joshua of this man's deceit but didn't name him. Joshua assembled all of the people and cast lots. Achan was taken. The Israelites took him and his family outside the camp and stoned them all to death. Thus was Achan pursued inexorably and dealt justice (Josh. 7:1-26).

Prayer of Application

Heavenly Father, thank You for Your grace. Because of it, I have hope in my death. There will be no condemnation for me, but rather treasures of grace beyond my understanding.

Leave the Inheritance of a Godly Life

A good man leaves an inheritance for his children's children, but a sinner's wealth is stored up for the righteous (Prov. 13:22).

One glance at this proverb will reveal it couldn't affect everyone. Some aren't blessed with children; others have no grandchildren. Good people may die penniless. And do we see sinners' wealth given to the just? We must look beyond the material to the spiritual to see the truth of the proverb.

The godly person, regardless of the children in his life, leaves an inheritance to future generations. The inheritance is his holy example, his godly walk in the reverence of his Lord, and the storehouse of intercessory prayer that has yet to be accomplished. All will benefit those generations yet unborn.

The wealth of the sinner stored up for the just is a common occurrence in the Old Testament. For example, we see Laban's going to Jacob (Gen. 31:1-16); the Egyptians' to Israel (Ex. 12:35-36); and Haman's to Esther and Mordecai (Est. 8:1-2). What wealth will today's sinner leave for the just? I believe it is the earth, which the meek will inherit when the Lord returns (Matt. 5:5).

Scriptural Examples

Abraham. God's covenant with Abraham was to be inherited by all generations. It was based on Abraham's faith in God's words. What a blessing this inheritance from a good man is for you and me, as we are heirs of the promise that was given to him so many years ago (Gen. 15; 17:7).

The Egyptians. As Israel was preparing to leave, Moses instructed the people to ask the Egyptians for silver and gold. God opened the hearts of the Egyptian people and they gave the Israelites great treasure (Ex. 12:35-36).

Caleb. The righteous Caleb received Hebron as his inheritance from the Lord. This land was passed on to many of this fine man's generations (Josh. 14:14).

Prayer of Application

Dear Lord and God, thank You for the inheritance You have given me in Christ Jesus. Lead me in a life that is pleasing to You, that my children and their children will be blessed by it.

Manage Your Resources Prudently

A poor man's field may produce abundant food, but injustice sweeps it away (Prov. 13:23).

This proverb brings to mind the collective farm system of the old Soviet Union that failed to feed their nation. Meanwhile, those who were allowed to plant a small, personal garden had great success. Because of personal incentive and personal responsibility, the individual farmers were able to out produce the large state farms. In some translations, "injustice" in the last phrase of this proverb is translated "want of judgment." In the Soviet Union, we saw both lack of judgment *and* injustice, and, of course, they are related.

All of us, farmers or not, have resources we need to manage. Some of us have jobs that require good administrative and supervisory skills. Others work in positions that require great manual skill in the assembly of a product. Whatever our occupation, we are given talents that need to be applied and managed if we are to be successful. We are also called to be good stewards of our material possessions, time, and our study of the Word. In all these things, God calls us to be wise, just, and faithful. All the resources and justice we need are in Him.

Scriptural Examples

Joseph. Joseph's prudent administration of Egypt's resources ensured that there would be much food in the time of famine in the land (Gen. 41:33-39).

Boaz. He is a fine example of a farmer who managed his people and his harvest with wisdom and prudence. He was well-respected by his employees and took an active role in the farm's administration (Ruth 2:4; 3:2).

Solomon. His wise management of Israel saw to it that there was peace and plenty during his reign (1 Kings 4:27-28).

Jesus. After feeding the 5,000, Jesus told the disciples to gather up the pieces so that nothing would be wasted (John 6:12).

Prayer of Application

Father, thank You that I am free to grow my own farm, business, or career. Give me diligence in management, Lord, and protection from those who would sweep it away unjustly.

Discipline Your Children in Love

He who spares the rod hates his son, but he who loves him is careful to discipline him (Prov. 13:24).

Discipline in the home should always be done from the perspective of love, seeking to put the child on a path of righteousness and purity. It should never be done hastily or in anger, or with the intent of revenge. The reason for the discipline should always be understood by the child and the application of a biblical principle should be made. Therefore, the discipline of our children must begin with our own self-discipline. Most of us hate pain and want no part of it. But discipline, while it may inflict a small amount of pain in the present, will prevent much greater pain in the future.

Every human being is a child of Adam, and is born with a predisposition to sin. We must lovingly and patiently combine teaching with physical discipline, if necessary, to encourage in our children a life of reverence for God and for His Word. Begin early and don't falter. No discipline is pleasant at the time, but in the end it produces a harvest of righteousness and peace for those who have been trained by it (Heb. 12:11).

Scriptural Examples

Eli and his sons. Hophni and Phineas sinned wickedly against the people and against the Lord. The Lord laid their sin at Eli's feet. He had failed to discipline them (1 Sam. 3:13).

David and Adonijah. Adonijah attempted to set himself up as king in place of his aging father. David had failed to restrict him or to interfere with his plans (1 Kings 1:5-6).

Our heavenly Father and us. God disciplines those He loves in order to give us wisdom, to instruct us in holiness, and to set our feet on a righteous path. We should view discipline as encouragement because God never disciplines those who just pretend to be His children (Heb. 12:5-9).

Prayer of Application

Heavenly Father, thank You for Your disciplining hand upon me. Help me to discipline my children in Your way of love with exactly what is appropriate for each of them.

Be Satisfied in God's Provision

The righteous eat to their hearts' content, but the stomach of the wicked goes hungry (Prov. 13:25).

Two lessons are here. First, God will providentially meet our every need (Phil. 4:19). Second, we have our appetites changed as we go through the process of sanctification. As they are moderated, our needs are more and more easily satisfied.

The wicked person is never satisfied (Eccl. 6:7). His needs keep growing and growing (Hab. 2:5). Because of this, he will always suffer want, while the mature follower of Christ will be content regardless of his circumstances (Phil. 4:11).

Christ said that life is more important than food (Luke 12:23). When He was hungry and tempted by Satan in the desert, He said that man does not live by bread alone, but by God's every word (Deut. 8:3; Matt. 4:4). Feed upon the Word until it becomes a part of you. How it satisfies as nothing else will!

Scriptural Examples

Jacob. In God's providence, he and his family were allowed to settle in Goshen, the best spot in Egypt, and were provided with food (Gen. 47:1-13).

The Israelites. In the wilderness, God provided the people with manna from heaven in the morning and quail in the evening (Ex. 16:4-15). But soon the wicked among them began to crave other food and to complain about God's provision (Num. 11:4-6).

Elijah. God sent him to a brook in the Kerith Ravine where he could drink, and sent ravens to feed him. Later, when the brook dried up, God sent Elijah to a widow in Zarephath. She had only a handful of flour and a little oil, but the Lord graciously caused it not to be used up (1 Kings 17:1-15).

Jesus. He miraculously provided for the needs of the multitudes. Learn the lesson that went over the heads of the disciples: God provides for all your needs (Matt. 14:19-21; 15:36-39).

Prayer of Application

Sovereign Lord, how gracious is Your provision for my life. Give me the faith to trust You more and sanctify me through Your Spirit and Word, that my needs would be moderated.

Chapter Fourteen

The Fear of the Lord

Four proverbs in this chapter speak of the fear of the Lord: Proverbs 14:2, 16, 26, and 27. The phrase "fear[s] the Lord" or "fear of the Lord" occurs 20 times in Proverbs. It is obviously important. What does it mean to "fear the Lord"? Can we define it precisely? Let me try.

I have created an acronym—F*E*A*R—to help us. First, "F" stands for "Faith in the Facts." We must know who the Lord is. He is the God-man, the Creator, the Great Judge, and the great and coming King. He is the way, the truth, and the life. He is Jesus Christ. Second, "E" stands for "Enjoyment." He is our sure foundation, our security and satisfaction, our rest and confidence, and our eternal hope. The Lord is our salvation, our wisdom, and our treasure. We enjoy His many benefits. Third, "A" stands for "Active obedience." Jesus said, "If you love me, you will obey what I command" (John 14:15). We must desire to follow His leading. Fourth, "R" stands for "Reverential awe." He is the thrice holy God of Isaiah 6:3. He is the Ruler of all creation and we worship Him in His might and majesty.

At its core, for the person who is saved by the Lord, to "fear" Him is to love Him. That is the first and greatest command: "Love the Lord your God with all your heart…" (Matt. 22:37).

Women, Build Your Home in the Love of Christ

The wise woman builds her house, but with her own hands the foolish one tears hers down (Prov. 14:1).

A wise woman blesses her family. She will order her household with diligence and raise up her children in loving discipline and in the wisdom of Christ and His Word. The foolish woman, on the other hand, tears her house down, even though she may do it inadvertently. She may be given to idleness, waste, and love of pleasure. She may neglect the spiritual and even the physical needs of her children, not disciplining them. She may be contentious toward her husband, failing to submit to his leadership, as unto Christ (Eph. 5:22). Without Christ, she may have the appearance of a model wife and mother, but she is doomed to ultimate failure.

The choice of a marriage partner is one of the weightiest decisions anyone can make in this life. In your choice, discount such things as birth, money, accomplishments, education, looks, etc. Instead, pray God will send you a partner with godly wisdom. How all other qualities of character and desirability pale in comparison to that one!

Scriptural Examples

Hannah. Hannah prayed for her son, Samuel, and gave him up fully to the work of the Lord. God, throughout Scripture, honors women who honor Him (1 Sam. 1:27-28).

Jezebel. Ahab, king of Israel, married this non-Israelite woman in direct defiance of God's will. Ahab later reaped the bitter fruit of his rebellion (1 Kings 16:31; 21:25).

The wife and mother of Proverbs 31. Here is a wonderful picture of a godly wife and mother. She earned the respect and admiration of all in her community (Prov. 31:10-31).

Eunice. Paul told us of the faithfulness of Timothy's mother (and grandmother Lois) to raise her boy in the nurture and admonition of the Lord (2 Tim. 1:5; 3:15).

Prayer of Application

Lord, make me the person You want me to be through the sanctification of washing by the Word. Help me to love, respect, and support those in my family, dying daily for them.

Prove Your Faith by Your Walk

He whose walk is upright fears the Lord, but he whose ways are devious despises him (Prov. 14:2).

James speaks to this principle in James 2:14-26. What kind of faith is it that is not backed up by works? James is not saying that we are saved by good works, but that saving faith, if it is real, produces works of righteousness. What kind of faith is it that has no works? It is a dead faith, and hence no faith at all.

The second part of this verse in Proverbs should send a shiver down our spines. How often do we realize when we are even slightly perverse in our way—a lustful glance, a hateful thought against our neighbor, a greedy decision, or a prideful word—we are showing a disposition to despise God. Immediately ask forgiveness, and the God who is faithful and just to forgive you (1 John 1:9) will place your feet back on the path of righteousness. Our upright walk proves our love for Him.

Scriptural Examples

Cain and Abel. Abel was a righteous man of faith (Matt. 23:35; Heb. 11:4) who worshipped God with a proper sacrifice. Cain, on the other hand, brought a sacrifice that was not pleasing to God. Cain murdered Abel and truly hated his Creator. If he could have gotten his hands on God he would have killed Him too (Gen. 4:1-8).

Haman and Mordecai. Haman tried to exterminate God's people. He showed by his actions that he despised God. Mordecai, on the other hand, walked in humility with God and refused to honor the vile Haman. God worked through Mordecai and Esther to foil Haman's plot against the Jews (Est. 3:8).

The scribes and Pharisees. The Jewish leaders of Jesus' day seemed to walk in the fear of the Lord. But their uprightness was superficial. Jesus denounced their legalism and they despised Him for it. They then sought for a way to kill the same Messiah they pretended to be so eager to greet (Matt. 26:4).

Prayer of Application

Father, I do love You but I know I have a disposition to deviousness. Point out areas of my life that are lacking that I might confess any sinfulness and be restored to uprightness.

Seek a Tongue of Humility

A fool's talk brings a rod to his back, but the lips of the wise protect them (Prov. 14:3).

The tongue, along with the eyes (Prov. 30:17), is the window to a person's heart. What a person says springs up from that fountain. The fool does not revere God in his heart, but speaks swelling, self-confident words. The KJV renders the "rod" here as a "rod of pride." Truly, the tongue of the fool is a rod of pride. He alone is the "master of his fate, the captain of his soul."

The wise person is one who understands his depravity and weakness, and speaks accordingly. He is dependent upon the grace of his God. He has been bought with a price (1 Cor. 6:19-20), the precious blood of the Lord Jesus. He confesses with his tongue that Jesus is Lord and believes in his heart that God has raised Him from the dead, and is thus protected (Rom. 10:9).

In the real estate business, the three basic characteristics of good real estate are "location, location, and location." St. Augustine said similarly that the three distinguishing characteristics of the Christian are, in essence, "humility, humility, and humility."

Scriptural Examples

Pharaoh. This prideful king lashed out at the true God. "Who is the Lord that I should obey him and let Israel go?" he asked. His pride brought him the rod of death (Ex. 5:2; 12:29-30).

Sennacherib. While attacking Jerusalem, he laughed at the God of Israel. Later, with 180,000 of his men dead, he withdrew in defeat, whipped by the rod of his own mouth (2 Kings 19:10).

Jeremiah's enemies. They plotted against Jeremiah, attacking God's prophet with their tongues to discredit him. Their tongues rod returned to their own backs (Jer. 18:18).

Paul. Paul had once lashed out at Christians with a rod of pride, but his encounter with Jesus changed him. Humbled, he counted his past but loss and spoke with humility and faith (Phil. 3:4-9).

Prayer of Application

Lord, allow me to see myself as I truly am so that You will be exalted in my thinking and I will be abased. Help me to speak from that understanding of my dependence upon You.

Honor God by Your Industry

Where there are no oxen, the manger is empty, but from the strength of an ox comes an abundant harvest (Prov. 14:4).

God formed man from the dust of the ground and returned him to it to till it for food (Gen. 3:23). We are required to work for a living, although it is God at work behind the scenes who provides for our needs. The psalmist speaks of God's providence, that He gives us food and satisfies our desires (Ps. 145:15-16). Jesus continues this theme in Matthew 6:26-33.

So in life a partnership exists between God and us. Each has a role to play. Our responsibility is to labor in the field, while God provides the field, sends the rain and the sunshine, creates the botanical system, etc. God has also created helps for our use, such as the ox in this proverb. Without oxen, one may have a clean stall but no dinner on the table.

This partnership is also at work in spiritual things. Although God saves us by His sovereign power, we have the responsibility of faith and of diligently devoting ourselves to study the Word, and than to make application of our Bible study to life. Whatever our role, let's honor God with our industry.

Scriptural Examples

Jacob. Jacob worked laboriously for Laban for many years and saw his own wealth increase by it (Gen. 30:29-30, 43).

Joseph. Joseph's administration of Egypt's storehouses filled them to overflowing. Then, when the famine came by God's providential hand, there was plenty for the people to eat. Joseph's industry and willingness to follow God figured prominently in the foundation of Israel (Gen. 41:49; 45:5-7).

Elisha. Elijah found him industriously plowing his fields using twelve yoke of oxen. He called him from the field to the service of God. Ultimately, Elisha became heir to the Spirit that rested upon the prophet of God (1 Kings 19:19-21).

Prayer of Application

Father, thank You for Your great provision for every part of my life. Give me the strength to be industrious in whatever You call me to do, to the end that You will be glorified in my life.

Honor the Truthful Witness of the Two Words

A truthful witness does not deceive, but a false witness pours out lies (Prov. 14:5).

At first glance, this proverb seems to be a simple truism. But on closer examination great wisdom is to be found. A false witness is not such simply because he lies. He lies because he is a false witness. He can do nothing else (Rom. 3:10-18). People sin because they are sinners by nature.

On the other hand, the truthful witness does not deceive. It is not in his nature to lie. Of course, the supreme truthful witness is God, who has spoken to us through His only begotten Son, our Lord Jesus Christ (Heb. 1:2), and through His everlasting and perfect Word, the Bible. As His children, we are charged with the responsibility of bearing witness to the truth which God has given us. It is our responsibility first to believe God's two Words—Christ and the Bible—then to sow them throughout the world.

Who then is the liar and false witness? Anyone who denies that Jesus is the Christ (1 John 2:22). Paul states that it is anyone who preaches a different gospel than the one of Scripture (Gal. 1:7-8), or who denies the truth of God's Word and hinders its communication. People like that should be condemned.

Scriptural Examples

Satan. He is the father of all liars (John 8:44) and the chief false witness. He cast doubt upon the truthfulness of the Word of God when he lied to Eve in the Garden of Eden (Gen. 3:1).

Ahab's false witnesses. Coveting Naboth's field, Jezebel, Ahab's wife, brought liars to testify that Naboth was a blasphemer and an anarchist. On their testimony, Naboth was stoned to death. Ahab got his field until God's justice intervened (1 Kings 21:13, 16-19).

The Sanhedrin's false witnesses. In Jesus' trial, the San-hedrin brought false witnesses forward to accuse Jesus of saying that He was going to destroy God's temple (Matt. 26:59-61).

Prayer of Application

Heavenly Father, thank You for Your Word and for its rule over my life. Help me to rightly handle it and to be a faithful witness to its truth in all of my thoughts, words, and deeds.

Find the Key to Wisdom in Obedience

The mocker seeks wisdom and finds none, but knowledge comes easily to the discerning (Prov. 14:6).

Jesus states in the Sermon on the Mount that everyone who seeks will find (Matt. 7:7). In the verses above we are told that the mocker seeks wisdom and doesn't find it. A contradiction? Not at all. The fault isn't in Jesus' words. The failure is in the heart of the mocker, who doesn't seek wisdom in readiness to obey it.

The scorner seeks wisdom, but for his own purposes and sinful interests. He reads the Bible to prove his own presuppositions rather than to seek what God really has to say. He never searches intending to obey the truth even if he finds it. Therefore, God does not reveal the truth to him.

The true seeker of godly wisdom does so with singleness of mind and purpose, that he might be obedient to it. Otherwise, he'll just be puffed up by it. But godly wisdom is meant to be put to work on a daily basis. Those who search for this reason are certain to find the wisdom they seek.

Scriptural Examples

Azariah and Johanan. These men pretended to have wisdom but called God's prophet a liar. They disobeyed God and moved to Egypt. The Lord told Jeremiah that Nebuchadnezzar would surely find them there and kill them (Jer. 43).

The Pharisees and Herodians. These men called Jesus a teacher of the truth but asked questions only to trap Him, and not so that they might obey (Matt. 22:15-17).

Simon the sorcerer. Simon offered Peter and John money if they would give him the Holy Spirit. Peter rebuked him for desiring the Spirit for his own selfish interests (Acts 8:18-24).

The Ethiopian eunuch. Philip shared the Word of God with this man, who immediately obeyed in repentance and faith and requested to be baptized (Acts 8:30-36).

Prayer of Application

Lord God, help me to study Your Word diligently, and always with the motive of obedience. I pray that my lack of faith will not inhibit the Spirit's work in teaching me wisdom.

Beware of the Fellowship of Unbelievers

Stay away from a foolish man, for you will not find knowledge on his lips (Prov. 14:7).

We are called by Christ to be the salt of the earth and a light unto the world (Matt. 5:13-16), but we are warned to avoid being drawn back into its ways. The Israelites were warned about intermarrying with the nations that they would drive out of the Promised Land. They disobeyed, and we can see the consequences of their disobedience throughout the Old Testament. Their foreign wives dragged them into idolatry. Paul warns believers many times about fellowship with unbelievers, as does Peter in 2 Peter 3:17, and John in 2 John 9-11.

We must recognize our responsibility to give out the gospel to unbelievers. In some cases we do this through "friendship evangelism." But we must be careful of drawing too near, lest we be drawn astray by foolishness. This is particularly true of the new believer who runs the risk of being drawn back into the life he just left.

How do we know when to avoid close fellowship with someone? When we discern that he does not speak with the wisdom of Christ. How do we get that discernment? Through a knowledge of God's Word.

Scriptural Examples

Delilah and Samson. Samson's problem was that he did not heed the principle found here and through his lusts got himself unequally yoked with this foolish woman (Judg. 16).

Hezekiah and the Babylonian envoys. Hezekiah befriended them and showed them Judah's treasury. Ruin and slavery was to come because of the king's foolishness (2 Kings 20:12-18).

Judas. Jesus put up with Judas because he had a specific role to play in the atoning work of Christ. Otherwise, he is the classic example of an unbeliever whose presence in the fellowship of believers is unwholesome (Matt. 26:23-25).

Prayer of Application

Father, help me to avoid any relationship that would lead me away from my daily walk with You. At the same time, help me to give out the gospel to unbelievers in friendship and love.

Understand the Will of God for Your Life

The wisdom of the prudent is to give thought to their ways, but the folly of fools is deception (Prov. 14:8).

Every thoughtful Christian has asked, "How can I know the will of God for my life?" The most obvious answer is, "Ask Him!" (James 1:5). Next comes study of the Word of God (2 Tim. 3:15-17), which is able to make one wise in many ways. Along with seeking and studying, one needs to obey God and He will lead you in the right path (Prov. 3:5-6).

The prudent person will also give thought to his fitness for a particular calling. What are your gifts? Your strengths and weaknesses? What do you enjoy doing? What subjects did you particularly enjoy at school? God has created you as a unique individual and much of who you are will indicate where God wants you to go and what He wants you to do. Then step out in faith, watching in anticipation as God directs your steps.

The unbeliever, on the other hand, practices deceit which manifests itself in his rejection of the Word and of God. Whatever path he takes, apart from repentance and faith, is the wrong one. So even though he may be wise and prudent in his own eyes, his wisdom is foolishness to God (1 Cor. 3:19)

Scriptural Examples

Moses and Joshua. While Joshua fought the Amalekites, Moses prayed on the top of a nearby hill. Each man knew the role to which he was called by God (Ex. 17:10-11).

Daniel's accusers. Their deceit got them thrown into the same lions' den from which Daniel had earlier emerged unscathed. Their deception proved their undoing (Dan. 6:24).

Paul and Peter. Paul was called by God to bring the gospel to the Gentiles, while Peter preached among the Jews. Both understood the similarity, yet the separateness, of their different callings as each gave thought to his way (Gal. 2:7).

Prayer of Application

Dear God, I can't see what's ahead of me in life, so I can only trust in Your guidance. Help me to obey Your Word, that my every step would be directed from above. Thank You, Lord.

Warn Others of Sin's Consequences

Fools mock at making amends for sin, but goodwill is found among the upright (Prov. 14:9).

The non-Christian hates the idea of a personal God who holds people accountable. Most people keep out of trouble because they know that if they break the law and get caught, they can be punished. But the idea of a personal God who will judge by His perfect law is unthinkable.

These people mock the notion of eternal justice. They mock it in their lives by willful sin. They mock it with their lips by denying the truth of God's Word and by slurring the name of Him who calls them to free salvation. How will they escape if they disregard the many warnings of God (Heb. 12:25)?

We are called by God to warn everyone of His wrath (Mark 28:19). But for His grace we would be just like the mockers, unable to realize the real trouble we're in. Likewise, we need to warn ourselves and other believers of taking our sin lightly, for we all must stand before His judgment seat (Rom. 14:10), even though we will escape condemnation.

Scriptural Examples

Lamech. This great-grandson of Cain murdered a man then boasted that if Cain was avenged seven times, he would be avenged 77 times. What foolishness to boast of one's sin (Gen. 4:23-24).

The people of Ephraim and Manasseh. Couriers were sent throughout Israel to exhort the people to return to the Lord. These people mocked the messengers (2 Chron. 30:10).

The soldiers at Jesus' trial. They mocked the King of Kings by putting a crown of thorns on His head, spitting on Him, and striking Him again and again (Matt. 27:28-30).

The Athenians. These people listened to Paul preach about the resurrection. Some sneered at such absurdity, but others wanted more information (Acts 17:32). It's the same way today.

Prayer of Application

Search me, Lord God and try my heart. Point out where sin still has a place and cleanse me of it. Give me the strength and the courage, Lord, to warn others of sin's consequences.

Know the Joy of Christ Who Knows You

Each heart knows its own bitterness, and no one else can share its joy
(Prov. 14:10).

At the annual Spring Sing, my college dorm sang a song that said, in essence, "no one is an island, no one stands alone." But in one sense every one of us truly stands alone. For who can know the bitterness, or the joy, of an individual, but that individual himself (1 Cor. 2:11)? While we may imagine what our friend's grief in the loss of her husband must feel like, we cannot truly know it. We cannot climb into her brain and experience her pain. In so many ways, even the closest loved ones are strangers.

But there is a Friend who is closer than a brother (Prov. 18:24b). He knows our souls in adversity (Ps. 31:7). He knows our afflictions and our cries for help (Ex. 3:7). He is our refuge and strength (Ps. 46:1). He binds up our wounds and heals our broken hearts (Ps. 147:3). He turns our mourning into joy (Jer. 31:13), and comforts us (Matt. 5:4). He is the Lord Jesus Christ, who indwells the heart of every believer. We can trust Him in our bitterness and in our joy and know that we always have a Friend nearby who understands perfectly (Heb. 2:18).

Scriptural Examples

Michal and David. She once loved David (1 Sam. 18:20), but now despised him as he danced in the streets of Jerusalem. She could not understand the joy that was in his heart. Only God could discern it, and He honored David for it (2 Sam. 6:16).

The Shunammite and Gehazi. Her son dead, and her heart in deep distress, the Shunammite sought Elisha. Gehazi began to push her away, but Elisha rebuked him and testified to the Lord's ability to tell him of her distress (2 Kings 4:27).

Job and his friends. Job's friends sought to comfort him, yet wound up causing him more distress than if they had been silent. Only God knew the facts of Job's situation (Job 13:4-5).

Prayer of Application

Dear Lord, thank You for the Friend that I have in Jesus. Thank You also for the joy of fellowship with other brothers and sisters in Christ, who give me comfort and understanding.

Walk by Faith, Not by Sight

The house of the wicked will be destroyed, but the tent of the upright will flourish (Prov. 14:11).

The non-Christian sees the things of this earth as his inheritance, so he builds his house on its foundation. He settles down and seeks to satisfy all the desires of his heart in earthly things. In the end, his house will be overthrown (Matt. 7:24-27).

The Christian, on the other hand, sees himself as a stranger and a wanderer on the earth. He is looking for a heavenly country (Heb. 11:16). He doesn't build his house on earthly foundations but lives in a "tent," waiting for a home with a better foundation. By faith, he lays up possessions that he will not see until after death.

The non-Christian views the Christian with contempt. He mocks with words like: "How can you be so sure?" and "Pie in the sky by and by!" In a way, the non-Christian has a point. There is no absolute certainty that we will ever inherit our great hope. That is why we walk by faith toward an unseen and future hope (Heb. 11:1). Without such faith it is impossible to please God (Heb. 11:6). Walk by faith.

Scriptural Examples

Noah and the pre-Flood people. Noah built an ark to the scorn of the people. They trusted in the earth and its ability to provide for them and were wicked in all their thoughts (Gen. 6:5). Noah had faith in God and was saved with his family, while the wicked people were drowned (Gen. 6:7-8).

Pharaoh and Moses. Pharaoh was blinded to the power of God through the hardness of his heart. Moses had little earthly power, but trusted in God and walked by faith. The house of the wicked Pharaoh was destroyed (Ex. 6-14).

Jericho and Joshua. Joshua and the Israelites walked around Jericho for seven days before its fortress walls crumbled as God said they would. It was truly a walk of faith (Josh. 6:1-20).

Prayer of Application

Father, grant me the grace to walk as Abraham, Moses, Joshua, and all the other great men and women of faith. Keep my eyes fixed on Jesus, the Author and Perfector of my faith.

Trust in Christ Alone, Not in Your Good Works

There is a way that seems right to a man, but in the end it leads to death (Prov. 14:12).

Most people believe in both heaven and hell but think that they are personally destined for the former. The non-Christian sees himself as a basically good person whose good deeds will outweigh the bad and he will be welcomed into heaven.

But God doesn't grade on a curve. God's law is the absolute standard (Ps. 119:1-8). The Bible is equally clear in stating that all have sinned and fall short of God's perfection (Rom. 3:23). If a person commits just one little sin, he is guilty of breaking the whole law (James 2:10). What then can we do?

There is nothing we can do except to put our faith in the One who did live a sin-free life then bore our sins on the cross in payment for the justice that God required (Rom. 5:6-21). He offers to all the free gift of salvation (John 3:16) and insists that Jesus is the only way (John 14:6). Trust Christ alone, not your own good works, baptism, sacrament, or book, and leave the way that leads to death.

Scriptural Examples

Cain and Abel. Cain brought an unacceptable sacrifice of the works of his hands. Abel brought the bloody sacrifice that God required and that spoke of Christ (Gen. 4:3-5).

David. This great king of Israel, whom God called "a man after my own heart" (Acts 13:22), clearly trusted only in the grace of God to deliver him from his sins (Ps. 51:9-10).

Isaiah. This great prophet of God spoke of the coming King who would also be a lamb who would suffer and be slain for the transgressions of mankind (Isa. 53:1-12).

Paul. He was a man who claimed to have kept the law of God meticulously and said he was blameless in legalistic righteousness. Yet after his encounter with Christ he was able to see the foolishness of trusting in his works (Phil. 3:4-11).

Prayer of Application

Father, thank You for sending Jesus to die for me so I would not have to trust in my feeble works. Strengthen me, that I might warn others of the foolishness of self-salvation.

Seek the Everlasting Joy of Christ

Even in laughter the heart may ache, and joy may end in grief
(Prov. 14:13).

Comedy clubs have become popular in recent years. The laughter of the non-Christian just briefly covers over the fear in his heart. It might be likened to putting a bandage on skin cancer. Modern people, as well as those of ages past, have sought happiness in alcohol, drugs, parties, jokes, and various diversions.

The spiritual person seeks eternal happiness, not by superficial cover-ups but by trusting God and by obeying His commandments. Often, living for righteousness' sake will bring momentary sorrow, but ultimate and lasting joy is promised. As the psalmist says in 30:5, "Weeping may remain for a night, but rejoicing comes in the morning." So the everlasting joy of Christ comes to us not on the wings of revelry and coarse joking (Eph. 5:4), but in following the steps of the Savior who endured suffering for the joy set before Him (Heb. 12:2).

Scriptural Examples

Israelites. While Moses was on the mountain with God, the people talked Aaron into fashioning a golden calf. Then they began to party. God was sorely angered. About 3,000 of them died that day (Ex. 32:1-28).

Belshazzar. This king of Babylon threw a party where wine flowed freely and idolatry was practiced. A human hand wrote on the walls of the palace. The king was so frightened that his knees knocked together. That night, in accordance with what the hand had written, Belshazzar was murdered and his kingdom given to someone else (Dan. 5:1-30).

Herod. Dressed in his royal finery, Herod joyfully accepted the people's acclaim as a "god and not a man." But God struck him down and he was eaten by worms. So will joy turn to grief for all who fail to give glory to God (Acts 12:21-23; Rom. 1:21).

Prayer of Application

Father, thank You that the happiness I find in this life is only a down payment on the joy that will be mine in the life to come. This gives me strength when trials and difficulty arise.

Be Content in the All-Sufficient Christ

The faithless will be fully repaid for their ways, and the good man rewarded for his (Prov. 14:14).

A backslider ("the faithless") is one who has turned from his first love and gone back to the ways of the world. Backsliding is a willful step but often subtle. Soon, however, the backslider returns to self-sufficiency and prayerlessness. If the person who chooses this path is saved, it will be a time of great discomfort for him because his heavenly Father will not allow it to happen without His loving discipline.

The "good man" finds all of his needs satisfied in the Lord. The Holy Spirit dwells within him as a spring of living water (John 7: 38). The Christian rejoices in the Spirit's testimony (Rom. 8:16), a clear conscience (2 Cor. 1:12), and an assurance of future glory and eternal reward (Col. 1:27). The good person does not seek independence but is a slave of righteousness (Rom. 6:19), depending upon God to meet his every need.

Scriptural Examples

Solomon. God gave three laws for future kings of Israel. They were not to collect many horses, which were utilized for offensive warfare. They were not to take many wives, nor were they to accumulate large amounts of silver and gold. Backsliding Solomon broke all three of these regulations. As a consequence, upon his death his kingdom was divided (Deut. 17:14-17; 1 Kings 10:14; 10:26; 11:1; 12:4; 14:25-27).

Jonah. This backslider was thrown overboard and swallowed by a large fish God had prepared for that occasion. Later, Jonah repented and went to Nineveh (Jonah 1:3; 3:3).

The Galatians. Paul was puzzled by their turning away and backsliding from contentment with the gospel (Gal. 4:9-11).

Demas. Demas was a first-century backslider who loved the things of the world and deserted Paul (2 Tim. 4:10).

Prayer of Application

Father, thank You that I have been called to rest in You. Keep me from falling back into the ways of the world. You are the source of all, and I should be content in Your providence.

Be Strongly Grounded in Your Faith

A simple man believes anything, but a prudent man gives thought to his steps (Prov. 14:15).

The Christian faith is not a blind faith. It is a faith based on solid historic fact that is backed up by the testimony of eye witnesses and millions of believers down through the centuries. It is a faith grounded in truth that was recorded in God's Word over thousands of years by various authors, yet with one basic message and no contradictions or errors. Furthermore, the Bible has a quality called "perspicuity." That is, its basic doctrines are essentially clear and understandable by anyone who wants to diligently study it and seek its truth (2 Tim. 3:16).

The simple person is tossed to and fro by every wind of doctrine and by the cunning craftiness of deceitful people (Eph. 4:14). Be careful not to let this happen to you. Prayerfully ground your faith in the lifelong study of the Word. It is a book that is sufficient for life and doctrine, and does not need any other book or priesthood to interpret it. Consider carefully each doctrine you hear and discern whether or not it is true by testing it against the revealed Word of God. Be cautious of the teachers you follow and of the church you join. Build your profession of faith on the solid rock of God's Word, not on the shifting sand of another person's opinion (Matt. 7:24-27).

Scriptural Examples

Eve. Acting out of emotion and self-will, rather than of faith in what God had said, Eve was beguiled by Satan and ate the forbidden fruit. Her rebellion started, as rebellion always does, with a questioning of the revealed Word of God (Gen. 3:1-6).

Timothy. Paul commended Timothy, who from infancy had known the Holy Scriptures. Those Scriptures are able to make one wise unto salvation and are useful in equipping everyone for God's purposes (2 Tim. 3:14-17).

Prayer of Application

Father, how I love Your Word, which is trustworthy, true, sufficient, and profitable in all ways for my life and walk with You. Help me to be firmly established in it.

Fear God and Depart from Evil

A wise man fears the Lord and shuns evil, but a fool is hotheaded and reckless (Prov. 14:16).

The non-Christian either denies the existence of God or he fashions God in his own image. His god perhaps wound things up eons ago, and sat down in his big easy chair to watch history unfold. This person confidently goes his own self-willed way, often hotheaded and reckless because he has no ultimate authority on whom to call or who will call him to account.

The Christian, on the other hand, has an understanding of the sovereignty of Almighty God and that He is working all of the circumstances of this world toward the accomplishment of His purposes and for His glory (Phil. 2:12-13). As the book of Job shows, God is even able to bring good out of evil. He has granted us a free will that will ultimately be confronted with judgment (Acts 17:31). So the Christian flees from evil, knowing the terror of the Lord (2 Cor. 5:11). The wise person knows all sin is vanity anyway, and will only disappoint in the end (Rom. 6:21).

Scriptural Examples

Rehoboam. Solomon's reckless son had confidence in the foolish advice of his young friends. He plunged onto a course that would lead ultimately to his own destruction and to the division of Judah and Israel (1 Kings 12:13-15).

Sennacharib. This self-confident Assyrian king mocked the name of the Lord. In response to Sennacharib's insults and foolish provocation, God sent His angel through the Assyrian camp and destroyed 185,000 men (2 Kings 19:28-37).

Zacchaeus. This wealthy tax collector had cheated many of the citizens of Jericho. But on his encounter with Jesus, the fear of the Lord came into his heart. He repented and offered to give half of his possessions to the poor, and to pay back those he had cheated by four times the amount he had stolen (Luke 19:1-10).

Prayer of Application

Father, show me the sin that remains in my life and give me the strength to avoid even the slightest deviation from Your holy way. May I warn others of the foolishness of evil ways.

Practice Spirit-Control and Honesty

A quick-tempered man does foolish things, and a crafty man is hated
(Prov. 14:17).

Many non-Christians, in their misconception that the events of this world are not subject to the government of God, react angrily in situations that do not please them. In doing so they prove their foolishness. Further, some people plan wicked or crafty schemes to cheat others, not understanding the Lord knows their every thought.

Christians should understand the Lord is working all events and circumstances out for His glory and for the ultimate good of His own (Rom. 8:28-29). The worldview of the Christian provides no room for hasty anger, even though sometimes events seem to warrant it. When we feel provoked, we are to prayerfully seek the control of the Spirit.

The person of God will not be crafty or dishonest, knowing the omniscience and holiness of his Lord. This should be self-evident, but we should understand it applies to every detail of life. The Christian should always seek to conduct his affairs in the reverence and awe of a Holy God.

Scriptural Examples

Balaam. Balaam's donkey saw the angel of the Lord and lay down on the trail. Venting his temper, Balaam beat the animal. But his eyes were then opened, and he, too, saw the angel (Num. 22:27-31).

Asa. Hanani, a seer, came to this king of Judah and condemned him for trusting in others, rather than in the Lord God. Asa was enraged and had Hanani thrown into prison. The king continued to oppress his subjects (2 Chron. 16:7-10).

Jesus. When falsely accused and beaten at His kangaroo court trial, He stood in silence. If the Creator of the universe can maintain such self-control, how can we mere creatures do otherwise (Matt. 27:12-14)?

Prayer of Application

Dear Lord, by Your Spirit working in me, help me to control my anger in situations where I am tempted to strike out at others. Help me also to speak the truth even when it hurts.

Be Crowned with Knowledge

The simple inherit folly, but the prudent are crowned with knowledge
(Prov. 14:18).

Just as I inherited my facial features from my mom and dad, I also inherited a propensity toward folly that has been handed down through generations since Adam's sin. This folly is the sin nature that has resulted from that sin (Ps. 51:5). For over 33 years I walked in folly without understanding. Then God put His knowledge into my heart; the knowledge that the end of such folly is death, but the gift of God is eternal life through Jesus Christ (Rom. 6:23). I was saved.

From that moment, God began to work in me a principle of obedience that leads to righteousness (Rom. 6:16). He began to place the knowledge of His Word in me. Then in excruciating heat and screeching of brakes, He turned me from the ways of folly to the ways of wisdom. If you have been saved as an adult, God must wean you from lifelong sinful habits. It is a difficult yet blessed road. This sanctification process is a lifelong journey, and I still must live with the old nature in this earthly body (Rom. 7:21-23). But soon, I will be eternally set free of it! Thanks be to God, who is able to rescue us (Rom. 7:24-25) and set our feet on the path leading to crowns of life (Rev. 2:10) and righteousness (2 Tim. 4:8) in the life to come.

Scriptural Examples

Adam and Eve. The first couple coveted the knowledge of good and evil and rebelled against God in their desire for it. What began as a search for wisdom and knowledge ended in folly and death (Gen. 2:9, 17; 3:6, 22).

Noah. This patriarch refused to be swept along by the folly of the pre-Flood world. In God's knowledge, he built an ark and preached to the simple in their folly, but no one responded. Only Noah and his family were saved (Gen. 6:5-22).

Prayer of Application

Dear Father, what folly it is to walk in my own power, trusting in my own righteousness. Help me to turn from sin to Your knowledge, not in my power, but in that of Your Spirit.

Be Prepared to Judge the World

Evil men will bow down in the presence of the good, and the wicked at the gates of the righteous (Prov. 14:19).

We rarely see the wicked bowing down to the righteous. We normally see men like Lazarus bowing at the gates of the wicked rich man (Luke 16:20). But this will not always be the case. Every person will one day bow the knee to Christ (Rom.14:11; Rev. 3:9). Even angels will be judged by His people (1 Cor. 6:3). They will bow down at the "gates of the righteous," which in biblical days was where judges sat (Deut. 21:18-19).

How then can we prepare for this certain event? Paul says in 1 Corinthians 6:1-6 that we need to judge between believers who are disputing with one another. We should be peacemakers (Matt. 5:9; James 3:18). We should train to be discerning, rightly dividing truth from error (2 Tim. 2:15 ; Heb. 5:14). By rightly understanding and applying the Word of God (2 Tim. 3:16-17; 2:15) we can help others to grow in faith and maturity.

Scriptural Examples

Joseph's brothers. They wickedly sold their brother Joseph into slavery. Later, they bowed down to him as the supreme ruler of Egypt, just as he had said they would (Gen. 37:5-8; 42:6).

Pharaoh. Following God's plagues upon the Egyptians, he bowed down to Moses and asked him to remove the plagues. Then, following the madness of his heart, he bowed to God in death as the Red Sea swept him away (Ex. 8:8; 9:27-28; 11:8; 14:28).

Saul. Saul pursued David to take his life. David found Saul in a cave, but rather than killing him, he cut off a piece of the king's robe. Later, Saul bowed before David as the man who would assume the leadership of Israel (1 Sam. 24:3-4, 16-21).

The Philippian magistrates. They had Paul and Silas stripped, beaten, and thrown in prison. When the apostles claimed Roman citizenship, the magistrates apologized profusely (Acts 16:20-39).

Prayer of Application

Sovereign Lord and God, though at the present we see many of the wicked in apparent power, I know that it is You who sits enthroned. Help me to prepare to judge the world with Christ.

Befriend the One Who Will Never Leave You

The poor are shunned even by their neighbors, but the rich have many friends (Prov. 14:20).

One is tempted to conclude from this verse that a person is better off rich than poor. But further thought brings us to question the apparent advantage of the rich. I am reminded of the silent screen stars who were on top of the world with their entourage of followers and friends. But when "talkies" came along, the money stopped flowing for many and their fame came to an end. Their "friends" vanished.

We have a Friend who sticks closer than a brother (Prov. 18:24). He will never leave us or forsake us (1 Chron. 28:20; Ps. 27:10; Heb. 13:5). He is the Lord our God. He is Jesus, who, while we were yet poor sinners and destitute of His riches of righteousness, died that we might be made eternally rich (Rom. 5:8).

And what should our response be to God's marvelous grace? We should emulate Christ, sticking close to our brothers and sisters regardless of their circumstances.

Scriptural Examples

Ruth. She stayed by Naomi's side in poverty and affliction. Ruth committed to adopt Naomi's people and her God. Because of her faithfulness, the Lord blessed her richly (Ruth 1:14-18).

Jonathan. The son of Saul was commanded by Saul to kill David, but Jonathan loved David and stuck close to him in his affliction, helping him escape the king (1 Sam. 19:1-7).

Job. In his misery and destitution, Job cried out in pain that all his friends had forsaken him. God did not (Job 19:14; 42:5).

Jesus. Jesus found His friends among the poor and it was to them that the good news was preached, not to those who had no need of a Savior (Matt. 11:5).

The disciples. Their hearts shattered, they deserted Jesus in His time of sorrow, affliction, and death (Matt. 26:56b).

Prayer of Application

Dear Father, Your desire is that Your children be conduits of the supplies which You so graciously provide. Help me to be a brother or sister to those in need, and not to prefer the wealthy.

Treat Everyone with Dignity and Kindness

He who despises his neighbor sins, but blessed is he who is kind to the needy (Prov. 14:21).

R. C. Sproul asks this: "What is the one question to which everyone will answer 'Yes?'" The question is: "Do you want to be treated with dignity?" Every person is created in the image of God (Gen. 1:27). While sin has defaced that image, people deserve proper respect because of it (1 Peter 2:17). Christ came to seek and to save the lost, such as these (Luke 19:10).

We are often tempted to despise our neighbor who is poor or different (Prov. 14:20). But we must not forget that the gap between them and us is infinitely more narrow than is the gap between Christ and us. He made Himself poor, that we might become rich in heavenly things. By being merciful, we remember Christ's sacrifice for us and so honor Him.

But another reason for mercy is here. We are promised that our mercy will bring us blessedness. Our Lord even compared acts of kindness toward the poor as commensurate with doing the same thing for Him (Matt. 25:34-40). The blessings of the Lord will abound to him who shares his food with the hungry and provides the homeless with shelter (Isa. 58:6-8).

Scriptural Examples

Job. Job said that it was his business to be kind to the poor, to be a father to the needy, eyes for the blind, and feet for the lame. Job took up the cause of the stranger (Job 29:11-16).

Cornelius. This Roman centurion was blessed by an angel of God for his prayers and for his generosity toward the poor. The angel then told him to send for Peter to tell Cornelius of the saving gospel of Christ (Acts 10:1-5).

The church at Antioch. Following a prophecy by Agabus, these people collected a generous offering for the saints in Judea and sent it via Barnabas and Paul (Acts 11:28-30).

Prayer of Application

Lord, help me to treat everyone with dignity, especially those who are poor in this world, serving them physically and telling them of the One who came to enrich them eternally.

Make Plans to Do Good

Do not those who plot evil go astray? But those who plan what is good find love and faithfulness [KJV: "mercy and truth"] (Prov. 14:22).

Actually committing sin is wickedness, but it is even greater wickedness to sin in premeditation. We know first-degree murder carries a much stiffer sentence than that of murder in the second degree—without "malice aforethought." God hates the heart of the wicked schemer who plots evil (Prov. 6:16-18).

As children of God, our planning should be for the good. Just as the wicked person's plan heightens the sin, so the plan of the righteous person for good heightens the righteousness of the deed. In fact, though the fruit of our work is often frustrated, God honors our righteous plans. God is interested more in the condition of our hearts than in our outward success.

And what is the reward for those who plan to do good? It is to find mercy and faithfulness or "truth." And what is this mercy and truth? It is none other than the blessedness of the Lord Jesus Christ. For as the Law came through Moses, grace (mercy) and truth came through Jesus Christ (John 1:17).

Scriptural Examples

David. David planned to honor God and build the temple in Jerusalem. God denied David that right, but told him his son Solomon would build it. David was honored in mercy and truth by his plans, even though he never lived to see the ultimate fruition of them (1 Chron. 28:2-5; 1 Kings 8:18).

David. In contrast, David sent for Bathsheba in an adulterous plan. When she became pregnant, David plotted to get her husband to sleep with her, so he would think the child was his. When this failed, David planned to cover up his sin. He had Uriah killed. David paid a great price for the rest of his days (2 Sam. 11:3-17).

Prayer of Application

Dear Lord, guide me in the making of plans to further Your kingdom. I know such plans will be ultimately successful, regardless of whether they bear fruit I can see or not.

Labor in the Calling that is Always Profitable

All hard work brings a profit, but mere talk leads only to poverty (Prov. 14:23).

There are situations in life where this proverb, taken too literally, is incorrect. If we labor in sin, for instance, that is not profitable for anyone (Rom. 6:21). In the same way, the teaching of our lips can be extremely profitable (Prov. 10:21).

But this proverb is really a contrast between industry and diligence on the one hand, and slothfulness on the other. We are to labor to support our families and to help others. We find fulfillment in labor as we utilize God-given talents. So honest labor is a blessing. Jesus tells us that we are not to work just for treasure that spoils, but for treasure that endures to eternal life (Matt. 6:19-20). We are to labor in the study of the Word, in prayer, and by helping meet the needs of others. This work is always profitable.

Unprofitable talk seems to be of two kinds. First, there is the idle talk of busybodies and gossips (1 Tim. 5:13). Then there is the lip service of people's mouths that is not backed by a heart that is right before God (Isa. 29:13). The Christian is called to speak the truth in love. That is always profitable for everyone.

Scriptural Examples

Adam. Following Adam's sin in the Garden of Eden, God cursed the ground and caused it to produce thorns and thistles. Adam was told that by the sweat of his brow he would get food to eat. So labor with frustration began (Gen. 3:17-19).

Jesus. He labored with His father as a carpenter, then labored tirelessly in teaching, healing, exhortation, and prayer. He labored on the cross, and now risen, He still labors as our Advocate and the Sustainer of all things (Heb. 1:3; 8:1-2).

Paul. Paul labored ceaselessly in the service of Christ's gospel. He charged others to be diligent in their labor, providing for their families and for their needy brothers (Acts 20:35).

Prayer of Application

Sovereign Lord, thank You for the blessings of work. Help me to labor in the work of Christ, knowing that none of my labor is in vain. You will make it all profitable.

Use Earthly Wealth to Honor God

The wealth of the wise is their crown, but the folly of fools yields folly (Prov. 14:24).

In Old Testament days, God gave material blessings to the obedient (Deut. 28; 1 Kings 3:13). Even today, honestly gained wealth is a blessing when used conscientiously. Abraham was crowned with wealth as were Job, David, and Solomon.

What a contrast are these men to other examples of foolish men and women throughout Scripture whose earthly possessions became not their crown, but their folly. Their riches were used to gratify selfish desires, not to bring honor to God. Fools do not understand that true riches come only from God.

God promises every believer riches beyond comparison, but we will not see all those riches in this life. Far better, Jesus tells us, are the riches stored up for eternity (Matt. 6:20). We have a crown of righteousness awaiting us (2 Tim. 4:8). We will be joint heirs with Christ (Rom. 8:17). Then God will be honored in all and by all. Honor God now with your possessions by acknowledging Him as their only source.

Scriptural Examples

The Israelites. When Moses was gone so long on Mt. Sinai, receiving the Law, the people feared he would not return. The Israelites and Aaron foolishly fashioned a golden calf and idolatrously gave it credit for bringing them out of Egypt and bondage (Ex. 32:1-6).

The Israelites. Upon escaping Egypt, the Israelites were given untold wealth by the Egyptian people (Ex. 12:35-36). The Israelites later wisely brought their riches to build the tabernacle, until no more was needed (Ex. 35:5-9; 36:5).

Joseph of Arimathea. This wealthy man loved Christ. After the crucifixion, he went to Pilate and requested permission to bury Jesus' body in his own tomb, rather than in a common grave (Matt. 27:57-60; Isa. 53:9).

Prayer of Application

Father God, who so graciously provides for all I need, help me to keep my eyes fixed on Christ and not on this world's riches. Give me the wisdom to use earthly wealth for His glory.

Be a True Witness for Christ

A truthful witness saves lives, but a false witness is deceitful
(Prov. 14:25).

God pledged death to any prophet who attributed falsehood to Him (Deut. 18:20). Today, there are lots of false prophets in the world. Some of them come in the name of Christ and deceive many (Matt. 24:5). They come refuting the inerrancy of Scripture or denying the Trinity. They say salvation is by works, not solely by God's grace. They, too, are promised death unless they repent of their lies and follow Christ in truth.

We who are saved are appointed as ambassadors for Christ (2 Cor. 5:18-20). As such, we need to be faithful witnesses for our Savior in this fallen world. We need to carry on our ministry in the power of the Holy Spirit, who is able to work the gospel into the hearts of people. In that way, our witness will truly save lives.

As a part of this ministry we need to pray for and financially support men and women who hold forth the whole counsel of God, helping those who teach Christ to a lost world.

Scriptural Examples

Miriam and Aaron. Moses' brother and sister began to question his sole right to speak the truth of God. God condemned their deceitful testimony, saying it was to Moses whom He spoke face-to-face, and not in dreams or visions (Num. 12:6-10).

Job's Friends. Eliphaz, Bildad, and Zophar were scolded by God for their deceit about His character and Job's condition. Then He accepted Job's prayer on their behalf (Job 42:7-9).

John the Baptist. John is called the greatest of the Old Testament prophets (Matt. 11:11). He pointed the way to the truth of Christ, as did all the true prophets of old (Matt. 11:10).

Jesus. Here is the true witness (Rev. 3:14). Jesus' testimony that He is the Way, the Truth, and the Life (John 14:6) was confirmed by His miracles and gifts from God (Heb. 2:3-4).

Prayer of Application

Lord, You have given me life in Your Son and have called me to be a witness to His truth. Empower me to be bold. May my whole life be a testimony to the saving power of Christ.

Find Strength in the Lord, Your Refuge

He who fears the Lord has a secure fortress, and for his children it will be a refuge (Prov. 14:26).

How can "fear" and "security" operate together? We usually think of them as opposites. Fear would normally mean lack of security and vice versa. Here, however, we are told the fear of the Lord leads to the security of a fortress. The answer lies in our understanding of the phrase "the fear of the Lord." This is not the fear perfect love casts out (1 John 4:18), but the fear that love brings in. It is the reverence a child has for his father, and that prompts the child to obey his father regardless of the circumstances. Fear of the Lord is taking delight in what God commands us to do (Ps. 112:1). We *fear* the Lord, but we're not *afraid* of the Lord. His fear in us gives us boldness and strength, and, in fact, strong confidence and security. We find such confidence in bold and faithful prayer.

When we were not yet God's children we fled from His presence. Some of us hid in alcohol, some in religion, some in our work, some in our denial of His very existence. But now, by His grace, we flee toward Him in prayer and intimacy. God is our refuge and strength (Ps. 46:1). Even in the face of death we have confidence in Him as our ultimate refuge.

Scriptural Examples

Abraham. When God commanded Abraham to take Isaac to Mt. Moriah and offer him as a sacrifice, the two set out in fear, yet in faith. Abraham, in his fear of God, knew even if he were required to sacrifice Isaac, God had the power to raise his son from the dead (Gen. 22:2-14; Heb.11:17-19).

Stephen. As the Sanhedrin began to stone him, Stephen looked to heaven and saw his refuge opened before him. He expressed confidence in his heavenly advocate Jesus, whom he saw standing at the right hand of the Father (Acts 7:55-60).

Prayer of Application

Father, I thank You that because of Jesus' finished work on the cross, where He reconciled me to You, I have found refuge from my fear of death. Help me to find a daily refuge in You.

Have Faith in God, Who Turns You from Sin

The fear of the Lord is a fountain of life, turning a man from the snares of death (Prov. 14:27).

Before we feared the Lord we clung to sin in the snares of death (Rom. 6:23). How then do we escape sin and death? Do we just make up our minds not to sin? No, for we are slaves to sin (Rom. 6:6). What then can set us free? The Fountain of Living Waters, Christ Jesus our Lord (John 4:14).

Christ's atoning work not only broke sin's yoke upon us but He took upon Himself our curse of sin. Christ experienced death and hell for us so we might experience life and heaven with Him. Now we have the liberty to turn from sin.

The Holy Spirit working in us makes it possible to resist temptation. We are always given a way of escape (2 Peter 1:3-4). We are to drink of the living waters of God's Word and fix His Word in our hearts (Ps. 119:11). Then we need to humbly confess our powerlessness over the sinful habits in our lives and prayerfully seek deliverance. He is faithful, who has begun His good work in you, to complete it (Phil. 1:6).

Scriptural Examples

Joseph. Because of his reverence for God, Joseph fled Potiphar's wife. His was the right response to sin: flee from it. I think Potiphar did not put Joseph to death because he knew he was dealing with a righteous man (Gen. 39:9).

Job. This righteous man feared God and shunned evil. Even in his anguish brought on by Satan, but allowed by God, he did not sin against God. He said even though God may slay him he would trust Him (Job 1:1; 42:7; 13:15).

Zacchaeus. On meeting the Lord Jesus, this once greedy tax collector repented of his deceit. Jesus confirmed salvation had come to Zacchaeus' household that day, as evidenced by his turning from sin (Luke 19:2-9).

Prayer of Application

Father, thank You for Christ's saving work and the freedom from slavery to sin. Grant me the discernment to recognize sin in its seduction and the strength to flee from its power.

Leaders, Know the Source of Your Authority

A large population is a king's glory, but without subjects a prince is ruined (Prov. 14:28).

For kings, or for anyone in a position of authority, there is only one source of that authority: the Lord God Almighty (Rom. 13:1). God sets up and tears down kings and governments. He does it in His church as well. We dare not forget it.

But a secondary source of authority also exists. Without the consent of his subjects, the prince is soon destroyed. History, if not common sense, should tell us this. Recall the recent coup attempt in the Soviet Union. The coup failed because the people stood against it. Jesus stated it this way: "Every household divided against itself will not stand" (Matt. 12:25).

Jesus also stated this principle of leadership another way: "If anyone wants to be first, he must be the very last, and the servant of all" (Mark 9:35). That is, you must find out what your people need and then get it for them. Jesus knew precisely what His people needed and He got it for them. Let those of us who are leaders become servants, even as Christ served us.

Scriptural Examples

Saul. The Lord rejected Saul as king because Saul failed to obey Him. Saul did not kill all of the Amalekite animals. He had also engaged in the sins of divination and idolatry and had built a monument to himself (1 Sam. 15:12, 23).

Absalom. This son of David attempted to steal the hearts of the people from his father and then set himself up as king (2 Sam. 15:1-10). His power play was to prove unsuccessful, and he was eventually slain by David's forces (2 Sam. 18).

James and John. Their mother asked Jesus to place them at His right and left hand in the kingdom of heaven that was to come. Jesus replied with the principle that whoever wants to be great must be the servant of all (Matt. 20:20-28).

Prayer of Application

Sovereign Lord, teach me to pray for those in authority over me. And, Lord, when I am called upon to lead others, may I lead with the same humility that was exemplified by Christ.

Be Patient, for Your God is Sovereign

A patient man has great understanding, but a quick-tempered man displays folly (Prov. 14:29).

The non-Christian may act patient for fear of reprisal or he may be just apathetic. But the Christian has a deep principle from which to draw. His God is sovereign over His creation, and is working all things out for His own glory and for the ultimate good of those He has called (Rom. 8:28-29). Therefore, the Christian doesn't need to "stuff" his feelings, which only leads to more anger later. Conversely, this principle dissipates anger, and allows the love of Christ to shine through the most difficult circumstances.

We are not to repay evil for evil but to try to live at peace with all people, leaving revenge to God. We are to treat our enemies with kindness, repaying evil with good. Then we may "heap burning coals on his head" (Rom. 12:17-21), coals which may bring repentance when he sees our understanding.

This is not to say that there is not a time for righteous anger. But there is a vast difference between a temper tantrum and godly anger which does not sin (Eph. 4:26). Godly anger seeks to be controlled by reason, not passion. It doesn't seek anyone's harm, but rather the correction of injustice in a godly manner.

Scriptural Examples

Balaam. This false prophet angrily cursed his donkey for lying down in the trail (Num. 22:27-29).

Asa. He was enraged by Hanani's reproof and threw him into prison. Soon after, Asa was stricken with a disease. He failed to seek God's healing, and died (2 Chron. 16:7-14).

Jesus. Our Lord had both the right and the power to save Himself and avoid the cross, but He patiently endured all these things to bring salvation to His people (Heb. 5:7-10).

The prophets. These men were examples of patience in the face of injustice, suffering, and oppression (James 5:10).

Prayer of Application

Father, how easily I get angry when I sense injustice. Help me to patiently understand that You are in control of all things, and that You are working every event toward Your glory.

Seek a Healthy, Selfless Heart

A heart at peace gives life to the body, but envy rots the bones
(Prov. 14:30).

Heart disease is the number one cause of death in the United States. But there is another heart disease that is rampant. It is the disease of a selfish heart. Out of this heart flows envy and anger and murder and theft and every evil work (Matt. 5:19). This heart disease will not only bring rottenness to the bones, but rottenness of the soul as well (Gal. 5:21).

When God invades a heart with His "triple bypass," He turns that heart from self-centeredness to God-centeredness. This new heart may bring good health in this life but is imperative for the life to come. You must be born again (John 3:3).

How does one get this new heart? Simply ask God for it and be prepared to turn from your sin in repentance and faith in Christ. He will be faithful to replace your heart of stone with a heart of flesh and put His Holy Spirit in you (Ezek. 36:26-27). Thereafter, God's Spirit will work in you to produce the sound heart God seeks in those who worship Him.

Scriptural Examples

Joseph's brothers. These men hated Joseph because they were envious of his close relationship with their father, Jacob. They sold him into slavery for some silver (Gen. 37:4, 28).

Jonathan. King Saul's son loved David even though David presented a threat to take the throne which would have naturally gone to Jonathan. Study Jonathan's life (1 Sam. 20).

Korah, Dathan, and Abiram. They became envious of Moses and Aaron, and in doing so they treated the Lord with contempt. It "rotted their bones" (Ps. 106:16; Num. 16:30-32).

Jesus' accusers: the scribes and Pharisees. We are told that Pilate knew that it was because of envy that these men handed Jesus over to him for trial (Matt. 27:18).

Prayer of Application

Dear God, thank You for taking out my old heart of stone, and implanting a heart of flesh. Work in me, Lord, to change it from self-centeredness to a heart that is centered on You.

Glorify God by Having Mercy on the Poor

He who oppresses the poor shows contempt for their Maker, but whoever is kind to the needy honors God (Prov. 14:31).

The Westminster Shorter Catechism asks in Question 1, "What is the chief end of man?" The answer: "To glorify God and to enjoy Him forever." And how do we glorify, or bring honor, to God? One answer is found in the verse above. We bring honor to God by having mercy on the poor.

God has made both the rich and the poor for His eternal purposes (1 Sam. 2:6-7). Each is made in his Creator's image. The rich person often looks with scorn upon him whose lot it is to be poor, calling him lazy, indolent, and worthless. To be sure, sloth can bring poverty (Prov. 20:4), but sloth does not explain the vast majority of the people on earth who are poor. Whoever shows them contempt also shows contempt for God.

Jesus came to this earth at the poverty level, and throughout His life He walked with the poor. He brought honor and dignity to the poor through His ministry to them and even claimed to be one of them: meek and lowly (Matt. 11:29 KJV). He said that to treat one of these poor brothers or sisters with kindness was to do that kindness for Him personally, an act that will carry with it everlasting rewards (Matt. 25:34-40).

Scriptural Examples

The people of Sodom. One of the many sins of Sodom was that she did not help the poor while she herself was arrogant, overfed, and unconcerned. Sodom died in a fury and lives on in infamy (Ezek. 16:49-50).

Dorcas. This godly woman whom Peter raised from the dead was known for her kindness to the poor (Acts 9:36).

Cornelius. This Roman centurion was greeted by an angel who told him that Cornelius' gifts to the poor had been received as a memorial offering to God (Acts 10:4).

Prayer of Application

Father God, there are many poor people in our community, many even without homes and in need of clothes. Help me to be a blessing to them, and in turn bring glory to Jesus.

Be Clothed in the Burial Suit of Christ

When calamity comes, the wicked are brought down, but even in death the righteous have a refuge (Prov. 14:32).

My mom used to kid my dad about his one good suit of clothes he didn't wear often. That suit was to be reserved for his funeral so he would look good in the casket. When the day came—almost 40 years ago—the kidding didn't seem so funny. He wore that suit and he looked all right, but more importantly, my dad had on another suit that day. This one was only apparent to God. Years earlier Dad had put on the righteous garments of Christ, who alone stands justified before God by works, and by whom we must be saved (Acts 4:12).

The Bible speaks of a day of calamity for those who, like the Pharisees, consider themselves righteous but have failed to hide themselves in Christ from the wrath of God. They hope in their own good works and will consequently be driven away into outer darkness (Matt. 7:22-23). The firm hope of salvation belongs to those who have put their hope not in their own good works, but in Christ's work alone (Matt. 25:34). They have become clothed in Christ's burial suit.

Scriptural Examples

Abraham. Abraham bargained with God over the city of Sodom. God said He wouldn't destroy Sodom if He could find 50 righteous people among the wicked. Abraham got Him down to 10 righteous, which was probably the number of Lot's family, but God could not even find 10 (Gen. 18:20-33).

David. David trusted in the covenant God had set up. He recognized it was God who would make his salvation sure and not his own good works (2 Sam. 23:5).

Peter. Peter spoke of being born again into a living hope that had at its foundation the resurrection of Christ. There was an eternal inheritance waiting for him in heaven (1 Peter 1:3-5).

Prayer of Application

Dear Lord, some time ago I requested that You save me and come into my heart by Your Holy Spirit. Thank You for clothing me in the alien righteousness of Christ, my Savior.

Let Christ's Wisdom Rest in Your Heart

Wisdom reposes in the heart of the discerning and even among fools she lets herself be known (Prov. 14:33).

I am in the habit of reading the morning newspaper early in the day. Sometimes I wonder why I waste my time because it seems that every day it's the same old stuff. There's little wisdom there. Most of it is just the foolishness of fools made known. A politician seeks another pragmatic solution. A judge allows a woman to abort her child. A man murders his family, then turns the gun on himself. A businessman deceives his stockholders and employees. The list goes on and on.

But true wisdom rests in the Word of God, and because God has given me that understanding, I try to spend most of my early morning time there. I want that wisdom to rest in my heart, to convict me of the foolishness that remains in me, and to rule over me. True wisdom *is* Christ, who rests in my heart by faith. Oh, for a closer walk in utter dependence upon His wisdom and grace.

Scriptural Examples

Saul. Although chosen by God to be Israel's king, true wisdom never seemed to rest in Saul's heart. Rather, it was his foolishness that was consistently manifested (1 Sam. 20:30-34).

Nabal and Abigail. This man made known the foolishness within him. His wife, Abigail, let her wisdom be known as she treated David and his men in kindness (1 Sam. 25:10-11, 223-28).

Jesus. Wisdom rested without measure in the heart of the One who literally was the Wisdom of God. His life and His words poured forth the essence of who He was, as those who walked with Him beheld His glory as that of the only begotten of the Father, full of grace and truth (John 3:34; 1:14; Luke 2:47; John 7:46).

David. After Saul, God anointed David as king in Israel. Unlike Saul, David was a man after the Lord's own heart, and in whose heart rested the wisdom of God (Acts 13:22).

Prayer of Application

Father, You have called me into the rest that is in Christ Jesus. I pray His wisdom would always rest in my heart and that I might let it be known, even to fools like I was.

Pray and Work for Revival in America

Righteousness exalts a nation, but sin is a disgrace to any people (Prov. 14:34).

Alexis deToqueville, in his 19th century work *Democracy In America*, stated "When America ceases to be good, America will cease to be great." Apparently he knew the proverb above. A nation's prosperity is inextricably linked with its righteousness.

Some politicians understand this principle on a practical level, knowing that crime, drugs, civil disobedience, and the like can bring a nation down. But most fail to link these violations of the nation's laws with open rebellion against God. Only God exalts nations, and then only when the people of that nation exalt Him in their minds and hearts by following His ways.

America is on a downward path. We have been riding on the coattails of our ancestors, whose exaltation of God and His principles caused God to exalt America (Ps. 112:1-2; Ex. 20:5-6). America's only hope for future prosperity is in prayer, repentance, humility, and seeking God's face (2 Chron. 7:14).

Scriptural Examples

Israel. Throughout its history a cycle of elevation followed by disgrace may be seen. Seeking God's righteousness, the nation was exalted and lived in peace. Then they would turn to other gods and sin. Famines would then occur, as well as defeat at the hands of enemies. The cycle began in the wilderness with their seditious lack of faith and continued through the destruction of the temple in A.D. 70 (Deut. 28:13; with Matt. 24:1-2).

Nineveh. Its people and king repented of their sin and found grace in the eyes of God. They turned from their evil ways and God did not destroy them (Jonah 1:2; 3:5-10).

Rome. Although the city is not specifically mentioned, Romans 1:22-32 aptly describes the sexual sins that prevailed in Rome at that time, and which led to its eventual destruction.

Prayer of Application

Lord, America has fallen so far. Revive and restore us to the teaching of our ancestors who set You and Your ways first. May revival come and begin with my own house first.

Serve the Great King in Wisdom

A king delights in a wise servant, but a shameful servant incurs his wrath (Prov. 14:35).

As an employer, I know how this proverb applies in business. Employees are hired to solve problems, not to create them. On several occasions I have been forced to discipline and even terminate a shameful employee. Most sought their own selfish interests rather than the benefit of the company.

God calls upon all people to repent, to bow down and serve His Son whom He raised from the dead (Acts 17:30-31). And what does it mean to serve Him? First, it means to believe in the One sent by God (John 6:29). Then, we will follow Christ's example and be obedient to His commands (John 14:15). Someone has said that it's not so much that we "believe in" Jesus, but that we "believe" Jesus (Gen. 15:6). To obey Him is all important.

If we love Christ, we will be drawn to serve Him in the wisdom that only He can give. Don't be deceived. God is not mocked. Whatsoever a person sows, that will he also reap (Gal. 6:7).

Scriptural Examples

Joseph. Joseph served both the king of Egypt and the King of Creation in wisdom and honor. He delighted them and was exalted by each (Gen. 41:39-41).

Daniel. Daniel was in exile in Babylon and served in the palace of a foreign monarch. He, too, served wisely, and was blessed by both earthly kings and the heavenly King (Dan. 2:48; 6:22-23).

The faithful servants. In Matthew 25:14-30, Jesus told the parable of three servants, two who were wise and one who caused shame. The master of these men brought honor to the wise and faithful servants, but his wrath rested upon the third, who hid his master's money and did not step out in faith.

Judas. This shameful man betrayed the King into the hands of murderers. God's wrath will be upon him forever (Matt. 26:24).

Prayer of Application

Father, give me strength to serve You with consistency and faithfulness. Teach me from the great examples of saints throughout the ages who have given their all for the great King.

Chapter Fifteen

Knowing God: His Omniscience

Proverbs 15:3 states about God: "The eyes of the Lord are everywhere, keeping watch on the wicked and the good." The verse speaks to God's omniscience—His perfect knowledge of all facts and events. God is infinite and is aware of everything that goes on. He understands and comprehends it perfectly. Nothing surprises God. He knows the future as well as the past, and even our present thoughts. He doesn't have to wait for something to happen to understand it. All knowledge lies open and revealed before Him. Because of His omniscience, God is able to ensure that His plans will prevail. For instance, Romans 8:28 is one of the greatest and most comforting promises in the Bible. It states, "And we know that in all things God works for the good of those who love him, who have been called according to his purpose." If God couldn't see and direct the future, how could He make good on the promise that all things will work for our good? And we see in the second part of the verse that our calling is "according to his purpose." Our future is in the hands of our omniscient God, who loves us and will not forsake us.

What joy for the believer! But what a fearful thing for the non-believer to be unable to hide from the all-seeing eye of God. God knows all the facts, and is able to judge the world with perfect justice.

Seek a Gentle Tongue

A gentle answer turns away wrath, but a harsh word stirs up anger (Prov. 15:1).

Words of mercy and kindness are the water that quenches the fire of anger, while harsh words are the fuel that keeps the fire going. Our natural bent is to add fuel to the fire, but God's wisdom is like water. How natural for us to want our own way, to "get the last word in," and to think that we are justified in our anger. Sometimes it is as if we'd rather lose a friend than to miss the opportunity to "zing" that person one more time.

But the gospel gives us the example of Christ's mercy, His Spirit imparts the love that "is not easily angered" (1 Cor. 13:5). Each person is created in God's image, therefore we must treat others without malice or contempt. Let us love others as Christ loved us. If others try to cause trouble, may our patient forbearance and humility—fruits of His Spirit—speak healing words that give us the victory, not only over our neighbor, but over ourselves, too.

Scriptural Examples

Jacob with Esau. Fearing his brother's anger, Jacob prepared a large gift, and rehearsed words of conciliation. But Jacob found Esau had already forgiven him (Gen. 32 – 33).

Aaron with Moses. On Nadab and Abihu's death, Moses was angry because the sin offering was not eaten by Aaron's other sons. Aaron appeased him with soft words (Lev. 10:16-20).

Reubenites with their brothers. The Israelites took offense at the tribes of Rueben, Dan, and the half-tribe of Manasseh for their construction of an altar at the Jordan, until it was patiently explained to them that the altar was a witness between the Reubenites and the rest of Israel (Josh. 22:15-34).

Gideon with the men of Ephraim. The Ephraimites resented Gideon's refusal to call them to battle. He calmed their sharp criticism with complimentary words (Judg. 8:1-3).

Prayer of Application

Father, may Your Holy Spirit cause my speech to be always full of mercy and love for others, and may I with Your help, Lord, lay aside every temptation to sarcasm and anger.

Seek a Tongue of Wisdom

The tongue of the wise commends knowledge, but the mouth of the fool gushes folly (Prov. 15:2).

A person's tongue is the window into his heart. The wise person commands his tongue, while the fool's tongue commands him. Wisdom is displayed not in the sum total of the knowledge one has but in how that knowledge is applied to life's situations. Where it is not applied, knowledge is wasted. Jesus displayed this wisdom time and again in commanding the respect of the people, in silencing His opponents, in teaching His disciples, and in winning sinners to Himself. A tongue of wisdom is a gift from God. It is His Spirit working in us to show forth the wisdom of Christ.

On the contrary, the fool "says in his heart there is no God" (Ps. 14:1). All of his thoughts are foolishness, leading ultimately to despair, the grave, and eternal loss. The non-Christian seeks not the things of God; therefore his lips speak only foolishness.

Scriptural Examples

Joseph with Pharaoh. Joseph gave witness to Pharaoh of the power of God to interpret dreams and to give people wisdom for planning the future (Gen. 41:16, 25-39).

Solomon. God gave Solomon a wise and discerning heart, which he displayed in his judging of the women who disputed over who was the mother of a child (1 Kings 3:12, 16-28).

Sennacherib. The Assyrian king boasted foolishly that the God of Israel was impotent. The angel of death proved him very wrong (2 Kings 18:26-29; 19:35-36).

The priests of Baal. Baal's worshippers foolishly shouted in vain for Baal to send fire upon the altar. Nothing happened until Elijah in wisdom called on God (1 Kings 18:25-38).

Daniel. As with Joseph, God gave Daniel extraordinary wisdom to discern Nebuchadnezzar's dream and its interpretation—an ability to prophesy of coming events in Babylon (Dan. 4).

Prayer of Application

Father, give me wisdom that I might serve You and Your kingdom, and bring glory and honor to Christ. May my every word pour forth from a heart of godly wisdom.

Live a Joyful Life Under the Gaze of God

The eyes of the Lord are everywhere, keeping watch on the wicked and the good (Prov. 15:3).

The non-Christian rebels at the notion that God sees every detail of his life. This fact shouldn't surprise the Bible student. We see it in the Garden of Eden immediately following the Fall, when Adam and Eve tried to hide from their Creator, covering their nakedness with leaves (Gen. 3:7-10). But God has perfect knowledge. There is no escape from His constant gaze.

We who have been reconciled to God through Christ (Eph. 4:24) should have no fear in standing naked before Him. He is our great High Priest who cleanses our defilements and covers us, as He did the first couple with righteous garments (Heb. 4:13-14). R. C. Sproul calls us to live our lives "Coram Deo"—under God's gaze. For the child of God, the gaze is no threat. Rather, it is a promise of safekeeping, that God will keep us in His tender care and work out all the circumstances of our lives to His great glory and our eternal benefit (Rom. 8:28-29).

Scriptural Examples

Hagar. Mistreated by Sarai and left alone in the desert, Hagar was comforted by God's angel. She gave God the name, "You are the God who sees me" (Gen. 16:6-15).

Moses and the people of Israel. At the burning bush, Jehovah told Moses that He had seen His people's suffering in the land of Egypt and had heard their cries of anguish (Ex. 3:7).

Gehazi. Elisha's servant sought to profit secretly from Naaman's healing. God, through Elisha, accused Gehazi and transferred Naaman's leprosy to him (2 Kings 5:19-27).

Nathanael. Jesus displayed His omniscience by telling Nathanael where He saw him, sitting under the branches of a fig tree. Nathanael, because of this miracle of Jesus' omniscience, recognized Jesus as the promised Messiah (John 1:48-49).

Prayer of Application

Lord, may the knowledge of Your constant gaze into my life purify me from sin, comfort me in times of trouble, and bring me the joy that only comes from loving Your mighty power.

Speak Healing Words

The tongue that brings healing is a tree of life, but a deceitful tongue crushes the spirit (Prov. 15:4).

Our Lord came to this world to heal affliction. It seems He spent a majority of His time healing those who were lame, blind, and sick. He also spoke words of healing, words that continue to heal us today. His greatest healing ministry was and is that of healing the deep wound of sin that separates the creature from his Creator (Luke 16:26). He commanded us to speak as His ambassadors and to make our speech "seasoned with salt" (Col. 4:6) as we live lives pleasing to Him.

The Genesis Tree of Life stood in the center of the Garden of Eden. When Adam and Eve were evicted from the garden, cherubim with a flaming sword were sent in to guard it (Gen. 3:24). In the book of Revelation, we see another "tree of life" in our eternal home (Rev 2:7; 22:2, 14, 19), the leaves of which are for the "healing" of the nations. We will be invited to eat of it then in the joy of being clothed in the righteousness of Christ, who is that Tree of Life to us.

Scriptural Examples

Elisha. In Jericho, Elisha pronounced healing upon the bad waters, making them pure and productive. The waters were healed according to the prophet's word (2 Kings 2:21-22).

Job's friends. Job's three friends sat with him during his time of suffering and trial and offered long, flowing speeches. But their "wisdom" was not wisdom at all and did not bring healing for their friend Job (Job 13:1-5).

Peter and John. Hauled in as prisoners before the Sanhedrin, and asked by whose authority they were preaching and working miracles, the apostles stated it was by the name of Christ. They argued they could do nothing but speak of the things they had seen and heard—the healing words of Christ (Acts 4:1-20).

Prayer of Application

Father, may the fruit of my lips bring healing to others. May I be bold in my witness of Your life-giving grace in all my conversation, and may many gladly receive Your free healing.

Obey All in Authority

A fool spurns his father's discipline, but whoever heeds correction shows prudence (Prov. 15:5).

The first of the Ten Commandments that speak of human relationships commands we honor our father and mother (Ex. 20:12). Parental authority is representative of the authority of God. How can anyone who despises his earthly father's teaching pay attention to that of his heavenly Father?

God has also provided the Church with leaders who are to have authority over us (Heb. 13:17). We are to seek their counsel, heed their advice, accept their reproof, and submit to their godly teaching. Our nature is to do the opposite, but God commands us to submit ourselves to those in authority over us.

In the same way, we are to submit to the authority of the Word of God. Through it, the Holy Spirit convicts us of specific sin in our lives that may never be noticed by our parents, teachers, or elders. The writer to the Hebrews tells us our Father in heaven also disciplines us for our good (Heb. 12:7-11). Let us submit to His discipline and live.

Scriptural Examples

Hophni and Phineas. These sons of Eli refused their father's rebuke and despised his instructions as they committed abominable sexual immorality and other sins (1 Sam. 2:22-25).

Solomon. Wise as no other man, he listened to and heeded his father David's advice, as in these verses that speak of the temple's construction (1 Chron. 22:11-13; 28:9-20).

Jesus. Although He Himself was able to teach—even to command—His parents Joseph and Mary, He subjected himself to their authority (Luke 2:49-51).

The prodigal son. Jesus told the parable of this young man who, against his father's wishes, went to a "far country" and spent his inheritance on wild living. (Luke 15:11-32).

Prayer of Application

Father, take away my natural desire to go my own way and instead give me the grace to submit to Your Word and to the godly advice and rebuke of all in authority over me.

Store Up Eternal Treasures

The house of the righteous contains great treasure, but the income of the wicked brings them trouble (Prov. 15:6).

Although there is nothing inherently wrong with earthly wealth, you should know the ground rules and pitfalls before making its accumulation a goal in your life. First, earthly wealth is an elusive treasure that often takes wings and flies away. Second, earthly wealth can become an idol and the root cause of other sins (1 Tim. 6:10). Third, earthly riches bring more accountability before God (Luke 12:48). Fourth, earthly riches can trouble one's household because of covetousness, envy, and pride. Fifth, earthly riches never seem to satisfy. The more you have, the more you need. Sixth, and finally, there is no correlation between how hard you work, or how smart you are, and how rich you will become. All wealth comes from God, and if He doesn't want you to have it, you won't get it (Ps. 75:7).

On the other hand, the home filled with the riches of Christ is infinitely wealthy. Our heavenly Father promises to meet all of our needs through His riches in Christ Jesus (Phil. 4:19). These vast, precious riches are in the house of the righteous, His heart. They are eternal, and as such cannot be stolen or corrupted. And, they are only the down payment of the promised treasure of our heavenly home; treasure infinitely superior to that of a mere Rockefeller or Trump or Gates (1 Cor. 2:9).

Scriptural Examples

Abraham's riches. Abraham had immense wealth but his earthly walk was characterized by trusting God (Gen. 13:2).

Job's riches. Job was exceedingly rich yet he did not set his heart on his earthly treasure. Instead, Job's treasure was in knowing the One who gave it to him (Job 1:3).

The man who found a treasure. Jesus likened the kingdom of heaven to a treasure in a field which, on finding it, a man sold all that he had and bought that field (Matt. 13:44).

Prayer of Application

Lord, help me to see that Your eternal treasures are so much more valuable than fickle earthly wealth which can injure so many in its seeking. May I look only to You for all my needs.

Sow the Seeds of Righteousness

The lips of the wise spread knowledge; not so the
hearts of fools (Prov. 15:7).

The wise person first stores up knowledge (Prov. 10:14), then disperses it out of its storehouse. So we are to first get wisdom and understanding (Prov. 4:5) then disperse it to fellow sinners.

The parable of the talents in Matthew 25:14-30 speaks of the principle of sowing seed. The individuals who received five and two talents increased their master's wealth because they sowed that seed money, using it as capital for a business that returned them a profit. In the church, we may apply this principle of seed-sowing to utilizing our gifts in the advancement of God's kingdom. We first sow the seeds of the gospel, expecting a harvest. Then we sow the seeds of God's Word that produce growth in the new Christian. That's the Great Commission (Matt. 28:19-20)! That's our business!

Notice in the parable that the servant who was given one talent buried it, then accused his master of being a wicked man. His master took the talent from this foolish servant who had not invested wisely, and gave it to one who had been faithful. Lord, help us all to be doers (and distributors) of the Word and not hearers only (James 1:22).

Scriptural Examples

Noah. He dispersed the knowledge of God's anger and pending judgment to the pre-Flood generation. He preached for years and had no converts. The hearts of the foolish fail to seek the knowledge of salvation (Gen. 6:22; 2 Peter 2:5).

Jesus. Our great example spread His gospel throughout Israel. Ironically, few seeds sprouted at first, as His own people rejected Him. Later, of course, those seeds would spring up as a great plant filling the earth (Matt. 4:23; 9:35).

John the Baptist. This greatest of prophets spread the message of repentance and the coming kingdom (Luke 3:3).

Prayer of Application

Father, open my lips that I may tell others of Your love. Give me the strength to be a witness for You in the midst of adversity in my family, among my friends, and at my place of work.

Worship God by Pursuing Righteousness

8) The Lord detests the sacrifice of the wicked, but the prayer of the upright pleases him. The Lord detests the way of the wicked but he loves those who pursue righteousness (Prov. 15:8-9).

A misconception among some professing Christians is that believing a set of facts about Jesus automatically brings eternal life. Others who profess Christ believe that baptism alone opens heaven's doors. Yet many of these people continue to live without any evidence of the Spirit's leading to godliness. They have a form of godliness, but deny its power. Paul says we are to "have nothing to do with them" (2 Tim. 3:5).

John tells us that whoever claims to be a Christian must walk as Jesus did (1 John 2:6). This theme is repeated often in Scripture, even by the Lord Himself, as in John 14:6. At the new birth, God's Spirit comes to reside in the heart of the believer. The Christian then seeks a life of righteousness by faith in the One who has given him eternal life. This is pleasing to God (Heb. 11:6), who accepts the prayers and worship of this righteous One. We are not righteous of ourselves, but only through faith in the One who shed His blood for us.

Scriptural Examples

Daniel. Daniel purposed in his heart not to defile himself before God. Through Gabriel, God told Daniel that both he and his prayers were highly esteemed (Dan. 9:23).

The Pharisee and the tax collector. The praying Pharisee commended himself but condemned the tax collector. But the tax collector confessed that he was a sinner, and begged for mercy. Jesus tells us that it was the tax collector who was justified before God (Luke 18:10-14).

Eunice and Lois. Paul commended Timothy's mother and grandmother for their sincere and active faith. They lived their faith and taught young Timothy to do the same (2 Tim. 1:5).

Prayer of Application

Dear God, guide me in the paths of righteousness to which You have called me. May every thought be acceptable in Your sight and may I worship You in spirit and in truth.

Willingly Submit to God's Discipline

Stern discipline awaits him who leaves the path; he who hates correction will die (Prov. 15:10).

No one likes discipline. For both the Christian and non-believer alike, it is a tough thing to endure. But there the similarity in undergoing discipline ends. Discipline turns the follower of Christ back to the correct way, humbled and yielding more to the Spirit (Rom. 8:29). He sees its reason. God only disciplines those He loves, not for revenge but for their eternal benefit (Heb. 12:6).

The Lord disciplines as a surgeon wounds those he treats as a condition of their ultimate healing. We need to seek our Father's favor rather than our own ease, and understand and submit to the sanctifying power of His rod. Then, through true repentance, we like David shall sing that the bones which God has broken now rejoice (Ps. 51:8).

Scriptural Examples

Pharaoh. God caused Pharaoh's heart to harden against the Israelites, because the king hated God's reproof. This led to grief for the Egyptians, and later to Pharaoh's death (Ex. 10:24-29).

The Jews. Time and again Israel forsook their Deliverer for other gods. God would discipline them with the oppression of another nation before they would cry out to Him in anguish, seek forgiveness, and be restored (the book of Judges).

Ahab. This wicked king of Israel hated the rebuke of God and was called to account by Elijah. Many prophets of Baal were slain, and later Ahab, too, died at the hand of God (1 Kings 18).

Peter. The Lord rebuked him for denying that He would be crucified (Matt. 16:23), and for insisting that he would never forsake his Lord (Matt. 26:34). Peter later repented.

Paul. He accepted his "thorn in the flesh" as the discipline of God working for his greater good. Paul had asked God to remove it, but God had refused (2 Cor. 12:7-9).

Prayer of Application

Loving Father, it is painful to undergo Your disciplining rod of correction. Yet how blessed to know that You use the rod for a purpose: to mold me into the likeness of Your Son.

Let Purity Dominate Your Thought Life

Death and Destruction lie open before the Lord—how much more the hearts of men! (Prov. 15:11).

There is no place in all of creation that is not open and visible to our omniscient, omnipresent God. He sees into the hearts and minds of every man and woman. The non-Christian scoffs at such a notion and goes on thinking sinful thoughts.

In contrast, the child of God understands that God has access to his thoughts. He seeks to allow God to control his thoughts (Gal. 5:16-18), for he knows that thoughts precede actions. The impurities that remain remind the Christian of his sinfulness and urge him toward closer fellowship with Christ.

How do you allow God to control your mind? One way may be to think of your mind as a blackboard. Ask God to write on it only thoughts that are pleasing to Him. What thoughts are pleasing to God? Whatsoever is true, noble, right, pure, lovely, admirable, excellent, or praiseworthy, think on such things, "and the God of peace will be with you" (Phil. 4:8-9).

Scriptural Examples

Aaron. His rebellious thoughts were known to God as surely as were Moses' angry words and swift rod at the waters of Meribah (Num. 20:12, 24).

Nebuchadnezzar. This Babylonian king wanted his wise men not only to interpret his dream but to tell him exactly what the dream was. God gave Daniel the dream that the king would not tell anyone, thereby allowing Daniel to witness to the omniscience of Almighty God (Dan. 2:29).

The Jews. Jehovah said that He would punish those Hebrews who even thought that He would not act (Zeph. 1:12).

The Pharisees. Jesus knew the evil thoughts these adversaries harbored in their minds. He read their minds like a book and often answered them before they spoke (Luke 5:22).

Prayer of Application

Dear Lord, purify my thoughts. May every one of them come into subjection to Your will. Search my mind, O Lord. See if there are any wicked thoughts there and purify me.

Submit to the Rebuke of Wise Men

*A mocker resents correction; he will not consult
the wise* (Prov. 15:12).

The mocker's big problem is he is full of rationalizations and self love. He has flattered himself for so long he is unable to receive any criticism or rebuke which seeks to tear away his carefully constructed façade. The wise person who would tell him the truth is no friend, but an enemy (Gal. 4:15-16). The mocker will avoid the light of truth at all costs (John 3:20). This is why the Word of God is so despised by the world. It sheds light upon the darkness of people's hearts (John 3:19).

As Christians, we need to seek the faithful rebuke of our righteous brothers and sisters, so we will continue to walk in the light. Each Christian should be accountable in his life to at least one other Christian so sin may not be allowed to gain the slightest foothold (Heb. 3:12-13). At the same time, we need to study, meditate upon, and memorize the Word of God, which is able to instruct us in the way of righteousness, so we will be furnished for every good work (2 Tim. 3:17).

Scriptural Examples

The Israelites. At Kadesh-Barnea, two of the 12 spies (Joshua and Caleb) who had gone in to look at the Promised Land exhorted the Israelites to go in and, by faith, take it. The people instead rebelled against their wisdom and sought to stone the pair (Num. 14:6-10).

Herodias. John the Baptist rebuked Herod for living with his brother's wife, Herodias. This mocker was so incensed by this rebuke she sought John's murder (Mark 6:19).

The Pharisees. Jesus rebuked the Pharisees for their love of money and for justifying themselves in the eyes of others. They sneered at His reproof and later brought about His death on a Roman cross (Luke 16:13-15).

Prayer of Application

Heavenly Father, grant me the grace to seek out and act upon godly rebuke from Christian brothers and sisters. And help me to ingest Your Holy Word, so sin might not gain a foothold.

Let the Joy of Christ Reign in Your Heart

A happy heart makes the face cheerful, but heartache crushes the spirit (Prov. 15:13).

This is body language as taught in the Holy Scriptures. The face, and indeed the whole body, mirrors what is going on in the heart. The spirit that is broken and sorrowful is carried in a body that slumps over and walks slowly with a downcast face. On the other hand, a joyful heart is reflected in a smile, an upright posture, and a quick step.

From time to time Christians go through sorrow. But Scripture is clear that rejoicing, not sorrow, is to be our normal condition (Rom. 12:12). By God's grace, He makes us brothers and sisters of our risen Savior and joint-heirs with Him (Rom. 8:17)! If that doesn't make your heart sing, nothing will.

We must be careful not to fake our joy, however. False joy is clearly seen. If you are sorrowful, don't try to cover it up. But go to the Word. Receive God's promises all over again and let the joy of knowing Him and His salvation reign in your heart.

The secret of joy in the Lord is in thanksgiving. We are called to give thanks in all circumstances of our lives (1 Thess. 5:18). Thanksgiving when the going is rough casts our cares upon God's providence and brings us joy (1 Peter 5:7).

Scriptural Examples

Hannah. Childless and in bitter despair, Hannah received Eli's blessing and smiled. She joyfully knew that God would answer her prayer and open her womb. He did (1 Sam. 1:12-20).

Saul. Saul's heart was broken because of worldly sorrow. There was no joy. His kingdom was to be taken from him and given to David (1 Sam. 28:15-17).

Stephen. The Sanhedrin looked upon Stephen's angelic face as they prepared to stone him to death. The first martyr knew God's joy even as the stones rained down (Acts 6:15; 7:59-60).

Prayer of Application

Father, You have brought me into a joyful relationship with Your Son. Although sorrow may come, may I then be restored to the joy of my salvation that I may bring You glory.

Search Diligently for the Knowledge of God

The discerning heart seeks knowledge, but the mouth of a fool feeds on folly (Prov. 15:14).

The desire to know God is implanted in the heart of the believer at regeneration, and its fruit should be a lifelong study to know Him. The reason we seek to know Him is to be changed into the likeness of Christ (Rom. 8:29) and bear His fruit. Knowledge without fruit-bearing puffs up, like the Pharisees and Sadducees who were puffed up by their learning (Matt. 23:5-7). But knowledge that builds consistency, completeness, and understanding, that teaches, encourages, and witnesses for the truth, is a worthy goal for each of us.

The non-Christian delights in the knowledge of this world, which is at best fleeting and not able to edify for eternity. Today, worldly knowledge is exploding. There is a temptation for the child of God to keep up with this knowledge explosion. While we do need some of it in our jobs or businesses or to invest our resources appropriately, it is in large measure not worthy of our time and energy. How much better to study the Word of God, which is beneficial for this life and for the life to come.

Scriptural Examples

The Queen of Sheba. She came from far away to hear the godly wisdom of Solomon (Matt. 12:42; 2 Kings 10:1-13).

Nicodemus and Mary. They both had a heart that sought understanding of God. They sat at the feet of the Master to learn from Him, and neither was disappointed (John 3:1-2; Luke 10:39).

The Ethiopian eunuch. He asked Phillip to explain the Scriptures, and his eyes were opened to the truth of God. With godly knowledge the eunuch asked to be baptized (Acts 8:30-38).

The Bereans. They searched the Scriptures diligently, to see if the things being taught by the apostles were true. How we need to be like the Bereans in our own day (Acts 17:11).

Prayer of Application

Father, give me a hunger to know Your Word and to know You through it. May I not be puffed up with knowledge, but may my life reflect the life of Christ so that He will be glorified.

Worship the Lord with Rejoicing

All the days of the oppressed are wretched, but the cheerful heart has a continual feast (Prov. 15:15).

The natural person's afflictions caused by his sin or the sin of others bring him only grief and bitterness. There is a sense in which the unsaved person never has a good day. Even on days when things seem to be going his way, he is only storing up wrath for himself against the day of God's wrath (Rom. 2:5).

Even though the Christian may go through difficult problems and circumstances, deep within there should be a peace and a joy that passes understanding (Phil. 4:7). There is a sense in which the Christian never has a bad day, because he knows all things, even those circumstances that are hurtful and bitter at the time, are the work of his Sovereign Lord in his life. They are designed by God for his ultimate good (Rom. 8:28-29).

Therefore, Paul is able to say whatever the circumstances that surround him, he has learned to be content (Phil. 4:11). And Nehemiah, when instructing the people, said they should not grieve, for the joy of the Lord was their strength (Neh. 8:10). Ours is a joyful feast that will never end, thanks to the finished work of our Savior. Worship Him with rejoicing!

Scriptural Examples

Job. Stripped of his earthly possessions and his children dead, Job praised his Lord anyway. Later he said even if the Lord killed him he would trust Him (Job 1:21; 13:15).

Habakkuk. The prophet Habakkuk cried out that even if all the crops failed and the cattle died he would rejoice in the Lord who was his strength. Oh, to have the faith of Habakkuk, giving thanks in all things (Hab. 3:17-19).

Paul and Silas. In Philippi, Paul and Silas were thrown into prison and put into stocks. But even locked up they sang hymns to God, rejoicing in their afflictions (Acts 16:16-34).

Prayer of Application

Our Father, help me to see the truth when I am going through trials in this life. Give me faith to trust You fully in these times of confusion and to worship You with rejoicing.

Prefer Poverty and Peace to Treasure and Trouble

16) Better a little with the fear of the Lord than great wealth with turmoil. 17) Better a meal of vegetables where there is love than a fattened calf with hatred (Prov. 15:16-17).

Have you ever seen the bumper sticker, "He who dies with the most toys wins"? Some yuppie is saying that success comes from the accumulation of stuff. But Jesus said that a person's life does not consist in the abundance of his possessions (Luke 12:15). All of the treasure in this world will not satisfy a worldly person (Eccl. 1:8), yet a very small portion of this world's goods will satisfy a person who fears the Lord.

Notice that the sources of the merry heart of verse 15 are the fear of the Lord (v. 16) and love for others (v. 17). For the person who has these attributes by the Spirit of God, life should be a continuing feast, regardless of external circumstances.

On the other hand, in a house filled with great treasure, yet where sin abounds, there is trouble. Oh, there may be a superficial peace, but underneath that façade is rebellion against God that can only mean big trouble in an ultimate sense.

Scriptural Examples

Saul. David was invited to come to King Saul's feast but no love was there. Saul in his anger and jealousy even hurled his spear at his own son Jonathan (1 Sam. 20:24-34).

Absalom. Plotting revenge for his sister Tamar, Absalom invited Amnon to dinner. After the rapist was filled with wine Absalom had him killed. Here was a house of great treasure and great power, but with much trouble (2 Sam 13:28-29).

Jesus. The disciples enjoyed a simple meal of fish and bread. It wasn't fancy cooking in a palace, but with the risen Lord and with His love it was a joyful feast (John 21:10-14).

The apostles. The new church led by these men met joyfully in homes to share their simple food (Acts 2:46).

Prayer of Application

Father, help me to fix my eyes on the true riches of holy reverence for You, love for others, and the peace that passes all understanding. Thank You for the many blessings You bring.

Be a Peacemaker

A hot-tempered man stirs up dissension, but a patient man calms a quarrel (Prov. 15:18).

Our very salvation comes as a result of God's being slow to anger (2 Peter 3:15). Patience and self-control are fruits of the Spirit of God (Gal. 5:22). So we who bear that Spirit in our hearts are called by Christ to be peacemakers (Matt. 5:9).

We often think, when confronted with an unjust situation, we need to give full vent to our feelings and stand up for our rights. But God requires we overcome evil with good (Rom. 12:21). We are to live godly lives in witness of the One who truly brings peace. Anger and wrath do not bring about the righteousness of God (James 1:20). We live a supernatural existence and we are called to reflect a higher wisdom than the natural person. We are called to lives of patience.

But how do we put this principle into shoe leather? First, we need to rely fully on the work of the Holy Spirit in our lives to control our temper and anger. Second, we need to realize God is sovereign in all things and we can submit to the circumstances of our lives knowing He will never leave us nor forsake us. Finally, we need to have firmly planted in our minds and hearts that a hot temper is a reflection of our depravity, and like sin it does not bring unity.

Scriptural Examples

Abraham. When his herdsmen and those of Lot began to quarrel over pastures, Abraham suggested they part company so that there would be pasture land for all (Gen. 13:7-9).

Isaac. Gerar's servants quarreled with Isaac over the ownership of a well. Isaac moved his flocks to another well, then another, until peace was restored (Gen. 26:19-22).

Jephthah. He was driven from his home by his half brothers. Desiring peace, he settled in the land of Tob (Judg. 11:1-3).

Prayer of Application

Lord, You have called us to be reflections of You, and as such to be peacemakers. Help me to do this by acknowledging You as sovereign Lord and trusting only You for justice.

Live Diligently by Faith

The way of the sluggard is blocked with thorns, but the path of the upright is a highway (Prov. 15:19).

In the Western U.S. there is a common hedge called a "natal plum." Its thorns are very sharp. The sluggard, lacking faith, grows in his own mind a barrier like this kind of hedge that hinders him from seeing life as a highway. At Kadesh Barnea, God sent 12 spies into the Promised Land. Although they liked what they saw, 10 of the spies grew such a hedge. The people grew a hedge, too. By their unbelief in the power of God, they refused to go in and take the land. Only Caleb, Joshua, and a few others believed God would give them the victory (Num. 13:26-30).

The faithful person's path is not an easy one, but it is a highway not blocked by a fear that enslaves. Notice that the proverb speaks of the "upright" person and not the "diligent." The upright person follows his Lord's commands. He continues steadfast in prayer, for which he expects an answer. The upright person believes God and acts upon God's Word without delay. To call a person "upright" is to claim diligence for him as well.

Scriptural Examples

The wife and mother of Proverbs. She was industrious and blessed, overseeing her household with diligence (Prov. 31:27).

The Sodomites. God condemned this wicked city, noted for its evil, arrogance, and apathy (Ezek. 16:48-50).

The slothful and diligent servants. The lazy servant buried his talent, but the faithful servants, entrusted with more, diligently put their master's money to work (Matt. 25:24-30).

Some Thessalonians. Paul said that he heard of some among them who were slothful, disorderly busybodies. He rebuked them for their lack of diligence (2 Thess. 3:10-12).

The young widows. Paul criticized the young widows in the church who were gossips and busybodies (1 Tim. 5:11-14).

Prayer of Application

Dear Lord, keep me on the path of faith. I humbly ask for Your leadership and the strength to follow You. Let me not build up a hedge of unbelief that blocks the highway before me.

Honor God by Honoring Your Parents

*A wise son brings joy to his father, but a foolish man despises
his mother* (Prov. 15:20).

The greatest joys in life, and the deepest hurts, are both experienced by parents. What a delight it is to have a son or daughter whose trust is in the Lord and who is prospering in the true way. Conversely, what great pain and unrest lie in the heart of the Christian parent whose child is headstrong and disobedient and who rejects the Lord.

The unselfish love of a mother is a tiny glimpse for us humans into the heart of God. For God has truly given us His only Son, the most expensive gift imaginable, that we might have eternal life. So, too, our dear mothers give of themselves without thought of repayment, to give us life and then sustenance on this earth. The child who despises such great love surely deserves the title of "fool. "Bring joy to your parents.

Scriptural Examples

Ruth. Witness the love of Ruth for her mother-in-law, Naomi. What joy the widow found in the Moabitess' faithful companionship. And what a reward God had in store for the beautiful Ruth, as she brought Him honor (Ruth 1:16-18).

King David. Much of the trouble David reaped in his sons was due to his own sin against Bathsheba and her husband. In 1 Kings 1:48, however, David rejoices and worships God because his wise son Solomon has been placed on the throne.

King David. David wept over the death of his rebellious son Absalom who wanted to be king. Absalom's horrible death shows how seriously God views the parent/child relationship. He will not let the rebellious go unpunished (2 Sam. 18:33).

Mary. The epitome of motherhood, Mary's joy and pain certainly exceeded the boundaries of normal human experience (Luke 2:19, 34-35).

Prayer of Application

Dear Father, You gave me parents for my great benefit and I thank You for them. Help me to always honor them, for in doing so I bring honor and glory to You.

Walk Joyfully in the Wisdom of God

Folly delights a man who lacks judgment, but a man of understanding keeps a straight course (Prov. 15:21).

We in America live in a society that takes great joy in the pleasures of the flesh. Many men and women live to party and to seek thrills from drugs, alcohol abuse, and sexual encounters. The Bible declares clearly that without Christ we are slaves to sin (Rom. 6:12; 7:24-25). Those who seek their joy in the flesh hate the gospel because it would turn them from their folly (Acts 3:26). But employment of godly wisdom brings a profoundly greater joy and delight without the hangover of sin.

Christ brings wisdom and understanding. The person with the Spirit seeks the things of God and is turned from the ways of the flesh. He gives himself to the authority of the Word of God and is freed from habitual sin into a deeper walk with the God who saved him. Now, only in the things of Christ does he find delight as he seeks to obey the Word and the Savior who calls him to such obedience (John 14:15).

Scriptural Examples

Joseph. He fled Potiphar's wife and the folly of sinning against God, whose provident eye guarded him (Gen. 39:7-12).

The Israelites. They came out of Egypt under the miraculous acts of an omnipotent God. Although led by His presence daily, they turned to folly (Ex. 32:5-6, 25).

Nabal. Abigail's foolish husband, Nabal, first insulted David and his men, then he went home and got drunk, not realizing that his days on earth were numbered (1 Sam. 25:10-11, 36-38).

Haman. Apparently on course to destroy all the Jews in Babylon, Haman reveled in his folly. His joy soon turned to fear, however, as he wore the noose he prepared for Mordecai (Est. 5:9).

Stephen. The first martyr of the early church, Stephen, was a man of understanding who delighted in God (Acts 6:8-10).

Prayer of Application

Dear Jesus, thank You that You won the victory over sin and death. But, Lord, I continue to struggle. Hold me up and strengthen me with Your grace that I might walk worthily.

Seek the Wisdom of Godly Counsel

Plans fail for lack of counsel, but with many advisers they succeed (Prov. 15:22).

If the beginning of wisdom is the fear of the Lord (Ps. 111:10), then wisdom's first small step is the distrust of one's own judgment. Our fallen nature is weak and untrustworthy. We need to feed upon the Word of God, to pray for wisdom from above (James 1:5), and to seek the advice of godly men and women. To learn from the experience and study of others is much less costly than learning lessons first-hand.

In business, I have learned that the best counselors are one's customers. A good businessperson is continually seeking feedback from those who are purchasing and using his product or service. It is of utmost importance that he be aware of their changing needs.

Likewise, we should seek the counsel of those whom we strive to serve, to ensure against failing to meet their needs. We lay people also need to listen carefully to the counsel of our teachers, elders, and pastors as they lead us in the wisdom of God's Word. To do so exhibits the wisdom of this proverb.

Scriptural Examples

Rehoboam. As king he rejected the godly advice of the elders for justice and mercy and followed his own course instead, scourging the people of Israel (1 Kings 12:8-19).

Ahab. This wicked king listened only to advice he liked, not God's Word. He represents so many today who reject the advice of the Word, ultimately to their great peril (1 Kings 22:18-39).

David. David rejected Joab's advice and ordered a census of his fighting men. God punished the nation most severely because of this breach in David's trust. (2 Sam. 24:1-4, 15).

Paul and Barnabas. These godly men journeyed to Jerusalem and sought the counsel of the apostles and elders in the disagreement about circumcision (Acts 15:1-22).

Prayer of Application

Dear Father, You have promised wisdom to those who ask. Help me, Lord, not to trust in my own wisdom, but to seek it daily from Your Word, Your Spirit, and from godly Christians.

Speak Timely Words

*A man finds joy in giving an apt reply—and how good is
a timely word!* (Prov. 15:23).

Martin Luther said that the word of a brother or sister which
is backed by Scripture and spoken in a time of need carries tremendous weight. Scripture is filled with such examples, such as
in Genesis 45:4-7 when Joseph dealt with his brothers.

Speaking timely words of wisdom brings joy to the speaker
and healing to the hearer. Timeliness is all-important. Words that
bring healing when spoken in private may bring irritation in public.
Sometimes the reverse is true. The general rule is to give reproof
privately except when the occasion calls for public rebuke. Use
kind words without condescension, and only after determining
the proper place and time. "The wise man's heart discerneth both
time and judgment" (Eccl. 8:5 KJV).

This same principle of timing holds true in giving words of
encouragement. Often, we can embarrass others by acknowledging
their work in a public setting. Instead, a simple personal note is
suitable. Other times, the public setting is very appropriate. Ask
God for a sense of good timing in your speech.

Scriptural Examples

Manoah's wife. Samson's mom upheld her husband's reeling
faith with a timely word. When he feared death because they had
seen the angel of the Lord, she calmed him (Judg. 13:1-23).

Abigail. This woman saved her wicked husband, Nabal, with
words of wisdom spoken at the proper time (1 Sam. 25:32-33).

Naaman's servants. When Naaman refused to wash in the
Jordan to be cured of leprosy, his servants spoke timely words of
wisdom that saved his life (2 Kings 5:13-14).

Paul. An earthquake caused the prison doors to pop open.
The jailor started to commit suicide. Paul's words stopped him,
then Paul led him and his family to salvation (Acts 16:27-31).

Prayer of Application

Father, my timing in giving encouragement and reproof is
all important. By Your Spirit, help me to develop a real sense of
timing that my words might carry the appropriate message.

Walk the High Road of Faith

The path of life leads upward for the wise to keep him from going down to the grave (Prov. 15:24).

An old Scottish ditty goes something like this: "Oh, you take the low road and I'll take the high road, and I'll be in Scotland afore ye." In a certain sense, every day of our lives we are choosing roads to take. Which road will you follow today?

There is also a sense in which every person is a pilgrim on this earth. Both saved and unsaved have only a temporary home here and each walks down the path that leads to his eternal home. For some it will be a home in the presence and joy of Christ, while for others the path leads only to the grave, destruction, and hell beneath. We who are Christ's should fix our eyes upon Him and upon His eternal things (2 Cor. 4:18-5:2). We should walk daily toward the high ground where our hope is (2 Cor. 5:1-5); where our treasure is (Matt. 6:20); where our eternal home is (2 Cor. 5:6-8); and where our Savior is (Col. 3:1). Our true fellowship is not of the earth, but upward in heaven (1 Cor. 15:47).

Scriptural Examples

Enoch. Enoch pleased God by his faith and therefore he did not experience death. Enoch walked the high road of faith and right on into heaven (Gen. 5:24; Heb. 11:5).

Abraham. He left home by faith in the promise of God. Then he trusted God's promise of a son, even though he and his wife Sarah were too old. God reckoned Abraham's high road of faith as righteousness (Gen. 15:6; Heb. 11:8-12).

Lot. Lot was a saved man, but his walk with God is not recommended. Read Lot's story to see what the low road of faith looks like (Gen. 19; 2 Peter 2:7).

Stephen. He died with his eyes fixed skyward on Jesus, submitting his earthly life to the One who gives eternal life, and died forgiving those who were murdering him (Acts 7:55-60).

Prayer of Application

Dear Lord, establish my feet on the rock of Your Word and guide them on the high road that is pleasing to You. Keep my eyes fixed on Jesus, the author and finisher of my faith.

Humbly Come to the Aid of the Needy

The Lord tears down the proud man's house but he keeps the widow's boundaries intact (Prov. 15:25).

God reigns supreme over this world, a fact suppressed by the natural person (Rom. 1:18-21), who does as he pleases without regard to eternal consequences. But the person who lifts himself up in pride and treason against his Creator will destroy not only himself but his whole house as well. Pride is, in many ways, the chief of sins because it elevates self over all.

God upholds the cause of the widow, the orphan, and all who are downtrodden. The early church established the office of deacon specifically to care for those in need (Acts 6:1-3). We, too, are enjoined to take up the widow's cause (James 1:27). God is their Friend and Benefactor. He establishes their boundaries.

But proud scoffers beware! Do not be deceived. If you fail to honor God with your riches and share your blessings with those in need, know this: God does not settle all of His accounts in this life. Read Jesus' story about Lazarus and the rich Dives in Luke 16:20ff., and tremble.

Scriptural Examples

Naomi and Ruth. God provided for these widows. Naomi was blessed by her faithful daughter-in-law. God blessed Ruth through Boaz, her kinsman-redeemer (the book of Ruth).

The prophet's widow. This woman cried out to Elisha as her dead husband's creditor came to enslave her two sons. Elisha told her to gather up jars, into which God poured oil. She sold the oil to pay the debt she owed (2 Kings 4:1-7).

The Shunammite. After restoring her son's life, Elisha told her to avoid the coming famine by going to Philistia. Seven years later, she returned to Israel at precisely the time the king was being told of Elisha's miracle. The king gave her back her land and seven years' income from it (2 Kings 8:1-6).

Prayer of Application

Father, in the riches of Your grace You take up the cause of the poor and powerless. Give me a real heart for the needy so I may become a representative of Your love for them.

Let God's Word Purify Your Thoughts

The Lord detests the thoughts of the wicked, but those of the pure are pleasing to him (Prov. 15:26).

The secret place of the mind, where plans are devised and where secret sins are harbored, is not really secret at all. It is laid wide open before the Lord, to whom all people must give account (Heb. 4:13). The natural person has shut God out of his thinking and his heart has become darkened (Rom. 1:21). That person's thoughts are detested by God, no matter how righteous the person may think they are.

But for the child of God, who by the grace of God has received salvation through faith in Christ, the Holy Spirit invades his heart through the medium of his mind and begins a process of purification (Rom. 12:2). How does it happen?

When snails are readied for the table, they are taken from their natural setting and fed only corn meal or another such pure food. Over time, their flesh loses its wild taste and becomes purified and cleansed. Similarly, the Christian is called to feed upon God's Word, which can cleanse and purify the thoughts, words, and way of the child of God (Ps. 119:9).

Scriptural Examples

The pre-Flood generation. God saw that the hearts and thoughts of pre-Flood people were wicked all the time. These men and women followed the abominable thought patterns of their father, Cain, and gave expression to them in violent ways. God sent the flood waters to destroy them from the face of the earth. Only the godly Noah and his family survived, and that was only by the grace of their Creator God (Gen. 6:5).

Tychicus. Paul commended his brother Tychicus to the church at Ephesus, knowing that he would encourage all the saints there and speak to them words of comfort, which flowed from the pure thoughts of his heart (Eph. 6:21-22).

Prayer of Application

Heavenly Father, put a real desire in my heart for holiness. I pray that the Holy Spirit purifying me through the Word might transform me into the person You want me to be.

Look to God as Your Only Source

A greedy man brings trouble to his family, but he who hates bribes
[KJV: "gifts"] will live (Prov. 15:27).

I can speak from personal experience as to how greed brought
trouble to my house. The details, related elsewhere in these pages,
resulted from various business speculations. While it seems unfair
that my family should suffer for my misdeeds, that is the way life is. I
tried to play God, to force the circumstances of the world to submit
to my will. I learned that I am but a cork floating in a raging sea,
small and without propulsion or rudder. But Christ, who promises
and delivers greater treasure than I ever imagined, allowed me to be
buffeted for a season, then lifted me up to a more solid path.

Jesus promises that if we seek His Kingdom and its righteousness, all of our material and spiritual needs will be met (Matt. 6:33).
The world's gifts are temporary, fleeting, and not really gifts at all,
but they do carry a price tag. In some countries bribes, or secret
gifts, are a way of life. God hates that kind of business. God's gifts
are so much better: eternal in nature and free for the asking. Seek
God's gifts. They bring peace, joy, fulfillment, and contentment.
They are truly worth seeking.

Scriptural Examples

Lot. Abraham's nephew chose the well-watered plain of the
Jordan, leaving the hill country to his uncle. He settled in the sinful city of Sodom. The decision, probably rooted in greed, was to
be his family's undoing (Gen. 13:10-11).

Abraham. He refused to accept gifts from the king of Sodom
following their joint victory in battle. Their acceptance would
somehow credit the king with winning the victory, which was in
reality a gift of God (Gen. 14:22-23).

Achan. After the battle of Jericho, Achan greedily hid some
of the devoted spoils of war in his tent. He was found out and his
whole family punished for his sin (Josh. 7).

Prayer of Application

Sovereign Lord, teach me to trust You for all my needs and
those of my family. Forgive me, Lord, for putting my trust in
other things when You are the source of every good thing.

Desire a Disciplined Tongue

The heart of the righteous weighs its answers, but the mouth of the wicked gushes evil (Prov. 15:28).

How often I have wanted to swallow words spoken in haste. Even though much good treasure may be stored up in the Christian heart, we must tend the door to it with care because of the wickedness that is still there. Sanctification never really weeds out all of the old person. It only suppresses him.

God has provided the medium of prayer for the tongue's discipline. James 1:5 gives us the principle of getting wisdom by asking God for it. In our speaking, we need to seek wisdom from God before opening the floodgates. Prayerfully seek to avoid answering on impulse.

The natural person may have no such desire for restraint in his speech. He multiplies his words and is consumed by his own lips (Eccl. 10:12-14). He doesn't know that he shall give account to God for every idle word that he speaks (Matt. 12:36). But we Christians need to prayerfully ask God for the wisdom of a disciplined tongue.

Scriptural Examples

Moses. The Gadites and Reubenites expressed a desire to settle on the east side of the Jordan. Moses delivered a hasty and scathing sermon to them about their lack of commitment to the rest of the Israelites. He was later appeased when he heard their further testimony (Num. 32:1-22).

Joshua. Fearing Israel's wrath, the Gibeonites played a trick on them. Without consulting the Lord, Joshua and the leaders of Israel made a hasty pact with them in opposition to God's will which had been clearly revealed to them (Josh. 9:14-15).

Nehemiah. He followed the proverb above, praying to the King of heaven before answering the king of Babylon (Neh. 2:1-6).

Peter. When Jesus told of His pending execution, Peter spoke hastily and foolishly (Matt.16:22).

Prayer of Application

Father, You have promised us wisdom if we ask. May Your wisdom guide my speech and my actions, to the end that I would only speak words that are pleasing to You.

Pray to Your Father Who Hears You

*The Lord is far from the wicked but he hears the prayer of
the righteous* (Prov. 15:29).

God's presence fills the universe, so in that sense He is equally
near every person on the planet (Acts 17:27-28). But in His gracious favor, He hears and answers the prayers of believers. At the
crucifixion of Jesus, the curtain of the temple was torn in two
(Matt. 27:51) and the way into God's presence was opened for
us. What a great privilege we have in prayer!

Our duty as Christians is to pray always (1 Thess. 5:17). Our
heavenly Father will not bar access to His seeking child. Rather,
He is only too willing to give us the things we ask of Him, in His
timing and in accordance with His will. Let your prayers have a
definite object in mind. Then make sure your motives are right and
that you are not praying selfishly to bring yourself pleasure, with
no profit for others or for God. Finally, have full confidence in
the One who hears and responds. The prayer of faith is powerful
and effective (James 5:17).

Scriptural Examples

The Israelites. The Lord turned a deaf ear to the people of Israel
following their decision at Kadesh Barnea to fight the Amorites
in their own strength. God wouldn't bless their works done in the
flesh (Deut. 1:45).

The enemies of David. David praised the Lord for deliverance
and recounted how his enemies and Saul prayed to the Lord but
were not heard (Ps. 18:40-41).

David. David testified that the Lord had heard his prayer and
had delivered him from trouble (Ps. 116:1-7).

The saints who prayed for Paul. Paul was delivered from
sickness and death and gave testimony to the effectiveness of the
prayers of the saints who stood with him, and to the graciousness
of the Lord in answering them (2 Cor. 1:9-11).

Prayer of Application

Father, teach me what it means to pray in faith, persistently
believing that You will answer my prayer. Create in me a prayerful
spirit, that I will thankfully bring all things to You.

Rejoice Both to See and Hear God's Truth

*A cheerful look brings joy to the heart, and good news gives
health to the bones* (Prov. 15:30).

With our eyes we feast on God's creation and are told of His
eternal power and godhead (Rom. 1:20). With our ears we hear
the glorious gospel of our Lord Jesus Christ (Rom. 10:17). Both
the beauty and majesty of God's creation, and of His holy and
perfect Word, confirm His existence and His holy character.

We see in creation that God is omnipotent and the Bible
confirms it. We see He has put all things in perfect order, and the
Bible confirms that, too. But His Word goes further. It tells of His
omniscience, of His unchanging nature, and of His love for us;
that while we were yet sinners Christ died for us (Rom. 5:6). It
speaks of His incredible grace that turns us from His enemies to
His friends.

And so, as we cheerfully view the created order and hear of
His grace on the pages of Scripture, let us give out the good news
of the gospel of Christ. Let us wear the cheerful look of one who
is heir to the riches of our wonderful God.

Scriptural Examples

Jacob. The aging patriarch feasted his ears on the good report
that his long lost son Joseph was alive (Gen. 45:26-28).

Jacob. Again, upon his arrival in Egypt, Jacob feasted his eyes
on the son of his beloved wife, Rachel (Gen. 46:29-30).

David. The great king exulted in the creative powers of his
God. The voice of creation literally shouts of the glory and majesty
of the Creator. No one can miss it (Ps. 19:1-3).

The shepherds. The shepherds at Bethlehem left their flocks
to feast their eyes on the One of whom the angels had spoken to
their hearing ears (Luke 2:13-17).

The two Marys. On that resurrection morning they were
filled with joy as they both saw the Lord and heard His words of
comfort and reassurance (Matt. 28:8-10).

Prayer of Application

Sovereign Lord, how I rejoice in the beauty of Your creation.
Thank You for opening my eyes and ears that I might see the
beauty of Your Word and know also the beauty of Christ.

Appreciate the Faithful Word of Rebuke

31) He who listens to a life-giving rebuke will be at home among the wise. 32) He who ignores discipline despises himself, but whoever heeds correction gains understanding (Prov. 15:31-32).

The natural person puts up a wall around himself that rejects godly reproof. He prefers words of flattery or encouragement that only serve to justify himself to himself. When the Spirit of God comes into our hearts, He brings humility and wise self-knowledge. Our hearts are open to the rebuke of the Spirit through His Word or through fellow Christians. This teachableness always results in greater understanding.

The chief place we should seek this rebuke is in the Word of God. Here in the book of Proverbs we are forced to examine every issue of our lives against the backdrop of God's righteousness. Let us accept rebuke from its pages and from those who shepherd. Although sometimes painful, it is not nearly so painful as the rebuke of actual experience. Remember, God only rebukes those He loves (Heb. 12:6).

Scriptural Examples

David and Nathan. After David's sin against Bathsheba and Uriah, Nathan rebuked him. The king acknowledged his sin and repented of it. David showed by his acceptance of God's rebuke that he was His child (2 Sam. 12:1-13).

The Pharisees and Jesus. Jesus rebuked them with seven woes but His reproof fell upon hardened hearts (Matt. 23).

Peter and Jesus. Following the resurrection, Jesus gently rebuked Peter for denying Him. In newness of understanding, Peter "fed the sheep" for the rest of his life (John 21:14-19).

Peter and Paul. Paul confronted Peter because of the latter's hypocrisy (Gal. 2:11-14). The Bible doesn't give Peter's reaction, in that context, but later reveals that Peter viewed Paul's words as Scripture (2 Peter 3:15-16).

Prayer of Application

Father, by Your Spirit working within me, help me to hear the faithful rebuke of the Word of God and of those who shepherd my life in the church, and act upon it to glorify You.

Humble Yourself in the Sight of the Lord

The fear of the Lord teaches a man wisdom, and humility comes before honor (Prov. 15:33).

One scriptural example of this principle stands far above the rest. Our Savior, exalted in heaven as the great and mighty God, Creator and Sustainer of the universe, humbled Himself to the estate of a common human child, and died a criminal's death in order that we might be exalted. Although His self-humiliation was far greater than we can even imagine, we are to have the same mind that was in Christ (Phil. 2:5) and humble ourselves in the sight of the Lord (James 4:10).

The fear of the Lord speaks of the reverent awe in which we are to hold our God. Humility is seeing ourselves as we really are, warts and all. This is the instruction of wisdom. It begins with submitting to His gospel, knowing there is nothing in and of ourselves that recommends us to Him. It continues with submission to the authority of His Word, the application of which sanctifies us. In the end, when we leave the earth, we will be exalted with our Savior, joint heirs with Him of the eternal treasures of God. Unthinkable! Unimaginable! But true!

Scriptural Examples

Joseph. Sold as a slave into Egypt, he was humbled for years before he was exalted by God to the throne of Egypt. Joseph's humility flowed from his fear of God (Gen. 39:9).

Moses. Humbled by God for 40 years in the desert, he left his sheep as God exalted him to the leadership of Israel. Even in that position Moses remained humble (Ex. 2–3).

Gideon. Gideon described himself as the "least of the families of Israel." God lifted up this humble man to be the judge and leader of all of His people Israel (Judg. 6–8).

David. A mere humble shepherd boy at the time, David was chosen by God to be the king of Israel (1 Sam. 16:1-13).

Prayer of Application

Dear God, help me to see myself by the light of Your Word, that I might be humbled in Your eternal wisdom. How I look forward to that day when I shall see my Lord face-to-face.

Chapter Sixteen

Knowing God: His Omnipotence

Two verses in the sixteenth chapter stand out among several in revealing the omnipotence of God: verses 4 and 33. Verse 4 says, "The Lord works out everything for his own ends—even the wicked for a day of disaster." Verse 33 states of God, "The lot is cast into the lap, but its every decision is from the Lord." To be omnipotent is to be in absolute power. God is all powerful. Nothing in all of His creation stands beyond the limits of His control.

Being omnipotent also means no created thing can restrict or restrain God's power and control. He cannot give up His omnipotence, just as He cannot cease being God. A less than omnipotent God is no God at all. Yet His power is restricted by who He is. God cannot sin, for instance. He cannot die or do anything that would contradict His perfect nature.

God's omnipotence means the same power that created the universe will be able to work all things out for our good (Rom. 8:28), and fulfill His promise of eternal life in our resurrected bodies. Our God is "A Mighty Fortress." As Martin Luther wrote in his wonderful hymn of that name, "And tho' this world, with devils filled, should threaten to undo us, we will not fear, for God hath willed His truth to triumph through us."

Praise God for His Marvelous Grace

To man belong the plans of the heart, but from the Lord comes the reply of the tongue (Prov. 16:1).

The King James Version's rendering of this verse is significantly different: "The preparations (or "disposings") of the heart in people, and the answer of the tongue, is from the Lord." In other words, while the NIV seems to say that only the reply of the tongue comes from God, the KJV says that both the tongue's reply and the plans of people are in the Lord's hands. I believe that the King James translation makes the most sense.

There are differences of opinion in the evangelical world regarding the grace of God. Is it a "prevenient grace" that God gives to everyone on the planet in hopes that some will come to Him for salvation? (John 3:16). Or is His saving grace for those whom He foreknew before the foundation of the world (Rom. 8:29) and whom He actually saves by it (John 6:65)? In other words, which comes first: the new birth or saving faith? Perhaps it's a question that has never entered your mind. Talk to your pastor about it.

Meanwhile, all evangelical Christians agree that we are saved only by the grace of God and that God gives His grace to undeserving sinners like you and me. By His grace, He both guides the plans of our hearts and the replies of our tongues. Who among us will admit that they are smarter, better, or more spiritual than their unsaved friends? Either way, it is our responsibility to believe in Jesus for salvation. He is worthy of our praise for His marvelous grace.

Scriptural Examples

Peter. After his confession of Christ, Jesus said that the truth of His Lordship was revealed to Peter by the Father (Matt. 16:17).

Lydia. This woman of Thyatira, a dealer in purple cloth, had her heart opened by the Lord, which enabled her to respond positively to Paul's gospel message (Acts 16:14).

Prayer of Application

Lord Jesus, thank You for the grace by which You save undeserving and hell-bound sinners. May I be a fervent sower of gospel seed that people everywhere might believe in You.

Cling to the God Who Forgives

All a man's ways seem innocent to him, but motives are weighed by the Lord (Prov.16:2).

The natural person may confess to some minor peccadillos, or even to serious sin, but he would quickly add that his virtues more than outweigh his vices. He judges himself and others—whom he uses as his yardstick—by actions and not by principles. But in the eyes of God his every motive is sinful.

When God's Law was given to the people of Israel, God was serious about their obedience to it. However, He knew at the same time that they could not keep it. He never intended the keeping of the Law to be the path to reconciliation. Rather, it was to be a mirror into which a person could look and discover that he was not innocent. Humankind was to see his sinfulness and come pleading to God for His mercy and grace.

The forgiveness of God through His grace has always been available to anyone who would ask for it. The sacrifices of His Law were to portray this grace of God, which is found in Christ. Have you trusted Christ for the forgiveness of your sin and rebellion against God? Don't trust in your own good works.

Scriptural Examples

Saul and David. Rejecting Saul as king, God ordered Samuel to go to the house of Jesse to select David as the new king of Israel. God gave this principle to Samuel: that He judges the heart of a person and not his outward appearance or actions (1 Sam. 16:7).

Pontius Pilate. This wicked ruler washed his hands, declaring himself clean in *his own* eyes. He failed to understand that only cleanliness in God's eyes counts (Matt. 27:24).

Paul. He declared his blindness in persecuting the saints while foolishly thinking that it would preserve the purity of the Jewish faith. Before his encounter with Christ, Paul was innocent in his own eyes (Acts 26:9-11).

Prayer of Application

Father God, thank You for Your grace that so freely acquits and removes the guilt and penalty of my sin. Help me to tell of Your love to the lost who are trusting in their own innocence.

Rest in the Providence of God

Commit to the Lord whatever you do, and your plans will succeed (Prov. 16:3).

Paul enjoins us in Philippians 4:6-7 not to be anxious about anything but to pray with thanksgiving that our hearts may be guarded with the peace of God that passes all natural understanding. The key to this peace is absolute trust and confidence in God. Proverbs 3:5-6 is another example of this principle of rest in God.

First, we must understand the God in whom we are called to trust. He is absolutely sovereign and is able to do much more than that for which we give Him credit. He is subordinate to none. Second, the faith we have in God must be an active faith. It is praying with thanksgiving and believing God hears us, that whatever it is we ask of Him, He can do (Mark 11:24). Finally, it is a faith that steps out with humble trust in the love, power, and provision of God. It is a faith that prays, then goes to work.

The person who commits the works of his hands, mind, and heart to the glory and honor of the Lord Jesus knows that his steps, plans, and even his every thought will be established and rewarded with eternal treasure in heaven (1 Cor. 3:11-15).

Scriptural Examples

Eliezer. Abraham's servant searched for a bride for Isaac. He committed his way to the Lord and his plans succeeded. He found and brought back Rebekah for his master's son (Gen. 24).

Nehemiah. He prayed that God would help in obtaining approval to rebuild Jerusalem. God established Nehemiah's way and work, and the city was restored (Neh. 1:4-11).

Daniel. Daniel purposed in his heart not to defile himself with the king's table but to follow the ways of his God. God caused the officials in the king's palace to show favor to Daniel and his friends Shadrach, Meshach, and Abednego. Because of their faith in the God of Israel, their ways were established (Dan. 1:8-20).

Prayer of Application

Provident Lord, help me to trust You fully in all things. I often want to trust in my own resources, and that is idolatry. Cause me to pray fervently and then to work just as fervently.

Let Your Purpose Be the Glory of God

The Lord works out everything for his own ends—even the wicked for a day of disaster (Prov. 16:4).

God is not the author of evil. How could a God of goodness give birth to wickedness (Matt. 7:18)? And yet God allows evil to exist for His purposes. He will be glorified by the wicked on the day of evil (Rom. 9:22-23). God's glory shines forth most strongly out of the black backdrop of the evil that people do.

Oh, to be able to understand the mind of God! How can God, who allows humankind the freedom of will to sin and to commit all manner of evil, work out of that same evil both His eternal glory and the eternal benefit of those whom He has called (Rom. 8:28)? Yet we are culpable for our actions. Every person will be judged by God according to his works (Acts 17:31; 2 Cor. 5:10).

As impossible as this "doctrine of concurrence" is to understand, we must be assured by faith that it is true. Otherwise, God would be powerless to achieve His eternal purposes. He would be, as it were, wringing His hands in worry, wondering how history would all turn out. What then should our purpose be? It should be to align our every thought, word, and deed with the purpose of God—His eternal glory. This leads to our eternal joy.

Scriptural Examples

Joseph's brothers. Although they were guilty of selling their brother into slavery, Joseph saw in their evil deed the providence of God at work. He told them that even though they meant to harm him, God worked it out for good (Gen. 50:20).

Pharaoh. Paul says that God raised up Pharaoh and hardened his heart so that God's glory and power might be revealed (Rom. 9:17). God gave Pharaoh over to the natural love of evil. God restricts the unrighteousness of people by the power of His Spirit which, if withdrawn, would allow people to destroy themselves just as Pharaoh did (Ex. 6-14).

Prayer of Application

Father, my finite mind cannot understand all of Your infinite mind. Help me to accept by faith what I cannot understand and give me the strength to warn others of Your wrath.

Beware of Secret Pride

The Lord detests all the proud of heart. Be sure of this: They will not go unpunished (Prov. 16:5).

Scripture warns often about the proud look and of the foolishness of pride. Here, we see that even the secret pride of the heart is an abomination to the Lord, who searches our hearts and knows all things. Pride is the root sin of most all other sins. To persist in it is to be certain of receiving the punishment of God.

We humans are proud of our position in society, our wealth, our race or nationality, our knowledge, our beauty, our talents, our strength and power, and our supposed goodness of heart. We would have none of these things if our Creator Jesus had not bestowed them upon us (Jer. 9:23-24; 1 Cor. 1:28-29). Everything we possess we owe to Him, whether or not we admit it.

As children of God, let us keep in mind who we really are: sinners snatched from the fire by God's grace. Then let us give the glory to Christ, without whom we would be destitute of all things, even life itself. With Him we are now heirs of all things because He loved us enough to die for us.

Scriptural Examples

Men of Babel. These prideful men built a tower that was to reach to the heavens. But God dispersed them throughout the world and confused their languages (Gen. 11:1-9).

Ben-Hadad. This Aramean king pridefully boasted of his coming victory over Israel, then proceeded to get drunk in his tent. His troops were soundly defeated (1 Kings 20).

Hezekiah. This king of Judah pridefully boasted of his treasure to Babylonian envoys. He let them see it all. They returned following his death to carry both the treasure and the people away (2 Kings 20).

Haman. Exalted in his own eyes, Haman was brought down by his own pride and punished by God (Est. 7).

Prayer of Application

Heavenly Father, remove any traces of pride from my evil heart. Make me ever mindful that except for the riches of Your grace towards me, I would have nothing, and be nothing.

Live Out the Gospel of Christ

*Through love and faithfulness [KJV: "mercy and truth"] sin
is atoned for; through the fear of the Lord a man avoids
evil* (Prov. 16:6).

Our "mercy and truth" and "love and faithfulness" don't amount
to a hill of beans. Only by God's mercy and truth, the God-man
Jesus Christ, can our iniquity be purged, our sin atoned for. People
seek to expunge sin through outward ceremonies and the doing
of good works, but God does it with the once-and-for-all sacrifice
of His Son (Heb. 7:27).

Does one whose debt to the Law of God is paid continue to
habitually practice sin? God forbid (Rom. 6:2)! The new birth
places in us a reverential fear of God and a hatred of sin, so that
the child of God *must* depart from evil. Will he therefore become
perfect and never sin again? No. As long as he is in an earthly
body there is always occasion to sin, but not the habit of it. Sin is
crowded out by a desire to live for God.

What, then, ought we to do, knowing that the gospel of Christ
is our only hope? We need to follow Christ's command to give out
the gospel to our neighbors (Matt. 28:19), and most importantly,
to *live out* the gospel each day of our lives.

Scriptural Examples

David. David cried out to God to purge his iniquity. He saw
himself as a sinner since his conception. Only the mercy and truth
of God could cleanse him. Cleansed, he desired to depart from
evil and teach others the fear of the Lord (Ps. 51:5-13).

Saul/Paul. Saul said he kept the law of God perfectly, yet he
later counted all his law-keeping as garbage (Phil. 3:6-8). On the
road to Damascus, an alien righteousness was given to him (Phil.
3:9), and he began to live a life of faith, not of works, giving out
the gospel of Christ and personally pressing on to the prize of the
high calling of Christ Jesus (Phil. 3:13-14).

Prayer of Application

Sovereign Lord, how I thank You for saving me through Christ.
Give me strength and courage that I might tell others of Your love.
May Your glory be known throughout the world.

Please the Lord by Your Faith

When a man's ways are pleasing to the Lord, he makes even his enemies live at peace with him (Prov. 16:7).

How do we please the Lord? We do it by faith. We must believe God exists and that He rewards those who diligently seek Him (Heb. 11:6). Faith that pleases God is an obedient faith (James 1:22), a faith that moves out and does something because God said to do it. Believe on the Lord Jesus Christ, then obey His commandments and follow His ways. That faith pleases God and causes one's enemies to live at peace.

But Jesus said that we would be persecuted for our faith (Matt. 5:11). A person's enemies would be in his own household (Matt. 10:36). But God restrains even these enemies and they can do no more to the believer than what God chooses to allow. In the ultimate sense, even the evil murder of a saint of God is an act which works to the saint's greater welfare. For as Paul tells us in Philippians 1:21, to die would be great gain for him.

Whatever your circumstances, whether your enemies are at peace with you or in outright warfare, remember that all circumstances of your life are conforming you to the image of Christ (Rom. 8:28-29), who has preceded you in death and bodily resurrection (Heb. 6:19-20). Each of us who is in Christ has this hope as the anchor for our soul.

Scriptural Examples

Esau. Esau forgot his enmity against his brother Jacob and embraced him upon his return to the land (Gen. 33:4).

Israel. God required its people to go up and worship three times a year. He promised that while they were away from home no other nation would attack their land (Ex. 34:23-24).

Job. God put a hedge around Job and his household. He wouldn't let him be harmed by the power of Satan without the prior approval of God Himself (Job 1:9-12).

Prayer of Application

Father, may my ways please You. May the faith that You have given me continue to grow, and may I live my life by that faith so that even my enemies will live at peace with me.

Seek Righteousness Before Riches

*Better a little with righteousness than much gain
with injustice* (Prov. 16:8).

The problem with riches is they are not what they seem to be. They promise enjoyment, but deliver sleepless nights (Eccl. 5:12); security, but fly away at a moment's notice (Jer. 17:11); contentment, but bring the need to accumulate more and more (Eccl. 5:10). And riches gained by injustice will bring eternal loss (James 5:1-4). Besides that, riches only bring increased accountability to God (Luke 12:48).

In the Sermon on the Mount, Jesus warned of the deceitfulness of riches (Matt. 6:19-24), and commanded His followers to seek after righteousness instead (Matt. 6:33). You see, it's easy for us to bend the rules a little in an effort to gain wealth. Injustice will bring failure and loss, both temporal and eternal.

The righteous person, regardless of his outward circumstances, has true riches that can never be lost. He is aware that his heavenly Father knows of his needs even before they arise (Matt. 6:8). What confidence we have in knowing the surety of these truths. Earthly riches, if withheld from us by our Father, are withheld not for our harm but for our eternal good.

Scriptural Examples

The Zarephathian widow and Jezebel. This poor widow was in a position to receive blessings from God through Elijah, while Jezebel, in her wealth gotten in sin, was to be condemned by God and slain (1 Kings 17:10; 2 Kings 9:32-37).

Elijah and Ahab. Elijah shared in the provision of God while his earthly nemesis, King Ahab, suffered death at the hands of God for his ill-gotten gain (1 Kings 17:5-6; 21:19).

Zacchaeus. This wealthy tax collector was captivated by Christ, and repented of his unjust riches. Jesus said salvation had come to his household that day (Luke 19:2-9).

Prayer of Application

Dear God, who provides for all my needs, may I be content in seeking righteousness and in serving You. Father, give me the faith, I pray, to trust boldly in Your provision for me.

Don't Worry, God Is in Control

In his heart a man plans his course, but the Lord determines his steps (Prov. 16:9).

Do people have free will? They do indeed have freedom of choice, for God could not hold them responsible for their decisions if they did not. And yet we can do nothing to thwart the purposes of God. People may make their plans, but in the final analysis it is God's will that will be done (Matt. 6:10). How different this concept is from the popular song that God is "watching us from a distance." Others believe in a kind of "dualism" in which Satan is free of the absolute control of God. But even Satan is a mere creature, subject to God's control.

Our free will consists in the ability to choose. Before we are saved, all of our choices are sinful. But God, who is all-powerful and all-seeing, directs the course of our free will to achieve His own eternal purposes. He even uses our sin to glorify Himself. Think of Pharaoh. God said that He had raised up Pharaoh in order to display His power and to proclaim His name (Ex. 9:16; Rom. 9:17).

Because God sits enthroned in power over the events of the universe, and the circumstances of our everyday lives, it is the obligation of every Christian to trust Him for the future. We are to rest from worry, which is sin. Our God is in absolute control.

Scriptural Examples

King Xerxes. Because of his sleepless night, the plot by Haman against Mordecai and the Jews was foiled. You guessed it! It was God who caused his sleeplessness (Est. 6:1).

Onesimus. This slave ran away from his master but his steps led right into the arms of Christ. Later, he returned to his master, but as his brother in the Lord (the book of Philemon).

Philip. Philip had been preaching to many in Samaria when the Spirit told him to go to a eunuch in the desert. His steps to that encounter were determined by the Lord (Acts 8:26).

Prayer of Application

Father, I pray that my heart may plan according to the leading of Your Spirit. But I know that You will use even my missteps to Your great glory. Thank You for such confidence.

Lead Others in Reverence and Righteousness

10) The lips of a king speak as an oracle, and his mouth should not betray justice. 11) Honest scales and balances are from the Lord; all the weights in the bag are of his making. 12) Kings detest wrongdoing, for a throne is established through righteousness. 13) Kings take pleasure in honest lips; they value a man who speaks the truth (Prov. 16:10-13).

God requires that kings, or anyone in authority over others, rule in righteousness and in the fear of the Lord (2 Sam. 23:3). A leader is obliged to seek God's wisdom and apply it diligently (1 Kings 3:9). The following four principles are drawn from God's wisdom in these verses:

1) In situations requiring a decision, the leader should weigh all the facts and reach a just judgment (vs. 10).

2) The leader should execute justice rightly, not showing favor to one party at the expense of another (vs. 11).

3) The leader should abhor all wickedness and not allow the presence of sin to reign in his administration (vs. 12).

4) The leader should surround himself with faithful advisers and value those who speak the truth (vs. 13).

Such leadership is honoring to God and leads to stability and peace. Christ's reign over this world is established and upheld in absolute righteousness (Isa. 9:7). How can we subscribe to anything less?

Scriptural Examples

Abimelech. Abimelech murdered the 70 sons of Gideon and declared himself king. But God sent an evil spirit between the men of Shechem and Abimelech, which led to Abimelech's downfall and death (Judg. 9).

Solomon. He was given wisdom by God in unparalleled measure. In one incident, he rightly judged between two women who contested the motherhood of an infant (1 Kings 3:16-28).

Prayer of Application

Dear Lord, anoint my leaders with a godliness and wisdom that helps them choose the righteous way, rather than the pragmatic or expedient way. And may I lead others in wisdom.

Seek the King's Favor

14) A king's wrath is a messenger of death, but a wise man will appease it. 15) When a king's face brightens, it means life; his favor is like a rain cloud in spring (Prov. 16:14-15).

The ancient kings held vast powers over their subjects. Wise people naturally would not want to anger the king but to seek his favor. They coveted his smile, not his scowl, which could mean immediate death at the hands of the executioners.

If only the non-Christian would see the angry, frowning countenance of the Almighty King who commands all people everywhere to repent and to seek His favor (Acts 17:30). How shall we mortals pacify such sovereign anger? We can't. But God in His grace sent His only Son as an atonement for us. Through Christ we are freely reconciled to the great King. In the light of His countenance, or the brightening of His face, is life indeed!

How then should we live who have been reconciled to our King? We should daily purpose in our hearts to please and glorify Him; to live by faith and in accordance with His commands. Surely the life of godliness in Christ is as refreshing as the spring rain.

Scriptural Examples

Esther. Esther went unsummoned into the presence of King Xerxes. She knew that only by his mercy she would not be put to death. Such was the power of the monarch. In Esther's case, she was received happily by Xerxes (Est. 4:11).

Jehoiachin. This king of Judah was granted mercy by Evil-Merodach, king of Babylon. He was released from prison and given a seat of honor at the king's table, a seat higher than all of the other kings who were in Babylon (Jer. 52:31-32).

Daniel. Following Nebuchadnezzar's edict that all of the court's wise men and astrologers be executed, Daniel went to him and appeased him. Daniel told the king God would reveal his dream and its interpretation (Dan. 2:15-16).

Prayer of Application

Lord Jesus, grant me the ability to love You from a sincere heart with an earnest desire to serve only You. May Your kingship of my life be evident in all of my relationships.

Desire Wisdom Before Wealth

How much better to get wisdom than gold, to choose understanding rather than silver (Prov. 16:16).

How different wisdom and wealth are. Wisdom is eternal, while worldly wealth is temporal and fleeting. Wisdom, even without wealth, is a treasure house for the whole community, while wealth without wisdom brings greed, theft, hatred, and every sort of evil (1 Tim. 6:10).

People labor day and night for gold and silver, yet the true treasure of life escapes them. Why? Because to their depraved minds, true wisdom has no value. But for those led by the Spirit of God, there is no greater treasure than godly wisdom. Jesus spoke of a man who found such a treasure in a field and went out and sold all that he had and bought that field (Matt. 13:44).

Now, there is no way that we can buy our salvation. Jesus' parable teaches that the value of wisdom greatly exceeds any temporal treasure. Even if someone would gain the whole world but lose his soul, what profit would there be? (Matt. 16:26). Wisdom is the gift of God (James 1:5), but unlike earthly wealth, which also comes from God, all who seek God's wisdom find it.

Scriptural Examples

Solomon. God asked Solomon what gift he would like. He asked for a wise and discerning heart. God opened his storehouses and gave Solomon the wisdom for which he asked, as well as the wealth and honor he had not requested (1 Kings 3:5-13).

Daniel. King Nebuchadnezzar recognized the wisdom of Daniel as 10 times greater than that of his own wise men. Daniel attributed his wisdom not to himself but to the gift of the sovereign God of Israel (Dan. 1:20; 2:23).

Joseph. Stephen spoke of the wisdom of Joseph and how as a result of the wisdom God gave to this patriarch, honor and wealth were his as well (Acts 7:9-14).

Prayer of Application

Heavenly Father, who graciously gives us all things for our benefit, equip me with wisdom that I may walk in Your ways and lead others to an understanding of Your truth.

Walk the Highway of Righteousness

The highway of the upright avoids evil; he who guards his way guards his life (Prov. 16:17).

When God saves us by His grace, He places our feet on the highway of righteousness. Although we sometimes stumble, God is faithful to forgive us (1 John 1:9) and to set our feet on the road of righteousness once again.

Dr. J. Vernon McGee told the story of the Prodigal Pig, who went with the prodigal son when he returned to his father's house. The pig was treated like royalty. He was washed and given new clothes and taught to eat with a fork. But the pig felt out of place and soon became homesick for his father's house, the pig pen. So he returned there (2 Peter 2:22).

Dr. McGee said life is like the Pasadena Freeway near his home. Some folks are going one way toward their father's house, and the rest are going the other way toward *their* father's house. We can't really know which is which. Only God knows for sure. But Jesus tells us that we may be pretty sure who is going where on the freeway of life by the fruits of their lives (Matt. 3:10; 7:16).

Scriptural Examples

Enoch. He walked on the highway of righteousness with his God, and God was so pleased that He snatched Enoch from the earth. He did not taste death (Gen. 5:24; Heb. 11:5).

Joseph. When he was tempted by Potiphar's wife, Joseph declared adultery would be a sin against God. Joseph understood the principle above. Any departure from the highway of righteousness is ultimately rebellion against God (Gen. 39:9).

Jesus. He lived a life of absolute righteousness and told His hearers to put His words into practice. Faith in Christ is not just intellectual ascendance to a set of facts about Him or the exercise of some sacrament like baptism or communion. It is a lifelong highway of obedience (Matt. 7:24).

Prayer of Application

Father, lead me in the path of righteousness for Your name's sake, and for Your glory. I know if I confess my sin You are faithful and just to forgive me and to cleanse me from it.

Walk in the Spirit of Humility

18) Pride goes before destruction, a haughty spirit before a fall. 19) Better to be lowly in spirit and among the oppressed than to share plunder with the proud (Prov. 16:18-19).

The person who lifts his eyes up in pride fails to watch the pathway beneath his feet and sets himself up for a fall. We need to focus our eyes on Christ, examining our secret faults in the light of His Word. Then we will have an accurate understanding of who we really are and won't be tempted to think too highly of ourselves. People don't need more self-esteem. We need more God-esteem, and less of self.

We need the attitude of the publican who beat his breast and cried out for mercy, rather than the Pharisee who tried to justify himself (Luke 18:10-14). Better, we need the attitude of Christ, who humbled Himself to be born a child, then sacrificially gave Himself over to His oppressors so that we, His brothers and sisters, might have eternal life (Phil. 2:5-9).

Scriptural Examples

Eve. Puffed up by Satan's swelling words, and desirous of gaining wisdom supposedly above and beyond that which came from God, Eve pridefully rebelled against God's command and then prompted Adam to do the same (Gen. 3:6-7).

Abraham. In humility, Abraham refused to take part in the division of the spoils of battle with the king of Sodom and others. Abraham made sure that all of the glory for victory belonged to God and not to people (Gen. 14:21-24).

David. He pridefully counted his troops, rather than giving the glory for his security to Almighty God (2 Sam. 24:1-10).

Amaziah. Following the defeat of the Edomites, this king of Judah set up his own gods and worshipped them. In his pride he refused to listen to the rebuke of a man of God and subsequently suffered defeat and destruction (2 Chron. 25).

Prayer of Application

Dear Lord, in Your tenderness help me to see myself as I really am. Teach me to walk humbly as one plucked out of the fire with no redeeming qualities, except that You saw fit to do it.

Exercise Wisdom Combined with Faith

Whoever gives heed to instruction prospers, and blessed is he who trusts in the Lord (Prov. 16:20).

If a person has true wisdom he will understand his natural, or earthly, wisdom cannot be trusted. He will realize his dependence upon his Creator, by faith acknowledging that true instruction and wisdom come from above (James 3:17).

And where does this heavenly wisdom lead? It leads to the qualities of Christlikeness that God desires us to exhibit. Faith leads to goodness, knowledge, self-control, perseverance, godliness, brotherly kindness, and love (2 Peter 1:5-7).

To fully lean upon God for all of our needs, just as a child relies completely upon his parents, is the key to blessedness in this life. Where then is anxiety or worry? Where is fear? These are all cast out by God's perfect love and provision (1 John 4:18). It's not easy. As a youth, I was encouraged to "stand on my own two feet" and be independent. Then, as a new Christian, I was faced with the obligation to trust God completely and not lean upon my own wisdom (Prov. 3:5-6). It is a formidable transition, one I have not begun to finish, but one well worth the trials involved in its accomplishment.

Scriptural Examples

Joseph. God's wisdom in a time of national emergency, a famine, worked through this man who trusted in God's leadership. God provided for Egypt and began the Egyptian formation of what was to become the nation Israel (Gen. 41:25-44).

Ahithophel. This man's advice was set aside by the Lord who intended to bring disaster upon Absalom. God's wisdom overcomes even the best human wisdom (2 Sam. 17:14).

The apostles. These men used godly wisdom in setting up the office of deacon and in selecting the men who would fill the office (Acts 6:1-7).

Prayer of Application

Lord God, increase my wisdom in the daily struggles that are set before me, and increase my faith and trust in Your provision for my every need. Blessed is he who rests in You.

Speak Sweetly from a Heart of Wisdom

The wise in heart are called discerning, and pleasant words promote instruction (Prov. 16:21).

Wisdom that is only in your mind and not in your heart causes conceit. Merely knowing what to do doesn't assure that you will act wisely. But wisdom that is seated in the heart provides consistency for your daily walk and has great practical value.

Jesus told the Pharisees that out of the overflow of the heart the mouth speaks (Matt. 12:34-35). So, too, He said that we shall recognize the essence of a person's character by his actions and fruits (Matt. 7:15). The person who has the wisdom of God dwelling in his heart will be known by his prudent life and by the sweetness of his speech. Conversely, the rebellious man will be known by his foolishness and godless chatter.

One specific way today's Christians need to put this principle to work is in our practice of discernment. Often the enemy is from within the visible church, which is being buffeted by both new and ancient heresies. We need to pray for both wisdom and sweetness in dealing with those who espouse philosophies and practices that contradict the Word of God

Scriptural Examples

Jethro. Moses' father-in-law gave him prudent advice in the matter of selecting competent men to aid in the administration of justice for Israel in its wilderness journey. Moses selected 70 leaders who could assist him (Ex. 18:17-23).

Abigail. With sweet wisdom and pleasant words, Nabal's wife pacified the anger of David and prevented him and his men from destroying her household (1 Sam. 25:18-31).

Paul. Paul told the Corinthians that his message and preaching came not through his own mind and wisdom but from the power of the Holy Spirit. The sweet Spirit that spoke through the great apostle still speaks to us today (1 Cor. 2:1-4).

Prayer of Application

Father, make my life and speech prudent and sweet through Your wisdom, and let not my mind be puffed up in fleshly pride. Rather, seat Your wisdom down deep in my heart.

Let Your Understanding Refresh Everyone

Understanding is a fountain of life to those who have it, but folly brings punishment to fools (Prov. 16:22).

There is a wide gap between head knowledge and real understanding. Some people have the knowledge of the way of truth but not the understanding. An example is Balaam. Peter calls people like him "springs without water," and warns us of their empty, boastful words (2 Peter 2:15-18). Of what value is a spring or well without water? There is only promise and no refreshment.

But true understanding from the Holy Spirit becomes a spring of water welling up unto eternal life (John 4:14). A person that has understanding should be like a lamp that gives light unto all the house (Matt. 5:16) and like salt that preserves food and makes it tasty (Matt. 5:13).

In contrast, the fool who says "No" to God (Ps. 14:1) teaches only folly. How readily this is seen today in liberal churches that have departed from the Bible to follow false doctrines. Truth to them is ever-changing, depending upon the latest whim of the majority. Such foolishness will bring God's punishment.

Scriptural Examples

Moses and the waters of Marah. This bitter wellspring in the desert was made sweet by God as Moses threw wood into it. The wood speaks of the person and work of Christ, who was hung on a tree of wood and gave to all who would believe on Him the true fountain of eternal life (Ex. 15:22-25; John 3:16).

Paul and Barnabas. With godly understanding welling up from their hearts, these apostles encouraged and strengthened the disciples (Acts 14:21-22).

The Hedonists. Paul said he fought the fight of faith because of the water of eternal life. Otherwise, he might as well teach the foolishness of the Hedonists—that people should eat, drink, and be merry for tomorrow they die (1 Cor. 15:32).

Prayer of Application

Dear Lord, increase my understanding of Your holy Word so that I might be a fountain of life for others. May I always be ready to share the reasons for the hope within me.

Allow Your Heart to Instruct Your Lips

A wise man's heart guides his mouth, and his lips promote instruction
(Prov. 16:23).

The mind is the seat of reason, and the heart the seat of affection. A person may have a great knowledge of God in his mind but, if none of it is transferred to his heart, his vast knowledge has no practical effect upon his life for righteousness. On the other hand, knowledge and understanding enter the heart through the mind.

Both the mind and heart of people are desperately wicked (Gen. 6:5; Rom. 3:9-23). Unchanged by the power of God, a person's heart in this wicked state teaches his lips only foolishness, regardless of his mind's knowledge. Only through the Spirit of God, circumcising his heart with the new birth (John 3:5), can a person's mind and heart be transformed to the pattern of righteousness (Rom. 12:2). Then, and only then, will a person's heart guide his lips in righteousness and holiness, setting them apart for God's service.

Scriptural Examples

The Pharisees. Jesus charged them with having evil hearts, out of which flowed the evil of their lips (Matt. 12:34-35).

Peter. The impetuous disciple had spoken foolishly on an earlier occasion, but by the Spirit of God he later spoke with discernment about Jesus' identity (Matt. 16:16-17) and preached with power at Pentecost (Acts 2:14-41).

Paul. This brilliant Pharisee did not have true wisdom in his heart until he met Christ on the Damascus road (Phil. 3:4-11).

The nation Israel. Their hearts were always going astray. They did not rest in God by faith, and hence their mouths complained and murmured against Him (Heb. 3:10).

Balaam. Balaam was a seer who knew *of* the God of Israel, but didn't know *Him*. His mouth betrayed his lack of wisdom as he spoke to the donkey in his madness (2 Peter 2:15-18).

Prayer of Application

Lord, You have given us many examples in Scripture of people who were wise in heart and who used that knowledge to instruct others in Your way. Help me to follow their example.

Speak Words of Sweetness and Health

Pleasant words are a honeycomb, sweet to the soul and healing to the bones (Prov. 16:24).

Honey is a food that is mentioned often in Scripture. God promised the Israelites a land flowing with milk and honey. John the Baptist ate a diet of locusts and wild honey. Honey from the honeycomb is both sweet and nutritious. The soul is satisfied with its taste, and the bones with its nutrition.

In the verse above, pleasant words are likened to the honeycomb. Words of counsel, sympathy, and encouragement both satisfy the soul of the hearer and "strengthen his bones" (KJV).

Solomon exhorted his son to listen closely to his words for they would be life to him and health to his whole body (Prov. 4:20-22). The words of God are like that. In them we find life that is eternal, a sweetness that surpasses any earthly pleasure, and a strengthening and encouragement that brings joy and contentment in the midst of trial, sorrow, and difficulty.

Scriptural Examples

Jonathan. Jonathan was strengthened and given energy by the honeycomb. He ate, ignorant of the foolish order his father had given the army of Israel (1 Sam. 14:24-30).

David and Jonathan. Later, with sweet and healthy words, Jonathan strengthened and encouraged his friend in the matter of Saul's envy and attempted murder (1 Sam. 23:16-17).

Cleopas and companions. They met the risen Lord but did not recognize Him immediately. He spoke to them of the sweet Scriptures. Later, their eyes were opened (Luke 24:13-31).

Philip and the Ethiopian eunuch. In the eunuch's chariot, Philip explained the sweet, healthy Word of God. The eunuch received Christ by faith and was baptized (Acts 8:35-36).

The Philippian jailor. Paul and Silas spoke words of life as they gave the gospel to this man following an earthquake (Acts 16:25-34).

Prayer of Application

Lord, thank You for the sweet and healing words of the gospel of Christ, which You have applied to my heart. Help me to speak these same sweet words to others as I walk in this life.

Warn Yourself and Others of Self-Delusion

There is a way that seems right to a man, but in the end it leads to death (Prov. 16:25).

Since Adam's fall, people's hearts have been radically affected. Although we think we know what is good for us, the Bible says we are blind (John 12:40; 2 Cor. 4:4) and cannot know the truth. Jesus described the Pharisees as "blind guides" who taught self-salvation. Their teaching didn't come from God.

Today, many in the visible church are being led by modern "blind guides." They are deluded into thinking that the way to reconciliation with God is through their good works or the taking of some external sacrament. Others teach that it's not important what people believe about God, as long as their belief is sincere. There are many such ways that lead to death, but Jesus says He is the only way to life (John 14:6). A person must be regenerated, or born from above (John 3:3). Only then is blindness healed and spiritual truth discerned (Acts 9:18).

Every manmade religion in the world is what may be termed "auto-soteric." That is, if you want to reach heaven you must do it yourself. This seems so right to fallen people, but leads to death. Only biblical Christianity is different. It is "hetero-soteric." The saving is done by God through Christ's atoning work on the cross. Ours is an alien righteousness (Rom. 3:21-26).

Scriptural Examples

Lot. After Lot and Abram's herdsmen argued over grazing land, the two agreed to part company. Lot decided to settle in the land that looked best to him, down by Sodom. It was a way that seemed right to Lot, but in the end brought trouble (Gen. 13:7-12).

Saul. In opposition to the Word of the Lord, Saul did what he thought best and did not kill all of the captured sheep and cattle. Samuel rebuked him for going his own way. Ultimately he was stripped of his kingdom (1 Sam. 15:20-22).

Prayer of Application

Dear Father, thank You for sending Your only Son as an atoning sacrifice for our sins. He is the only way to reconciliation with You. Help me to be a true witness of His gospel of grace.

Be Blessed in Your Work

*The laborer's appetite works for him; his hunger
drives him on* (Prov. 16:26).

Adam was created to tend and enjoy the magnificent garden God had given him. When he sinned, God turned the first couple out of the garden to a frustrating soil that bore thorns and thistles (Gen. 3:17-19).

While our frustration may be part of God's curse, there are also blessings that come from our work. We have the satisfaction of filling our family's physical needs, which drives us on. There is also the joy of helping others and filling community needs. Also, there is a real joy in diligently using the talents and brains God has given us in a useful way.

We need to be careful, however, that our work is not done in vanity (Hab. 2:13) or for evil covetousness (Isa. 5:8; Hab. 2:9), and therefore labor toward our own ruin. Nor should it occupy so much of our time that we have no time or energy left for our families or for the worship of God and the study of His Word (John 6:27). All our work should be centered in the One who truly supplies all our needs. We should find our true reward there, as we labor to honor God.

Scriptural Examples

Boaz. He blessed his workers and they blessed him. He worked alongside them in the fields and even slept beside them during the time of harvest (Ruth 2:4; 3:7).

Jeroboam. Solomon observed how well this young man did his work, so he put Jeroboam in charge of a large labor force. Jeroboam was blessed by his godly diligence (1 Kings 11:28).

Paul. Paul was determined to work at a trade, even though he was in "full-time ministry." He was a tentmaker who supplied his own needs and was not a burden on anyone (Acts 18:3; 20:33-34).

Prayer of Application

Heavenly Father, thank You for my work. In it I am given satisfaction and fulfillment, yet also frustration, difficulty, and conflict that show me my faults and aid in my sanctification.

Beware of the Ungodly Slanderer

27) A scoundrel plots evil, and his speech is like a scorching fire. 28) A perverse man stirs up dissension, and a gossip separates close friends. 29) A violent man entices his neighbor and leads him down a path that is not good. 30) He who winks with his eye is plotting perversity; he who purses his lips is bent on evil (Prov. 16:27-30).

James has much to say about the tongue being full of poison, a burning fire (James 3:5-8). In Proverbs 6:16-19 we find the tongue at the foundation of four of the seven things that are detested by God. Of course, the ungodly tongue is the manifestation of an ungodly heart (Matt. 12:34-35).

Beware of the gossip who is clothed in apparent righteousness, but who whispers half-truths and even lies against a neighbor. If there were a Sin Hall of Fame, these people would hold a place of honor. God hates slander and gossip which turn brother against brother and cause division.

Scriptural Examples

Hanun's advisors. David sent a delegation to express his sympathy to Hanun in his father's death. Hanun's advisors accused the men of being spies. Because of the advisors' slander, Hanun sent the men back to David in shame (2 Sam. 10:2-4).

Sheba, Son of Bicri. This slanderer caused the men of Israel to desert David their king (2 Sam. 20:1-2).

Jeremiah's enemies. These men devised plans against Jeremiah, whom they also slandered. They also shut their ears to what he said and hence to God's words (Jer. 18:18).

Jesus' accusers. The chief priests and the Sanhedrin sought false witnesses to testify against Jesus . They came up with two such ungodly men who had half-truths to tell (Matt. 26:59-61).

The false apostles. They pretended to follow Christ, just as Satan masquerades as an angel of light (2 Cor. 11:13-15).

Prayer of Application

Lord God, deliver us from the tongues of wicked people bent on division and deception. There are many who slander Your Word. Shut their mouths, Lord, and still their tongues.

Honor the Elder Saints in the Church

Gray hair is a crown of splendor; it is attained by a righteous life (Prov. 16:31).

Some years ago when my beard became mostly white, I let it grow, and have sported a white beard since that time. I call it my "menopause folly." I like my white beard because it reminds me of how short a time I have before I leave this life to (hopefully) receive a real crown of splendor from the Lord.

There is a tendency today to serve youth and to discount the value of age. But God likens respect for the aged with reverence for Himself (Lev. 19:32). He commanded the Israelites to rise in the presence of the elderly, showing them respect.

The gray head is a crown of splendor (or "glory" KJV) to the righteous, but a crown of pending doom to the old man or woman who has rejected Christ. Each day, he or she waits for time on earth to end and eternity to begin, having only laid up for that eternity a store of God's wrath (Rom. 2:5).

On the other hand, the elderly saint of God will never be closer to hell than he is on this planet. Each day speaks of the nearness of his face-to-face meeting with the Ancient of Days. He will complete the redemption that God began so long ago.

Scriptural Examples

Rehoboam. He rejected the godly advice of elderly advisors and followed that of youth. His kingdom was forever divided between north and south (1 Kings 12:13-20).

Elisha. God's prophet was accosted by a gang of youths who jeered at him about his balding head. Elisha called down a curse upon them (2 Kings 2:23-24).

Simeon. This aging saint praised God as he held the baby Jesus in his arms. God let him see His salvation (Luke 2:28-35).

Anna. This old widow also served in the temple, fasting and praying. She, too, praised God for Jesus (Luke 2:36-38).

Prayer of Application

Sovereign Lord, forgive us for failing to honor the aging saints in our congregations. Help us to see that within the gray head of the elderly saint resides much godly wisdom.

Submit Your Anger to the Spirit's Rule

Better a patient man than a warrior, a man who controls his tem- per than one who takes a city (Prov. 16:32).

There is a battle going on in the heart of every Christian that the world knows nothing about. It is a battle that will continue until the saint's death. It is the Christian's battle against spiritual forces and enemies and against his own flesh (Eph. 6:12).

The Christian has yielded his body as an instrument of righteousness (Rom. 6:13-14). Sin is no longer his master, but much of the warfare against sin is waged on the field of the tongue (James 2:2-12). If we can control our tongues, James says, we will control the battle. "But who is equal to such a task?" he asks. No one is. But we have a very powerful Ally who is!

Paul speaks of this Ally in Romans 8:37. He is an Ally who makes us more than conquerors, even over our tongues, our anger, and our passions. Who is this Ally of such power? He is none other than the Lord Jesus Christ, who by His Spirit lives in the heart of every believer. Yield today to His rule over your life, your death, your anger, and even your tongue.

Scriptural Examples

Simeon and Levi. These two sons of Jacob became greatly angered over the seduction of their sister Dinah. They went beyond justice and killed all of the people of Shechem, bringing great disgrace upon their father (Gen. 33:18–34:31).

Gideon. Sharply criticized by his brothers the Ephraimites for going to battle against Midian without them, Gideon had every opportunity to get angry with them, but controlled his tongue and brought peace among the brothers (Judg. 8:1-3).

Saul. King Saul's anger controlled him. In one instance, he was so angry with his beloved son Jonathan for supporting his rival David, that he hurled his spear at him, attempting to kill his own son (1 Sam. 20:30-33).

Prayer of Application

Father God, by Your Spirit, help me to refrain from sinful anger and to control my tongue from bitter words. But also, Lord, help me to know when righteous anger is appropriate.

Worship God in His Sovereignty

The lot is cast into the lap, but its every decision is from the Lord (Prov. 16:33).

Some Christians think of God as a disinterested observer of this world. Others view Him as a sort of glorified errand boy who is waiting to serve their every whim. But the biblical picture of God is as Sovereign Lord, who is working out His purposes in the history of this planet in detail.

Historians can't tell us much about the "lot" in terms of what it looked like, but its purpose was to aid in making decisions. I've always envisioned a pair of dice when I hear the term "lot." The dice players in Las Vegas say, "Luck be a lady tonight." But the Bible teaches that there is no such thing as "luck."

While we don't know much about the lot, I think we have a better way today for good decision-making. First, let's seek to know the Word of God (2 Peter 1:19). Then, trust fully in the One who wrote it (Prov. 3:5-6), resting in His providential care. Next, seek the godly advice of others. Finally, let's make our decisions and step out by faith in the sovereignty of the One who created and sustains all things by His powerful Word (Heb. 1:3). Worship God by faithfully resting in Him.

Scriptural Examples

Joseph. He was cast into a pit by his brothers at precisely the same time a caravan of Ishmaelites went by. Joseph wound up as a slave in Egypt. Later, in power there, Joseph told his brothers that they had meant his slavery for evil but God had intended it for good (Gen. 37:25; 45:4-8).

Jonah. The sailors on the ship carrying Jonah cast lots to see who was responsible for the storm that threatened their ship. The lot fell upon Jonah, so they cast him into the sea at precisely the same time that a great fish, which God had prepared, swam by and swallowed him. Luck? No way (Jonah 1:7, 17).

Prayer of Application

Father, help me always to rest in You. Your power to control every detail of Your creation is too high for me to understand, but by faith I can find my rest in it and please You.

Chapter Seventeen

Knowing God:
His Justice

Proverbs 17:5 states, "He who mocks the poor shows contempt for their Maker; whoever gloats over disaster will not go unpunished." God's justice focuses on His righteousness. As Abraham said in Genesis 18:25, "Will not the Judge of the earth do right?" God "will judge the world with justice by the man [Jesus] he has appointed" (Acts 17:31). Every person will receive what is due him on the day of judgment. God will settle all of His accounts then.

But for those who have fallen down at the foot of the cross and received the grace of the Lord, God's justice has already been served. Christ paid the infinite penalty due us for our sins, so that we might be reconciled to God. "[God] did it to demonstrate his justice at the present time, so as to be just and the one who justifies those who have faith in Jesus" (Rom. 3:26).

But if God only saves some and not all, isn't He being unjust? That is an objection sometimes raised to the particular versus the universal call of God to salvation. Those who ask the question are confusing justice with grace. If God chose to save no one He would be just in doing so. All people deserve hell. But since God extends His saving grace to some, is He required to save everyone? No. Then grace would no longer be grace, but would be required by justice.

Prefer Peace to Plenty

Better a dry crust with peace and quiet than a house full of feasting, with strife (Prov. 17:1).

How many of us have experienced this? At a family get-together, where the house is overflowing with food and drink, some prideful relative begins to snip, backbite, and criticize, and soon the feast is ruined. Much better to have stayed home and had a peanut butter and jelly sandwich in peace and quiet.

How joyful it is when Christian brothers and sisters can feast together around the person of their Lord! Whether we're feasting on a Thanksgiving turkey, on the Lord's Supper, or on His powerful Word, how sweet is the unity that is there.

Christ calls us to contentment and to reliance upon His provision for our lives. He also calls us to peace and to the avoidance of silly arguments (1 Thess. 4:11). For whatever we have on the table, is it not more than we really deserve? Let's consistently follow the example of the Savior, who in everything gave thanks to His Father and loved His brothers and sisters.

Scriptural Examples

Laban and Jacob. Jacob got a little of his own deceitful medicine as he was tricked into working seven years for Leah instead of her sister Rachel, whom he loved. Here was a house of plenty that was probably filled with strife (Gen. 29-31).

Barzillai and David. This old man brought food to David's men in the desert. David invited him to Jerusalem, but the old man declined David's invitation, saying that he would prefer the peace of his hometown (2 Sam. 19:31-39).

Jesus and the Pharisee. At dinner, a woman who had lived a sinful life anointed Jesus with perfume and washed His feet with her tears. The host was indignant and accused Jesus of consorting with sinners. In the midst of plenty at the Pharisee's table there was strife because of pride and an unforgiving spirit (Luke 7:36-50).

Prayer of Application

Father, thank You for Jesus, who brings us peace. Help me to reflect His peace wherever I go and in whatever I do. Let there be no room in my life for pride, covetousness, or unforgiveness.

Be a Wise Servant...and Child

A wise servant will rule over a disgraceful son, and will share the inheritance as one of the brothers (Prov. 17:2).

Although Scripture contains many examples of disgraceful sons and wise servants, there is no literal example of this actual exchange taking place. Joseph and Daniel are examples of wise servants who were set over "sons" within the kingdoms of Egypt and Babylon, respectively. Nadab and Abihu are but two examples of "foolish sons" who caused their father, Aaron, shame. Perhaps the best example is not individuals but vast numbers of "children and servants"—the Jews and Gentiles.

The servant who is promoted over a child causes envy (Dan. 6:3-5). This is what Paul hoped would happen to his people, the Jews, as he preached to the Gentiles (Rom. 11:14). Later on in the same chapter, he exhorted the Gentiles, who had become God's children, not to become conceited because ultimately God would lift the spiritual blindness that had come upon the Jews. They, too, would be saved (Rom. 11:25-26).

Scriptural Examples

Eliezer and Abraham. Abraham had no son, so he intended to leave his estate to his wise servant. But God told Abraham that he would have a son from his own loins (Gen. 15:3-4).

Jacob and Laban. Jacob served Laban wisely and Laban's wealth grew. So Jacob renegotiated his contract, probably at Laban's sons' displeasure (Gen. 30:27-34).

The prodigal son. This disgraceful son was prepared to go back to his father's house as a servant. When he returned home, his father was joyful. The display of the father's love and forgiveness did not bring joy to the elder son (Luke 15:19-20, 28-30).

The ingrafted branches. Paul speaks of the natural branches, Israel, being broken off, while those of a wild olive shoot, the Gentiles, have been grafted in (Rom. 11:17-21).

Prayer of Application

Father God, You have saved me and caused me to be a child and a joint-heir with Christ in the Kingdom of heaven. Thank You for Your unspeakable grace. May I now be a wise servant.

Submit to God's Furnace of Purification

The crucible for silver and the furnace for gold, but the Lord tests the heart (Prov. 17:3).

To refine silver and gold, the ore is subjected to tremendous heat and the precious metal is separated from its impurities. God uses this same principle in people. He does it both to the natural and spiritual person, but for different reasons.

God uses such "heat" to reveal the evil that is in the hearts of those who refuse His grace. He will judge those same hearts in justice by Christ whom He has raised from the dead (Acts 17:31). God uses the heat to try, but also to refine the heart of the child of God. He melts away our slag of rebelliousness and purifies our hearts to produce the precious gold He desires. The heat is for our sanctification, to conform us to the image of His Son (Rom. 8:29). God disciplines those He loves (Heb. 12:7-8).

There is no easy way; the child of God must go through the heat. But thank God that there is a purpose for it, that He is producing in us the gold that will last through eternal life.

Scriptural Examples

Abraham. God tested Abraham severely in the matter of offering up for sacrifice his only son, Isaac. Although ultimately God stopped Abraham, God told him that He'd given him the trial to test him (Gen. 22:12).

David. David was put through the heat of God's furnace on many occasions. In Psalm 139:23-24, David acknowledged the leadership of God in the testing and purification of his heart.

Hezekiah. When the envoys from Babylon came to Hezekiah, God said He left this king of Judah in order to test him and to see what was in his heart (2 Chron. 32:31).

Jesus. Jesus was tested by Satan, by the Pharisees, by the crushing crowds, and finally by the cross. Even He learned obedience from what He suffered (Heb. 5:7-9).

Prayer of Application

Thank You, Lord, for revealing to me in Your Word that You use the heat in my life for Your eternal purposes: to try my heart, to purify it, and to cause me to bear abundant fruit.

Shut Your Ears to Wickedness

A wicked man listens to evil lips; a liar pays attention to a malicious tongue (Prov. 17:4).

We've all heard the old saying, "Misery loves company." In the verse above we're told "evil loves company." A wicked person will listen to evil because he wants to believe it, for in evil his own wickedness is approved. In the same way, the liar loves the wicked tongue because it confirms the liar in his sin.

There is another old saying that fits here: "Birds of a feather flock together." Why? For mutual comfort and security. Jesus said evil people hate the glaring light of truth, preferring darkness (John 3:20). Paul also warned against approval of those who practice deceit and every kind of wickedness (Rom. 1:32).

The message to Christians is clear. We are to walk in the light of God (Ps. 56:13; 89:15; 1 John 1:7) and to avoid even listening to the words of evil people (Ps. 1:1).

Scriptural Examples

Ham to Shem and Japheth. Ham was apparently amused by the sight of his father lying naked in his tent. Then he gossiped to his brothers about what he had seen. Shem and Japheth were not amused, and covered Noah (Gen. 9:20-27).

Jonadab to Amnon. Jonadab told David's son Amnon how to lay a trap for Amnon's half-sister, Tamar, whom Amnon desired. Their wicked conversation led to Tamar's rape (2 Sam. 13:5).

Jezebel to Ahab. She schemed to get Naboth's vineyard for her husband, Ahab. She planned a day of fasting in which two false accusers paved the way to stone Naboth to death, opening the way for the confiscation of his vineyard (1 Kings 21:4-15).

Demetrius and the men of Ephesus. Concerned that Paul's preaching might harm his business of making shrines for the goddess Artemis, Demetrius' evil and false words to those men of Ephesus started a riot among the people (Acts 19:23-29).

Prayer of Application

Father, You have saved me out of the evil of this world. Even though I am still in the world, I am to be separate from the world's evil. Lord, keep me from the snares of wicked people.

See God's Providence in the Trials of Others

He who mocks the poor shows contempt for their Maker; whoever gloats over disaster will not go unpunished (Prov. 17:5).

In an attempt to elevate themselves in their own eyes, some people mock those they consider less than themselves. I remember growing up in Tennessee when African-Americans were looked upon as almost subhuman by many whites, including some who called themselves Christians. Racial discrimination still goes on, and it is a reproach and sin against our Maker.

The spiritual person should see God in control of every circumstance. Where there are poor people, it is not necessarily due to their bad fortune or laziness, so much as it is to the providence of the God who made them (1 Sam. 2:7). He who laughs at the condition of the poor utters treason against God. This is particularly true when calamity befalls them.

Rather, the Bible teaches that we are to sympathize with the victims of calamities, lifting them up in prayer and providing for them in acts of loving-kindness (Prov. 24:17; 25:21; Rom. 12:20). The Bible teaches that every person is made in the image of the Creator (Gen. 1:26) and is an eternal being. Although fallen, each person should be treated with dignity and respect.

Scriptural Examples

Moses. He led the Israelites who sang of the defeat of Pharaoh. They were not gloating but were bringing honor and glory to the Lord God who had done it (Ex. 15).

Shimei. As David fled from Absalom's conspiracy, this Benjamite cursed him and pelted him with stones. David held his peace, for he said that the Lord may be instructing Shimei to curse him. Or maybe the Lord would see David's distress and repay him with good for the curses (2 Sam. 16:5-13).

Job. Even in his distress, Job said he never sinned against God by rejoicing at his enemy's misfortune (Job 31:28-30).

Prayer of Application

Sovereign Lord, You have made all people for Your glory and eternal purpose. Help me to respect every person, to right the wrongs I can right, and to attend to the needs of the poor.

Parents and Children, Bless Each Other

Children's children are a crown to the aged, and parents are the pride of their children (Prov. 17:6).

This proverb speaks to what should be and not to what always is. So often in Scripture we see the son turning away from the instruction of his righteous parents, or conversely, the parents bringing shame upon their children. Here we see that a person's children's children are a crown to him. What a delight to be a grandparent!

God created the family as our first social structure, an institution created for our blessing and well-being. When a man and woman leave their parents and cleave to one another (Gen. 2:24), a family is created. If God's will is such, children will come. Parenthood is a great joy, yet a profound responsibility. But blessing and responsibility are also implied for the children here. They are to honor their parents (Ex. 20:12), who in turn are to raise their children in the nurture and admonition of the Lord (Eph. 6:4). The Christian home should be a great blessing for all who dwell in it.

Scriptural Examples

Adam and Cain. Adam lived to see many generations of his son Cain. God would ultimately destroy them in the Flood. Cain was not a blessing but a curse for Adam. Neither did Cain glory in his father (Gen. 4; Jude 11).

Adam and Seth. God had promised a deliverer to Adam and Eve, and although the first couple may have thought Him to be Cain, it was from the godly line of Seth that He was to come. Adam was surely blessed by Seth's children (Gen. 5).

Timothy. Paul spoke of the excellent witness and faith that lived in Timothy's grandmother Lois and his mother, Eunice, and which now lived in him. Surely Timothy was the crowning glory of their lives, as they were of his (2 Tim. 1:5).

Prayer of Application

Oh, Sovereign Lord, may I be a blessing to my children, raising them with love for You so that they may one day say I have been their glory. Lord, that will be glory for You.

Speak Words of Excellence and Truth

Arrogant lips are [KJV: "excellent speech is"] unsuited to a fool— how much worse lying lips to a ruler (Prov. 17:7)!

My parents used to say, "What you are speaks so loudly I can't hear what you say." What it meant was that you could tell loads about a person even before he opened his mouth. How much more is that true when he does open it and out flows garbage. Such is the speech of a fool. Words of hate, slander, lying, abuse, filth, gossip, and all sorts of depravity may pour forth.

The ruler or prince, on the other hand, should employ words in keeping with his position. The lying prince will be ultimately humbled with the fool. If excellent speech does not become a fool, nor lying lips a prince, neither does foolish talk or deceit become the child of God. It's like putting overalls on a ballerina, or a tutu on a farmer. There's just not a fit. We need to follow the example of our Lord Jesus, who spoke fitting, wise, and beautiful words, and who taught us that by our words we would be justified or condemned (Matt. 12:37).

Scriptural Examples

Saul. This king lied about the total destruction of the Amalekites. He had preserved some of the animals he had captured for sacrifices (1 Sam. 15:1-26).

Job's friends. Although they gave long and flowing speeches regarding Job's afflictions, these men spoke foolishly and not according to the truth of the matter (Job 42:7).

Herod. On meeting the wise men, this prince lied to them and asked them to return his way, so he, too, might worship the Child who had been born (Matt. 2:8).

The Philippian slave girl. She followed the apostles shouting, "These men are servants of the Most High God, who are telling you the way to be saved!" Tiring of her devilish sarcasm, Paul cast out a demon from her (Acts 16:16-18).

Prayer of Application

Help me, Father, to speak only those things which are true and beneficial to others. Help me to lift others up with my speech, to edify them, and encourage them in all things godly.

Beware of Men Bearing Gifts

A bribe is a charm to the one who gives it; wherever he turns, he succeeds (Prov. 17:8).

Paul says the love of money is the root of all kinds of evil (1 Tim. 6:10). In the verse above we see the power of money: a precious gift or bribe in the hands of a person who would pervert justice. The politician who gives favors for secret campaign contributions, or a policeman who tears up a ticket for a few dollars secretly passed to him, are examples of the bribe.

The Christian should not have his eyes focused on money, but on the eternal things of Christ. We need to be careful that we avoid situations where we are obliged to do things for money that offend our Lord. How can we, under the obligation to serve and follow the One who has saved us, depart from Him to serve the base desires of people because of a gift? You cannot serve God and money (Matt. 6:24).

Scriptural Examples

Balaam. This false prophet was motivated by the "wages of wickedness" (2 Peter 2:15) when he was bribed by Balak to prophesy against the people of God (Num. 22:7-8).

Ziba. Ziba bribed the great king David with donkeys, bread, raisins, and wine, and David gave him that which belonged to Mephibosheth, Jonathan's son (2 Sam. 16:1-4).

Daniel. The king of Babylon offered gifts and power to Daniel if he deciphered the wall's handwriting. Daniel declined the king's gifts, but interpreted the writing (Dan. 5:17).

Judas. For thirty pieces of silver, this disciple of Jesus delivered the Lord into the hands of the authorities who falsely accused, tried, and put Him to death (Matt. 26:14-16).

Felix. Governor Felix heard Paul's testimony about the events in Jerusalem and Paul's faith in Christ. He probably would have released him, but he was hoping Paul would offer him a bribe. So he kept Paul in prison (Acts 24:26).

Prayer of Application

Heavenly Father, help me to live in control of my finances so that I will never be placed in a position of being tempted to compromise my Christian principles for money.

Overlook Small Offenses

He who covers over an offense promotes love, but whoever repeats the matter separates close friends (Prov. 17:9).

Jesus' primary role on this earth was to show forth the love of God. He exhibited that love in His perfect life and ultimately in dying for lost sinners. He provided a covering for our sins against God. Jesus doesn't overlook sins (1 Peter 4:8), but we are called to overlook small offenses against us.

But what about major offenses? In that case, we are to humbly go to our neighbor and tell him of the matter (Matt. 18:15). If he seeks forgiveness, we are then obliged to forgive him, up to an innumerable number of times (Matt. 18:22). This should restore an atmosphere of love between brothers and sisters.

The absolutely wrong thing to do is to go and tell others about your neighbor's sin without first seeking him out. If he does not ask for forgiveness, you are to go to him a second time, this time with two or three witnesses. If he still won't listen, then bring the matter up before the church-at-large. If, after all of this, he still will not listen, we are to expel him from church membership (Matt. 18:16-17). All of this is not to punish our sinning brother or sister. Rather, it is to reconcile him to fellowship.

Scriptural Examples

David and Mephibosheth. David, in spite of the injustices rendered to him by Saul, desired to show kindness to the house of Saul for Jonathan's sake. So he befriended Jonathan's son, Mephibosheth, who was crippled since childhood, and took him into his palace. David restored all of his grandfather's land to him (2 Sam. 9).

Ziba and Mephibosheth. Ziba slandered Mephibosheth, the invalid grandson of King Saul, by telling David that he was awaiting ascension to Saul's throne. This deceit damaged the friendship of David and Mephibosheth (2 Sam. 16:3-4).

Prayer of Application

Heavenly Father, help me to reflect the love of Christ in all of my relationships with others. Help me to overlook small offenses, as I hope others will overlook mine against them.

Be Discerning in Your Rebuke of Others

A rebuke impresses a man of discernment more than a hundred lashes a fool (Prov. 17:10).

This proverb speaks of a wide disparity in forms of discipline. For the wise person, a gentle or mild rebuke is all that's necessary to set matters right. But for a fool, 100 lashes (more than double the number that would probably kill him) are needed to create a heart of obedience. In other words, even 100 lashes will not impress a fool.

We are commanded to give reproof to others who offend us (Luke 17:3), but we are also taught that the effectiveness of that reproof will depend upon the heart of the receiver. In some cases, such as the fool here or the one in Proverbs 27:22, it won't do any good no matter what form the rebuke takes.

Scriptural Examples

Pharaoh. Time after time the Lord brought disaster upon Pharaoh and the Egyptians, yet the foolish king continually hardened his heart against the Lord's reproof (Ex. 7-15).

David. David's stony heart became fleshly at the wise rebuke of Nathan in the matter of Bathsheba and Uriah. David confessed his sin before God and repented (2 Sam. 12:1-7; 13).

Ahaz. This wicked king of Judah was disciplined by God for his foolishness and worship of idols. But the rebuke didn't humble Ahaz; he became more unfaithful (2 Chron. 28:22).

Israel. Isaiah begins his book with a scathing reprimand of Israel. They had been beaten and scourged. Their land was left desolate. God pled with them to come and reason with Him. He offered them forgiveness and healing (Isa. 1).

Peter. Peter needed only a look from our Lord to break his heart because he remembered Jesus' prophecy that before the cock crowed Peter would disown Him three times. It happened just as the Lord had said it would (Luke 22:61-62).

Prayer of Application

Lord, give me understanding so that I will be neither too harsh nor too light in the rebuke of others. May I do it in love, that the one reproved would be edified and encouraged.

Warn the Rebellious of God's Revenge

An evil man is bent only on rebellion; a merciless official will be sent against him (Prov. 17:11).

God exhorts us to be loyal to Him, and to those He has put in authority over us (Ex. 22:28; Rom. 13:1, for instance). But the evil person, whose desire for autonomy won't be subdued, rebels against such authority. Saul was rejected as king because of his arrogant rebellion (1 Sam. 15:23). The nation of Israel rebelled again and again. It is a common theme of Scripture.

Just as God rewards loyalty, so He also repays rebellion. There is no secret rebellion, because the hearts of people lie wide open before the great Judge (Heb. 4:13). There is no hiding place or safe refuge from the wrath of Almighty God. Except one.

What about the one who forsakes his rebellion and who seeks to be reconciled with God? Will God still seek revenge on him? No. Although that person may be forced to suffer the temporal consequences of his sin, such as a prison sentence or even execution, God seeks these people to come to the repentance and faith in Christ that leads to salvation (2 Peter 3:9-15). Christ is the one refuge to which the sinner may run and be saved.

Scriptural Examples

Korah and his followers. These Levites rose up against the authority of Moses and Aaron. God opened up the earth, which swallowed both the Levites and their families (Num. 16).

Absalom. He rebelled against his father David, and thus against God, seeking the kingdom for himself. God confused his mind in listening to Ahithophel's wise advice and as a result he suffered defeat and death (2 Sam. 15-18).

Sheba. This son of Bicri led a host of Israelites in rebellion against David. Joab pursued Sheba to Abel Beth Maacah where a wise woman persuaded the townspeople to throw Sheba's head from the city wall (2 Sam. 20:1-22).

Prayer of Application

Heavenly Father, seek in me any rebellious spirit, no matter how small, and root it out. Give me strength to warn the unsaved of Your terrible revenge to come. Thank You for Jesus.

Beware the Uncontrolled Malice of a Fool

Better to meet a bear robbed of her cubs than a fool in his folly (Prov. 17:12).

A mother bear, robbed of her cubs, is synonymous with a fierce and dangerous fighter. But a person is better off to meet one of these savage beasts than to meet a fool whose anger is out of control. These people seem to abound in our society today.

In Southern California it seems that these malicious people are multiplying rapidly. Hardly a day goes by that we don't read of a drive-by shooting on the freeway or an argument in some bar that leads one person to murder another.

Jesus recognized the malice thrust at Him by the Pharisees to be that of their father, the devil (John 8:44). We children of God are to put off all malice and take vengeance on no one because we recognize that vengeance belongs to the Lord (Rom. 12:19). Rather, we are called to be peacemakers (Matt. 5:9) who repay insults with blessings (1 Peter 3:9).

Scriptural Examples

Simeon and Levi. These sons of Jacob plotted revenge against their sister's seducer. They went way overboard in their revenge and Jacob was shamed by them (Gen. 34:25-29).

Saul. Saul accused Ahimelech and his priests of siding with David and had Doeg slay 85 priests of God. Then he put the entire town of Nob to the sword, all of its women and children and all of its livestock (1 Sam. 22:17-19).

Nebuchadnezzar. He was so angry with Shadrach, Meshach, and Abednego that he foolishly heated the furnace seven times hotter than normal and threw them into it. Their executors were the only ones burned up (Dan. 3:13-22).

Herod. On learning that he had been foiled by the Magi, who failed to return to tell him of Jesus, he gave orders to kill every male child in Bethlehem and vicinity under two years old (Matt. 2:16).

Prayer of Application

Father, people have grown cold to Your truth and many are running uncontrolled. Keep our families safe from these madmen, while at the same time we give them the gospel.

Flee from Ingratitude

If a man pays back evil for good, evil will never leave his house (Prov. 17:13).

At the heart of people's rebellion against God is ingratitude (Rom. 1:21). Fallen man pays back evil for God's goodness, yet blames God for all of the ills that befall him. God hates this, and repays the ingrate with evil which will never leave his house.

Ingratitude is also a common sin in our relationships with other people. How often do we see children ungrateful to their parents, who in selfless love have provided them with good things. Employees murmur and complain against employers and vice versa. Husbands repay loving wives with infidelity, and wives repay faithful and loving husbands with sloth or attempts to dominate.

Christians should be known for thanksgiving. We are commanded to give thanks in all things (1 Thess. 5:18), because we know our loving heavenly Father is working out His purposes in us (Rom. 8:28-29). Grab hold of that worldview! Your heart will be thankful for all things that come your way, and you'll find yourself repaying evil with good.

Scriptural Examples

Adam to God. Man was made in God's image, and God called him "good." But the first man rewarded God's good with evil. Surely this proverb speaks directly to Adam, as evil has never departed from his house (Gen. 3:5-6).

David to Uriah. In an attempt to cover up his liaison with Bathsheba, David had the loyal Uriah brought in from Israel's army camp in hopes of luring him to sleep with his wife. Uriah refused to go in to her, so David had him killed in battle. Evil filled David's house for the rest of his days (2 Sam. 11:6-17).

The Jews to the prophets. Jesus scathingly denounced Israel's treatment of God's prophets. Later, He, too, would be slain. Evil will never leave those who reject Him (Matt. 23:32-39).

Prayer of Application

Father, help me to major in thanksgiving, giving You thanks for every circumstance of my life. Help me also to show my gratitude to others who will be encouraged by it.

Nip Strife in the Bud

Starting a quarrel is like breaching a dam; so drop the matter before a dispute breaks out (Prov. 17:14).

This verse makes me think of the young man in Holland with his finger in a dike that had sprung a leak. His finger, in effect, was keeping the entire North Atlantic out of the fields of his homeland. Were a small hole to be left unattended, it would increasingly widen until the whole dike was breached and the land was flooded.

The proper time to correct a relational problem is at the beginning of the problem. The longer it is allowed to fester, the more serious it becomes. A phrase I like says that we should "keep short accounts." This is particularly important in the context of marriage. We should not let the sun go down on our anger (Eph. 4:26). To the good advice to "kiss and make up" should be added this: "Do it quickly."

Scriptural Examples

Abram and Lot. Abram's herdsmen argued with Lot's about space to graze their herds. So Abram suggested a peaceful plan to part company. Lot chose first and took the plain near Sodom, while Abram stuck to the hill country (Gen. 13:8-9).

Israel and Sihon. Israel sent an envoy to the Amorites, seeking passage through their country. Sihon, the Amorite king, refused and attacked the Israelites, only to be soundly defeated. He could have saved himself much trouble and anguish by simply fulfilling their request (Num. 21:21-24).

The disciples and Jesus. The disciples had been arguing about who would be greatest among them. Jesus defused the argument quickly by telling them that whoever wanted to be first among them must be the servant of all (Mark 9:33-35).

Paul and Barnabas. These great men argued about taking Mark with them on a journey. Ultimately peace was restored, even though it meant parting company (Acts 15:36-40).

Prayer of Application

Help me, Lord, to solve my relational problems with others quickly and before they get too large and out of control. Particularly help my marriage, where the stakes are so high.

Flee from Injustice

Acquitting the guilty and condemning the innocent—the Lord detests them both (Prov. 17:15).

Our God is just and He is tremendously concerned that justice be done on the earth. Over and over again He speaks of the rights of the widows and the fatherless (Ex. 22:22; Deut. 10:18, for example). God hates injustice. The judge who acquits the guilty or condemns the innocent is an abomination to Him.

Every day we exercise discernment in our treatment of others and we're not to show favoritism to the rich man (James 2:1-7) or to despise the poor man. We are in training in this life to be judges in the next. Don't you know that the saints will judge the world? We'll even judge angels (1 Cor. 6:2-3).

Someone asks, "But what about God? Doesn't He acquit the guilty?" Yes, He does. But God acquits, or justifies, us according to justice, never injustice (Rom. 3:25-26). We are saved by grace in which He freely justifies—but it wasn't free. His own Son, our Lord Jesus, paid the penalty for our sins.

Scriptural Examples

Joel and Abijah. Samuel's sons turned to dishonesty and injustice. They had become an abomination to the Lord, so the people of Israel cried out for a king (1 Sam. 8:3-5).

Herod the Tetrarch. He perverted justice by having John the Baptist imprisoned, then beheaded. He made a frivolous oath to the daughter of Herodias, which he thought to be of greater value than the prophet's life (Matt. 14:1-11).

Pontius Pilate. He self-righteously washed his hands of the blood of Jesus, all the while consenting to the execution of the only truly righteous man who ever lived (Matt. 27:11-26).

Pontius Pilate. The same day he condemned the just Jesus, he released the anarchist Barabbas, thereby also acquitting a wicked man. In one day injustice was perfected (John 18:40).

Prayer of Application

Righteous Father, help me to treat fairly everyone with whom I have contact. Give me a discerning heart, Lord, so that I will be able to judge rightly, in accordance with your Word.

Warn Others About the Peril of a Hard Heart

Of what use is money in the hand of a fool, since he has no desire to get wisdom? (Prov. 17:16).

God has given every person some of the "money," or where-withal to get the wisdom that leads to salvation. Specifically, He has revealed Himself in His creation, showing through natural or general revelation His eternal power and godhead (Rom. 1:20). Additionally, we in America have been given specific revelation in spades. Bibles are everywhere. Many churches preach the gospel freely and openly, and the Word of God is going out all the time on radio, television, and in the printed media. Yet, fools still reject it. Why? Certainly they have the knowledge, or "money." The problem is, they don't have the heart for it. Their hearts are stone cold dead (Eph. 2:1).

Thank the Lord daily that He turned your heart of stone into a heart of flesh (Ezek. 11:19), enabling you to cast off the bondage of Satan (Eph. 2:1-2) and freely come to Christ.

Scriptural Examples

The ten tribes. Hezekiah sent messages inviting the people to come to Jerusalem for Passover. Although they had the knowledge of God, they scorned the messengers. Only a few men from three tribes humbly responded (2 Chron. 30:1-11).

The Gadarenes. When Jesus cast demons out of the Gadarene demoniac and into a herd of pigs, these people hardened their hearts and told the Savior to get out of town (Matt. 8:34).

Korazin and Bethsaida. Jesus pronounced a "woe" upon these cities that rejected the Kingdom. Wicked Tyre and Sidon will be better off in the judgment than they (Matt. 11:21-22).

The rich young ruler. He asked the Savior what to do to inherit eternal life. Sadly, he loved his riches more than the riches of Christ, so not having the heart, he rejected the Word. He had lots of money, but what use was it? (Mark 10:17-22).

Prayer of Application

Heavenly Father, thank You for preparing my heart to receive Your gospel. Help me to be a conduit for Your message of reconciliation, warning others to beware of a hardened heart.

Emulate the Unfailing Friendship of Christ

A friend loves at all times, and a brother is born for adversity (Prov. 17:17).

I am reminded again of the champion boxer who, as long as money and fame are flowing, has lots of friends. But let him lose his skills and his championship, and his entourage disappears. So it is with worldly friends.

But true friends love you regardless of your circumstances and are, in fact, born for adversity. Where do we find such a friend? One is right beside you. He is the living Savior. He says that He will never leave you nor forsake you (Heb. 13:5).

In light of Christ's unfailing love for us, what kind of friends should we be? We should emulate Him who calls us to reflect His love (Gal. 2:20). To visit a friend when he is sick, or when disaster strikes, is to represent Him. To share with our friends their joys and victories, as well as their sorrows and defeats, is to be the kind of friend that Jesus exemplifies.

Scriptural Examples

Joseph and his brothers. Even though they had sold him into slavery and hardship, Joseph loved his brothers with a Christ-like love. When they came to Egypt seeking food, he opened his arms and received them with tears of brotherhood, forgiveness, and friendship (Gen. 45:5).

Ruth and Naomi. The young widow Ruth stuck by her mother- in-law and vowed to stay with her regardless of the circumstances or consequences (Ruth 1:16).

Jonathan and David. This friendship withstood the ravages of Saul's hatred and jealousy of David (1 Sam. 18:3).

John and Mary. At Jesus' request on the cross, John took His mother into his home to care for her (John 19:27).

Paul, Priscilla, and Aquila. Paul's friends stuck with him when the going got tough, risking their lives (Rom. 16:3-4).

Prayer of Application

Father, thank You for the friend I have in Christ. Oh, that I would be more like Him, and carry the message of His love to my unsaved friends who need His friendship so much.

Beware of Risky Contracts

A man lacking in judgment strikes hands in pledge and puts up security for his neighbor (Prov. 17:18).

A wise rule in business that will never fail you is, "Never sign personally on a loan." That is, don't secure a loan with your personal net worth, but solely with the collateral for which the loan is being used. If you default, the lender can look only to the collateral for repayment and not to you personally.

This is particularly true if you are asked to become surety for someone else. Although we Christians are called to bear one another's burdens (Gal. 6:2), we must be careful not to put our family at risk out of kindness to others. We can't see what the future holds. Therefore, we should beware of any contract that risks our family's future welfare unnecessarily.

When you are tempted to enter a business deal, make a large purchase, co-sign a promissory note with a friend, or any such obligation where you are called upon to provide personal surety, ask yourself what your motive really is. Is it greed, covetousness, or to gain popularity? If so, graciously decline.

Scriptural Examples

Judah. Judah guaranteed his father, Jacob, that he would be surety for Benjamin's safety in Egypt. Later, when Benjamin was accused of stealing, Judah offered to take Benjamin's punishment upon himself (Gen. 43:8-9; 44:33-34).

Israel and the Gibeonites. Filled with fear when they heard of the fall of Jericho, the Gibeonites pretended to be a people from far away, come to make peace. Without seeking God's guidance, Israel swore an agreement with them (Josh. 9).

Jesus. On the cross, Jesus willfully became our surety and risked everything—by faith—for His family. Did He violate the principle? No. As God, He saw the end from the beginning and completed the work He was sent to do (Col. 2:14-15).

Prayer of Application

Father, thank You for Your wisdom that can keep me from stumbling. I pray You would infuse me with good judgment for my family's financial well-being. And thank You for Jesus.

Open Wide the Gates of Love

He who loves a quarrel loves sin; he who builds a high gate invites destruction (Prov. 17:19).

If you are like me, you hate to argue and will do almost anything to avoid conflict, unless your principles and convictions are being compromised. But there are people who love a good quarrel. They seem to flourish in strife because they love it. These are the people of whom this proverb speaks.

These lovers of strife have as their basic problem the sin of pride (Prov. 13:10). They build a high gate between themselves and those around them. Their superiority demands that everyone else see things their way, even though it may not be backed with the authority of Scripture. They are self-willed, not God-willed, and rarely resist any opportunity for conflict.

The Bible is very clear in condemning the sin of pride and its fruits of hatred, discord, dissensions, factions, and the like. Paul says that people who live like that will not inherit the kingdom of God (Gal. 5:19-21). As the apostle Paul commands in Romans 12:18, "If it is possible, as far as it depends on you, live at peace with everyone." Open the gates of love.

Scriptural Examples

Gerar's herdsmen. These men quarreled with the herdsmen of Isaac over water rights. They were Philistines who seemed to love to fight, particularly with the people of God. Later, there were to be many battles between the two nations (Gen. 26:20-22).

The Benjamites. Benjamites from Gibeah raped a visitor's concubine, who subsequently died. The Ephraimite cut her body into 12 pieces, sending one to each tribe of Israel. They rose up against the tribe of Benjamin that had "exalted his gate," refusing to bring the wicked men to justice. The incident precipitated the destruction of virtually the entire tribe of Benjamin at the hands of its brothers (Judg. 19:22-21:25).

Prayer of Application

Lord, help me to overlook the small things that can add fuel to an argument. But give me the strength to confront the person who sins against me, in a spirit of love and restoration.

Warn Those Perverse of Heart and Tongue

A man of perverse heart does not prosper; he whose tongue is deceitful falls into trouble (Prov. 17:20).

A common expression is "Have a good day." According to the Bible, that can never apply to a person with a perverse heart. While it *appears* that many with perverse hearts are prospering, a closer look shows appearances can be deceiving.

Romans 8:28 states all circumstances of life are working together for the good of those who love God and who are the called according to His purpose. While we see bad things happening to the children of God, what is at stake in this verse is their ultimate spiritual prosperity. Verse 29 tells us ultimate prosperity is to be conformed to the image of Christ.

But for the perverse of heart and tongue, none of the circumstances of his life are now working to his good, only ultimate trouble in final judgment. How can we recognize the natural person on whom rests God's judgment? Through the perverse and deceitful words he speaks (Matt. 7:15-20).

Scriptural Examples

The people of Babel. After the flood, perverse men in Shinar built a monument to themselves. God confused their tongues and scattered them to the four winds (Gen. 11:1-9).

The people of Sodom. The Sodomites had perverse hearts and practiced every kind of abomination. God did not scatter them as at Babel. He utterly destroyed them (Gen. 19:1-24).

The people of Jerusalem. As Jesus overlooked the city, He spoke of its perverse history of shedding innocent blood and its evil self-will, then prophesied the desolation of the city. That literally took place in A.D. 70. (Matt. 23:37-38).

The people of Corinth. Even in the church we may see evidence of the perverse heart and tongue. Paul rebuked those who caused divisions and strife there (1 Cor. 1:11).

Prayer of Application

Dear God, help me to warn men and women of Your coming judgment. Give me the boldness to share with them the gospel of Christ, who calls people everywhere to free salvation.

Pray for Your Children

To have a fool for a son brings grief; there is no joy for the father of a fool (Prov. 17:21).

A fool is a person who does not fear the God of creation (Ps. 14:1). What a painful thing it is for a person of God to have a child who thinks like this fool. If only we could inject our kids with the truth and have them become instant believers! But it doesn't work that way, as you well know. Ephesians 6:4 tells us to raise our children in the nurture and admonition of the Lord. Sometimes, even when we do that to the best of our ability, our children wander into the folly of unbelief. What can a parent do to find peace in the midst of such uncertainty?

First, be a godly parent who practices righteousness in all your affairs. Don't be too harsh with your children, nor too easy on them, but bring them up in a godly home that exposes their formative minds to the truth of God's Word daily.

Second, recognize that if the Spirit is to come into your child's heart, He will come as the sovereign act of God. The prayer of faith is your mightiest and most effective weapon. Pray without ceasing for your children.

Scriptural Examples

Hannah. Hannah prayed to the Lord for a son (1 Sam. 1:28). God granted her desire and she turned him over to Eli to be raised in the service of the Lord. In 1 Samuel 2:1-10, we are given insight into Hannah's prayer life. She sought God's help in raising one of the Bible's most godly men.

David. David prayed that his son Solomon, as king over Israel, would have peace with his enemies and be successful in building the temple of God. He prayed that his son might have wisdom and that he might keep God's law (1 Chron. 22:9-12).

Job. This godly man and devoted father made it a regular habit to pray for his children (Job 1:5).

Prayer of Application

Heavenly Father, thank You for my children. I pray that as I am in Your presence through the ages, they will be there with me. I love them, Lord, and humbly ask You for their salvation.

Be Cheerful Even in the Face of Trials

A cheerful heart is good medicine, but a crushed spirit dries up the bones (Prov. 17:22).

The "crushed spirit" spoken of here does not lead to salvation (Ps. 51:17), but that of selfishness and despondency. This is not the calling of the follower of Christ. At one time or another, each of us will suffer crushing blows. They may come with divorce, disease, the death of a loved one, or the loss of a job. For a season we may be in sorrow and even anguish, but those things are not to characterize our lives.

Beneath the surface turmoil of life, the Christian has an underpinning of hope that transcends even the most severe trial. Our Lord applies Isaiah 61:1 to Himself in Luke 4:17-18. He stops before quoting verses 2 and 3, which speaks of the Lord who will bring comfort to mourners, gladness instead of sorrow, and a garment of praise rather than a spirit of despair.

The next time you are tempted to wallow in a crushed spirit, consider the blessings of Christ. Put on the garment of praise, giving thanks for His wonderful grace. Your cheerful spirit in the face of trouble will be like a medicine to all.

Scriptural Examples

Saul and David. On hearing Goliath boast, Saul and the Israelites were terrified. But David's cheerful and believing heart convinced Saul he could defeat the giant. David brought victory to Israel that day (1 Sam. 17:11, 37).

Paul and Silas. They sang praises to God in spite of their chains. After an earthquake, they led the jailor and his whole family to the Lord. Their cheerfulness was like a medicine to those who heard them (Acts 16:25).

The martyrs. We're told of their steadfast faith and contentment in the face of death, not accepting deliverance, so they might obtain a better resurrection (Heb. 11:32-39).

Prayer of Application

Dear Lord, how often when trouble strikes I am tempted to wallow in self-pity. Show me the true way, Lord—to be content and joyful even when the events of my life say I shouldn't be.

Conduct Business Justly

A wicked man accepts a bribe in secret to pervert the course of justice (Prov. 17:23).

Our God is a God of absolute justice. To pervert the course of justice is to run diametrically opposed to His will. Here we see a man who does exactly that.

Suppose you are a purchasing agent and are trying to decide between two competing bids for a service your company needs. One company's sales rep sends you two tickets to a ball game and a free dinner. You accept the gift and thereby feel obligated to lean more heavily toward this sales rep's proposal. The fact that you let the gift even enter your mind for the purpose of making a decision violates Solomon's principle. The decision should be made in justice, solely on the merits of each competing bid, and not perverted by the acceptance of a gift which skewed the decision-making (judicial) process. God sees all such transactions of wicked people.

Scriptural Examples

Delilah. The Philistines bribed her with a large sum if she would find the source of Samson's strength (Judg. 16:5)

Joel and Abijah. Samuel appointed his sons as judges over Israel but they refused to walk in the honest ways of their father. Instead, they turned away to dishonest gain, accepting bribes and perverting justice (1 Sam. 8:1-3).

Ben-Hadad. Asa, king of Judah, sent a bribe of silver and gold to this king requesting that he break his treaty with Baasha, king of Israel, weakening Israel's forces. Ben-Hadad accepted the bribe, and Baasha withdrew (1 Kings 15:19-21).

Haman. This wicked strongman asked King Xerxes for 10,000 talents of silver to bribe the men who would carry out his plan to exterminate Mordecai and the Jews (Est. 3:9).

Prayer of Application

Sovereign Lord, in all my dealings with others in this world, keep me from this sin of showing favoritism and perverting justice because of some secret reciprocity.

Keep Focused on Christ and His Word

A discerning man keeps wisdom in view, but a fool's eyes wander to the ends of the earth (Prov. 17:24).

Have you noticed the number and velocity of fads in our land? As far back as I can remember, there have been fads in clothing, music, automobiles, lifestyles and, perhaps worst of all, fads in religion. We see some troubling fads today in the church, to which the wise person should not turn.

In his book *Our Sufficiency In Christ*, John MacArthur lists three prominent fads in the church today which go against the wisdom of Scripture. The first, he says, is "psychologism." We in the church have become infatuated with humanistic psychology and sometimes replace the wisdom of the Bible with it. The second is "pragmatism." Some churches water down the Word and conduct services that are entertaining to draw in the unsaved, catering to society's whims instead of following the Word of God. Third, Dr. MacArthur lists "mysticism." Many churches espouse experience, intuition, and personal revelation at the expense of biblical doctrine.

The discerning Christian will focus on Christ and His holy Word. The foolish person is ready to adopt any new teaching that comes along, even to the ends of the earth.

Scriptural Examples

The Israelites. Instead of focusing on the God who delivered them from Pharaoh, they set their minds on their life in Egypt and began to murmur and complain (Ex. 16:1-3).

Samson. Set apart since birth, Israel's judge seemed to fritter away his responsibilities in sexual encounters, riddles, and revenge, slipping farther away from God (Judg. 13-16).

The Galatians. Paul complained of their fickleness in turning away from the gospel to another gospel, which was no gospel at all, but a doctrine that led to death (Gal. 1:6-12).

Prayer of Application

Lord Jesus, Your Word is complete and worthy for our edification, rebuke, and training in righteousness. Help me to keep my eyes fixed on it and to resist the fickle fads of change.

Discipline Your Children in the Lord

A foolish son brings grief to his father and bitterness to the one who bore him (Prov. 17:25).

In verse 21 of this chapter we drew the principle that we are to pray for our children. Here is the other part. We are to work daily with them to discipline them and to train them in the things of God. If a child grows up to become President of the United States, yet denies Christ, he will surely bring grief to his godly parents. Prayer is a principal mode of transporting our children into the Kingdom, and this is the practical part. Without it our prayers are a mockery. But how do we do it?

It is never too early to start. Read them Bible stories, pray with them, hold regular family devotionals, and involve them in the church where they will be brought into contact with others who share a love for the Lord. Watch over what they are learning at school and ensure that they get a Christian perspective to offset the world's. Most importantly, be an example to them in your life, that they may see God in and through you.

Scriptural Examples

Cain. He was thought to be a son of promise who would deliver people from the curse, but he murdered his brother Abel and was sorrowful only about his punishment. Cain was truly a grief to Adam and a bitterness to Eve (Gen. 3:15; 4:1-16).

Esau and his wives. He brought much grief to Isaac and Rebekah. Esau even married Canaanite women, which displeased his father (Gen. 26:34-35; 28:8-9).

Absalom. In Absalom's treachery, he brought great grief to David, particularly in his own foolish death (2 Sam. 18:33).

Timothy. Here is a son that was a joy, and not a bitterness, to her that bore him. His mother, Eunice, evidently trained Timothy from infancy in the Holy Scriptures, and the result was the sincere faith of a man of God (2 Tim. 1:5; 3:15).

Prayer of Application

Lord, give me discernment in bringing up my children. May I always discipline them in the context of loving patience, remembering that my ultimate desire is for their salvation.

Respect Everyone, Chiefly Those in Authority

It is not good to punish an innocent man, or to flog officials for their integrity (Prov. 17:26).

The words "not good" represent a gross understatement. It would be better read "utter abomination," for both the ill treatment of the innocent and the assault upon righteous authority are abominations in God's sight (Prov. 17:15).

Every man and woman, rich or poor, slave or free, tall or short, fat or thin, be they black, white, brown, or whatever, is made in the image of God (Gen. 1:26). For that reason all are worthy of proper respect and just treatment. It is an honor to God to set the innocent free as surely as it is to condemn the guilty (Isa. 5:23). We honor the Creator by doing so.

It is particularly important to treat those in authority in the same way, whether in the home, the church, in business, or in the realm of politics. This is even more intensely true when these people rule in integrity. Our words should rather be offered to God in prayer for their strength, encouragement, and righteous administration (1 Tim. 2:1-2).

Scriptural Examples

Joseph and his brothers. They were jealous of his relationship to Jacob. He had "snitched" on them. But the sale of Joseph into slavery was total injustice. Not only did it punish Joseph unjustly, but also Jacob in the loss of his son (Gen. 37:18-24).

The prophets and Israel. They called out to God's people to repent and turn from their wicked ways, but the people of Israel treated them unjustly and killed them (Acts 7:51-52).

Paul and Ananias. When struck in the mouth by Ananias, Paul lashed back with a stinging rebuke of this Jewish leader. When he found out that it was the High Priest that he cursed, Paul apologized and quoted Exodus 22:28, that one is not to speak evil of the ruler of the people (Acts 23:2-5).

Prayer of Application

Lord, thank You for the dignity Your image brings. May I respect the dignity of every person and may those who exercise authority over me rule in integrity and in Your wisdom.

Seek a Restrained Tongue

27) A man of knowledge uses words with restraint, and a man of understanding is even-tempered. 28) Even a fool is thought wise if he keeps silent, and discerning if he holds his tongue (Prov. 17:27-28).

Normally I don't have a lot to say. But sometimes I run off at the mouth for no apparent reason. In the words of that modern proverb, I put my mouth in gear and leave my brain in neutral. Then these proverbs will generally pop into my mind. That's as it should be.

Our Lord had an amazing capacity to answer wisely and briefly. He exhorted us to be careful of casting our pearls before swine (Matt. 7:6), to be discerning in our speech when in the company of unbelievers. But it is in times of pressure, when the heat is turned up in our lives, that we most often need to remember to restrain our tongues. It is in precisely such times as these that Jesus portrayed for us what is exemplary conduct in God's sight. Have the wisdom to keep silent.

Scriptural Examples

The prophet to Amaziah. The prophet accused the king of idolatry. When the king threatened to kill him, the prophet wisely stopped speaking, stating only what God had determined to do (2 Chron. 25:15-16).

Nehemiah. The people complained that their wealthier brothers were foreclosing on their fields. Nehemiah was very angry. Rather than speaking harshly, he held back his anger and brought repentance and restoration (Neh. 5:1-12).

Jesus. The scribes and Pharisees continually tested Jesus with questions intended to trap Him. Jesus was astonishing in His succinct and restrained responses. When they asked for a sign from heaven, He said that Jonah was the only sign that their generation would get. When they asked Him if they should pay taxes to Rome, His answer amazed them (Matt. 16:1-4; 22:15-22).

Prayer of Application

Father, grant me the restrained and wise speech of Jesus. To the poor and afflicted He spoke words of loving-kindness, but to those who opposed Him, calm words of rebuke.

Chapter Eighteen

Knowing God: His Goodness

God's goodness may be seen in nature for anyone who cares to look. We see it in the beauty of the earth, in the tiny creatures that abound, and in the intricate design of flowers and crystals. We see it in the rainstorm that brings life to the plants of the fields, and the fresh air that God lets us breathe. In spite of the fact that people are innately God's enemies, He provides us with many good things. Many, though, "show contempt for his kindness, not realizing that God's kindness leads [them] toward repentance" (Rom. 2:4).

Proverbs 18:10 says of God's goodness, "The name of the Lord is a strong tower; the righteous run to it and are safe." God's goodness underlies His grace to those who run to Him for safety. God's "name" stands for the complete manifestation of God to His people. In other words, His name is who He is.

God's goodness refers to both His character and His actions. God always does what is good because He is good. He cannot be anything but good. As Jesus said, "Every good tree bears good fruit" (Matt. 7:17). My family began our children's dinnertime prayer with the words, "God is great, God is good." God is goodness and the fountain of all goodness. Everything God does is good. To accuse God of evil or anything short of perfect goodness is sin.

Beware the Opinions of the Selfish Fool

1) An unfriendly man pursues selfish ends; he defies all sound judgment. 2) A fool finds no pleasure in understanding but delights in airing his own opinions (Prov. 18:1-2).

Let me try to restate this proverb in a positive way: "A godly man pursues unselfish ends; he manifests sound judgment. He finds great pleasure in understanding and delights in the full counsel of God." The fool is exactly the opposite. He doesn't listen to the counsel of his Creator, but only to his own opinions. Why? Because he itches to pursue his own selfish purposes. He wants to be self-directed—autonomous.

The KJV says, "Through desire a man, having separated himself, seeketh and intermeddleth with all wisdom. A fool hath no delight in understanding, but that his heart may discover itself." There is a sense in which both the godly person and the fool seek to be separate—the godly person unto holiness and the fool unto selfishness. Why? Because the fool loves darkness and hates the light of God's Word (John 3:19-20). When you hear a fool's opinion, consider the source.

Scriptural Examples

The Nazirites. Separated unto the Lord, they were called to lives of abstinence and holiness. Samson was a Nazirite, as was Samuel, and apparently John the Baptist (Num. 6:1-21; Judg. 13:5; 1 Sam. 1:11; Luke 1:15).

The returning Israelites. The Israelites and others who returned to Jerusalem from exile in Babylon separated themselves from the unclean practices of their Gentile neighbors in order to celebrate the Passover and seek the Lord (Ezra 6:21).

The rich fool. He delighted himself in his selfishness and pride. He aired his own opinion that he had it made and could take life easy and "eat, drink, and be merry." But God had other plans for this foolish man (Luke 12:16-20).

Prayer of Application

Heavenly Father, bless those in pulpits who stand against the foolish, opinionated voices in America to teach the full counsel of God. Strengthen them and increase their number.

Warn Others of the Shame of Despising God

When wickedness comes, so does contempt, and with shame comes
disgrace (Prov. 18:3).

Wickedness has at its heart the contempt of God and His Word. From the beginning, Satan cast his shadow of doubt across the words of the Lord: "Did God really say…?" (Gen. 3:1). Even today, people calling themselves Christians echo this deceit in their denial of the objective truth of Holy Scripture. Mere humans add their words to the Word, subtract words from the Word, and twist the clear meaning of the Word to accommodate their own desires. Shame and disgrace await them.

Another way that people show contempt for God is in their denial of His gentle patience, love, and long-suffering, which is intended to lead them to repentance (Rom. 2:4). They deny the love and patient suffering of the Lord Jesus. Instead, His precious name has become a swear word and a thing of contempt. But just as God has grafted you and me as wild olive branches (Rom. 11:17), He can do the same for them. Warn people of the awful shame of the contempt of God and His Word.

Scriptural Examples

Adam and Eve. They met face-to-face with wickedness in the form of the serpent, who showed contempt for God's words. Their rebellion led first to shame as they hid from God, and then to disgrace as they were ushered out of their garden home into an unfriendly land of thorns and thistles (Gen. 3).

Cain. In contempt for God and his brother Abel, Cain murdered his brother. God brought shame upon the shameless Cain and exiled him to be a restless wanderer (Gen. 4:1-16).

Judas Iscariot. Judas walked with the Savior for three years and then contemptuously betrayed Him to His accusers for 30 pieces of silver. No name in history is viewed with more scorn and disgrace than the name of Judas Iscariot (Matt. 26:24).

Prayer of Application

Lord Jesus, thank You for Your grace that saved me. Give me the strength now to warn others of the fate that awaits those who hold You in contempt, that they also might be saved.

Let Your Words Spring from Depths of Wisdom

The words of a man's mouth are deep waters, but the fountain of wisdom is a bubbling brook (Prov. 18:4).

We have here the storehouse and the delivery of wisdom. As we mature in Christ, we store up the wisdom of God (Ps. 119:11). It becomes a deep reservoir of truth and "uncommon" sense, ready to spring forth when the need arises.

The words we speak reveal our heart. If it is filled with pollution, foolish words will gush out. If filled with the truth of God's Word, our words will be a well-spring of wisdom, bringing up life and truth for every situation and need.

First, our words will honor God, bringing glory to His name. They will point the way to His salvation and edify our brothers and sisters. Second, our words will heal, bringing justice, unity and peace to our neighbors. Third, our words will provide loving guidance and encouragement for others.

Pray that your words will be as a crystal clear mountain spring, welling up from a deep and ever renewed reservoir of the heart, bringing refreshment and life to those around you.

Scriptural Examples

Jethro. Moses' father-in-law saw that Moses' role as judge was too much for him, so he offered wisdom out of the depths of his understanding and advised Moses to appoint capable men to assist him in the task (Ex. 18:11-24).

Solomon. The queen of Sheba came to visit and brought with her some tough questions to test his wisdom. She was amazed at the depth of the wisdom she found (1 Kings 10:1-7).

Gamaliel. This Pharisee stood up in front of the Sanhedrin and wisely addressed them regarding the persecution of Christians. He said that if their teaching was of God, there was nothing they could do to stop it. I don't know whether Gamaliel ever became a believer, but he spoke with godly wisdom (Acts 5:33-40).

Prayer of Application

Father, how Your wisdom thrills my heart and satisfies my soul. Create in me a deep reservoir of Your love and truth, and let the words of my mouth give out that which is in my heart.

Seek Justice in a World of Injustice

It is not good to be partial to the wicked or to deprive the innocent of justice (Prov. 18:5).

God showed how deeply He is concerned with justice when He sent Jesus to the cross to pay the just penalty for our sins. He did not set aside justice in granting us mercy. That should strike terror in the heart of the non-believer. Without Christ, justice means eternal punishment. The examples below all surround events in and near a city of Manasseh, which had a history of injustice and brutality.

Scriptural Examples

Dinah and the Shechemites. The sons of Jacob dealt cruelly and unjustly with the people of Shechem following their sister's seduction by Shechem, son of Hamor (Gen. 34:1-30).

Joseph and Shechem. Jacob sent Joseph to the vicinity of Shechem to look for his brothers. On his arrival, they threw him into a well. They then plotted his death, but instead sold him into slavery to a passing caravan of Ishmaelites (Gen. 37:12-28).

Shechem: It was a "city of refuge" which would serve justice as a protection of those accused of murder, until their innocence or guilt could be proven (Josh. 20:7).

Joshua and Shechem. Joshua called the people there to decide if they would serve the Lord of justice or foreign gods. The people chose the Lord, so Joshua put up a monument against them should they prove to be untrue (Josh. 24:1-28).

Abimelech and Shechem. Gideon's son unjustly murdered his 70 brothers at Ophrah. He was crowned king by the people of Shechem before being mortally wounded (Judg. 9).

Rehoboam and Shechem. Solomon's son made himself king in Shechem and promised to deal unjustly with the people. The kingdom became divided (1 Kings 12:1-24; 14:21-31).

Murderers near Shechem. Hosea told of marauders who murdered people on the road to Shechem (Hos. 6:9).

Prayer of Application

Father, thank You for sending Christ to die on the cross to pay the penalty for my sins. Help me to emulate Your passion for justice, Lord, by living my life in obedience to Your Word.

The Fool's Tongue Will Self-Destruct

6) A fool's lips bring him strife, and his mouth invites a beating.
7) A fool's mouth is his undoing, and his lips are a snare to his
soul (Prov. 18:6-7).

Here is the litmus test of the fool. Listen to what he says. Is he looking for an argument? Do his words stir up anger? Is he asking for a punch in the kisser? If the answer is "Yes," it's a good bet you are listening to a fool. Fools love contention and will be afflicted by the very words they utter (Ps. 64:8; 107:17).

The spiritual person doesn't look for trouble. Strife arises out of fleshly lust (James 4:12) as the selfish heart seeks to expand its borders at the expense of others. But Christ calls us to love our neighbors as we naturally love ourselves (Matt. 22:39). To love one's neighbor means to seek what is best for him, even if it comes at the expense of our own selfish desires.

The natural person seeks to please himself. He wants to destroy God and anyone else who gets in his way with his weapon of choice, his tongue. In the end, it will prove to be a trap he set for himself, as he is judged by his own words.

Scriptural Examples

The men of Succoth and Peniel. Gideon's army was exhausted in their pursuit of the Midianites Zeba and Zalmunna. They stopped at Succoth and Peniel and asked for bread. Gideon was foolishly taunted and his request refused. After Gideon and his men had routed the Midianites and captured their two kings, he returned and took revenge (Judg. 8:4-17).

Daniel's false accusers. These men, plotting to bring Daniel down, caused King Darius to issue a decree that if anyone prayed to any god except the king he would be thrown in the lions' den. Then finding Daniel in prayer, they had him thrown in with the lions. But when he emerged untouched, Darius had Daniel's false accusers put on the lions' menu (Dan. 6).

Prayer of Application

Father, I have been assailed with the fool's tongue. Help me to respond in a godly way should it ever happen again. May Your Holy Spirit control my lips, giving me the words to say.

Speak Only Good of Your Neighbor

The words of a gossip are like choice morsels; they go down to a man's inmost parts (Prov. 18:8).

While I was in the army I took a course in first aid. I learned that the most fearful wound one could suffer in battle was a bullet or piece of shrapnel to the stomach. Not just painful, the stomach wound usually caused a torturous death unless hospital care was at hand. Such are the words of a gossip.

In another sense, the gossip's words go down to the stomach as food for the one who delights to ingest them. They become a part of him. Ultimately they are poisonous and will corrupt the hearer as surely as they do the speaker (Ps. 15:3).

In the film *Bambi*, Thumper the rabbit offered us this advice: "If you can't say anything good about somebody, don't say anything at all." Under normal circumstances, that is good advice. But there are times when we may have to warn our neighbor about an evil plot against him. Or perhaps that same neighbor's actions have been harmful to others and he needs our rebuke. In those instances, we must be absolutely sure of the accuracy of our information, and that our motives are pure. Our words must seek the ultimate benefit of all involved.

Scriptural Examples

Joseph. In spite of the overwhelming excellence of his life before God, Joseph sometimes came back from the fields and brought a bad report about his brothers to their father. As a consequence of Joseph's habit of tattling on them, his brothers built up resentment (Gen. 37:2).

Tobiah and Sanballat. This pair hired Shemaiah to convince Nehemiah to run to the temple and hide in fear of death at their hands. But Nehemiah realized they were behind Shemaiah's lies and had hired him as a talebearer to bring discredit upon those rebuilding the city of Jerusalem (Neh. 6:1-14).

Prayer of Application

Father, let my lips speak only loving words of truth and health. Let me only say what is necessary about my neighbor and then speak only words of peace, seeking the welfare of all.

Be Diligent in Your Work

*One who is slack in his work is brother to one
who destroys* (Prov. 18:9).

In St. Augustine's *Confessions*, he painfully recalls when he and some other boys stole some pears. The thing that troubled him deeply was he wasn't hungry. It was pure vandalism. In San Diego where I live, as elsewhere in our nation, vandalism is rampant. There are crushed mailboxes, graffiti, and broken windows. But what does this have to do with being diligent? The proverb says the person who is slothful is a brother to the vandal.

In the world today much more harm is done through sloth than vandalism. God has given each of us gifts and talents to employ. We need to honor God by diligently using them.

The same principle applies to our work in Christian service. We are called to diligence in worship (1 Chron. 22:19), to study the Word (2 Tim. 2:15), to obedience (Deut. 6:17), to striving after perfection (Phil. 3:13-14), to good works (1 Tim. 3:10), and to making our calling more sure (1 Peter 1:10)—indeed, in all areas of life.

Scriptural Examples

The wise and foolish servants. Jesus tells of a master who left various sums of money in care of his three servants. The first two put theirs to work immediately. When the master returned, they both showed excellent profits. The third servant buried his in the ground. Then he accused his master of injustice and excused himself on the grounds that he feared such injustice. He was cast into outer darkness (Matt. 25:14-30).

Apollos. This man taught boldly about Jesus. He was diligent in Bible study and in the way of the Lord (Acts 18:24-25).

Onesiphorus. Paul prayed to the Lord for mercy for this man's family. He had shown great diligence in searching for Paul in Rome and in meeting his needs in jail (2 Tim. 1:16-17).

Prayer of Application

Lord, I pray I might receive a real spirit of diligence in all of the tasks I am given to do. May I always remember to "bring my brain" to work, that I may use it as You intended.

Trust Only in the Riches of Christ

10) The name of the Lord is a strong tower; the righteous run to it and are safe. 11) The wealth of the rich is their fortified city; they imagine it an unscalable wall (Prov. 18:10-11).

In these two proverbs we are allowed to see a big difference between the spiritual person and the natural person. The natural person in verse 11 thinks what he sees is the real world. The spiritual person knows that the real world is that which is unseen (2 Cor. 4:18). One trusts in his bank account, his real estate, or his stock portfolio, while the other trusts in the name and the riches of the Lord.

The natural person can see only this world and structures his plans around his brief time here. He fears that he won't have enough to last, so he spends his energies storing up for the future. But the riches he seeks are fleeting; not really a sure bet for the here and now (Prov. 23:5), and meaningless at death.

God has exalted the name of Jesus above every other name (Phil. 2:9). Ultimately, every knee will bow to Him (Phil. 2:10). But presently, we don't see this happening (Heb. 2:8). The spiritual person accepts the Lord by faith, and his faith proves to him both the unseen and the future reign of his Savior (Heb. 11:1). He longs for another world wherein dwells righteousness (Heb. 11:16) and runs to the strong tower of Christ.

Scriptural Examples

The people of Babel. These people built a city with a prominent tower that reached to the heavens as their security and fortress. But God came down and confused their languages and scattered them to the four winds (Gen. 11:4-8).

Nebuchadnezzar. This king took pride in the city he had built for his own glory. But God had other plans for him. He sent him out of the city to eat grass like a wild animal, until the king acknowledged that only God is sovereign (Dan. 4:30-34).

Prayer of Application

Sovereign Lord, give me the faith to trust in You for my every need. I know that You are Lord of all of the wealth in the world. Keep me from trusting in this world's fleeting riches.

Beware of Pride that Goes Before a Fall

Before his downfall a man's heart is proud, but humility comes before honor (Prov. 18:12).

I lived through the truth of this verse. When I was saved in 1971, I was with a large commercial real estate brokerage firm. In 1972, I decided to leave that organization and start my own development company. God had been "real smart" to save me, and I was going to "cut a wide swath" for Him, making lots of money for His kingdom. My real motives, of course, were to pridefully create a name for myself, and to live a life of luxury.

Three years later I owed more money than I ever could hope to repay. I moved my family to Florida in order to earn a living. There, for the next five years, God continued to humble me. Returning to San Diego, I started a business in 1981 with only an idea and virtually no money. God has prospered that company and has allowed me to pay my development debts.

No longer does honor from others appeal to me. I have learned much in the school of God's discipline, the most important lesson being that one should live his life for God alone. If the Lord God wants to honor me, that's His business. My business is to humbly obey Him.

Scriptural Examples

Moses. We are told here that Moses was a very humble man, more so than any man who was on the earth. God lifted him up in high honor because of his meekness (Num. 12:3).

Uzziah. This king of Judah became very prideful. He entered the temple to burn incense to the Lord, an activity only allowed the priests, and God struck him with leprosy. He carried that disease until the day he died (2 Chron. 26:16-21).

Satan. Described in these verses as the "king of Tyre," Satan is said to have become proud of his beauty, so his wisdom was corrupted. God threw him out of heaven (Ezek. 28:11-17).

Prayer of Application

Heavenly Father, search my heart for the pride that it holds and remove it from me. Place in me a humble spirit that I might only boast in You, and of Your grace and providence.

Weigh All of the Facts

He who answers before listening—that is his folly and his shame
(Prov. 18:13).

Formerly when I read this proverb I thought it dealt with finishing other people's sentences. But there is a much deeper meaning here regarding proper judgments. The fool believes anything he's told (Prov. 17:4; 14:15), and because of his pride his mind is unlikely to be changed when faced with the facts.

Like any business organization, my company has had its share of rumor mongers in the past who stirred up dissension. During a siege of such gossip a few years ago, we established "Operation Truth," a program roughly derived from Matthew 18:15-18. When gossip is heard, the hearer is to take the talebearer to his immediate superior, where the tale is to be traced back to its beginning and the truth discovered. It has worked.

Listen carefully to all parties involved. Probe for salient facts as opposed to mere opinions. Apart from that depth of investigation, don't believe anything you hear from a gossip.

Scriptural Examples

Solomon. He listened carefully to each side disputing the motherhood of a baby. He asked a probing question, the answer to which made all the difference (1 Kings 3:16-28).

Zophar the Naamathite. Job's friends unjustly accused him regarding the source of his troubles. It was partly due to their failure to listen and weigh all of the facts (Job 20:1-3; 21:1-6).

The crowd in Jerusalem. Paul spoke to this hostile crowd. They listened quietly until he said that God had sent him to take the gospel to Gentiles, then they went berserk (Acts 22:1-23).

The Great Judge. God is patient and forebearing, but He is saving up our every word and deed (Matt. 12:36) for the day when He'll open up the books and call all of us to the eternal court of law (Heb. 4:13; Rom. 14:10b).

Prayer of Application

Lord, so often my sinful mind wants to judge something before I have weighed all of the facts. Keep me from prejudging, Lord, and help me to distrust any gossip I may hear.

Be Strengthened by the Indwelling Spirit

A man's spirit sustains him in sickness, but a crushed spirit who can bear (Prov. 18:14)?

The natural person's strength of spirit in infirmity is often amazing. Acts of heroism in battle, stoicism in the face of poverty, a resignation to pain and sickness—all of these speak to the strength that God puts in us. But it only goes so far. The Christian has far greater resources, particularly when the natural spirit within him lies crushed. A crushed spirit may sink the natural person, but the Christian has hope in it.

In today's world, depression, guilt, and shame send the natural person to his psychologist or psychiatrist. There he is given treatment that may help him temporarily. But the spiritual person has the additional power of Christ's strengthening Spirit within (Eph. 3:16). The Spirit heals our crushed spirits by taking us to the Cross, where we see ourselves as we really are: despicable and full of sin. There, by God's grace, while we were His enemies, Christ died for us (Eph. 2:5). Christ alone is the ultimate cure for the crushed spirit. Go to Him, confess your sin, be cleansed of guilt, and receive His healing (Isa. 53:5).

Scriptural Examples

Job. In the midst of infirmity Job still praised God. God allowed Satan to crush Job's spirit until he cursed the day of his birth. Later, Job had a renewed hope in God, saying, "Though he slay me, yet will I trust him" (Job 1:21; 3:1; 13:15).

Paul. He knew that the Spirit within was sufficient for all of the adversity he would ever face. He boasted in his infirmities so Christ's strength might abound in him (2 Cor. 12:9-10).

The martyrs. These men and women down through the ages have found peace in the arms of Christ and the hope they had in Him. They were more than conquerors (Rom. 8:37) because of the Spirit that was within them (Heb. 11:35-39).

Prayer of Application

Heavenly Father, thank You for Your Holy Spirit. Even though I may face a crushed spirit, which sinks me to the depths of mourning, I will not fear, for You will uphold me even then.

Diligently Seek the Knowledge of God

The heart of the discerning acquires knowledge; the ears of the wise seek it out (Prov. 18:15).

Notice that it is the *heart* of the discerning that acquires knowledge and not merely his mind. This is spiritual knowledge. It is the knowledge of God and knowledge that comes from God. Secular knowledge is important, but without knowledge of God, mere secular knowledge is "chasing after the wind" (Eccl. 1:16-17).

Those who get this knowledge thirst for more. In today's world, the Christian has a tremendous opportunity to gain scriptural knowledge. The person who sticks to a diet of milk and doesn't mature to solid food (Heb. 5:11-14) by acquiring and practicing the knowledge of God is without excuse.

But we must never forget its true source is God. We need to ask Him for it (James 1:5). Then we need to ask for proper application of it. Otherwise, knowledge just feeds a person's pride. The knowledge that comes from above is proven by the good deeds and humility of the one receiving it (James 3:13-17).

Scriptural Examples

Adam and Eve. The first couple sought knowledge apart from their Creator. They ate of the tree of the knowledge of good and evil and found it to be a curse, not a blessing (Gen. 2:9; 3:6).

Bezalel. This man was given by the Spirit the knowledge of how to make artistic designs and all kinds of crafts. Bezalel and his assistant, Oholiab, used this knowledge to glorify God in the construction of the tabernacle (Ex. 31:3-6).

Daniel and his friends. God gave them knowledge in all kinds of literature and learning. Also, to Daniel He gave the ability to understand visions and dreams (Dan. 1:17).

The disciples. Jesus testified that God had given these followers, and all believers, the knowledge of the secrets of the Kingdom (Matt. 13:11) and the knowledge of salvation (Luke 1:77).

Prayer of Application

Father, how I long for the knowledge and wisdom that only You can give. I pray that You will encourage my diligence in its acquisition and apply it to my heart by Your Spirit.

Use Gifts with Discretion

A gift opens the way for the giver and ushers him into the presence of the great (Prov. 18:16).

In Proverbs 17:8 and 23, we saw the destructive power of a gift (*sohad*) to pervert justice. The word for gift here is *mattan* and is probably not to be construed to mean a bribe. Gifts can also be in keeping with good social form, because they provide opportunity to show kindness, respect, and friendship.

The motive behind a gift is all-important. In my business I've always been distrustful of gifts. Perhaps I have just been overly-concerned with the giver's motive. We should use discretion and be sure our motives for bestowing a gift on someone are innocent and not for some hidden, selfish reason.

There is another way to view this proverb: as dealing with the gifts God gives us (1 Cor. 12:4-11; Rom. 12:6-8). The application of diligence to the development and perfection of our gifts from God will allow us to become of real value in this world, and cause us to stand before great people. We need first to identify God's gifts to us and then be diligent in perfecting them.

Scriptural Examples

Eliezer. Abraham's servant asked the Lord for guidance in finding a bride for Isaac. He gave Rebekah gold jewelry and was welcomed into Laban's house (Gen. 24:22-33).

Jacob. Jacob presented his estranged brother Esau with a peace offering because Jacob was not sure how his brother would receive him since he had stolen Esau's birthright (Gen. 32:17-21; 33:1-11).

Jacob. He sent some nuts, honey, balm, spices, and myrrh for the man who held the key to the food in Egypt, food which his family so desperately needed (Gen. 43:11).

Jesse. David's father told his son to take food to his brothers in the Israelite army's camp and at the same time gave him a gift of 10 cheeses for their commanding officer (1 Sam. 17:17-18).

Prayer of Application

Father, give me the wisdom to know when a gift would be appropriate. Keep my motives pure and allow me the practice only when it is fitting. Thank You for all of Your great gifts.

Listen to Both Sides of the Story

The first to present his case seems right, till another comes forward and questions him (Prov. 18:17).

If you have ever served on a jury you understand this principle readily. Following the prosecutor's presentation of his case, there may have been no doubt in your mind that the accused was guilty. But then the defense attorney began to present evidence which cast a doubt on your premature judgment. Later, justice was served because you and your fellow jurors weighed all the evidence in the case and made a fair and impartial decision based upon all the evidence.

To get all the facts is important in many human relationships. Counselors need to get each partner's story in order to help a rocky marriage. Parents need to be armed with all the facts before punishing a child. Employers should ensure against unfair discipline or termination. We all need to shun gossip that gives only one side of a story and seeks to harm its victim.

Scriptural Examples

Potiphar. He only listened to his wife's side of the story and sent Joseph to jail. A miscarriage of justice occurred because only her evidence was heard (Gen. 39:7-20).

Saul and Samuel. Saul told Samuel that he had destroyed the Amalekites, when actually he had spared their king and many sheep and cattle. Samuel's review of the evidence and some cross examination got to the truth (1 Sam. 15:7-24).

David, Ziba, and Mephibosheth. Ziba accused his master, Mephibosheth, of treason against King David, and on his testimony alone David gave him all of Mephibosheth's property. Later, David would see his error (2 Sam. 16:1-4; 19:26-30).

Solomon. Two women each laid claim to a small child. Weighing the verbal evidence before him, Solomon's wise decision was just (1 Kings 3:16-28).

Prayer of Application

Lord, keep me from prejudging any situation until I have all of the facts, and let my judgment be fair to all concerned. Give me discernment and wisdom to discover the truth.

Seek and Accept God's Will in Controversies

Casting the lot settles disputes and keeps strong opponents apart
(Prov. 18:18).

The lot was discussed in Proverbs 16:33 as a divine conduit of the will of God. Here we see it solving disagreements. The lot is no longer used. In fact, we don't even know what it originally looked like. We do know that it was used by God's people, the Babylonians (Est. 3:7), and other Gentiles (Jonah 1:7).

Today we have another way to seek God's will in controversies and to bring peace to the household of God. It is God's Holy Word (2 Peter 1:19). It is profitable for "teaching, rebuking, correcting, and training in righteousness"(2 Tim. 3:16).

This is one reason why it is extremely important not to be "unequally yoked" with unbelievers (2 Cor. 6:14). Between Christians, the Bible is the foundation of reconciliation. But what if one of the parties refuses to obey it? Then there may be no mutual solution. The Word says that righteousness and wickedness have nothing in common (2 Cor. 6:14).

Scriptural Examples

King Saul. Earlier, Samuel had cast lots among all the tribes of Israel in order to select a king from among the people. The lot fell to Benjamin. Then Saul was taken. By its use, sinful presumption and error were avoided (1 Sam. 10:20-24).

Saul and Jonathan. Jonathan didn't hear his father's order and ate some honey during the battle. He later was chosen by lot. The men of the army, however, would not let Saul slay his son, who had led them with courage and daring (1 Sam. 14:24-42).

Jesus. The lot was used by Gentile soldiers to divide Jesus' garments at the cross (John 19:23-24). Psalm 22:18 predicted they would do so hundreds of years before the actual event.

The disciples. Later, the lot was also used to fill Judas' vacated position among them. Matthias was chosen (Acts 1:26).

Prayer of Application

Father, help me to become more familiar with the practical teachings of Your Word, so that when disagreements arise I may be able to apply its righteous judgment and bring peace.

Seek Unity in the Household of God

An offended brother is more unyielding than a fortified city, and disputes are like the barred gates of a citadel (Prov. 18:19).

Bitter splits have been witnessed in the church through the centuries, where Christians are offended to such a degree that they set up barred gates between one another and close the citadel door to reconciliation. But God's will for His Church is that it should be unified, not divided (Rom. 15:5; Eph. 4:13).

Why has there been such disunity? The answer, I believe, is in a simple three letter word: sin. Major divisions can come as people turn away from the Word of God, stripping the Word of its authority. While many denominational differences seem minor, and even silly, sometimes pride keeps us separated.

How do we solve the problem? Paul says that the solution is in love (Col. 3:14). This is not love that seeks unity at any price, but the love that keeps short accounts, confronts in humility, listens carefully and humbly to the other person's position, forgives readily, and understands the Word according to its truth, with faith in its accuracy and sufficiency.

Scriptural Examples

Joseph and his brothers. Joseph offended his brothers by tattling to their father, Jacob. Then he implied that they would one day bow down to him. Years later, by the grace and purposes of God, there would be reconciliation (Gen. 37:2-11).

Israel and Judah. This split in the house of God would continue to divide God's people for years (2 Chron. 13:16-17).

Christians of Antioch. Circumcision sparked their debate. With the help of Paul, Barnabas, and Peter, reason and the grace of God brought peace (Acts 15:1-22).

Paul and Barnabas. Sadly, Paul and Barnabas also had a sharp dispute. It apparently ended with the brothers parting company and going their opposite ways (Acts 15:37-40).

Prayer of Application

Father, I pray that I might live in peace and unity with my Christian brothers and sisters. Help me to be a peacemaker in the house of God by humbly submitting to Your Word.

Speak Words of Life

20) From the fruit of his mouth a man's stomach is filled; with the harvest from his lips he is satisfied. 21) The tongue has the power of life and death, and those who love it will eat its fruit　(Prov. 18:20-21).

The old saying, "Sticks and stones may break my bones, but words will never hurt me" is about as far from the truth as a saying can get. Words can be devastating, even as we see in the verses above, unto death. Conversely, there are words of comfort, blessing, encouragement, and life. We need to speak those.

It might be revealing for each of us to carry along a tape recorder for a week. I know I say words I wish I could take back into my mouth. Like the prophet Isaiah, I think most of us would want to cry out, "I am a man of unclean lips" (Isa. 6:5).

As Christians, we have been entrusted with the true Word of Life (Phil. 2:16). In all of our speaking we need to hold forth the Word, so that we, as Paul exhorts us, may boast that our labor and sojourn on this earth were not in vain (1 Cor. 15:58).

But how do we do it? First, we are to diligently study the Word, making it a part of our daily lives (2 Tim. 2:15). Then we need to ask God to restrain our tongues, causing our lips to be consecrated to the One who is the Life, our Lord Jesus.

Scriptural Examples

Melchizedek. This king of Salem was priest of the Most High God. He blessed Abraham on his return from defeating the kings who had kidnapped Lot and his family. His words of blessing are followed in the text by Abraham's receipt of the promise of God for a son and offspring more numerous than the stars. God also gave Abraham the assurance of justification by grace, through faith. Surely the blessing of Melchizedek, a type of the High Priesthood and Kingship of Christ, were words of life to Abraham (Gen. 14:19–15:6; Heb. 5:6-10).

Prayer of Application

Dear Lord, create in me a tongue of life from which flows the blessings of the Word of God. May I seek only good for my neighbor, that I may be a true ambassador of Christ.

Choose Your Spouse with Great Care

He who finds a wife finds what is good and receives favor from the Lord (Prov. 18:22).

The key to this proverb is that a good wife, or a good husband, one who will provide mutual support, encouragement, sympathy, and love, is from the Lord's favor. A wife or husband who doesn't do these things isn't necessarily good at all, and in fact can make his or her spouse miserable.

How does one go about getting this favor from God? First of all, through prayer (Gen. 24:12-14), the medium God has given us to request blessings from Him. Second, we may receive a good spouse through the wisdom God gives us in His Word. We should marry only in the Lord and avoid being unequally yoked with unbelievers (1 Cor. 7:39). Third, we should be careful not to rely too much upon the physical attractiveness of a potential partner, but rather seek out qualities that may be seen in godly men and women in Scripture. Finally, as married people, we should always seek to bless our partner in all things, as heirs together of God's gracious gift of life (1 Peter 3:7).

Scriptural Examples

Manoah's wife. This woman, whose name Scripture does not give us, was the mother of Samson and a true blessing to her husband. When a visit from the angel of the Lord promised her a son, Manoah was afraid because they had seen God face-to-face. His wife uttered words of comfort and wisdom that calmed him (Judg. 13:1–14:3).

Boaz' wife. For me, Ruth is the finest example of womanhood in the Old Testament. Her loyalty, simplicity, beauty of soul, humility, obedience, faith, and love are exemplary (the book of Ruth).

Job's wife. In contrast, this godly man had a foolish wife. As her husband sat stricken in affliction, she urged him to "curse God and die" (Job 2:9-10).

Prayer of Application

Heavenly Father, help those who seek a spouse to do so prayerfully and with a sound mind, relying on You and Your Word. Thank You for my spouse, who is truly a gift of grace.

Even in Wealth, Be Dependent upon God

A poor man pleads for mercy, but a rich man answers harshly
(Prov. 18:23).

I was discharged from the Army and began my business career in 1964. I didn't really like the "dog-eat-dog" business world from the beginning, but stuck with it because I had a dream of financial independence.

The poor man in the verse above is dependent upon the rich man, who has no sympathy for his plight. He doesn't listen to his pleas for help and answers harshly. The rich man is selfish, which he thinks keeps him from becoming poor. How wrong he is.

The rich man fails to see he is totally indebted to God for every dime he has (Ps. 145:15-16; Matt. 6:26-33). When he dies, he will take none of it with him. If he is unsaved, he'll stand naked and penniless to face judgment (Acts 17:31). Then, though he may beg for mercy, he will not be heard (Luke 16:19-31).

In the years since 1964, I have seen that financial independence can be like a mirage that vanishes as you approach it. When we think we've got all the financial resources we need, we worry about losing them. We've just switched our dependence to a bank account. True independence, I've learned, comes from total dependence upon the living God. He is our stronghold and refuge, our very present help in trouble (Ps. 46:1).

Scriptural Examples

The prophet's widow and her husband's creditor. This poor woman asked Elisha to help her. Her dead husband's creditor was coming to take her two sons as his slaves. Through the providence of God her sons were not taken (2 Kings 4:1-7).

Lazarus and the rich man. Jesus told the story of a beggar who sat at the gate of a rich man. They both died. Lazarus entered "Abraham's bosom," but the rich man entered torment in hell. His trust in riches became a curse to him (Luke 16:19-26).

Prayer of Application

Dear Lord, thank You for the freedom and independence I have in my dependence upon You. You have given me Your Word, that I may know You and Your provision for me.

Be a Friend Like Our Heavenly Brother

A man of many companions may come to ruin, but there is a friend who sticks closer than a brother (Prov. 18:24).

Other translations state that the person who makes many friends invites destruction. Either way, we have real wisdom. In order to make friends, a person must reach out to others; but if he does so indiscriminately he invites problems. What good is it if a person's many friends desert him in times of trouble? He's worse off than the unfriendly person, because at least the latter knows where he stands. It is not the number of our friends that counts but the quality of such friendship.

As Christians, we need to seek true friendship only with those who share our faith. The bond that unites Christians is stronger than blood. My best friend in the Lord is also my natural brother. We are twice blessed.

But my brother and I have an even closer Friend. He is the Lord Jesus. He helps us in many ways: in escaping temptation (1 Cor. 10:13); in cheering us up (John 14:17); in comforting and healing us (Ps. 41:3); in dispelling our fears (Ps. 23:4); and in giving us the blessed hope of an eternal dwelling place with Him (John 17:24). Oh, to be like Him as a friend to others.

Scriptural Examples

Abishai, Benaiah, and Eleazar. While engaged in battle against the Philistines, David happened to mention how he would like some water from Bethlehem. These three slipped through the Philistine lines to get it for him (2 Sam. 23:13-17).

Eliphaz, Bildad, and Zophar. Job's three friends should be given some credit for sticking with him when he was down and out. We can't say the same for Job's wife and the rest of his family and servants (Job 2:9, 11-13; 19:11-13).

Priscilla and Aquila. These friends of Paul risked their lives for the great apostle (Rom. 16:3-4).

Prayer of Application

Dear Father, thank You for the Friend we have in Jesus. Strengthen me through His friendship, that I might be a true and trusted friend to those You have called me to serve.

Chapter Nineteen

God's Providence

God governs the universe "sustaining all things by his powerful word" (Heb. 1:3). God "gives all men life and breath and everything else" (Acts 17:25). We in the 20th century seem to have lost sight of this great truth of God's providential care for His creation. We speak of events happening by "chance" or "luck," as if those concepts really had any power of their own. But Jesus said "even the very hairs of your head are numbered" (Matt. 10:30). God governs His creation.

But, then, is God the author of sin? God forbid! We humans have been created with a will of our own and are responsible for our actions. We cause events but God makes the events we cause, even our sin, work to His glory. Proverbs 19:21 says, "Many are the plans in a man's heart, but it is the Lord's purpose that prevails." We may scheme and make plans, but it is God's will that will be done.

Consider Joseph's reaction to seeing his brothers who had sold him into slavery. Did he seek revenge for their actions against him? No. He knew God's providential hand was at work even in their sin. "Joseph said to them, 'Don't be afraid. Am I in the place of God? You intended to harm me, but God intended it for good to accomplish what is now being done, the saving of many lives' " (Gen. 50:19-20). Trust in the providential hand of the Lord.

Prefer Integrity to Riches

Better a poor man whose walk is blameless than a fool whose lips are perverse (Prov. 19:1).

In business as in life, a person is often faced with difficult decisions. For instance, suppose you found out that the company you manage uses a particular software on 10 computers, but has only purchased licenses for four. The chances that you will be discovered for this copyright infringement are slim indeed, and it will cost $2,100 to purchase the other six, which in turn will adversely affect the bottom line. What do you do? This proverb gives you the answer. Spend the money and let the bottom line suffer. Don't forfeit principle for pragmatism.

Wealth is honored more in our society than is the hidden heart of integrity. That's one reason why BMWs and big homes are popular. There's nothing wrong in owning a BMW or a big home, but in God's economy, the heart of integrity is worth much more. What good is it for a person to be rich in the things of the world but poor in the things of God? (Luke 12:21).

Scriptural Examples

Joseph and Potiphar's wife. What might have been viewed by some slaves as an opportunity for personal advancement, Joseph fled with his integrity intact (Gen. 39:8-12).

Shiprah, Puah, and Pharaoh. The midwives feared God more than they feared the perverse king, so they refused to commit sin by killing the newborn Hebrew boys (Ex. 1:15-19).

Peter and Simon Magus. Peter, in his integrity, rebuked Simon and his money and called upon him to repent of the perverseness and sin in his heart (Acts 8:18-23).

Paul, Barnabas, and the Lyconians. In Lystra, Paul healed a man who had never walked. The people called Paul and Barnabas "Hermes" and "Zeus" and proceeded to worship them. But the apostles would have none of it (Acts 14:8-15).

Prayer of Application

Father, sensitize my heart to keep Your commandments. Point out areas in my life that may deviate even slightly from truth, justice, or even the smallest breach of integrity.

Know God's Way First, Then Move Ahead

It is not good to have zeal without knowledge, nor to be hasty and miss the way (Prov. 19:2).

True integrity springs from the fear of the Lord, as does knowledge of Him (Ps. 111:10; Prov. 9:10). The person that lacks the knowledge of God is lost and is like the "beasts that perish" (Ps. 49:20). He has no proper direction for his life, no solution to his problem of guilt. He has no underpinnings of support in times of trouble, nor outside strength to bolster him. Principally, he lacks hope. Only the grave awaits.

But we who know God often act as if we do not. We may not apply His wisdom and commands to our lives (Heb. 5:12-14). We may act rashly and in haste, without thoughtfully and prayerfully seeking God's way. Carefully consider your actions and your words and compare them with God's Word. Then you won't be driven impulsively and won't need to apologize to others and to God for hasty and foolish behavior.

Scriptural Examples

Moses. He observed an Egyptian beating one of the Hebrew slaves and in rashness and haste murdered him, then buried his corpse in the sand. He fled Egypt (Ex. 2:11-15).

Joshua. Basking in the victories the Lord had delivered at Jericho and Ai, he acted rashly and hastily. Without consulting God, Joshua allowed the Gibeonites to live (Josh. 9:3-15).

David and Uzzah. When the ark of the covenant was recaptured, David put the ark on a cart, a hasty mistake as it was supposed to be carried between long poles (Ex. 25:27). The oxen stumbled and the ark began to fall. Uzzah reached out in haste to catch the ark, and God struck him dead (2 Sam 6:3-7).

The centurion on shipboard. Paul warned him that disaster awaited if they sailed on, but the centurion rashly decided otherwise. The ship was lost, yet without loss of life (Acts 27:6-22).

Prayer of Application

Father God, forgive me for my sometimes hasty words and actions. Strengthen me, Lord, in the knowledge of You through Your Word, that I might do Your will and not sin.

Beware of Accusing the Lord

A man's own folly ruins his life, yet his heart rages against the Lord (Prov. 19:3).

Here is a picture of the two-faced person. His own foolishness is the cause of his trouble, but he blames it on someone else, namely God. People who will not give God the time of day when things are going their way (Rom. 1:21), are the first to accuse Him when disaster or trouble strikes.

As Christians, we need to be careful not to accuse God of wrongdoing. By His grace He saved us; how shall He not freely give us all things? (Rom. 8:32). Every circumstance of our life is in perfect compliance with His will for us (Rom. 8:29-30) and is working to our ultimate benefit and to His glory.

All of this doesn't mean that nothing bad will ever happen to us. Many have lost children, jobs, loved ones or health, not understanding why God would let it happen to them. We may be tempted to blame God. But remember, God can see the end from the beginning and is working in all things according to His good purpose (Phil. 2:13). Therefore, let us trust Him in every circumstance, taking trouble and trial along with the blessings of life, and press on without murmuring (Phil. 2:14).

Scriptural Examples

Rachel. Rachel was jealous of her sister Leah and accused Jacob, screaming, "Give me children or I'll die." Her cry was really against God for her inability to conceive (Gen. 30:1-2).

The Israelites. Complaints against God began even before the people left Egypt (Ex. 5:21). They continued at the Red Sea (14:11-12); for lack of food (16:2-3); at the bitter waters of Marah (15:23-24); and for lack of water (17:2-3).

David. Following God's judgment upon Uzzah for steadying the ark of the covenant with his hand, David foolishly became very angry with the Lord (2 Sam. 6:7-8).

Prayer of Application

Lord, You have saved me by grace alone and are working all things out to the pleasure of Your will. Who am I to doubt and question You? Help me not to complain.

Beware of Economic Class Favoritism

4) Wealth brings many friends, but a poor man's friend deserts him. 6) Many curry favor with a ruler, and everyone is the friend of a man who gives gifts. 7) A poor man is shunned by all his relatives— how much more do his friends avoid him! Though he pursues them with pleading, they are nowhere to be found (Prov. 19:4, 6-7).

If you doubt the truth of these verses, try winning the lottery. "Friends" will come out of the woodwork. I once knew a man who became very wealthy. His gifts to charity were extraordinary. When the news broke that he was a fraud who was giving away his investors' funds, his "friends" sought to distance themselves far from him.

We sometimes think the salvation of a prominent person will greatly enhance God's work. That may or may not be true. God doesn't need anyone's money, social position, or popularity. God values people of faith who will humble themselves, pray, and serve others (Luke 22:26-27).

You might ask, "What about the Great Ruler, Jesus? Why don't more people curry His favor?" Good question. Christ holds out the riches of salvation to everyone free-of-charge. You'd think that people would be clamoring to receive them. But no! Why? Because most prefer riches to spend on their lusts (James 4:3).

Scriptural Examples

Elihu. This young man held his counsel until Job's friends had spoken. He said he would show partiality to no man because of his position. Why? Because he feared the Lord's retribution. Elihu was never criticized by God (Job 32:21-22).

The dinner party host. Jesus said we should not invite those from whom we seek favor or repayment. Then we will be repaid at the resurrection of the righteous (Luke 14:12-14).

Prayer of Application

Father, help me to look beyond the world's system of values to see the values You hold dear. All people, regardless of their place in society, have dignity because they are in Your image.

Beware the Consequences of the Selfish Lie

5) A false witness will not go unpunished, and he who pours out lies will not go free. 9) A false witness will not go unpunished, and he who pours out lies will perish (Prov. 19:5, 9).

Deceit is a common theme in Proverbs. Notice that in verse 5 the liar "will not go free," while in verse 9, we see his final forecast of doom. The truth is a fragile thing, and easily bent or broken. Shading the truth ever so slightly so the listener is deceived is a gross offense before God.

But what about times when lying actually preserves lives, such as those who protected Jews hiding from the Nazis before and during World War II? Is it always wrong to lie? Scripture itself has many instances where lies have been utilized for good and not for evil. I am reminded of the Egyptian midwives who lied to Pharaoh (Ex. 1:15-19). I think also of Ehud secretly presenting tribute to Eglon the Moabite king before dispatching him with a double-edged sword (Judg. 3:16-21).

The answer, I believe, lies in the motivation for the deed. If our motive is injustice, greed, convenience, or to elevate self, then lying is always wrong. But if our motives are selfless, we may find that, in wartime, deceiving the forces of evil is a weapon for good. But let's hope that we will never be forced to tell a lie.

Scriptural Examples

Pharaoh. Time after time Pharaoh lied as he promised to let God's people go. Only after the death of all the firstborn did Pharaoh do what he promised. But he was not to escape God's wrath. He soon went swimming in the Red Sea (Ex. 7-14).

The disobedient son. Jesus told this short parable. A man asked both his sons to work in his vineyard. One said "No," but then he later went to work. The second said that he would go, but never did. Which of the two did his father's will? The first. The second was a liar and a deserter (Matt. 21:30).

Prayer of Application

Sovereign Lord, keep my tongue from lies. Sometimes I am tempted to shade the truth just a little for a selfish motive. Strengthen me, Lord, that I may tell the truth in all such instances.

Find True Self-Esteem in Esteeming Others

He who gets wisdom loves his own soul; and who cherishes understanding prospers (Prov. 19:8).

What irony is here. We know wisdom begins with the fear of the Lord and ends in obedience to His commandments (Ps. 111:10). It is a path of selflessness, self-denial, and even self-loathing, not self-love (Luke 14:26). Yet the proverb says he who gets wisdom loves his own soul. How is this true?

As Jesus said, the person who seeks to save his life will lose it, and the one who seeks to lose his life for Christ's sake will find it (Matt. 16:25; Mark 8:35). Therefore, I find true love or esteem for my own soul, not through self-promotion, but through selfless devotion to the gospel and to others. Real "self-esteem," then, is really "other-esteem."

Our problem is not that we think too lowly of ourselves, but too highly. The Bible says people are desperately wicked (Jer. 17:9). We are dead in trespasses and sin (Eph. 2:1). But God, who is rich in mercy, makes us alive in Christ Jesus (Eph. 2:4-5). He opens our eyes to see our need for a Savior (Acts 13:48).

Receiving wisdom from God, the believer in Christ has a desire to walk according to his new nature. The new soul—regenerated by God—is to be loved, for it is the dwelling place of the Holy Spirit. This is the true wisdom which comes from God. The person who hates this wisdom harms himself and loves death (Prov. 8:36).

Scriptural Examples

Paul. Paul once put his confidence in the flesh and took pride in his fleshly wisdom. He claimed to be faultless in legalistic righteousness. He had very high self-esteem and loved his life as a zealous Jew. Then he had an encounter with Christ and his mind and heart changed. The things he formerly saw as wise, he now considered rubbish. He had found newness of life in Christ Jesus (Phil. 3:3-9).

Prayer of Application

Heavenly Father, thank You for the new heart You have implanted in me. By Your Spirit, help me to deny self and seek to obey Your command to love and exalt others.

Beware of Emulating the Exalted Fool

It is not fitting for a fool to live in luxury—how much worse for a slave to rule over princes! (Prov. 19:10).

In the life to come, government—indeed society itself—will exclude all fools. The righteous shall reign with Christ forever (2 Tim. 2:12). But such is not the case now. This sinful world is upside-down, and we see examples everywhere of fools who rise to the top of corporate ladders and to exalted positions in government while the righteous may be passed over.

We need to beware of such exalted fools, not as to what they might do to us but that we are not seduced into following them. It is easy to forget the promises of Scripture. When we see these fools exalted in the world, we may be tempted to emulate their tactics and strategies. Christian, resist the temptation. If you are called to wealth and high office, don't exalt yourself. Rather, exalt the One who put you there (Jer. 9:23-24)!

Scriptural Examples

Sheba, son of Bicri. This foolish servant sought to be king over Israel and led many of David's men to follow after him. Joab cornered the rebel in Abel Beth Maacah, a designated city of refuge. The people cut off Sheba's head and threw it down from the city wall to avoid disaster (2 Sam. 9:6-8).

Jeroboam. He was an enemy of Solomon in the latter's sinful, declining years. Jeroboam had been a diligent supervisor in the repair of Jerusalem's walls. Later, he became king and made two golden calves to keep the people from going up to Jerusalem to worship (1 Kings 11:26-28; 12:20, 25-33).

Zimri. One day, Elah, king of Israel, got drunk in the home of a subject. Zimri entered the home and assassinated him, setting himself up as king of Israel. He reigned seven days before he, too, was struck down by a fire that ironically had been set by his own hand (1 Kings 16:9-10, 15-19).

Prayer of Application

Lord, how I want to emulate Jesus and others who have emulated Him successfully down through the ages. Protect me from emulating those fools who are exalted by the world.

Turn Your "Rights" Over to God

A man's wisdom gives him patience; it is to his glory to overlook an offense (Prov. 19:11).

In Matthew 18:23-35, Jesus tells a parable about a servant who owed millions of dollars (10,000 talents) to his king. When he defaulted, the king ordered that he and his whole family be sold. The servant begged for mercy and was forgiven. Then, the servant went out, found those in debt to him and did not show them mercy. When the king found out, he threw the wicked servant to the torturers until he repaid all he owed.

Our debt to God because of sin has been forgiven by His grace. How can we who are forgiven fail to forgive others? Are we higher than God? Is our neighbor's meager offense against us greater than our infinite offenses against a righteous God? No.

We first need to understand the sovereignty of God in circumstances. He is using even the injustice against us to achieve His purposes. Understanding this, and that revenge is His, our anger should be assuaged. Overlook small offenses. If someone sins against you, you need to humbly bring it to his attention (Matt. 18:15). If he asks for forgiveness, you are to forgive him as God in Christ has forgiven us.

Scriptural Examples

Joseph. Joseph had every reason to be angry against his brothers, but in wisdom he confronted them. He told them not to be angry with themselves, but to know that God intended for good what they had planned for evil (Gen. 45:4-5; 50:20).

Jesus. He warned us about anger's kinship to murder (Matt. 5:21-22). He taught forgiveness and mercy, even toward enemies (Matt. 5:44-45). Most importantly, He lived a life that exemplified these qualities. When reviled and beaten He was calm, resting in His wisdom. On the cross He said, "Father, forgive them; for they know not what they do" (Luke 23:34 KJV).

Prayer of Application

Dear God, thank You for the forgiveness that is mine in Christ Jesus. Help me to be ready to forgive others by calmness in the face of injustice against me, knowing You are in control.

Flee the King's Wrath: Delight in His Favor

The king's wrath is as the roaring of a lion; but his favor is as dew upon the grass (Prov. 19:12 KJV).

The faithful king wants faithful subjects. His appropriate response to all who would rebel against his rule is wrath. The ancient kings were absolutely powerful. To incur their wrath was deadly—not unlike facing an angry lion. But the king's reward was as cool as the dew on a newly mown lawn.

You and I have a King like this. His name is Jesus and He seeks those who will share in His vision and purpose. But many under His reign rebel against Him and try to be their own authority. Their anarchy seeks to cast off His righteous restraint. They practice deceit and sin against Him constantly. His wrath will fall upon them with swift finality. But His favor is toward those who delight in doing His will. Surely His goodness and mercy shall follow them all the days of their lives and they will dwell in the house of the King forever (Ps. 23:6).

Scriptural Examples

King Xerxes. He threw a huge banquet to display his wealth and power. On the seventh day he sent for Queen Vashti to display her beauty. She refused to come. The king burned with anger. He banished Vashti from his presence forever. It was not a good idea to cross the ancient king (Est. 1:1-22).

King Xerxes. Following Vashti's departure, Esther became queen. She soon found herself in the position of having to seek an audience with the king. Anyone who did so risked immediate death, unless his golden scepter was extended to them. He did so. His favor was like dew on the grass (Est. 4:1-5:3).

King Xerxes. Haman found the full scope of the king's anger as he was hung on the same gallows that he had prepared for Mordecai (Est. 7:1-10). Mordecai, on the other hand, a loyal and worthy subject, found the king's favor (Est. 10:3).

Prayer of Application

Father, how I take joy in being included in Your Kingdom. Teach me to obey all of Your commands, dear Lord, that I might always find Your favor as fresh as dew upon the grass.

Seek the Lord's Blessing for Your Family

13) A foolish son is his father's ruin, and a quarrelsome wife is like a constant dripping. 14) Houses and wealth are inherited from parents, but a prudent wife is from the Lord (Prov. 19:13-14).

If the whole world stands in opposition to a person, yet he has a home that supports and honors him, he will be energized for the battle. But woe to the one who finds opposition both in the home and in the world. The foolish son can be a great calamity, but once old enough he can be tossed out on his ear. However, the contentious wife or husband must be endured.

The first phrase of verse 14 only emphasizes the second. While riches may be an inheritance from your father, a prudent wife or husband who supports, encourages, and loves his or her spouse is purely a gift from God.

Without God's rule over a household, life can be miserable. There may be peace for a while, but it is only a matter of time before situations develop that cause strain. Contentions like the continual dropping of a Chinese water torture may commence. Young single person, don't make the mistake of choosing the wrong spouse. Seek godliness in that person above all else.

Scriptural Examples

Ham: a foolish son. Ham's foolishness was a calamity to his father, Noah, and also to his son Canaan. What did Ham do? Noah got drunk and lay naked in his tent. Ham came in and saw him, then went out and gossiped to his brothers. They then backed into the tent and covered their father (Gen. 9:21-23).

Mrs. Lot: a contentious wife. When fleeing with her family from Sodom, Lot's wife looked back and was turned into a pillar of salt (Gen. 19:26). She was over-concerned with her possessions (Luke 17:30-32), and apparently looked back remembering the country club, her bridge club, and the garden parties of her favorite city (Gen. 19).

Prayer of Application

Dear Lord, thank You for the precious gift of faith. What a blessing it is to see this faith working itself out in godly families. Thank You for these oases in the midst of this sinful world.

Wake Up and Serve the Lord!

Laziness brings on deep sleep, and the shiftless man
goes hungry (Prov. 19:15).

It's no secret that slothfulness can result in poverty. The fate of the college freshman who parties all night should be no mystery to him. He will not be invited back for the second semester. The same is true of the worker who prefers sleep to earning a living for his family. He won't have a job very long.

But let's apply this proverb to our spiritual lives. Are we just going through the motions in God's service or is our faith a vibrant daily reality? Has spiritual sloth cast its deep sleep upon us so we are barren of fruit? Do we think laypeople simply hire pastors, then sit back and criticize them? If you are like me, those questions stir your conscience.

We need first the conviction that sloth or laziness in spiritual worship, prayer, Bible study, and service to God is utterly inconsistent with what the Bible teaches about personal godliness. Second, we need to ask God for forgiveness for our shortcomings in this area. Third, go on to the next proverb, 19:16, for the secret to successful Christian living.

Scriptural Examples

The Sodomites. God had a lot more against that city than sexual sin. They were prideful and arrogant. They ate too much and they practiced idleness in their apathy (Ezek. 16:49).

The Athenians. They heard Paul speak at the Areopagus. They spent their time doing nothing but talking and listening to the latest ideas. Let's avoid being like the Athenians and serve the Lord with enthusiasm (Acts 17:21).

Some Thessalonians. Paul had a word for these folks: "busybodies." It has been said that "some people in the church are about as active as termites and with the same result." Paul urged the Thessalonians to diligence (2 Thess. 3:11-13).

Prayer of Application

Father, forgive me for laziness. I know I have not served You as I ought. Empower me to please You in all things, wanting only Your glory and honor in all I do.

If You Love Christ, Obey Him

He who obeys instructions guards his life, but he who is contemptuous of his ways will die (Prov. 19:16).

Following His resurrection, Jesus asked Simon Peter three times, "Do you love me?" Each time after Peter had answered in the affirmative, Jesus said, "Feed my sheep" (John 21:15-17). Jesus was telling Peter his faith in Christ meant action. He was calling Peter and the others, as well as you and me, to be doers of the Word and not hearers only (James 1:22). Putting your faith to work is the secret of victorious Christian living.

Without Christ we can do nothing (John 15:5). Whoever lives by the truth comes to the light so it may be seen that his deeds have been done through God (John 3:21). He'll supply the opportunity, the strength, and the gifts to carry the work out through the power of the Holy Spirit working in us.

But what are Christ's commandments? Look first to Jesus' words in the four Gospels. Then observe the works of the apostles in Acts. Next, look carefully at the apostles' teachings in the books that make up the rest of the New Testament (John 14:26). Finally, compare all of this with the Ten Commandments (Ex. 20; Deut. 5) and the rest of the Old Testament. You will find that Christ's commandments don't omit any of the moral code found there but serve instead to crystallize it and enhance our understanding of it.

Scriptural Examples

Joshua. God commanded Moses that upon entering the land everyone living there was to be put to death. Moses passed this task on to Joshua, who carried it out, but not fully. The people later suffered for it (Josh. 10:40; 11:15).

The disciples. Jesus prayed for His disciples (and for the church) prior to His passion. He said He had revealed the Father to those the Father had given Him and they had obeyed the Father's Word (John 17:7).

Prayer of Application

Heavenly Father, I do love Jesus and I want to serve Him. By Your Word, teach me His commandments, then empower me by Your Holy Spirit to carry them out each day of my life.

Invest in the Poor

*He who is kind to the poor lends to the Lord, and He will reward him
for what he has done* (Prov. 19:17).

For those of you looking for a place to invest your money, what
safer place, or what greater return, than to invest in the poor? Your
investment will not be insured by the U.S. government but by
the Lord God Himself. He is surety for the poor. But there are a
few restrictions He imposes before He accepts your deposit in His
CD (Certificate of Devotion). First, you need a genuine pity and
open heart for the poor and dispossessed. Second, understand the
CD will not be liquid: you may not get your principal and interest back in this life. But get it back you will, and at great reward
(Matt. 6:19-21).

Jesus prophesied we would always have the poor with us (Matt.
26:11). The reasons are complex, of course. But one thing is sure:
as long as the poor are with us we are to declare our own personal
war on poverty, not relying on humanistic governments, but
revealing what is in our own hearts. Then when we meet Christ
on that day He will say to us, "Come, you who are blessed by my
Father; take your inheritance... For I was hungry and you gave
me something to eat, I was thirsty and you gave me something to
drink" (Matt. 25:34-35).

Scriptural Examples

The Samaritan. Jesus told of a man who took pity on one who
lay beaten and bleeding on the side of the road. The Samaritan
bandaged the man's wounds and put him on his own donkey, then
took him to an inn and paid the innkeeper to look after him. Jesus
said, "Go and do likewise" (Luke 10:33-37).

The deacons. In the early church a dispute arose about the
distribution of food to the poor. The disciples met together and
selected seven men to serve as deacons. The deacons were to ensure
that the poor were properly cared for (Acts 6:1-5).

Prayer of Application

Father, give me a real heart for the poor and needy, for those
who are homeless, and for those who languish in prisons. They
need both human kindness and Your words of mercy and hope.

Discipline Your Children Early

Discipline your son, for in that there is hope; do not be a willing party to his death (Prov. 19:18).

In the desert, a phenomenon called flash floods sometimes occurs. A little bit of rain can unleash a torrent of muddy water. It happens very quickly. If you are caught in a flash flood's path it will sweep you away. In a way, flash floods are like children. You bring the little tykes home one day and then, like a torrent of rushing waters, they are grown up. There is so little time.

Babies are precious but they have a predisposition to rebellion. They need to be taught immediately that the way of the flesh is the wrong way. Sometimes that includes physical punishment to get your point across. While discipline may be uncomfortable for all concerned, it is preferable to being a willing party to death. We parents have been entrusted with an eternal soul, and much of its future may rest in our hands.

Love your children. Spend quality time with them. Read to them. Share your life and testimony with them; your victories and defeats. (To share defeats is particularly important, especially how God worked in your life even then.) Sing songs with them. Pray with them. And don't neglect the discipline of the Lord, which leaves no room for the flesh.

Scriptural Examples

David. God called David a man after His own heart (1 Sam. 13:14). What made the difference in David's life, apart, of course, from the call of God? Much of the answer must lie in the 71st Psalm, where he speaks of having confidence in God since his youth, and how since his youth he had been instructed by his Father in Heaven (Ps. 71:5, 17).

Timothy. Here was a young man disciplined from infancy in the ways of the Lord. His mother and grandmother's early discipline helped change history (2 Tim. 1:5; 3:15).

Prayer of Application

Father, help us as parents to bring up our children in the ways and discipline of Your hand, so when they are grown they might follow after You in godliness and holiness.

Beware of a Hot Temper

A hot-tempered man must pay the penalty; if you rescue him, you will have to do it again (Prov. 19:19).

I once had a friend with a hair-trigger temper. Along with the temper he had the body of a 98-pound weakling—he couldn't fight a lick. So when he challenged some big guy to a battle, he was like a fog horn of a mouth backed up by a bag of bones. On more than a few occasions, my friends and I had to step in and rescue him from a sure pounding.

What creates such an explosive temper? I'm not a psychologist, but I would guess the cake recipe would look something like this: Take two scoops of pride and fold in three cups of selfishness. Add a dollop or two of guilt and hold all wisdom and understanding. Half-bake the whole mixture in a hot circumstance, then ice with a little jealousy. Instead of candles, add a short fuse. Then get far away from the poisonous mixture before it goes off, as it surely will.

There is but one sure cure for a hot-tempered person. Introduce him to the One who is meek and lowly in heart (Matt. 11:29). Help him to see God's eternal purposes and His sovereignty in all things. Then pray God's Spirit will enter the angry one's heart and mold him into the image of Christ.

Scriptural Examples

Cain. Beneath his hot temper lay pride and a desire to rebel against the command of God. Cain murdered his brother. We're not told much more about Cain, but I wouldn't be surprised if his temper got the best of him again (Gen. 4:5-16).

Simeon and Levi. After they overreacted to the seduction of Dinah, Jacob uttered a curse on them (Gen. 34). He said they were men of violence with whom he would not associate. They had killed men and cruelly cut the hamstrings of oxen. They were to be scattered and dispersed in Israel (Gen. 49:5-7).

Prayer of Application

Lord God, restrain my temper. Give me understanding that every circumstance of my life has been ordered for my sanctification and is molding me into the image of Christ.

Invest in Wisdom

Listen to advice and accept instruction, and in the end you will be wise (Prov. 19:20).

Some years ago my company established a 401(k) plan, by which savings may be deducted tax free from one's paycheck and then allowed to grow tax-free for retirement. How much retirement income an employee will have down the road depends largely upon how much he has contributed each month and upon how long he has participated.

Wisdom is like that 401(k) plan. If someone begins in his youth to make a daily deposit of godly counsel and instruction, in his latter years he will be filled to overflowing in the wealth of wisdom. However, the person who gets a late start will have trouble catching up. Therefore, it is important that we begin early and make those deposits on a regular basis.

How do we invest in wisdom? We should begin with a daily quiet time before God, praying for wisdom, worshiping and praising Him, and interceding for others. We need to daily read and meditate upon God's Word. Each Sunday should be devoted to God, to hear His Word from the pulpit and from wise Sunday School teachers. Finally, let's put God's wisdom into practice! This is the "solid meat" of the mature (Heb. 5:14).

Scriptural Examples

The scoffers. We met these mockers in the first chapter of Proverbs. Although wisdom cried out to them, they rejected such godly instruction. All who invest in wickedness and unrighteousness will reap its fruit in later life (Prov. 1:20-33).

The licentious young man of Proverbs 5. This young man wouldn't obey his teachers or listen to his instructors. He became licentious, went in to the adulterous woman and was trapped. At the end of his life he had come to utter ruin, his flesh and his body were spent, and his life had come to no good end (Prov. 5:7-14).

Prayer of Application

Dear heavenly Father, thank You for putting the desire for godly wisdom in my heart. Help me to store it up daily, that by it I might glorify You in every thought, word, and deed.

Be at Peace: Ultimate Victory Is Assured

Many are the plans in a man's heart, but it is the Lord's purpose that prevails (Prov. 19:21).

The natural person frets over the evening news wondering where this messed-up world is headed. He hopes that his "luck" holds long enough so that he can get through it. But the Bible denies that chance or luck exist. Instead, it teaches God is using all of life's circumstances toward the accomplishment of His purposes (Eph. 1:11; Heb. 6:17, for instance).

Since the Fall, people's devices and God's purposes have been in direct opposition. People worry this world will fall either to nuclear holocaust, pollution, over-population, global warming, AIDS, or some combination of those disasters. What they fail to understand is that if God had allowed sinners to reign over the world without His restraint, we would have destroyed ourselves by now.

We look at the wicked hearts of Adolf Hitler, Idi Amin, and Saddam Hussein and think they are aberrations in a world of pretty good people. In reality they represent every person (Ps. 14:1-3; 53:1-3), because each of us is capable of such lawlessness. Only the restraint of God, foiling the devices of people, and working out His own purposes, keeps us from plunging into the abyss. For those in Christ, victory is certain.

Scriptural Examples

Pharaoh. The Lord used Pharaoh's treachery for His own holy purposes. In hardening his heart, God removed any restrictions and let it seek the lowest depths of its own radically corrupt nature (Ex. 5-14; Rom. 9:17).

Sihon. This Amorite king was asked by Moses to merely allow the Israelites safe passage through his country. But God hardened Sihon's heart, and he sent out his army to attack the Israelites. They killed both Sihon and his army, and took over all of his territory (Num. 21:21-24; Deut. 2:30).

Prayer of Application

Dear Lord, thank You for the Word, where we understand You are overseeing the events of this world to the pleasure of Your will, for Your glory, and for our ultimate benefit.

God Honors Your Willingness

What a man desires is unfailing love; better to be poor than a liar (Prov. 19:22).

Even knowing the Lord's sovereignty, we Christians sometimes experience frustration. A few years ago, my brother Bill went to China on a summer mission. While there he received an appointment to teach English at the University in Qingdao. However, upon traveling to Hong Kong for further briefings, he was advised that the bureaucrats in Beijing had denied his appointment. He was greatly disappointed. God honored Bill's willingness to go and serve, but had another agenda for him. He would go on to Taiwan, meet his future bride, and then enroll in seminary in Mississippi.

God is interested in your heart (Jer. 17:10). To be poor and yet want to give richly to God is of great value in His sight. On the other hand, to be rich, but to withhold from God as if you were poor, is to be a liar. God covets our loyalty and our kindness to others. He judges us on that basis. God wants your heart. It is your faith that pleases Him (Heb. 11:6).

Scriptural Examples

Abraham. God commanded the patriarch to sacrifice Isaac. Ultimately, God stopped him and provided a ram as the sacrifice. But God honored Abraham because of his willingness to follow the command. He had proved his faith by the act (Gen. 22:2-14; Heb. 11:17-19; James 2:21-22).

David. He wanted to build the temple and God was pleased with the desire that was in his heart. Nevertheless, because of the blood that was on David's hands, God turned this duty over to David's son Solomon, who reigned after him (2 Chron. 6:8-10).

The poor widow. Jesus viewed her gift to the temple treasury as greater than all the others because she showed that she was willing to give all she had (Mark 12:41-44).

Prayer of Application

Dear Father, what a comfort to know that You look upon my heart and reward me for the desire that is there, regardless of the ultimate outcome. Help me to stick my neck out.

Fear God: Your Life, Satisfaction, and Security

The fear of the Lord leads to life: Then one rests content, un- touched by trouble (Prov. 19:23).

An old cigarette ad said something like "Smoke Chokers, they satisfy." I tried them and all they brought me was a persistent cough, wheezing lungs, and the promise of an early grave. On February 11, 1970, I quit smoking. So many things in life are like that ad. They promise satisfaction but deliver the opposite.

Sin promises us excitement, fulfillment, and even security, but delivers hangovers, guilt, disease, and bankruptcy. God is not like that. He delivers what He promises: every time, all the time. He promises life, and fulfills that promise with joy and peace. He promises satisfaction and He delivers the knowledge of Himself and the release of guilt and shame that truly satisfies the soul. He promises eternal security and guarantees in His Word that He will deliver that, too (Heb. 6:17-20).

Scriptural Examples

Noah and the pre-Flood crowd. The whole earth teemed with those who had no fear of God, who laughed at the giant ship Noah was building. Noah preached of God's righteousness (2 Peter 2:5), all the while preparing for the flood. When the rains began, and the earth belched forth waters from beneath the ground, those who had refused to fear God were visited with trouble, while Noah and his family lived (Gen. 6–8).

The Passover keepers. The final plague on Pharaoh and his people would kill all the firstborn in Egypt. But the angel of death would "pass over" the houses of those who feared and obeyed God. Those keeping the Passover were to prepare a lamb, roasting it over the fire and putting its blood on the doorframes and lintels of their homes. The Passover foreshadowed the sacrifice of the true Lamb of God, who died for us, and by whose blood keeps us from the evil day (Ex. 11:1-12:30).

Prayer of Application

Lord, by Your mighty power You saved me. How can I not then trust You for all things? Thank You for being my life, the satisfaction of my intellect and spirit, and my portion forever.

Live a Life of Self-Control

The sluggard buries his hand in the dish; he will not even bring it back to his mouth (Prov. 19:24)!

This verse presents a picture which would be very humorous were it not so tragic. The glutton has his hand in the mashed potatoes and gravy and is so sleepy from his overeating that he can't find the strength to take another bite. Tragically, he is so intent on consuming food that he is himself consumed.

God calls each of us to self-control and a life of spiritual fruit-bearing (Gal. 5:22-23). We need to eat for the sustenance of our bodies. Eating is pleasurable, but it can also be taken to extremes. There are many such pleasures in life that, while not expressly forbidden, are sin when taken to extremes. We are to avoid the sinful desires of the flesh that war against the soul. We are to do this as a testimony to the pagans, bringing glory to God (1 Peter 2:11-12).

God has given the Christian food unto everlasting life, even the Bread which comes down from heaven, our Lord Jesus (John 6:31-35). Those who come to Him will never be hungry or thirsty, neither will die (John 6:50). Feast on this Bread, and don't be consumed by the things of this world.

Scriptural Examples

Esau. He was so concerned with getting some food in his mouth that he sold his birthright as the first-born son to his younger brother, Jacob. The writer to the Hebrews said of Esau that he was a godless man (Gen. 25:30-34; Heb. 12:16).

The Israelite rabble. They complained about the manna God had so richly provided and began to crave other food they had enjoyed in Egypt. The Lord was angry with them for not trusting His provision (Num. 11:4-32).

The Cretans. Paul tells Titus about these men and their lazy and gluttonous lifestyles. He quotes one of the Cretans' own poets, Epimenides, to prove his point (Titus 1:12).

Prayer of Application

Dear Father, help me to live a life of self-control. Cause me to understand this life is best spent in the pursuit of spiritual things and not in the satisfaction of the lustful flesh.

Use Wisdom in Administering Rebuke

Flog a mocker, and the simple will learn prudence; rebuke a discerning man, and he will gain knowledge (Prov. 19:25).

Derek Kidner points out three kinds of minds here: the scorner, the simple, and the one of understanding (p. 135). The first mind, he says, is closed, or hardened. The second is empty. And the third is open. In the case of the scorner, there isn't much in the way of corrective action one can take to cure him of his closed mind. One hundred lashes won't impress a fool as much as a simple rebuke to a person of discernment (Prov. 17:10).

But the scorner's severe punishment is valuable to the simple mind. He needs a warning shot fired across his bow. God's law is full of examples of this wisdom in action, a few of which are examined below. I'm afraid that our criminal judicial system has lost sight of these truths in America today.

The man of understanding has an open mind and needs only a mild word of rebuke to correct the error of his ways. He responds to the Word of God applied to his sin by confessing the sin and repenting of it (2 Cor. 7:10).

Scriptural Examples

The idolater. The Law said that if a person enticed another to worship other gods, the people were to stone him to death so that all Israel might hear of it and be afraid (Deut. 13: 6-11).

The liar. In the same way, if a person took the witness stand and scornfully bore false witness against someone accused of wrongdoing, he was to receive the same punishment as the man he sought to harm would have received if guilty. This was done so the people would hear of it and be afraid (Deut. 19:16-21).

David. His great sin against Bathsheba and Uriah may have gone unpunished (on this earth) were it not for the admonition of God through a prophet named Nathan. Nathan rebuked the king, and David's heart softened (2 Sam. 12:1-13; Ps. 51).

Prayer of Application

Lord God, how wonderful is Your Law. Its quick and severe punishment deterred the simple mind from sin. Lord, give us understanding and wise judges in our courts.

Honor Your Father and Your Mother

He who robs his father and drives out his mother is a son who brings shame and disgrace (Prov.19:26).

This is a picture of corruption in its most radical form. Here is a son who is fed, educated, clothed, and kept in safety throughout his childhood and youth. He is nurtured, loved, and tenderly disciplined by this couple who disregard their own needs and comfort for him. Then, when he is an adult, he steals his father's home and possessions and evicts his mother, throwing her out on the street to fend for herself.

God commands that we honor our parents (Ex. 20:12). The command was placed before the commandment against murder and came with a promise. Those who kept it could expect long life in the land God was giving them. What of those who failed to keep it? Proverbs 30:17 gives us a picture of the punishment they could expect. Their eyes would be pecked out by the ravens. They would be consumed by the vultures.

Scriptural Examples

Cain. In Genesis 3:15, Adam and Eve were promised that an offspring (seed) of the woman would crush the serpent's head. I believe they thought Cain would be this one, not realizing that the promise would be fulfilled centuries later in Christ, the seed of Mary. What a shame Cain was to his father and mother who had expected so much (Gen. 4:1-16).

Absalom. Absalom's father was David. Absalom rebelled against his father and sought to set himself up as king over Israel (2 Sam. 15:1-14). He lay with his father's concubines in the sight of all Israel (2 Sam. 16:20-22). Ultimately, Absalom's death at the hands of David's army caused David tremendous pain and torment. Surely Absalom wasted his father (2 Sam.18:33).

Timothy. Timothy was a man who honored his mother, Eunice, and his grandmother Lois (2 Tim. 1:5).

Prayer of Application

Dear God, thank You for my parents and for their self sacrifice in raising me from infancy. They were not perfect, but they deserve my respect and love. Help me to honor them.

Listen to the Instruction of the Word

Stop listening to instruction, my son, and you will stray from the words of knowledge (Prov. 19:27).

The Word of God is true (John 17:17), complete (Rev. 22:18-19), sufficient for correct doctrine, and perfects our behavior in human relationships (2 Tim. 3:15-16). We are not to be led astray by every wind of doctrine that blows down the pike (Eph. 4:14). How do we protect ourselves from error? We are to chew on the solid food of the Word, putting it into practice, and thereby learning to distinguish good from evil (Heb. 5:14).

Throughout the history of the church and particularly in our day, people have brought in heresies that God calls destructive and damnable (2 Peter 2:1). Many even deny Christ is Lord. But we are called by Christ to be discerning (Luke 12:57). When we stand before Him to give account of ourselves (2 Cor. 5:10), we will each be held accountable for errors we have made in following false teachers. Therefore, let's do like the Bereans who didn't even take the apostle Paul's word for it. They searched the Scriptures to see if what he was telling them was so (Acts 17:10-11). Open your ears and eyes to the Word.

Scriptural Examples

Noadiah. Nehemiah prayed God would remember this false prophetess who had tried to intimidate him in rebuilding the walls of Jerusalem (Neh. 6:14).

Hananiah. He prophesied falsely that Babylon's yoke upon Israel would be broken and peace would be restored. Jeremiah told him because he had taught rebellion against the Lord he would die that very year. In the seventh month, Hananiah died (Jer. 28).

The Nicolaitans. These men compromised the teachings of Christ with those of the pagan world and taught both idolatry and immorality (Rev. 2:6, 15).

Prayer of Application

Dear Lord, thank You for giving me a mind that can discern truth from falsehood, and the living Word that is essentially clear in its teaching. Feed me from it that may I be steadfast.

Beware of the Ultimate Lie

28) A corrupt witness mocks at justice, and the mouth of the wicked gulps down evil. 29) Penalties are prepared for mockers, and beatings for the backs of fools (Prov. 19:28-29).

Even if the Bible didn't teach it, justice makes sense as an eternal concept. Otherwise, Adolf Hitler mocked justice when he committed suicide in his Berlin bunker. But he only fled the hands of angry people to fall into the hands of an angry God.

In the verses above we see the person who mocks justice by lying and who also "gulps down evil" (v. 28). All the while he sets a trap for himself. In the end, his contempt for justice will form the basis of his judgment because he scorns the free gift that God offers (Rom. 8:1).

Have you ever wondered what would be the biggest lie one could tell that would be a 15 on a scale of 1 to 10? John says one who claims to be a Christian but who does not do what Christ commands "is a liar and the truth is not in him"(1 John 2:4). I believe that to mock Christ's atoning work, all the while posturing as His follower, is the ultimate lie. Peter says it would have been better not to have known the way of salvation than to turn one's back on the Savior (2 Peter 2:21). Beware of mocking the ultimate Judge (Acts 17:31).

Scriptural Examples

Joseph's brothers. They lied to their father, giving him false evidence that Joseph was dead. They mocked judgment but received mercy at the hands of their brother and were spared (like us) the punishment they so richly deserved (Gen. 39:8-12).

The Pharisees and teachers of the Law. While posing as men of God, these men told the ultimate lie. They practiced godliness with their lips, but their hearts were far from God (Matt. 15:7-9). Jesus mocked these mockers, these "blind guides" who nibbled at righteousness but gulped down evil (Matt. 23).

Prayer of Application

Heavenly Father, may I never betray You by paying You lip service yet living a life that belies what I say. I can only do this through the power of Your Spirit sustaining me.

Chapter Twenty

God's Saving Grace

Proverbs 20:9 asks a rhetorical question: "Who can say, 'I have kept my heart pure; I am clean and without sin?'" The obvious answer is: No one who has ever lived...except one, the Lord Jesus Christ (Rom. 3:10-20). By God's saving grace, the righteousness of Christ, who lived the perfectly sinless life that Adam did not, is imputed to the believer. Also by God's grace, the believer's sinfulness was imputed to Christ. He bore our sins on the cross. It was a double imputation: our sin to Jesus; His righteousness to us. And it was all because of the saving grace of God.

God's saving grace stands in direct opposition to our merit. Grace is by definition an unmerited favor—it is undeserved. Even works that are said to be done with the assistance of God's grace are opposed to saving grace. Saving grace is based upon Christ's merit alone. That's why Paul said in Galatians 5:4, "You who are trying to be justified by law have been alienated from Christ; you have fallen away from grace." And the Apostle tells us again in Ephesians 2:8 and 9, "For it is by grace you have been saved, through faith—and this not of yourselves, it is the gift of God—not by works, so that no one can boast." Don't trust in your church membership, your loyal service, or any other thing for salvation. Trust in Christ alone.

Don't Be Deceived by Alcohol

Wine is a mocker and beer a brawler; whoever is led astray by them is not wise (Prov. 20:1).

Deceit occurs when promises are made that will not be kept. Beer commercials all promise fun, popularity, and peer bonding. There is an element of truth there, but for many the promise of alcohol reverses into a curse of pain and suffering. The beer commercial has sucked many into a life of pain.

Murders, drunk driving, child molestations, wife beatings, and other crimes are often committed by people who've been drinking. Much of the homelessness in America is due to alcohol abuse. Trouble dogs the trail of the compulsive drinker.

Nowhere in Scripture are we told not to drink alcohol. But we are warned often of its deceit and of the serious consequences of its misuse. Paul may have been thinking about alcoholic beverages when he wrote that although something may be lawful, it is not necessarily constructive or beneficial. He declined to be brought under the power of anything or let anything be his master (1 Cor. 6:12; 10:23). Alcohol will try to be your master. Don't be deceived by it.

Scriptural Examples

Noah. After the Flood, Noah planted a vineyard. He then got drunk and passed out naked in his tent. This led to Ham's sin and Noah's subsequent curse upon Canaan. Noah was deceived and his sin had lasting consequences (Gen. 9:20-21).

Lot. Lot also got drunk and lay in his tent—twice. Lot's daughters slept with their father, and the product of these incestuous unions were the Moabites and the Ammonites, two of Israel's most pestiferous enemies (Gen. 19:32-38).

Elah. He was partaking heavily of wine in the palace at Tirzah when Zimri, one of his cavalry officers, sneaked in and assassinated him, succeeding him as king (1 Kings 16:8-10)

Prayer of Application

Father, many of life's activities promise one thing but deliver the opposite. Give me the wisdom of self-control and moderation in all things, bringing glory to You in all I do.

Beware of Provoking the King's Anger

A king's wrath is like the roar of a lion; he who angers him forfeits his life (Prov. 20:2).

Going to the movies as a kid I used to enjoy the roar of the MGM lion. But his roar was not worthy to be compared with actually facing the king of the jungle on the African veldt where nothing would separate me from his fangs and claws but grass and air. That I would find very fearful indeed.

What provokes the human king to anger? Isn't it rebellion against his authority? One who raises himself up against the king's absolute authority had better be prepared to forfeit his life. To rebel against the Great King is utmost foolishness. No chance for success exists. Such rebellion forfeits eternal life.

The sinful person sets himself up as king of all he surveys, but rejects the Kingdom of God. God offers riches beyond measure as a joint-heir of His throne, but many refuse to give up control of their own puny thrones. What foolishness! Don't rebel against the King. Obey Him! Bow before Him! Submit to His reign and live.

Scriptural Examples

Pharaoh. In Exodus we have the story of two angry kings in what resembled a boxing match. In one corner was Pharaoh, lion of Egypt, and in the other, Jehovah God, Lion of Judah. God, the infinitely greater power, toyed with Pharaoh, backing him into a corner, before throwing the knockout punch at the Red Sea. Pharaoh's big mistake was in scheduling the bout. If he had really known the Lion with whom he was to spar, he would have never put a foot into the ring (Ex. 7-14).

Adonijah. This son of David tried to make himself king as his father lay dying. Anointing Solomon, David stopped Adonijah's plot. Solomon let him live, but later when Adonijah asked if he could marry David's concubine, the request angered the king and cost Adonijah his life (1 Kings 1:1-2:26).

Prayer of Application

Lord Jesus, thank You for reigning in my life by faith. Your sovereign rule is a great comfort to me. Help me to warn others of Your pending judgment at the Great White Throne.

Seek Peace, Not a Quarrel

It is to a man's honor to avoid strife, but every fool is quick to quarrel (Prov. 20:3).

Here again, the godly wisdom of Scripture is in direct opposition to the wisdom of the world. The natural person finds it necessary to defend his honor, while the spiritual person finds honor in not defending himself, seeking peace instead.

America has become an incredibly litigious society. Thousands of lawsuits are filed daily. Our Lord called us to agree quickly with those who oppose us and to try to avoid courts of law. You don't know what kind of trouble you might find there, particularly if you are paying your attorney by the hour. Overlook the offense. It will be to your glory (Prov. 19:11). Seek peace and pursue it (Ps. 34:14; 1 Peter 3:11).

Scriptural Examples

Isaac and the Philistines. The issue was water rights. Isaac would no sooner dig a fresh well than the Philistines would claim it as their own. Each time, Isaac would move his herds, and thus to his honor avoid strife (Gen. 26:17-25).

Gideon and Jepthah. Each handled a similar experience in different ways and achieved different results. Both men were called to go to war. In each case, they were accused by their brothers, the Ephraimites, of not calling them to join in the fighting. Gideon soothed the Ephraimites' anger and preserved the peace. Jepthah said he had called but they had refused to come. This remark brought great anger, and even began a battle between brothers (Judg. 8:1-4; 12:1-4).

Hanun and David. David sent an envoy of peace to Hanun to express sympathy on the occasion of his father's death. Instead of receiving David's men in peace, Hanun seized them, shaved off their beards, and cut off their garments at the buttocks, sending them home in shame (2 Sam. 10:1-7).

Prayer of Application

Sovereign Lord, You call the peacemakers "blessed" in Your Word. Give me the grace and understanding to pursue Your peace in a world that is in rebellion against You and Your Word.

Let's Stop Making Excuses

A sluggard does not plow in season [KJV: "by reason of the cold"]; so at harvest time he looks but finds nothing (Prov. 20:4).

It is estimated that in any given congregation, 10 percent of the membership does 90 percent of the work. Only four percent of the members of evangelical churches in America tithe. No wonder we can't reach the lost for Christ, with the vast majority of Christians riding their hot-air balloons of excuses.

We have in the verses above a picture of the would-be farmer who can't plow his fields because it's too cold. Frozen land is not the problem here. It's personal, not physical. He is just uncomfortable plowing on those cold March mornings. He's procrastinating. Come harvest time, he'll look out at his fields and they'll still be brown dirt and weeds. No crops will have grown.

For many of us, procrastination is a habit that needs to be overcome. Not only are our plans and dreams stifled by it, but it brings depression and guilt in its wake. Let's stop making excuses and get on with the work at hand.

Scriptural Examples

Aaron. When Moses climbed the mountain, he left Aaron in charge of the camp. The people began to party and Aaron made a golden calf. Aaron blamed his sin on the pressure of the people. He said the idol just popped out of the fire. Aaron is an example of our propensity to cook up an incredible excuse if a good excuse won't come to mind (Ex. 32:22-24).

Gideon. God chose Gideon to lead His people. But Gideon began coming up with excuses. He basically accused God of not being able to do what He said He would do (Judg. 6:12-17).

The unwilling disciples. These two men excused themselves from following Jesus. The first had to take care of his father and the second wanted to bid his family good-bye. They placed personal priorities above the Kingdom (Luke 9:59-62).

Prayer of Application

Father, forgive me for making excuses instead of being about Your work. Give me the wisdom to establish priorities, Lord, and then to make my priorities Your priorities.

Be Discerning of the Intentions of Others

The purposes of a man's heart are deep waters, but a man of understanding draws them out (Prov. 20:5).

I used to enjoy watching Perry Mason on TV because he was so discerning. Through his cross-examinations he could extract the truth from the depths of people's hearts.

I don't believe that we should think all people are out to take advantage of us, but we should realize that some are. We are to hide the Word in our hearts and use it as the basis for our discernment (Ps. 119:11). We are also to ask God for wisdom (James 1:5) as we use our God-given common sense.

Learn how to ask good "Perry Mason"-type questions that get to the heart of a matter. Develop a sense about certain things, such as "if it sounds too good to be true it probably is." Your spouse will often have intuition about a certain transaction or person that goes beyond your ability to properly discern. Finally, and above all, ask God and godly people for specific guidance. Make no major decision without prayer and the competent counsel of those you trust.

Scriptural Examples

David. One day Absalom approached David and asked to travel to Hebron for worship to fulfill a vow. It was a lie, but David did not discern his son's evil intent. Absalom went to Hebron and proclaimed himself king (2 Sam. 15:2-10).

Darius. The king of Babylon was hoodwinked by his advisors into signing a law that was designed to trap Daniel. Their deception backfired as the Lord protected Daniel (Dan. 6:4-9).

The Wise Men. Had not God intervened, they would have probably played into King Herod's hands. They failed to discern that it was his intention to kill the baby Jesus (Matt. 2:7-12).

Paul. He understood some of the intentions in the hearts of those who preached Christ. They taught out of selfish ambition and envy, not out of a heart of love and good will (Phil. 1:15-17).

Prayer of Application

Heavenly Father, grant me a discerning mind. Help me not to be cynical, but to keep a balanced view and to always give the other person the benefit of the doubt when I'm not sure.

Be Discerning of Professions of Faith

Many a man claims to have unfailing love, but a faithful man who can find? (Prov. 20:6.)

In the last proverb we saw the need to discern the intentions of the heart. Here is the same need for the lips. Most people claim to be good. This is directly opposed to the Word of God, which speaks of mankind's evil nature and alienation from God's goodness (John 2:23-25, for instance).

In the visible church today, many claim with their lips to have "unfailing love." But what do they do? Their "procession" often doesn't match their "profession." I spoke with an acquaintance the other day who is a professing Christian. During our conversation he revealed that there was a young woman sharing his bed, as if that were a perfectly normal thing to do outside of marriage. He was deceiving himself, and others, because of the dichotomy of what he claimed to believe and what he was actually practicing.

Scriptural Examples

Jehu. Jehu claimed to have great zeal for the Lord, and indeed he did show some zeal for killing, because he slaughtered the priests of Baal. But he worshipped the golden calves at Bethel and Dan. Jehu's talk did not match his walk (2 Kings 10:16-31).

The Pharisees. False prophets often come in sheep's clothing, professing to be something other than the wolves they really are. They perform their acts of righteousness, i.e., fasting, almsgiving, and prayer, in a public setting for all to see. They love to receive honor at banquets and to be given titles. Woe to those who have an outward profession of godliness but no inward reality (Matt. 7:15; 6:1-2, 5, 16; 23).

The Laodicean church. The Lord rebuked this lukewarm church. He wished they were either hot or cold. They professed to be in need of nothing, but they were "wretched, pitiful, poor, blind, and naked" (Rev. 3:16-18).

Prayer of Application

Lord, help me to back up my profession of faith with the reality of godly behavior that I would bring glory and honor to Your name. Help me not to be fooled by false professions.

Bless Your Children by Your Faithful Walk

The righteous man leads a blameless life; blessed are his children after him (Prov. 20:7).

What you are speaks so loudly to your children they often can't hear what you say. If you talk a good game, but don't walk in a manner that conforms to it, you are not practicing integrity. Integrity comes when one lives what he says he believes.

There is a very foolish belief in some evangelical circles today that since we are no longer "under law, but under grace" (Rom. 6:14), the Christian can do anything he pleases and be accepted by God. This is absolute nonsense. While grace is vulnerable to this kind of irresponsible presumption, it never teaches it. We are "under grace" inasmuch as we are able to choose integrity over and against hypocrisy. By God's grace, and the indwelling presence of the Holy Spirit, we are no longer slaves to sin, but rather slaves to righteousness (Rom. 6:16-19).

We parents are called to lead a blameless life. The parent who has been truly called of God will want to walk in integrity. If he doesn't, his children will see through the ruse quickly. Bless your kids and live what you say you believe.

Scriptural Examples

Adam. Adam sinned against God in eating the fruit forbidden by God's commandment. Adam's children have paid for his rebellion ever since (Gen. 4:8-12).

Abraham. Abraham was a man of integrity who walked in the ways of God. He walked by faith and God counted it to him as righteousness (Gen. 15:6). Abraham's faithful walk blessed his children after him (Gen. 17:19-21; 18:19).

Job. Job suffered greatly but remained steadfast in his integrity. The Lord blessed the final part of Job's life, giving him seven more sons and three more daughters. His daughters were declared to be the most beautiful in all the land (Job 42:12-14).

Prayer of Application

Heavenly Father, keep me in the way of righteousness by Your mighty hand. May my children see the evidence of Your hand upon me and be blessed, giving You the glory.

Warn Others of the Great King's Judgment

*When a king sits on his throne to judge, he winnows out all
evil with his eyes* (Prov. 20:8).

The word "winnows" here brings to mind the picture of a
farmer separating the interior kernel of wheat from the surrounding
chaff. In Old Testament days, threshing floors were typically on
top of a hill where the wind facilitated the work. In Judges 6:11,
however, Gideon threshed wheat down in a valley. Boaz' threshing
floor in Ruth 3:2-14 was probably on a hilltop as was certainly
that of Araunah the Jebusite, which was to become the site of the
temple (2 Sam. 24:21).

The natural person scorns the wrath of God but the Bible says
that all history is moving toward the final day of judgment when
the Great King will winnow out all evil with His eyes. Nothing is
hidden from His sight (Heb. 4:13).

The Christian awaits the Judge confidently (Rom. 8:1). He
is not confident in his own good works, which are in the eyes of
the Great King as filthy rags (Isa. 64:6). He has confidence in the
work of the same Great King, who saved him by grace.

Scriptural Examples

David. David was the great king of Israel. Except for a few
notorious lapses, he reigned in justice and in the fear of the Lord.
In Psalm 101:3-8, David poured his heart out to God that he
hated the deeds of unfaithful people, and would set his eyes on
no evil thing, cutting off every evil-doer from Jerusalem.

Jesus. David foreshadowed the Great King who will judge the
nations in righteousness and justice. Jesus told His disciples of the
day when He would separate the sheep from the goats. The sheep
will be invited to an eternal inheritance, but to the goats He will
say, "Depart from me into the eternal fires prepared for Satan and
his followers." Warn others of the judgment that is certain unless
they repent (Matt. 25:31-34, 41).

Prayer of Application

Great God and King, thank You that the Great Judge on that
day of wrath will also be my defense attorney, only because He
died for me on a Roman cross while I was still Your enemy.

Invite Others to the Lamb's Cleansing

*Who can say, "I have kept my heart pure, I am clean and
without sin"* (Prov. 20:9)?

Americans are historically very independent people and want
to do things for themselves. But can you imagine do-it-yourself
heart surgery?

There you are lying flat on your back on the operating table,
looking into a big mirror on the ceiling. Your scalpel is poised
on the line drawn on your chest. Beads of perspiration break out
on your forehead as you think of the pain that lies ahead, since a
general anesthetic would be out of the question. The only sound
you hear is that of the steady wheeze of the respirator and your
own sickly heart, beating uncontrollably.

Sound ridiculous? It's actually not as ridiculous as the heart
surgery that millions of people perform on themselves every day.
They say, "My heart is clean, I have made it pure." They don't
practice surgery, but self-deception. The heart they claim to make
pure by good deeds is their eternal soul.

Only one Surgeon can give you a clean heart that is sinless
and pure in the sight of God. His name is Jesus, the Lamb of God
slain from the foundation of the world. His heart was broken so
that many hearts could be eternally healed. Invite others to wash
their hearts in His cleansing blood.

Scriptural Examples

David. David was a sinner and acknowledged that fact. Even
a great king like David needs cleansing; he can't do it for himself.
In David's wonderful 51st Psalm he asked God to cleanse him
from his sin and wash away all his iniquity. He requested a pure
heart, freshly created by God, and that all of his past sins would
be blotted out of God's record book. Why would a just God do
this for King David and for you and me? For the purpose of His
own delight, pleasure, and glory (Ps. 51:1-19).

Prayer of Application

Heavenly Father, thank You for the cleansing blood of Christ
by whom every person must be washed if he is to be presentable
in Your sight and stand faultless before You.

Practice Absolute Honesty

Differing weights and differing measures—the Lord detests them both (Prov. 20:10).

If a someone owns a grocery store and permits its produce scales to weigh just a slight bit heavy, so that for every true pound of potatoes he is charging for 1.02 pounds, then he has stolen from his customer just as certainly as if he had pilfered the stereo from his customer's car. Actually, what the grocery owner has done may be worse than common burglary, because he has done it in the context of a seemingly honest business transaction in which an innocent party is tricked.

We Christians must practice squeaky-clean honesty in all our dealings. We must do this not just because we know that our God is omniscient and that His judgment is like a consuming fire (Heb. 12:29). We are to do it primarily out of love for Christ and a desire to see His name glorified in us.

Scriptural Examples

Satan. Called "the king of Tyre," it is nevertheless Satan who is described by Ezekiel. At one time a blameless and beautiful creature, Satan's heart became proud and he engaged in sins and dishonest trade. Satan is the father of lies (John 8:44), and the father of dishonest scales, too (Ezek. 28:12-19).

Jacob. Although Jacob used dishonest means to steal his brother Esau's birthright and in some of his dealings with his father-in-law, Laban, toward his latter years God changed him. When his sons returned from Egypt, Jacob insisted that they return the silver in their sacks (Gen. 43:12).

Judas. Judas complained to Jesus that the perfume lavished upon Him by Martha's sister Mary was a waste. He said its value could have been given to the poor. But Judas didn't care about the poor. He was a dishonest schemer who would probably have kept the money for himself (John 12:4-6).

Prayer of Application

Lord, every day I run into situations where my honesty is tested. It may be in financial matters, in my associations, or in my home. Help me, Lord, to be honest in every way.

Observe Your Children Closely

Even a child is known by his actions, by whether his conduct is pure and right (Prov. 20:11).

In computer lingo, we hear the acronym, "WYSIWYG." It stands for "What You See Is What You Get." What you see on the screen will be duplicated when it is printed on paper. Little children are like that. Not yet adept at masking their fears and feelings like adults, what you see is who they are.

A secular proverb says, "Large oaks from little acorns grow." A character flaw may begin as a little acorn. If left unchecked it will one day become a large oak. We as parents need to observe our children closely. When we see acorns of selfishness, vengefulness, pride, dishonesty, and the like, we need to stifle that trait's growth by discipline and fervent prayer before it forms into a settled habit.

Conversely, we are to encourage and seek to strengthen character traits in our kids that will mature into large oaks of righteous behavior. Don't forget to reaffirm correct behavior in your children. Train up your children in the Word of God and watch as it does its transforming work in their lives.

Scriptural Examples

Jacob. Jacob's character was seen very early when he came forth from the womb holding onto Esau's heel. It was a glimpse of the personal ambition and deceit that would mark his later life (Gen. 25:26; Hos. 12:3).

Samuel. The Lord's hand was upon Samuel from his youth, and Samuel's words were without defect. All Israel recognized that he was to be a prophet of the Lord (1 Sam. 3:19-20).

John the Baptist. The Spirit's hold upon John was evident even from within Elizabeth's womb (Luke 1:15, 44).

Jesus. Jesus' messianic mission was discerned by both Simeon and Anna as they served in the temple. His character and holiness were evident from His youth (Luke 2:25-52).

Prayer of Application

Heavenly Father, help us parents to be discerning of the character traits of our children even from birth, then help us to raise those children in the fear and discipline of the Lord.

Rejoice in the Grace of God

*Ears that hear and eyes that see—the Lord has made them
both* (Prov. 20:12).

Jesus called Lazarus from the tomb. He was stone cold dead
and had even begun to stink. He was just like you and me before
salvation. Could Lazarus have done this on his own? No, he was
dead. Dead men don't make choices (John 11:1-45).

Many believe they were merely sick when they chose to follow
Christ. But Ephesians 2:1 states that they were, in fact, dead in
trespasses and sins, blind and deaf to the things of the gospel. Can
dead bones live? Yes, but only by the grace and sovereign breath
of God (Ezek. 37:3-5).

Jesus says that the necessary condition of our salvation is to be
born again, or "from above" (John 3:3). What decision did you
have in your first birth? Absolutely none. And neither do we "decide" to be born again. We need God to breathe in us His breath
of life before we can either hear or see the gospel and respond to
it in faith, which is our part of the transaction. Rejoice that He
has chosen you and given you the power to believe (John 15:16;
John 1:12). Joyfully give God all the credit.

Scriptural Examples

Cleopas and companion. These men were walking along the
road to Emmaus discussing the events surrounding Jesus' death.
The resurrected Lord came and walked beside them but they
were kept from recognizing him. Jesus began to explain things to
them; then after breaking bread their eyes were opened and they
understood who He was (Luke 24:13-32).

Paul. On another road the great apostle was blinded. Soon,
he was to receive both hearing and sight (Acts 9:3-7).

Lydia. In Philippi, Paul's message caught the ears of a busi-
nesswoman from Thyatira. When the Lord opened her heart, she
responded to the gospel of Christ (Acts 16:13-15).

Prayer of Application

Amazing grace, how sweet the sound that saved a wretch like
me. I once was lost but now am found, was blind but now I see.
Father, I rejoice in Your sovereign grace that saved me.

Rise and Shine

Do not love sleep or you will grow poor; stay awake and you will have food to spare (Prov. 20:13).

"Rise and shine" were my mother's words as she made the rounds getting all of us sleepyheads out of the sack. It was a tough job. That bed was so warm and cozy. Just a few more minutes to roll over and drift back to sleep...but no: "Rise and shine!" Mom knew the secret. A day stood waiting to be conquered and every moment lost was a moment never to be regained.

The army changed me. As soon as my eyes opened in the morning, my feet would hit the floor. Now I love the morning. I guess I'm what you would call a "morning person." But let me confess that I am guilty of another form of sleepiness, a form which also can lead to a kind of poverty: spiritual drowsiness. I am sometimes a sleepyhead on matters of discernment. My eyelids often close when I should be watchful in prayer (Matt. 26:40). I need to awake to the "rise and shine" exhortation of Paul: "Wake up, O sleeper!" and live wisely, making the most of every opportunity, because the days are evil (Eph. 5:14-16).

Scriptural Examples

Samson. Samson slept both with his eyes and his mind as Delilah learned the secret of his miraculous strength and cut off the seven braids of his hair. Those eyes that longed for sleep would soon be put out by the Philistines (Judg. 16:19-21).

Israel's watchmen. The Lord spoke of these leaders of Israel who were blind and lacked knowledge. They loved to sleep and lie around all day dreaming, never satisfied as each sought his own way (Isa. 56:10-12).

Eutychus. This young man sat in a third-story window listening to Paul preach. Sleep overcame him and he plunged to his death. Paul rushed down to him and restored him to life. Let's not be like Eutychus; let's be watchful (Acts 20:9-12).

Prayer of Application

Father, teach me that I have only one life and it will soon pass; only what's done for Christ will last. Place my feet on the ground and give me the energy and strength to rise and shine.

Avoid Hypocrisy at All Costs

"Its no good, its no good!" says the buyer; then off he goes and boasts about his purchase (Prov. 20:14).

The hypocrite is deceitful. He says one thing with his lips, but his heart is in another place. Here we see a buyer who bad-mouths the seller's product, hoping to strike a better deal. So what he knows is good he says is bad. The seller, on the other hand, might attempt to deceive the buyer by claiming some benefit of his product that is beyond his product's ability to deliver. For the Christian application, we may talk the talk of faith, but fail to walk the walk. This is hypocrisy.

We live in a world of inconsistency. We are promised something verbally and yet on reading the fine print we find the opposite is true. Advertisements promise enjoyment for smokers but deliver cancer, emphysema, and heart disease. TV commercials promise fun and popularity for beer drinkers but often deliver broken lives and homes. The world offers fulfillment and satisfaction in so many of its ways, but in the end delivers guilt and shame. Only in Christ is found the consistency that brings full joy and peace and confidence. Follow Him and avoid the trap of the world's hypocrisy.

Scriptural Examples

The Israelites. Time and again they would honor God with their lips, yet their hearts and minds were unfaithful to His covenant with them (Ps. 78:34-38).

The adulteress. She promised the simpleminded youth enjoyment in her bed. It was safe. Her husband was on a long trip. He followed her, little knowing that while she promised sweetness and excitement she delivered death (Prov. 7:10-23).

The Pharisees. Jesus called them hypocrites (Matt. 15:7) and warned His disciples of their devious ways. They were false prophets who kept people from the Kingdom (Luke 11:39-52).

Prayer of Application

Father in Heaven, keep my life free from hypocrisy. As I grow in Christ, help me to follow His commands consistently, that my life will bear the fruit of which my lips speak.

Let Wisdom Be Your Wealth and Adornment

Gold there is, and rubies in abundance, but lips that speak knowledge are a rare jewel (Prov. 20:15).

Gold is known for its beauty, luster, permanence and weight, and is valued for its scarcity. Rubies are precious stones of rare beauty. Both gold and rubies are prized for their intrinsic value and for their beauty in jewelry. The world puts its trust and gives its honor to things like gold and rubies.

But there is jewelry of far greater value that is much more beautiful than mere gold or rubies: the lips that speak knowledge. This is not the world's knowledge but the knowledge of God, or divine knowledge, that transcends our ability to mine gold and rubies. It is a gift from God and must be sought from Him and His Word.

Isaiah 52:7 speaks of the beauty of "the feet of those who bring good news, who proclaim peace…who proclaim salvation." How feet and lips of beauty are needed in this world today. Let your trust and ultimate security rest in His knowledge, then let your lips be your precious adornment.

Scriptural Examples

Solomon. Solomon could have asked God for gold and rubies but he asked for wisdom to tell right from wrong and to govern God's people. Because of his request, the Lord also showered Solomon with wealth and honor (1 Kings 3:5-13).

The merchant and the pearl. Jesus told of a merchant who sold everything he had to buy a pearl. The pearl of wisdom was the key to the kingdom and was infinitely more valuable than all his other possessions (Matt. 13:45-46).

The rich young man. He asked Jesus how to inherit eternal life. Jesus discerned his covetousness and told him to sell his "gold and rubies" and follow after Him. The man was sad, seeing wealth of more value than eternal life (Matt. 19:16-22).

Prayer of Application.

Father, what a treasure is stored up for those who love You. Give us wisdom to use our lips to tell others of it, to the end that we might bring glory to You, wisdom's great Source.

Don't Be a Sucker

Take the garment of one who puts up security for a stranger; hold it in pledge if he does it for a wayward woman (Prov. 20:16).

We are warned many times in Proverbs about being surety for a stranger, as in co-signing a note at the bank (Prov. 6:1-5; 11:15; 17:18, for instance). Here we have a picture of a person who comes to you for a loan, the purpose of which is to pay "the debt of a stranger whose reliability is unknown, and the debt of a wayward woman whose unreliability is known" (NIV Study Bible notes, p. 974). This person foolishly does something that exceeds what Christian charity requires, and then asks you to join him in his foolishness. If you do make the loan, get collateral to back up the debt should he default. Don't be a sucker.

Often, Christians seem to be easy marks because of our desire to follow the Lord in doing good. But there is a limit to Christian charity. If people ask you to lend them money so that they can help a stranger, don't do it unless you can afford to lose what you have given. If you decide to go ahead, take collateral if you ever hope to see your money again.

Scriptural Examples

Joshua and the Gibeonites. This man of God and mighty warrior was suckered into believing the story of a group of Gibeonites. These men had heard of the victories of the Israelites over Jericho and Ai, so in their fear they resorted to a ruse to get out of a sticky situation. They pretended they were from a far country, put on old sandals and clothing, and carried cracked wineskins and moldy bread. They said they had come a long distance in order to make a treaty with the invading Israelites. Joshua and the men of Israel saw the Gibeonite "evidence" but didn't ask God for wisdom in the matter. They foolishly struck a binding treaty with men who actually lived in the land they had come to conquer (Josh. 9:3-26).

Prayer of Application

Heavenly Father, help me to be wise and to understand the limits to which I can go in Christian charity. At the same time, keep my heart and mind open to the real needs of others.

Beware the Aftertaste of Sin

Food gained by fraud tastes sweet to a man, but he ends up with a mouth full of gravel (Prov. 20:17).

The food gotten both honestly and deceitfully tastes sweet at first. The difference lies in the aftertaste. The sweetness of fraudulent food will turn to gravel in the mouth of the eater.

There are two principles at work here; natural and spiritual. The natural principle might be: "You have to live with the consequences of your actions." In other words, if you stay up late drinking wine, be prepared to have a hangover in the morning (Prov. 23:31-32). But some people seem to get away with sin. Enter the spiritual principle. Nobody gets away with sin. The Lord who sees all says, "It is mine to avenge, I will repay" (Heb. 10:30). Sin that tastes sweet always winds up as gravel.

As I was meditating on this proverb I thought of the food that endures to eternal life, our Lord Jesus (John 6:35). He is the food that comes in truth, always satisfying with never a bitter aftertaste. He bore our sins on the cross and "ate gravel" for us that we who are hidden in Him might never taste of it.

Scriptural Examples

Eve. Eve saw that the fruit was pleasing to the eye and looked nutritious. She wanted the wisdom that it held, even though she knew that it was off limits. The first bite must have been delicious. She gave some of it to Adam. Immediately thereafter its taste turned to gravel (Gen. 3:6ff).

Aachan. This man deceitfully hid some of the plunder from Jericho. Following the initial defeat at Ai, Aachan's sweet food of fraud became gravel in his mouth (Josh. 7:21-25).

Ananias and Sapphira. They sold some real estate and announced that they were going to give the entire proceeds to the common fund. But they kept back a portion for themselves. Shortly, they both ate the gravel of their sin (Acts 5:1-10).

Prayer of Application

Dear Lord, help me to resist the temptations in life that promise sweetness and deliver gravel. Rather, help me to walk in the righteousness that You have laid forth in Your Word.

Go to Battle Armed with Good Advice

Make plans by seeking advice; if you wage war,
obtain guidance (Prov. 20:18).

In my lifetime, I have seen our U. S. Presidents struggle often with decisions when war hung in the balance. I am sure any such decision is an agonizing one, and only made after the counsel of many advisers. I personally would not want to be faced with the responsibility of sending young men and women into armed conflict.

But every Christian is engaged in spiritual warfare (Phil. 1:30), so I see this proverb in that light. Each Christian needs to establish his personal strategy in the struggle against Satan and his minions who would make war with God. We should do this armed with godly counsel and advice. There are as many different roles in the battle as there are soldiers. Some will fight in foxholes along the front lines, while others will be engaged in supplying the front line troops with bread, prayer, and encouragement. God distributes different gifts to different people.

Each one's calling in the battle plan will be in accordance with the gifts God has given him, and should be established in the counsel of the Word of God. It should also be in the counsel of the wise advice of our pastors, elders, and other mature warriors of the faith.

Scriptural Examples

David. At war with the Philistines, David sought the counsel of God as to whether or not to attack. God said he should, so David attacked and was victorious. But then the enemy entered the Valley of Rephaim, David once more inquired of God. This time, the Lord gave him tactical instructions. David was to circle around behind enemy lines and as soon as he heard the sound of marching he was to attack. David defeated the Philistines again (2 Sam. 5:17-25).

Prayer of Application

Father, You have drafted me into spiritual warfare. Help me to take up Your battle cry and, armed with advice from Your Word and godly people, pitch daily into the fray.

Beware of the Person Who Talks Too Much

A gossip betrays a confidence; so avoid a man who
talks too much (Prov. 20:19).

Although the KJV uses the term "flatters" instead of "talks too much," Derek Kidner points out that the person in this proverb is one who babbles on like a fool, revealing secrets not so much from malicious intent but from an empty mind. We are to use caution in our conversations with a person like that because the next secrets to be revealed may be our own.

The Lord warns us in Matthew 12:36 that we shall give account on the day of judgment for every idle word that we speak. I've got some explaining to do! Sometimes I feel pressure to keep a conversation going and may say the first thing that comes into my mind without thinking. I didn't have a malicious purpose, it was just foolishness. Nevertheless, I need to confess it and seek the Lord's strength to prevent reoccurrence.

There are those to whom this foolish babbling or chattering comes naturally. They talk on and on about the neighborhood's latest juicy morsels without compunction. Normally we don't have to look far to find such a person. Apparently they do it because their idle minds have nothing else to do. It fills the time, and elevates the talker at the expense of others. Beware of people like these if you don't want your secrets spread all over town.

Scriptural Examples

The Thessalonian busybodies. They had nothing better to do than to go around being busybodies. They were evidently spreading gossip and revealing secrets of other members of the Christian community. Paul rebuked them (2 Thess. 3:11-12).

The young widows. Apparently, some young widows had traded their love for Christ for sensual desires. They went from house to house talking too much. They were gossips and busybodies. Paul condemned their activities (1 Tim. 5:11-15).

Prayer of Application

Lord God, help me to control my tongue and to speak only appropriate words of encouragement and truth. And, Lord, whenever I hear gossip being spread, help me to stop it.

Beware of Cursing Those in Authority

If a man curses his father or mother, his lamp will be snuffed out in pitch darkness (Prov. 20:20).

In this proverb, we see a person who is in total violation of the commandment in which God orders us to honor our parents and, indeed, all those in authority over us (Ex. 20:12). It is the first commandment with a promise attached, but the other side of the coin is here. The child who curses his parents will himself be cursed and will be left in "pitch darkness."

For the Jew, the blessing of God was seen as the light of God. In Numbers 6:22-26, God tells Moses how to bless the Israelites. The Lord's blessing was His face shining upon them. (See also Psalms 4:6; 31:16; 80:3, 7, 19; 104:15; 119:135.) On the cross, God the Father turned His back, as it were, on Jesus and darkness consumed the land (Matt. 27:45). Darkness, or the absence of light, is a manifestation of separation from God. In Matthew 22:13, Jesus tells of the uninvited wedding guests being thrown into obscure darkness. This is the fate of all those who reject the truth and despise authority (Rom. 2:8).

Scriptural Examples

The stubborn son. The parents of the disobedient and rebellious son were to take him to the elders and then to the men of the town, who were to stone him to death (Deut. 21:18-21).

Eli's sons. The sons of this man of God were disobedient, and a stench to their father's nostrils. They refused to listen to Eli's rebukes so the Lord put them to death (1 Sam. 2:22-25).

The Recabites. Jonadab, son of Recab, ordered his sons not to drink wine, build houses, or plant vineyards. When Jeremiah set bowls of wine in front of them they wouldn't drink, saying that they would rather honor the command of their father. God then contrasted their obedience with the disobedience of Israel, who shunned the authority of His Word (Jer. 35:1-14).

Prayer of Application

Dear Father, how we as humans are so quick to despise authority. Help me, Lord, to honor my parents and all those in authority over me, as all authority has been instituted by You.

Beware of Easy Money, Easy Salvation

An inheritance quickly gained at the beginning will not be blessed at the end (Prov. 20:21).

Some years ago, in a TV show called "The Millionaire," a rich man named John Beresford Tipton sent his employee to an unsuspecting family to give them $1 million. The show then told the story of how the windfall affected their lives. Most think a million dollars would be a blessing, but that show caused many to think otherwise. If one isn't accustomed to dealing with money, there can be many sorrows.

Christians are called to an inheritance that makes an earthly inheritance look measly. Jesus warned us in Matthew 13:20 -21 that there would be those who would receive the gospel with joy but have no root and last only a short time. When trouble or persecution comes, they fall away and lose the apparent blessing. He enjoins us to first sit down and count the cost , then take up our cross daily and follow Him (Luke 14:27-29).

Jesus also said that "he who stands firm [endures] to the end will be saved" (Mark 13:13). We are not saved by enduring to the end, but endurance is indicative of true salvation. Salvation is the free gift of God by faith and not of works (Eph. 2:8-9). But faith that is void of works is no faith at all (James 2:14ff). Beware of easy salvation.

Scriptural Examples

Naboth and Ahab. Naboth inherited and cared for a vineyard that had probably been in his family for centuries. Ahab coveted Naboth's vineyard, and deceitfully took both it and Naboth's life. God brought disaster upon Ahab's house because of his treacherous "inheritance" (1 Kings 21:1-29).

The prodigal son. He took some easy money from his dad and went off to the far country. He longed for the "good life" that his early inheritance could bring. Like many "rich kids" do, he got his whipping in the far country (Luke 15:12ff).

Prayer of Application

Father, thank You for the riches that are mine in Christ Jesus. Help me to rightly view my responsibilities, to the end that I would glorify You in my life and enjoy You forever.

Have Faith in God and His Justice

Do not say, "I'll pay you back for this wrong!" Wait for the Lord, and he will deliver you (Prov. 20:22).

One of the most cherished of all human lusts is the lust for revenge. When we sense we have been wronged, our first instinct can be to lash out in an attempt to see justice done. When we do so we sin, and the justice of God is not done. Throughout Scripture we see examples of this. Simeon and Levi sought vengeance for the seduction of their sister Dinah (Gen. 34). Moses murdered the soldier in Egypt (Ex. 2:11-14). Joab vengefully slaughtered Abner (2 Sam. 3:27).

Personal revenge is expressly forbidden by God (Lev. 19:18; Rom. 12:17). Why? Because God says He alone is the instrument of revenge (Rom. 12:19). He has established government to be his "agent of wrath" in administering justice (Rom. 13:4). Only God knows a person's motives, and since we are prejudiced toward our own position we will have a tendency to inflict worse punishment than justice calls for.

Paul says instead of repaying evil for evil, we are to repay evil with good (Rom. 12:20-21). In this way we will reflect the love of Christ and fulfill our position and calling as God's ministers of reconciliation (2 Cor. 5:18-21).

Scriptural Examples

Shimei and David. This relative of Saul sat by the side of the road and cursed David, pelting him with stones. Abishai suggested that Shimei's head be removed, but David said the Lord would see and bring justice (2 Sam. 16:5-14).

Herodias. Herodias married her brother-in-law, Herod, and received the scorn of John the Baptist. She held a grudge against John and looked for revenge. At a feast, her daughter danced for Herod and his guests and was given one request. At her mother's prompting, John was decapitated (Mark 6:19-24).

Prayer of Application

Lord God, often on the freeway I feel endangered by someone's erratic driving and want to exact revenge. Help me to be calm, to back off, and to let You and the police handle it.

Beware of Your Ability to Rationalize

The Lord detests differing weights, and dishonest scales do not please him (Prov. 20:23).

Whenever a verse is repeated we need to grasp the seriousness of its warning. This proverb's rebuke is heard four times in the book, twice in chapter 20 itself (Prov. 11:1; 16:11; and 20:10). God detests deceit, with a capital "D."

As heirs of the sin nature we can deceive not only one another but ourselves as well. Much of our self-deceit lies in our capacity to rationalize or to ascribe fictitious causes to our moral choices. Flip Wilson cried, "The devil made me do it!" We need to be suspicious of all our motives, filtering everything through the grid of God's Word and praying that the Holy Spirit will keep us away from the abomination of deceit.

The work of the Holy Spirit at regeneration put a desire in my heart to do what is pleasing in God's sight. But only through the Spirit of God working in my heart and mind, moment by moment, can I be empowered to do it and overcome the deceit that still lurks within me (Rom. 7:15-25).

Scriptural Examples

Shelemiah, Zadok, Pedaiah, and Hanan. These men were said by Nehemiah to be trustworthy so they were placed in charge of distributing supplies to their brothers (Neh. 13:13).

Elymas. This man, whose name means "sorcerer," opposed Paul and Barnabas at Paphos. The apostle called him an enemy of that which is right, full of deceit and treachery. Paul then proceeded to render Elymas blind for a season, a condition that matched his lack of spiritual sight (Acts 13:6-11).

The Jews. Paul described in Romans 10:2-3 what might be called "The Great Deceit." The Jews, like all people who do not know of the righteousness that comes from God, sought to establish their own, listening to the deceitfulness of their hearts.

Prayer of Application

Gracious God, You have called me to walk honestly in this world. Protect me from my own deceitful heart, which is able to rationalize, and excuse in me that which is morally wrong.

Live in Absolute Dependence upon God

A man's steps are directed by the Lord. How then can anyone understand his own way (Prov. 20:24)?

As men and women born under the curse of sin, we want to be in control. We want to be the "captain of our ship, the master of our fate." The notion of a holy God who controls our every step is unthinkable. Even many Christians want to believe that God depends on us, not the other way around. But God's Word tells us that we are absolutely helpless apart from Him. God is *the* "mover and shaker." There is no other.

Ironically, for the person who understands the absolute sovereignty of God, it is his "magna carta" of freedom. It is not a freedom to sin. God forbid! It is a freedom from worry, fear and anxiety, the false guilt of legalism, and from the necessity *to* sin. Are we free from personal responsibility? No. Our dependence does not imply passivity, but rather a call to diligence without presumption.

I challenge you to cast off any worldview that opposes the absolute sovereignty of God. Let the Bible speak to you and prostrate yourself before God in absolute dependence upon His mighty power and grace.

Scriptural Examples

Rebekah. She just "happened" to come out of her house at precisely the same time Eliezer finished praying God would deliver to him Isaac's wife-to-be (Gen. 24:12-15).

Joseph. He attested to the overruling sovereignty of God. His brothers had played into God's hands (Gen. 50:20).

Pharaoh's daughter. This woman just "happened" to be at the Nile when Moses was hidden. Then she just "happened" to select Moses' real mother as his nursemaid (Ex. 2:1-9).

Rehoboam. This young king's heart was turned against the people's advice. Why? It was to fulfill the word of God as spoken to Jeroboam through Ahijah (1 Kings 12:1-15).

Prayer of Application

Sovereign Lord, help me to understand clearly that I am at Your mercy. Thank You that by Your grace You reached down and saved me while I was yet Your bitter enemy.

If You Vow, Be Sure to Follow Through

It is a trap for a man to dedicate something rashly and only later to consider his vows (Prov. 20:25).

There is a saying in wartime that "there are no atheists in foxholes." Faced with the imminent prospect of death, many have made rash promises to God. The problem is not the voluntary promise or vow. The problem comes when we fail to follow through. We sin when we promise, to God or to others, without truly counting the cost first.

Solomon writes it is better to keep your mouth shut than to make a vow that you don't keep (Eccl. 5:4-5). Some, caught up in religious fervor, will make a rash vow to God without considering the cost (2 Peter 2:21-22). I have volunteered in ways that became a burden as I struggled to follow through. Better to say "No" than to have to back out later.

God is very serious about promises. He will deliver on every detail of every promise He has ever made and He expects no less of us. What a joy it is for the Christian to understand that He does so. But what an awesome responsibility it is to follow in His footsteps.

Scriptural Examples

Jepthah. Israel's judge made a rash vow that if God would grant him victory, whatever would come out of his house first upon his return home, he would sacrifice as a burnt offering. It was his daughter, his only child (Judg. 11:29-40).

The Israelites. The Benjamites were slaughtered by the other tribes. Then, they vowed not to allow their daughters to marry Benjamites. The tribe almost perished (Judg. 20–21).

Hannah. She made a vow to God that if He would give her a son she would dedicate him to His service. God granted her request, and as soon as the boy Samuel was weaned, she took him to Eli, following through on her vows (1 Sam. 1:11-24).

Prayer of Application

Precious Savior, thank You for following through on the promise that a sacrifice would be provided for my sins. Help me, in like manner, to follow through on the promises I make.

Leaders, Allow No Wickedness in Your Midst

A wise king winnows out the wicked; he drives the threshing wheel over them (Prov. 20:26).

A lack of discipline exists in the visible church today. Many congregations do not follow the rules set forth in Matthew 18 and 1 Corinthians 5. It is a serious fault, for by allowing gross sin to pass unpunished in our midst, we allow the message of the gospel to be stripped of its power.

A few years ago, I visited a church where a matter of church discipline was carried out. And it was on Easter Sunday! I had been a member of two congregations that had been torn apart as the rules of church discipline were disregarded. I was impressed enough by the exercise of God's rules of order to make the church that carried out discipline my permanent place of worship.

The visible church is composed of wheat and weeds (Matt. 13:24-30), and in most cases, only the Lord really knows which is which. That's not our business. But in matters where the commandments of God are violated in the church, He calls the leaders to a plan of action that will either restore the sinner through repentance or drive him out of the church. In either case, reconciliation should be our primary goal.

Scriptural Examples

Ananias and Sapphira. In a very severe disciplinary action, God called this couple on the carpet for not doing what they said they would do. In fact, they died on the carpet (Acts 5:1-11).

The Corinthians. A man in their congregation was guilty of immorality in the taking of his father's wife. And they were proud of it! Paul said they should have disciplined the man and removed him from among them (1 Cor. 5:1-13).

Hymenaeus and Alexander. In 1 Timothy 1:18-20, Paul spoke of these apparent blasphemers. He said he "handed [them] over to Satan" for their instruction and discipline.

Prayer of Application

Dear Lord, You have called our church leaders to give account to You for those under their care. Give them strength, Lord, to carry out Your will even when it is not easy or popular.

Welcome God's Lamp of Conscience

The lamp of the Lord searches the spirit of a man; it searches out his inmost being (Prov. 20:27).

God has placed a lamp of right and wrong in every person, making him a moral being. The natural person hates the light of God's lamp (John 3:20) and runs from it, preferring the darkness. Those who deny a Creator God usually say the conscience is a product of societal conditioning and that humankind must cast it off if he is to continue to advance as he evolves.

But the conscience is much more a part of us than mere societal conditioning. It is the lamp of God which searches out our inmost being and illumines sin. We can sear our conscience by repeated sin, but we cannot eliminate its witness against us in the final judgment, when Jesus Christ will judge the secret things of every person (Rom. 2:14-16).

Christians should see their conscience as a friend. We should seek to sensitize it by continuing to feed on the Word of God, which is its guide. Welcome God's lamp of conscience.

Scriptural Examples

Pharaoh. His conscience told him it was wrong to take Sarai into his household, so as soon as he learned who she was he told Abram to "take her and go" (Gen. 12:10-20).

Abimelech. The king of the Philistines had a similar experience with his conscience after the ruse of Isaac that Rebekah was just his sister and not his wife (Gen. 26:6-11).

Daniel. In the Babylonian courts, Daniel resolved in his heart not to defile himself with the king's food and wine. He sought to eat "kosher" for conscience sake (Dan. 1:8).

Nehemiah. Earlier kings of Judah had lorded it over the people and placed heavy tax burdens upon them. But Nehemiah's conscience told him that he could not govern that way. He was guided by God's lamp (Acts 8:9-24).

Prayer of Application

Creator God, thank You for my conscience. Help me to use it to keep from sin, not trusting it fully but only trusting in Your Word.

Leaders, Govern in Love and Faithfulness

Love and faithfulness keep a king safe; through love his throne is made secure (Prov. 20:28).

The Bible is full of examples of rulers who exhibited the antithesis of this principle in their administrations. From Pharaoh to Herod, many governments were characterized by egocentricity, idolatry, and wicked despotism. In the northern kingdom of Israel, not one king ruled in love and faithfulness, and only a precious few did so in Judah.

David was such a king. Although a sinner and imperfect, David was a good king. He pointed to the One who had established an eternal kingdom in love and faithfulness, a kingdom made forever secure for its subjects. Soon His truthful and merciful reign will be extended over all the earth as He returns to take His rightful place as King of Kings and Lord of Lords (1 Tim. 6:15; Rev. 17:14; 19:16).

As leaders in the home, the community, in business, and in the church, we are to govern in this same love and faithfulness. We are to seek the highest good for all those under our charge, serving out of a heart of truth and mercy. In this way, we will portray Christ's coming again in power, to rule the earth forever.

Scriptural Examples

Rehoboam. His reign was not one of safety and security, but of trouble and warfare (1 Kings 12-14).

Artaxerxes. This Gentile king showed more reverence for God than did the wicked kings of Israel who preceded him. He commissioned Ezra to rebuild the temple (Ezra 7).

Xerxes. Here again is a Gentile king who exhibited a high degree of love and faithfulness (the book of Esther).

The king of Nineveh. Here also is a Gentile king who heard the Word of God and repented of his evil deeds, leading his people toward a more righteous way (Jonah 3:6-10).

Prayer of Application

Dear God, thank You for those who rule in love and faithfulness. Bless our political leaders, too, that they will rule over this country in ways pleasing to You. Come, Lord Jesus!

Act Your Age

The glory of young men is their strength, gray hair the splendor of the old (Prov. 20:29).

In the summertime, our church has a regular Wednesday evening gathering at the beach for volleyball, horseshoes, worship, study, and prayer. Sometimes I will succumb to the temptation of playing volleyball with the young people. My problem is that once I get ready to play, I'm 21 again, diving to "dig out" low shots, leaping to "spike" a good set, and lunging to save an errant shot. It all came so easily 30 years ago. Now I just get sore muscles and joints. I forget to act my age.

Just as a firm body and athletic skills are the purview of young people, so wisdom and understanding should be that of their elders. That's why professional ball players are usually under 40 and their coaches and managers over 40. And so our roles in life, and in the church, are often defined by age.

In a spiritual sense, often the most zeal and energy in a congregation are seen among its young people. That's as it should be. But zeal without knowledge is not good (Prov. 19:2). There should be a partnership between the zeal and energy of youth and the wisdom of the older saints. As in any good partnership, one partner supplies what the other lacks.

Scriptural Examples

The young men of Helkath Hazzurim. Here is the antithesis of what this proverb teaches. Abner and Joab led the armies of Judah and Israel. They foolishly agreed that some of their young men should fight each other. Neither strength nor wisdom prevailed when 24 men died for nothing (2 Sam. 2:13-16).

Rehoboam. This foolish young king listened to the young men in his court rather than to those who had gray hair. The result had a lasting effect because the kingdom was divided, never to be glued back together again (2 Chron. 10:6-14).

Prayer of Application

Father, help our young people to gain wisdom to match their zeal for You. Strengthen those of us who have more knowledge that our zeal for You and Your Word would not flag.

Receive Cleansing from the Wounds of Christ

Blows and wounds cleanse away evil, and beatings purge the in- most being (Prov. 20:30).

What a marvelous double meaning we find here. Christians are cleansed and healed because of the wounds that Christ suffered on Calvary (Isa. 53:5; 1 Peter 2:24), and we also receive cleansing and healing from the wounds that He inflicts upon us in His discipline (Ps. 51:8; Prov. 3:12).

Our Lord went to the Cross voluntarily, submitting to the wounds and stripes of the authorities. He did it that He might suffer condemnation for us and atone for the sins of His people. He made us whole, purging evil from our inmost being.

In God's sanctification process, it is sometimes necessary for us to receive discipline. This discipline of the Lord is not to punish us but to help us to turn from our wicked ways to ways that reflect His righteousness. No discipline is pleasant but the end result of the wounds we receive at the hand of our Lord is a harvest of righteousness and peace (Heb. 12:11).

Scriptural Examples

David. David was Israel's greatest king. But David was not without sin, and in fact, he sinned greatly in the matter of Bath-sheba and Uriah the Hittite. He penned Psalm 51 in retrospect, crying out to God for mercy and renewal. David wrote, "Let the bones you have crushed rejoice." God had "crushed" David's bones in discipline, but David knew that those wounds meant hope for him. David had been a shepherd as a young man and he knew that shepherds would sometimes be forced to break the leg of an habitually wayward lamb, then carry that little lamb on his back while its leg healed. In that way, the lamb would bond with the shepherd and would never stray from its master again. It is for this same purpose that our Master wounds those sheep who stray from Him (Ps. 51:8).

Prayer of Application

Lord Jesus, thank You for going to the cross to take the punishment for sin that should have been mine. And thanks also for the faithful wounds of discipline for my sanctification.

Chapter Twenty-one

God's Sovereignty

Someone might ask at this point, "The chapter headings have covered God's omnipotence and His providence; what's the difference between those characteristics of God and His sovereignty?" My short answer would be that omnipotence deals with God's ability to rule His creation, providence deals with God's work in ruling His creation, and sovereignty deals with God's will in ruling His creation. Ability, work, and will.

Notice as you read through Chapter 21 that three verses stand out that speak of God's will to rule—His sovereignty. The first is verse 1: "The king's heart is in the hand of the Lord; he directs it like a watercourse wherever he pleases." What God pleases to do, He does. He is the great King of Kings, and the sovereign Lord. Verse 30 says, "There is no wisdom, no insight, no plan that can succeed against the Lord." This verse speaks of the wills of men or angels set up against the will of God—the creature versus the Creator. It is no contest. What God wills is what happens. Finally, verse 31 states, "The horse is made ready for the day of battle, but victory rests with the Lord." Again, humans plan and prepare, but God's will is done. Victory and defeat are in His hands. The battle belongs to the Lord. What a wonderful truth we have in knowing that our God is sovereign.

Beware of Your Innate Independence

The king's heart is in the hand of the Lord; he directs it like a watercourse wherever he pleases (Prov. 21:1).

East of my home the mountains drop down quickly into the Imperial Valley. Much of this parched desert land was transformed into a garden earlier in this century by the introduction of irrigation. Now farmers water their fields simply by opening and closing gates in water ditches or sluices. This is the picture we have in the verse above. God opens and closes sluice gates directing the king's water into the fields of God's own choosing.

It is a very appropriate illustration in another sense as well. The flow of the water is naturally under the control of the king. The moral liberty of his own volition is not impaired by God; he is culpable for his actions. But the results of those actions all belong to God. Notice God is directing the course of the water, not its flow. And what more forceful illustration than of a king's heart, who in that day ruled others with absolute power.

Dr. J. Vernon McGee points out that in America we have a Declaration of Independence but today it seems to be used to declare our independence from God (p. 71). People seek to do whatever pleases them. But if the King of Kings directs the ordinary king's watercourse, will He not also direct the steps of everyone on earth? What we need in America, Dr. McGee states, is a "Declaration of Dependence" upon the Living and True God. Watch your own sinful desire to be independent of God. Trust in the One who controls the direction of all things.

Scriptural Examples

The Kings. The Bible is full of kings. There are good kings and bad kings, honest kings and lying kings, godly kings and wicked kings. But all of these men have this one thing in common: each one fulfilled the purposes of Almighty God, whether that was his express intention or not (Rev. 17:16-17).

Prayer of Application

Father, it is a mystery how I have moral responsibility for my choices yet You direct all results by Your providential oversight. Help me to trust fully in Your divine power.

Beware of Rationalization

*All a man's ways seem right to him, but the Lord
weighs the heart* (Prov. 21:2).

Most all Christians have what might be called their "life verse." But can you name the verse in Scripture that frightens you the most? For me that verse is Romans 2:1, where Paul argues, "You, therefore have no excuse, you who pass judgment on someone else, for at whatever point you judge the other, you are condemning yourself, because you who pass judgment do the same things." Paul is saying we justify the same activity in ourselves that we condemn in others. We have an uncanny ability to do this. It's called rationalization and we are all by nature good at it. But the person who dies without Christ will be judged by the same law he laid down for his neighbors.

The average person flatters himself into believing that the things he does are all right. But God looks on his heart and says it is "deceitful above all things and beyond cure. Who can understand it?" (Jer. 17:9). If my heart only deceived others, that would be one thing. But my heart deceives itself. The first thing we need to learn about human nature is we cannot trust ourselves (Prov. 28:26). We need to rely rather upon the Word of God as it is applied to our hearts by the Holy Spirit.

Scriptural Examples

James and John. When news came that Jesus and His disciples were not welcome in a Samaritan town, these "Sons of Thunder" asked, "Lord, do you want us to call fire down from heaven to destroy them?" Jesus rebuked them. Their zeal for Jesus hid a pair of murderous hearts (Luke 9:51-55).

The rich young ruler. This self-righteous fellow had a covetous heart that deceived him. When Jesus zeroed in on it, the young man went away sad, probably rationalizing Jesus didn't recognize purity when He saw it (Matt. 19:16-22).

Prayer of Application

Great Lord and God, forgive me for the motives of my heart that are not right in serving You. Help me to understand that I need my wicked heart purged to serve You out of a pure heart.

Beware of Superficiality in Worship

To do what is right and just is more acceptable to the Lord than sacrifice (Prov. 21:3).

The Hebrew word here for "sacrifice" is *zebach*, which means the slaughter of an animal in ritual sacrifice. Animal sacrifices were established by God and were pleasing to Him (Gen. 4:4; 8:21). Yet Solomon is saying that there are things we can do that are much more pleasing to God.

The sacrifices established by God were to point to the great sacrifice of the Lord Jesus Christ. But they were detestable to Him if valued only for themselves and not for the One to whom they pointed: the righteous and just One. Righteousness and justice are the reality, while animal sacrifices were but a shadow of that reality (Heb. 10:1-2).

People throughout the ages have deceived themselves into thinking that mere superficial observance of some religious ritual can please God (Prov. 21:2). The practice of church sacraments without a corresponding and underlying true repentance and faith is detestable to God (Ps. 51:16-17). What God demands is a living sacrifice! He wants your whole being! All of you! That is your acceptable worship (Rom. 12:1).

Scriptural Examples

Cain. Cain brought a sacrifice to God but it was superficial. God looked upon Cain's heart and saw that he had not brought his heart to the altar as his brother Abel had (Gen. 4:3-7).

Solomon. No man sacrificed more animals to God than this king of Israel. But underlying them were wisdom and the practice of justice and mercy in his kingdom (1 Kings 3:4; 8:64).

The Pharisees and teachers of the law. These men were scathingly rebuked by Jesus for their superficiality. Our Lord raked them over the coals for neglecting the more weighty matters of justice, mercy, and faithfulness (Matt. 23:23).

Prayer of Application

Lord, I see much of the Pharisees' superficiality in myself. Forgive me and cleanse me from it. Help me to present my body daily as a living sacrifice to You for Your glory.

Beware of the Pride that Blinds

Haughty eyes and a proud heart, the lamp of the wicked, are sin (Prov. 21:4).

The KJV translates "lamp" here as "plowing" or "tillage." The confusion lies in a vowel. The Hebrew *nir* means "plowing," and *ner* means "lamp." I'd like to use both words to illustrate what I believe to be the full meaning of the proverb.

Plowing seems to indicate an industrious person whom the proverbs would normally seek to elevate. But we must remember that anything the unsaved person does is sin (Rom. 8:5-13; Eccl. 7:20; Eph. 4:17-22). While the unsaved person's gifts to and activities on behalf of charity seem to be good, the Bible tells us that if the action does not seek God's glory through Christ, it is all sin (Rom. 14:23). Whatever we do we are to do in humility to the glory of God (1 Cor. 10:31).

The word "lamp" seems to best tie in the first phrase of the proverb. A wicked person's eyes and heart are his "lamp." Jesus uses this motif in Luke 11:34 when He says, "The eye is the lamp of the body." He goes on to say that good eyes let light in so that your body is full of light. Bad eyes or lamps see only darkness. Here we see those "bad eyes" of which our Lord spoke. They are haughty eyes, lifted up in pride. They look only upon darkness and eternal judgment. Beware of the pride that blinds.

Scriptural Examples

Hezekiah. He became ill and prayed to God for healing. When God healed him, proud Hezekiah did not give thanks. God's wrath was on him until he repented (2 Chron. 32:24f.).

The King of Assyria. God said that He would punish him for his proud heart and haughty eyes. The king bragged of his accomplishments and wisdom, his conquering armies, and his power and might. He denied the One who establishes all rulers by the power of His might (Isa. 10:12-14).

Prayer of Application

Father, take away any desire to be raised up in honor without giving You all the glory due Your name. Without Your uplifting hand I couldn't do anything, even take a breath.

Beware of Hasty Shortcuts

The plans of the diligent lead to profit as surely as haste leads to poverty (Prov. 21:5).

Early on in my real estate career I tried to score hasty "touch-downs" by going after big deals that were risky although they appeared to be "slam dunks." Most turned out to be "strikeouts" (to complete my all-season mixed metaphor). The only things slammed were my wallet and my foolish pride.

Life should be viewed as a long distance race (Heb. 12:1). Such a race is run aerobically. That is, a runner's lungs process the air he breathes and don't build up an oxygen debt. In the 100-yard dash, run anaerobically, the runners catch their breath after the tape. Running sprints in a marathon is stupid.

Just as we need to avoid get-rich-quick schemes, we also need to avoid the other side of the coin. We can study an opportunity so long that it vanishes. In so doing we may just be afraid, excusing our fear by calling it diligence. Jesus tells us that we are to weigh the cost of what we do, including the act of becoming His disciples (Luke 14:28-33). Then, after deciding to move ahead, we should work our plans with energy, discipline, and patience, dedicating the results to the glory of God.

Scriptural Examples

Saul. Because he wanted a quick victory over the Philistines, Saul gave a foolish order that his men were not to eat on the day of battle. This hasty command caused all kinds of problems in the conduct of his troops and, most importantly, in his relationship with his son Jonathan (1 Sam. 14:23-45).

The shallow soil. In this parable, our Lord described one of four soils as rocky and shallow. The seed that was sown there sprang up quickly but died when the sun scorched the plants. So it is with some who receive the news of the Kingdom with joy but fall away when persecution comes (Matt. 13:5-6, 20-21).

Prayer of Application

Oh, Sovereign Lord, help me always to count the cost before undertaking a major decision. And Lord, keep me from hasty shortcuts and help me to take the long view of life.

Beware of the Snare of Hasty Wealth

6) A fortune made by a lying tongue is a fleeting vapor and a deadly snare. 7) The violence of the wicked will drag them away, for they refuse to do what is right (Prov. 21:6-7).

We see in these verses a man who in his haste to be rich used a "forked tongue." The fortune that he made with his misrepresentations vaporized as quickly as it was gotten and became in the end a death trap (Rom. 6:23). P.T. Barnum, the founder of the Barnum and Bailey Circus, is supposed to have said, "There's a sucker born every minute." What P.T. probably didn't understand is that the real "sucker" is the guy who tries to make one of others.

Examples of this type of behavior abound. A segment on my local TV news focuses on consumer issues. The reporters point out the most recent scams that prey upon the elderly and unsuspecting. We only need to go back a few years to remember the savings and loan scandal that rocked the nation. What has become of the fortune of those who lied? It has vanished in a fleeting vapor while they spend years in the slammer.

Scriptural Examples

Zacchaeus. He was a wealthy tax collector who extorted his riches. That is, he used his office to collect more from the taxpayer than was owed and he kept the difference for himself. The Lord Jesus walked through Zacchaeus' hometown one day and spotted the little man perched up in a tree. Jesus proceeded to call him by name, telling him to come down, that He would be spending that day in his house. Zacchaeus, who was probably used to being shunned by the people, was overjoyed by the Lord's greeting and offered to pay back by four-fold anyone he had ever cheated. Jesus remarked that salvation had come to Zacchaeus' house that day. He had been saved from the deadly snare he had been laying up for himself (Luke 19:2-9).

Prayer of Application

Lord God, help me to commit to You that I will never use my tongue for illicit gain. Rather, may I focus on the riches of Christ and not do anything that would violate Your Word.

Praise God for His Marvelous Grace

The way of the guilty is devious, but the conduct of the innocent is upright (Prov. 21:8).

The first line of this proverb speaks of every person on earth, unless by a miracle of God's grace he or she becomes innocent. The former's lifestyle is characterized by deviousness, while the latter practices uprightness.

The word "guilty" in line one of the NIV version may be more appropriately rendered "guilt-laden. "This describes all those whose sins have not been forgiven and the eternal consequences of those sins not lifted by the blood of the Savior. Most, if not all, natural people would take umbrage at that statement and argue that their behavior is mostly moral and upright. But they use the world's standard, not the Word of God. Ethics today are determined by majority vote. If 80 percent of unmarried college students are sexually active, then it must be all right. After all, the humanist manifesto calls man the measure.

But by God's marvelous grace He saves some people. Those saved are then innocent in God's eyes and their subsequent walk will be characterized by purity and uprightness. No longer will the Christian walk according to his old boss, Satan (Eph. 2:1-3), but in step with his newfound friend, Jesus (Eph. 4:22-24). What you do demonstrates who you are. Praise God for the new you (2 Cor. 5:17)!

Scriptural Examples

The false prophets. In the Sermon on the Mount, Jesus warned us of these men and their devious walk. Outwardly they look moral and upright, but inwardly they are ferocious wolves. We would recognize them by their fruit. An apple tree doesn't bear oranges. Watch and see what characterizes a person's life. There are many of these deceivers out there today. Don't be drawn away from the truth of the Word of God because of them. (See Matt. 7:15-20.)

Prayer of Application

Father, thank You for saving me. When I was dead and guilty in trespasses and sins You made me alive and innocent in Christ Jesus. I have no reason to boast. You deserve the credit.

Married Couples, Love One Another

Better to live on a corner of the roof than share a house with a quarrelsome wife (Prov. 21:9).

A young man was asked about his recent marriage. He said, "I didn't know what happiness was until I got married. And then it was too late."

The homes of the desert region of Palestine had flat roofs with a parapet wall. They were often used for sleeping, particularly when the weather was hot. But the idea in the verse above is of a permanent situation. Lacking a small guest room, a man's stay there would have been subjected to wind, rain, and snow. Even that most uncomfortable predicament would be preferable to being warm and toasty with a quarrelsome spouse.

Men are not innocent of a quarrelsome spirit. The root of such contentiousness is sin, expressed in pride and selfishness that seeks its own way. The love that seeks to exalt one's partner at the expense of self is missing. That is the agape love of Christ which every believer should portray in marriage.

A bigger problem may exist when a Christian is "unequally yoked" (2 Cor. 6:14) with an unsaved spouse. While the Christian seeks to honor and serve the Lord, his spouse is embarrassed by his enthusiasm for Christ. It can be an awful situation, because as one grows closer to God, the other, unless saved, grows more distant. Single man or woman, don't even date non-believers. You might wind up on the corner of a rooftop.

Scriptural Examples

Mr. and Mrs. Job. Job received battering after battering at the hands of Satan. Sitting in despair on a pile of ashes, scraping at his boils, Job didn't need to hear his wife's nagging. She said, "Are you still holding on to your integrity? Curse God and die!" Job rebuked her. He asked, "Shall we accept good from God, and not trouble?" I'm sure her words added greatly to Job's suffering (Job 2:7-10).

Prayer of Application

Dear God, we have in our marriages a wonderful opportunity to show forth Your love. Help me to exemplify Christ in my marriage, in the good times and bad, through thick and thin.

Seek Only Good for Your Neighbor

The wicked man craves evil; his neighbor gets no mercy from him (Prov. 21:10).

This proverb reminds me of a short story that was written in the form of a diary. A man moved into a new neighborhood and proceeded to destroy the relationships there in any way he could. Through innuendo, deceit, gossip, slander, and vandalism, longtime friends were at each other's throats. Marriages were destroyed and children were disregarded. After the wreckage was complete, the man placed one final entry into his diary: "Time to move."

The wicked person "craves evil" in that he lives for himself. He doesn't necessarily act in the manner of my short story example, but even when he does something seemingly out of a genuine love and concern for his neighbor, an underlying principle of selfishness is at work.

Some self-esteem advocates would teach us to first love ourselves, then we will be able to love our neighbor. But the Golden Rule actually teaches that we are to give the same priority to our neighbor's well-being that we would naturally give to our own. We don't need to be taught to provide for our own needs. That just comes naturally. Only through the Spirit of God working through us will we learn to put the law of love to practice in our neighborhoods.

Scriptural Examples

Nabal. This descendant of the righteous Caleb should have been more like his ancestor. But when David asked Nabal for food, the wicked man repaid David's earlier kindness with evil (1 Sam. 25).

Paul. Paul cried out regarding his own wickedness. He said, "For what I want to do I do not do, but what I hate I do." He concluded only the Lord Jesus could rescue him from his body of death, his sin nature (Rom. 7:15-25).

Prayer of Application

Heavenly Father, help me to practice Your principle of agape love in all I do, seeking the highest and best for my neighbor and expecting nothing in return.

Learn from the Lord's Instruction

When a mocker is punished, the simple gain wisdom; when a wise man is instructed, he gets knowledge (Prov. 21:11).

Here again are the three students: the mocker, the simpleton, and the wise man (Prov. 19:25). The person who mocks wisdom gets a rod on his back, but as we're told in Proverbs 17:10, even 100 lashes won't teach him much. But the blow that strikes the mocker should teach the simple.

In earlier years punishment of criminals in many societies was carried out in public places. The idea behind this sort of demonstration was to teach a lesson to the simple. After witnessing an execution the simple should have said, "Wow, I don't want that to happen to me!" God instituted stoning in Israel as a public capital punishment. It both punished the sin and served as an example to others. Unlike the mocker, the simple may become wise through example.

The wise man learns by instruction. He never stops learning and acquiring knowledge. Let's keep on learning until the end of our days and use the knowledge God gives us to glorify Him in all we think, say, and do.

Scriptural Examples

The blasphemer. The son of an Israeli and an Egyptian got into a fight and blasphemed God's name. The Lord instructed Moses to have the entire assembly stone the mocker to death. Today, God's name is mocked around the world. More than a stoning awaits those mockers (Lev. 24:10-16).

The people of Laish. These simple people apparently did not have a leader to teach them the elementary principles of defense. Some Danites robbed Micah of his idols and family priest, then went to Laish and torched it. How much better to have gained wisdom through instruction rather than through actual experience (Judg. 18:27-28).

Prayer of Application

Dear Lord, thank You for Your Word, which when applied to our hearts through Your Holy Spirit, guides us into all truth. By it, help me to avoid the pitfalls in life that trap others.

Look at Justice as an Eternal Concept

The Righteous One takes note of the house of the wicked and brings the wicked to ruin (Prov. 21:12).

The wicked do sometimes get their comeuppance in this life, but volumes could be written about those who don't.

For centuries, philosophers have sought to give rational (extra-biblical) evidence for the existence of God, one of which has to do with our principle. There are basically five such arguments. The ontological argument, principally of St. Anselm, holds that people can have the idea of a perfect and supreme being, the greatest being imaginable. Since, according to Plato, existence or reality is an essential quality of being, that absolutely perfect and supreme being must logically exist. The cosmological argument states what exists as an effect must have had a primary cause, and that cause had to have the power of being in itself. The teleological argument sees the intelligence and order of the universe as proof of a great architect. The historical argument looks at people's religiosity, and posits a being who created people with that innate calling.

Ironically, a central proponent of the moral argument was Immanuel Kant—himself an agnostic—who thought people should live as if there was a God. Kant argued since there is a disparity between what most people deserve and what they get in this life, justice must be eternal in nature. In order for justice to be applied there would have to be a judge who was omniscient and who was also powerful enough to carry out the sentence. This is exactly what the Bible and this proverb teach.

Scriptural Examples

Job and his friends. Their basic argument was Job must have done some evil to bring about his disaster. Job contended he was innocent and scorned the very counsel of the wicked. Behind the scenes we see God in control. His justice ultimately prevailed (the book of Job).

Prayer of Application

Heavenly Father, thank You for your eternal government over human affairs. Most of all, Lord, thank You for sending Your Son to die for me and to cancel the debt of sin in my life.

Beware of Shutting Your Ears to the Poor

If a man shuts his ears to the cry of the poor, he too will cry out and not be answered (Prov. 21:13).

In my city, as in other communities across the nation, the problem of feeding the poor and homeless has become widespread. Our government's welfare system has historically locked the poor into a system of handouts and provided little incentive or ability to find meaningful employment. Such welfare is a sinful system that has recently experienced many major overhauls on federal, state, and local levels.

I believe the cry of the poor is not so much "give me something to eat," as it is "give me a job to do." Educational systems and standards should be established that will prepare those not currently employable for meaningful jobs in the future. This is the proper way to permanently hear the cry of the poor: give them work to do that is honorable and fulfilling.

My church is active in a rescue mission that gives food, clothing, and a gospel message to all who come. Other Christian works help the needy in our society. They should be supported with our money and our time. Beware of the proverb's warning. To shut one's ears to the cry of the poor will bring God's judgment. We will cry out to Him, but we will not be heard.

Scriptural Examples

Job and Eliphaz. Job's friend Eliphaz accused him of shutting his ears to the poor (Job 22:7) and ascribed part of the reason for the calamity that had come upon Job to that sin. Job was confident he was innocent of the charges (Job 31:7).

The rich man and Lazarus. For years, the beggar Lazarus had lain at the gate of the rich man, who wouldn't give the poor homeless man the time of day. Both died. The rich man cried out from hell for Lazarus to put only a drop of water on his tongue. His cries for mercy went unanswered (Luke 16:19-31).

Prayer of Application

Dear Lord, make me more sensitive to the needs of the poor in our society. Help me to serve them to the end that Your Kingdom will be advanced and Your Name honored.

Let Your Anger Be Soothed by God's Gifts

A gift given in secret soothes anger, and a bribe concealed in the cloak pacifies great wrath (Prov. 21:14).

As a husband approaches his home he hides a bouquet of flowers behind his back. He and his wife had an argument before he left for work and he is bringing a peace offering. As she opens the door, out come the flowers. Quickly, the morning's argument is forgotten in the beauty and aroma of a dozen red roses. It works, guys!

This proverb employs both the word "gift" and the word "bribe." Sometimes the line between the two is fuzzy. We need to be careful in our gift-giving, because to cross the line into bribery or to use a secret gift to pervert justice is sin (Ex. 23:8; Deut. 16:19; 27:25). But to use a gift to melt the anger of a loved one may be a courteous and effective way to say, "I'm sorry, let's make up," and restore the relationship.

Most people are prone to anger, particularly when our "rights" have been trampled on, or when we don't get our way. Such unrighteous anger is not honoring to God. At the times when anger lures us we need to consider God's gifts to us, His Word and His only Son, who when He was mistreated responded in love. Therefore, we are called to follow Him in humility and love of others. We are not to seek revenge.

Scriptural Examples

Jacob. He brought a gift to his brother Esau to appease the split he had caused many years earlier. Jacob didn't hide the herds he brought but they were secret inasmuch as they were a surprise (Gen. 32:1-23; 33:1-17).

Samuel's sons. Joel and Abijah didn't walk in their father's ways. They accepted bribes, perverting justice (1 Sam. 8:1-4).

Abigail. Nabal's wife showed great wisdom in bringing gifts to David and his men, thereby assuaging their anger following the rebuff of her wicked husband (1 Sam. 25:14-34).

Prayer of Application

Father God, thank You for the gifts of Your Word and Your Son. Your Word says He is Lord of all. Take my anger, Lord, and replace it with Your patient love and forgiveness.

Let Your Conduct Bring Both Joy and Terror

When justice is done, it brings joy to the righteous but terror to evildoers (Prov. 21:15).

A man joined a golf foursome that included Billy Graham. Following the round, the man was asked what it was like to play golf with Billy. He replied it had been an awful experience. The evangelist was a Bible-thumping bully, he said, and used every opportunity to make him feel guilty. Pressed about specifics, he confessed Graham hadn't said one word about God. Graham's mere presence had caused him extreme discomfort.

The word "justice" in the verse above seems to be better rendered "right conduct" (Kidner, p. 143). Right conduct in our lives brings joy to us and to fellow believers, such as our pastor and elders. Jesus said His yoke was easy and His burden light (Matt. 11:30). Jesus is a loving and forgiving Master. Faithful service to Him is something His sheep will want to do. It is a joy. But that same conduct brings terror to the unsaved. Why?

Paul says Christians are the odor of God both to those who are saved and to those who are perishing. To one, we are the putrid smell of death and to the other, the fragrant aroma of life (2 Cor. 2:16). If you have been criticized by those outside the church, seemingly without reason, you will know what this means. For the unsaved person, joy comes only in sin. To see a life of righteous conduct is anathema to him. Let your right conduct in Christ be a terror to those who do evil and reject God's grace.

Scriptural Examples

The Old Testament saints. They were tortured and faced jeers and floggings. They faced all kinds of persecutions, but their right conduct was commended by God (Heb. 11:35-39).

The prophets. They spoke for God and called Israel to leave the idolatry and sins of the pagan nations. They were ridiculed, beaten, and mocked as they suffered for the Lord (James 5:10).

Prayer of Application

Our Father, we are sinners and we live in a world of sinners. Help us to remember that if we are called to suffer with Christ now, we shall not suffer the wrath to come.

Stay on the Path of Understanding

A man who strays from the path of understanding comes to rest in the company of the dead (Prov. 21:16).

Derek Kidner points out the irony of this verse (p.144). Here is a fellow, he says, who desires independence and a more exciting life so he strays from the clear path of understanding. What happens to him is exactly the opposite of what he seeks. He loses his mobility and independence as he comes to rest in a congregation of others. The company he comes to keep is dead.

To stray from the path of understanding requires only a small step at first. Soon, though, the true path is left far behind as the wanderer shows his real character and home. I don't believe a true believer can stray permanently into the company of the dead (John 10:27-28). But, I believe a make-believer can. What we have here is the test between the two.

The wife of a man I know left him and moved herself and their child out of the country. Although she professed Christ and had much biblical knowledge, she showed her true colors when she left the path. Paul tells us to work out our salvation in "fear and trembling" (Phil. 2:12). We are to have absolute trust in God but absolute distrust of self and the wandering nature within us.

Scriptural Examples

The thorny ground. In Jesus' parable, the fellow represented by the thorny ground leaves the path of understanding. Why? The desires for other things like wealth choked the Word and made him unfruitful (Mark 4:18-19).

The prodigal son. This young man seemed to stray into the company of the dead, but was drawn back to his own father's house. So it will be with all who are truly saved (Luke 15:11-23).

The man in the mirror. He took a look in the mirror of God's law but drifted away, forgetting what he looked like, a sinner condemned by his own wandering (James 1:23-24).

Prayer of Application

Father, thank You for the assurance we have in Your Word, that Jesus the Great Shepherd will not lose one of the sheep You have given Him. Keep me on the right path.

Beware of the Love of Pleasure

He who loves pleasure will become poor; whoever loves wine and oil will never be rich (Prov. 21:17).

God has created many things in this world for our pleasure and enjoyment. Wine and oil are among them. Oil here probably connotes the finer things in life. There is nothing intrinsically wrong with either commodity, as God has given us these things to enjoy. The problem comes when we begin to love them and live for them and not for God. To love them is to give them top priority. The proverb says that will lead to poverty.

In a physical sense the excessive love of these things may cause us to neglect our responsibilities or to live beyond our means. There is a real sense in which we will suffer spiritual poverty as well when we seek after such pleasure. Jesus said in Matthew 6:33 we are to seek first the Kingdom of God and His righteousness. We are to make that our top priority and God will enrich us in all things. If we replace our search for God and His righteousness with the search for wine and oil, that will surely cause us to become poor in the riches of God.

Scriptural Examples

Samson. This most enigmatic of men sought the company of prostitutes and women outside Israel. He was apparently much in love with "wine and oil" even though set apart by God as a Nazirite. He became an object of mockery (Judg. 16:1-21).

The drunkard. He consumed so much wine he suffered a tremendous hangover. He also suffered from a guilt trip and bloodshot eyes. His head whirled around in confusion and he saw visions of strange sights. His stomach felt like he was on the top of a mast on a sailing ship in a winter storm. To feel better, he took a little "hair of the dog," another drink to help him in his pain. It would be easy to see how a fellow like this could be brought to rags. It happens all the time (Prov. 23:29-35).

Prayer of Application

Heavenly Father, the things of the world can be appealing in many ways. Keep my eyes upon Jesus, seeking to live my life for Him, and away from yielding to the temptations of the flesh.

Hide in Christ, Your Ransom

The wicked become a ransom for the righteous, and the unfaithful for the upright (Prov. 21:18).

What irony! Jesus, the Righteous One, gave His life as a ransom for many (Matt. 20:28), the Upright for the unfaithful. How then can the wicked become a ransom for the righteous; the unfaithful for the upright? As a God of absolute righteousness and justice, God cannot overlook sin and demands that a ransom or payment be made. Interestingly, there are instances in redemptive history where the wicked have become such a ransom for others.

When Moses went up on the mountain to meet God, the people talked Aaron into fashioning a gold idol. When Moses came back, he told the Levites to go through the camp with their swords and kill their brothers, friends, and neighbors. About 3,000 people died. Later, God also struck the people with a plague for their sin. But Aaron did not die by the sword or in the plague. God's anger against this "righteous" man was assuaged in the ransom paid by those who did die (Ex. 32:1-33: 6).

Paul tells us the righteous Jesus became a curse for us that we might be redeemed (Gal. 3:13). He who knew no sin became sin so we might become the righteousness of God in Him (2 Cor. 5: 21). Those who are hidden in Him and in His ransom will avoid the punishment reserved for the wicked.

Scriptural Examples

Aachan. He hid some of Jericho's plunder for himself, so the Israelites stoned Aachan and his family to death. They were a ransom assuaging God's fierce anger (Josh. 7:24-26).

Egypt and Ethiopia. They were ransom for Jerusalem as God turned Sennacherib from the city (Isa. 43:3-4; 2 Kings 19:7-9).

The firstborn of Egypt. These people, many perhaps mere babies, were used as a ransom for the deliverance of God's people from Egypt (Hos. 11:1; Ex. 11:4-8; 12:29-36).

Prayer of Application

Dear Lord, thank You for sending Jesus to the cross to pay the ransom for the sins of all who would be saved. Thank You, Lord, that it was effective, and secured my salvation.

Live in Peace with Your Spouse

*Better to live in a desert than with a quarrelsome and
ill-tempered wife* (Prov. 21:19).

The desert that lies 70 miles east of San Diego can be a very inhospitable place. There are lots of ways to die out there, including dehydration, sunstroke, and rattlesnake and Gila monster bite. But even a hot, treacherous desert is better than a cool beach house with a quarrelsome and ill-tempered spouse.

We can substitute "husband" for "wife" here. Wives do not have a corner on being contentious and angry. No situation on earth is more difficult for a person than to be the spouse of someone like this. Even the desert will look good.

Our goal in marriage should be to live at peace with one another. Husbands and wives should be the best of friends, putting the other before self. It is in this way we honor God in our marriages and reflect Christ in the world.

Scriptural Examples

Zipporah. Moses' wife showed her bent for contentiousness in an incident involving her husband's religious practices. But Moses was not without fault (Ex. 4:25-27).

___**Nabal and Abigail**. Nabal is the biggest jerk in Scripture, with the possible exceptions of Ahab and Haman. His wife Abigail was a woman of enormous patience to be able to abide his contentiousness, stubbornness, and bad temper. David saw that quality in her, I'm sure, and following Nabal's demise, he took her to be his wife (1 Sam. 25:2-39).

Michal. This daughter of King Saul and wife of King David contentiously chided her husband for dancing in the streets of Jerusalem following the return of the ark of the covenant. She called him vulgar and undignified. God rebuked her for such contentiousness with barrenness for the remainder of her days (2 Sam. 6:16; 20-23).

Prayer of Application

Dear Father, give us attitudes that reflect the humility and love of Christ. Help us to avoid quarrelling and strife and instead seek peace and pursue it, making it a top priority.

Store Up the Treasures of Christ

20) In the house of the wise are stores of choice food and oil, but a foolish man devours all he has. 21) He who pursues righteousness and love finds life, prosperity and honor (Prov. 21:20-21).

Jesus said, "Do not store up for yourselves treasures on earth" (Matt. 6:19). But here we see the wise man's house containing choice treasure and that of the foolish man nothing. How are we to resolve this apparent contradiction?

Jesus was not telling us to stop planning for the future. The prudent person will lay up a storehouse for future contingencies and needs. The difference lies in the placement of trust. The wise man will recognize God is the source of all material and spiritual blessings. Even though he wisely stores up for the future, the wise man does not put trust in his earthly stores.

The foolish man uses up his treasure through his appetites. He may be a drunkard, a gambler, or one who lives beyond his means, but he is not prudent in his handling of money.

The real treasure of this life and the next is Jesus Christ. His is the righteousness and the love we are to pursue with all of our heart, mind, and strength (Deut. 6:5; Luke 10:27). The rewards of His treasure house are mind boggling and eternal (Matt. 6:20). Store up His treasures.

Scriptural Examples

Job and Abraham. They were two of the richest men who ever lived. God delighted to honor them for their faithfulness, righteousness, and kindness to others (Gen. 12:1f.; Job 1:1-3).

Ruth. She didn't have much of this world's treasures, but she pursued righteousness and love. She was blessed by God with the life, prosperity, and honor promised here (Ruth 3:10ff).

Paul. He pressed on in pursuit of the high goal toward which Christ had called him. Forgetting what was behind, he set his sights on an eternal prize (Phil. 3:12-14).

Prayer of Application

Lord, help me to be a good steward over all You have placed in my hands. May I trust only in Your sovereign power to sustain me and in the hope of Your treasures in heaven.

Prepare to Wage Spiritual Warfare

A wise man attacks the city of the mighty and pulls down the stronghold in which they trust (Prov. 21:22).

Superiority in battle lies not so much in numbers as it does with the strategies and tactics employed and with the preparation of the troops and their equipment. A wise commander can defeat a substantially larger force. The invasion of Normandy in 1944 is a good example of that.

Even though Christians live in the world we do not wage war like the world does (2 Cor. 10:3-5). With our weapons we are able to demolish all arguments and pretensions that set themselves up against the knowledge of God. We are to put on the whole armor of God (Eph. 6:10ff). The only offensive weapon Paul speaks of is a sword, which is the Word of God. This is the power by which we attack the "city of the mighty." The problem is most of us aren't fighting with a very big sword.

R.C. Sproul often laments the "fideism" of today's Christian community. *Fides* is Latin for "faith," as in *Adeste Fidelis*. Much of today's church, he says, has a "faith in faith" and lacks a rational and biblically sound understanding of why they believe what they do. The Bible is our foundation. We need to take up that sharp, double-edged sword (Heb. 4:12) and pull down the secular strongholds that abound in our culture. Along with prayer, we have the keys to victory in the war we're called to fight.

Scriptural Examples

Joshua at Ai. Joshua led a force against the city of Ai, using tactics that were brilliant in both their planning and execution. The mission was a huge success and Ai fell (Josh. 8:1-29).

The poor city dweller. There was a poor man who lived in a city under siege by a powerful king. By his wisdom the man saved the city. Though no one remembered him, Solomon concluded "wisdom is better than strength" (Eccl. 9:13-16).

Prayer of Application

Dear Father, thank You for Your Word. Help me to understand its depths, Lord, to the end that I may be able to take my place in the spiritual battle that rages on this planet.

Keep Close Rein on Your Tongue

He who guards his mouth and his tongue keeps himself from calamity (Prov. 21:23).

When my brother and I were kids we couldn't wait for Saturday afternoon matinees. The main feature was typically a "shoot-em-up" western that starred singing cowboys like Gene Autry or Roy Rogers and always had a scene featuring a runaway wagon. The heroine would be imperiled as the frightened horses bolted when the reins were dropped.

The hero would then try to get up on one of the lead horses to gain control of the team or just grab the heroine and let the rig go over a cliff. Either way, a runaway team always promised calamity and kept us glued to our seats. The Bible tells us that the human tongue can be like those horses (James 3:1-8).

How do we rein in this troublemaker before we are carried over the precipice? First, we need to be keenly aware of the tongue's ability to dispense poison. Second, we need to speak only after careful reflection. Is what we intend to say true, pleasant, helpful, kind, and edifying? Does it submit to God's law of love? If not, don't say it! Ask God to help you control your tongue. He's more powerful than a zillion cowboys.

Scriptural Examples

Hezekiah. Hezekiah received messengers of the king of Babylon and proceeded to babble on about the great fortune he held in Jerusalem. His tongue brought great calamity on Judah. Isaiah foretold that all of Judah's treasures would be carried off to Babylon. That's exactly what happened (2 Kings 20:12-17).

Peter. When Jesus told His disciples how He must go up to Jerusalem and suffer, die, and rise again, Peter rebuked Him saying, "Never, Lord! This shall never happen to you!" Jesus then rebuked the impetuous Peter for his foolish words spoken in haste, calling him "Satan" (Matt. 16:21-23).

Prayer of Application

Father, how often have I put my tongue in gear while my brain remained in neutral? Help me, Lord, to keep a close check on all my words that they might always reflect glory to You.

Warn Others of Mocking God

The proud and arrogant man—"Mocker" is his name; he behaves with overweening pride (Prov. 21:24).

What is the most arrogant statement imaginable? I think it is: "There are many ways to God, Jesus is only one of them." Ironically, the Christian is accused of this same arrogance by claiming there's only one way to be saved (John 3:36).

But can you imagine standing before Almighty God and telling Him this: "Your only Son is not a good enough Savior for me! I am the one to determine how I ought to be saved, thank you"? That is exactly what people are saying when they say that all ways are valid in seeking God. They trust in their good works. Every religion in the world, except historical Christianity, teaches this "self-salvation." Mocker is their name.

Today's culture reeks with relativism. People say there is no such thing as objective truth. One of the most fundamental laws of logic, non-contradiction, is broken all the time. This law states that two opposing statements cannot both be true at the same time and in the same relationship. Both can be false, or one may be true and the other false, but not both true.

Jesus said, "I am the way and the truth and the life. No one comes to the Father except through me" (John 14:6). Now someone may deny Jesus said that. He may think of Him as a madman for saying it, or as a liar and a fraud. But he needs then to prove his case. To pay Christ lip-service by saying He was a "great teacher" or "a wonderful example for all people" and then to call Him a liar is the utmost mockery. We need to warn people everywhere of this deadly practice.

Scriptural Examples

The scribes and Pharisees. These men stared truth in the face and mocked it. They heard the words of the Savior and saw the authenticating miracles that He performed, yet their pride wouldn't allow them to see the truth (Matt. 23).

Prayer of Application

Lord, thank You for opening my spiritual eyes and ears. Help me to show others the fatal error of their thinking, to the end that they would turn to Christ in repentance and faith.

Let's Grow Up!

25) The sluggard's craving will be the death of him, because his hands refuse to work. 26) All day long he craves for more, but the righteous give without sparing (Prov. 21:25-26).

The sluggard would rather wish than work. His inaction ruins him because his cravings continue unabated. On the other hand, the diligent, righteous person sees giving as more important than getting. His cravings are regulated and restrained by the Holy Spirit. His generosity reveals, at least in part, his righteousness. He steps out in faith. He sets his mind to something and then goes for it, leaving the results to God. The sluggard only wants the path of least resistance, the easy money. He wants something for nothing. The church today has more than its share of spiritual sloth.

We want to be "fed" but don't want to work for our spiritual food. We wander from church to church, from self-help book to self-help book, looking for a "quick fix." We crave the fruit of spiritual maturity but we don't want to pay the price required to get it. Therefore, we have many spiritual "babies" (Heb. 5:12-13) who are being fed strained peas and formula.

As "the righteous give without sparing" (v. 26), so the diligent Christian will seek to feed others without sparing in his holy example and through the gifts of the Spirit. Let's grow up, then let's roll up our sleeves and get to work.

Scriptural Examples

The baby Corinthians. They thought they were "super saints" but they hadn't even begun the growth to maturity. They were still arguing with one another and going off on pointless tangents. They were not ready for solid food (1 Cor. 3:1-23).

The baby Hebrews. They were chided for their love of milk. The time had come to eat solid food by constantly using what they had already learned (Heb. 5:11-14).

Prayer of Application

Gracious God, enable me to set an example of diligence and righteousness by helping others to grow in Your Word through the exercise of my spiritual muscles. Help me to grow up.

Beware of Worship Without Repentance

The sacrifice of the wicked is detestable—how much more so when brought with evil intent! (Prov. 21:27)

I am reminded of a scene in one of the *Godfather* movies where the Mob goes to church so that the Robert DeNiro character could get baptized. Here he was, a man who earned his living breaking every commandment of God, being given the sign of God's covenant people. The very thought of such a thing is detestable to God, and particularly when it is done with such evil intent to deceive others in order to rob them. The Mob and their leader went out of the church and back to business as usual, raping and pillaging the community, selling drugs, and extorting money. They made a mockery of the sacrament.

James says, "Religion that God our Father accepts as pure and faultless is this: to look after orphans and widows in their distress and to keep oneself from being polluted by the world" (James 1:27). David's prayer of confession states, "The sacrifices of God are a broken spirit; a broken and contrite heart" (Ps. 51:17). These are the sacrifices that are acceptable to God. Sacrifices, and hence worship, given without a corresponding change of heart in genuine repentance and turning from sin are detestable to God.

Scriptural Examples

Balaam. This wicked false prophet offered sacrifices to God. At the same time he conspired with Israel's enemy Balak to curse God's chosen people. What idiocy, to offer sacrifices with an evil intent. He didn't get away with it (Num. 23:1-3, 13).

Absalom. This son of David offered animal sacrifices in Hebron after deceiving his father as to his evil intent. He really went to Hebron to establish himself as king over Israel. He sought to overthrow the kingdom that was instituted by God (2 Sam. 15:7-13).

Prayer of Application

Sovereign Lord, forgive me for the times I have tried to worship You with a heart hardened to You and Your Word. Create in me a heart devoted to You in repentance and faith.

Beware of False Witnesses

A false witness will perish, and whoever listens to him will be destroyed forever [KJV: "but the man who heareth speaketh constantly"] (Prov. 21:28).

As you can see by the differences between the KJV and the NIV in the second line of this verse, there has been some difficulty in translation. Noting the verse's obscurity, Derek Kidner sides with the KJV and sees the one who listens as being the one worth listening to (p. 146). Either way, false witnesses are to be shamed and faithful witnesses are to be heard.

Jesus calls us to be His witnesses (Isa. 43:10,12; Acts 1:8). What does it mean to be a witness? When a lawyer adroitly questions witnesses (i.e., TV's Perry Mason) he hopes to establish his case in the minds of the jury. A faithful witness will tell the truth. A false witness alters or obscures the truth. Jesus calls each of His followers to tell the truth about Him.

Our Lord said many false witnesses would go out into the world (Matt. 24:5) claiming to be Christ. They would deceive many. Not only will they perish (1 Peter 2:1-3), but those who follow them will also perish. Another type of false witness claims Jesus is worthy of our respect but that He is certainly not God. John says these are antichrists (1 John 4:2-3). Paul would say, "To hell with them!" (Gal. 1:9).

Scriptural Examples

Jesus and the false witnesses. These men lied at the "trial" of the Lord. Can you imagine that on your record? They will be destroyed while the Faithful Witness they tried to murder will reign eternally with His own (Matt. 26:59-61).

Stephen and the false witnesses. False witnesses were also called in to accuse the faithful Stephen. The Pharisees again twisted God's law that calls for true witnesses (Ex. 20:16). They then stoned Stephen to death (Acts 6:12).

Prayer of Application

Precious Savior, help me to be a faithful and trustworthy witness for You. Give me strength to testify of what I know to be true, that You are the Christ, the Son of the Living God.

Make All Your Ways Pleasing to God

A wicked man puts up a bold front [KJV: "hardeneth his face"], but an upright man gives thought to his ways (Prov. 21:29).

I once saw a photograph of a man who was running for mayor of a small town. He was in shorts and a T-shirt, and punching a body bag. There was a scowl on his face and his T-shirt pictured a skeleton's face with a cigarette dangling out of its mouth. On it were the words, "Who wants to live forever anyway?" It reminded me of the first phrase of this proverb.

The natural person has every reason to suspect God will one day call him into account (Rom. 1:18-23). But because of the hardness of his heart, the unregenerate person puts up a bold front, casting aside the revelation of his Creator in Jesus Christ. He hardens his face in a fearless scowl and chooses to live his life any way he pleases. But as Derek Kidner writes, "A bold front is no substitute for sound principles" (p. 146).

The upright person seeks to live a life of obedience to God. He gives thought to his ways and his entire lifestyle, and seeks to please God in all he thinks, says, and does. The upright person takes the Word of God seriously and applies its truth to all areas of his life, asking the Holy Spirit to assist him in carrying out its demands. Mostly, the upright person lives a life of faith, submitting his body as a living sacrifice to God (Rom. 12:1).

Scriptural Examples

Abraham. What a contrast we see in this upright man. God told him to take Isaac to a mountain and offer him as a burnt sacrifice. Believing God would either stop him or raise Isaac from the dead, Abraham obeyed (Gen. 22:2-14; Heb. 11:17-19).

The adulteress. This woman was loud and defiant as she looked for a simpleton to lure into her bed. With a brazen or hardened face she even talked of making offerings to the God she so flagrantly disobeyed (Prov. 7:10-14; Luke 12:5).

Prayer of Application

Dear Lord, thank You for rescuing me from my rebellion when I, too, set my stony face against Your Word and Your Son. Help me, Lord, to live a life pleasing to You in every way.

Don't Fight With, or Without, the Lord

30) There is no wisdom, no insight, no plan that can succeed against the Lord. 31) The horse is made ready for the day of battle, but victory rests with the Lord (Prov. 21:30-31).

My dad loved to watch prizefighting. When I was in high school we used to watch the "Friday Night Fights" on TV together almost every week. Many of the fights were well-matched and featured premium boxers of the day, but some fights were clear mismatches. One fighter would pummel the other until a merciful knockout punch was delivered.

The proverbs above teach us if we were to put Plato, Aristotle, Kant, and all of the world's philosophers into one corner together with all the other secular "movers and shakers" who have ever lived, and the living God in the other corner, it would be the most lopsided mismatch conceivable. Fight promoter Don King wouldn't touch it with a 10-foot pole! Joe Louis vs. Woody Allen would be a better fight. Hear this: There is no wisdom, no philosophy, no insight, no religion, no plan, that can have success against the purposes of God.

All too often we Christians want to trust in "horses" rather than in the God who has saved us. We trust Him for eternity, how about for our daily battles? Worry is an insult to God. It says, "I alone can do something about my problems, Lord. I don't trust You." When we worry we fight the Lord, when the only way to real victory is to rest in Him by faith (Heb. 4:11).

Scriptural Examples

Solomon and his horses. God commanded that a king was not to acquire great numbers of horses for himself. Solomon collected 12,000. Did he sin? If he acquired the horses to trust in them rather than in the deliverance of God, it was sin. While we need to be prepared for war, to trust ultimately in weapons rather than God is idolatry (Deut. 17:16; 1 Kings 4:26).

Prayer of Application

Father, the wisdom of this world is foolishness to You. People make their plans but nothing can prevail against You. Help me to live daily in this blessed assurance and hope.

Chapter Twenty-two

Proverbs and the Business of Life

In 1981 I started a business that grew rapidly throughout the 1980's. Before long I had over 100 employees and precious little training or experience in managing them. But I figured that if I just went by the Golden Rule and treated my employees and customers the way I like to be treated, I'd be OK. It turned out that I was right, but I also found out along the way that the Bible has a lot to say about managing a business, as well as a home or any endeavor. Proverbs takes a leadership role in solid advice for managers.

Much good counsel is to be found in the 22nd chapter. For instance, in 22:13 we find the sluggard saying, "'There is a lion outside!' or 'I will be murdered in the streets!' " We are taught that diligence requires that we stick our necks out and not become trapped in irrational fears. Verses 26 and 27 speak to borrowing practices: Don't sign personally on a note. Verses 24 and 25 advise on whom to avoid as potential friends or employees. Verses 22 and 23 caution the businessperson against exploiting his customers and employees. Verse 10 speaks about terminating the employee with the bad attitude who is creating problems. Verse 4 teaches that humility is foundational to success in business and in life. Finally, verse 1 reveals what the real goal of any enterprise should be.

Desire a Good Name from God and Others

A good name is more desirable than great riches; to be esteemed is better than silver and gold (Prov. 22:1).

Riches are nothing to sneeze at, particularly when they are used for God's kingdom. But even great riches are surpassed by a good name. To have great riches and a bad name may mean that one acquired his wealth by devious or selfish means. Such wealth is worthless (Prov. 11:4). Likewise, to have a good name before others but not before God is a hollow sham, because a good name in God's sight is infinitely more valuable. To think you can obtain a good name before God, without one before others is to be self-righteous like the Pharisees, who put heavy burdens upon people for their own aggrandizement (Luke 11:46).

To be esteemed by both God and others is true riches. But the greatest wealth imaginable is to have your "good name" written in God's Book of Life (Rev. 20:15; Ps. 69:28). It is a good name only by the grace of God, and for those whose names are listed there it is a reason for great joy, much greater joy than mere earthly power or wealth could ever bring (Luke 10:20).

Scriptural Examples

The Babel builders. You'll never acquire a good name their way. They wanted nothing to do with God. They built a city with a high tower to make a name for themselves (Gen. 11:4).

Absalom. This wicked son of David erected a monument to himself. This is another way people try to get a good name for themselves, by using their wealth to buy it (2 Sam. 18:18).

Job. This wealthy man was blessed with a good name before God. God said His servant Job was a blameless and upright man who feared God and shunned evil (Job 1:8).

Cornelius. This Gentile centurion had a good name before the Jews who knew him. He loved the Hebrew nation and had even built a synagogue for them (Luke 7:4-5).

Prayer of Application

Father, help me to live my life seeking a good name from You alone. The fallout of a life that is pleasing to You should produce a good name in the sight of others.

Enter into God's Rest

Rich and poor have this in common: The Lord is the Maker of them all (Prov. 22:2).

The Lord is not only the Maker of all people as their Creator, but He makes them rich and He makes them poor (Prov. 10:22). He saves some people while some he allows to continue on down their self-willed promenade to the grave and hell (1 Cor. 1:18). Christians have trusted our eternity to God. Why is it so difficult to trust Him with today?

The nation Israel was brought out of Egypt by God's mighty power, but almost as soon as the Israelites were out of danger, they began to grumble about God's provision. "We'd be better off if we had stayed slaves in Egypt!" they cried. God brought forth water for their thirst. He sent manna and quail for their hunger, but still they didn't trust Him. He promised them victory over their enemies and entrance into the Promised Land, but they trembled in fear and refused to go in. Therefore God swore they would never enter His rest (Num. 14:21-23; Deut. 1:35). He let them wander aimlessly in the desert for 40 years until everyone except Caleb and Joshua died.

The writer to the Hebrews picks up this theme saying the person "who enters God's rest also rests from his own work." We are to "make every effort to enter that rest," and to avoid a "sinful, unbelieving heart that turns away from the living God" (Heb. 3:7-4:11). What is "rest" but a simple childlike faith in God to keep His promises? Is God a liar? By no means! Is God unjust? Absolutely not! Is God unable to keep His promises because He lacks the power? No!

Brothers and sisters, commit today and all of your tomorrows to God's tender loving care. Our worry over the future and our complaining against Him is very displeasing to Him. Do we really believe God? Then let's live like it. Otherwise, our "faith" is just lip-service and our trust in other things is idolatry.

Prayer of Application

Father, thank You for the great and precious promises in Your Word. Give me the faith to trust You fully in every circumstance and to rely on Your power, not on any idol.

Walk Prudently and Take Refuge

A prudent man sees danger and takes refuge, but the simple keep going and suffer for it (Prov. 22:3).

The prudent person will foresee difficulty in the road ahead and plan for it. The simple person, on the other hand, just keeps on truckin' down the road fearing nothing. The older we get the more clearly we ought to see danger ahead, but how often we are "cockeyed optimists." Some of life's troubles may blindside us, as when a quarterback gets sacked by the linebacker he doesn't see. But most problems are foreseeable if we just take the time to hear wise counsel and plan ahead.

There is danger in spades for many on this planet who are walking down the road of life, whistling a happy tune. It is the sure judgment and wrath of God (Heb. 9:27; Acts 17:31). There is only one refuge from His wrath: Jesus Christ. He offers His covering and protection from the coming judgment free-of- charge to anyone who comes to Him in faith (Rev. 22:17; Rom. 6:23; Eph. 2:8; Isa. 55:7), trusting in His blood shed on the cross as a sacrifice for sin. If you have never trusted Christ for His refuge, do so today.

Scriptural Examples

The Israelites. God warned them He would send one final plague upon the Egyptians. The households which had not prepared by placing the blood of a lamb on the lintel of their doorway would lose their firstborn son. The Israelites believed God and escaped the danger ahead (Ex. 12).

Noah. Noah was warned about the Flood and built a huge ship. Meanwhile, for more than 100 years he preached to lost souls of the coming doom. No one came forward to set foot on the ark. The Flood came, as God said it would, and swept them all away except Noah and his family. Noah's faith condemned the world and made him an heir of righteousness (Heb. 11:7).

Prayer of Application

Lord, Your Word is a lamp unto my feet and a light unto my path. Help me to see its warnings of trouble ahead, and trusting fully in Your ability and desire to deliver me, move out in faith.

Walk Humbly and Fear the Lord

Humility and the fear of the Lord bring wealth and honor and life (Prov. 22:4).

Sit back for a second with me, close your eyes, and try to imagine what the perfect life would be like. What follows is an imaginary interview with someone who has done that.

"OK, let's see. First, there would be lots of money. I could use it to help my church build that new sanctuary and to help missionaries and others in ministry. There's also that new home I've always hankered after." What else? "Well, I'd like to have some recognition. I was never a star athlete or student, and have never received much in the way of earthly honors." OK, what else? "Well, I'd like a fulfilling life, an enriching and meaningful occupation, a life with a big family and lots of friends, that is filled with excitement and good health, with love and contentment."

Now open your eyes and let me tell you about a life that's more than all that. It is the Christian life, a life of humility and the fear of the Lord. Humility is coming to grips with who we really are: totally depraved and lost without Christ. We are not as bad as we could be, but only because of the restraining power of God. Next, it is understanding God is holy, righteous, just, omniscient, omnipresent, omnipotent, etc., yet loving, kind, and merciful. Then, to realize what He has done for us through the Lord Jesus is to fall trembling at His feet in thanksgiving, adoration, and awe: the fear of the Lord.

Christians have riches beyond understanding. Your heavenly Father knows your needs and has promised to provide all things richly to you for your benefit (Rom. 8:28-32; Matt. 6:25-34; Phil. 4:19). They are riches which will endure (Rom. 8:17), never to spoil or be taken away (Matt. 6:20). They are treasures of glory and honor and life. The Christian life is a life that will surpass any of your wildest dreams.

Prayer of Application

Dear Lord, thank You for eternal life. Help me to see this life began the moment I trusted You. Give me the strength to live it to the fullest now. Help me live above my circumstances.

Make Level Paths for Your Feet

In the paths of the wicked lie thorns and snares, but he who guards his soul stays far from them (Prov. 22:5).

Proverbs 1:17-18 speaks of how the net a wicked person spreads for others only traps himself. But there are other "thorns and snares" that lie in the weeds along the path of the wicked. The following is a short and incomplete list.

There is the trap of disease and sudden death caused by sin. I think of the horrors of AIDS and the terrible effects of crack cocaine. There is the snare of unfulfilled lust from being addicted to pornography. There is the disappointment that comes when sin doesn't deliver what it promises. There are relational problems like divorce and child abuse. Finally, there is unrelenting guilt and the bondage of the fear of death (Heb. 2:15).

"Well, I'm a Christian," someone says, "and my life hasn't exactly been a bed of roses!" I understand. I, too, have had many troubles as a Christian. But the trials the Christian suffers are purposeful. He is given the sure hope that God's sovereign purposes are being worked out in his life. In guarding our souls we avoid the consequences of sinful habits and life-styles. We have the forgiveness of a loving Father who removes our fear of death. We need to cling to Him by faith and walk on paths made level for our feet (Prov. 4:26; Heb. 12:13).

Scriptural Examples

Job. Job suffered greatly, but his trials give us a behind-the-scenes look into God's providence. Perhaps Job never understood what God's purpose was, but he guarded his soul and was rewarded with doubled prosperity (the book of Job).

The wicked prophets of Samaria. Jeremiah told of these godless men who followed evil and used their power unjustly. The Lord said that He would make their paths slippery. They would be banished to darkness and disaster (Jer. 23:10-13).

Prayer of Application

Father, keep my feet on level paths that avoid the traps and snares of the unbeliever. Thank You for Your wonderful and loving providence that assures me of a safe journey home.

Dedicate Yourself and Your Kids to the Lord

Train a child in the way he should go, and when he is old he will not turn from it (Prov. 22:6).

The Hebrew word *chanak*, translated here as "train," is translated elsewhere in Scripture as "dedicate" (Deut. 20:5; 1 Kings 8:63). There is a sense in which we parents dedicate ourselves to the solemn responsibility of training up our children. Certainly, the emphasis here is on our responsibility.

I believe that Dr. J. Vernon McGee hit the nail on the head when he said, "The way the child should go is the way God wants him to go" (p. 76). From an eternal perspective, there are really only two ways to go: the way of righteousness or the way of wickedness. How do we ensure that our kids will go the right way?

There is no certain way but I believe that God honors the sincere attempts of godly parents to bring their children up in the training and admonition of the Lord (Eph. 6:4). Parental training should adopt at least this three-pronged approach. First, children should be grounded in the Word of God. Read it to them. Teach them its stories. Tell them of the sin problem and its remedy in Christ. Second, as you admonish them in issues of sin, rebellion, and obedience, make the Word of God come alive by making practical application of it to their lives. Show them how the Word speaks directly to them.

Finally, and most importantly, it is imperative that you teach them by your own godly example. Charles Bridges says that "the child learns more by the eye than by the ear" (p. 404). The other two methods will be rendered ineffective if hypocrisy is seen in the teacher. Pray with your children. Confess your own shortcomings to them and tell them how God is working in your life. Take them with you to a Bible-believing church where they can meet other godly men and women. Dedicate both yourself and your kids to the Lord.

Prayer of Application

O Sovereign Lord, help godly Christian parents everywhere to dedicate their children to You, that they might give top priority to their instruction in righteousness.

Get Out of Debt

The rich rule over the poor, and the borrower is servant to the lender (Prov. 22:7).

Have you seen the bumper sticker that reads, "I owe, I owe, so off to work I go"? The American way seems to be to load ourselves up with a mountain of debt as we seek the "good life" here and now, not understanding its ultimate toll on us as we become enslaved to the payments.

Christian economist and financial advisor Larry Burkett includes this principle as a common thread throughout his advice to clients: get out of debt, particularly consumer debt or debt that has been encountered in the purchase of rapidly depreciating assets. He views those assets differently from a house, which should have a measure of price stability.

The Christian who has indebtedness beyond a modest or necessary house payment is seeing his money go to interest each month that could otherwise be put to work in the Lord's service. Our credit card debt then becomes a two-edged sword. It cuts us in the direction of our servanthood to the lender, and then in our lack of servanthood to the Lord (Matt. 6:24). The best way is to be debt-free, if you can pull it off. That should at least be a very practical goal for every Christian.

Scriptural Examples

The Egyptians. God honors the payment of debt. While in bondage to this nation of people for 400 years, the Israelites were owed plenty. On leaving, they got repaid, as their prior captors reached down deep in the family jewels (Ex. 12:36).

Slavery and the debtor's prison. In former times, and certainly in Old Testament times, actual slavery might be imposed on a debtor should he default. In some civilizations debtors' prisons were common. Jesus alluded to this type of prison in Matthew 5:25-26. Debt creates a different form of slavery today.

Prayer of Application

Heavenly Father, help me to live within my means, giving back to You my tithes and offerings and being cautious in taking on any debt which could enslave me.

Don't Use Your Freedom to Enslave Others

He who sows wickedness reaps trouble, and the rod of his fury will be destroyed (Prov. 22:8).

John Michener's *Chesapeake* is an historical novel dealing with the Chesapeake Bay and the states that border it. One of the most tumultuous periods of which he writes was the mid-1800s prior to the Civil War. In one scene, as Southern plantation owners and slave holders were trembling at the prospect of a potential revolt among their subjects, they hired a preacher to preach to the slaves against revolt.

The preacher, who was well paid for his efforts, gave the slaves an impassioned plea describing torture in hell for those who ran away and consequently "stole themselves." He equated their escape to God's commandment not to steal (Ex. 20:15). The irony of this misuse of the Word of God to keep others in bondage was that he was preaching to the wrong audience. It was the plantation owners who should have heard a sermon, one based on this text in Proverbs.

"What does this have to do with me?" you ask. Just this. We who have been made rich in the things of God should not use our wealth to place others in spiritual bondage. We should not twist the Word of God to support our own fallacious principles and legalistic practices. That is what the Pharisees did in Jesus' day and what the Judaizers did in Paul's. They made up their own rules while they missed the grace of God (Gal. 5:1; Heb. 12:15). Neither should we use our freedom as a license to sin (Rom. 6:15-16). Sin will only enslave the sinner.

Scriptural Examples

The false teachers. They apparently claimed to be Christians but were adulterous, greedy, and never stopped sinning. They promised people freedom but they were themselves slaves to depravity. Peter denounced them severely (2 Peter 2:10-22).

Prayer of Application

Dear God, there are still those who use their Christianity as a cloak to deceive and enslave others. Put a stop to their evil ways and help those under their teaching to escape the error.

Use Your Freedom to Enrich Others

A generous man will himself be blessed, for he shares his food with the poor (Prov. 22:9).

In stark contrast to the slave holders of Michener's novel, *Chesapeake*, were the Quakers and others who risked their lives and property to help slaves find freedom. They formed the Underground Railroad, which transported runaways north to Canada and other places of refuge. What principles guided people like these who generously risked everything for the freedom of some poor slaves? I, of course, can't answer for all of those who helped, but I suspect many understood the principle I have drawn from this proverb.

What makes a person truly generous, to the extent he would give his very life for people he's never met? While noting the courage of some secular people, I believe it is freedom in Christ that does it. Not being enslaved by covetousness or fear of death, a generous person is free to share all he has with those in need. He has put his trust in his heavenly Father to fill all his needs (Matt. 6:25-34; Isa. 58:7-11; Phil. 4:19). Such a generous person will be blessed in this life (Mark 10:29-30), and with eternal blessings at the hand of his Creator.

Scriptural Examples

Abraham. He cherished the son God had given him and Sarah in their old age. When God told him to go and sacrifice Isaac at Mt. Moriah, Abraham obeyed. His trust in the Living God gave Abraham a freedom that allowed him to risk everything (Gen. 17:19; 22:2-14; Heb. 11:17-19).

The poor widow. This woman came to the temple while Jesus and His disciples were there. She put two small copper coins into the treasury. It was all she had to live on. Her extreme generosity must have been a sign of the freedom that was in her heart, a heart that trusted in the Lord God (Mark 12:41-44).

Prayer of Application

Heavenly Father, thank You for the freedom we have in Christ Jesus. It is a freedom from sin's bondage which allows us to give freely and generously of all that we have and are.

Get Rid of that Bad Attitude

Drive out the mocker, and out goes strife; quarrels and insults are ended (Prov. 22:10).

In Matthew 5, we have what are known as "The Beatitudes." In the verse above we have the "Bad Attitudes." God's warnings against strife, quarrels, and insults are loud and frequent in Scripture. How can we recognize, then get rid of, a bad attitude?

Isaiah says that "the wicked are like the tossing sea, which cannot rest, whose waves cast up mire and mud. 'There is no peace,' says my God, 'for the wicked'" (Isa. 57:20-21). This verse is often taken to mean that God will allow the wicked no peace. But the context seems to say that the wicked want no peace for others. A bad attitude is one that disturbs the peace. Its cause is always the same: pride. When pride comes, peace departs.

The bad attitude is easy to recognize but a lot more difficult to cure. As an employer, I know that an employee with a bad attitude is a double-edged threat. If you allow him to stay on the job he will spread his poison through others in the company, threatening everyone's livelihood. On the other hand, if you fire him, he may file a lawsuit. In my opinion, the latter option is always preferable. Just make sure you document the causes and employee warnings well.

Matthew 18:15-20 speaks of dealing with bad attitudes in the church. For a bad attitude in a child, see Proverbs 22:15. The best remedy for the bad attitude, and the only one that truly lasts, is to introduce the one with a "bad attitude" to the Savior and let the Savior change it and him, if He will.

Scriptural Examples

Paul. Paul had been a mocker, a blasphemer, and a violent man. But he was shown mercy so that the Lord might display his unlimited patience. The grace of God made all the difference in Paul's bad attitude (1 Tim. 1:13-16).

Prayer of Application

Dear Lord, may my life reflect the humility, peace, patience, and love of Christ, who became a servant of all so that men and women everywhere might be saved.

Befriend the King

He who loves a pure heart and whose speech is gracious will have the king for his friend (Prov. 22:11).

The story of Robin Hood is well-known. While his friend King Richard is off fighting the Crusades, Robin Hood and his merry men fight Richard's evil brother, who aspires to Richard's crown, and his wicked co-conspirator, the Sheriff of Nottingham. In the end, Richard arrives back in England and dubs Robin a knight, honoring him for his loyalty and courage. Robin showed himself faithful in his king's absence.

In the same way, our King has left this world and an impostor wants to put himself on the throne: the evil conspirator Satan. Like Robin, we are to arm ourselves for battle. Our basic armament may be summed up in this proverb: We are to love a pure heart, and have gracious speech.

To love a pure heart is not necessarily to have a pure heart (Matt. 5:8), but to aspire to one (Phil. 3:12-15). It is a love of truth, a love of righteousness and holiness, and a desire to put God first. It is a love for God that loves others. Coming from a heart that cherishes purity, our speech will reflect the graciousness of Christ.

Oh, for that blessed day when the King shall return and set all things right, deposing the wicked imposter and bestowing upon all His friends who eagerly await Him a crown of righteousness (2 Tim. 4:8). Befriend the King!

Scriptural Examples

Ezra. He was a godly man of purity and grace who found the friendship of a king. King Artaxerxes of Babylon gave Ezra authority to return to Jerusalem, reconstruct the temple, and rule over all the people there (Ezra 7:6, 21-25).

Daniel. Daniel served before two monarchs of Babylon. He was given lofty positions by each because he led a life dominated by purity of heart and gracious speech (Dan. 6:3, 28).

Prayer of Application

Great King, thank You for changing my heart in friendship when I was yet an enemy, and placing me on a pathway toward Your purity. May my speech reflect Your graciousness.

Put Your Trust in the Enduring Word of God

The eyes of the Lord keep watch over knowledge, but he frustrates the words of the unfaithful (Prov. 22:12).

Jesus said, "Heaven and earth will pass away, but my words will never pass away" (Matt. 24:35; Mark 13:31; Luke 21:33). By God's omniscience—His watchful eye—not one jot or tittle will pass from the Word of God until all is fulfilled (Matt. 5:18), nor until heaven and earth disappear. Jesus confirms the Lord will "keep watch over knowledge."

Down through the ages, the Bible has come under more attacks than any other document in human history. Yet it has survived those ravages with a degree of accuracy unsurpassed by any other document. How this has happened is a worthy study for everyone, but why it happened is no mystery. God has kept watch over it for His eternal purposes (Ps. 119:152). He has not allowed sinful people to have their way with it. By now there would be little left, as scissors in sinful hands snipped away at its truth.

In Isaiah 55:11, God said the word that goes out of His mouth would not return void, but it would accomplish the purpose for which it was sent. One of God's purposes was to save me. I trust that one of those purposes was to save you, too, dear reader. For each of us who names the name of Christ has been "born again," not of perishable seed but of imperishable, through the "living and enduring Word of God" (1 Peter 1:23). This is the icing on the cake, the final proof in the pudding. Besides our objective knowledge of its truth, we know its truth subjectively because God's Spirit makes it real to us.

The unfaithful, however, are like the grass of the field. They wither and fall, "but the Word of the Lord stands forever" (1 Peter 1:24-25; Isa. 40:6-8). People may try to disavow the Bible in their vain philosophies and attempts to explain it away, but God will frustrate their every word. Only His Word is perfect. Trust only in the perfect and enduring Word of God.

Prayer of Application

Sovereign Lord, thank You for Your enduring Word. Its truth is a lamp unto my feet and a light unto my path. I pray it will accomplish Your purposes through me.

Flee the Faithless Alibi of the Idle

The sluggard says, "There is a lion outside!" or, "I will be murdered in the streets!" (Prov. 22:13).

If this fellow put as much energy and imagination into meaningful labor as he does in creating excuses for its avoidance, he'd be a rich man. Rather, he's a biblical "couch potato" who imagines all kinds of perils awaiting him should he get up from his easy chair in front of the TV set. "I might get killed on the freeway!" "Someone might come in to where I work and shoot me!" Funny, but you probably won't hear any concern that his ice cream or popcorn might be poisoned.

Christian faith is committing oneself to the care of the Living God, then getting up and doing what God says. Faith expresses itself in active love by helping others (Gal. 5:6). Difficult situations in life are opportunities to exercise faith, not to stifle action. The sluggard's idleness is due to a lack of faith.

What the sluggard doesn't realize is there is an armed person looking for him. His name is Poverty (Prov. 6:11). There is also a lion in the streets seeking sluggards to devour, right in their easy chairs. His name is Satan (1 Peter 5:8). Don't follow the way of the sluggard. Obey Christ and live by faith. It is the only way that is pleasing to God (Heb. 11:6).

Scriptural Examples

The Israelites. The 12 spies brought back a glowing report of a land filled with milk and honey. But they also reported the fierce fighting men they saw. In faithlessness, the people chickened out and turned away. That generation would never enter the land (Num. 13:27-14:10).

David. David told King Saul that Goliath would be just like the lion and the bear he had once killed. Armed only with a simple sling, five smooth stones, and the might of the Lord God, David slew the giant (1 Sam. 17:33-36; 13:14; Acts 13:22).

Prayer of Application

Father God, make me a person of faith to step out and express my faith in action like David did. Unlike the Israelites, I want to trust You, so that by my faith You will be glorified.

Beware the Deep Pit of God's Wrath

The mouth of an adulteress is a deep pit; he who is under the Lord's wrath will fall into it (Prov. 22:14).

One of the most popular TV shows of the '80s and early '90s was the sitcom *Cheers*. The series took place in a basement bar in Boston whose denizens included a bartender/owner named Sam Malone. Sam was a former Red Sox pitcher who was more famous for his exploits in bed than for those on the mound. In many respects, Sam's promiscuity represented the ethos of our culture, i.e.: "Sex is fun. It feels good so it must be good. Get sex whenever and wherever you can."

But the warning of this proverb is anything but funny. All who succumb to the mouth of the adulteress are under the wrath of an angry God. God gave humankind the gift of sexual intercourse to be enjoyed only in the context of the heterosexual marriage union (Gen. 2:20-25; Heb. 13:4). What a testimony it is to man's depravity that this greatest of life's physical pleasures should be used to mock the Creator who gave it.

The bottom line is this: all sin is insanity. Called to choose heaven, people choose hell. Only by the grace of God available in the work of the Savior can anyone be saved. But God's love to sinners is deeper than the deepest pit leading to hell. There is no sin so grievous as to restrict God's mercy. God's call is to repent from it and believe in the One who can fully save (1 Tim. 1:16; Isa. 45:22; Acts 2:21).

Scriptural Examples

The Corinthian adulterer. The believers in Corinth had a man in their assembly who was sleeping with his stepmother. And they were proud of it! I'm sure that they were like the many Christians today who laugh at shows like "Cheers" but fail to see God's wrath overriding any humor in adultery. Paul told the Corinthians to expel the sinner from their midst (1 Cor. 5:1-3).

Prayer of Application

Father, thank You for the gift of sexuality. Lord, people have perverted Your gift and cheapened it in sin. Help America to forsake sexual sin and turn to You for grace.

Spare the Rod and the Child Will Stay Spoiled

Folly is bound up in the heart of a child, but the rod of discipline will drive it far from him (Prov. 22:15).

Some years ago there was a popular novel and motion picture called *Rosemary's Baby*. In it, a woman conceived the child of Satan. As the happy parents-in-waiting made preparations for the blessed event, the Antichrist was forming in Rosemary's womb. In one central respect, "Rosemary's Baby" is a snapshot of every woman's baby. We are all born children of Satan (John 8:44) and slaves to sin (Rom. 6:15-17).

From the day a child is born, the struggle begins to determine who is in control, his parents or him. His wickedness must be driven out by the rod of discipline. In today's society children are "innocent" and only become "bad" through societal conditioning. Now that may be a nice sentiment, but it cannot stand up under rigorous investigation. The truth of this proverb, however, may be demonstrated universally. It's not just some who sin, everyone sins. Sin is grounded in our nature (Ps. 51:5).

What type of "rod" do we use? My dad used to take off his belt and use that on my rear end. I don't necessarily recommend that rod, though it did leave a lasting impression on me. I think whatever the rod may be, from physical punishment to the withholding of toys and treats, it must not be done from revenge or in passion, but in tenderness and compassion and out of love for the child. To allow a child to go his own way, without the rebuke of punishment for the sins he commits, is to destine him for a life of selfishness and conflict.

As parents, the most important thing for us to understand is this: If you spare the rod, you won't spoil your child. He's spoiled even before the doctor slaps his little fanny. Only the rod of discipline in your hand can turn him from his natural bent to rebellion. It's a big responsibility, and one the neglect of which we are seeing today throughout America.

Prayer of Application

Father, I pray every parent in America could understand this principle. People are sinners from birth and can only be turned from their wicked ways by Your grace and the parents' rod.

Beware of These Roads to the Poorhouse

He who oppresses the poor to increase his wealth and he who gives gifts to the rich—both come to poverty (Prov. 22:16).

Karl Marx spoke of a day when the masses would revolt against their rich oppressors and form a classless society. Well, the classless society never happened. The Russian proletariat who revolted in 1917 merely traded their Czarist oppressors for Communist ones. Ultimately, both systems have tumbled and have been reduced to poverty.

Many of us are familiar with the beautifully ornate Faberge eggs of the former Czarist rulers of Russia. These stunning works of art each contain a hidden treasure intended to delight its recipient. They were gifts royalty gave to royalty for their pleasure, while the people were starving to death. Like the Bolsheviks after them, the Czars came to ruin.

If you are an employer, these verses will speak to you about paying your employees fairly. While profit is desirable and, yes, even mandatory for any business, excess profits that exploit others will work to your ruin. God, who has given us the stewardship of material possessions on this earth, holds us accountable. He is the protector of laborers, widows, fatherless, and aliens (Mal. 3:5) and will bring down the house of those who treat them unfairly.

Scriptural Examples

The money changers. Jesus displayed His righteous anger at those who made huge profits by imposing false rates of exchange and overcharging for animals to be used in sacrifice. They themselves would pay heavily (John 2:14-16).

The rich. James spoke of those who withheld the wages of the poor while they lived in luxury and self-indulgence. A day of misery was coming. Their wealth had rotted. They had only been fattened for their own slaughter (James 5:1-5).

Prayer of Application

Dear heavenly Father, help me to treat others less fortunate than myself with dignity and justice. Place in my heart Your love which reaches out to others in kindness and humility.

Listen to What Not to Do

17) Pay attention and listen to the sayings of the wise; apply your heart to what I teach, 18) for it is pleasing when you keep them in your heart and have all of them ready on your lips. 19) So that your trust may be in the Lord, I teach you today, even you. 20) Have I not written thirty sayings for you, sayings of counsel and knowledge, 21) teaching you true and reliable words, so that you can give sound answers to him who sent you (Prov. 22:17-21)?

Solomon begins a different form of address to his listeners in this section entitled "Sayings of the Wise," which extends through 24:22. He leaves the Hebrew parallel style and begins to address us directly, telling us what *not* to do.

The phrase most commonly used in "Sayings of the Wise" is "do not." It appears 25 times in the NIV text in these verses. Even though the phrase "do not" is one of the most frequent combinations of words in the Bible, its use here greatly exceeds elsewhere in Scripture. Per my calculations, if one were to apply the frequency with which "do not" appears in these verses to the entire Bible, there would be over 12,000 uses, or over nine times its current usage.

These five verses are a mini-introduction, much like we had in the first nine chapters of the book. In verse 17, we are enjoined to pay attention and apply the words to our lives. Learning without practical application only brings pride. Then in verse 19 he tells us why: "So that your trust may be in the Lord." They are words of counsel and knowledge (v. 20). Again, we have here the revealed will of God: divine counsel and knowledge of the Holy One set forth in His Word.

Finally, they are true words—words of reliability—given that we might be able to answer to the One who sends us forth into this world to obey Him. By that obedience, may the pagans see our good deeds and glorify God on the day He visits us (1 Peter 2:12).

Prayer of Application

Dear Lord, thank You for Your Word which is so beneficial in its boundless truth and wisdom. Help me to apply it to every area of my life that I might live my life in obedience to it.

Do Not Exploit or Oppress the Poor

22) Do not exploit the poor because they are poor and do not crush the needy in court, 23) for the Lord will take up their case and will plunder those who plunder them (Prov. 22:22-23).

Our Lord was asked, "Teacher, which is the greatest commandment in the law?" Jesus replied, "Love the Lord your God with all your heart and with all your soul and with all your mind. And the second is like it: Love your neighbor as yourself" (Matt. 22:36-40). The proverbs above are not just a warning against a minor breach of these two great commandments but against an absolute and utter violation of them.

We see the poor here being exploited because they are poor, and therefore easy prey. We break the commandment to love our neighbor when we do not help the poor and needy, when it is within our power to do so. Here, the poor are being exploited, which is far worse. Even more contemptible is the judge who crushes the needy in his courtroom. That is a person who uses his God-given position to oppress the poor. Not smart!

God is on the side of the poor and needy. When someone attempts to exploit and oppress them, he is openly attempting to exploit and oppress Almighty God, for He is their champion.

Scriptural Examples

The poor man and his lamb. Nathan told David this story of a rich man who took the only little lamb of a poor neighbor and cooked it. David burned with indignation and said the rich man deserved to die. Nathan then equated the rich man with David, and the king was humbled (2 Sam. 12:1-13).

Job's friends. Zophar and Eliphaz brought this charge against their suffering companion. According to them, he had obviously oppressed the poor and had received his just reward in his tortures. It was a lie (Job 20:19-23; 22:5-10).

Prayer of Application

Father, by taking up the cause of the poor You give us a picture of Your mercy and grace. But it also points out You are a God of ultimate justice, who will not stand for oppression.

Do Not Befriend a Hot-Tempered Man

24) Do not make friends with a hot-tempered man, do not associate with one easily angered, 25) or you may learn his ways and get yourself ensnared (Prov. 22:24-25).

Years ago, there was a popular TV show called *The Honeymooners*. Jackie Gleason played Ralph Cramden, a bus driver in the big city with a temper as expansive as his prominent waistline. The target of his temper tantrums were his wife, Alice, and the dim-witted, sewer worker Norton, played by Art Carney. The show continued for years. Isn't it ironic that many of the popular TV shows display a human activity or habit that is anathema to God? In the case of *Cheers* it was adultery (see Prov. 22:14). In *The Honeymooners* it was the hot temper. How many more shows feature violence, murder, oppression, covetousness, and like sins?

What is it about the hot-tempered, angry person that is offensive to God? First, he is selfish through and through. Second, he may get angry because his overweening pride gets stepped on and he wants to strike back. Third, he is a person who is out of control. He lacks self-control and wisdom. And fourth, when he gets angry he is really angry at God for not making him the center of the universe. He lacks understanding.

We are not to befriend such a person. His pride and covetousness may rub off on us (1 Cor. 15:33). That's one reason we need to be careful of which TV shows we watch. We might get ensnared by the sin they promote.

Scriptural Examples

Jonah. Following his visit to Nineveh he became sullen and angry. He was angry with God for not destroying the Ninevites and for causing his vine to wither. God said that Jonah was selfishly more concerned with his own welfare than with the welfare of the 120,000 people of the city (Jonah 3:10-4:11).

Prayer of Application

Lord, keep me from pride that elevates self, and when self does not get its way, bursts forth in anger. Help those who have this life-dominating sin, showing them the calmness of Christ.

Do Not Pledge All of Your Assets

26) Do not be a man who strikes hands in pledge or puts up security for debts; 27) if you lack the means to pay, your very bed will be snatched from under you (Prov. 22:26-27).

Suppose you and a friend decide to go into business together, wholesaling "widgets" to hardware stores. You handle sales and your partner administers the office and warehouse and does the bookkeeping. It will take about $100,000 to get off the ground, including inventory, vehicle, and working capital. You have $20,000 in savings and your friend can put up $10,000. The bank will lend you $70,000 in a line of credit.

As collateral, the bank wants full security of equipment and receivables. Additionally, they get separate guarantees from the partners. They get all your assets in case of default.

The business is a success right from the start, thanks to your sales efforts. Then one day you come in and find a note from your partner, saying he had to leave town. He leaves no forwarding address. The bank account is empty, the line of credit is drawn down to zero, and you owe for orders to manufacturers totaling tens of thousands of dollars. Your "partner" has turned his $10,000 into $150,000 and left you holding the bag.

The bank seizes all the collateral and you are out of business. Then, in place of the $50,000 payment still owed, they take your car, your savings and securities, and finally your home and the very bed in which you used to sleep at night.

This story is not farfetched. It happens all of the time. People sign personally on notes only to find creditors knocking on the door when a partner defaults. Through no fault of yours you have lost all you own, and you and your family are left bankrupt. Derek Kidner says (p. 71) these warnings against pledging assets do not banish generosity, but rather gambling. Be careful. Don't "strike hands in pledge or put up security for debts." More than a good night's sleep is at stake.

Prayer of Application

Dear Father, help me to avoid the traps that set themselves up for the unwary. I know indebtedness is one such trap, particularly in guaranteeing the indebtedness for another.

Do Not Stray from the Apostles' Teaching

Do not move an ancient boundary stone set up by your forefathers
(Prov. 22:28).

Since satellites are now used in precise survey work and title insurance is available, real estate boundary-stone movement isn't the crime it used to be. But in spiritual things, boundary-stone movement is a thriving business.

Back in the 16th century, the Roman Catholic church accused the Reformers of moving the "ancient boundary stone," by which they meant their traditions. In reality, it was Rome who had, by her traditions, moved the boundary stone established by God; principally the rock of salvation by faith alone. That was a boundary stone that had been established as early as God's dealing with Adam and Eve (Gen. 3:15, 21) and Abraham (Gen. 15:6; Rom. 4). Rome displaced the pure doctrine of grace (Eph. 2:8-9) for one of grace plus works.

Other false doctrines were brought in. The once-and-for-all sacrifice of Christ for His people (Heb. 10:12-14) was moved aside in favor of a mass where Christ is brought down and sacrificed over and over again. They denied the Christian's blessed assurance (Isa. 12:2; Rom. 8:35-39) and brought in doubt with their extra biblical notion of purgatory.

I have a great deal of heaviness in my heart for those sitting under the teaching of the "boundary-stone movers." But Rome isn't the only culprit. Many who call themselves Protestant are equally at fault. Turn to Proverbs 23:10-11 for more.

Scriptural Examples

Paul. The great apostle condemned anyone who would preach another gospel than the one he preached. In these verses he didn't say it just once, he said it twice. "If anybody is preaching to you a gospel other than what you accepted, let him be eternally condemned" (Gal. 1:6-10).

Prayer of Application

Father, thank You for the gospel of salvation by grace alone. It offers salvation without cost to any who would receive it. Help people escape the teaching of those who have changed it.

Honor God in Your Work

Do you see a man skilled in his work (KJV, "diligent in his business")? He will serve before kings; he will not serve before obscure men (Prov. 22:29).

When we are introduced to someone the first question usually asked is, "What do you do?" Our identity is often tied to what we do for a living. People are workers, the creation of a working God who established the sanctity of labor in the first chapters of Genesis. There we read of God's own labor in Creation. Adam tended the garden and became the first scientist as he gave names to living things (Gen. 2:19).

In the Roman Catholic Church of the Middle Ages, work was divided into two classes. The sacred calling was to serve in the church, while everyone else did profane, secular work. But Scripture doesn't teach such dualism. On the contrary, we find that all work is sacred (Eph. 4:28; 1 Thess. 4:11-12; Ex. 23:12; 34:21). The curse following the Fall added frustration to work.

Throughout Scripture we see godly people honored by secular powers and communities for their diligence in business or in the work of their hands. Those like Joseph and Daniel are examples of how God honors the labor of our hands and brains. We need to be faithful to God in the work He has given us on the job, at home, or in the church. We bring honor and glory to Him by being faithful at that work.

Scriptural Examples

Joseph's brothers. Pharaoh put Joseph's brothers who had special abilities in charge of his own livestock. These men would serve the king, not obscure men (Gen. 47:6).

Bezalel and Oholiab. These men were filled with the Spirit of God and given skill, ability, and knowledge in the crafts that were used in the construction of the tabernacle, in its furnishings, and in the priestly garments (Ex. 31:1-7; 35:30).

Prayer of Application

Dear Lord, help me to honor You in my work. I thank You, Lord, that You have given me meaningful and fulfilling work to do and that You have given me the skills with which to do it.

Chapter Twenty-three

Proverbs and Life's Traps

The number one trap humans face in life is their own sin. Way back in Chapter One the father warned his son about not joining with those who try to entrap others. Verses 17 and 18 said, "How useless to spread a net in full view of all the birds! These men lie in wait for their own blood, they waylay only themselves!" Sin traps the sinner. But not all of life's traps involve one's own sin. Traps are also set by the wicked for the unwary. Chapter 23 speaks of several types of traps.

We are warned to beware of the deceitful host who has something up his sleeve beyond the delicacies he's offered you (vv. 1-3, 5-7). Beware of the trap of fleeting riches (vv. 4-5). The scornful fool lies in wait for your wisdom in verse 8. Beware of the trap of trying to take candy from a baby. His Defender stands ready to pounce on you (vv. 10-11). Look out for the trap of the undisciplined child. It will spring shut sooner than you think (vv. 13-14). Watch out for the traps of envy (vv. 17-18), drunkenness and gluttony (vv. 19-21), scorn of parental guidance (vv. 22-25), adultery and fornication (vv. 26-28), and finally, the trap of drunkenness, which is revisited in verses 29 through 35. But the key verse for avoiding all these traps is in verse 26: "My son, give me your heart and let your eyes keep to my ways." God wants to be the treasure of your heart (Matt. 6:21).

Do Not Be Deceived by Impressive Food

1) When you sit to dine with a ruler, note well what is before you, 2) and put a knife to your throat if you are given to gluttony. 3) Do not crave his delicacies, for that food is deceptive (Prov. 23:1-3).

To be invited to a dinner party at the sumptuous home of a rich and influential person may flatter us, causing us to succumb to a little "social climbing." We may be overly impressed with the lavish banquet spread out before us. The wine and the delicacies may cause us to overindulge and forget our manners or position. We may begin to envy the host and hostess, forgetting wealth is not all it's cracked up to be.

Remember, the Christian needn't take a back seat to anyone in any situation. You are an ambassador of the King of Kings and Lord of Lords. You are one of His personal representatives on this earth. Your position in Christ is exalted beyond any mere earthly throne. But as ambassadors of Christ, we are called to humility and service, to modesty and good manners, to simplicity and to truth.

James says that we who are of humble circumstances ought to take pride in our high position in Christ. Likewise, the brother or sister who is rich should take pride that he has been brought low, for the rich and powerful of the earth will fade away and be destroyed (James 1:9-11). Don't envy the rich. Exemplify to them the Christ who brings us riches no ruler of this world ever imagined (1 Cor. 2:6-8).

Scriptural Examples

Daniel. He never forgot his roots as a child of the King. When the king of Babylon ordered Daniel to eat the royal "delicacies," Daniel asked for a special diet for himself and his friends. After a trial period of 10 days, these four men were better nourished than any of those who ate the king's food. They were not deceived by the rich Babylonian fare (Dan. 1).

Prayer of Application.

Father, help me to remember I am an ambassador of the King of Kings. Keep me from being overly impressed with earthly wealth and power and help me to exemplify Christ in all I do.

Do Not Worship the Fickle Idol of Wealth

4) Do not wear yourself out to get rich; have the wisdom to show restraint. 5) Cast but a glance at riches and they are gone, for they will surely sprout wings and fly off to the sky like an eagle (Prov. 23:4-5).

In the 17th century "Enlightenment" movement, secular philosophers like David Hume and John Locke made a watershed impact on Western thought by reducing what could be known about anything, to that which could be observed by sight, touch, taste, or hearing. For these men, and the many who have followed them, the supernatural realm was left totally unknowable, the chasm too wide to jump.

Their empiricist thinking dominates our culture today. One area that is especially touched is economic materialism. We have lifted covetousness to an art form. Greed is our creed. Even Christians have been swept up into its vacuum. We honor the rich man in our midst and pour contempt upon the poor man who is rich in faith (James 2:1-7). But the wisdom of the world is foolishness in God's sight (1 Cor 1:20).

God says that it is a person's faith that counts (Heb. 11:6; Gal. 5:6). Faith deals in the realms of the unseen and the future (Heb. 11:1), not in the material of Hume and Locke. To attribute power to earthly riches and to bow down to them is idolatry. We are called instead to trust in God for all our needs (Matt. 6:28-34). He will not fly away like the eagle of verse 5 here. His riches are permanent and eternal. Trust in the eternal riches of Christ, not in the fleeting idol of materialism.

Scriptural Examples

The rich fool. Jesus told a parable of a rich man who relied on his earthly wealth, yet was not rich toward God. In his case, his own life took wings and flew away. God called him a "fool" because he trusted in the wrong treasure (Luke 12:15-21).

Prayer of Application

Dear Lord, You promised to supply all my needs through Your riches and You've done it. Keep me from the idolatry of materialism and focused upon the eternal riches of Christ.

Do Not Trust the Kindness of a Greedy Man

*6) Do not eat the food of a stingy man, do not crave his delicacies; 7)
for he is the kind of man who is always thinking about the cost. "Eat
and drink," he says to you, but his heart is not with you. 8) You will
vomit up the little you have eaten and will have wasted your
compliments* (Prov. 23:6-8).

The stingy man's heart is not with you but with himself.
Although he wears a smile and invites you to "eat and drink," he
has a mental calculator that's adding up the bill. After dessert, he
will hand you the check, and the total will make you sick. Appearing to be sincerely interested in you, this man's only interest
is in what you can do for him. Don't desire his delicacies. In the
end, you'll pay much more than they're worth.

What a marked difference we see in the One who invites us to
the feast of wisdom. (See Prov. 9:1-6.) He is not stingy or interested
only in Himself. On the contrary, His invitation is freely given and
without cost to you. The bread is eternal and wholesome, the wine
of the finest vintage, and the check was picked up by your Host
nearly 2,000 years ago. One warning: you may leave the banquet of
wisdom hungry—for more of your Host's grace and righteousness.

Scriptural Examples

Pharisee host #1. Jesus sat down at his table without washing
His hands first. The Pharisee noticed the omission and called it to
Jesus' attention. Jesus saw right through to his covetousness and
scolded him, saying something like, "It's what's on the inside that
counts… Give what is inside the dish to the poor, and everything
will be clean for you" (Luke 11:37-44).

Pharisee host #2. On another occasion, Jesus noticed a
Pharisee's guests were taking the best seats at their host's table. The
Lord said to him he should give banquets for the poor and
those who couldn't afford to repay (Luke 14:12-14).

Prayer of Application

Sovereign Lord, keep me from the greedy man who is only
interested in himself, and keep me from becoming like him. May
I be one who freely and cheerfully gives to those in need.

Do Not Cast Your Pearls Before Swine

*Do not speak to a fool, for he will scorn the wisdom of
your words* (Prov. 23:9).

In the Great Commission, Jesus hires you and me to be His
"Ambassadors of Reconciliation" (2 Cor. 5:18). The commission
has two parts. First, we are to "go and make disciples of all nations,
baptizing them in the name of the Father and of the Son and of the
Holy Spirit." Second, we are to "[teach] them to obey everything
I [Christ] have commanded you." Finishing our commissioning
ceremony, Jesus added, "Surely I am with you always, to the very
end of the age" (Matt. 28:18-20).

Each believer is given, as it were, a bag of pearls and individual
instructions in distributing them. We cast the pearls of the gospel
before the unsaved and expect a harvest of souls. Sometimes the
message is greeted with enthusiasm, often with disinterest, and
occasionally with anger and rancor. It is in these last areas that we
need to exercise great prudence. But, as Charles Bridges appropriately points out, "we should never make the rule of prudence
an excuse for indolence" (p. 427).

Sometimes the casting of pearls may be downright unsafe. In
such instances, we should proceed cautiously, and perhaps even
cease to witness to those we fear may be "swine." Our Lord stopped
speaking in the two examples below.

Scriptural Examples

The Nazarenes. Jesus' hometown folks exhibited a total lack
of faith. At one point they even tried to kill Him. Jesus didn't
hang around too long (Luke 4:16-30; Matt 13:54-58).

The Gadarenes. Jesus cast a multitude of demons out of a man
in their territory and into a herd of pigs. The Gadarenes pleaded
with Jesus to leave their land. Can you imagine telling the Lord of
the universe to "Get out of town"? Who was more like the swine,
the pigs or their owners? (Mark 5:1-19).

Prayer of Application

Father, give me a real passion for sharing the gospel with the
lost. At the same time, help me to know the words to say, and take
care that I do not waste wisdom on the scornful fool.

Do Not Add to What Is Written

10) Do not move an ancient boundary stone or encroach on the fields of the fatherless, 11) for their Defender is strong; he will take up their case against you (Prov. 23:10-11).

Here again we have a boundary stone, and here, too, is deep spiritual ground. Jesus said if anyone were to cause any of His little children to sin, he would face serious consequences (Matt. 18:5-7). I believe many "little children" are being led into sin today in Protestant circles by false teachers.

First, there are many televangelists who preach about a god who is tantamount to a "heavenly butler," ready to fetch whatever is commanded of him. There are other "Christian" teachers who say the Bible merely "becomes" the Word of God as each individual understands it existentially. They say it's our acceptance that counts, not what God has said. There are those who deny the miraculous works of our Lord and teach a Bible devoid of any act not demonstrable in a scientific laboratory. Calling themselves "Christians," they deny even the resurrection of Christ. And there are many others.

The boundary stone being moved today is the very Word of God. Brothers and sisters, it is not "God said it, I believe it, that settles it." It's "God said it—that settles it!" You and I are idolaters at heart, and given the opportunity we will try to alter our view of God to accommodate the flesh. But the "Defender" of the faith is a God of ultimate power and wrath. He will take up the cause of these "little ones," the "fatherless." Beware of His holy judgment, all you who would move His ancient stone.

Scriptural Examples

Pharisees and teachers of the Law. These men moved the boundary stone by adding to the Law of God a plethora of picayune prohibitions. Jesus said, "Woe to you" as He scathingly rebuked those who would alter God's Word (Matt. 23).

Prayer of Application

Lord God, Defender of the powerless, confuse those who would change the Word of God to fit their purposes. Thank You for pastors and teachers who are true to Your Word.

Do Not Neglect to Study the Bible

Apply your heart to instruction and your ears to words of knowledge (Prov. 23:12).

Lately I've been doing some reading into the many and varied religions and cults in America. It is amazing how many different "gospels" there are today. How do we know that we have the right one? How do we know for sure that salvation is by faith alone in Christ Jesus? We can know for sure by adhering to this proverb and applying our hearts to the instruction and knowledge of God's Word.

Few Christians regularly dwell in the Word, particularly the Old Testament. Some pay attention to the pastor's sermon on Sunday, and some may join a Bible study or attend Sunday school. But in many of today's churches, laypeople have given up rigorous Bible study, deferring to the seminary-trained "professional." I thank God for our evangelical seminaries and for those who have undergone their godly disciplines. But the Bible deals with matters of eternal consequence, and I want to know the truth for myself. Furthermore, if you and I are to grow in Christ, we need to know the Word and to put it into practice every day (Heb. 5:11-14).

Each Christian, by the illumination of the Holy Spirit, can be like the Bereans of Paul's day who "examined the Scriptures every day to see if what Paul said was true" (Acts 17:11). Indeed, it is our responsibility before God (2 Tim. 2:15).

Scriptural Examples

Ezra. This man had God's gracious hand upon him because he devoted himself to the study and observance of the law of the Lord and taught others to do the same (Ezra 7:10).

Apollos. We're told in Acts of this man's knowledge of the Old Testament. He was a great help to many in the early church and is mentioned often by Paul (Acts 18:24, 27; 1 Cor. 3-4).

Prayer of Application

Lord, You have given us Your Word so that we may know of Your power and trustworthiness. Give me a hunger for Your Word and a thirst for the righteousness that is mine through it.

Parents: Do Not Withhold Discipline

13) Do not withhold discipline from a child; if you punish him with the rod, he will not die. 14) Punish him with the rod and save his soul from death (Prov. 23:13-14).

My mom used to recite this homegrown proverb occasionally: "Every old crow's little baby is white as snow." I finally figured out that she wasn't speaking of large black birds, but of mothers who thought their children were without flaw.

Because of our tendency to overlook faults, we parents will sometimes withhold discipline. We're afraid we'll hurt their little egos, damage their "self-esteem," or restrain their creativity. We fear that the rod might cause them to grow up hating us, sabotaging an adult relationship with them later on. But the wisdom of God tells us exactly the opposite. Discipline for the child brings his little ego into submission to the truth and gives him the only self-esteem that is worth anything, the kind that comes from knowing God. Proper discipline will ensure a healthy, lifelong relationship with your child.

But discipline must be done in love and not anger. Discipline is not incessant fault-finding. It shouldn't be stern and severe. We should follow the counsel of Paul and not exasperate our children, but bring them up in the training and instruction of the Lord (Eph. 6:4). Let our discipline be given in a spirit of hope and love, not in chastisement and retaliation.

Scriptural Examples

Paul. He claimed to be "father" of the saints of Corinth through the gospel. Like normal children, they were infants in their understanding of the Word. Paul saw the need for discipline and administered some healthy doses of it (1 Cor. 4:15).

Our heavenly Father. God disciplines us because He loves us. If we aren't disciplined we are illegitimate. If God disciplines His children, how can we not discipline ours (Heb. 12:4-11)?

Prayer of Application

Father, thank You for Your disciplining hand. Although it is not pleasant at the time, it produces a harvest of righteousness and peace. Help parents to also discipline their children in love.

Children: Do Not Grieve Your Parents

15) My son, if your heart is wise, then my heart will be glad;
16) my inmost being will rejoice when your lips speak what is
right (Prov. 23:15-16).

The Bible speaks of the heart of people as being the very locus or center of their character. Our Lord testified that out of a person's heart flows all sorts of evil words and deeds (Matt. 15:19-20). Indeed, out of the heart are the very issues of life.

The heart is also the residence of joy (Ps. 4:7) and of deep sorrow (Ps. 13:2). The word "heart" is used 107 times in the Psalms. This shouldn't surprise us, for in the Psalms we find the deep longings, joys, and sorrows of a person's heart in his thirst to know God. David, the great king and psalmist, was a man after God's own wise heart (Acts 13:22).

The wise heart is the heart instructed by the wisdom of God. For Christian parents, all other hopes for their children dim in comparison to the hope that their children will be wise in heart. The child of the Christian parent may grow to achieve worldly greatness and to be highly honored among others. But if that child does not obey the One True God, there is a heaviness in the heart of his mom and dad. Young person, bring joy to your parents in the wisdom of a heart that loves God.

Scriptural Examples

The prodigal son's dad. The prodigal son, who had grieved his father, decided to leave the pigsties and go home. On seeing his son coming from a distance, the father's heart leapt for joy. He ran out to meet the lad and received him back into his household with thanksgiving (Luke 15:13-24).

Paul. In 1 Thessalonians 2:19-20, we see Paul as a father to a church, this time in Thessalonica. Far from his scathing discipline of the Corinthians, he expresses to the Thessalonians that they are his glory and joy.

Prayer of Application

Lord, what a great joy are the children You give to us. But, at the same time, what great heartache lurks for parents whose children do not obey You. May I bring joy to my parents.

Do Not Take Your Eyes off of the Eternal

17) Do not let your heart envy sinners, but always be zealous for the fear of the Lord. 18) There is surely a future hope for you, and your hope will not be cut off (Prov. 23:17-18).

There is an old saying that goes "He is so heavenly-minded that he's no earthly good." But for every Christian of whom that may be said, there must be 10 who are so earthly-minded they are no heavenly good. Why? Because many of us have succumbed to the attractions of this world. We want a temporal reward rather than an eternal one.

Our envy stems from both admiration and resentment. The Christian may feel sorry for himself. He has to play by a different set of rules. He is disciplined by God for something sinners do with applause from others. We are preoccupied with ourselves and with this world. But this world is a will-o'-the-wisp, a fancy that will soon pass away (1 Cor. 7:31).

Jesus commands us to lay up for ourselves eternal treasures in heaven (Matt. 6:19-21). God calls us to a life in this temporal world that is characterized by faith (Rom. 1:17), zealously walking in the fear of the Lord. Sinners work to receive a crown that will not last, but those who are zealous for the fear of the Lord will get a crown that will last forever (1 Cor. 9:25). It is a crown that will be bestowed by the Lord Jesus Himself. But it is a crown that we will have to die to get.

Scriptural Examples

Elijah. In an amazing story of a man of God who was always zealous in the fear of the Lord, this prophet kept on working for God right up to the time that God took him up to heaven in a whirlwind (2 Kings 2:1-12).

Asaph. In Psalm 73, Asaph tells us of his envy of the wicked. His feet had almost slipped. But he concludes God is "the strength of my heart and my portion forever."

Prayer of Application

Father, thank You for Your eternal hope, a hope that will never be cut off. Help me, Lord, to keep my eyes fixed on Jesus, who assures me His promise of reward will come to pass.

Do Not Cross the Line of Intemperance

19) Listen, my son, and be wise, and keep your heart on the right path. 20) Do not join those who drink too much wine or gorge themselves on meat, 21) for drunkards and gluttons become poor, and drowsiness clothes them in rags (Prov. 23:19-21).

Driving home the other day, I saw three men dressed in rags. As I drove by, one of the men raised a quart of beer to his lips and took a big swig. Sadly, it was a perfect picture of this proverb's message to us. Even sadder is the fact that this scene is repeated many thousands of times across our country today.

I believe that Scripture teaches beneficial aspects of alcoholic beverages (1 Tim. 5:23), used as intended and in moderation (Titus 1:7). Certainly meat, or food, is a necessity of life. We'd starve to death if we didn't eat. But to cross the line into drunkenness and gluttony by letting a substance control our thoughts and actions is expressly forbidden by Scripture.

George Lawson says it like this: "Although we do not dethrone reason by drinking, yet if we impair the vigor of it, and render ourselves less fit for the business of life, and the service of God, than we are at other times, by the free use of the bottle, we are wine-bibbers" (p. 407). In other words, if our use of alcohol or food ever leaves us feeling less fit for the service of others and of God, then it has become our master.

Scriptural Examples

Jesus. His enemies called our Lord a wine-bibber and a glutton. They had earlier criticized John the Baptist, who "came neither eating nor drinking" (Matt. 11:18 KJV), of having a demon. While Jesus was a friend of sinners, like those homeless men in the illustration above, He was never guilty of this or any sin (John 2:1-11).

The Corinthians. Some of the converts in Corinth were overindulging in food and wine at church dinners. Others in their midst had nothing to eat or to drink (1 Cor. 11:20-22).

Prayer of Application

Father, there are many things in this life that can become my master if I let my guard down. Help me in all ways to keep my eyes fixed on You and fit for service in Your kingdom.

Children, Buy the Truth and Do Not Sell It

*22) Listen to your father, who gave you life, and do not despise
your mother when she is old. 23) Buy the truth and do not sell it;
get wisdom, discipline and understanding. 24) The father of a
righteous man has great joy; he who has a wise son delights in him.
25) May your father and mother be glad; may she who gave you
birth rejoice! (Prov. 23:22-25).*

Of course, no amount of money can buy ultimate truth, that
of salvation. Its value surpasses anyone's ability to pay. And even
if one could buy it with money, who would be willing to do so
(Rom. 3:10-12)? Jesus said, "I am the way, and the truth, and the
life" (John 14:6). Salvation is "the gift of God—not by works, so
that no man can boast" (Eph. 2:8-9).

But once a person is saved, he begins to "buy" the truth by
investing in diligent prayer, Bible study, and meditation. I believe
that Jesus 'parables of the hidden treasure and the pearl speak to
this principle (Matt. 13:44-46). The treasure and the pearl are
God's wisdom and truth, which are more valuable than any earthly
treasure.

The parents of the person who "buys" the wisdom and truth of
God will rejoice greatly. It is in practicing the truth that the fifth
commandment is most fully obeyed. And who would sell such a
rich treasure? The answer goes without saying.

Scriptural Examples

The rich young ruler. This man was asked by Jesus to "buy"
the truth. But he esteemed the riches of this present world of
greater value than heaven's treasures (Luke 18:18-23).

Moses. On the contrary, Moses was a wealthy man who
"bought" the truth. He regarded disgrace for the sake of Christ
as of greater value than the treasures of Egypt (Heb.11:24-26).

Esau. Esau was a man who was willing to "sell the truth." He
sold his birthright for a bowl of lentil stew (Heb. 12:16-17).

Prayer of Application

Dear God, thank You for Your great gift of salvation. And
thank You for the truth of your Word. Help me to be diligent in
its study, and with Your help, practice its truth in all that I do.

Do Not Give Your Heart to Any But God

25)   My son, give me your heart and let your eyes keep to my ways, 26) for a prostitute is a deep pit and a wayward wife is a narrow well. 28) Like a bandit she lies in wait, and multiplies the unfaithful among men (Prov. 23:26-28).

Solomon steps directly into the role of Divine Wisdom and speaks as if the words come right from the lips of God. "Give me your heart," God says. He wants it all, not just a part. "God loves a broken heart, but can't abide one that is divided" (Bridges p. 439). God's demand on everyone is, "Give me your heart."

There are three other suitors for the heart. First and second are the devil and the world. Satan said to Jesus, "If you worship me, [the world] will all be yours." Jesus replied, "It is written: 'Worship the Lord your God and serve him only'" (Luke 4:5-8). The third suitor is the flesh. In these verses, we see the fleshly call of sin in the prostitute and wayward wife. Like all idols, these women lie in wait to ensnare their victim. These three suitors promise happiness and fulfillment, but when the chips are down, they deliver frustration and death.

To give one's heart to God is a moment-by-moment occurrence. It is our proper spiritual worship (Rom. 12:1-2). As St. Augustine said, "Our hearts are restless until they rest in Thee."

Scriptural Examples

Lot's wife. Just as Tony Bennett left his heart in San Francisco, she left hers in Sodom. She looked back longingly at her first love. God turned her into a pillar of salt (Gen. 19:26).

The Pharisees. Quoting Isaiah, Jesus said, "These people honor me with their lips, but their hearts are far from me." To pay lip service to God is not a good idea (Matt. 15:1-8; Isa. 29:13).

David. He was a man after God's own heart, fully devoted to the Lord. But even so, his heart went out to a beautiful woman. A time of confession and repentance restored the joy of his fellowship with God (Acts 13:22; Ps. 51).

Prayer of Application

Dear Sovereign Lord, You have promised that You would not let me be tempted beyond that which I am able to resist. Thank You, Lord. Keep my heart steadfastly upon Christ.

Do Not Linger over Wine or Strong Drink

29) Who has woe? Who has sorrow? Who has strife? Who has complaints? Who has needless bruises? Who has bloodshot eyes? 30) Those who linger over wine, who go to sample bowls of mixed wine. 31) Do not gaze at wine when it is red, when it sparkles in the cup, when it goes down smoothly! 32) In the end it bites like a snake and poisons like a viper. 33) Your eyes will see strange sights and your mind imagine confusing things. 34) You will be like one sleeping on the high seas, lying on top of the rigging. 35) "They hit me," you will say, "but I'm not hurt! They beat me, but I don't feel it! When will I wake up so I can find another drink?" (Prov. 23:29-35).

Here is a man who has gotten drunk and has a major hangover. He wakes up with a headache, a queasy stomach, and a mouth full of cotton. Getting slowly out of bed, he peeks in the mirror and sees a couple of bloodshot eyeballs staring back at him.

Alcohol, consumed to excess, clouds the mind and confuses the thought patterns (v.33). The KJV renders "strange sights" as "strange women." That makes sense, inasmuch as alcohol lowers the inhibitions and causes one to imagine sexual situations. The drunk's stomach reels like a ship caught in a storm (v. 34). He feels like he's been beat up, but doesn't remember much (v. 35). All he knows is that he's going to get himself another drink (v. 35). He thinks a "pick-me-up" will make his hangover subside, but it'll just get him a little deeper in trouble.

Scriptural Examples

Belshazzar. This Babylonian king gave a great banquet in which he used the sacred articles of the temple in Jerusalem to serve wine and to get drunk. Suddenly, the finger of a human hand wrote on the wall of the palace, "God has numbered the days of your reign and brought it to an end." Belshazzar's fright at seeing the hand is reminiscent of these verses (Dan. 5).

Prayer of Application

Father, thank You for the Holy Spirit who controls me. May I find joy and gladness in life only in You and Your Word, and in the fellowship of my brothers and sisters in Christ.

Chapter Twenty-four

Proverbs and the Sluggard

The slothful person or sluggard is a major theme of Proverbs. The sixth commandment says in part, "Six days you shall labor and do all your work." Paul said, "If a man will not work, he shall not eat" (2 Thess. 3:10). Sloth is a very serious sin in God's eyes.

In verses 30 through 34 we are given a clear picture of the results of sloth. "I went past the field of the sluggard, past the vineyard of the man who lacks judgment; thorns had come up everywhere, the ground was covered with weeds, and the stone wall was in ruins. I applied my heart to what I observed and learned a lesson from what I saw: A little sleep, a little slumber, a little folding of the hands to rest—and poverty will come on you like a bandit and scarcity like an armed man."

Notice first that the sluggard lacked judgment. He failed to tend his vineyard and so allowed it to go to seed. Not a very good environment for producing fine wine! He had permitted the stone wall around his property to fall into ruin, which allowed goats and cattle to come in and eat his plants. The result of all this is clearly seen. His slothfulness will earn only poverty. He will go out to harvest his crop and discover that he can't find enough fruit to make a little box of raisins. Such is the trap that the sluggard sets for himself.

Follow the "Foolishness" of God

1) Do not envy wicked men, do not desire their company: 2) for their hearts plot violence, and their lips talk about making trouble (Prov. 24:1-2).

In 1 Corinthians 1, Paul speaks of two kinds of foolishness: the "foolishness" of God and the foolishness of the world. In verse 18 he says that the message of the Cross is "foolishness to those who are perishing," but through it (v. 20b) "God [has] made foolish the wisdom of the world." He goes on to say, "For since in the wisdom of God the world through its wisdom did not know him, God was pleased through the foolishness of what was preached to save those who believe" (v. 21).

In the world's "wisdom," it is foolish to seek one's treasure in a future life. In the wisdom of God, it is foolish to seek one's treasure in the here and now (Matt. 6:19-20). Jim Elliot, a missionary who was martyred in the jungles of Ecuador, loved this proverb: "He is no fool who gives what he cannot keep to gain what he cannot lose." The wisdom of God and the wisdom of the world are diametrically opposed to one another.

This is why we are not to envy the wicked when they seem to prosper in this life. They have the short view, which is the foolish view in God's sight. All that the wicked do is sin (Rom. 3:12-18). On the other hand, the Christian takes the long view. He begins to seek after the things that please God, not himself. No longer is the Christian's primary interest in building his own estate, but the estate of God among others. To the natural person, nothing could be more foolish. To God, nothing could be wiser.

Scriptural Examples

Moses. He was an heir to the kingdom of Egypt. He received the finest education, wore the finest clothes, and held the highest offices and honors. Yet Moses chose to forsake all of that for the disgrace of Christ. Why? Because he had the long view (Heb. 11:24-26).

Prayer of Application

Father, sometimes I am tempted to envy the wealth and fame of the lost. Then I think of Your gracious promises and am brought back to rest in You. Thank You, Lord, for Your wisdom.

Build Your House on the Rock of Christ

1). By wisdom a house is built, and through understanding it is established; 4) through knowledge its rooms are filled with rare and beautiful treasures. 5) A wise man has great power, and a man of knowledge increases strength; 6) for waging war you need guidance, and for victory many advisers (Prov. 24:3-6).

In homebuilding, the wicked person's short view is like constructing an igloo in Arizona in August. At sunrise, the igloo would start to melt, and by noon there would be nothing left except cracked desert soil. Not a home to be envious of.

The way of wisdom uses a different construction code: the Word of God. It leads to an eternal dwelling place filled with rare and beautiful treasures.

Paul calls the church in Corinth "God's building" (1 Cor. 3:9-16). Paul laid a foundation of the gospel message on which someone else will build. Different kinds of building materials are used: "gold, silver, costly stones" on the one hand, but "wood, hay and stubble" on the other. By the wise use of the better materials, a builder (such as you and I) will fill the rooms of his house with rare and beautiful treasures: heavenly rewards. Otherwise, our work will be burned up when its quality is tested by the fire of Christ's judgment.

The wise man will build for the long haul, and with the guidance of many counselors. Build on the only secure foundation — the Lord Jesus Christ. And then build with the best materials, using the building code of the ages: the Word of God.

Scriptural Examples

The wise and foolish builders. I once built high-rise condominiums on the coast of Florida. We drove pilings deep into the sand and anchored to them. Nearby, other buildings did not use pilings. Some day a hurricane will move them across the street. These two biblical examples also had different results because of the different codes to which they adhered (Matt. 7:24-27).

Prayer of Application

Father, thank You for the Word of God which gives us the guidance needed for the construction of a permanent dwelling, and for Christ's foundation that is so firm and secure.

Let Your Wisdom Shut the Mouths of Fools

Wisdom is too high for a fool; in the assembly at the gate he has nothing to say (Prov. 24:7).

In biblical days, the gate to the city was where the elders sat and dispensed justice (Deut. 21:18-20, for instance). The fool in the verse above may have been accused of a crime, and the evidence against him is so weighty that he has no wisdom to draw upon to defend himself. Or, perhaps he aspires to a seat among those who rule the town, but doesn't have the wisdom required for the job. It is too high for him. It's not that he lacks intelligence. Rather, he does not have the moral character to seek wisdom. He's speechless. That, by the way, is an unusual circumstance for a fool.

Peter tells us that we are to live our lives in such a way that although the pagans may accuse us of wrongdoing, they will see our good deeds and glorify God on the day He visits. We are to silence the mouths of fools by good works (1 Peter 2:12, 15).

To paraphrase the words of movie character Forrest Gump, "Wisdom is as wisdom does." James says that we deceive ourselves when we merely hear words of wisdom but don't act upon them (James 1:22). But the person who practices wisdom is the person who does the will of God and who will shut the mouths of foolish people. At the last judgment, the fool will have no excuse or defense. In fact, he won't have a word to say.

Scriptural Examples

Job. He sat at the gate of the city, but he wasn't speechless. (Note the lengthy discourse between Job and his three friends.) But then God entered the conversation and Job shut up. In the same way the fool will be speechless before God (Job 29; 38–42).
Jesus. He said to the Pharisees and teachers of the Law, "Do not believe me unless I do what my Father does." Because Jesus did precisely the will of His Father, He shut the mouths of these foolish false teachers (John 10:37-38).

Prayer of Application

Lord, help me to live in such a way as to shut the mouths of those who oppose Your truth. We Christians prove the truth of Your Word by our actions. Help me to live consistently with it.

Detest the Schemes of the Mocker

8) He who plots evil will be known as a schemer. 9) The schemes of folly are sin, and men detest a mocker (Prov. 24:8-9).

Ever seen a movie or read a book where the "perfect crime" is planned? You know, a squad of schemers meet in a smoky room and plan to steal some fabulous treasure. They devise intricate strategies to get into the museum by lowering a guy dressed in black on a rope. In great suspense, he snatches the jewel out of its case and then make his escape.

Funny, isn't it? If these schemers spent half the time and energy planning a legitimate business they would avoid 20 years in prison and sleep much better to boot. But you see, they like to do it. And they never think they'll be caught. Little do they suspect that an all-seeing God knows their every move, their every thought. Of course, they mock at the notion of a personal God who holds them accountable. But with God, they don't just face a 20-year prison term. They face eternal fire.

The wicked schemes of mockers are legion. A wife conjures up a way to have an affair with another man. An employee seeks to be fired so he can sue his employer. An employer looks for devious ways he can cheat his customers. The list could go on and on. Detest such schemes. They are on the way to death.

Scriptural Examples

The great multitude. The Bible is full of schemers, people who lie on their beds plotting evil: women like Jezebel, Delilah, and the prostitute of Proverbs 5, and men like Cain and Balaam and Judas. I could fill this book with this multitude of schemers. But, instead, I list next the granddaddy of them all.

Satan. He is also the prince of mockers. He schemed to elevate himself above the throne of God (Isa.14:13-14). He schemed to deceive Eve (Gen. 3: 1). But God knows his schemes and has already defeated this king of schemers (Rev. 20:10).

Prayer of Application

Father, though mockers scheme against You, You sit on high and laugh at them. May I only plan for good, to the end that You will be glorified and evil schemers will be mocked.

Prepare for the Judgment Seat of Christ

10) If you falter in times of trouble, how small is your strength! 11) Rescue those being led away to death; hold back those staggering toward slaughter. 12) If you say, "But we knew nothing about this," does not he who weighs the heart perceive it? Will he not repay each person according to what he has done (Prov. 24:10-12)?

Incredibly, many Christians think that they will not be held accountable for what they do. But Paul says, "For we must all appear before the judgment seat of Christ, that each one may receive what is due him for the things done while in the body, whether good or bad. Since then, we know what it is to fear the Lord, we try to persuade men" (2 Cor. 5: 10-11; Rom. 14:10-12). There *will* be a judgment day for believers: not unto condemnation (Rom. 8:1), but unto rewards. Believers who have by their faithfulness laid up "treasures in heaven" (Matt. 6:19-20) will be rewarded, while others will suffer loss (1 Cor. 3:12-15).

The verses above teach about an omniscient Judge who sees through our excuses. When we get out of our "comfort zone" (Prov. 24:10), we may shrink back. We say, "That's not my responsibility," or "I'm not gifted in that direction." We may follow only those commandments we find enjoyable. We may plead ignorance (v. 12), but that's a flimsy excuse which God sees through.

Paul says, "Wait till the Lord comes. He will bring to light what is hidden in the darkness and will expose the motives of men's hearts" (1 Cor. 4:5). Trust in God. He gives us the strength to overcome our fears and weaknesses (2 Cor. 12:9).

Scriptural Examples

Faith's hall of fame. Hebrews 11 gives a glowing record of men and women of faith. Note particularly Moses who looked forward to his reward, and also those saints who refused to be released from torture to obtain a better resurrection. Surely they were all prepared for Christ's judgment seat.

Prayer of Application

Heavenly Father, Your grace is overwhelming. We not only are given heaven but treasures beyond imagining. Help me to desire a better reward and not to shrink back in faithlessness.

Taste the Sweetness of God's Hope

13) Eat honey, my son, for it is good; honey from the comb is sweet to your taste. 14) Know also that wisdom is sweet to your soul; if you find it, there is a future hope [KJV: "reward"] for you, and your hope will not be cut off (Prov. 24:13-14).

From the instant that Adam and Eve sinned, people have been hiding from God (Gen. 3:8-10). We don't hide literally in the bushes anymore, but in things like religion, our own good works, the denial of God's self revelation (Rom. 1:18-21), and in other devious ways. Sweetness to the natural person is having autonomy— to call his own shots. He wants nothing at all to do with God and creates his own gods that he can control.

Autonomy is freedom without accountability. We see it throughout America today. People want the freedom to have sex without the responsibility of raising a child. Some hide in "victimhood" because victims are not accountable for their actions. The drunkard becomes an alcoholic, the victim of a disease and not morally accountable. Such is the "sweetness" of the world's wisdom, but it leads to death (Prov. 14:12).

But the wisdom that comes from above begins with the "fear of the Lord" (Ps. 111:10; Prov. 1:7; 9:10). Our hearts are quickened by God and made alive from their deadness in sin. We begin to run toward Him, not away from Him. His words become sweet to our souls (Prov. 16:24) as we discover His grace that covers our many sins and gives us hope.

God promised the Israelites a land flowing with milk and honey (Ex. 3:17). In the New Testament, milk is sometimes used as a synonym for the Word of God (1 Peter 2:2). Here, I believe honey is used in the same sense. Its sweetness lies in our humble dependence upon the One who wrote it and the hope of resurrection that it teaches. It is a hope that will not be cut off, a sure hope, a hope that is but a sweet taste of the real thing. What joy and sweetness there will be when we enter God's Promised Land!

Prayer of Application

Lord, the hope of resurrection is sweet, removing my fear of death and judgment. But still lurking within is the desire to have my own way. Keep me in utter dependence upon You.

Do Not Forget God's Deliverance

15) Do not lie in wait like an outlaw against a righteous man's house, do not raid his dwelling place; 16) for though a righteous man falls seven times, he rises again, but the wicked are brought down by calamity (Prov. 24:15-16).

Have you ever experienced trouble so deep that you could see no avenue of escape? If so, you were exactly where God wanted you to be. In such times God reveals His mighty power.

Back in the 1970s, I was in Florida preparing to build homes on some golf course lots. As I was about to take out building permits, interest rates began to rise. Seeing trouble, I made the decision to sell the lots and move my family back to California. I settled into a lonely house by myself and tried to sell the lots. Several months went by and the lots went into foreclosure. I had only two weeks before the bank took them back. I sat in that empty house, lonely, frightened, and sad. All I could do was pray. My back was to the wall.

Then the phone rang. On the other end was an investment banker in Los Angeles whom I knew slightly. His wealthy aunt had called him with a desire to buy some Florida lots. She had specified that they had to be on a golf course! I flew to L.A. the next day, and the deal was closed in less than two weeks.

I've had my back to the wall more times than seven (v. 16). Each time God has delivered me. I pray that I've learned more of His wisdom, so not to get myself into trouble like that again.

Scriptural Examples

The many examples. Men like Joseph, David, Gideon, and Paul, and women like Esther, Ruth, Rahab, and Mary are examples of those whose backs were to the wall, yet who experienced God's deliverance. On the other hand, many in the Bible like Haman, Sennacherib, Jezebel, and Michal, found only calamity. Trust in God and remember His deliverances. He'll do it again and again.

Prayer of Application

Dear Lord, thank You for the many times that You have picked me up after I have stumbled and fallen. Thank You for your rescue from the ultimate peril I face: death and judgment.

Do Not Delight in Your Enemy's Trouble

17) Do not gloat when your enemy falls; when he stumbles, do not let your heart rejoice, 18) or the Lord will see and disapprove and turn his wrath away from him (Prov. 24:17-18).

Human beings delight in revenge. Almost every movie deals with the subject of justice. I remember as a kid going to the Westerns. We would always "boo" the bad guys and then explode in a rousing cheer when the guys in white hats swept in and saved the day. We delighted in seeing justice done.

There is nothing wrong with justice unless you happen to be on the receiving end. I want mercy, don't you? I've found that mercy in Christ. How then can I rejoice when my enemy stumbles and falls? In his shoes, but for God's grace, go I.

Jesus tells us to "love your enemies and pray for those who persecute you" (Matt. 5:44). That is diametrically opposed to the message of the movies: "Laugh and cheer when those who persecute you and treat you unfairly receive their just desserts." The world says, "Vengeance is sweet." God says, "Vengeance is mine" (Ps. 94:1). We who are recipients of His mercy must want all people to come to a knowledge of Christ.

We will ultimately cheer for the justice God will bring at His judgment throne. But in this world, let us love our enemies and fear the One who disapproves of our boasting (Rom. 11:17-21).

Scriptural Examples

David. When David heard that Saul and Jonathan were dead, you might expect a sigh of relief. But instead, David and his men tore their clothes and wept openly. Someone might say that David wept because Jonathan had been killed. Others might claim that David wept over the destruction of the Israelite army. Both options are tenable. But I believe David knew of this proverb's principle and was sorely afraid that if he took to gloating, Saul's fate awaited him (2 Sam. 1:11-12).

Prayer of Application

Dear God, how tempting it is to cheer and gloat at the defeat of the wicked. Help me instead to pray for my enemies, and to hope that they, like I, would receive Your free salvation.

Do Not LookBack

19) Do not fret because of evil men or be envious of the wicked, 20) for the evil man has no future hope, and the lamp of the wicked will be snuffed out (Prov. 24:19-20).

Christians are tempted to look at rich, successful, and famous people and envy them. Those of us who were saved later in life may look back on our former lifestyles and secretly wish to be up to our old tricks again. When we look back, we momentarily adopt the "short view" of life. When this occasionally happens to me, I lose my contentment in Christ Jesus and need to repent for restoration of His "long view."

If God has given you the eternal perspective; i.e., the long view, don't look back. Keep your eyes focused on Jesus, the author and finisher of your faith (Heb. 12:2). Don't envy the wicked. True prosperity is in the salvation of God.

Scriptural Examples

Lot's wife. Lot hurried his wife and daughters out of town toward a future hope. On the trail, Mrs. Lot took a short look back, remembering all she was leaving behind. It was the last look back she would ever get (Gen. 19:15-26).

The Israelites. At Kadesh-Barnea, the spies brought back glowing reports of the land God had promised. But the people began to grumble. They took a look back at Egypt and cried out for a leader who would lead them there (Num. 13:25-14:38).

The rich man and Lazarus. Here is the Bible's most poignant story of the long and short views of life. The beggar Lazarus sat at the rich man's gate and longed for something to eat. He died and went to heaven. Meanwhile, the rich man took the short view and enjoyed himself in the here and now, not giving a hoot for the needs of the old beggar at his gate. When the rich man died, his perspective changed and he finally got the long view. But it was too late (Luke 16:20-31).

Prayer of Application

Heavenly Father, how magnetic are the things of this world which try to pull us back to our old ways. Keep me in Your long view, that I might live in steadfast love and devotion to You.

Beware the Consequences of Lawlessness

19) Fear the Lord and the king, my son, and do not join with the rebellious, 22) for those two will send sudden destruction upon them, and who knows what calamities they can bring (Prov. 24:21-22)?

Rebel against the Lord's and the king's law and you can expect calamity and sudden destruction. Peter picks up this theme in 1 Peter 2:17. Paul, of course, devotes a healthy part of Romans 13 to it. We normally would apply these verses to the secular government. But I think an even clearer application may be made to the church. Hebrews 13:17 tells us to obey our church leaders and submit to their authority. They are charged with giving account to God for our actions.

I once knew of some members of a local congregation who rose up against their godly pastor. They sought to have him removed from office and lobbied the other members to do so. Their actions split the church right down the middle. Were there calamities wrought against that group? I don't know, but I wouldn't want to be in their shoes.

Scriptural Examples

Korah and his followers. They tried to usurp Moses' authority. God put a calamitous end to their rebellion as the ground split open and they were swallowed alive (Num. 16).

David and Saul. Even though Saul tried to kill him on several occasions, David had respect for his king, and would not take advantage of him (1 Sam. 24:6).

David and the Amalekite. Conversely, David brought sudden destruction on this young man, who claimed to have ended Saul's life with the sword (2 Sam. 1:1-16).

Absalom. Rebelling against the king isn't safe even if he's your dad. This youth discovered the truth of these verses the hard way, as he dangled from a tree by his hair (2 Sam. 15:1-18:15).

Prayer of Application

Dear Lord, thank You for the godly people who govern our local churches. Strengthen them to the task that is before them and help those of us under their care to support them fully.

Exercise Authority in Justice and Truth

23) These also are sayings of the wise: To show partiality in judging is not good: 24) Whoever says to the guilty, "You are innocent"— peoples will curse him and nations denounce him. 25) But it will go well with those who convict the guilty, and rich blessing will come upon them. 26) An honest answer is like a kiss on the lips (Prov. 24:23-26).

Someone says, "Wait a second, I'm not a judge! I don't have any authority over people! How does this principle apply to me?" I'm glad you asked. Are you a parent? Elected to an office at school or church? Supervise others at work? A hospital volunteer? Virtually every person in the world exercises some kind of authority over others at one time or another. These proverbs are aimed at that rather large group of people.

From almost the moment we are able to speak, we humans know the words, "That's not fair!" We all have an innate sense of fair play and when it is offended we get very upset. I believe God is calling us in these proverbs to a strict duty of fair play, without partiality, where the guilty party gets justice.

God wants us to be a people of justice and truth. Whatever your position or calling, honest and forthright dealing with those under your authority is always the best policy. In fact, an honest and upright policy is just like a kiss on the lips.

Scriptural Examples

Joel and Abijah. These sons of Samuel accepted bribes and perverted justice. The people of Israel were very angry and cried out against their unrighteous rule (1 Sam. 8:1-3).

David's oracle. His last words bring tribute to those who reign in righteousness and in the fear of God (2 Sam. 23:1-4).

Job. Job sat by the city gate in the place of judgment and was revered by the people. He said, "I put on righteousness as my clothing and justice was my robe and my turban" (Job 29:7-17).

Prayer of Application

Father, how often it seems that fair play turns unfair under the influence of sin. Help me to be fair in every way, particularly when You put me in a position of authority.

Put First Things First

Finish your outdoor work and get your fields ready; after that, build your house (Prov. 24:27).

Whenever I read this proverb, I always think of the pioneer family who comes upon a plot of land and decides to settle down. They sleep in their covered wagon until they get the corn crop planted down by the river. Then they begin to build their home on high ground above the flood plain. But most of us aren't pioneers. How do these verses apply to us?

Kidner and Ironside both see "house" here as referring to a family. They say the verse is telling us to get financially and emotionally stable before getting married. That's exactly what the pioneer family was doing, although in another context. They planted the field so they would have something to put on the table when they built a house for the table. They put first things first. They had their priorities straight.

Actually, the verse above could have read, "First, get your medical degree, then do brain surgery." Or, "First, get your high school diploma, then join the Navy." How about, "First, save the cash, then make the purchase." The principle is the same in all of these cases. Be sure you have what it takes to advance to the next step in your life, then go ahead.

Scriptural Examples

The tower builder. Our Lord told of the man who wanted to build a tower. He said the smart thing to do was to sit down and figure out how much it was going to cost, and then if he had the cash, go ahead and start building (Luke 14:28-30).

The church builder. In building the Lord's church the principle is the same: First, know your foundation is solid, then build on it. Paul tells us that this foundation is none other than Jesus Christ Himself and the gospel of salvation through faith alone (1 Cor. 3:10-15; Eph. 2:8-9).

Prayer of Application

Father God, help me to get my priorities straight. Remind me daily that my first priority is to seek Your glory and righteousness. Then, all else I need will be added unto me.

Love Your Neighbor as Yourself

28) Do not testify against your neighbor without cause, or use your lips to deceive. 29) Do not say, "I'll do to him as he has done to me; I'll pay that man back for what he did" (Prov. 24:28-29).

Our principle here is also a direct command of Jesus that is found three times in Matthew (5:43; 19:19; 22:39), twice in Mark (12:31, 33), and once in Luke (10:27). Paul speaks of the commandment twice, in Romans 13:9 and Galatians 5:14, where he adds that it summarizes the entire law. James calls it "the royal law" (James 2:8). In Leviticus 19:18 it appears in this same context, that of not seeking revenge against another.

Why doesn't God want us to seek revenge when we are wronged by someone? I believe the answer is threefold. First, we don't know all the facts. We cannot see into our neighbor's heart and judge his motives. Second, our judgment is always perverted by sin in our own hearts. Romans 2:1 speaks of this tendency every man has to judge others for the same offenses he overlooks in himself. Finally, that same sinfulness also prohibits us from making the punishment fit the crime. We will tend to err on the side of harshness.

But perhaps the overarching reason for loving our neighbor is that we are called on this earth to reflect the love and mercy of God. We have no inherent "rights" as such. All rights are God's rights, so in any sin He is the offended party, not us. Therefore, it is God's right only to seek revenge. We who have been loved by God have been forgiven much. How can we not, therefore, wish what is best for our neighbor?

Scriptural Examples

Stephen. As the stones rained down upon his dying body, the first Christian martyr did not seek God's revenge upon those who unjustly executed him. Rather, he sought God's forgiveness of their sin (Acts 6:5–7:60).

Prayer of Application

Our Father in heaven, take the desire for personal revenge from me, and replace it with a genuine love for all. Help me to be a true representative of Your grace and mercy on this earth.

Ponder the Results of Sloth

30) I went past the field of the sluggard, past the vineyard of the man who lacks judgment; 31) thorns had come up everywhere, the ground was covered with weeds, and the stone wall was in ruins. 32) I applied my heart to what I observed and learned a lesson from what I saw: 33) A little sleep, a little slumber, a little folding of the hands to rest — 34) and poverty will come on you like a bandit and scarcity like an armed man (Prov. 24:30-34).

Some time ago, my daughter and I took a trip up through the Napa and Sonoma valleys, noted for their rolling vineyards and fine wines. We drove past mile after mile of beautiful vineyards, with brightly painted fences and precise stone walls. What a contrast to the vineyard in these verses. As Solomon says, "[I] learned a lesson from what I saw." Let's do the same.

Just like a healthy garden requires persistent effort in its care and maintenance, so does every part of one's life. I wonder also about this sluggard's home, his job, his marriage, and his family. Would we see the same crumbling walls?

One relationship where sloth is often found is between ourselves and the Lord. Consistent Bible study, a vibrant prayer and devotional life, regular church attendance, participation in the Lord's Supper, and fellowship with other believers are of inestimable worth if the Christian's "vineyard" is to bear fruit. Neglect it and don't be surprised to see the thorns and thistles grow up to choke out its fruitfulness. Ponder the results of sloth and of slothful Christianity.

Scriptural Examples

The Lord's vineyard. Isaiah wrote of a day when the Lord's vineyard would bear much fruit because the Lord Himself would watch over it. No briers or thorns will grow there. It will be a day when Jacob will take root and all Israel will bud and blossom and fill the world with its fruit (Isa. 27:2-6).

Prayer of Application

Father, how easy it is to slide back to old lazy ways. Help me to be more diligent in my relationship with You. That will bear godly fruit and all my other relationships will blossom, too.

Chapter Twenty-five

Proverbs and the Tongue

The tongue is another central theme of the book of Proverbs. James has much to say about our speech in the New Testament. He says that "the tongue…is a fire, a world of evil among the parts of the body. It corrupts the whole person, sets the whole course of his life on fire, and is itself set on fire by hell" (James 3:6). Proverbs also warns of the traps set by our tongues. Here in chapter 25 we see prideful tongues (v. 6), hasty tongues (v. 8), gossiping tongues (vv. 9-10), boastful tongues (v. 14), lying tongues (v. 18), inappropriate tongues (v. 20), sly tongues (v. 23), and quarrelsome tongues (v. 24). But we also see a measure of righteousness in the use of the tongue.

Verse 11 speaks of "a word aptly spoken" being "like apples of gold in settings of silver." The next verse tells us of the high value of the wise man's rebuke. Verse 13 exalts the "trustworthy messenger" who uses his tongue to "refresh…the spirit of his masters." We see the power of the gentle tongue in verse 15. Finally, the tongue that carries "good news from a distant land" is compared to "cold water to a weary soul" in verse 25.

The tongue may be used for evil or for good. God exalts the use of the tongue for righteousness sake but condemns the sinful words that so easily spring off of it.

Worship God: Honor the King

*1) These are more proverbs of Solomon, copied by the men of
Hezekiah king of Judah. 2) It is the glory of God to conceal a matter;
to search out a matter is the glory of kings. 3) As the heavens are high
and the earth is deep, so the hearts of kings are unsearchable* (Prov.
25:1-3).

Here begins the third major division of the book of Proverbs,
copied out by the men of Hezekiah, who reigned from 715 to 687
B.C. Note, God honors not only Solomon, but also his publisher
and his employees. There is nothing done in service to God that
is too small to escape notice and reward. Remember that the
next time you change a dirty diaper in the nursery on Lord's Day
morning or set up chairs for a Sunday school class.

God and kings are contrasted. God conceals Himself from us
just as He concealed His face from Moses and the Israelites (Ex.
33:20-23). God reveals Himself partially in His creation, in His
Word, and in Christ. "Now we see in a glass darkly," Paul writes,
"but then face to face"(1 Cor. 13:12). Our understanding of God
is limited by our humanness, sinfulness, and God's own timing.

Earthly kings are God's representatives for law and order.
Where God reveals and conceals, kings search. For example, they
search for the truth to make right judgments and for good people
to serve them. Ironside likens them to believers (p. 346). We, too,
are God's representatives. We, too, search for truth.

Scriptural Examples

Manoah and wife. Samson's parents asked the angel of the Lord
His name. He replied, "Why do you ask my name? It is beyond
understanding." Likewise, God is unsearchable (Judg. 13:17-18).

Solomon. A good example of a king who sought the truth.
With two prostitutes and a baby, he displayed wise creativity in
getting to the heart of the dispute (1 Kings 3:16-28).

Prayer of Application

Father, thank You for revealing Yourself to us in Your Word,
by Christ and through the Spirit's illumination. Help me to learn
of You, to the end that I will reflect Your Son.

Keep Looking Up!

4) Remove the dross from the silver, and out comes material for the silversmith; 5) remove the wicked from the king's presence and his throne will be established through righteousness (Prov. 25:4-5).

In the last verses, we saw that it was to the glory of a king to search out a matter. Here we see why the godly king searches: that his throne be established in righteousness.

To remove the dross—its slag or scum—from silver, the refiner applies a lot of heat. The silver ore is melted. Its impurities then float to the surface where they are skimmed off. In this same process the king above searches out the wicked. He applies the heat and the wicked are revealed.

Our Great King is now on His throne applying heat to this world. One day, He will remove all the wicked from this planet, skimming them off into a fire that will never be quenched (Isa. 66:24). At the same time, He is in the process of removing wickedness from His children (Heb. 2:17-18) by applying the heat of discipline in our lives, sanctifying and purifying us (Heb. 12:10-11; 1 Peter 1:6-7).

There is wickedness everywhere we look. Indeed, all creation displays the many effects of sin (Rom. 8:22). We groan, awaiting the redemption that draws nearer with every passing day. This is our great hope in which we are saved (Rom. 8:24), and we are to wait patiently for it. Keep looking up! Your redemption draws nigh (Luke 21:28).

Scriptural Examples

Solomon. Just before David died, he gave a charge to his son who was to succeed to the throne. David exhorted him to follow the Law of the Lord and to rid the kingdom of the wicked who would hinder the proper establishment of a righteous reign. Joab, Shimei, and others were subsequently slain by Solomon as he brought the heat to bear (1 Kings 2).

Prayer of Application

Lord God, one day soon the history of this world will be invaded once again by Jesus. This time He won't come as a little child, but as the conquering King of Kings! Hallelujah!

Imitate Christ's Humility

6) Do not exalt yourself in the king's presence, and do not claim a place among great men; 7) It is better for him to say to you, "Come up here," than for him to humiliate you before a nobleman (Prov. 25:6-7).

God chose to reveal Himself to us in His Son, "who being in very nature God, did not consider equality with God something to be grasped, but made himself nothing, taking the very nature of a servant, being made in human likeness. And being found in appearance as a man, he humbled himself and became obedient to death—even death on a cross (Phil. 2:6-8)!"

There is a wonderful old hymn that goes like this: "Out of the ivory palaces, into a world of woe." The song tells the story of Jesus, who in unfathomable humility came to this earth to die for the sins of people like you and me. In doing so, He revealed God's character of ultimate humility, grace and love.

How much different we are. We who are nothing seek to elevate ourselves in the eyes of others and will use every trick in the book to do it. How foolish we are and what a glaring difference between our character and that of the Living God. Humble yourself after the example of Jesus.

Scriptural Examples

The disciples. They argued among themselves as to who was the greatest. They didn't get it, did they? Jesus said, "If anyone wants to be first, he must be last" (Mark 9:33-35).

The Roman centurion. He asked Jesus to heal his servant, but said he didn't deserve Him under his roof. Jesus lauded his faith and appreciated his humility as well (Luke 7:2-10).

The party guest. Jesus attended a party once where guests sought places of honor, so He told a parable about a man who didn't heed this proverb. The man was humiliated when his host asked him to move to a lesser seat (Luke 14:7-10).

Prayer of Application

Dear God, how far I am from the excellence of Your divine nature. I can taste it, but I can't duplicate it. Help me to grow more in the likeness of Your Son to bring Him glory.

Don't Be Quick to Judge Your Neighbor

8) What you have seen with your eyes do not bring hastily to court, for what will you do in the end if your neighbor puts you to shame? 9) If you argue your case with a neighbor, do not betray another man's confidence, 10) or he who hears it may shame you and you will never lose your bad reputation (Prov. 25:8-10).

Frances got off the city bus just as rays of morning sunlight streamed through the trees on Elm Street. Working the graveyard shift was tough, but it was a job. As she neared her home, she saw a man backing a green Chevrolet out of the driveway at Erma Smith's house. She stopped in her tracks. "Erma is having an affair," Frances said half-aloud.

She was soon on the phone calling Gretchen Latimer. A sleepy woman's voice answered and Frances vomited out what she had seen. "Well, don't tell anybody," Gretchen said, "but I've suspected Erma of cheating on her husband for years!" Within an hour Frances had called all of her friends.

In a few minutes the phone rang. The voice on the other end was spewing bullets. "Frances, this is Erma Smith. What's the big idea of spreading a story of my having an affair? The man you saw was my husband's brother James, visiting us from Pittsburgh." Frances hastened to retreat. "Well, I didn't think there was anything wrong, but Gretchen Latimer told me that you had been cheating on George for years."

Relationships are destroyed because of a rush to judgment. Derek Kidner wisely points out that a woman like Frances: 1) didn't know all the facts, 2) didn't interpret the facts correctly, and 3) had impure motives (pp. 157-58). She also divulged secrets to clear herself of blame (Lawson, pp. 441-42).

I believe Jesus would have instructed Frances to solve the matter privately (Matt. 18:15). As it was, she probably lost two friends, Erma and Gretchen, and got a very bad reputation, one that she may never lose (v. 10, above).

Prayer of Application

Father, keep me from judging quickly, but to always give the other person the benefit of the doubt. Help me never to spread gossip about anyone or betray the confidence of a friend.

Be an Encourager

11)   A word aptly spoken is like apples of gold in settings of silver. 12) Like an earring of gold or an ornament of fine gold is a wise man's rebuke to a listening ear (Prov. 25:11-12).

We don't grow many golden apples locally, but we do have golden oranges. However, the allusion here seems to be to apples of the precious metal gold. Perhaps they are set in a silver ring. The idea is that a word aptly spoken is like a precious and choice jewel in a setting that complements its value and charm.

With your permission, I'd like to change the word "rebuke" in verse 12 to "encouragement" and look at the verses in that light. Actually, even rebuke should be encouragement. When we gently rebuke someone, such as our children, our motive should be to encourage them to be their very best.

If you are looking for a job to do in your local congregation, why not set yourself up as president of the "Encourager's Club"? There are no dues or by-laws, and it's OK if you are the only member. All you have to do to get started is to find someone who needs encouragement and encourage him! Someone whom you know is hurting may need a kind word and an assurance that you are standing with him. You could send notes of encouragement to the sick. Or you just might write about how you appreciate the other person. Use your imagination!

In the next proverb, 25:13, we'll look at those who should be number one on your list of people to encourage: your pastor and his wife.

Scriptural Examples

Boaz. Boaz noticed Ruth as she gleaned in his field and encouraged her to stay and gather much. He commended her for her love for Naomi and gave her his blessing (Ruth 2:8-12).

Barnabas. This companion of Paul was a great joy to him. Even his name means "son of encouragement" (Acts 4:36).

Prayer of Application

Heavenly Father, help me to encourage others. I know from my own experience how sweet a word of encouragement is from a brother or sister. It seems to breathe new life into me.

Encourage Your Pastor and His Wife

Like the coolness of snow at harvest time is a trustworthy mes- senger to those who send him; he refreshes the spirit of his masters (Prov. 25:13).

Harvest time is the hottest time of the year in many places. The faithful messenger is like a frosty snow cone on a day of harvesting. Doesn't that describe your faithful pastor?

The encouragement we receive from the faithful preaching of the Word of God is far better than a cold drink on parched lips. It reaches down deep into one's soul and refreshes like nothing else can. When we are going through times of trial, the Word is especially encouraging. Without it we might give up.

But you know your faithful pastor feels the "heat" for his entire congregation. When one of his flock is hurting, he hurts with them. When someone is in grief, the pastor grieves, too. He needs everyone's encouragement. And don't forget his wife. She needs a special portion of encouragement as she seeks to fulfill her difficult role in his life and in the life of the church.

Here's a short list of ways you can encourage your pastor and his wife, although I'm sure you can think of many more: (1) pray for them daily; (2) attend church regularly; (3) ask how you can shoulder some of the heavy load; (4) send them notes of encouragement; (5) remember their birthdays and their anniversary; (6) invite them out to dinner; (7) above all, imitate Christ in all that you do. They will then be encouraged as they see the fruit of their ministry being borne out in your life.

Scriptural Examples

Jahaziel. Facing a war with the Ammonites and Moabites, the Israelites and their king, Jehoshaphat, were encouraged by this little-known man (2 Chron. 20:14-17).

Priscilla and Aquila. This couple encouraged Apollos, a bold preacher of the gospel of Christ (Acts 18:24-28).

Prayer of Application

Father, thank You for the encouragement of my pastor and his wife. May I in turn encourage them and become for them what they are for me, the coolness of snow at harvest time.

Flee from the Barrenness of Idolatry

Like clouds and wind without rain is a man who boasts of gifts he
does not give (Prov. 25:14).

Proverbs 25:13 speaks of the refreshment given to people by the faithful messenger. Here is the unfaithful messenger, someone who promises gifts but never delivers. Rain that would refresh the earth and bring forth fruit never comes. Here is a covetous rich person who announces that he's going to give a big gift to the church, but somehow the money never arrives. He may be the one who promises to enter an agreement but never goes through with the deal. (Sound familiar, salespeople?)

But I believe that there is a wider application here—idolatry. We are Idolators because of the sin that is in our hearts. Given the chance, we often run to the first promise that looks good, forsaking the promises of God. And when we place our hope in anything over and above the promises and providence of God, we are into idolatry. And exactly what is the idol to whom we will run? It is someone or something which boasts of gifts that he or it does not give.

God is the One who brings all good gifts. There is no other ultimate Giver (James 1:17). He gives us new life and sends the rain to refresh us and cause our fruit to grow. Hope in God and God alone for every good and perfect gift.

Scriptural Examples

Satan. This deceiver boasted of gifts he did not give as he misled the first couple. Instead, he brought death (Gen. 3:3-5).

Idols. The Israelites often worshiped the gods of the other nations. But these "gods" were only wood and stone. People like idols because idols put no demands on them.

False teachers. Both Peter and Jude speak of these men as "clouds without rain" and "springs without water." How different they are from faithful pastors (Jude 11-13; 2 Peter 2:17).

Prayer of Application

Lord, keep me from idolatry. I become enamored easily with the ways of this world. Help me to put all my confidence in You, Lord, as the source of every good and perfect gift.

Fight with Patience and a Gentle Tongue

Through patience a ruler can be persuaded, and a gentle tongue can break a bone (Prov. 25:15).

Back in the days of Napoleon and the French Revolution, when heads were rolling in the streets of Paris, a man across the English Channel was waging a different kind of warfare. His name was William Wilberforce and his enemy was the English slave trade. For over 40 years, this devout Christian politician exercised patience and a gentle tongue and won the battle to emancipate all of the slaves in the British Empire. What a contrast to the blood that flowed in America in our own Civil War fought over the same issue. And what a contrast to the way we typically wage our little everyday wars.

My mind goes instinctively to 1 Peter 3:1-2 when I think of the proverb above. There, women who are married to unbelievers are given instructions about how they are to graciously live with their husbands. Peter might just as well have quoted this proverb, applying it to unbelieving husbands. Nagging and belittling and arguing over doctrine never won anybody to the Lord. But patience and a gentle tongue have persuaded many.

Let us follow Christ's example. Whether the battle that rages around you is in your home, at your job, in your school, or at your church, use the weapons of patience and a gentle tongue. God is in control.

Scriptural Examples

David and Saul. While Saul was waging war with the tools of the world, David used a gentle tongue. At one juncture, Saul killed 85 priests of God in his vehement wrath. But twice when he had Saul cornered, David refused to take his life. Instead, David spoke to him with patience and gentleness. Saul was forced to confess, "May you be blessed, my son David." And David was blessed (1 Sam. 24:8-20; 26:17-25).

Prayer of Application

Dear God, I am often tempted to raise my voice in anger when confronted with wickedness and violence in the world. Help me to use the weapons of patience and a gentle tongue.

Don't Overdo a Good Thing

If you find honey, eat just enough—too much of it, and you will vomit (Prov. 25:16).

As a child I loved pears. One day, a friend and I found a pear tree with some juicy ripe fruit on it. Before long, I was sick of pears and my stomach was reeling. I didn't eat another pear for years. Such is the penalty we pay when we overindulge in the otherwise good things that God has given us to enjoy.

Today, I am tempted by peanut butter, mayonnaise, sour-dough bread, cookies, and ice cream, just to mention a few delicacies. I'm not really afraid of vomiting after eating any of these foods: I guess I've outgrown that phase. But I am afraid of the pounds they add to my frame. It's food you can wear.

We are tempted to overindulge with our eyes, feasting on too much TV. We're tempted to listen to too much secular music or too many talk shows on the radio. These things aren't necessarily wrong in and of themselves, but too much of them will begin to show up in a flabby spirituality and walk with God.

Of God's honey, no amount is too much. We are called to feed on the Word of God, to desire its sweetness, and to be gorged on its power (1 Peter 2:2; James 1:25). We are to put the Word into practice as we grow from spiritual babies to mature Christians (Heb. 5:11-14). Feast on the honey of the Word of God and go easy on the honey of the natural world. God has prepared a place for us that is overflowing with the milk and honey of an eternity with Him.

Scriptural Examples

Samson. He killed a lion with his bare hands, leaving its carcass to rot on the ground. Sometime later he saw that it housed a hive of bees. He scooped out some of the honey and went on his way, dreaming up a riddle about it. Samson was a man who always seemed to overindulge in sensual pleasures. Ultimately, it got the best of him (Judg. 14:1–16:31).

Prayer of Application

Lord, thank You for the many pleasures You give me freely to enjoy. But help me to not let any have power over me. Although all things are legal for me, all things are not expedient.

Practice Moderation in Visiting Others

Seldom set foot in your neighbor's house—too much of you, and he will hate you (Prov. 25:17).

Back in the late 1940s, TV was just getting under way and my family didn't have one. Our neighbors bought a Hoffman that had a small green screen set high in the middle of a dark brown wooden cabinet. It looked like a brown Cyclops.

My brother Bill and I were always sneaking over there to watch the wrestling matches featuring Gorgeous George vs. Mr. Moto. Frankly, we would have watched the test pattern if they'd have let us. I have often wondered what our neighbors must have thought of those Beasley boys coming over night after night to eat their popcorn. They must have gotten pretty sick and tired of us.

I had a friend in high school who used to hang around our house all the time. It got so bad that we finally took to hiding from him when the doorbell rang. Like my brother and I, he had never read this proverb and didn't know better. We need to be careful that we don't overstay our visit and wind up hated by our host. My mom used to say, "After three days, fish and houseguests start to smell." Let's not wear out our welcome.

Of course, God's door is always open, and He never tires of us. Ironside says, "More time spent in secret with God, and less spent in gadding about among men, would result in far greater profit for our souls, and bring much more glory to our Lord Jesus Christ" (p. 354). Oh, that more of us would spend our time seeking the company of our Heavenly Father.

Scriptural Examples

The young widows. They were chided by Paul for their habit of going about from house to house, being busybodies and gossips. How much better it would have been for them, Paul said, to get married, have children, stay home, and manage their own households (1 Tim. 5:13-14).

Prayer of Application

Dear Lord, create in me a heart that wants to dwell in Your presence. But may I practice moderation in visits to others. Father, thank You for the sweet fellowship I share with You.

Speak the Truth in Love

Like a club or a sword or a sharp arrow is the man who gives false witness against his neighbor (Prov. 25:18).

In the motion picture *Braveheart*, the arrows flew and the swords sliced. The picture was bloody indeed as brave Scots fought for the freedom of their land. In the verses above, swords and sharp arrows are used as similes for lies.

Words hurt deep down, in the same way a sword or an arrow might hurt. And the hurt stays with you. My wife finished a course in calculus as part of a master's degree program. It's amazing that she even embarked upon the program. For years, the words of a third-grade teacher haunted her: "Amy, you'll never be good at math." For years she avoided math classes, only braving the master's program after much encouragement. She passed the course with flying colors.

But this proverb is about lies. What if someone says something negative but true? I believe that negative words are always false in this sense: the speaker never has all the facts to make a true summary judgment. Amy may have done poorly in the third grade, but what her teacher said has proven to be untrue. She was a false witness. How much better if the teacher had remained silent or encouraged Amy to keep on trying.

If you need to criticize someone, always do it in a loving, encouraging, and positive manner. Never give way to the sinful propensity to cough up a false summary judgment. Speak the truth in love (Eph. 4:15) that all may be built up.

Scriptural Examples

Jael and Sisera. Fleeing from Barak, Sisera thought he'd hide in the tent of Jael, wife of Heber the Kenite, a friend of his boss. Jael greeted him warmly, giving him a glass of milk and a place to sleep. Later, Sisera would find her false words as deadly as the tent peg she drove through his temple (Judg. 4:17-21).

Prayer of Application

Father, my tongue is capable of deadly poison. Keep me from uttering false and hurtful words. Rather, let me be a source of encouragement and edification to everyone.

Be Faithful in Your Service to Others

Like a bad tooth or a lame foot is reliance on the unfaithful in times of trouble (Prov. 25:19).

I have been a businessman most of my adult life and have had a few employees who were unfaithful. As long as things are going smoothly, everything's peachy. But bring on the tough times, and these folks become like the bad tooth or the lame foot described in the verse above. Of course, bosses can be faithless, too, and fail to serve those under us as we should.

You never know the true character of a person until the chips are down, until trouble ("the heat") comes. Then what's inside us becomes visible. God uses trouble in our lives to give us a glimpse of what is lurking down there in the recesses of our hearts. Often, it's not pretty.

But Christ calls us to obedience and to lives of service to one another. In a large sense, we carry out His orders in the context of the local church. Too often, however, we Christians want to be served, rather than to serve others. Then we are like the abscessed molar or the broken toe. Encourage your pastor by your faithful service to him and to others.

Scriptural Examples

David. In Psalm 55, David's lament focuses on a man he had at one time considered his close friend, with whom he had enjoyed sweet fellowship in the temple of God. He may well have had in mind his own sons, Adonijah or Absalom, who both turned against his leadership and tried to establish their own thrones. But God was also giving us a glimpse of a future act of faithlessness, when Judas would deliver his friend, our Lord, to those who would crucify Him.

John Mark. When Paul sailed from Paphos to Perga, John Mark left him and returned to Jerusalem. Later, Paul refused to take Mark because of his earlier desertion (Acts 13:13; 15:37-38).

Prayer of Application

Father, thank You for our faithful friend Jesus. And thank You for those brothers and sisters who imitate the Lord in faithfulness. Help each one of us to be reliable at all times.

Rejoice with the Joyful; Mourn with Mourners

Like one who takes away a garment on a cold day, or like vinegar poured on soda, is one who sings songs to a heavy heart (Prov. 25:20).

I had a little wooden boat as a child. It had a paddle wheel on its stern, which was made to propel the boat as vinegar was poured on a cache of soda in its tiny hold. I'm no chemist, but I believe a reaction between an acid (the vinegar) mixed with a base (the soda) gave off carbon dioxide gas. Likewise, a cheerful song sung to a heavy heart fizzles and makes gas.

To take a garment from someone on a cold day was greatly discouraged by the Law of Moses (Deut. 24:10-13). What purpose would it serve, but to cause discomfort and even illness in the one with the missing garment? In the same way, a song sung to a person in misery just adds to the mourner's sorrow.

It's not easy to know what to say to those who are going through times of grief and sadness. I've never been real comfortable at funerals, have you? But I've found it's not what you say, as long as you show up. Being there says you care. You don't even have to open your mouth. Just let those who mourn know you are standing with them in their grief.

Scriptural Examples

The captives. While their captors demanded songs of joy, those from Zion wept over Jerusalem. They said, "How can we sing songs of the Lord while in a foreign land?" (Ps. 137:1-6).

The Good Samaritan. He tended his neighbor's wounds not with vinegar and soda, but with wine and oil (Luke 10:34).

Christ Jesus. In greeting the church in Corinth, Paul and Timothy testified of God's comfort which overflowed to them. Such comfort came through the sufferings of Christ, which also overflowed to them, producing the patient endurance that enabled them to comfort others (2 Cor. 1:3-7).

Prayer of Application

Father, help me to be a comforter to those who mourn and are heavy in heart. And what greater comfort, Jesus, than to remind them of You who suffered and died for us.

Witness with the Kindness of Christ

21) If your enemy is hungry, give him food to eat; if he is thirsty, give him water to drink. 22) In doing this, you will heap burning coals on his head, and the Lord will reward you (Prov. 25:21-22).

Many years ago, in a far-off land, a man laid down his life for his enemies. Very few of us would dare to even lay down our lives for a friend, yet we're told that while we were His mortal enemies, Christ died for us (Rom. 5:6-8). Almost 2,000 years later this former enemy of Christ felt these "burning coals" and my heart melted in receipt of the gift which Christ's life, death, and resurrection brought.

Someone says, "I've lived a good life. I don't have any enemies." But if your life is "hidden with Christ" (Col. 3:3), you have a world full of enemies. Whoever is an enemy of Christ is also your enemy. Our enemies are right next door, and perhaps within our own homes (Matt. 10:36). It is these people whom Jesus would call us to love, pray for, and treat with the kindness most of us reserve for our closest friends.

Many of us do have enemies, however, and of the type created by our sin, not by our devotion to Christ. It is with these people that this command gets very difficult. We just want to erase their memories from our minds. But I believe that Christ calls us to treat them with an extra-special kindness and desire for reconciliation. It is a powerful witness of His saving grace, as the coals that would melt sinful hearts are heaped high. God will reward us greatly (Matt. 5:11-12).

Scriptural Examples

Stephen and Saul. In mortal persecution, something which few of us will be asked to endure, Stephen cried out, "Lord, do not hold this sin against them." Standing nearby was a young man named Saul, who though perhaps not perceiving it, then got a load of burning coals heaped upon his head (Acts 7:59-60).

Prayer of Application

Dear God, give me the courage to be a bold witness of the saving grace of Jesus Christ. Help me to pray for my enemies, and by my kindness to them may they come to know You.

Meet a Slanderous Tongue with Anger

As a north wind brings rain, so a sly tongue brings angry looks. [KJV: "The north wind driveth away rain, so doth an angry countenance a backbiting tongue."] (Prov. 25:23).

The NIV has the rains coming with the north wind. The KJV has the north winds driving the rain away. (In Israel, the west wind brings the rain.) Regardless of the divergent translations, the point is the same. If you are approached by someone with slander on his tongue, fend it off with godly anger.

The slanderer is a character assassin, a murderer of good names and reputations. In his ugly backbiting, the slanderer harms more than just the object of his libel. He hurts himself, and he hurts his hearers. If the slanderer happens to be part of a church, add the holy name of God to that list (Bridges, p. 478). This proverb shows us that the best way to stop slander is with an angry countenance, added to a few words of rebuke.

The worst thing to do is to stand with a smile on your face and drink the poison in. That does nothing but encourage it. How much better to suggest going directly to the victim and force the slanderer to face his target. That will shut him up quickly. Whatever approach you use, always seek reconciliation and truth, never allowing separation and lies to win the day.

Scriptural Examples

Moses. Moses showed righteous anger as he brought the Law down from the mountain, only to find his people partaking in wicked idolatry, enabled by his own brother Aaron. Moses smashed the tablets on the ground (Ex. 32:19).

Jesus. Jesus displayed His anger in dealing with the money changers in the temple courtyard (Matt. 11:15-17). He was also angry at the stubborn hearts of the Pharisees and teachers of the law (Mark 3:5). Finally, in Mark 8:33, Jesus rebuked Peter in no uncertain terms when the disciple suggested an easy path.

Prayer of Application

Father, help me never to slander anyone. If I do hear gossip or lies about a fellow human being, give me the courage to confront the slanderer with an angry look and the truth.

Wives, Submit to Your Husbands

Better to live on a corner of the roof than share a house with a quarrelsome wife (Prov. 25:24).

The principle here is in Ephesians 5:22. Actually, the word for "submit" does not occur in the Greek text. It's in verse 21: "Submit to one another out of reverence for Christ." The word *hupotassomenoi* is a plural passive participle meaning "subject or subordinate yourselves" one to another.

The husband's responsibility is spelled out in Ephesians 5:25-26. "Husbands, love your wives just as Christ loved the church and gave himself for her." Think for a second, guys, about how Christ loved the church. He humbled Himself so His church might be exalted. He went to His death for His bride. Does that sound like He would bully His bride, boss her around, restrict her freedom, and withhold His love? No. Just as Christ submitted to the Father, so we are to submit to Him.

Notice, this proverb is repeated verbatim from 21:9. When Scripture repeats, it's important. The quarrelsome wife is one who defies God's law and refuses to submit to His foundational principles for the home. She wants her own way and will stop at nothing to get it. But it could be she's responding that way because her husband is not submissive to Christ.

For some wives, no amount of self-sacrificing love would ever be enough to soften her quarrelsome manner. Her husband will have to satisfy himself with the corner of a rooftop.

Scriptural Examples

Jezebel and Ahab. This couple exhibited the antithesis of God's rule for the home. Ahab was a sniveling rodent who submitted only to evil and the rule of his wife over him. Jezebel's name is synonymous with the rebellious and arrogant wife. She nagged her husband to greater acts of evil for which they would both pay with their lives (1 Kings 21:25).

Prayer of Application

Lord God, thank You the design of the marriage relationship, which allows for mutual respect. And thank You for Christ, who leads both of us. May we both grow in the likeness of Your Son.

Drink the Living Water of the Word

*Like cold water to a weary soul is good news from
distant land* (Prov. 25:25).

When I was in college, I spent summers working on construction projects in San Diego. On one job I was to dig wooden sleepers out of concrete with a pick. It was hot, dusty work, and to make matters worse there was a desert wind that took temperatures into the high 90s. I have never been thirstier. That drink of cold water at break time was the best I ever had!

Good news from a distant land is like that drink of cold water. Because it comes from afar, its refreshment seems to be magnified. It's news from home! But this proverb's not just a statement comparing a cold drink to good news from home.

The Christian's true home is in a better land, the eternal city of God (Heb. 11:9-10). And we are not without news from that wonderful place! It is the fountain of living water, whereby we are cleansed and prepared for our journey (Eph. 5:26). It is the living and eternal Word of God. Sit at the feet of your pastor and drink deeply from the cool, clear gospel reservoir. Take joy in the one who brings you the Good News, and in the knowledge of the One who has sent it to you.

Scriptural Examples

The angels. What Good News was announced that first Christmas in the hills of Bethlehem! Excited and refreshed by it, the shepherds ran off to find the Babe (Luke 2:8-16).

The prodigal's dad. What good news for a father to see his son coming home! He didn't wait. Refreshed in his soul, he ran toward his son and embraced him (Luke 15:20).

The Thessalonians. The good news brought by Timothy was that the Thessalonians, who had been visited by Timothy, were standing firm in the Lord. Paul rejoiced and was refreshed by the news from his missionary field (1 Thess. 3:5-8).

Prayer of Application

Dear Lord, thank You for the Word of God that refreshes my weary soul and causes me to look up in expectation of Your deliverance. Thank You for my pastor, who teaches me its truth.

Let Clear, Living Water Flow from You

Like a muddied spring or a polluted well is a righteous man who gives way to the wicked (Prov. 25:26).

In the arid, sandy deserts where the Bedouins drive their flocks and herds in search of forage, water is a most welcome sight. Imagine a shepherd driving a flock of sheep all day under a hot sun. At nightfall, he reaches an oasis, but does not find the clear spring of water bubbling up. The spring is polluted and undrinkable. You can understand his frustration.

Jesus said in John 7:38, "Whoever believes in me, as the Scripture has said, streams of living water will flow from within him." The righteous man of this verse is one who has trusted Christ for his salvation, but his stream of living water has become polluted with sin. He's lost the refreshing quality of his counsel and fellowship, useless for satisfying the thirst of others. How did he get that way? He began to give in to the way of wicked people. Can he be restored to fellowship and become a clean, fresh spring once again? A most emphatic, "Yes!"

Scriptural Examples

The waters of Marah. After leaving Egypt, the people began their trek across the wilderness sands. They became thirsty at Marah, but the water there was polluted. The Lord showed Moses a piece of wood. When Moses threw it into the water, the water became sweet and drinkable. The wood speaks of the Body of Christ, who offered Himself on a wooden cross. He is able to restore all who come to Him in repentance (Ex. 15:22-25; 1 John 1:9).

Peter. Peter denied that he knew Jesus three times before the sun rose. Peter gave way before wicked people by not acknowledging his Savior. Did Jesus restore Peter? Yes, and made him a great apostle (Matt. 26:69-72).

Demas. Paul was deserted by him because Demas loved the world and gave way to the wicked (2 Tim. 4:10).

Prayer of Application

Lord, I praise You that You are the God of the second chance, the God of many chances. If You did not forgive sin, who could stand? Help my spring to be clear and refreshing.

Seek Only the Honor and Glory of God

It is not good to eat too much honey, nor is it honorable to seek one's own honor (Prov. 25:27).

Just as the sweet taste of honey is naturally desirable to most of us, so we all want others to like us and include us in their lives. The urge to be admired and respected is good in moderation, but like honey, desiring too much of it is not good.

First of all, we need to realize we have no control over the minds of others. If we seek honor among others, we may wind up making them sick to their stomachs. We will suffer the same fate as the presumptuous dinner guest of Proverbs 25:6-7. Second, we need to understand we have absolutely no claim upon honor. All the honor and glory of this universe belongs to God, and it is His glory we are to seek (1 Cor. 10:31). Indeed, it is to be our life's purpose. Finally, we need to understand "God opposes the proud but gives grace to the humble" (1 Peter 5:5). The proud person will be destroyed (Prov. 16:18) but the humble will be lifted up (1 Peter 5:6).

Lay lecturer Os Guinness uses the phrase "The Audience Of One" to illustrate the correct focus of our lives. We should play out each moment of each day for the Audience of One, the Lord God, and not be overly concerned with what others think about us.

Scriptural Examples

Solomon. The Lord asked the new king what he wanted as a gift. Solomon asked for wisdom and the ability to rule his people wisely. Because Solomon did not ask for wealth or honor, God gave him the wisdom he desired along with a substantial amount of honor and wealth (1 Kings 3:5-13).

The hypocrites. Jesus spoke of these people who indulged in the normally pietistic activities of prayer, fasting, and tithing, but did so in order that people could see them. He said because they sought and received their reward from others, none would be forthcoming from God (Matt. 6:1-8, 16-18).

Prayer of Application

Lord and God, only You are worthy of honor and glory and praise. Sometimes I sinfully want to share in Your glory. Lord, take this desire from me and let me give all the honor to You.

Practice Self-Control

Like a city whose walls are broken down is a man who lacks self-control (Prov. 25:28).

In the ancient world and through the middle ages, cities were fortified with walls against the potential attack of invading armies. Sometimes, other barriers such as moats and pits were also constructed, but the walls of a city were its ultimate protection. A breach in the city's walls during a siege meant disaster, as the invaders poured into the city.

We, too, have walls like those ancient cities and enemies who seek to break through the weak spots to destroy us. How do we keep our walls from being breached? First, let's admit our weaknesses. Do a complete self-inventory just as Nehemiah inventoried the walls of Jerusalem that had been broken down (Neh. 2:3-5). Second, humbly submit to God's Spirit in prayer, asking for strength to reinforce those weaknesses (Matt. 26:41). Third, share your weaknesses with close friends, asking them for prayer and support. There is strength and encouragement in numbers, particularly in times of temptation.

What are the results of the breach of a personal wall? A witness for Christ is limited or destroyed. A life of service is hobbled or even shut down. The joy of purity is extinguished in guilt and sadness. Families are broken apart. There is loss of heavenly reward (1 Cor. 9:27). Watch your walls with care and prayer. A breach in your walls can be devastating.

Scriptural Examples

Paul. Paul boasted in his weaknesses. Why? Because he realized that it was through his weakness that the Lord's strength could be manifested. When he complained to God about a certain thorn in his flesh, the Lord said, "My grace is sufficient for you, for my power is made perfect in weakness." This same power is available to each of us (2 Cor. 12:7-10).

Prayer of Application

Father, thank You for the power to live my life in a way that is pleasing to You. But I have weaknesses in my walls that need constant attention. Help me to be strong by relying on You.

Chapter Twenty-six

Proverbs and the Fool

The so-called "fool" is mentioned in all of the first eleven verses of this chapter. He is a common subject of the book of Proverbs. Throughout the book he's also referred to as the "simple" or as the "scoffer" (also "mocker" or "scorner"). Who is this fellow?

Derek Kidner gives us some insight into the character of the three on pages 39-42 of his book, *Proverbs*. Kidner says the "simpleton" is gullible and irresponsible. He's lazy and thoughtless and empty-headed. He's fodder for temptation. He's unstable but prefers that to the life of discipline. The "fool" is the simple one's big brother. He has a deep-rooted spiritual problem. "He has no preference for the truth, preferring comfortable illusions" (p. 40). The fool is a menace in society and will stop at nothing to get his own way (see Prov. 17:12). One of the Hebrew words for "fool" is *nabal*. You might recognize that name as that of Abigail's husband who played the role perfectly (1 Sam. 25). Finally, Kidner says the scoffer "makes it… clear that mental attitude, not mental capacity, classifies the man." He doesn't do "the random mischief of the ordinary fool, but the deeper damage of the 'debunker' and deliberate troublemaker (21:24; 22:10; 29:28)." He'll ultimately get his own medicine as "[the Lord] mocks proud mockers" (Prov. 3:34).

Do Not Give Honor to a Fool

Like snow in summer or rain in harvest, honor is not fitting for
a fool (Prov. 26:1).

The next twelve verses speak of the fool. The fool does not lack mental prowess, but moral character. As Ironside writes, "Fools are those who make a mock of sin, rejoice in iniquity, and refuse to heed the voice of wisdom" (p.361). The fool says in his heart, "there is no God," or says "No" to God (Ps. 14:1). Either way, he exhibits his lack of wisdom.

Snow is great in winter. It brings moisture to the fields and keeps the seed sown in the fall from freezing. But snow in the summer would be out of place. It would break the leaves off the maturing plants and wreak havoc. So also, rain in harvest not only restricts the activity of the harvesters, it can ruin the crop which is so close to going into the barn. So it is with fools. They are completely out of step with reality, out of season with the wisdom of God. For this reason, they should not be honored.

One doesn't have to look far to see fools being honored in America. Movie stars and musicians are but examples. This is the true measurement of any society: the people it holds in respect. America has sunk to real depths of depravity. Don't be a part of giving honor to fools. Rather, honor the godly men and women who seek to bring glory to God, who hate sin, and who rejoice in righteousness.

Scriptural Examples

Nebuchadnezzar and Daniel. The former was a foolish king who had a dream. He sent for a wise Jew in exile named Daniel to interpret the dream for him. Daniel saw in the dream that God would humble Nebuchadnezzar and send him out into the fields like a wild beast. Daniel's interpretation came to pass about a year later as the foolish Nebuchadnezzar reveled in his own exalted state. After a season as an animal, the king was restored to his throne, but this time he was worshiping God (Dan. 4).

Prayer of Application

Father God, how low we have sunk in our worship of fools, rather than exalting You, the Living and True God. Heal our land and restore in us the desire to honor those who honor You.

Do Not Fear the Superstition of Fools

Like a fluttering sparrow or a darting swallow, an undeserved curse does not come to rest (Prov. 26:2).

New Orleans historians tell of a voodoo practitioner named Marie Laveau who once held the town captive, arousing great fear among the local politicians lest they cross her and come under her curse. Laveau died many years ago, yet those modern people she fooled with her legacy of black magic still pay homage at her tomb.

Every spring the swallows return to San Juan Capistrano in California. These little birds tear around in the sky like they're going to rip your head off, but in fact, they wouldn't harm a hair on it. So it is with the curse of a fool: it does not come to rest. It has no real power.

What the cursed fool doesn't realize is that a real and powerful curse is upon him. It is the curse of God and it is not undeserved. The fool makes light of the Creator, instead giving himself over to the worship of animals and money and voodoo dolls (Rom. 1:18-23). He is therefore under an eternal curse.

But thanks be to the God of mercy and love, who has extended His grace to all those who would simply believe on the name of His Son. The fool can come and receive mercy from the God who took the curse upon Himself (Gal. 3:10, 13). The Cross is where the curse came to rest. Come, as this fool did, to the Cross and avoid the only curse with any real power.

Scriptural Examples

Balaam. Although paid by Balak to put a curse on Israel, even this false prophet knew that he could not say anything effectual without the approval of God (Num. 22:38; 23:8).

Goliath. This behemoth cursed the boy David by his gods, and made threat after threat against the youthful shepherd. But his curses were meaningless. David, guided by God, put his stone where Goliath's "mouth was" (1 Sam. 17:43-44, 49).

Prayer of Application

Dear Lord, thank You for Your absolute control over events and that nothing happens without Your prior consent. The powers of Satan are limited by Your divine providence.

Spare the Rod and Encourage the Fool

A whip for the horse, a halter for the donkey, and a rod for the back of fools (Prov. 26:3)!

The halter and the whip seem to be placed on the wrong animals here. But ancient Assyrian asses were apparently less stubborn than their more fleet-footed counterparts, Assyrian horses. The point here is that both the horse and the ass need a measure of physical stimulation to cause them to go in the direction the rider desires. In the same way, it takes a rod to drive the fool away from his foolishness.

Remember the young American who was arrested in Singapore and sentenced to receive a certain number of strokes from a bamboo rod? We are beginning to hear much more about corporal punishment for law breakers in America. Legislatures are working on bills that would bring public floggings back to the courthouse steps. When parents will not supply the rod, the state will ultimately need to wield it. Currently there is very little rod-wielding going on in our communities as people walk away from felonies with little more than a slap on the wrist. Is this verse suggesting that we encourage our legislators to bring about public whippings of the lawbreakers in our midst? What do you think?

Scriptural Examples

Pharaoh. He is arguably the biggest fool in the Bible. Like all fools Pharaoh sorely needed a dose of humility, and God gave it to him. After repeated warnings and consequent plagues upon His people—God's rod for Pharaoh's back—the Egyptian king met a liquid grave (Ex. 10).

The citizens of Succoth and Peniel. All Gideon wanted from these folks was some bread for his fighting men. These fools wouldn't part with even a meager crust, so Gideon laid a heavy rod on their backsides (Judg. 8:5-16).

Prayer of Application

Father, America is weighed down with criminals who plea bargain their way to freedom and laugh at the judicial system. Show our courts and lawmakers a better way, Lord.

Use Discretion When Answering a Fool

4) Do not answer a fool according to his folly, or you will be like him yourself. 5) Answer a fool according to his folly, or he will be wise in his own eyes (Prov. 26:4-5).

Many ancient rabbis saw contradiction in these verses that made some question the canonicity of the book of Proverbs. But what we have here is the inspired wisdom of God's Word, showing us that there is a "time to be silent and a time to speak" (Eccl. 3:7).

One way a fool displays folly is in a display of anger. Let's suppose you are in a discussion with a fool. Suddenly, he begins to get angry and starts to shout. Verse 4 here should be applied immediately. Maybe the best thing to do is to walk away in silence. If you shout back, you will "be like him yourself."

But folly is also manifested in irrationality. Some deny the very basic laws of logic. For instance, the fool may say that the Islamic faith and the Christian faith are both true, when in actuality they are poles apart. Logically they could both be false, but not both true. In this situation, the fool needs to be challenged in his folly, lest "he...be wise in his own eyes."

Scriptural Examples

Hezekiah's men. Before attacking Jerusalem, the king of Assyria sent his field commander forward to talk the leadership of the city into surrendering. This fool railed against God and against Hezekiah, king of Israel, saying that the people had no hope short of capitulation. Hezekiah ordered his men not to answer the fool and they obeyed (2 Kings 18:16-36).

Nehemiah. When the fool Sanballat accused the Jews of plotting a revolt, Nehemiah spoke up. He responded in writing with a firm denial of the charges (Neh. 6:5-8).

Jeremiah. After the foolish Hananiah broke the wooden yoke off of Jeremiah's neck, he uttered a false prophecy. Instead of contradicting him, Jeremiah walked away (Jer. 28:10-11).

Prayer of Application

Heavenly Father, give me wisdom and discretion as I speak to people who do not know You. Help me to respond in ways that are pleasing to You, and in conformity with Your wisdom.

Beware of Putting a Fool into Godly Service

6) Like cutting off one's feet or drinking violence is the sending of a message by the hand of a fool. 7) Like a lame man's legs that hang limp is a proverb in the mouth of a fool. 8) Like tying a stone in a sling is the giving of honor to a fool. 9) Like a thorn bush in a drunkard's hand is a proverb in the mouth of a fool (Prov. 26:6-9).

These four verses speak of elevating a fool to the role of pastor or Bible teacher. Fools in pulpits and on TV screens are "cutting off the feet and doing violence" (v. 6) to those deluded by their message. The "limp legs of a lame man" (v. 7) exhibit the worthless fools who attempt to explain God's wisdom.

To let a fool teach is like "tying a stone in a sling" (v. 8), because the sling's purpose is to release the stone. Finally, we have the picture of a drunk in a thorn bush. He's too smashed to get up and too full of pain to lie there. He's between a rock and a hard place, as are you if you give credence to a fool.

The following examples were provided by Ironside (pp. 364-366) as representative of the four verses here.

Scriptural Examples

Jonah (v. 6). He was sent by God to Nineveh to deliver the Word of God to those people. But Jonah had other ideas, and his shipmates nearly had "their feet cut off" (Jonah 1).

Saul (v. 7). The king of Israel took off his clothes before Samuel and others and lay down for a day and a night. He prophesied to the prophets like a lame man (1 Sam. 19:24).

Herod (v. 8). The people gave honor to Herod, calling him a "god." The fool believed them and refused to pass on the glory to God. He died and was eaten by worms (Acts 12:20-23).

Shemaiah the Nehelamite (v. 9). He incurred the wrath of God because he prophesied a lie to Jeremiah. His punishment was to be far worse than a few thorns (Jer. 29:30-32).

Prayer of Application

Lord God, send revival to our land today and a return to the full counsel of the Word. Build Your church by establishing the pulpits of righteous people, and tearing down those of fools.

Interview Prospective Employees Carefully

Like an archer who wounds at random is he who hires a fool or any passer-by (Prov. 26:10).

If you are ever placed in a position where it is your responsibility to hire new employees, approach that task with all the diligence you can muster. It is most critical in any business and can literally mean the difference between success or failure. To just pick the first person who walks in the door, whether the job is for janitor or chief executive officer, is like walking in front of a machine gun nest. It is fraught with peril. And in today's society of frivolous lawsuits, it's even much more critical than when this proverb was written.

I once had a very good employee quit. She had been the receptionist, secretary, accounts receivable clerk, bookkeeper, and girl Friday all rolled into one. I (stupidly) was in a panic to hire someone to fill her shoes. I interviewed a few people and then chose a woman I hoped would fit. It didn't take long to find out she was a disaster. Her foul language and rough manner alienated both customers and other employees alike. I am thankful she did not sue us following her termination.

Almost every month or so we hear of a gunman who opens fire in a crowded subway, on a college campus, or in a restaurant. This proverb compares that gunman with the hiring of a "fool or any passer-by." Be selective in your hiring. Remember, the prospective employee will never look better than during the interview.

Scriptural Examples

The vineyard laborers. Jesus likened the kingdom of heaven to a landowner who hired laborers. He didn't interview them, he just called them in. Careful study reveals the landowner was God, and He doesn't need to interview. He's omniscient. We are not omniscient! Interview carefully! (Matt. 20).

Prayer of Application

Father, thank You for the responsibility of choosing others as employees. But I cannot always see through the smile and the résumé. Help me to choose those who will succeed.

Recognize a Fool by His Actions

As a dog returns to his vomit, so a fool repeats
KJV: "returneth to"] his folly (Prov. 26:11).

The dog returns to its vomit because that comes naturally. The fool also returns to what he does naturally. Peter quotes this proverb in 2 Peter 2:20-22, where he refers to those who have claimed to be believers but who have returned to a life of sin. Better that they had never heard of the gospel of Jesus Christ than to turn their backs on it (2 Peter 2:21; Acts 17:30).

Can a person lose his salvation? If a person were saved by good works, then later evil works would very well cause him to lose his standing before God. But we are saved by grace, not works (Eph. 2:8-9), so works can't get us "unsaved." That would make God a liar and take away the efficacy of His free grace. Since we know that God only speaks the truth, it is impossible to lose one's salvation!

Dr. J. Vernon McGee believed in the security of the believer, but he also believed in the insecurity of the make-believer. There are many who merely claim to be Christians. They may have even taught a Bible study or filled a pulpit. But if they are fools, sooner or later they'll return to their folly.

Who's saved and who's not isn't our business. That's God's business. Our business is to sow seed and to feed the sheep. But occasionally, when we see someone fall back into a life of sin, we wonder. It could be just a dog returning to its vomit.

Scriptural Examples

Peter and Judas. Each denied the Lord Jesus. But Peter found restoration and healing at the hand of his Lord. Judas, on the other hand, went to his death unrepentant. Was his the example of a man who was saved earlier, then lost his salvation somehow? No. Jesus knew all along of the one who would betray Him. Judas was always a wolf (dog?) among the sheep (Matt 26:21-25, 33-35, 46-50, 69-75; 27:3-5; John 21:2-19).

Prayer of Application

Father, thank You for the assurance of Your salvation which comes to those who do Your will. Keep me from sin, Lord. Only Your mighty hand will cause me to persevere until the end.

Beware of "The Wisdom of the Wise"

Do you see a man wise in his own eyes? There is more hope for a fool than for him (Prov. 26:12).

The fool who is ignorant is far better off than one who prides himself on his wisdom. The former has the hope of gaining real wisdom, while the latter shuts his mind to it altogether. I marvel at fools who revel in their wisdom. In the "Jesus Seminar," people have taken scissors to the Scriptures, clipping out those words of Christ that don't fit their agenda. What foolishness!

But God sits in His heaven and laughs (Ps. 2:1-6), saying, "I will destroy the wisdom of the wise; the intelligence of the intelligent I will frustrate. Where is the wise man? Where is the scholar? Where is the philosopher of this age? Has not God made foolish the wisdom of the world?" (1 Cor. 1:19-20)

The wisdom of God and the world's wisdom are direct opposites. People say, "I am the captain of my ship, the master of my fate." God said, "Every knee will bow before me; every tongue will confess to God" (Rom. 14:11). People say, "There are many paths to God." Jesus said, "I am the way and the truth and the life. No one comes to the Father except through me" (John 14:6).

Submit to the Word of God as your only sourcebook of truth, evaluating all "facts" through its grid. We are so profoundly affected by sin that God's truth is easily obscured. Let your wisdom be God's wisdom, and walk humbly with Him.

Scriptural Examples

The Pharisee and the Publican. They went up to the temple to pray. The self-righteous Pharisee commended himself to God. But the Publican beat his breast and begged for mercy. Jesus said the latter went home justified (Luke 18:10-14).

The Laodiceans. They were rebuked for lukewarmness and for their pride in earthly wealth and wisdom. They were really wretched, pitiful, poor, blind, and naked (Rev. 3:16-18).

Prayer of Application

Dear God, thank You for the wisdom that comes from above. Your wisdom has been hidden from the wise and learned of this earth, but revealed to those who are simple and needy.

Flee from Spiritual Sloth

13) The sluggard says, "There is a lion in the road, a fierce lion roaming the streets!" 14) As a door turns on its hinges, so a sluggard turns on his bed. 15) The sluggard buries his hand in the dish; he is too lazy to bring it back to his mouth. 16) The sluggard is wiser in his own eyes than seven men who answer discreetly (Prov. 26:13-16).

Derek Kidner says the sluggard of Proverbs is faithless (13), feckless (14), foodless (15), and foolish (16). He neglects his responsibilities to his family, work, and friends, and you can be certain he will neglect his larger spiritual duty to God. Let's see how these verses describe the spiritual sluggard.

First, in verse 13, he is spiritually faithless. He won't step out in faith to do anything. He always has an excuse. There may not really be "a lion in the road," but something is always standing between the sluggard and his duty.

Second, in verse 14, he is spiritually feckless, or irresponsible. A door never leaves its door jamb. In the same way, the sluggard's life is going nowhere. He is without goals or the strategies for attaining those goals. He likes his soft bed, but can doze just as easily in a pew on Sunday morning.

Third, in verse 15, the sluggard is spiritually foodless. While he may know some Christian jargon, the deep things of Christ are avoided. He's a spiritual baby, feeding on baby food and milk, not able to chew on the real meat of the Word (Heb. 5:13-14). Why? Because a deeper knowledge of God may convict him of his sloth and awaken him from his slumber.

Finally, in verse 16, the spiritual sluggard is foolish. He is puffed up in pride. He bluffs his way through life, not understanding that his superficiality is as plain to others as the nose on his face. Don't join the spiritual sloth. Rather, flee from sloth and join with those who, in humility and diligence, work out their salvation with fear and trembling (Phil. 2:12).

Prayer of Application

Father, keep me from spiritual sloth. I know how easy it is to forsake Bible study, prayer, and reflection, and instead seek my own pleasure. Help me to live faithfully before You.

Mind Your Own Business

Like one who seizes a dog by the ears is a passer-by who meddles in a quarrel not his own (Prov. 26:17).

I remember a photograph of President Lyndon Johnson holding up one of his hound dogs by its ears. There were screams of protest from the SPCA. But in ancient Syria, only President Johnson's welfare would have been at stake. Their dogs were not hound dogs, but wild beasts that often roamed in packs. You wouldn't have wanted to seize one by the ears.

Policemen say the most dangerous part of their job is marital disputes. They arrive at the scene to find the troubled couple screaming at each other. Stepping between the feuding pair, they find themselves the focus of a new quarrel, as the warring husband and wife join forces. It is a very tough job. Lawmen are paid not to mind their own business.

Proverbs often reminds us of the sinfulness of quarrelling. (Prov. 17:14 and 19, for instance.) And those are our own quarrels! How much more should we avoid a quarrel that doesn't concern us. The best idea is to mind your own business and not be sucked into a disagreement in which you don't have a stake. The trick is to know the difference.

Scriptural Examples

Moses. Moses went out to see the Hebrew people at hard labor and saw an Egyptian beating one of them. He killed the Egyptian. That was his first mistake. Then he went back to the scene and found two Hebrews fighting each other. Stepping into the quarrel, he was rebuked for it. At least he found out word that he had murdered the Egyptian was out, so he fled the country (Ex. 2:11-14).

The busybodies. Paul warned of these folks who made it their business to be in everybody else's business. They were gossips who went from house to house doing things they had no business doing (2 Thess. 3:11; 1 Tim. 5:13).

Prayer of Application

Lord, keep my nose out of areas that don't concern me. But some of the things that concern my fellow Christians are my concern. Help me to discern what is my business and what is not.

Beware of Excusing Evil as a Joke

18) Like a madman shooting firebrands or deadly arrows 19) is a
man who deceives his neighbor and says, "I was only joking!"
(Prov. 26:18-19)

These verses really convict me of some of the stunts I was a
party to in college. Some were not only done in jest, but were
downright dangerous. I remember someone bringing a crossbow
on campus. We tried to penetrate closed doors with its arrows.
Suppose another student had walked out of one of those doors
and had taken an arrow in the chest. The "deadly arrows" of verse
18 would have ceased to be metaphorical. Can you imagine our
trying to explain we were "only joking"?

The words "shooting firebrands" remind me of a "joke" that
was played on me. I was taking a shower one morning when a
guy took a drawer full of my clean shirts and wedged it between
my shower door and the bathroom wall so that I could neither
escape nor throw water on him. Then he proceeded to shoot a
stream of flaming lighter fluid onto the rear wall of the shower
stall. He laughed the whole time. Though I was not hurt, I failed
to see any humor in it.

Perhaps the worst offender is he who deliberately deceives his
neighbor, then excuses himself by saying it was a joke. Beware of
the "practical lie" and the practical joke which can harm your
neighbor. God doesn't think them funny in the least.

Scriptural Examples

Pharaoh. Although the Bible doesn't say so, he must have
chuckled at his own deceit. He viewed the plagues as magic, so
he kept on lying, thinking it was all a joke (Ex. 7-12).

Aaron. When Moses came down from the mountain to find
the people worshipping a golden calf, Aaron lied, saying that the
calf had just "jumped out of the fire." Later Aaron might have
told his brother, "You know, I was only joking" (Ex. 32:1-24).

Prayer of Application

Dear God, Your Word tells us it is our responsibility to love
You and to love our neighbors as ourselves. Help me never to treat
my neighbor in an irresponsible way.

Beware the Words of the Gossip and Flatterer

20) Without wood a fire goes out; without gossip a quarrel dies down. 21) As charcoal to embers and as wood to fire, so is a quarrelsome man for kindling strife. 22) The words of a gossip are like choice morsels; they go down to a man's inmost parts. 23) Like a coating of glaze over earthenware are fervent lips with an evil heart. 24) A malicious man disguises himself with his lips, but in his heart he harbors deceit. 25) Though his speech is charming, do not believe him, for seven abominations fill his heart. 26) His malice may be concealed by deception, but his wickedness will be exposed in the assembly. 27) If a man digs a pit, he will fall into it; if a man rolls a stone, it will roll back on him. 28) A lying tongue hates those it hurts, and a flattering mouth works ruin (Prov. 26:20-28).

The gossip and flatterer are one and the same. He stirs up the pot with his gossip (v. 20), and tries to bring strife between brothers (v. 21). To the naive and unsuspecting, his words are swallowed hook, line, and sinker (v. 22). The gossip's words are as smooth as glass (v. 23) and always seek to build up his listener, while tearing down his victim (v. 24). Deep in his heart, there is malice toward all except himself (v. 25). Rest assured that he will be discovered eventually for what he really is (v. 26), because he is just setting a trap for himself (v. 27). Finally, the gossip hates all who listen to his words, as well as those who are his victims (v. 28). He is operating in exact antithesis to the law of love, which seeks no harm for its neighbor (Rom. 13:10).

Why does the gossip and flatterer do what he does? Why do these "abominations fill his heart" (v. 25)? He is simply attempting to elevate himself in the eyes of others. He is a victim of his own pride and is self-deceived. The wise person will see right through his smooth words to the malicious schemes and treachery in his heart.

Prayer of Application

Dear Lord, help me never to utter words detrimental to another person. And keep me from flattery to gain some kind of advantage. Rather, Lord, help me to expose this kind of evil.

Chapter Twenty-seven

Proverbs and the Family

Proverbs has much to say about life in the family. Our relationships with others begin there as children and continue throughout our lives. Family ties can be extremely close and life in the family a joy. But sin can intrude and make life miserable. Two particular proverbs regarding family life stand out in Chapter 27.

Verse 8 says, "Like a bird that strays from its nest is a man who strays from his home." (This proverb is an example of emblematic parallelism.) America is deeply troubled by this situation today: husbands and/or wives straying from their rightful place in the home, leaving behind those who need their nurture and physical support. Enticements of sin and excitement are often the culprit as spouses leave their homes in search of something "better."

One reason for the straying spouse might be found in verses 15 and 16. "A quarrelsome [spouse] is like a constant dripping on a rainy day; restraining her is like restraining the wind or grasping oil with the hand." (Notice another example of emblematic parallelism, this time a double one.) A quarrelsome spouse usually indicates one who wants his own way and will make life miserable for everyone else until he gets it. Quarreling is not patient leadership that builds relationships. Quarreling is the dynamite that destroys relationships.

Do Not Boast of Something You Don't Have

Do not boast about tomorrow, for you do not know what a day may bring forth (Prov. 27:1).

Three different roads are here. First, we see the "trail of the talker"—the ambitious person who thinks he can control the future. Second, we find the "walkway of worry" and look at those who worry about problems that never arrive. Finally, we may choose the "pathway of procrastination," where those who can never seem to get a "round tuit" walk. In a sense, these folks are all boasting of something they don't have.

James rebukes businessmen who boast about the money they will make in a new city (James 4:13-16). He's not talking about planning, but their unwillingness to understand tomorrow is under God's control, and to bow to His will and trust in His providence for what will happen in the future.

Jesus denounces worry (Matt. 6:25-34), which shows our lack of trust in God's provision. Rather, we are boasting in our own ability to control outcomes. God may supply our needs but He may not supply our wants, so we place our will above His.

Finally, we boast when we put today's work off until tomorrow. Jesus tells of ten virgins. Five are wise and have their lamps filled with oil when the bridegroom shows up. But five have procrastinated, boasting they had plenty of time tomorrow (Matt. 25:1-13). The latter five are left out in the cold.

Scriptural Examples

The rich fool. Jesus spoke of this man who built larger barns to hold the grain for a comfortable retirement, but his treasures were useless when his soul was required of him. His big "tomorrow" never came (Luke 12:16-21).

Felix. Paul witnessed to this ruler about the kingdom of God, but Felix decided to put off his decision. One wonders if another day ever arrived for this procrastinator (Acts 24:24-25).

Prayer of Application

Lord, You control tomorrow. How foolish we are when we don't confess it is so, then trust You in all things. The future is in Your hands and, praise Your name, so am I!

Seek Only the Praise of God

Let another praise you, and not your own mouth; someone else, and not your own lips (Prov. 27:2).

In Proverbs 27:21, we'll see that praise from others is like a hot crucible used to refine metal. In the verse above, praise from others is better than self-praise, which is condemned in Scripture (2 Cor. 10:18). But if we want praise without potentially disastrous results, we will seek praise only from the Lord.

Is it wrong for Christians to praise one another, to encourage each other in the faith? No, encouragement is very beneficial. We are commanded to do it (1 Thess. 5:11; Heb. 3:13; 10:25). But this proverb is not about giving praise, it's about seeking praise.

If we seek praise from our own lips, it is self-righteous and cheap. People see right through it. On the other hand, if we seek the praise of others, we may become like the Pharisees who "loved the praise of others more than the praise of God" (John 12:42-43). Our motivation is all-important. If we do good works only to be praised by others, their praise is the only reward we'll ever get (Matt. 6:1-6).

How much better to seek our reward and praise from God. The "another" or "someone else" in Proverbs 27:2 should be Christ. How will He reward you? With a joy and peace that pass all understanding, and with a treasury of eternal riches laid up for you in heaven; it's the only praise worth having.

Scriptural Examples

Goliath. What a contrast in this boasting Gentile. While the boy David approached, he praised himself and boasted of his ability to carve the lad up and feed him to the birds. A few seconds later, the giant lost his head (1 Sam. 17:41-51).

The centurion. This Gentile was a humble man. He asked Jesus to heal his servant, adding that he was unworthy for Christ to come into his house. He was praised by the elders of the Jews and later by Jesus Himself (Luke 7:3-9).

Prayer of Application

Lord God, keep my eyes focused on Jesus. Let me seek praise from no one else, as I seek to bring glory not to myself or to any other, except to Him who saves me and makes all life possible.

Cast Off the Heavy Burden of Pride

3) Stone is heavy and sand a burden, but provocation by a fool is heavier than both. 4) Anger is cruel and fury overwhelming, but who can stand before jealousy? (Prov. 27:3-4)

During the course of my college summers, I pushed a lot of concrete buggies full of cement, stone, and sand, and carried plaster on my shoulders to the waiting trowels of journeymen. Those were heavy loads. But this proverb tells us of something heavier: the provocation—or wrath—of a fool.

Let's start at the beginning and see how this came to be. What sin got Satan into trouble, and also plunged the human race into enmity with God (Gen. 3:5-6; Ezek. 28:12-19)? It was the sin of pride. Webster defines the pride God hates like this: "A high or inordinate opinion of one's own dignity, importance, merit, or superiority: conceit; arrogance." In other words, the sin of pride ascribes to oneself the honor and glory due only to God.

The prideful fool seeks to elevate himself at the expense of others. This breeds hatred and contempt of those who would thwart his ambition, or who he perceives to be higher up the ladder he's climbing. From hatred and contempt flow gossip and lies (Prov. 26:20-28), anger and wrath.

The Christian is called to forsake the sin of pride and respond in Christ's humility. We are to love our neighbor and seek his highest good. The burden of love is light (Matt. 11:30).

Scriptural Examples

Joseph's brothers. These men hated their brother Joseph because he was loved by Jacob, and because he prophesied of a higher position of honor than they. Ultimately, the fury of their envy was manifested (Gen. 37:3-28).

Cain. The end of the fool's wrath is murder. Because his deeds were evil and his brother's righteous, Cain murdered Abel. Cain's fury could not be contained (1 John 3:12).

Prayer of Application

Father, how can I possibly claim to follow Jesus if I lift up my nose in pride? Lord, keep me from pride and the envy it brings, and rather seek the humility and unselfishness of Christ.

Be an Honest, Open, and Gentle Friend

5) Better is open rebuke than hidden love. 6) Words from a friend can be trusted, but an enemy multiplies kisses (Prov. 27:5-6).

Have you ever been to an Alcoholics Anonymous meeting? I've attended several of AA's open meetings, and although I don't agree with their "higher power" concept, nor with their "disease" model, I found that the meetings I attended shared a unique and refreshing spirit.

Typically, there are many speakers during an AA meeting. Each gets up in front of the assembled crowd and tells about his weakness for alcohol and how he has stayed sober. No one is afraid to share weaknesses and failures. No one is judgmental, and all are willing to help a fellow drunk stay sober.

In the church, it seems that we all go to great lengths to keep our dirty laundry secret. Is it because we want to appear to be "super-saints"? Are we afraid that we won't be accepted? I'm not sure. But James 5:16 tells us to "confess your sins to each other and pray for each other so that you may be healed." I believe this is telling us that in order to be good rebukers, we first need to be good confessors.

Be open and honest about the sin still stirring within, confessing it to a friend. Then like an honest, open, and gentle friend, encourage him to greater godliness as well.

Scriptural Examples

Judas. These proverbs remind me of that night when he greeted Jesus with that infamous kiss. Are we like Judas? Do we care more about our stature in the Christian community than about the condition of our walk with Jesus (Mark 14:43-45)?

Paul. The great apostle corrected entire churches in a spirit of openness, honesty, and gentleness. On one occasion, he even rebuked his friend and fellow apostle Peter for conduct unbecoming a minister of the gospel (Gal. 2:11-14).

Prayer of Application

Father, rebuke is a very difficult thing for me to do. Help me to develop deep and solid friendships where confession and gentle rebuke are welcomed and refreshing. Thank You, Lord.

Hunger for Righteousness

He who is full loathes honey, but to the hungry even what is bitter tastes sweet (Prov. 27:7).

Think back to that last Thanksgiving dinner when you ate too much turkey, mashed potatoes, and gravy. One last piece of pumpkin pie looked good, but you knew that it would only add to your growing discomfort. You wanted to be hungry again, didn't you?

Most Americans have been gorged with belongings and food. We seek larger homes and fancier cars. We long for more exotic foods, and wilder entertainment to satisfy our jaded tastes. All along the Mexican border, many illegal immigrants cross the border at night, hungrily seeking the jobs that would be beneath most of us. What is bitter to us is sweet to them.

For the man or woman whose spiritual eyes have been opened, a hunger begins for the things of God: His Word and His righteousness. Then, after time, sometimes this hunger has a way of abating. The person may feel full and no longer in need of the pure food of the Word (Heb. 5:13). He grows spiritually slothful and fat, satisfied with far less than God has for him. Have you been "spiritually stuffed"? I know I have.

But Jesus says, "Blessed are they who hunger and thirst after righteousness, for they shall be filled" (Matt. 5:6). We need the Word to convict us of sin and to convince us of our need for its healing and sustaining power. Perhaps we should not pray for more food. Perhaps we should pray for hunger.

Scriptural Examples

The sinful woman. Jesus welcomed the hunger of this woman. While she washed His feet and anointed them with perfume, His hosts complained of her presence (Luke 7:47).

The Laodiceans. These self-satisfied churchgoers thought they had it made. But Jesus rebuked them, saying, "You are wretched, pitiful, poor, blind and naked" (Rev. 3:17-18).

Prayer of Application

Father, thank You for the Word which helps me to grow in righteousness, as I am guided by Your Spirit. I confess that sometimes I feel stuffed and unwilling to eat. Make me hungry.

Pick a Church Home and Stick with It

Like a bird that strays from its nest is a man who strays from his home (Prov. 27:8).

The bird's nest is for protection from predators and shelter from the elements. It is for the raising of a family in security. So, too, is the Christian's church home a protection from the world's buffeting and the deceitfulness of sin (Heb. 3:13). We need one another, and we need deep and continuing relationships that will foster mutual accountability and aid spiritual growth. For us to flit from place to place wreaks havoc on God's Church.

The central reason for the wandering eye of the ecclesiastical tourist is his preoccupation with being served. He's there on Sunday morning to be spoken to, complimented, entertained, and coddled. He gives no thought to what he can do for others in attendance, or for the real purpose of being there—to worship the God who created and sustains him.

When searching for a church home, find one that has opportunities for service in areas where your spiritual gifts can be utilized effectively. If you want to teach, find a local congregation that needs teachers. Then stick with it.

What encouragement to the pastor who hears the words, "We're thinking about joining your congregation. Are there any opportunities to serve others here?" Be careful if you switch church homes. Be fully assured that the reason for your move is not selfish, or due to your desire to escape responsibility.

Scriptural Examples

Dinah. This daughter of Jacob wandered from her nest and precipitated a horrible massacre of the citizens of Shechem. The incident maligned the name of her father (Gen. 34).

Jonah. Instead of going east to Nineveh, Jonah's wandering eye took him out upon a sea he knew the Lord controlled. It took a large fish to get him back on track (book of Jonah).

Prayer of Application

Father, thank You for the church home where people continue to uphold me in prayer and fellowship. When I was grieving, You used the same brothers and sisters there to encourage me.

Find Joy in the Counsel of a Friend

Perfume and incense bring joy to the heart, and the pleasantness of one's friend springs from his earnest counsel (Prov. 27:9).

Looking back on my life, one mistake I have made that is predominant over all the rest is of not always seeking the earnest counsel of godly friends. Of course, this one error can lead to countless other troubles and trials, and that's another reason why I would place it at the top of the list.

I fancy myself an entrepreneur, an innovator, a person who likes to tread ground on which no other has tread before. If I had been born 100 years earlier, I would probably have been a pioneer in a wagon train. Someone once told me a pioneer is a person with arrows in his backside. Then "pioneer" describes me well, because I've taken lots of arrows there. Some of them went pretty deep and were very painful.

A friend is someone who loves you and wants to see you succeed in life. He earnestly seeks what is best for you. His counsel will therefore be honest and based upon his own experience and education. He may have blind spots, but chances are his blind spots will not be your blind spots. And so he can help you to see the pitfalls you can't see for yourself.

Scriptural Examples

Mary, Martha, and Jesus. These sisters threw a dinner party for Jesus. Martha served while Mary anointed the Lord's feet with expensive perfume. Here is friendship at its finest. The joy Mary had known as she learned at her Master's feet was now returned by her lavish gift (John 12:1-7).

Peter and Andrew. Peter received joyous counsel from his brother Andrew as the latter ran to find him with the good news that he had found the Messiah. What greater joy can we bring to a friend than to introduce him to the Savior of mankind (John 1:40-41)?

Prayer of Application

O Lord, thank You for the wise counsel of friends and godly people of the church. Help me to humbly submit to their sincere rebuke and advice, earnestly seeking it and acting upon it.

Treasure Lasting Friendships

Do not forsake your friend and the friend of your father, and do not go to your brother's house when disaster strikes you—better a neighbor nearby than a brother far away (Prov. 27:10).

God intends the church to be a place of service, not entertainment. Each Christian should decide upon a church home and then stick with it (Prov. 27:8). This proverb gives us a further reason. We need to send down roots of friendship. One reason is so we will have trusted advisors and counselors (Prov. 27:9). The other reason is here. God wants us to have a solid underpinning of support when trouble or disaster strike. The support network we seek is not just for ourselves, but for our children and their children as well.

My brother lives 8,000 miles away. While I can pick up the phone and talk to him for counsel and encouragement, he's not going to be much physical help if I fall down the stairs and break my leg. I need a friend close by on whom I can call in times of physical need. What better place to find that circle of friends than my church home. A single phone call to a friend can start a prayer chain or bring physical help. Invest time and energy into friendships. They are a rare treasure.

Scriptural Examples

Solomon and Hiram. When Solomon succeeded David on the throne, Hiram, King of Tyre, sent an envoy. Hiram wanted his friendship with David to carry over to his son. Solomon sent back word of his decision to build a temple for the glory of God. Would Hiram supply the cedar for it? You bet Hiram would! He supplied all the wood Solomon needed (1 Kings 5:1-10).

Rehoboam and the elders. It's a pity that Solomon's son didn't have his father's wisdom. When Rehoboam became king, he sought the advice of Solomon's friends and advisors, but then rejected it, to his ultimate regret (1 Kings 12:6-19).

Prayer of Application

Dear God, thank You again for the church home to which You have called me, and for the many friends who would stop whatever they are doing to come to my aid if I am in need.

Bring Joy to Your Teachers and Parents

*Be wise, my son, and bring joy to my heart; then I can answer
anyone who treats me with contempt* (Prov. 27:11).

Most of the men and women who teach school are in the
profession to play a part in shaping the lives of young people.
They face many problems in this task. Often, parents are not sup-
portive and refuse to get involved in the child's formal education.
(This proverb refers specifically to parents, many of whom have
relinquished their responsibility to schools.) Much of a teacher's
classroom time is spent in disciplinary matters and not in teaching. Like front line soldiers in warfare, teachers bear much of the
heat of battle.

What a joy it is for a teacher to be part of training a young
man or woman who achieves success. But like parents, they also
face words of contempt when their charges fail. It is the responsibility of the student to both his parents and his teachers, to bring
them joy, not contempt.

In a spiritual sense, what a joy it is for a pastor to see those
under his care grow in the nurture and admonition of the Lord
(Eph. 6:4). Like the child's parents, pastors and teachers in the
church also have a stake in the future of each child placed in their
care. How diligent we need to be in order that "their work will be
a joy, not a burden" (Heb. 13:17).

Scriptural Examples

Simeon and Levi. They dealt harshly with the people of
Shechem after the seduction of Dinah. Jacob was very angry and
accused them of bringing upon him the contempt of his
neighbors. Jacob saw clearly how people will accuse the fathers
for the children's' sins (Gen. 34:30).

David. David's sin with Bathsheba and Uriah the Hittite
brought contempt upon David's heavenly Father from His enemies
(2 Sam. 12:14).

Prayer of Application

Heavenly Father, thank You for devoted teachers, parents, and
pastors who are serious in the training of their young people. Help
their students bring them joy and not contempt.

Prepare for Change

The prudent see danger and take refuge, but the simple keep going and suffer for it (Prov. 27:12).

God has reiterated this verse because it is extremely important. Back in Proverbs 22:3 we applied its truth to salvation and how the simple keep marching right on to destruction. While many specific applications might be used, I have chosen one that is universal: providing for future needs.

Today's world is becoming increasingly complex. Someone has said in one year, the computer business sees more changes than a normal business sees in seven years. But all businesses are affected and the changes are becoming increasingly intense. If you are counting on having your current job until retirement, think again. If you are just beginning, you may have as many as five different careers. People who are prudent will learn to adjust rapidly to change.

What can we do to prepare? The first thing that should be done is to seek the Lord's help. He and He alone will provide for all our needs. But does that fact obviate our need to be wise? An emphatic "No!" First, discover any gifts, talents, and interests which you may not be using currently. How can they be used in the future? What training can you invest in now that will pay dividends later on? Seek counseling. Whatever you do, don't hide your head in the sand. Technological advances and change are here to stay.

Scriptural Examples

The inhabitants of Jerusalem. Jesus warned of a day when Jerusalem would be totally destroyed . The event occurred in 70 A.D. when Titus besieged the city and leveled it. The Christians who lived there and who heeded the warnings escaped. The simple- minded who refused to see the danger ahead came into unbelievable suffering and death (Matt. 24:15-21).

Prayer of Application

Dear Lord, thank You we do not have to worry about the future. But, we are to make godly plans for our family's welfare. Help me to diligently prepare for the days ahead.

Don't Let Kindness Overshadow Prudence

*Take the garment of one who puts up security for a stranger; hold it in
pledge if he does it for a wayward woman* (Prov. 27:13).

Charles Bridges says, "Kindness loses the name of virtue,
when shown at the expense of prudence" (p. 514). In other words,
kindness loses its goodness when it loses sound judgment. Again,
the verse above is repeated because it's important (Prov. 20:16).
Let's look at it from another angle here.

The Bible enjoins us to be kind to others, particularly the
poor and needy (James 1:27; Deut. 10:18). We are also given the
Great Commission (Matt. 28:18-20). We act prudently when we
combine these tasks. When we feed the poor, we also need to give
them the gospel. To feed a poor person physically without feeding
him spiritually, or to feed him spiritually and not physically, is to
greatly weaken or even destroy our testimony.

I walk for exercise, and my walks usually take me through
urban areas where I'm accosted by homeless panhandlers. I rarely
give them any money. While my one dollar gift may seem kind,
it may just fuel an alcohol habit. If it does, my kindness loses its
goodness and becomes instead a stumbling block. However, if I
give money to Christian missions, to my local church's deacon
fund, or carry granola bars and gospel tracts to give to the homeless, I will be helping fill both spiritual and physical needs.

Whether we are lending money or giving it away, we need to
do it with prudence and in keeping with the knowledge that we
will one day have to give an account to God (Rom. 14:12).

Scriptural Examples

Jesus and the multitudes. Jesus practiced this principle in all
of His activities. When He gave a sermon it was often followed by
free food (Mark 6:34-42). He healed the multitudes and spoke
of the Kingdom of God. Let's follow His example and prudently
make our kindness count for eternity.

Prayer of Application

Heavenly Father, thank You for material blessings. Help me
to make wise giving decisions that will at the same time benefit
people physically and lead some into Your Kingdom.

Beware of Flattery

If a man loudly blesses his neighbor early in the morning, it will be taken as a curse (Prov. 27:14).

Imagine that it is 4:00 in the morning and you are tucked safely into bed in your upstairs bedroom which overlooks the front lawn. Down below stands your next-door neighbor in his pajamas, shouting up at your window about what a great person you are, what a super golfer you are, how good you are to your kids, and on and on. This fellow is not being a blessing to you. Instead, given the hour and the tone of his voice, you wonder if he has been hired by someone to drive you crazy, or out of town, or both. He is not a blessing, he is a curse.

Ironside quotes an old Italian proverb that goes like this: "He who praises you more than he is wont to do, has either deceived you, or is about to do it" (p. 387). We need to be extremely careful in the face of flattery. The greatest curse it carries is we might begin to believe it (Prov. 27:21). To that thought McGee adds the proverb, "Flattery is like perfume. The idea is to smell it, not swallow it" (p. 92).

So what do we do about this neighbor of ours and his wee hour rampages of flattery? I suppose the best thing would be to go downstairs and invite him in for a morning cup of coffee. We could then explain to him how much we appreciate his enthusiasm, then introduce him to the only One worthy of any praise, the Lord Jesus Christ.

Scriptural Examples

Absalom and the people of Israel. While his father, David, sat on the throne of Israel, this wicked son went through the nation flattering the citizens with his political promises and kisses. In this way he stole the hearts of the people of the country. Elevated in his own eyes, he began a campaign to unseat his dad and soon became a curse to everybody, including himself (2 Sam 15:1-6).

Prayer of Application

Father, help me to see myself as I really am, a hell-bound, rebellious sinner saved only by Your grace. May I give all the glory to You for anything others see as good within me.

Don't Be a Quarrelsome Spouse

15) A quarrelsome wife is like a constant dripping on a rainy day; 16) restraining her is like restraining the wind or grasping oil with the hand (Prov. 27:15-16).

This is the fourth time we have encountered the quarrelsome wife (Prov. 19:13; 21:9, 19). She's like the Chinese water torture, where drips of water upon a person's forehead gradually drive him insane. In these verses, the quarrelsome woman has become uncontrollable. To try and gain the upper hand is like trying to stop the wind from blowing, or changing the oil in your car by carrying it in your hands.

But why is she uncontrollable? First, the home is run by her timetable and plans or there is trouble. Second, she is not willing to change her preconceptions. Third, she will not listen to reason and will throw reason back into her husband's face. He gets buried by the words of his argumentative spouse and there is no peace. What a difference between this woman and the woman of Ephesians 5:22, who is submitted to her husband as he is submitted to the Lord.

But wives do not have a corner on the quarrelsome market. Overbearing, hard-headed husbands are legendary, and so I have alluded to them in the principle above. Husbands and wives, submit to one another and love one another. Be forgiving of one another and do not drive your partner to an early grave.

Scriptural Examples

Queen Vashti. King Xerxes summoned his wife to appear before him, but she refused to come. Enraged with anger, and concerned that her contentiousness might cause the other women of the nation to despise their husbands, too, Xerxes proclaimed that henceforth Vashti would be dethroned and never again be allowed to enter his presence. The submissive Esther took her place eventually (Est. 1:10-20).

Prayer of Application

Father, the family is Your oldest institution. Help us to follow the guidance of Your Word to the end that we would live peacefully with one another and bring glory to Your name.

Brothers and Sisters, Disciple One Another

As iron sharpens iron, so one man sharpens another (Prov. 27:17).

Back in 1980, a friend of mine and I began a businessmen's Bible study. Recently, a young man joined our study. One morning he told us why he had come. "I just like the openness of this group," he said. "I feel free to share my troubles and heartaches here, and to receive help from teaching, prayer, and godly advice." This is foundational in the Christian life—teaching and encouraging one another (Col. 3:16; 1 Thess. 5:11).

The Christian life needs to be lived in intimate fellowship with others who share our precious faith. The writer to the Hebrews enjoins us to "encourage one another daily," to the end that "none of you may be hardened by sin's deceitfulness" (Heb. 3:13). This can be done neither in the context of a "loner" mentality nor that of a large group. There has to be personal intimacy, and this is only possible in the small group or in one-on-one discipling relationships.

If you are not involved in a small group or discipling ministry of some kind, I urge you to get involved. The only requirement is to be serious about living for and glorifying the Lord Jesus, and a consequent desire to be sharpened in your walk with God and to sharpen others.

Scriptural Examples

Job. Eliphaz the Temanite spoke of his friend Job's discipling ministry. Job's words had supported those who had stumbled and had strengthened those who had faltering knees. What a blessing to be a person like Job (Job 4:3-4)!

The men on the Emmaus Road. After the crucifixion, two men were walking from Jerusalem to Emmaus when a stranger appeared and spoke to them about the prophecies that had been fulfilled in Christ. Later, they recognized the stranger as the Lord Jesus, who had just discipled them (Luke 24:13).

Prayer of Application

Father God, thank You for my brothers in Christ, who share common experiences on the road of faith. Help me to take seriously my responsibility to encourage and disciple others.

Do Your Work as Unto the Lord

He who tends a fig tree will eat its fruit, and he who looks after his master will be honored (Prov. 27:18).

Back in my college summers I worked as either a laborer or carpenter. My dad would say to me as I went to work, "Make a profit for your employer today." I found that he meant if my hard work made a profit for my employer, I'd make a profit, too.

The wise employee who tends to his employer's needs will himself be honored and enriched. At least that's the way it is supposed to work. Books could be filled with tales of unscrupulous employers who failed to pay the worker his wages or who absconded with the company's pension funds.

As Christians, we need to understand that it is our heavenly Father who signs our paychecks. Everything we have, or ever will have, comes from His hand. Somehow, we have lost confidence in the providence of God over all our affairs. But that doesn't make it less true.

What it boils down to is this: If you are seeking justice in the work you perform every day in your employer's service, or even working for yourself, look to the One True Employer to provide it (Col. 3:22-24).

Scriptural Examples

The faithful servants. In this story, Jesus illustrates the rewards given out in the kingdom of heaven to those who have been good and faithful servants. We need to work for the reward that never perishes, laboring in the field of the Lord for His glory and profit and for our eternal joy (Matt. 25:14-23).

The fig tree. In order for a fruit tree to bear fruit, it needs attention. Jesus spoke of a man telling his servant to cut down an unproductive fig tree. The man begged to be allowed to dig around the tree and fertilize it. The owner honored his servant's wish and gave the tree one more chance (Luke 13:6-10).

Prayer of Application

Oh, Father, whatever I do, help me to do it unto You and for Your glory. Lord, I thank You that every calling is a sacred calling and all labor has its focus in Your honor.

Look into Your Own Heart and Know Everyone

As water reflects a face, so a man's heart reflects the man (Prov. 27:19).

One Sunday, a young man complained to his mom saying, "I don't want to go to church today! I mean, it's boring and the people there are all a bunch of hypocrites. I'm just not going to go!" His mother responded, "But son, you have to go!" "Give me one good reason!" he demanded. "You're the pastor," she said.

The point is, when your pastor has just finished scolding you from the pulpit for your pet sin, and you begin wondering how in the world he found out about it, stop wondering. Chances are that he simply looked into his own heart and came to know what was in yours, too.

Like looking in a mirror and seeing my face, by looking into the thoughts and intents of my heart (Heb. 4:12), I can get a pretty clear picture of my character. When contrasted to the perfect Word of God, I have to admit that it is ugly. But, in the proverb's larger sense, I am looking at the heart of every man and woman who has ever lived, save One. We are all corrupted, none of us seeks after God. No one does good. No, not even one (Ps.14:1; Rom. 3:9-18).

But the search awakens in me a deeper understanding of the love of a Savior who, while I was yet His enemy and dead in trespasses and sins, died for me (Rom. 5:6). I need to hear the gospel of Jesus Christ every day. But I cannot appreciate its truth completely until I have understood the depths of my own sinfulness, and therefore the heights to which I am called heavenward in Christ Jesus (Eph. 2:6).

Scriptural Examples

Paul. Paul searched his heart and saw in it two contrasting principles at work. On the one hand, he wanted to follow God, but on the other hand, his sin nature kept pulling him in the opposite direction. Isn't Paul's experience yours (Rom. 7)?

Prayer of Application

Father, how can I ever thank You for sending Christ to die for me and to pay the price of my redemption. Now saved, I long for the day when I shall meet Him face to face.

Find Satisfaction in Christ Alone

*Death and Destruction are never satisfied, and neither are
the eyes of man* (Prov. 27:20).

I recently attended an annual automobile show. There, shining
brightly beneath flood lamps were new cars from all over the
world. Hundreds of us "lookieloos" feasted our eyes on
glistening new paint and soft leather bucket seats. Such are the
eyes of people. We see it and we want it.

The main force that keeps the automobile industry churning
out new models every year is the truth of this verse. People want
something newer and prettier and more expensive than our neighbor's. It is what has built American industry. But it is a treadmill to
nowhere. Its end apart from God is "Death and Destruction."

Augustine said, "O, Lord, thou hast made us for thyself, and
our hearts are restless until they rest in thee." Christ is where the
"buck" of restlessness and dissatisfaction stops. We will never find
peace and contentment (Phil. 4:11-13) until we find it in Him.
What is it about Christ that beckons us?

Christ gives us a new perspective on life, a new sense of purpose, and a faith in the Sovereign God that submits to His reign
over our lives. By faith, we enter the rest of God and find a peace
that passes understanding (Phil. 4:7). Let us make every effort to
enter that rest (Heb. 4:10-11) and be satisfied in the One who
gives us all things freely to enjoy (Rom. 8:32).

Scriptural Examples

The woman at the well. Jesus approached this Samaritan
woman and asked her for a drink. He then spoke of her lover
and five former husbands. Why do you suppose she had had
five husbands and was now living with a man? Could it be that
she wasn't satisfied? Christ spoke to her of her thirst and how by
normal water it is never satisfied. Only He could give her living
water, the drink which satisfies eternally (John 4:5-26).

Prayer of Application

Lord, the blessings of plenty can become a curse if they become an end in themselves. Help me to tell others of the genuine
satisfaction in Christ.

Use Care in Giving and Receiving Praise

The crucible for silver and the furnace for gold, but man is tested by the praise he receives (Prov. 27:21).

Part of God's testing us involves praise, both its giving and receiving. Derek Kidner says an alternate reading might be, "we stand revealed by what we praise" (p. 168).

If you are anything like me, you like to have others say nice things about you. Honest praise lifts us up and puts a spring in our step. We feel accepted. Praise is okay as long as we maintain a proper perspective and are not puffed up by it. Charles Bridges says, "It is a dangerous crisis when a proud heart meets flattering lips" (p. 521). The heart is deceitful beyond imagining (Jer. 17:9) and often flattery or the praise of others is its fuel.

How do we avoid the temptation of becoming a legend in our own mind? One way—not recommended—would be to marry the quarrelsome and critical spouse (Prov. 27:15 -16). But there is a less painful way. Remember to "live your life for the Audience of One," to borrow a phrase from Os Guinness. Let God be the source of your praise, if you qualify for any. Live to please God and not others. Then, by seriously attempting to match your life against God's Word, you will be kept in humble submission to His grace.

Scriptural Examples

The Pharisees. Some say none of the Jews believed in Jesus. Oh, but they did! In fact, many of the Jewish leaders believed in Him, but were afraid to confess Him because they loved the praise of others more than the praise of God. Don't get caught in their trap (John 12:42-43).

Paul and Barnabas. With their popularity they could have started their own TV ministry and cashed in on their stardom! But no. They were eager to give all credit to God. Like them, let's live for our Audience of One (Acts 14:11-15).

Prayer of Application

Lord, I need the gospel every minute. First, to remind me I am dead and without hope except through You. Then to remind me who You are a holy, all-powerful, and loving God.

Only God Can Grind Sense into a Fool

Though you grind a fool in a mortar, grinding him like grain with a pestle, you will not remove his folly from him   (Prov. 27:22).

My parents once took us on a trip to the Grand Canyon. We also saw the Wupatki National Monument near Flagstaff, which is the site of ancient Indian ruins. There, we saw the foundations and subfloors of ancient houses that had crumbled in the rush of years and harsh elements.

Everywhere we looked, we saw smooth concave holes in the venerable stone floors. These, the guide explained, were mortars, where grain was ground with a pestle. By crushing the grain between the movable pestle and the immovable mortar, the chaff was removed and the edible portion of the grain was exposed. Then the grain was ground to meal under the same pressure. The mortar and pestle is a great tool for processing food, but that same tool is useless for processing fools.

Charles Colson founded Prison Fellowship because he knew that if people were to be truly penitent for their sins, they needed to be reconciled to God. Today, in prisons across America, men and women are meeting the Savior in their jail cells because of the work of prison ministries. No, you'll never remove the folly of a fool by grinding him with a mortar and pestle. But God can do it by Him who was ground to death for our folly, and raised again for our justification (Rom. 4:25).

Scriptural Examples

Ahaz. This foolish king of Judah suffered bitterly because of his unfaithfulness. But after it all, "in his time of trouble, Ahaz became even more unfaithful to the Lord" (2 Chron. 28:22).

Manasseh. Again, a foolish king brought trouble upon himself and his kingdom. Unlike Ahaz, Manasseh called upon the Lord and the Lord delivered him from it (2 Chron. 33).

Prayer of Application

Dear Lord, thank You for all prison ministries. The gospel is the only real hope and the only way that folly can ever be removed from a fool. Give them grace to continue their work.

Prepare for the Future in Diligence and Faith

23) Be sure you know the condition of your flocks, give careful attention to your herds; 24) for riches do not endure forever, and a crown is not secure for all generations. 25) When the hay is removed and new growth appears and the grass from the hills is gathered in, 26) the lambs will provide you with clothing, and the goats with the price of a field. 27) You will have plenty of goats' milk to feed you and your family, and to nourish your servant girls (Prov. 27:23-27).

I don't own any flocks or herds, not even a single goat. I do have a modest portfolio of common stocks, but I never made it to the goal of "financial independence." I like to say that I could retire tomorrow, but only if I were to die next week.

The wealth of this world is fickle and fleeting (Matt. 6:19), and in the final analysis, cannot be relied upon to provide us with so much as a cup of coffee in the future. We are to rely upon God as the ultimate source of all we have. He is absolutely reliable, and our hearts can rest content in the knowledge that if all our investments flop, and our pension plan goes bankrupt, and if the Social Security system fails, God will provide for all our needs (Isa. 58:11; Phil. 4:19). But does this knowledge preclude us from being diligent about providing for the future? These verses pronounce an emphatic "No!"

Scriptural Examples

Jacob. Jacob diligently tended Laban's flocks and then carved out of them massive flocks and herds of his own. When he returned to his homeland, he had plenty to take with him. By his careful preparation Jacob ensured food for his large family and nourishment for his servant girls (Gen. 30 and 31).

Boaz. Boaz personally looked after his flocks and his fields. He exercised diligence in his work and in his provision for the future (Ruth 2:1-16; 3:6-13).

Prayer of Application

Dear Heavenly Father, help me to trust You alone as the Great Provider of all things. But then help me to do my part in providing for my needs and for those of my family.

Chapter Twenty-eight

Proverbs and the Christian Life

Proverbs 28:9 should be memorized by everyone who embraces the name "Christian." It states simply, "If anyone turns a deaf ear to the law, even his prayers are detestable." What arrogance to think that we can disregard God's precepts—His law—and believe that He will regard our prayers. Some teach that a person can be saved and yet continue to live in a state of sin. Now while it is true that we all sin (1 John 1:8), 1 John 2:6 says, "Whoever claims to live in [Christ] must walk as Jesus did." That is, the believer must walk in righteousness, leaving old habits and patterns of sinful behavior in the past.

Repentance is crucial to the Christian life. Take a look at the back of your hand. Pretend for a moment that the back of your hand is the practice of sin in your life. Now turn your hand over and look at your palm. We'll call the palm side of your hand the Christian life. Just as when we turn our hand toward its palm the back of our hand turns away, so when we turn to Christ we turn away from the practice of sin. That is what repentance is. When we are saved and encounter the righteous and holy God, we should want nothing to do with sin. Yet sin is still "at work within [our] members" (Rom. 7:23). Paul cries out with us, "Who will rescue me from this body of death? Thanks be to God, through Jesus Christ our Lord" (Rom. 7:24-25).

Be Bold in the Righteousness of Christ

The wicked [KJV: "lawless"] flees though no one pursues, but the righteous are as bold as a lion (Prov. 28:1).

I love the 23rd Psalm, particularly the verse that says, "Surely goodness and mercy shall follow me all the days of my life." The man or woman of God, who like David has been made righteous by the righteousness imputed to him by Christ, confidently expects the goodness and grace of the Lord to follow him everywhere he goes (Rom. 8:28). The natural person should expect exactly the opposite. He should look over his shoulder, anticipating only wrath and anger (Rom. 2:8).

We're told by modern psychologists that humankind's problems stem from a guilt complex. If we could only get rid of our guilt, we'd be able to toss off our fears and anxieties, our phobias and our psychoses. But the Bible says that our guilt can only be washed away by the blood of Christ. Guilt is real, and its cause is self-seeking sin and the rejection of the truth of God.

Throughout Scripture, the Messiah is known as the Lion of Judah (Gen. 49:9 ; Hos. 5:14 ; 11:10; Rev. 5:5). Christ is that Lion and His righteous ones may be as bold as He is. No longer beset with guilt that causes him to fear, the Christian can look forward with confidence (Phil. 3:13). His Master and Brother is not just king of the jungle but King of Kings.

Scriptural Examples

Adam and Eve. Following their sin they hid in the garden. Why? Because they were afraid. Although they were naked before the Fall, it was the shame and guilt of their sin that exposed their nakedness to their eyes, and brought fear (Gen. 3:9-10).

Caleb and Joshua. While the other 10 spies at Kadesh Barnea were fearful of giants, these men were bold as lions and confidently argued for an immediate attack and occupation of what God had promised (Num. 14:6-10).

Prayer of Application

Sovereign Lord, you are truly the Lion of Judah. Even today You are in control of all things. Make me bold, Lord, in the knowledge that through Your strengthening, I can do all things.

Beware of the Anarchy of Sin

When a country is rebellious, it has many rulers, but a man of understanding and knowledge maintains order (Prov. 28:2).

God established government for the purpose of maintaining law and order (Rom. 13:1-5). The word anarchy is from the Greek *anarchia* meaning lack of a leader. It is a state or society without government or laws. Anarchy is opposed to God's will.

In *Anarchism: Left, Right, and Green*, (City Light Books; San Francisco), Ulrike Heider interviewed leaders of three wings of anarchism: the left wing, or radical Communists; the right wing neo-Nazis; and the green wing of the "eco[logical]-anarchist" Green Party. Anarchism is rampant, because people delight in doing their own thing without governmental interference.

But this proverb also speaks of the anarchist that resides in all of us. Countries are rebellious because people are rebellious. Without God at the control of our lives through the power of His Spirit, sin can gain control. If we allow "the man of understanding and knowledge"—the Lord Jesus Christ—to be dethroned from His position of authority in our lives, we are then slaves to "many rulers"—the manifold nature of sin.

Sin can creep into our lives even in things that are neutral (1 Cor. 6:12). We need to be constantly on guard that it does not lead us away from God, lest we become enslaved to its rule.

Scriptural Examples

Rehoboam and Israel. Rehoboam began his reign by angering the people. He listened to his young, rebellious friends while refusing to listen to the wise counsel of the elders. This split the kingdom, as 10 rebellious tribes refused to follow him. Only Judah and Benjamin remained loyal to the house of David. Interestingly, the Davidic dynasty lasted 350 years, but the rebellious people of the other tribes had many rulers: nine different dynasties in about 200 years (1 Kings 12:16-21).

Prayer of Application

Father, inside me there remains a seed of rebellion. Help me to live only for Your glory and honor, forsaking all other paths, and living under the authority of Your Word and by Your Spirit.

Beware of Your Propensity to Betray Trust

A ruler [KJV: "poor man"] who oppresses the poor is like a driving rain that leaves no crops (Prov. 28:3).

The Hebrew words *geber ras*, translated "ruler" by the NIV, actually mean "poor man." Apparently the NIV translators "corrected" the text by inserting the (apparently) more logical word. But the simile suggests otherwise. As a rainstorm approaches, the farmer says, "Oh, boy! This is good. The rain will help the crops grow." But the driving rain destroys his crops in its ferocity and the farmer is left poorer yet. Isn't this what can happen when a poor man comes into power?

One needs only to think of the French Revolution, the Russian Revolution, and Adolf Hitler to find examples of poor people who oppressed those they came to serve. The powerful poor person may have no comprehension of the nature and requirements of his position, and in his fearful mistrust of all, seek to rule with an iron fist. His own poor roots have become the seed of his betrayal of those who brought him to power.

Likewise, we need to watch carefully our own faithfulness to those who have put us in authority. If you are elevated in your church, your community, your business or organization, or your family, be careful that you do not forget your poor roots and betray the very ones who trusted you to serve them.

Scriptural Examples

Scribes and Pharisees. These hypocrites oppressed others. Jesus said that they sat in Moses' seat and "tie[d] up heavy loads and put them on men's shoulders, but they themselves are not willing to lift a finger to move them." How very different Jesus was (Matt. 23:1-4).

Zacchaeus. Jesus called to him and invited Himself to dine at Zacchaeus' home. Confessing his sin of oppressing the poor, Zacchaeus found forgiveness that day (Luke 19:2-9).

Prayer of Application

Lord, Your Word says that You are very concerned about our treatment of the poor. Help me to lead others in humility and the fear of the Lord, and not to oppress in any way.

Conform to the Standard of God's Law

4) Those who forsake the law praise the wicked, but those who keep the law resist them. 5) Evil men do not understand justice, but those who seek the Lord understand it fully (**Prov. 28:4-5**).

During the Reformation, Roman Catholics brought charges of lawlessness against those who said "justification is by faith alone." They claimed this "legal fiction" led to lawlessness, and insisted people need to be conformed to the law of the church in order to be saved. But to those who truly understand God's grace, their only response to His free gift of salvation can be to obey His law. Protestant justification is by faith alone, but it is not a faith that stands alone. True faith produces obedience.

Jesus said, "By their [people's] fruit you will recognize them" (Matt. 7:16). And what are the fruits of lawless people? Two such fruits are listed above. In verse 4, the lawless praise those who are also lawless. In verse 5, wicked people do not comprehend justice, or judgment. (See Romans 1:18-32 for more fruits.)

The lawless have this in common with all lawbreakers: they are openly hostile to God. They do not submit to God's law, nor can they (Rom. 8:7). Hostility loves company. Their numbers give each a sense of strength. They even know their actions deserve death, but that doesn't stop them (Rom. 1:32).

But the man or woman who has been saved by God's grace warns others about the dead end of lawlessness and seeks instead the godly life which is aligned with the law of Christ.

Scriptural Examples

Noah. Living in an era of unbridled lawlessness, this godly man preached of the coming judgment. The lawless around him joined hands and mocked him. But the ark's doors were shut and God's wrath was unleashed upon them (Gen. 6:9-7:6; 2 Peter 2:5; Heb. 11:7). (Notice in this last reference that Noah was an heir of the righteousness that is by faith.)

Prayer of Application

Father, I love You because You first loved me and sent Your Son to die that I might be justified in Your sight, saved only by the blood of Jesus. Because of this, I obey You.

Be Careful of Equating Wealth with Blessing

Better a poor man whose walk is blameless than a rich man whose ways are perverse (Prov. 28:6).

I recently read of a survey taken in San Diego where wealthy people in an affluent bedroom community were interviewed regarding the source of their riches. An overwhelming majority of those interviewed said they definitely believed they were rich because God had blessed the character and content of their lives with material prosperity. Now they were right in assuming God allowed them to become wealthy, but they were not necessarily right in assuming their wealth was a blessing of God. It could be a curse.

Jesus said, "It is easier for a camel to go through the eye of a needle than for a rich man to enter the kingdom of God" (Matt. 19:24). His disciples were astounded. They carried with them the belief God must have enriched the rich man because of his piety or excellent character. But as James tells us, "Has not God chosen those who are poor in the eyes of the world to be rich in faith and to inherit the kingdom he promised those who love him?" (James 2:5) The rich person who has the short view and whose ways are perverse is infinitely poorer than the poor one who has Christ.

Scriptural Examples

Dives and Lazarus. By all earthly appearances, the wealthy and high living Dives was blessed of God in his riches, while the homeless beggar Lazarus was the scourge of the earth. But in the final analysis, their roles reversed. Lazarus found himself in Abraham's bosom while Dives was in torment (Luke 16:19-31).

The poor widow. While rich men were putting their 10 percent into the temple treasury, this woman gave 100 percent—all she had. Her trust was rightly grounded in the Living God and not in her meager coins (Luke 21:1-4; Matt. 6:3).

Prayer of Application

Father, thank You for providing my material needs. But they pale in comparison to my need for salvation. Thank You for sending Your Son to shed His blood for my eternal need.

Don't Be Sucked in by Peer Pressure

He who keeps the law is a discerning son, but a companion of gluttons [KJV: "riotous men"] disgraces his father (Prov. 28:7).

Bill Smith (we'll call him) was a junior in high school and was exulting in the fact that it was Friday—no more school for two days—and summer was just around the corner. The phone rang. Swigging on an open milk carton, Bill picked up the receiver and flopped down on the couch in one fluid motion.

"Hey Bill, it's Fred," came the voice. "We got two kegs for the party tonight. Gonna tap 'em soon as it's dark. You coming?"

"I don't think so, Fred. Mary and I are going to the movies."

"Well, go to the movies early and then come down to the beach. It ought to be a wild evening. We're expecting 100 kids."

"No thanks, Fred. I'm not interested in drinking anymore."

"Yeah," Fred responded, "I've noticed you avoiding the guys lately. Don't tell me you went and got religion."

"Let's put it this way, Fred," Bill answered. "I'm just following a new leader these days: Jesus Christ."

Fred muttered a few expletives before saying, "I never figured you for one of those pantywaist Christians; that you would fall for all that pie in the sky, bye-and-bye B.S."

"Actually, Fred, I've never been happier or more excited about life. I just don't feel any need to get drunk anymore."

"Well, it won't last long." Fred hung up.

Young man or woman, you don't have to succumb to the pressure of those who would lead you into sin. Once in a group like that, it's difficult to extricate yourself. God gave us the Law as an example of His grace and of His love for us. When we keep on its path, we live abundantly satisfying lives of joy and avoid the traps of evil people. Follow God's Law for His glory and for your own benefit. Listen to and honor your godly parents, and beware of the company you keep.

Prayer of Application

Father, when we are converted we often bring along ungodly entanglements. Help us all to avoid that which prompts us to sin and, instead, seek to follow Your Law in all that we do.

Be a Distributor, Not an Accumulator

He who increases his wealth by exorbitant interest amasses it for another, who will be kind to the poor (Prov. 28:8).

The Law of Moses let the Israelites charge interest to foreigners, but not to brothers (Deut. 23:19-20). As Derek Kidner points out, the Hebrews were a family. Charging interest would be like a physician charging his own children for his services (p. 170).

But this proverb speaks to more than just the sin of usury. The KJV renders the first line "He that by usury and unjust gain increaseth his substance." The idea is that any unjust means of accumulating wealth brings judgment. We in business need to be especially watchful. Are we willing to cheat just a little bit in order to improve quarterly profits? If we do, we will pass on our ill-gotten gains to someone who will be kind to the poor.

Material wealth in this life brings with it increased responsibility. "From everyone who has been given much, much will be demanded" (Luke 12:48). God will call us to account for what we did with the resources He gave us. We Christians should not be in the accumulation business. We should be in the distribution business, distributing the gospel, our knowledge, encouragement, gifts, joy, and our material wealth to anyone in need.

Scriptural Examples

The Jewish brothers. The pilgrims sent up a loud cry against their brothers who had been charging them interest during times of famine and excessive taxation. Immediately, the practice was brought to a halt (Neh. 5:1-13).

The righteous man and his violent son. Some signs of a righteous man include: not taking excessive interest, withholding his hands from doing wrong, and judging fairly between other men. On the other hand, the righteous man's wicked and violent son does the opposite of his dad. The son, the Lord concludes, will be put to death for his own sins (Ezek. 18:1-13).

Prayer of Application

Lord, help me to understand that true wealth is in trusting You. May I be a distributor of Your wealth, forsaking usury and unjust gain, and clinging rather to justice and equity.

Beware of Mocking God

*If anyone turns a deaf ear to the law, even his prayers
are detestable* (Prov. 28:9).

Prayer is an unspeakable privilege. As those words flow from my fingers to the computer screen, I am shivering inside. Oh, that I were more a man of prayer. I must confess that I am not nearly what I should be. But I know that when I pray, God is faithful to hear and answer my prayer because I revere His Law and try to apply it consistently to my life. Do I always do so? No, sadly I do not, but I want to (Rom. 7:15-21).

This proverb addresses the person who will not even listen to the Law of God. That is, he will not open God's Word and read it, and then prayerfully seek to make it the grid through which all his thoughts, words, and actions are judged. In short, he couldn't care less about what God has to say, although ironically he thinks God should care about what he has to say. He wants the benefits of knowing God with none of the responsibility. The prayers of a person like this are detestable to God.

Are you like the person who turns a deaf ear to God? If so, you might like to know of the exception to the rule of the proverb above. God will hear the prayer of the repentant heart. Confess your idolatry to God and He will hear from heaven and forgive you (1 Kings 8:33-39; 2 Chron. 7:14).

Scriptural Examples

The elders of Israel. These men came to Ezekiel to seek the Lord. The Lord would not allow them to inquire of Him because the idolatry of their fathers was continuing (Ezek. 20).

Simon the sorcerer. This man was practicing witchcraft in Samaria when he heard the gospel through Philip. When Peter and John came up from Jerusalem, Simon, wishing to use the Holy Spirit as a tool to increase his sorcery business, offered to pay for the gift of the Spirit. Peter rebuked his idolatry (Acts 8:9-24).

Prayer of Application

Dear God, thank You for the privilege of prayer. Help me, Lord, to be a man of much prayer. But I understand that if I won't listen to You and Your Law, neither will You listen to me.

Beware of Evil Pathways

He who leads the upright along an evil path will fall into his own trap, but the blameless will receive a good inheritance
(Prov. 28:10).

I always equated the "evil path" as one of physical sin like adultery, murder, or theft. But I believe the main evil path is a path away from God and His Word. There are many false spiritual paths out there. Let's look at a few.

First, there is the path of unbelief. People are leading others to distrust the Word of God. Second, there is the path of tradition. Many traditional dogmas conflict with the revealed truth of the Scriptures. Third, people say that doctrine is unimportant. What is important is our experiential contact with God, not His Word. Finally—but not exhaustively—people are being drawn down the path of gopherism. People teach that God is a heavenly gopher... "go fer this, go fer that." He is reduced to their servant, not vice versa.

Each evil path seeks to discredit God and His Holy Word, and instead to elevate the creature: us humans. Watch out for these paths. Look forward instead to the inheritance of those who have been found blameless, saved through the Word of God taught by godly people (Rom. 10:14), justified before God by faith alone in the precious blood of Jesus Christ (Heb. 10:19).

Scriptural Examples

Satan. He is the chief of deceivers. He laid out the evil path in Eden and continues his deceit today (Gen. 3:1-6).

Balaam. This deceiver tried to lead the Israelites onto evil paths of sexual immorality and idolatry (Num. 31:16; Rev. 2:14).

Men of the last days. Paul spoke of their radical departure from the ways of God to the folly of the evil path (2 Tim. 3:1-9).

The false teachers. They try to lead God's people astray with their heresies. But God has ordered swift destruction for them. They will fall into the pit they dig for others (2 Peter 2:1-22).

Prayer of Application

Heavenly Father, shut the mouths of false teachers and allow instead the pure truth of Your Word to go out unfettered into this world. Help me to warn others of their evil paths.

Do Not Equate Wealth and Wisdom

A rich man may be wise in his own eyes, but a poor man who has discernment sees through him (Prov. 28:11).

We often elevate the rich and famous to pedestals of honor. They speak at banquets and conventions and we come in droves to hear them, hoping a little of their wisdom will rub off on us. Remember the smug saying "If you're so smart, why aren't you rich"? It's as if those who possess the world's riches are models of moral excellence, far exalted above mere mortals.

But far too often, the rich person is what he is because of greed and treachery, not because of high ethical standards and a keen sense of fair play. And even if wealth is gained in a morally upright way, does not its possessor often see himself as "self-made," independent of God? Is he not "wise in his own eyes"?

I know a few rich people who see their wealth as a gift from God. Their riches are not the result of their personal accomplishment, but God's accomplishment in them. They don't trust their wealth to deliver them in time of trouble, but trust instead in the foundation of all wealth, the Lord Jesus Christ.

The poor man will not be seen on the dais of this world's "rubber chicken" circuit. Why? Because the world worships wealth and fame and power. The poor man with discernment worships the One with whom the world wants nothing to do.

Scriptural Examples

Naaman and his servants. Wise in his own eyes, he rejected the advice of Elisha to wash in the Jordan River to be healed of his leprosy. But his servants saw through his arrogance and advised him to follow Elisha's command (2 Kings 5:9-14).

The ruler of Tyre. This city was a center of commerce in the ancient world. Its prince had become wise in his own eyes because of his great wealth. He failed to honor God, who promised him a violent death in the same sea on which his ships sailed (Ezek. 28:1-8).

Prayer of Application

Dear Savior, I know that wealth only brings increased accountability before You. Help me to use any riches that may come my way for Your glory and honor, not selfishly.

Look Up! The Triumph Is Coming!

When the righteous triumph, there is great elation; but when the wicked rise to power, men go into hiding (Prov. 28:12).

There is a sense in which all Christians are "in hiding" today. We don't cower in caves, afraid to come out for fear of being mocked or murdered. No, we are all hiding in bodies of clay, waiting for the glory of Christ to be revealed (Isa. 40:5; Rom. 8:18-24a). Then, "[He] will transform our lowly bodies so that they will be like his glorious body" (Phil. 3:21).

What a glorious day that will be! No longer will sin be found in our mortal bodies! No longer will the wicked rule! No longer will the glory of Christ be hidden by our sin natures! The Lord Jesus Christ, the Righteous King of Kings, will reign eternally and we will reign with Him (2 Tim. 2:12).

God has given us a firm hope, although it is a hope which we cannot see or touch. But we wait patiently for it (Rom. 8:24- 25) and in it we are purified (1 John 3:3). A day is coming soon when "the Lord himself will come down from heaven, with a loud command,…and the dead in Christ will rise first. After that, we who are still alive and are left will be caught up together with them…to meet the Lord in the air. And so we will be with the Lord forever" (1 Thess. 4:16-18). Keep looking up! "Your redemption is drawing near" (Luke 21:28)!

Scriptural Examples

The ancient witnesses. For thousands of years, people of God have been persecuted in this sinful world. Read Hebrews 11:35-40. These verses speak of the faithful witnesses of antiquity, who looked forward, as do we, to the resurrection of their bodies. They suffered punishment and indignities of every kind, and this world was not worthy of them. They did not see Jesus' day, the day of which "God had planned something better for us, so that only together with us would they be made perfect (v. 40)."

Prayer of Application

Father, the first time Christ visited this earth, He came in humility to save His people from sin. This time, He will come in power and great glory to take us all home. Praise His name!

Both Confess and Forsake Your Sins

*He who conceals his sins does not prosper, but whoever confesses
and renounces them finds mercy* (Prov. 28:13).

Charles Bridges comments that both God and people cover
sin. God covers sin in free unbounded grace, and people in shame
and hypocrisy (p. 538). You can do it, or you can let God do it,
but you cannot have your cake and eat it too.

The mature believer is not someone who never sins. Rather,
he has become acutely aware of his sin and is humbly dependent
upon God for mercy and forgiveness. Many seem to be preoccupied
with their image and don't want anyone to think they struggle
against sin. But we all do. Each of us needs to confess our sins to
God (1 John 1:9), and to one another (James 5:16), and thereby
encourage each other toward purity of life.

Bridges goes on to say that "while the hypocrite confesses
without forsaking, the hearty forsaking here is the best proof of
sincere confessing" (p. 540). In other words, to confess without
forsaking is a sham. If we do sin, we must forsake it anew each
time, asking the Spirit to work His righteousness in us.

Scriptural Examples

Adam and Eve. They attempted to cover themselves with fig
leaves, but God provided them with the skins of animals He
slew as a testimony that without the shedding of blood there is
no forgiveness (Gen. 3:7-21; Heb. 9:22).

Saul. God told him to completely destroy the Amalekites—
their men, women, children, sheep, and cattle. But Saul
disobeyed and tried to cover his sin, saying that he'd kept some
animals to sacrifice to God (1 Sam. 15:1-23).

The woman's accusers. When the Pharisees brought a woman
caught in adultery to Jesus, He wrote something in the sand and
the people quietly disbursed. Did Jesus write, "Adulterer,"
"Murderer," "Blasphemer"? (John 8:1-11)

Prayer of Application

Father, thank You for the grace that removes each blot of sin
from my life and imputes to me Christ's righteousness. Help me
to confess and forsake any remaining sin in my life.

Thrive on the Law of the Lord

Blessed is the man who always fears the Lord, but he who hardens his heart falls into trouble (Prov. 28:14).

What does it mean to "fear the Lord" on a consistent basis? I believe it begins with an understanding of the gospel: who I am and who God is, and the great gulf between us that has been bridged by Jesus Christ. It means to live in utter dependence upon Providence, and to trust God's Word to guide us. It means to love His law and to obey it (Ps. 119:97, 113, 163, 165).

We who have been born again never need to fear the Lord's condemnation (Rom. 8:1). We are given a desire to serve and please Him that brings us liberty. No longer is God's Law understood to be a taskmaster that we must keep perfectly in order to be saved. (The law never saved anyone.) Rather, the Law has become an expression of God's grace and we love it.

The person who fears the Lord wants to keep the moral law for two basic reasons. First, he stands in awe of his God and he wants to please Him. Second, he realizes that God, in His infinite wisdom, has given people His Law as a guide to a happy, fulfilling, and productive life. The Christian puts God's wisdom above his own and relies completely upon God's judgment.

Hardness of heart is simply unbelief (Heb. 3:15-19). Those who turn their backs on God's way fall into trouble, just as the Israelites who refused to trust and believe God in the wilderness. Don't be like them. Fear the Lord and thrive on every word that proceeds from His mouth (Deut. 8:3).

Scriptural Examples

Shadrach, Meshach, and Abednego. These men feared the Lord much more than they feared the flames of the king. They were blessed of God as they survived the furnace without so much as a singed beard. They declared that even if they died, they wouldn't let their hearts be hardened, but would trust God (Dan. 3:16-18).

Prayer of Application

Father, thank You for the Law, which provides a lamp for my eyes and a path for my feet, keeping me from sin and trouble. May my feet never stumble into pathways of unbelief.

Husbands, Lead Your Homes in Love

15) Like a roaring lion or a charging bear is a wicked man ruling over a helpless people. 16) A tyrannical ruler lacks judgment, but he who hates ill-gotten gain will enjoy a long life (Prov. 28:15-16).

Derek Kidner says the tyrannical leader is subhuman (15), stupid (16a), and short-lived (16b) (p. 171). That brings to my mind a picture of old Archie Bunker, who in the 1970's TV sitcom *All in the Family*, ruled his household from a self-styled throne of malicious accusations, thoughtless insults, and self-indulgent despotism. But his program was not short-lived. In fact, on the contrary, it set records for longevity. Why? I believe one reason was many saw their own fathers in Archie Bunker. The show allowed them to laugh at some very painful memories of their childhood.

The Bible condemns Archie Bunkerism. Just because God has given men the responsibility of leadership in the home doesn't give them a license to be tyrants. Men are commanded to love their wives "just as Christ loved the church and gave himself up for her" (Eph. 5:25). Was Christ a tyrant? Did He come to bully the Church? No. He came to serve and tenderly shepherd His people. He came to die for them and to save them.

Scriptural Examples

The seventy judges. At his father-in-law's suggestion, and with the Lord's approval, Moses appointed men to help him rule the Israelites. Their qualifications? That they feared God, were trust-worthy, and hated dishonest gain. All of the people, the family of God, would then be satisfied (Ex. 18:21-23).

The beasts of Daniel's vision. Daniel had a vision of four beasts coming out of a troubled sea. They represented the tyrannical rule of four major kingdoms that were to come on earth, which would ultimately be burned up (Dan. 7:1-12).

Prayer of Application

Our Father in heaven, in Your wisdom and providence You have given men the role of family leadership. Help all of us in that role to lead in love and in the grace of Christ.

Do Not Stand in the Way of Justice

A man tormented by the guilt of murder will be a fugitive till death;
let no one support him (Prov. 28:17).

We have gotten used to seeing news reports of candlelight vigils outside penitentiaries where a death row inmate is to be executed for his crime. Many today consider themselves more compassionate than God, and therefore protest the taking of anyone's life, even one who butchered his victims. But God says that a murderer shall die (Num. 35:16 ; Ex. 21:14).

Most arguments against capital punishment surround the notion that it is not a deterrent. But God does not demand capital punishment on its use as a deterrent. Rather, He commands it because we are made in the image of God. Even in a fallen state, humans have great intrinsic worth in God's sight (Gen. 9:6). The murderer has sinned against God more than he has sinned against the corpse.

Most murderers will be tormented by the guilt of their deed right to their grave. In some cases, it is perhaps more merciful to execute them. Some murderers have committed suicide rather than to face the terrible guilt. Judas Iscariot is a foremost example of that. God will exact His penalty, one way or another.

Scriptural Examples

The cities of refuge. God established six such cities where a person accused of murder could flee to escape the "avenger of blood." The avenger could kill the accused on sight outside the confines of a city of refuge. They provided a safe haven for the accused until he could receive a fair hearing (Num. 35).

Paul and the snake. Even the pagan mind had a sense of the justice of God. Shipwrecked on the island of Malta, Paul had a viper bite his hand, only to shake it off into the fire without ill effect. But before he did so the islanders said, "This man must be a murderer; for though he escaped from the sea, Justice has not allowed him to live" (Acts 28:1-5).

Prayer of Application

Father, many claim to cherish human life, but in their practice degrade it. You have commanded in your Word that whoever takes a life will forfeit his own. Return us to Your Law.

Walk the High Road of Moral Purity

He whose walk is blameless is kept safe, but he whose ways are perverse will suddenly fall (Prov. 28:18).

While we may want to see believers in line one of this proverb, and unbelievers in line two, I want to apply it just to believers. One Christian steers a course of integrity and the other a course of compromise. They both may be heading for heaven, but one is on the high road and the other on the low.

The higher path is not necessarily the easier path. Believers are called to suffer pain in this world and oftentimes the most blameless suffer the most (Job 1:1). But God draws a great distinction between different reasons for suffering (1 Peter 2:20-21). Suffering for righteousness' sake is praiseworthy, but suffering for sin is not. Let's look at two biblical examples of men who took opposite paths.

Scriptural Examples

Two patriarchs: Abraham and Lot. Both of these men trusted God for salvation (2 Peter 2:7). But Lot went down to wicked Sodom with his family, while Abraham stayed in the hills. The destruction of Sodom broke Lot's family apart. On the other hand, God never had one word of rebuke for the righteous Abraham. He trusted God and His promises, and although he saw his share of trouble, he became the ancestor of all who would receive God's free gift of salvation (Gen. 12–15, 19).

Two prophets: Daniel and Jonah. Both of these men were called to serve God outside of the nation Israel—Daniel in Babylon and Jonah in Nineveh. Daniel served with integrity, and even though he suffered, God carried him through it to safety. Jonah, on the other hand, refused God's orders. He was thrown from the ship for his sin and only by God's grace rescued by a giant fish. God brought Jonah through his trials also, but was not pleased with his ways.

Prayer of Application

Dear heavenly Father, keep my feet on the high path of Your law, for I am powerless to follow it unless Your Spirit provides strength and stability for my daily walk.

Set Realistic Goals and WorkToward Them

*He who works his land will have abundant food, but the one who
chases fantasies will have his fill of poverty* (Prov. 28:19).

A good farmer will have his whole year planned. He knows
exactly when to plow and sow and harvest and mend the fences
and feed the animals. He has daily, weekly, monthly, and yearly
goals that he sets for himself and his helpers. Then he gets up in
the morning with one thought in mind: to accomplish what he
has planned. He sets realistic goals and then goes to work. Each
day he accomplishes just a little, so at harvest time his family's
table is set for another year.

The "one who chases fantasies" (or rainbows) believes that
money grows on trees. A man moved to Los Angeles because he
had heard that money flowed freely in L.A. He got off the bus,
saw a $100 bill lying on the sidewalk, and said to it, "You're just
gonna have to lie there, $100 bill. I'm not gonna work my first day
in Los Angeles." This fellow will chase whatever looks promising
at the time without regard for setting reasonable, attainable goals
and then working toward them. As a consequence, his table is
always bare.

Set for yourself worthwhile goals in your business, family,
physical, and spiritual lives, then work toward them diligently.
God honors goals and will take you places with them you never
thought possible.

Scriptural Examples

Solomon and the Temple. Inheriting David's goal for the
construction of a dwelling place for God, Solomon finished the
drawings, planned the work, and built the temple that his father
had longed to see (1 Kings 5:1-6:38).

Paul. Paul was a great goal-setter, and was undoubtedly the
greatest church planter who has ever lived. How did he plant all
those churches? One believer at a time.

Prayer of Application

Dear Lord, it seems so simple, but realistic goals are powerful.
Thank You for setting the goal of the Cross for Jesus, and for His
work in marching toward that dark yet joyous hour.

Walk the Path of True Riches

A faithful man will be richly blessed, but one eager to get rich will not go unpunished (Prov. 28:20).

A person doesn't need to live long to discover the god so many are serving: "the almighty buck." Of course, God commands us to earn a living for our families (1 Tim. 5:8). And note in this proverb riches are not in question. The contrast is that of the faithful person versus the one who is "eager to get rich." The latter wants his dollars now and he doesn't care how he gets them. He will not go unpunished.

The faithful person is the person who seeks to please God. He puts the Word of his Lord into practice. He "pursue[s] righteousness, godliness, faith, love, endurance and gentleness" (1 Tim. 6:9-11). In contrast to this man who dwells safely (Prov. 1:33), is the man who chases "the almighty buck." He "fall[s] into temptation and a trap…into ruin and destruction" (1 Timothy 6:9).

Notice in 1 Timothy 6 money is not the root of all evil, it is the *love* of money. To desire to get money more than to desire to please God means trouble. Many have stumbled at this point, because their greed has led them to unfaithfulness.

God controls all of the riches in the world. If He wants you to have it, you'll get it. If He doesn't, all the work, plans, and chasing in the world won't make you rich. The secret of real wealth, whether one is rich or poor, is to be faithful to God.

Scriptural Examples

The covetous capitalists. Isaiah warned those who would accumulate great tracts of farmland. Although desiring to be rich, their greed would only impoverish them. Their mansions would become desolate and their fields barren (Isa. 5:8-10).

Zacchaeus. He was wealthy due to his penchant to steal. But an encounter with Christ changed his heart, and his eternal destiny as well (Luke 19:2-10).

Prayer of Application

Father, I have followed the quick road to wealth, and it led to ruin and pain. I've found the riches You give are much more valuable and lasting than money. Thank You, Lord.

Beware of that First Step on Greed's Path

To show partiality is not good—yet a man will do wrong for a piece of bread (Prov. 28:21).

In this verse we have the first step down the path to destruction (Prov. 28:20). It's just a little step, but left unchecked it will establish a habit, a character, then ultimate ruin.

God's Law deals heavily with the sin of perverting justice by favoring one person over another (Lev. 19:15, for instance). The problem is most often associated with judges, but no one is exempt from its practice. The first step is to do a small favor for someone as a bribe of "a piece of bread."

A headwaiter accepts a $20 tip from someone and gives your reserved dinner table to him. A policeman tears up the speeding ticket of a prominent businessman with connections at City Hall. A preacher favors a parishioner because of his large contributions. A senator accepts the gift of a trip to South America by oil interests there.

Not amazingly, I suppose, the national economies of some countries are based on a system of bribes and payoffs. U.S. businesspeople doing business abroad are often faced with the moral dilemma of either paying a bribe or returning home empty-handed. Mexico is one such country. There, the practice is called *mordida*. The giving and receiving of bribes is commonplace there. Mexican economic perils are also common knowledge. Could it be that Mexico is but a national example of someone who took the first step along the path of greed and is now reaping the whirlwind?

Scriptural Examples

The false prophetesses of Israel. The Lord told Ezekiel to speak out against these women who prophesied out of their imaginations. Their goal was to ensnare people with lies about God. They profaned Him for a few scraps of bread and treated the people unjustly. Destruction lay ahead (Ezek. 13:17-19).

Prayer of Application

Dear Lord, many are those who are ensnared in this lethal game of bribe giving and taking. I pray that its practice will not overtake America, as it has other nations, to their great peril.

Beware the End of Greed's Rainbow

A stingy man [KJV: "he that hath an evil eye"] is eager to get rich and is unaware that poverty awaits him (Prov. 28:22).

We conclude here the trilogy which began at verse 20 and see that the pot at the end of greed's rainbow is not filled with gold, but with poverty. How ironic that the eagerness for riches leads to the exact opposite. And it's not just monetary wealth that this "pot of poverty" is missing. Lacking also is the sweet fellowship of friends, the joyous peace of knowing God, and the sure foundation of faithfulness and service to Him.

But the pot of poverty isn't entirely empty. There are two consolation prizes for the person with the "evil eye." First, there are reams of regret. He will look back and see how his life was wasted by his foolish search for the elusive buck. Second, he'll find cartons of condemnation. For eternity he will try to flee from the God he snubbed on earth, but he'll never be able to escape His fury.

Christian, what business do we have being stingy, we who have been justified by Jesus' blood? Let's lay up instead treasures in heaven which cannot vanish like the wind (Matt. 6:19-20). The Christian who eagerly pursues only temporal riches will find only loss, when he unwittingly exchanges the eternal for the temporal (1 Cor. 3:15). Follow instead the rainbow of God's true riches.

Scriptural Examples

The rich young ruler. Jesus' words struck right to the heart of this young man's problem. His eyes were on greed's rainbow. He rejected Jesus' advice and went away sad (Matt. 19:16-26).

The rich men. They had fattened themselves at the expense of others. But they were fattened in anticipation of their own slaughter. Their wealth was rotten and corroded. It would testify against them and eat their flesh like fire (James 5:1-5).

Prayer of Application

Father, You are the source of all riches. Help me to freely use all You have given me to bring honor to Your name and to further Your Kingdom on earth. Keep me from stinginess, Lord.

Consider the Long-Term Value of Rebuke

He who rebukes a man will in the end [KJV: "afterward"] gain more favor than he who has a flattering tongue (Prov. 28:23).

I must confess that I am not very adept at rebuke. I would rather not take the chance of harming a friendship, so many times I just let the opportunity pass. Do you have that problem too? If so, this proverb is ours to study, chew over, and act upon.

The flattering tongue brings momentary pleasure perhaps, but in the end leaves a bitter aftertaste (Prov. 26:28; 29:5). The gentle rebuke may bring momentary bitterness, but afterward it produces a harvest of righteousness and peace (Heb. 12:11). If we could only see the long-term benefits of rebuke we would be more receptive to encouraging others in righteousness.

A non-believing friend of mine once commented that he couldn't understand why some studied the Bible constantly. I told him that the Bible was written to rebuke us in our sin and to lead us to the gospel of Jesus Christ (2 Tim. 3:15). After we're saved, it is to teach and rebuke us, to correct us, and to train us in righteousness (2 Tim 3:16).

Likewise, we need to rebuke others for sin in their lives. We should never do it to show some supposed superiority. Conversely, we are to approach others humbly and prayerfully, knowing that we share the same weaknesses.

Scriptural Examples

Peter and Paul. In 2 Peter 3:15, Peter speaks of his "dear brother Paul." The rebuke which Peter had suffered from Paul is recorded in Galatians 2:11-19. Peter proved the truth of this proverb through this incident.

The Corinthians and Paul. He rebuked them for allowing a member to live in sin with his father's wife. Later, we find that the church had set the matter straight. Paul did not overlook sin, but rebuked his converts (1 Cor. 5; 2 Cor. 2:1-10).

Prayer of Application

Dear Lord, thank You for Your Word, which is profitable in every way for our edification and rebuke. Thank You also for the godly rebuke of faithful Christians who care for me.

Care for Those Who Cared for You

He who robs his father or mother and says, "It's not wrong"—he is partner to him who destroys (Prov. 28:24).

God takes our relationship with our parents very seriously. Parents have the awesome responsibility of raising their children (Eph. 6:4). But He has given equal responsibility to children. We are to honor our mothers and fathers, to respect and obey them (Ex. 20:12; Eph. 6:1). To steal from them is a gross violation of the fifth commandment. But then to say, "It's not wrong," or "It's perfectly legal," is to compound the sin's seriousness. Interestingly enough, the Bible records a perfect example of this sin in both Matthew 15:1-9 and Mark 7:1-13.

Some Pharisees and teachers of the Law accused Jesus' disciples of not washing themselves prior to eating. Jesus returned their accusation, saying that they had overturned the Law of God by teaching regulations made up by humans.

He said that instead of honoring their parents by supporting them in their old age, they had created a loophole in the law. If they devoted a certain possession to God, then the possession was called *corban*, and thus excluded from what was owed to the provision of their parents. They were stealing from their parents what was properly due them and calling it legal. Do you think these hypocrites ever read this proverb?

Many of my friends are faced with the prospect of aging parents. Our generation, like all those before it, needs to realize that God requires that we be faithful to them (1 Tim. 5:4-8). Those who rob their parents are vandals in God's sight.

Scriptural Examples

Jacob's sons. They wronged Joseph by selling him into slavery. But consider the calamity it brought their father, Jacob, who grieved at length for the son he was told had died in the jaws of a wild animal. These boys stole more than money from their dad (Gen. 37).

Prayer of Application

Father, thank You for my parents. They are with You now, but I have many friends whose parents are living. Give them the grace not to forsake those who lovingly cared for them.

Trust God for True Prosperity

25) A greedy man stirs up dissension [KJV: "strife"] but he who trusts in the Lord will prosper. 26) He who trusts in himself is a fool, but he who walks in wisdom is kept safe (Prov. 28:25-26).

The greedy man doesn't always stir up trouble; only when he doesn't get his way. But don't let him be the boss and the fur begins to fly. The greedy man trusts in his wealth, his position, his manipulating and negotiating skills, and his intellect. In other words, he trusts in himself. He is a fool.

On the other hand, the person who trusts in the Lord and walks in His wisdom prospers and is kept safe. In what ways will the faithful prosper? The fool sees prosperity in a large bank account, a privileged position, an exalted title or lifestyle. But for the child of God, these are secondary to his real interests.

The person who trusts God prospers beyond the fool's understanding. True prosperity is the assurance and peace that God is his friend and loves him (Phil. 4:7). It is confidence that God has prepared a place for him in eternal mansions (John 14:2-3), and will meet his every need in this life (Matt. 6:30). It is the joy of knowing the Creator intimately through His Holy Word.

True prosperity is a clear conscience, and the certainty of His forgiveness when we slip (1 John 1:9). It is freedom from slavery to sin (Rom. 6:18). Finally, true prosperity is in the fellowship of the Holy Spirit and of fellow believers.

Scriptural Examples

Haman and Mordecai. What a contrast ! Haman stirred up strife for the Jews in his greedy pride, yet was thwarted by the wisdom of the humble Mordecai. In the end, Mordecai was elevated to the position that Haman vacated (book of Esther).

Diotrephes. The visible church is not without its fools. John tells of this man who stirred up strife because he wanted to have preeminence in a local congregation (3 John 9).

Prayer of Application

Dear God, You are the source of all that is. They are fools who think they can find joy, peace, or prosperity apart from Your hand. Thank You, Lord, for Your exceeding goodness.

Let's Get Rid of the Fear of Poverty

He who gives to the poor will lack nothing, but he who closes his eyes to them receives many curses (Prov. 28:27).

The person who freely gives to the poor will lack nothing, but woe to him who closes his eyes. The Lord is very serious about sharing our material possessions with the poor. It is an oft-repeated theme of Scripture. (James 5:1-4, for instance.)

I'm afraid that we who are so willing to "share our faith" with an unbeliever, or to "share a verse" with a hurting friend, don't want to share our possessions with the poor. Now I'm no expert on fear, but I've looked into my own heart and come up with the title principle above. I think it is the fear of being poor that causes us to "close our eyes" to those in need. If I give too much, I'll have nothing left for myself. Do you ever feel that way? We know intellectually that only God can provide for our needs, but we won't put it into shoe leather and make it real.

In Acts 4:32-37, men and women sold their real estate and other possessions and shared with everyone in the church, as each had need. How about putting those verses of Acts into action in our lives? After all, what we "own" is only lent to us by the Lord to be stewarded according to His will. This proverb is a clear expression of that will, and it contains two promises. If we give generously, God will take care of us generously. If we don't, we bring upon ourselves many curses. Let's quit fearing and start giving! Let's trust in the Lord with all our hearts (Prov. 3:5-6), and with our bank accounts.

Scriptural Examples

Nabal. He was asked to share a few of his belongings with David and his men. He refused, and spent what he had on himself. In a few days, he felt the curse of God (1 Sam. 25).

The rich young ruler. This fellow didn't have money—it had him. He was so concerned with having enough, he refused the only thing worth having (Luke 18:18-27).

Prayer of Application

Dear Lord and Supplier of all my needs, forgive me for not trusting You more fully for all that the future will bring. Help me to live by faith and be an example to others in trusting You.

Become Involved in the Political Process

When the wicked rise to power, people go into hiding; but when the wicked perish, the righteous thrive (Prov. 28:28).

In Proverbs 28:12, we saw almost this same verse and drew a spiritual, end-time principle. But what specific message does this verse have for us today? How can we learn from it and put what we learn into action? I've drawn a principle which I hope will help us to do that.

The popular end-time view called "dispensational premillennialism" teaches that the rapture of the church will come seven years before Christ's ultimate return. I believe that this view has had the effect of causing some to say, "Why should I get involved? Let's just pray for the rapture and quit trying to be 'light and salt' " (Matt. 5:13-14). The problem is that when we do that, we get "trampled under the feet of men."

Now, granted, the abortion issue has struck a nerve in the Church and has caused many to get involved. Unfortunately, some have become like those they wish to stop. But if a righteous government had been in power in the 1960s, appointing righteous men and women onto the Supreme Court, the *Roe v. Wade* decision of 1973 that brought wholesale abortion upon us might have never been made. Think of all the murders that would have been prevented by a few properly persuaded votes! If we don't get involved in electing men and women of faith to power, and in supporting fervently those who are already elected, we may really have to "go into hiding," looking back on the days of abortion as the "good old days."

Scriptural Examples

Haman and the Jews. Mordecai and Esther got involved in the political process back in Babylon, and Haman's plot that caused the Jews to go into hiding was stopped short. Righteous rule was restored and the people celebrated (Est. 8).

Prayer of Application

Dear Lord, thank You for the freedom we have in the United States. Revive us, Lord, and allow this country to thrive once again as "the land of the free and the home of the brave."

Chapter Twenty-nine

Proverbs and Anger

When the subject of anger is broached in a class or at a conference, I am invariably asked, "Isn't some anger good?" Usually the person who asks the question is thinking of the anger our Lord displayed while cleansing the temple of money-changers (John 2:13-16). Yes, some anger is good. The crucial difference between good anger and sinful anger is the fruit each yields. Righteous anger yields a motivation to act righteously, while unrighteous anger "stirs up dissension" (Prov. 29:22). We must be careful not to lead ourselves to believe we are being righteous when our "righteous anger" is really a mask for spiritual pride that separates us from others. Abortion and euthanasia should make us angry, and our anger should lead us to participate in the fight against these evils.

Proverbs 29:11 speaks to what is usually true about anger: "A fool gives full vent to his anger, but a wise man keeps himself under control." But won't "stuffing" anger lead to serious physical problems like a heart attack? Perhaps. But the wise person doesn't stuff his anger. His would-be anger is dissipated by his understanding God is in control of every situation. He relies fully on the sovereign Lord of the universe to avenge him. The wise person understands that a hot temper is the province of the fool (Prov. 29:22).

Beware of a Spiritual Stiff Neck

A man who remains stiff-necked after many rebukes will suddenly be destroyed—without remedy (Prov. 29:1).

Sometimes when I get up in the morning, this old grey head is being held up by a very stiff neck. But the spiritual stiff neck is not the result of sleeping in a contorted fashion—it is the result of living that way. Its remedy is not chiropractic help or a muscle relaxant, but repentance and submission to the Lord.

Our God is very gracious and compassionate, slow to anger and abounding in love, a God who relents from sending calamity (Jonah 4:2). I'm afraid that because He is the God of "many rebukes," some think that He lacks either the power or the resolve to punish sin. As Paul says in Romans 2:4, people "show contempt for the riches of [God's] kindness, tolerance and patience, not realizing that [His] kindness leads [them] toward repentance." The "rebukes" in this verse are manifestations of God's kindness. But His kindness has its limits.

And you who call yourself a Christian, are you living in sin? Are you consistently violating God's commandments? Know that God is not mocked, that He will not allow your sin to continue, but will visit His quick and sure discipline upon you. Your loss, even though perhaps not of salvation itself, will be eternal, and also beyond recapture (1 Cor. 3:15).

Scriptural Examples

The people of Nineveh. How different were these Gentiles, who, upon hearing a few sermons by that stiff-necked prophet Jonah, humbled themselves in sackcloth and ashes and softened their necks in repentance and faith (Jonah 3:6-10).

The people of Israel. They were often backslidden. The Lord even calls them "stiff-necked" in Exodus 32:9. But the nation Israel foreshadows the church, and so we, too, need to beware that we do not fall after the example of their rebellion (Heb. 3:7-15).

Prayer of Application

Father, You have called us who have trusted Christ for salvation to a life of obedience. Help me, Lord, by the power of Your Spirit, to live that life. Help me also to teach it to others.

Get Involved in World Missions

When the righteous thrive, the people rejoice; when the wicked rule, the people groan (Prov. 29:2).

Even though the natural person will badmouth Christianity, he relishes the thought of living in a land where the Word of God reigns over the lives of its citizens. He wants God's benefits, but rejects His requirements. In most countries of the world today, the wicked are ruling and the people are groaning. The suffering of the people gives evidence of the leader's sin.

Political solutions rarely work. Typically they just cause more problems. The only solution is to change people's hearts, because that is where the problem has its root. I know of only one person who can change hearts: the Lord Jesus Christ. Only Christ, working through the media of the Holy Spirit, the Word of God, and even people like us, can change hearts.

God's "kindness, justice, and righteousness" (Jer. 9:23-24) are to be transported throughout the world (Matt. 28:19-20). How? By people like you and me. Now, we can't all go to the foreign field, but we can pray for and financially support those who can go and who are called to go. Get involved in world missions, to the end that the righteous everywhere will thrive and the people will rejoice.

Scriptural Examples

The Romans. The ancient Roman world was a paradigm of pagan wickedness and immorality. The rulers were egocentric and corrupt and treated people with cruelty and disinterest. But one day, a small home church was planted in Rome. I suspect Paul had something to do with converting the people who went to Rome, starting this mission by long distance. Within a few centuries, Rome became a thriving center for the Christian faith. Even the government became ostensibly Christian following the emperor Constantine's conversion (Rom. 16).

Prayer of Application

Lord God, You have commanded us to take Your gospel message to a lost and groaning world. Show me where I can help and let me have a part in bringing rejoicing to the world.

Bring Joy to Your Heavenly Father

A man who loves wisdom brings joy to his father, but a companion of prostitutes squanders his wealth (Prov. 29:3).

Here again is an oft-repeated proverb. The child who rejects wisdom, and instead loves fleshly things, saddens his godly parents and squanders the wealth that could be his.

Our ultimate parent is God. He is the Father of all in the sense that all are created in His image (Gen. 1:26). In reality, He is the Father only of those who believe (Rom. 4:11). It may surprise some to think that God experiences joy, but it is true. He rejoices over the works of His hands (Ps. 104:31); His bride, the church (Isa. 62:5); Jerusalem and its people (Isa. 65:18-19); and over those His hands have been mighty to save (Zeph. 3:17). These are but a few examples, but they all point to the one cause of God's rejoicing: He rejoices in those who do His will.

Jesus said, "If you love me, you will obey what I command" (John 14:15). In other words, Jesus is saying that "love" means nothing unless it is expressed in good works. The person who loves wisdom puts wisdom into practice. This brings God joy.

On the other hand, it might be said that a "companion of prostitutes" or thieves or drunkards loves foolishness. What a man loves is exhibited in his daily life. It's as simple as that. Jesus said, "You shall know them by their fruit" (Matt. 7:16).

Scriptural Examples

Reuben. Jacob's firstborn son slept with Jacob's concubine, an act which caused Jacob much grief. As Jacob was about to die, he reminded Reuben of his sin and chastened him. His wealth went to another (Gen. 35:22; 49:3-4).

Jesus. What joy was brought to the Father's heart as His only begotten Son fulfilled the work which He was sent to do. Jesus, as God incarnate, set His face toward the cross to redeem the lost, and to experience the "joy set before Him" (Heb. 12:2).

Prayer of Application

Sovereign Lord, I want to bring You joy. But I know that I fail You and do not love You as I ought. Continue to make me more like Your precious Son, my Lord Jesus Christ.

Beware of Self-Interest Before Justice

By justice a king gives a country stability, but one who is greedy for bribes tears it down (Prov. 29:4).

Special interest groups wield extraordinary power in America today. Across our land, people are paid to lobby our elected officials for the benefit of "single issue" organizations. There's nothing wrong with this, but if they do it at the expense of justice for all, then it will ultimately tear America down.

Maybe I've become cynical, but there seems to be one question in legislators' minds today: "How will my vote help or hurt my chances for reelection?" Now I realize that's a generalization, but I don't think I'm far from the truth. Even if a military base is totally superfluous, the chances of the hometown legislator supporting its closure are slim and none.

Let's rewrite this proverb: "By justice a Congress gives America stability, but those whose main ambition is to be reelected tear it down." You may disagree with the words, but the voice of the proverb is unchanged in its rewriting.

This proverb applies to all of us as citizens and parents, employees or employers. The foundation of society is justice, and the foundation of justice is the Lord God (Jer. 9:24). All who fling justice aside for self-interest are destroying our country.

Scriptural Examples

The king the people wanted. The Israelites clamored for a king. The Lord told them what life would be like under such a king. He would demand their sons and daughters, fields and olive groves, cattle and donkeys, and their servants for his own use. They themselves would become his slaves (1 Sam. 8:11-19).

The kings the people got. Space does not permit a list of all the kings of Judah and Israel. But very few, David and Solomon among them, ruled in justice. The vast majority of their kings tore the countries down in greed, as the Lord said they would.

Prayer of Application

Father, thank You for the men and women in our government who serve selflessly and in justice. Help us to weed out those who care only for self-benefit. Revive America, Lord.

Beware of Flattery's Trap

Whoever flatters his neighbor is spreading a net for his feet
(Prov. 29:5).

I'm sure you, like I, have had a friend like "Florence the Flatterer." She (or he) phones you and spends the first several minutes telling you how much you are admired and respected, how beautiful your children are, etc. You can almost feel the spring being stretched tight. At last, the trap is sprung. "Oh, by the way, would you do me a little favor?"

We all want to be praised and encouraged. There's nothing wrong with that unless we seek praise in an inordinate fashion. But the flatterer preys upon this natural human propensity. The term "flattery" connotes insincere or exaggerated praise, like the honey of Proverbs 25:16, which makes you sick to your stomach. If you begin to believe it, the trap is already closing down upon you (Prov. 27:14).

The best answer to flattery is, "Let all the praise go to Jesus, because without Him I'm nothing." By deflecting someone's insincere praise onto Christ, you avoid the trap that the flatterer seeks to spring, and may provide an opportunity to witness.

Scriptural Examples

Ziba and David. Ziba flattered David with words and gifts, and then sprung his trap. He lied about his boss Mephibosheth, and the king bought it hook, line, and sinker. He gave Ziba all that had belonged to his master (2 Sam. 16:1-4).

Ahab and the false prophets. The wicked king was flattered by the false prophesies of his "yes" men. Micaiah had the true Word of the Lord in his mouth and told the king that which he did not want to hear (1 Kings 22:9-23).

The smooth talking Romans. These flatterers plotted to deceive the minds of naive people. Paul warned the Roman church about the obstacles these men put up which were contrary to pure doctrine (Rom. 16:17-18).

Prayer of Application

Father, help me to see through the plans of the flattering tongue and avoid its trap. I am a sinner saved only by Your grace. Without Jesus, I couldn't even take my next breath.

Know the Joy of Peace with God

6) The evil man is snared by his own sin, but a righteous one can sing and be glad. 7) The righteous care about justice for the poor, but the wicked have no such concern (Prov. 29:6-7).

Verse 7 is merely an illustration of the truth of verse 6. We've all seen evil people merrily singing, but their gladness is shallowly anchored in mud: they live only for themselves. They go their merry way, unaware of the trap being set. On the other hand, the righteous are anchored on the Rock, the sure hope of salvation in Jesus Christ (Heb. 6:18-20). Their song of gladness stems from their being at peace with God. Because of this peace, they care about justice. Their gladness will be eternal.

How does peace with God manifest itself now? First, there is a sense of harmony between the Christian and God. Fear has lost its grip. He is calm and stable, no longer at war with God or his neighbor. Second, the Christian has a sense of adequacy, of knowing that Christ has promised to fill all of his needs and never to leave or forsake him. Third, there is a sense of freedom, as he is no longer enslaved by sin. He has a clear conscience and knows that God has forgiven him and has the power to keep him from falling. Finally, there is an overarching sense of purpose to his life. He knows that every moment has eternal consequences, so he is not lost in meaninglessness. He therefore seeks justice for the poor.

Scriptural Examples

The blessed of the Father. Jesus told of a day when His sheep would be separated from the goats. Then the blessed of His Father would be given their long-awaited inheritance. These are they who fed and clothed Him, who visited Him in sickness and in prison. "When did we do this Lord?" they will ask. He will respond, "Whatever you did for one of the least of these brothers of mine, you did for me" (Matt. 25:34-40).

Prayer of Application

Lord, before I knew You I reveled in shallow self-interest. But You opened my eyes to the trap. Thank you for the peace that floods my heart, and grows more each day as I learn of You.

Be Ready to "Stand in the Gap"

Mockers stir up a city, [KJV: "Scornful men bring a city into a snare"]
but wise men turn away anger (Prov. 29:8).

Ezekiel penned these words of God: "The people of the land practice extortion and commit robbery; they oppress the poor and needy and mistreat the alien, denying them justice. I looked for a man among them who would build up the wall and stand before me in the gap on behalf of the land so I would not have to destroy it, but I found none. So I will pour out my wrath on them and consume them with my fiery anger...declares the Sovereign Lord" (Ezek. 22:29-31).

The mocker who stirs up the city is the person who rejects God and serves himself. He plays by the rules of society only because he's afraid of getting punished, or as the rules serve his needs. He may seek justice for others, but not because it honors God. America is full of these people. They want God's benefits, but they don't want to know or serve Him. Because of this, God's wrath will surely come. Unless...

Unless the people of God stand in the gap in prayer and full commitment to Him. He stands ready to respond. Pray for revival in your own heart, your church, neighborhood, city, state, country, and world. We need the grace of God shed on every heart, so that His fiery anger doesn't consume the land.

Scriptural Examples

Moses. Following the Israelites' sin against God in the wilderness, the Lord was ready to destroy the entire nation and start over again. But Moses stood in the gap and pled with the Lord for the people's lives. The Lord relented and let them live (Ex. 32:10-14).

The king of Nineveh. He believed Jonah's report and issued a declaration. He called for all people to repent and to call upon God. "Who knows?" he said, "God may yet relent and...we will not perish." God heard their prayers (Jonah 3:6-10).

Prayer of Application

Heavenly Father, thank You for the unspeakable privilege of prayer. Help me to pray more. Forgive my lack of faith and lack of love that often causes my prayerlessness.

Don't Try to Argue with a Fool

If a wise man goes to court [KJV: "contendeth"] with a fool, the fool rages and scoffs, and there is no peace (Prov. 29:9).

I once had a disagreement over a sewer line. The sewer contractor argued that the problem was poor soil compaction. I argued he used faulty installation procedures. We went to arbitration. The disagreement was settled in equity and in a calm, sincere manner. The contractor was an honest man who was ready to accept the arbitrator's decision.

The fool is different. He doesn't care about rational argument and will use any method at his disposal to win. Some use intimidation. They shout with rage at your reasonable approach. They may attempt to confuse things by logical fallacy or specious arguments. They may throw accusations in your face to keep you off balance. The fool will laugh at you, shout at you, mock you, accuse you, bully you, and maybe even punch you, but he will not calmly face you in logical debate. Unless, of course, he's right and you're wrong. It's wise to avoid any contact with a fool, but that's pretty tough in this world. My advice, if you find yourself in a dispute with one, is cut your losses and try to extricate yourself any way you can. An argument with a fool is tough to win.

Scriptural Examples

Nehemiah and Sanballat. Sanballat mocked those who were rebuilding Jerusalem, accusing them of rebellion against Babylon. With Tobiah, he laughed at the efforts of the Jews and even threatened them. But Nehemiah refused to be drawn into their spurious scheme, and rather trusted God to see the work through to its completion (Neh. 2:10,19; 4:1-10; 6:1-9).

Stephen and the Synagogue of Freedmen. They could not stand up against Stephen's wisdom. So they resorted to the arguments of fools. They falsely accused him of blasphemy and stirred up the people against him (Acts 6:8-14).

Prayer of Application

Dear God, protect me and my family from the scornful folly of fools. This is a litigious world, but I thank You for Your ability to shut the mouth of the raging and scoffing fool.

Be Prepared to Suffer for the Gospel

Bloodthirsty men hate a man of integrity and seek to kill the up- right [KJV: "but the just seek his soul"] (Prov. 29:10).

From the beginning, the upright person—made so only by the grace of God—has been the focus of the scorn and hatred of bloodthirsty people. Why? Because in their hatred of the Creator, people also hate His children. We are a constant reminder of their own sinfulness and ultimate destruction. Brothers and sisters, there's a war going on, and every person on this planet is involved. You are either a hater of the True God and therefore hate His people, or you love the True God and His people. The latter group seeks the best for the former group, but the former seeks to kill the latter. Think of the example of Jesus.

Christians are their "brother's keepers" (Gen. 4:9). Ironside says, "This concern for the blessing of those about him is one of the first and strongest evidences that a man has been born of God" (p. 419). Paul says, "God did not give us a spirit of timidity, but a spirit of power, of love and of self-discipline. So do not be ashamed to testify about our Lord, or ashamed of me his prisoner. But join with me in suffering for the gospel, by the power of God" (2 Tim. 1:7-8). Have you suffered for the gospel? If not, perhaps you haven't lived for it.

Scriptural Examples

Cain and Abel. The stage was set from the beginning when Cain murdered his brother Abel. Cain's own thoughts and actions were evil, and his brother's righteous (Gen. 3:15; 1 John 3:12).

Jezebel and Elijah. Jezebel vowed to hunt Elijah down and kill him. The prophet ran for his life, hiding in caves and rocks until his spirit was strengthened by his God (1 Kings 19:2-18).

Herod and John the Baptist. Herod hated John and kept him in prison. One day the wicked king responded to a request of his queen and chopped John's head off (Matt. 14:3-11).

Prayer of Application

Heavenly Father, thank You for the ministry of reconciliation. But the gospel message is like a sword, and many of us will suffer for it. Give us strength that we may be bold for You.

Let Wisdom Overcome Your Anger

A fool gives full vent to his anger, but a wise man keeps himself under control (Prov. 29:11).

Derek Kidner points out that the verb translated "keeps" has the sense of "anger overcome, not merely checked" (p. 175). The wise man is not so just because he can hold his tongue. No, the wise man has learned to deal with anger at its root cause.

Pride is the root of sinful anger, along with greed, jealousy, and envy. It comes from frustration, when things aren't going one's way. Whatever the proximate cause of anger, at its heart is self-interest that shuts out the interests of others. Modern psychiatry says that venting one's anger is healthy, because it lowers the blood pressure. While that may be true, how much better it would be never to be bothered with anger in the first place. But is that just wishful thinking?

I don't believe it is. First, we must understand that God is in absolute control of every detail of this universe. Nothing escapes His eye, and all history is part of His plan for the ages. Second, God must put His love in your sinful heart, a love that disregards self. Anger springs from self-love. If you get your mind off of yourself and on to others, out goes anger and its ally, fear. Finally, you must understand that nothing ever happens to a Christian that is not for his ultimate good (Rom. 8:28-29). Even seemingly awful circumstances have at their center a loving, caring Father who has our best interests at heart.

Scriptural Examples

Joseph and his brothers. Joseph had every "right" to be angry with his brothers who sold him into slavery. Instead, he saw the hand of God at work in the whole matter. He had compassion on them and knew that God had all their best interests at heart. God had taken their sin and turned it around for their ultimate benefit (Gen 42-45; 50:20).

Prayer of Application

Lord, thank You for gradually taking anger from me over the years. I still have problems on the freeway when people follow too closely. Help me to pray for them, and get out of the way.

Do Not Manipulate Others

If a ruler listens to lies, all his officials become wicked
(Prov. 29:12).

The sinful underlings of a ruler have a tendency to change into whatever the ruler wants them to be. If he wants to hear lies, they will tell him what he wants to hear. If he wants to be flattered, they will flatter him. They will do whatever is necessary to shore up their position in his court. They will try to manipulate him to control the situation.

Were you ever on a date and sensed you were being manipulated? The person was warm one week and cold the next, playing hard to get. You sensed that your date controlled every situation by his or her mood changes. I once had a high-ranking employee who would say in meetings whatever he thought I wanted to hear. Then, when he went back to his desk, he would do just the opposite. Eventually, I had to fire him. He was manipulating me.

Be yourself! Treat your boss, your spouse, your friends, your employees, and every one else in the same way: openly and honestly. Be transparent. Don't be like a chameleon who changes "colors" in order to deceive and manipulate others.

Scriptural Examples

Jehoshaphat, Ahab and his prophets, and Micaiah. Judah and Israel joined forces to make war on Aram. Ahab summoned 400 prophets who told him the lie he wanted to hear. But Jehoshaphat insisted on a prophet of the Lord. Ahab reluctantly sent for Micaiah, who was no chameleon. He spoke openly and honestly before the kings, correctly predicting failure (1 Kings 22:6).

Shadrach, Meshach, and Abednego. Nebuchadnezzar ordered all in his kingdom to fall down and worship the image he had made of himself. These Jews refused, openly declaring their allegiance to God. They were thrown into the fiery furnace for refusing to perjure themselves to please the king (Dan. 3:1-20).

Prayer of Application

Jesus, You never change: the same yesterday, today, and forever. May I never alter my behavior to manipulate or control situations or people. Help me to trust You for all outcomes.

Treat the Poor with Justice and Equity

13) The poor man and the oppressor have this in common: The Lord gives sight to the eyes of both. 14) If a king judges the poor with fairness, his throne will always be secure (Prov. 29:13-14).

At first glance, these proverbs seem to deal with two different issues. The first says that God has made all people equal in His sight (Prov. 22:2), while the second instructs kings how to maintain their thrones. But their real commonality is that they both deal with ways of treating the poor. In verse 13, the poor are oppressed. In verse 14, they are treated fairly.

One thing characterizes the poor of every generation: their disenfranchisement. They have very little power in making social change. If oppressed, they rarely have an alternative but to bear it. What their foolish oppressor fails to realize is that the poor are his equals in God's sight. God gives sight, and life, to all. The only real difference is the disparity of wealth and position, both of which are also gifts of God. So, what we have is a man who foolishly uses his God-given power to oppress those who have no power. This is utmost foolishness.

Conversely, the wise king sees the poor as his brothers and as his responsibility before God. He therefore treats them as God would lead him to treat them: with justice and equity. He is blessed by God and reigns securely.

Scriptural Examples

King Solomon. He asked the Lord for a discerning mind, so that he would be able to apply just principles in his reign. His reign is a type of the reign of a King who will come again to bring judgment upon all oppressors (2 Chron. 1:9-13).

King Jesus. It is King Jesus who sits upon that throne. What Solomon could not do because of his weakness, Jesus will do forever in perfect righteousness and justice. Foolish oppressors beware, even now He reigns! (Ps. 9; Heb. 1:8-9; Rev. 22).

Prayer of Application

Lord, thank You that Jesus reigns, and will reign eternally. We see much injustice toward the poor. Help me to move counter to this world's ways and be a representative of the King.

Spare the Rod and Spank the Parents

15) The rod of correction imparts wisdom, but a child left to himself disgraces his mother. 17) Discipline your son, and he will give you peace; he will bring delight to your soul (Prov. 29:15, 17).

The book of Proverbs consistently repeats a warning to parents (Prov. 13:24; 17:21; 19:18; 22:15; 23:13-16). Something will be broken in your home; either your child's will, or your heart. The stripes from the rod of correction will either land on your child's rear end, or on your own (Bridges p. 573). If it is the latter, then both you and your child will feel the pain.

Parents, don't neglect to learn from these examples God has given us in His Word. Here are a just few of them:

Scriptural Examples

Abraham. God chose Abraham to be a blessing to all the nations on the earth by directing "his children and his household after him to keep the way of the Lord by doing what is right and just" (Gen. 18:18-19).

Eli and his sons. Hophni and Phineas sinned wickedly. The Lord laid their failing at Eli's feet. He had failed to restrain and discipline them, and paid the consequences (1 Sam. 3:13).

David and Adonijah. Adonijah tried to set himself up as king, because his father failed to restrain him (1 Kings 1:6).

Paul. He argues from his position as spiritual father of the saints in Corinth. Like regular children, these saints were infants in their understanding. Paul saw the need for discipline, and in his letter to them, administered it (1 Cor. 4:15).

Timothy. This young man was disciplined from infancy in God's ways by his mom and grandmother. I'd say he turned out rather well (2 Tim. 1:5; 3:15)!

Our heavenly Father. He disciplines us because He loves us. If He doesn't, we are illegitimate. Since God disciplines His children, how can we fail to discipline ours? (Heb. 12:4-11).

Prayer of Application

Father, help us parents to deal with our children in the same way You deal with us. In Your love, You test us and strengthen us and cause us to grow in the likeness of Your Son.

Rejoice to Be on the Winning Team!

When the wicked thrive, so does sin, but the righteous will see their downfall (Prov. 29:16).

Back in my college days, the New York Yankees were a perennial powerhouse. I had been a Chicago Cubs fan from my youth. The Cubbies were perennial losers. I hated the Yanks, but my best friend loved New York. One day I asked him why. "Because they are winners," he replied, "and I like winners." I thought that made sense, so that day I became a Yankees fan…well, at least until the Dodgers and Sandy Koufax moved to L.A.

If one could count up the apparent score in the game of life today, it would appear that the "wicked" are ahead "60-zip." Our cities teem with crime. Sin abounds. People reject God and cling to worthless idols. We might be tempted to think that the battle was over, and that the righteous have been defeated, conquered by the hosts of evil. But the Bible says the game isn't over.

Jesus said that it will not be the strong or the rich or the super intelligent who will inherit the earth. No, He said that it will be the meek (Matt. 5:5). Who are the meek? The meek are those who have humbly put their trust in Jesus Christ, that through Him the victory over sin and evil has been won. The game clock is still ticking, and those who are Christ's are down in the trenches getting dirty. But one day soon, the whistle will blow and the game will be over. On that day, the righteous meek will witness the downfall of the wicked.

Scriptural Examples

The pre-Flood people. Their millions were teamed up against God and a man named Noah. It looked like they would prevail until it began to rain (Gen 6–7).

The Babel builders. These guys were the "movers and shakers" of their day. The only problem was that they liked to do their moving and shaking in opposition to God (Gen. 11:1-9).

Prayer of Application

Father, thank You for the Cross. It is foolishness to a world that seems to be winning now, but when Christ returns in power, they will cringe in fear and find no place to hide.

Covet Divine Instruction

Where there is no revelation, the people cast off restraint; but blessed is he who keeps the law (Prov. 29:18).

The KJV translates the first line of this verse: "Where there is no vision, the people perish." That translation has led many to think it's speaking of a vision for the future. But the proverb's "vision" is really divine revelation, or more precisely, "instruction." The Hebrew word *para* is the word used in Exodus 32:25 when the Israelites "cast off restraint" (see below). This is emphasized by the antithetical parallelism of the second phrase: "but blessed is he who keeps the law."

When the Ten Commandments were ripped from the walls of our public schools in America, the skids were greased for America's descent into lawlessness. This act of violence against God's Law has had exactly the result predicted by this proverb. Our public schools have disintegrated, and with them the moral and spiritual character of our nation.

The school bulletin board is not the only venue where God's instruction has been thrown out. In many churches across America, the clear teachings of God have been set aside in favor of "politically correct" human teachings (1 Tim. 4:3). If that happens in your church, you can be sure that your congregation is in decline as people begin to cast off restraint.

Scriptural Examples

The Israelites. When Moses returned from the mountain with the first tablets of the Law, he found the people had "cast off restraint" and were "running wild." Aaron had succumbed to the demands of the evil crowd and had constructed a golden calf for the people after the desires of their own evil hearts (Ex. 32:19-25).

The Israelites. The prophet Hosea spoke of a time when the people of God would be destroyed for lack of knowledge as they rejected the divine instruction of God (Hos. 4:1-6).

Prayer of Application

Father, thank You for Your Word, a gracious gift to us. We need Your counsel before us on a consistent basis. Without its clear moral instruction, restraints are removed.

Back Up Your Words With Action

A servant cannot be corrected by mere words; though he understands, he will not respond (Prov. 29:19).

The godly servant should respond to the words of his master without delay. But alas, such is not our natural inclination. Most will not respond to mere words. To prove my point, get out on a freeway. How fast is everyone going without regard to the threat of a speeding ticket? I rest my case.

Mom tells little Johnny to take out the trash. Johnny refuses. Mom raises her voice, but still no action. Finally she says, "Young man, you just wait until your father gets home!! You'll get it then!" But Johnny knows he won't "get it." Sure enough, dad comes home and takes the trash out himself.

"The heart is deceitful above all things and beyond cure" (Jer. 17:9). Left to ourselves, we are "beyond cure." But God has provided the cure in the person of Jesus Christ and His atoning work on the cross. The new birth gives people a desire to do God's will. As His servants, we should respond to God's words without delay. If we don't, guess what. Our heavenly Father stands ready to back up His words with swift but loving discipline (Heb. 12:5-11).

Scriptural Examples

Joseph. Sold into Egypt, Joseph found himself a servant. His service was exemplary and rejected the sexual advances of his master's wife. He suffered for his loyalty to God, but in due time was raised to great heights (Gen. 37; 39; 41).

Job. Job was a servant of God and a master of men. But following his beating at Satan's hands, he complained, "I summon my servant, but he does not respond, though I beg him with my own mouth" (Job 19:16).

Jonah. He claimed to be God's servant, but when given God's instructions to go to Nineveh and preach there, he headed off in the opposite direction (the book of Jonah).

Prayer of Application

Father, help me as a leader to stand ready to back up my words with actions. But also help me to willingly follow Your commands and the commands of those in authority over me.

Beware of "Foot in Mouth" Disease

Do you see a man who speaks in haste? There is more hope for a fool than for him (Prov. 29:20).

"Foot in mouth" disease is closely related to that common ailment "diarrhea of the mouth," and should be avoided like the plague. Its symptoms occur first in the mind. A sufferer begins to think he knows pretty much everything about everything. Suddenly his mouth opens, and before he can get his brain in gear, out comes a gusher of words. No tourniquet or coagulant yet devised can stop the oral bleeding that ensues. On most occasions, these outbursts are followed by a reddening of the facial skin tissues as the sufferer's foot glides slowly from the ground to his mouth and becomes firmly imbedded between his upper and lower jaws. Those so infected should go on a strict diet of humble pie until the symptoms disappear.

I confess I am sometimes susceptible to this disease, and am forced to ask God to forgive me. I pray He is cleansing me of it, but just when I think I'm healed, it's b-a-a-a-ck. Do you have this problem? We need to weigh carefully the words that we speak, and avoid "foot in mouth" disease.

Scriptural Examples

Jephthah. This judge of Israel rashly vowed to sacrifice the first thing that walked out the door of his house when he returned from battle. Sadly, it happened his daughter was first out of the door (Judg. 11).

Saul. In his conceit, Saul spoke in haste on the day his son Jonathan brought victory to the army of Israel over the Philistines. Were it not for the intervention of the troops, Saul would have put his son to death for eating a little honey (1 Sam. 14).

The Lord God. The words of God are never spoken in haste, nor need to be taken back. On the contrary, the words of God are flawless, like silver refined in the furnace (Ps. 12:6).

Prayer of Application

Dear Lord, keep me from putting my foot in my mouth by speaking before my brain is in gear. I am your representative, Lord, and I need to choose all my words with care.

Beware of Expectations and Entitlements

If a man pampers his servant from youth, he will bring grief in the end (Prov. 29:21).

In 1981 I started a company which grew to 120 employees in seven years. During that time, I sometimes made the error of promising my employees more than I could deliver. I didn't do it deceitfully or to manipulate them. I was naively optimistic. But whether the promises were fulfilled or not isn't the point. I should have managed their expectations more carefully.

If an employee, or a family member, is allowed to have his or her expectations grow beyond reality, when disappointments come, you are sure to get grief. When tough times hit, and expectations are not met, morale goes south. How much better to manage the expectations of those under your authority. Then when those tough times come, they are more acclimated to taking lumps with you. When times get better, that fat bonus comes as a welcome surprise.

A regular gift to someone, even though done out of kindness, may quickly become in his eyes an entitlement. If the gift is then withheld in the future, its withdrawal becomes an injustice. Also, if you pamper your employee and never hold him accountable, he will begin to expect the same in the future. The point is, we need to be careful in raising the expectations of others, because they will come to view our hopeful promises or current treatment of them as an entitlement.

How do we avoid this trap? The best way is to set goals and put them in writing. Hold everyone who is looking to you for leadership accountable for his actions, whether he is an employee or your child. Make sure everyone understands that this year's bonus is given only because the company made certain financial goals. Tell them not to expect it next year. Condition others to expect reality and they won't be disappointed and give you grief.

Prayer of Application

Dear Father, thank You for Your many precious promises. You will never fail us. But help those of us in authority to help others see reality in their expectations of You and of us.

Beware the Root of Pride that Brings Anger

22) An angry man stirs up dissension, and a hot-tempered one commits many sins. 23) A man's pride brings him low, but a man of lowly spirit gains honor (Prov. 29:22-23).

Not all anger is sinful. But this kind of anger is sinful through and through. What causes it? Verse 23 answers that point-blank: Sinful anger has as its root the sin of pride.

The prideful person has many reasons to be angry. First, his "rights" are higher and wider than anyone else's and are easily stepped on. Second, his understanding is deep, so conflicts easily arise. Third, his needs are greater than others' and always less satisfied. Fourth, his ambitions are greater and easily thwarted. The prideful person tends to live in a state where anger is always lurking just below the surface.

Peace lives in the person of "lowly spirit"(Matt. 5:3). First, this person understands that we are to subordinate our "rights" for the glory of God. Second, he realizes there is much that he does not know. Third, he is interested mainly in the needs of others. Fourth, his only ambition is to please God, so he cannot be frustrated if money, position and power are denied him. Finally, unlike the prideful, the person of lowly spirit has peace with God. Any honor he has is imputed to him only by the One to whom all honor belongs: the Lord Jesus Christ.

Scriptural Examples

Haman and Mordecai. Haman stirred up dissension as a hot-tempered man full of pride and ambition who hated the Jew Mordecai. Haman's pride brought him low, while the lowly Mordecai was exalted to a position of honor (Est. 8:1-2).

The prodigal's brother. While his brother was taught a lowly spirit in the far country, this man stewed in his prideful anger. He refused to join in the celebration welcoming his prodigal brother home (Luke 15:28-32).

Prayer of Application

Lord, keep me from the pride that goes before a fall. Unrighteous anger shows our pride, but the fruits of humility are love, joy, peace, and all the other traits of the lowly spirit.

Beware the Threefold Trap of an Accomplice

The accomplice of a thief is his own enemy; he is put under oath and dare not testify (Prov. 29:24).

Way back in Proverbs 1:10-19, we saw the trap set by those who lie in wait to steal or shed innocent blood. The trap would catch only themselves. This proverb gives us a glimpse of the threefold trap that awaits those who fail to obey chapter one's warnings, and so become accomplices of the criminal.

Suppose I decide to join some guys who are burglarizing houses in my neighborhood. I am asked to wait outside the victim's home and give a signal if danger nears. Pretty easy, huh? But something goes wrong. A secret alarm alerts the police who catch my companions red-handed. I am called to testify in court as a witness. My problems have just begun.

What do I do? I have three choices. I can (1) keep my mouth shut, (2) perjure myself by lying, or (3) spill my guts and tell the truth. The first alternative violates a command of God regarding testimony: "If a person sins because he does not speak up when he hears a public charge to testify regarding something he has seen or learned about, he will be held responsible"(Lev. 5:1). Perjury also breaks the direct command of God (Mal. 3:5; 1 Tim 1:10), and carries with it penalties in the human court. The third alternative gets me a prison term, and perhaps even more fearful, the eternal malice of the other burglars.

The best alternative is to never become the accomplice to a thief or any lawbreaker. Even if one is never caught, the God who sees all things will repay him according to his sin.

Scriptural Examples

Jesus. He was put under oath and refused to testify. But Jesus' failure to testify was in accordance with the prophetic words of Isaiah 53:7. He had done nothing worthy of punishment. In silence He set His face like flint toward Calvary refusing to answer the charges laid against Him (Matt. 26:63).

Prayer of Application

Dear Father, to break the law of God or the government ever so slightly is foolishness. I thank You, Lord, that You have set my feet on a straight path. Give me power to live a life of obedience.

Fear God Alone: He Will Keep You Safe

Fear of man will prove to be a snare, but whoever trusts in the Lord is kept safe (Prov. 29:25).

An entire book would not suffice to tell all the stories Scripture gives us of the men and women who exemplified both the thesis and antithesis of this principle. Here are but a few.

Scriptural Examples

Noah. He preached righteousness and built a huge ship, all to the taunts of people who were to die. Noah and his family were kept safe (Gen 6:5-7:7; 2 Peter 2:5).

Joseph. He did not fear the fury of Potiphar's wife, but said, "How can I sin against God?" God prospered him (Gen 39:9).

Aaron. He bowed to the demands of the Israelites and made them a golden calf to worship (Ex. 32:22-24).

Joshua and Caleb. They trusted God while the other spies feared the "giants" in the land. God honored these men, while the others were snared in unbelief (Num. 13:30-31; 14:22-24).

Saul. He told Samuel he failed to follow God's command to destroy all the cattle of the Amalekites because he was afraid of the people and gave in to them (1 Sam 15:24).

Pilate. He feared the people and the loss of his position, so he allowed the Son of God to be executed (John 19:1-16).

Peter. He succumbed to the fear of people in denying his Lord (Matt 26:75), and accommodating the Judaizers (Gal 2:11-14).

Moses. He feared God rather than the power of Pharaoh and God kept him safe. "He regarded disgrace for the sake of Christ of more value than all the riches of Egypt" (Heb. 11:26).

Brothers and sisters, how we need to follow the example of Jesus, "who endured such opposition from sinful men," yet was faithful to the Father, even to death on the cross (Heb. 12:1-3). Others have no power over us that is not allowed them by our God. "If God is for us, who can be against us?" (Rom. 8:31).

Prayer of Application

Heavenly Father, thank You for Your providential care for Your people. You alone are to be feared. Let no Christian be intimidated by what others can do to him. Rather, let all fear You.

Have Confidence in God Alone

Many seek an audience with a ruler, but it is from the Lord that man gets justice (Prov. 29:26).

This principle builds upon the previous one. We need to fear God and have complete confidence in God alone. People, try as they may, can never take the place of our God.

Take our federal government for instance. It has become in the eyes of many the all-seeing, all-knowing father. It promises to provide for our needs and to eliminate all the problems that beset us. Many politicians have set themselves up as gods, controlling the purse strings and morals of the nation.

The government has declared war on poverty, crime, drugs, illiteracy, and on and on. But poverty, crime, drugs, and illiteracy go on and on. The Social Security system is going bankrupt. Medicare is toppling. Welfare rolls continue to grow. Meanwhile, the government is being revealed for what it is: mere fleshly humans attempting to solve what only God can solve.

Only Almighty God deserves our confidence. Only He has proven consistently trustworthy. Have you ever tried to get an audience with the President of the United States? God is available to you at this very moment, wherever you are. He answers our prayers with justice; with your best interests at heart. If you were to get a few minutes with the president, would you get satisfaction or only a few promises and some excuses? I think you know the answer.

Scriptural Examples

Felix. This deceitful ruler kept Paul in prison for two years hoping to please the Jews on the one hand and to extract a bribe from Paul on the other (Acts 24:25-27).

The rulers of this age. Paul wrote of these crucifiers of Christ as coming to nothing. While here, they act either wittingly or unwittingly as servants of God. But ultimately, God is in control of all governments (1 Cor. 2:6-8).

Prayer of Application

Dear Lord, thank You for hearing and answering prayer. And thank You for treating Your subjects in justice and mercy, so unlike the treatment most of us get from our governments.

Hate Sin, but Love Sinners

The righteous detest the dishonest; the wicked detest the upright (Prov. 29:27).

In the introduction I spoke of the polarity between the "righteous" and the "wicked." No middle ground exists. One must score 100 percent to be counted in the realm of the righteous—a score impossible for people—but not for God (Mark 10:27).

By His grace alone, God saves some. They are regenerated, given new hearts of flesh (Ezek. 11:19; 36:26). Though justified in His sight, we still carry the stain of sin. Those "born from above" (John 3:3) are armed with the gospel and sent out to the ends of the earth to gather His people together (Matt. 28:19-20).

Everyone should be confronted with the gospel of Christ in love. There, but for the grace of God, go we. Their sin is despicable, but we need to love them enough to give them the opportunity to be freely saved. Others may hate us and revile us and say all manner of evil against us falsely, yet we are to pray for them and do good to them (Matt. 5:44-45).

I believe Proverbs 29:27 will reach its full application in the age to come, following the judgment. Then the wicked in hell will be truly detested by the righteous, as they come under the permanent wrath of God. Then they will be hated, even as they also hate the righteous in heaven. God will bring glory to those who reached out to them in love.

Scriptural Examples

Cain and Abel. The wicked's hatred of the righteous came early in history. Righteous Abel was murdered by Cain. This bloodshed is but a foreshadowing of the evil done by the wicked upon the righteous ever since (Gen 4:8-10; 1 John 3:12-13).

Paul. Paul wept over his Jewish brothers who would not respond to the gospel he preached. He loved them and even wished that he could be judged in their place (Rom. 9:1-3; 10:1).

Prayer of Application

Father, thank You for saving me and imputing to me the righteousness of Christ. Help me to fulfill my role in the Great Commission, so that all may hear of Your salvation.

Chapter Thirty

The Sayings of Agur

If I was asked to choose a favorite chapter of Proverbs, I would be hard-pressed to decide between chapter 9, the calls of wisdom and folly, and chapter 30, the sayings of Agur. Agur calls himself "the most ignorant of men" (v. 2), but don't you believe it. His wisdom is far-reaching and eternal. For instance, Agur knew the Creator God who controls the wind and waters and who "established all the ends of the earth" (vv. 3-4). He knew that the Holy One has a son (v. 4c), and might have known that it was He "who has gone up to heaven and come down" (v. 4a).

Agur knew the "flawless" Word of God (vv. 5-6). His prayer of verses 7-9 is a classic and worthy of repetition every day of our lives. He knew of the destructiveness of pride (vv. 11-14), and of the disparity between giving and taking (vv. 15-16). Agur saw that God's creation was incomprehensible (vv. 18-19), and knew the inherent deceitfulness of sin (v. 20). He witnessed the irony of ill-fitting occupations (vv. 21-23), and found the gospel of God expressed in the little creatures (vv. 24-28). Finally, Agur saw the difference between stately bearing and foolish pride, between rightful honor and self-honor (vv. 29-33). I pray that as you study the sayings of Agur, you, too, will come back again and again for refreshment.

Know the Creator in Humility and Reverence

1) The sayings of Agur son of Jakeh—an oracle: This man declared to Ithiel, to Ithiel and to Ucal: 2) "I am the most ignorant of men; I do not have a man's understanding. 3) I have not learned wisdom, nor have I knowledge of the Holy One. 4) Who has gone up to heaven and come down? Who has gathered up the wind in the hollow of his hands? Who has wrapped up the waters in his cloak? Who has established all the ends of the earth? What is his name, and the name of his son? Tell me if you know!" (Prov. 30:1-4)

For eons, sinful people have tried to explain the universe apart from the Bible's God. If there is no personal Creator, there is no need for a Savior. No Creator requiring righteousness, no future punishment. So, those who desire autonomy attack Christianity right at its foundation; they deny the God that made them (Rom. 1:18-20). Despite the humble statement of verses 1-4, Agur knew of Him.

There are but three scenarios that could account for the existence of the universe: 1) A Supreme Being who has the power of existence within Himself, and who has existed eternally created it; 2) The universe created itself. To create itself, the universe would have had to exist prior to itself, which is a rational absurdity. 3) The universe has always existed. But which part of the universe has the power of existence within itself? The universe is an effect and all effects have causes. God is not an effect, but the Causer. The rational mind must believe that if something exists now, something must have always existed. In Latin the phrase is: *ex nihilo, nihil fit.* Out of nothing, nothing comes.

Scriptural Examples

Jesus. He controlled the wind and the waves. He ascended into heaven and sustains all things by His powerful Word. He is the Creator God, the Self-Existent One, the Holy One who is from of old (Matt. 8:26; 14:32; John 1:1-3, 14; Heb. 1:3).

Prayer of Application

Father God, thank You for the beauty of Your creation that speaks of Your glory and power. We humans are so sinful that without Your illumination we refuse to tie the two together.

Trust Every Word of God

5) "Every word of God is flawless; he is a shield to those who take refuge in him. 6) Do not add to his words, or he will rebuke you and prove you a liar" (Prov. 30:5-6).

Satan's prime target is the Christian's trust in the sufficiency and trustworthiness of the Bible. Many either deny the Bible's trustworthiness by denying its verbal inspiration by the Holy Spirit, or deny the Bible's sufficiency by adding human words to the very words of God. God will rebuke these people and prove them to be liars.

Agur, who wrote the verses above, believed in the Word of God. He says in verse 5 that "every Word of God is flawless." Those of us who flee to God and His Word for refuge find that He is trustworthy to shield us from the ultimate tragedy of eternal judgment. He provides for our future security and His words are able to make us wise unto that salvation (2 Tim. 3:15).

In verse 6 above, Agur speaks of the sufficiency of Scripture. Many would add to the words of God by other writings and by their traditions. The Jews in Jesus' day were guilty of this error by their Talmud, or oral tradition, which they held to be equal with God's Word. Jesus told them on one instance, "You nullify the word of God for the sake of your tradition" (Matt. 15:6). Today, the Roman Catholic Church has built up a huge body of tradition by which God's Word is erroneously augmented. For example, they teach of a place called "purgatory," which has no biblical basis. When people do this, they deny that the Scripture is sufficient (2 Tim. 3:16-17).

Scriptural Examples

Satan. Behind all the Bible-bashing in the world is Satan. In the Garden, he first tempted Eve by questioning God's Word. Don't follow him. Follow God by trusting in His perfect Word that He has provided for your refuge (Gen. 3:1-6).

Prayer of Application

Lord, thank You for the trustworthiness and sufficiency of the Bible. Help me to read it in sincerity and faith, seeking to do what it says, and enjoying its refuge and sure salvation.

Pray for God's Control over Your Life

7) "Two things I ask of you, O Lord; do not refuse me before I die: 8) Keep falsehood and lies far from me; give me neither poverty nor riches, but give me only my daily bread. 9) Otherwise, I may have too much and disown you and say, 'Who is the Lord?' Or I may become poor and steal, and so dishonor the name of my God" (Prov. 30:7-9).

Because Agur says in verse 7, "before I die," it seems to me that this was Agur's "life prayer." Do you have a "life prayer" like you may have a "life verse"? If not, you might want to adopt Agur's. He asks for only two things. First, he asks to be kept from falsehood and lies. The world system is a system of lies, and of self-seeking deception. It says it will do what only God can do and leads many astray. How different is God's way, the way of humility and truth. Agur is a man of humility and we see it clearly in his prayer.

The second part of Agur's prayer is strange indeed. How many folks do you know who pray that they may be kept from riches? Not many I'm sure. Most of us see riches as a blessing from God. But Agur knew that often the more material wealth a person has, the less he thinks he needs God. Then in verse 8 he asks that he also be kept from poverty. He feared he would become a thief under those circumstances.

Agur wants simply to bring honor to the name of his God (v. 9). This should be the motivating force behind every Christian's life (1 Cor. 10:31; Phil. 2:11). All of us should pray that God will control every detail of our lives, then submit fully to His providential care. That is the need of every Christian.

Scriptural Examples

Jeshurun. The name "Jeshurun" is a pseudonym for Israel. In Deuteronomy 32:15 we find that Jeshurun grew fat and sleek and was filled with food. He abandoned God his Savior, which is exactly what Agur had feared in his prayer.

Prayer of Application

Lord, I want to adopt Agur's prayer as my own. I have seen what riches can do to people and I'm afraid of that prospect. Control every part of my life, that I might walk in Your ways.

Don't Criticize the Roles of Other Christians

"Do not slander a servant to his master, or he will curse you, and you will pay for it" (Prov. 30:10).

In my business, we keep a notebook of letters from customers who compliment our employees. We celebrate these letters loudly. On the other hand, sometimes we get complaints. Although difficult to receive, these are really of more value than the others. Why? Because management is made aware of a problem and can take steps to correct it. But this proverb is speaking of slander, half-truths, innuendo, and gossip that is intended to harm, not build up.

As Christians, we are each the servant of our Master Jesus Christ. He gives each of us our marching orders, and each set of orders is different from all the others. The Christian's servanthood with his God is a very individual relationship, and we must be careful that we do not impose our own orders upon others.

Please understand that I am not talking about the "thou shalt nots," or negative commandments. I'm speaking of the positive commands which are open-ended, and to which every Christian must conform as he is personally led by the Spirit. Each part of the Body of Christ has a different role to play (1 Cor. 12:14-20). To criticize another unfairly may equate to slander in the Lord's eyes. After all, Jesus is his Master, not you and I.

Scriptural Examples

Abraham and Abimelech. Abraham complained to Abimelech about the latter's servants, who had seized his well. It was a valid complaint, and the two men made a covenant between them that brought peace (Gen. 21:25-26).

Doeg and David. On the other hand, this Edomite told half-truths to King Saul about Saul's servant David. For the awful consequences of his act, Doeg came under the curse of God (1 Sam. 22:9-10, 16-19; Ps. 52:1-5).

Prayer of Application

Father, help me to realize that I am responsible to You for my own marching orders, not those of others. Enable me to give solid advice to other Christians, but never to criticize them.

Beware the Arrogance of the Contemptuous

11) "There are those who curse their fathers and do not bless their mothers; 12) those who are pure in their own eyes and yet are not cleansed of their filth; 13) those whose eyes are ever so haughty, whose glances are so disdainful; 14) those whose teeth are swords and whose jaws are set with knives to devour the poor from the earth, the needy from among mankind" (Prov. 30:11-14).

Here, Agur gives us a simple statement of fact. There are many folks like this. They are arrogant, self-serving, disrespectful of authority and of other people in general, and ready to take advantage of those who can't fight back. In these four verses a detailed picture emerges. They are arrogant people who are contemptuous of everybody but themselves.

Their contempt for others apparently got an early start in life: "They curse their fathers and do not bless their mothers" (v. 11). By this, they show contempt for the command of God that parents be honored (Ex. 20:12). Parents are representatives of God in the life of the child, and represent all authority on earth. Those who hate their parents will hate all authority, in particular the authority of God.

They are filthy, but they see themselves as pure and clean (v. 12). Notice their eyes are haughty (v. 13). Back in 6:17 we learned that this is "Sin #1" on God's "Hate List." Beware of the jaws and teeth of people like this, but don't be afraid of them. Rather, fear you might be one of them and not realize it.

Scriptural Examples

Pharisees and teachers of the law. Proverbs 30:11-14 describes this generation of vipers perfectly. Jesus accused them of the same failings seen in these verses. They loved the place of honor and exalted themselves at others' expense. Jesus called down many woes upon them and termed them "whitewashed tombs" (Matt. 23).

Prayer of Application

Father, only by Your grace am I not listed among those who lift up their eyes against You. I have nothing to offer You, only my filthiness. Thank You for cleansing me in Jesus' blood.

Be Satisfied with the Riches of Christ

15) "The leech has two daughters. 'Give! Give!' they cry. There are three things that are never satisfied, four that never say 'Enough!':
16) the grave, the barren womb, land, which is never satisfied with water, and fire, which never says 'Enough!'" (Prov. 30:15-16).

The old Tarzan movies starring Johnny Weissmuller were great. When he swam across a jungle river a couple of leeches regularly attached to his arms and back. Those blood suckers made us squirm in our seats as Tarzan pulled them off. The leech has two suction cups with which it extracts blood from its victims. In the verses above, these suckers are called "daughters," each screaming "Give!" They are never satisfied.

We have seen the three/four construction of verse 15b before (Prov. 6:16), and we'll see it again. This formula says, "Here are four specific instances, but the list is not exhaustive."

The grave has stood with its yawning mouth since the Garden of Eden. "Gimme more," it cries. The barren womb will not be satisfied until full with child. Witness the cries of Rachel (Gen. 30:1) and Hannah (1 Sam. 1:1-19), who thought it better to be consumed by the grave than to languish with a barren womb. In California, we have a lot of land that is never satisfied with water in the dry summer months, so year after year brush and forest fires consume thousands of acres. "Enough" is not in the vocabulary of the fire.

People are like those fires. But Jesus said in John 10:10, "I have come that they may have life, and have it to the full." Jesus came to fill up His people with life. He fills us to overflowing with His Spirit (Eph. 5:18), with joy (2 Tim. 1:4), with righteousness (Matt. 5:6), and with every good and perfect gift (James 1:17). I believe that St. Augustine said it best: "Thou hast made us for thyself, and our hearts are restless till they rest in thee." Only Christ satisfies. Only Christ stops the raging fire within and brings peace. Be satisfied with the riches of Christ.

Prayer of Application

Sovereign Lord, how blessed is the peace that comes from the rest to which You have called me. How sweet it is to pursue the things of Christ that are eternal and eternally satisfying.

Beware of a Mocking and Scornful Eye

"The eye that mocks a father, that scorns obedience to a mother, will be pecked out by the ravens of the valley, will be eaten by the vultures" (Prov. 30:17).

With the previous verses, I related squirming in the movies at the sight of leeches sucking blood. But those scenes were nothing compared to those in which the cavalry soldiers got captured by the Apaches and were staked half-naked to an anthill. This is a horribly uncomfortable predicament, but the real enemy lurked overhead, lazily circling in the hot desert sky. As the sun burned down upon the hapless soldiers, the vultures and ravens waited to tear into their flesh. Barring reinforcements, the birds eventually attacked. Eyes were the first target. A slow death followed. Only bleached skeletons remained.

The fifth commandment is "the first commandment with a promise—that it may go well with you and that you may enjoy long life on the earth" (Eph. 6:2-3; Ex. 20:12). These verses say that it is also the first commandment with a punishment specifically prescribed to it. And it's not very pretty! Is God trying to say something to us?

The eyes that mock and scorn parents are also set against all in authority. God hates the arrogant and scornful eye that lifts itself up in pride to mock those in authority.

Scriptural Examples

Absalom. He was loved by his dad, but Absalom mocked and scorned David. His long hair was caught in the limbs of a tree where he died, and his corpse thrown mercifully into a pit, perhaps to spare the king's son the sharp beaks of the vultures that probably soared over the battle (2 Sam. 18:9-17).

The rebellious son. The law provided death for the son who rebelled against the authority of his parents. He was to be taken from the camp and stoned to death (Deut. 21:18-21).

Prayer of Application

Father, sometimes parenthood seems to be a thankless job when children seek to have things their own way. I know that You hate this rebellion against parenthood.

Marvel at God's Creation

18) "There are three things that are too amazing for me, four that I do not understand: 19) the way of an eagle in the sky, the way of a snake on a rock, the way of a ship on the high seas, and the way of a man with a maiden. 20) This is the way of an adulteress: she eats and wipes her mouth and says, 'I've done nothing wrong'" (Prov. 30:18-20).

Notice again the three/four construction in these and in the following three groups of verses. These are not all-inclusive. Here, we are given a fifth thing more amazing than the rest.

When I lived in Florida some years back, I would often watch the pelicans catching the updraft in front of our condominium. They floated effortlessly, expertly riding the sea breeze. The snake has no feet like other animals, yet it moves with speed and grace as it slithers over the rocks—another of God's marvelous creations. It always amazed me how the same principles of aerodynamics that the pelican uses also drive a sailboat into the wind. How does the centerboard on a sloop push against the tons of water that slide by above it and counterbalance the force of the wind against the sails? Beats me.

In God's final act of creation, He created man and woman. The word translated "maiden" here is the Hebrew *almah*, which does not necessarily mean virgin, but a young woman who is sexually ready for marriage (*Expositors,* p. 1124). Human sexuality and marital love are two of God's greatest mysteries. Who can understand romantic love? Who knows the way between a man and a maiden?

But the most amazing of all these things is that anyone could see all the other marvels, and yet choose to toss aside the God who planned and created them. The adulteress amorally shrugs off her sin and says, "I've done nothing wrong." In doing so, she denies the very God who created the beauty and mystery of marital sex which she so blatantly mocks.

Prayer of Application

Creator God, how Your ways are unsearchable and Your paths beyond finding out. Yet Your mark on creation speaks loudly of Your eternal power and Godhead. No one can miss it.

Avoid Those Too Big for Their Britches

21) "Under three things the earth trembles, under four it cannot bear up: 22) a servant who becomes king, a fool who is full of food, 23) an unloved [KJV: "odious"] woman who is married, and a maidservant who displaces her mistress" (Prov. 30:21-23).

My dad would say of someone whose estimate of himself was too high, "That guy's too big for his britches." Today we might say, "He's a legend in his own mind."

Are these people really "earth shakers"? The first is a servant who becomes king. History is full of those who have risen from the mail room to president, or from shepherd boy to king. Some do a good job. But for many, abilities and moral character lag behind ego and ambition. Their reign is marked by tyranny, deceit, and bloodshed. Hitler is a good example.

The second is a fool who has become wealthy and "full of food." He considers himself wise, but as a matter of fact he's the same old fool he always was. He struts and crows and throws his money around to get his way.

The third is an odious woman who rules her household with an iron fist, including her hen-pecked husband (Prov. 21:9, 19). Finally, there's the maidservant who charms her master and he falls for it. He then boots his wife out the door and replaces her with the servant girl. As you can understand, these are all folks you and I would do well to avoid.

Scriptural Examples

Zimri. This servant aspired to be king. He made it, but only for seven days, after he murdered his boss (1 Kings 16:1-18).

Nabal. This fool was rich and full of food to boot. He shunned David's request and ate his final meal (1 Sam. 25).

Jezebel. She was history's most odious woman. Her tyrannical rule over her household, her husband, and her land earn her a spot in the Bible's Hall of Shame (if there was one) (2 Kings 9:30-37).

Prayer of Application

Father, some of the people I meet in life are impossible to like. Help me to pray for those I don't like and, out of love for You, hope they will blessed even as You have blessed me.

567 We met the industrious ant in Proverbs 6:6-8.

Learn the Gospel from the Little Creatures

23) "Four things on earth are small, yet they are extremely wise:
24) Ants are creatures of little strength, yet they store up their food in
the summer; 26) coneys are creatures of little power, yet they make
their home in the crags; 27) locusts have no king, yet they advance
together in ranks; 28) a lizard can be caught with the hand, yet it
is found in kings' palaces" (Prov. 30:24-28).

We met the industrious ant in Proverbs 6:6-8. It is featured again here, along with three other small yet wise members of the animal world: the coney, or rock badger; the locust; and the lizard, or gecko. Let's see what these half-pints have to say to us about eternal matters.

The ant understands the need to provide for the future. Each ant works within the colony to store up food for the coming bitter cold of winter. We humans fret about future physical needs, but how few of us give thought to preparing for life beyond the grave. The ant speaks to us of the provision of salvation while the days allow it.

The rock badger is a rabbit-like animal that cannot burrow into the ground for protection. It runs to safety in the crags, or rocky outgrowths. We learn that the way to eternal safety is in the Rock of Ages, the Lord Jesus Christ. We hide in Him.

As Christians, we join an army advancing together, but without an apparent leader or king. The locusts have no cellular phones yet they rise together like a cloud, blotting out the sun. So, too, Christians appear to be leaderless. Yet each in the vast army receives his marching orders from the Holy Spirit and advances together with his brothers and sisters.

Finally, the lizard represents the life of faith. The gecko has sticky fanlike feet that can climb slick walls and hang suspended from the high ceilings of kings' palaces. It reminds us of the faith that holds onto the promises of God and that enters into heavenly places (McGee, p. 101).

Prayer of Application

Father, thank You that by Your grace I have become part of a vast body of believers marching onward toward the precious hope of an eternity with You. Help me to march worthily.

Walk with a Royal Stride

29) "There are three things that are stately in their stride, four that move with stately bearing: 30) a lion, mighty among beasts, who retreats before nothing; 31) a strutting rooster [KJV: "greyhound"], a he-goat, and a king with his army around him" (Prov. 30:29-31).

Here are three more members of the biblical zoo, and a kingly fourth. Do you remember the Wizard of Oz? The Cowardly Lion hoped the wizard could give him courage. Christians are to walk courageously by faith.

The NIV's "rooster" is translated "greyhound" in the KJV and "horse" in other versions. The Hebrew word literally means "girded to the loins." In other words, this animal is a swift and sure runner. Like him, we are called to run the race set before us (Heb. 12:1-2).

The "he-goat" is, of course, a ram. In the desert mountains of San Diego county, one may easily see these sure-footed climbers scaling the rocky desert peaks. Like rams, we are climbers as well, as we negotiate the lofty peaks of our faith.

Finally, like kings, we have been called by God to reign with Christ. We walk by faith, but we walk with a royal bearing. We are not ashamed of the gospel of Jesus Christ (Rom. 1:16).

Scriptural Examples

The ram. God prepared a ram to replace Isaac. The ram was emblematic of the Lamb of God who would one day lay down His life in sacrifice on that very same hill (Gen. 22:13).

The lion. Christ is the Lion of Judah. In Jacob's blessing, he said the Redeemer would come from Judah (Gen. 49:9-10).

The horses. If we cannot keep up with mere people, how shall we run with the horses? We need to keep spiritually and physically in shape for the tasks before us (Jer. 12:5).

The king. The little baby Jesus, born in poverty and humility, rose physically from the tomb. One day, He will return as King of Kings with a great army (Rev. 19:11-16).

Prayer of Application

Father, You have called me to walk in humility and sacrifice. But I am more than a conqueror through Him who loved me and gave Himself for me. May I walk worthy of You.

Bring Unity in Humility and Righteousness

32) "If you have played the fool and exalted yourself, or if you have planned evil, clap your hand over your mouth! 33) For as churning the milk produces butter, and as twisting the nose produces blood, so stirring up anger produces strife"
(Prov. 30:32-33).

Augustine said that humility is the central defining characteristic of the Christian. It is the mark of a lifestyle that leads to peace and unity among brothers, and the mark of the life of our Lord and Savior Jesus. The opposite pathways of pride and self-exaltation lead to anger and strife.

If you were to stand at the doorway to your local supermarket and take a poll of the people coming out, you probably wouldn't find one in 10 who thought that there was any connection between their disposition or lifestyle and the strife they encounter in life. We are a nation of "victims" who blame someone or something else, but only we are to blame.

It takes no talent to stir up anger. Anger comes naturally to everybody. Rare indeed is the person who is not easily provoked (1 Cor. 13:5). At the end of anger's path is trouble, while at the end of humility and patience is peace and unity.

An interesting play on words is in verse 33. The ancient Hebrews spoke of a man with patience as being "long of nose." Their word for anger was literally "short nose." But we see here a bloody nose made out of the raw material of sin.

Scriptural Examples

Sihon. This Amorite king did more than just open his mouth foolishly. He waged war against the wandering Israelites. He was to suffer more than a bloody nose (Num. 21:21-24).

Job. God spoke to Job out of the storm. Job was almost speechless. He said, "I am unworthy. . . I put my hand over my mouth." Job knew when to shut up. Do we? (Job 40:1-5).

Prayer of Application

Dear Lord, those who walk in pride are on a collision course with others, and more importantly, with You. Help me to be an example of humility and the fear of the Lord.

Chapter Thirty-one

The Wisdom Woman

The majority of Chapter 31 is the epilogue description of the "wife of noble character" (v. 1). My wife, Amy, and I collaborated on a book regarding the woman in Proverbs 31. It is entitled *Wisdom for Women*. Here is some of what we said in the preface of that volume:

"Who is this Proverbs 31 woman, and why is she so important? She seems so 'perfect' it's discouraging…could anyone ever do all the things she does?

"…Frankly, we think if anyone tried to copy her life exactly she would go nuts. But we are not to imitate her activities. Rather, we are to imitate her character. She is a model woman who embodies the righteous characteristics of Christ. Because we are called to imitate Christ (1 Cor. 4:16-17; Eph. 5:1), we may use her example as a guide for the Christian life.

"…As you will see, the woman of these verses isn't restricted. Quite the opposite, she's a vital, fulfilled, joyful, multi-dimensional woman. Her life has been defined by God, who has set her free in Christ Jesus to be the woman He intended her to be. Just like her, our study of and meditation upon the Word of God sets us free to live a life pleasing to God—the most wonderful life imaginable."

Mothers, Teach Your Children the Right Path

*1)   The sayings of King Lemuel—an oracle his mother taught him:
2) O my son, O son of my womb, O son of my vows, 3) do not spend
your strength on women, your vigor on those who ruin kings. 4) "It is
not for kings, O Lemuel—not for kings to drink wine, nor for rulers to
crave beer, 5) lest they drink and forget what the law decrees, and
deprive all the oppressed of their rights. 6) Give beer to those who are
perishing, wine to those who are in anguish; 7) let them drink and
forget their poverty and remember their misery no more. 8) Speak up for
those who cannot speak for themselves, for the rights of all who are
destitute. 9) Speak up and judge fairly; defend the rights of the poor and
needy" (Prov. 31:1-9).*

There never was a king of Israel named Lemuel, so this is
perhaps a nickname given to Solomon by his mother Bathsheba.
"Lemuel" literally means "under God or with God." Bathsheba
treasured her son, particularly after the loss of her first child (2
Sam. 12:19). Perhaps she taught him this oracle trusting that he
would be king one day. If so, he would need protection against
three opponents: wine, women, and song.

She knew firsthand of David's affinity for the opposite sex.
She joined God in warning against a multiplicity of wives (Deut.
17:17). Eventually, Solomon would take 700 wives and 300 concubines (1 Kings 11:1-3).

Next, she warned her boy about the damaging effects that
alcohol can have. With all of the responsibilities they hold, kings
don't need to be anesthetized. They need to bring proper justice
and equity to their subjects.

Finally, Bathsheba warned him against frivolity and
favoritism. Instead, he should take up the cause of the poor and
destitute, not just the cause of the established and affluent.

Mothers, your sons and daughters need oracles from you, too.
What greater legacy than a guide to the right pathway?

Prayer of Application

Father, thank You for mothers who provide godly guidance
to their children. May Bathsheba's oracle provide an outline for
modern day moms who want their children to walk with You.

Finally, Learn the ABCs of Wisdom's Walk

10) A wife of noble character who can find? She is worth far more than rubies. 11) Her husband has full confidence in her and lacks nothing of value. 12) She brings him good, not harm, all the days of her life (Prov. 31:10-12).

Beginning here, the wisdom of Proverbs is summed up in the person of "The Wife of Noble Character." But these final verses are not just for you, ladies. This wisdom is for everyone.

"The Wife of Noble Character" is a picture of an idealized wife (or person), and not necessarily a model against which all women should be viewed. Most could not emulate her lifestyle because of their different circumstances. For instance, she is married and has children. She is wealthy and capable of entering into business deals involving real estate, agriculture, trade, and other enterprises. Finally, she has a multiplicity of talents, plus more energy than any five people I know.

These final 22 verses are arranged alphabetically in an acrostic. The first letter of each verse starts with a different letter of the Hebrew alphabet, all arranged sequentially like our ABCs. (Ps. 119 is another example of this type of Hebrew poetic literature.) Its domestic setting helps to bring out the variety of ways that wisdom should be shown in our daily lives. In "The Wife of Noble Character," wisdom is seen in a balanced lifestyle of industry and charity.

In these first three verses, we see first that the noble character is rare, worth far more than rubies, which are even more precious than diamonds. Her husband, and all who come in contact with her, trust her implicitly. She is "love" incarnate. Why do I say that? Because in verse 12 we see that every day of her life she brings good and not harm. That is what love does. Turn in your Bible to 1 Corinthians 13 and read God's definition of love. It is the most precious, rare, and valuable commodity on the face of the earth.

Prayer of Application

Lord, thank You for this picture of wisdom incarnate. It is a picture up against which all Christians should place their own lives—a goal to set before us in our daily walk with You.

Finally, Learn the Freedom of Wisdom

13) She selects wool and flax and works with eager hands. 14) She is like the merchant ships, bringing her food from afar. 15) She gets up while it is still dark; she provides food for her family and portions for her servant girls. 16) She considers a field and buys it; out of her earnings she plants a vineyard. 17) She sets about her work vigorously; her arms are strong for her tasks. 18) She sees that her trading is profitable, and her lamp does not go out at night. 19) In her hand she holds the distaff and grasps the spindle with her fingers. 20) She opens her arms to the poor and extends her hands to the needy (Prov. 31:13-20).

In the ancient world, women were often regarded as chattel. The pretty ones were ornaments, rarely thought of as bright entrepreneurs of substance and integrity. Even today the ancient error is made. It is a lie which these verses demolish.

Christianity has been accused of restricting women unduly. But Christ was a champion of equality! I believe it all stems from a restriction upon women against serving as elders (hence, pastors) in the church (1 Cor. 14:34-35; 1 Tim. 2:11-12, etc.). So people conclude that women are second-class citizens in God's eyes. Nothing could be further from the truth! Here's a story that may help us to understand.

Jephthah lived during the times of the judges (Judg. 11). His mother was a prostitute, which made him a bastard. The law prohibited bastards from entering into the assembly of the Lord (Deut 23:2). Jephthah wasn't even allowed to go to church, much less govern it! But Jephthah is listed in God's "Hall of Fame!" (Heb. 11:32).God blessed him in spite of the restriction.

We err when we think the commands of God to be punitive. Restrictions are not the negation of His blessing, but are ultimately meant for our freedom and for our own good. Jesus said that He had come to provide "freedom for the prisoners" (Luke 4:18). Read the verses above carefully. Is this a woman who is restricted?

Prayer of Application

Father, help all of us to get a new view of Your Law, that it is ultimately freeing and not restrictive. Only in Christ do we have the freedom to be who You created us to be.

Finally, Learn the Joy of Wisdom

21) When it snows, she has no fear for her household; for all of them are clothed in scarlet. 22) She makes coverings for her bed; she is clothed in fine linen and purple. 23) Her husband is respected at the city gate, where he takes his seat among the elders of the land. 24) She makes linen garments and sells them, and supplies the merchants with sashes. 25) She is clothed with strength and dignity; she can laugh at the days to come. 26) She speaks with wisdom, and faithful instruction is on her tongue. 27) She watches over the affairs of her household and does not eat the bread of idleness (Prov. 31:21-27).

The sluggard is a person who lacks freedom. Ironically, his restrictions are self-imposed. On the other hand, the person of discipline, integrity, strength, and love is free to experience the joy and excitement of an unrestricted life.

In verses 13-20 we see this woman is as at-home in the wool market as she is in her own home. She goes to the supermarket and prepares her food in the early hours. She's an entrepreneur who dabbles in real estate and agriculture. She works hard. Even though her charity starts at home (v. 21), she doesn't forget the poor and needy of her community (v. 20).

Notice in the verses above that she provides for her family in the winter, when it snows, so her mind is free from worry. She dresses in fine clothes and her husband is happy. This woman is full of joy! She is one happy camper because she doesn't eat the "bread of idleness" (v. 27).

One seems to know intuitively that the kind of love this woman displays for others is the very essence of *agape* love. Ironically, although Christian love does not start out with a self-serving motive, the ultimate beneficiary of love is not just the receiver, but the giver as well. In Acts 20:35 we are told, "It is more blessed to give than to receive."

Prayer of Application

Dear Lord, how precious is Your joy. But in disobedience, joy quickly turns to pain and I lose my vision and my strength. Instill in me discipline and love that keep me on track.

Finally, Learn the Reward of Wisdom

28) Her children arise and call her blessed; her husband also, and he praises her: 29) "Many women do noble things, but you surpass them all." 30) Charm is deceptive, and beauty is fleeting; but a woman who fears the Lord is to be praised. 31) Give her the re- ward she has earned, and let her works bring her praise at the city gate (Prov. 31:28-31).

Whoever is placed next to the "Proverbs woman" will suffer in comparison. That's because she is an idealized woman given to us as a goal. Matching her abilities, energy, and grace isn't the bottom line. That is in these last four verses.

Notice that she is praised by the people who know her best. Although she is praised at the city gate, it is praise from her children and her husband which really counts. One may receive praise from friends or acquaintances, but have a spouse and children who remain silent. Here, the people who know this woman best rise and call her "blessed." But you know, sometimes we can do our best at home and never get this kind of praise. Perhaps you are in that situation and feel cheated or defrauded. If so, read on.

I believe this woman is a metaphor for Christ's bride—His Church. The church is comprised of people with different gifts and energy levels. There is only one Husband, Jesus Christ, and one bond of marriage, the new birth (John 3:3, 29). Our Husband knows us far better than we know ourselves. After all, He created us. It is only from Him that we should seek praise.

As we began our study, we read that the "fear of the Lord is the beginning of wisdom" (Prov. 1:7). Here at last, we see that this woman fears the Lord. So the fear of the Lord is also wisdom's ultimate destination. It isn't your charm, talent, energy, service, or intelligence that count. The bottom line is: Do you fear the Lord and allow Him to shape your life as He pleases? Live only for Christ, and look for your reward only in Him. That, beloved, is ultimate wisdom.

Prayer of Application

Father God, Proverbs has taught me that the pinnacle of wisdom is in the person of the Lord Jesus. Knowing Him and His righteousness is the only wisdom worth having.

Bibliography

Aitken, Kenneth T. *Proverbs*. Philadelphia: Westminster, 1986.

Alden, Robert L. *Proverbs*. Grand Rapids: Baker, 1983.

Beasley, Bob and Amy. *Wisdom for Women*. San Diego: Legacy Press, 1997.

Bridges, Charles. *A Commentary On Proverbs*. Carlisle, PA: Banner of Truth, 1987. (First published in 1846.)

Gaebelien, Frank E., Gen ed. *Expositor's Bible Commentary*. Grand Rapids: Zondervan, 1991.

Ironside, H. A. *Proverbs and the Song of Solomon*. Neptune, NJ: Loizeaux Brothers, 1989. (First published in 1908.)

Kidner, Derek, *Proverbs*. Downer's Grove, IL: InterVarsity Press, 1975.

Lawson, George. *Commentary On Proverbs*. Grand Rapids: Kregel, 1980. (First published in 1829 by W. Oliphant, Edinburgh.)

McGee, J. Vernon. *Thru The Bible*. Pasadena: Thru The Bible Radio, 1982.

Nave, Orville J. *Nave's Topical Bible*. Grand Rapids: Baker, 1984.

Voorwinde, Stephen. *Wisdom for Today's Issues*. Phillipsburg, NJ: P & R, 1981.

34495593R00329

Made in the USA
San Bernardino, CA
29 May 2016